D0612990

Lyrics from English Airs
1596—1622

Edited and with an Introduction by
Edward Doughtie

Harvard University Press
Cambridge, Massachusetts 1970

Publication of this book has been aided by a grant from the
   Hyder Edward Rollins Fund

Library of Congress Catalog Card Number 78-115474
SBN 674-53976-1

To Andrea

Preface

  This edition brings together the verses from all those sixteenth- and seventeenth-century songbooks which contained "airs," with the important exception of the works of Thomas Campion. Thus all of the lute-song books included in Percival Vivian's edition of Campion's *Works* (Oxford, 1909) and in Walter R. Davis' more recent edition (New York: Doubleday, 1967) are omitted: *A Booke of Ayres* (1601) by Campion and Philip Rosseter, *The Discription of a Maske . . . in honour of the Lord Hayes* (1607), *Two Bookes of Ayres* (c. 1613), *The Description of a Maske . . . At the Mariage of . . . the Earle of Somerset* (1614), *The Third and Fourth Booke of Ayres* (c. 1617), John Coprario's *Songs of Mourning* (1613), and *Ayres Sung and Played at Brougham Castle in Westmerland in the Kings Entertainment* (1618) by George Mason and John Earsden. The decision to omit these was made some time ago because it was then understood that Vivian's edition was being revised by Catherine Ing, and that to include them would be an unnecessary duplication of effort and would add to the cost of what promised to be an expensive book to produce. Oxford has recently reprinted the 1909 edition of Vivian's Campion without changes, though I am told that the revision will eventually be published. In the meantime, the gap has been filled by the welcome appearance of Professor Walter R. Davis' edition. Although it is a great improvement on Vivian's text and provides such bonuses as music for some of the songs and translations of a number of the Latin verses, it is still not the "definitive" edition proclaimed on the dust-jacket. It has little of the bibliographical apparatus scholars have come to expect in a full-dress edition. For example, there is no indication that copies were collated for press-corrections, and the names of the printers of the originals cannot be found in the volume. But Davis' edition fills a genuine need, and I hope the present edition will not be an unworthy companion to it.

This edition is most unabashedly "full-dress," and I have risked racking the butterfly-wings of these songs with the weight of variant readings and footnotes mainly in the hope that no one will have to do it again. New sources for the poems will be discovered, editorial procedures will become more refined, and—alas—mistakes will be found in this edition, but not enough, I hope, to make anyone else go through all that collation.

Another edition of these poems, Fellowes' *English Madrigal Verse* as revised by David Greer and F. W. Sternfeld (Oxford), has recently been published. The revised and enlarged *English Madrigal Verse* is welcome and useful because it contains verses from both madrigals and airs. But it is a modernized text with limited space for apparatus and commentary. The present edition is for those scholars, students, and critics who need more than a modernized text but less than several copies of the originals, and who would be interested in details about manuscript versions, textual matters, and sources.

I have omitted yet another volume which is included among the airs in *English Madrigal Verse*, Walter Porter's *Madrigals and Ayres* (1632). This book contains no lute songs; moreover, both the music and the poetry are of a later generation. Porter was a pupil of Monteverdi, and composed settings of poems by Carew, King, and Strode.

Although the errors and shortcomings of this edition are my own, any virtues it may have are not. If it had to depend entirely on my own labors, it would be thin and poor indeed, and I would be trembling under the shadow of the late Hyder Edward Rollins even more than I am now. My debt to Professor Rollins (whom I unfortunately never knew) is enormous, not only because of the common ground between the songbooks and the poetical miscellanies he edited with such care and erudition, but also because of the fund he left to help subsidize publications such as this. Many other scholars have contributed to the information gathered in the notes and elsewhere, and the debts I have accumulated are so numerous as to make adequate thanks impossible. But it is with pleasure and gratitude that I make the attempt. The more personal debts involving encouragement and help beyond the call of duty are even harder to repay. My wife, who typed almost all of this horribly exacting manuscript while raising two pre-schoolers, must have done so for love, for she says no one could have paid her enough money to do it. All I could do in return was to dedicate the book to her. Many thanks are due to Professors Herschel Baker and John Ward of Harvard University, who read parts of the edition in its pupa stage as a dissertation, and gave helpful criticism on a draft of the introduction. Mrs. Diana Poulton has been a source of sweetness and light during lute lessons in London and during a long and fruitful correspondence. David Greer kindly let me see the typescript of his notes to *English Madrigal Verse* and provided me with other information. My colleagues at Rice University, especially Carroll Camden, Robert Cox, Stewart A. Baker, and Joseph L. Battista, have been generous with help and advice. Rice University has supported my study with summer grants and subvention for publication. I am also grateful to the United States Educational Commission for the Fulbright grant which enabled me to work in British libraries and to enjoy many profitable talks with Professor Bruce Pattison. The American Philosophical Society recently provided me with a grant for another project, but it enabled me to do some last-minute checking for this edition and should be acknowledged here. The director and staff of Harvard University Press have been exceptionally helpful and patient, especially my editor, Mrs. Phyllis Cooper. I should also like to thank Professors William Blackburn, W. H. Bond, Edgar Bowers, John P. Cutts, Walter R. Davis, Francis Fabry, Albert B. Friedman, James Haar, the late W. A. Jackson, James G. Mc-Manaway, T. J. Mattern, Ruby Mimser, James M. Osborn; Messrs. Ian Harwood, Donald S. Pirie, Robert Spencer, Fürst Alexander zu Dohna-Schlobitten, Miss Katharine F. Pantzer, and Mrs. Charlena Williams.

I am particularly grateful to the knowledgeable and helpful staffs of the following libraries: Fondren Library, Rice University; Widener, Isham, and Loeb libraries, Harvard University; University of Texas Library; Boston Public Library; Newberry Library; University of London Library; Royal College of Music; Gonville and Caius College, Cambridge; Glasgow University Library; Manchester Public Library; Liverpool Public Library; and Lincoln Cathedral Library. I should also like to thank the cooperative staffs of the following institutions, and to thank their governing bodies for permission to publish material under their jurisdiction: the Houghton Library, Harvard University; Folger

Shakespeare Library; Biblioteca Estense, Modena; Music Division, New York Public Library; Murhardsche Bibliothek der Stadt Kassel und Landesbibliothek; Cambridge University Library; Bodleian Library, Oxford; Huntington Library, San Marino, California; Pierpont Morgan Library, New York; Victoria and Albert Museum; Yale University Music Library; Provost and Fellows of King's College, Cambridge; Master and Fellows of St. John's College, Cambridge; Master and Fellows of Trinity College, Cambridge; Governing Body of Christ Church, Oxford; Board of Trinity College, Dublin; Warden and Fellows of St. Michael's College, Tenbury Wells; Chapter of Carlisle Cathedral; Trustees of the National Library of Scotland; Trustees of the British Museum; Dulwich College; John Rylands Library, Manchester; Inner Temple Library; and the Philip and A. S. W. Rosenbach Foundation, Philadephia. Mr. Henry Nyburg of Caux, Switzerland and Fürst Alexander zu Dohna-Schlobitten of Lörrach, Germany have generously allowed me to publish parts of works in their possession; and Professor James M. Osborn has allowed me to quote from a manuscript in the Collection of Marie-Louise M. and James M. Osborn, Yale University Library. I gratefully acknowledge permission to publish excerpts from works originally published by Oxford University Press; Oliver and Boyd, Limited; Rutgers University Press; Valentino Bompiani, Milan; the Lute Society; and Yale University Press. Permission to include material that originally appeared in *Anglia* (Band 82) and *Renaissance News* (XVII and XVIII) has been granted by Max Niemeyer Verlag, Tübingen, and the Renaissance Society of America.

Houston, Texas   E. D.
December, 1969

Contents

Abbreviations for Works Cited

References to works by Shakespeare are to the edition of W. A. Nielson and C. J. Hill (Cambridge, Mass.: Houghton Mifflin, 1942). References to the classics are to the editions in the Loeb Classical Library (Cambridge, Mass.: Harvard University Press).

A	Altus
Arber	Arber, Edward, ed. *A Transcript of the Registers of the Company of Stationers of London; 1554–1640.* 5 vols. London, 1875–1894.
At1622	Attey, John. *The First Booke of Ayres.* 1622.
B	Bassus
BM	British Museum, London
Bod.	Bodleian Library, Oxford
Bond	Bond, R. Warwick, ed. *The Complete Works of John Lyly.* 3 vols. Oxford: Clarendon Press, 1902.
Boyd	Boyd, Morrison C. *Elizabethan Music and Musical Criticism.* Philadelphia: University of Pennsylvania Press, 2nd ed. 1962.
Bt1606	Bartlet, John. *A Booke of Ayres.* 1606.
Bullough	Bullough, Geoffrey, ed. *Poems and Dramas of Fulke Greville.* 2 vols. New York: Oxford University Press, 1945 (reprint of edition of 1939).
By1596	Barley, William. *A New Booke of Tabliture.* 1596.
C	Cantus
C2	Cantus Secundus
1, 2 Camp[1613]	Campion, Thomas. *Two Bookes of Ayres.* N. d., *c.* 1613.
3, 4 Camp[1617]	Campion, Thomas. *The Third and Fourth Booke of Ayres.* N. d., *c.* 1617.

Cav1598	Cavendish, Michael. *14. Ayres.* 1598.
Ck1610	Corkine, William. *Ayres, To Sing and Play to the Lute and Basse Violl.* 1610.
Ck1612	Corkine, William. *The Second Booke of Ayres.* 1612.
Collier	Collier, John Payne, ed. *Lyrical Poems, Selected from Musical Publications between the Years 1589 and 1600.* London: the Percy Society, 1844.
Cop1606	Coprario, John. *Funeral Teares.* 1606.
Cop1613	Coprario, John. *Songs of Mourning . . . Worded by Tho. Campion.* 1613.
Ct	Countertenor
Dan1606	Danyel, John. *Songs for the Lute Viol and Voice.* 1606.
Davis	Davis, Walter R., ed. *The Works of Thomas Campion.* Garden City, N.Y.: Doubleday, 1967.
DNB	*The Dictionary of National Biography,* ed. Sir Leslie Stephen and Sir Sidney Lee. 22 vols. London: Oxford University Press, 1917–.
Do1597	Dowland, John. *The First Booke of Songes or Ayres.* 1597.
Do1600	Dowland, John. *The Second Booke of Songs or Ayres.* 1600.
Do1603	Dowland, John. *The Third and Last Booke of Songs or Aires.* 1603.
Do1612	Dowland, John. *A Pilgrimes Solace.* 1612.
Einstein	Einstein, Alfred. *The Italian Madrigal,* trans. A. H. Krappe, Roger Sessions, and Oliver Strunk. 3 vols. Princeton: Princeton University Press, 1949.
ELS	*The English Lute-Songs,* formerly *The English School of Lutenist Song Writers,* ed. E. H. Fellowes, now being revised and continued by T. Dart *et al.* London: Stainer & Bell. Series I: 17 vols. 1920–1959; Series II: 19 vols. 1925–1966.
EM	*The English Madrigalists,* formerly *The English Madrigal School,* ed. E. H. Fellowes, under revision by T. Dart *et al.* 36 vols. London: Stainer & Bell, 1913–1924.
EMV	*English Madrigal Verse,* ed. Edmund H. Fellowes. 3rd ed. revised by F. W. Sternfeld and David Greer. Oxford: Clarendon Press, 1967. (A few references specify the 2nd. ed., 1929.)
Fd1607	Ford, Thomas. *Musicke of Sundrie Kindes.* 1607.
Fer1609	Ferrabosco, Alfonso. *Ayres.* 1609.
Folger	Folger Shakespeare Library, Washington, D.C. (STC books in the Folger are catalogued by the STC number.)
Forbes	Forbes, John (printer). *Cantus, Songs and Fancies.* With an Introduction to Music by Thomas Davidson. Aberdeen, 1662 (2nd ed., 1666; 3rd ed., 1682).
Gardner	Gardner, Helen, ed. John Donne. *The Elegies and The Songs and Sonnets.* Oxford: Clarendon Press, 1965.
Gr1604	Greaves, Thomas. *Songes of sundrie kindes.* 1604.
Grierson	Herbert J. C. Grierson, ed. *The Poems of John Donne.* 2 vols. Oxford: Oxford University Press, 1912.
Grove	Grove, Sir George. *Dictionary of Music and Musicians.* 5th ed., ed. Eric Blom. 10 vols. London: Macmillan, 1954–1961.

HAH	Hughey, Ruth, ed. *The Arundel Harington Manuscript of Tudor Poetry.* 2 vols. Columbus: Ohio State University Press, 1960.
Han1609	Handford, George. *Ayres.* 1609. Trinity College, Cambridge, MS R.16.29.
Harl.	Harleian MSS, British Museum.
Hu1605	Hume, Tobias. *The First Part of Ayres.* 1605.
Hu1607	Hume, Tobias. *Captain Humes Poeticall Musicke.* 1607.
Hughes-Hughes	Hughes-Hughes, Augustus. *Catalogue of Manuscript Music in the British Museum,* 2 vols. London, 1906–1908.
Huntington	Henry E. Huntington Library and Art Gallery, San Marino, California.
Ing	Ing, Catherine. *Elizabethan Lyrics.* London: Chatto & Windus, 1951.
JAMS	*Journal of the American Musicological Society*
Jo1600	Jones, Robert. *The First Booke of Songes or Ayres.* 1600.
Jo1601	Jones, Robert. *The Second Booke of Songs and Ayres.* 1601.
Jo1605	Jones, Robert. *Vltimum Vale.* 1605.
Jo1609	Jones, Robert. *A Musicall Dreame.* 1609.
Jo1610	Jones, Robert. *The Muses Gardin for Delights.* 1610.
Jonson, *Works*	Herford, C. H., and Percy and Evelyn Simpson, eds. *Ben Jonson.* 11 vols. Oxford: Clarendon Press, 1925–1952.
Kerman	Kerman, Joseph. *The Elizabethan Madrigal.* New York: American Musicological Society, 1962.
Kökeritz	Kökeritz, Helge. *Shakespeare's Pronunciation.* New Haven: Yale University Press, 1953.
LSJ	*The Lute Society Journal*
M	Medius or Meane
M & L	*Music and Letters*
Ma1611	Maynard, John. *The XII. Wonders of the World.* 1611.
MB	*Musica Britannica.* 24 vols. London: Stainer & Bell for the Royal Musical Association, 1954–.
McK. & F.	McKerrow, R. B. and F. S. Ferguson. *Title-page Borders used in England and Scotland 1485–1640.* London: The Bibliographical Society, 1932.
McKerrow or McK.	McKerrow, Ronald B. *Printers' & Publishers' Devices in England & Scotland 1485–1640.* London: the Bibliographical Society, 1913.
MGG	Blume, Friedrich, ed. *Die Musik in Geschichte und Gegenwart.* 13 vols., in progress. Kassel and Basel: Bärenreiter, 1949–.
MLN	*Modern Language Notes*
Mo1600	Morley, Thomas. *The First Booke of Ayres.* 1600.
MP	*Modern Philology*
N & Q	*Notes and Queries*
Nichols, *Progresses of James I*	Nichols, John. *The Progresses, Processions, and Magnificent Festivities, of King James the First.* 4 vols. London, 1828.
NLS	National Library of Scotland, Edinburgh
Obertello	Obertello, Alfredo. *Madrigali Italiani in Inghilterra.* Milan: Valentino Bompiani, 1949.

OED	*Oxford English Dictionary*
Pattison	Pattison, Bruce. *Music and Poetry of the English Renaissance.* London: Methuen, 1948.
Pi1605	Pilkington, Francis. *The First Booke of Songs or Ayres.* 1605.
Plomer	Plomer, Henry R. *English Printers' Ornaments.* London: Grafton, 1924.
PRMA	*Proceedings of the Royal Musical Association*
Puttenham	Puttenham, George. *The Arte of English Poesie,* ed. Gladys Willcock and Alice Walker. Cambridge: University Press, 1936.
Q	Quintus
RAAD	Rollins, Hyder E., ed. *The Arbor of Amorous Devices.* Cambridge, Mass.: Harvard University Press, 1936.
Rawl.	Rawlinson MSS, Bodleian
RBBD	Rollins, Hyder E., ed. *Brittons Bowre of Delights.* Cambridge, Mass.: Harvard University Press, 1933.
RCM	Royal College of Music, London
RD01610	Dowland, Robert. *A Musicall Banquet.* 1610.
Reese	Reese, Gustave. *Music in the Renaissance.* New York: W. W. Norton, revised ed., 1959.
REH	Rollins, Hyder E., ed. *England's Helicon.* 2 vols. Cambridge, Mass.: Harvard University Press, 1935.
RES	*Review of English Studies*
Ringler	Ringler, William A., ed. *The Poems of Sir Philip Sidney.* Oxford: Clarendon Press, 1962.
RN	*Renaissance News*
Ros1601	Rosseter, Philip (and Thomas Campion). *A Booke of Ayres.* 1601.
Rosenbach	Philip and A.S.W. Rosenbach Foundation Museum and Library, Philadelphia
RPN	Rollins, Hyder E., ed. *The Phoenix Nest.* Cambridge, Mass.: Harvard University Press, 1931.
RPR	Rollins, Hyder E., ed. *A Poetical Rhapsody.* 2 vols. Cambridge, Mass.: Harvard University Press, 1931–1932.
Rubsamen	Rubsamen, W. H. "Scottish and English Music of the Renaissance in a Newly-Discovered Manuscript," *Festschrift Heinrich Besseler.* Leipzig: Institut für Musikwissenschaft, 1961, pp. 259–284.
Seng	Seng, Peter. *The Vocal Songs in the Plays of Shakespeare.* Cambridge, Mass.: Harvard University Press, 1967.
Simpson	Simpson, Claude M. *The British Broadside Ballad and Its Music.* New Brunswick: Rutgers University Press, 1966.
SR	Stationers' Register. *See* Arber.
SR	*Studies in the Renaissance*
STC	Pollard, A. W. and G. R. Redgrave, *A Short-Title Catalogue of Books Printed in England, Scotland, and Ireland 1475–1640.* London: The Bibliographical Society, 1926.
Stevens	Stevens, John. *Music and Poetry in the Early Tudor Court.* London: Methuen, 1961.
T	Tenor

Tenbury	St. Michael's College, Tenbury Wells
Tilley	Tilley, Morris P. *A Dictionary of the Proverbs in England in the Sixteenth and Seventeenth Centuries.* Ann Arbor: University of Michigan Press, 1950.
Tx	Triplex
Vivian	Vivian, Percival, ed. *Campion's Works.* Oxford: Clarendon Press, 1909.
Warlock	Warlock, Peter (pseud. for Philip Heseltine). *The English Ayre.* London: Oxford University Press, 1926.
Williams	Williams, Franklin B., Jr. *Index of Dedications and Commendatory Verses in English Books before 1641.* London: The Bibliographical Society, 1962.

Lyrics from English Airs

Introduction
The Composers
Editorial Procedure

Nquiet thoughts your ciuill slaughter stint, & wrap your wrongs

within à pensiue hart: And you my tongue that maks my mouth a minte, & stamps my

thoughts to coyne them words by arte: Be still for if you euer doo the like, Ile cut the

string, ij. that maks the hammer strike.

But what can staie my thoughts they may not start, How shall I then gaze on my mistresse eies?
Or put my tongue in durance for to dye? My thoughts must haue some vët els hart wil break,
When as these eies the keyes of mouth and harte My tongue would rust as in my mouth it lies
Open the locke where all my loue doth lye; If eyes and thoughts were free and that not speake.
Ile seale them vp within their lids for euer, Speake then and tell the passions of desire
So thoughts & words and looks shall dye together, Which turns mine eies to floods, my th oghts tofire

Introduction

During the years between the time Joyce's Stephen Dedalus took pleasure from the "grave and mocking music of the lutenists" and the time Kingsley Amis' Lucky Jim painfully faked the tenor part of one of Bartlet's airs (Bt1606.III), many of the poems in this collection, as well as their musical settings, have become so familiar as to need little introduction. But the reader who is not a music historian might not object to a brief consideration of the musical context and some reminders of the parallels between music and poetry during the sixteenth and early seventeenth centuries. The obvious place to begin is with a definition of the air: it is generally regarded as a solo song with lute accompaniment. Although this was perhaps the most usual mode of performance, what distinguishes the air is the presence of a dominant melodic part, which *may* be accompanied by the lute. Actually, the accompaniment may take many forms.

Although four airs with bandora accompaniment had been published in 1596 by William Barley, the first book of airs printed in the format that became standard until 1622 was John Dowland's *First Booke of Songes or Ayres of fowre partes with Tableture for the Lute: So made that all the partes together, or either of them seuerally may be song to the Lute, Orpherian or Viol de gambo* (1597). As the full title indicates, the purchaser of the book could perform the songs in several possible ways. He could sing the Cantus part as a solo, accompanying himself on the lute, orpharion, or viol; or he could, with three friends, sing the songs as *a cappella* part-songs, because tenor, bass, and alto parts were arranged on the page facing the Cantus and tablature so that all the singers sitting around a table could read from one book; or the part-singers could be joined by instrumentalists. The title pages of later collections show that some composers intended that both the lute and the viol should accompany the solo voice, while some also indicated that a consort of viols could play the accompanying voice parts. Some performers may have played the songs on instruments alone, for the title pages of some fifteen sets of madrigals stated that they were "apt for both Viols and Voyces," and there is no reason to suppose airs would be treated differently in this regard.

It is necessary, however, to make some distinctions between airs and other vocal forms such as madrigals, canzonets, ballets, and chansons, since these frequently involve differences in the nature of the lyrics. In Italy, the madrigal developed from the relatively simple four-part songs of the early sixteenth century to elaborate, subtle compositions of five or six parts in which each voice is of more or less equal importance and in which great pains were taken to enhance and illustrate the sense and emotions of the words through the music. The great master of this later style is Luca Marenzio (1553–1599). English madrigalists such as Morley, Wilbye, and Weelkes usually wrote in a style roughly corresponding to Marenzio's, but were never so adventurous; the popularity of the rather old-fashioned madrigals of Alfonso Ferrabosco the elder was a conservative influence. The experimental and mannered styles of such early seventeenth-century Italian composers as Gesualdo and Monteverdi find few parallels in England.

The madrigals of the English composers could be both chordal and contrapuntal, but are not, like the air, accompanied melody. The texts of madrigals are usually single stanzas; if the poem had more than one stanza, it was set straight through, not strophically like the air. In the English madrigal at least, the texts are often inconsequential as poetry because their main function was to provide syllables for singing, words simply naming a mood or action or emotion that the composer could exploit. Since the different voices were often singing different words simultaneously, the sense of the words was frequently obscured to all but the singers themselves. This is not said to condemn the madrigal but to define its appeal, which is mainly musical; like other chamber music, it was composed for performers rather than for audiences. The air, especially when performed as an accompanied solo, is more likely to be sung to an audience. It appeals to literary as well as musical interests because the music allows the words to be heard and understood, and because the words are frequently more satisfying as poetry than the madrigal verses. Composers of airs may have been influenced, as we shall see later, by humanistic and Reformation theories about the relationship of words and music, but practical considerations apply as well. If the words deserve to be heard, a composer is likely to be moved to set them to music which will allow them to be heard; conversely, if a composer prefers musical forms in which the words can be heard, he will probably select words he thinks worth hearing. The generalization that poetry in the books of airs is more interesting does not always hold, of course, but I think it is true enough to justify the attention they receive in this edition.

Although Thomas Morley had published original madrigals in the Italian style three years before Dowland's airs, the latter represent the older tradition in England. The immediate ancestors of the air were the homophonic part-song and the solo song accompanied by a consort of viols.[1] The "consort song" is strophic, and typically consists of a melodic vocal line free of written out embellishments and usually with only one note per syllable of text, to which the accompanying parts provide a polyphonic foundation, moving more rapidly and filling in rests between the phrases of the voice. Some of the surviving consort songs date from as early as the 1560's (*e.g.*, "Pandulpho" by Robert Parsons, who died in 1570).[2] Other examples may be found in the only English secular songs printed between 1530 and 1588, Thomas Whythorne's *Songes, for three, fower and fiue voyces* (1571); in the secular volumes of William Byrd (1588, 1589, and 1611); and here and there among the madrigal volumes, *e.g.*, "If floods of tears" in Thomas Bateson's *Second Set of Madrigals* (1618), No. XII. Some of these consort

---

[1] For full references to many of the items cited in these notes see the list of abbreviations above. The background of the air is discussed by Pattison, pp. 113–140; Reese, pp. 815–819, 835–841; and Denis Stevens in *A History of Song* (London: Hutchinson, 1960), pp. 79–86. See also Ulrich Olshausen's *Das Lautenbegleitete Sololied in England um 1600* (Frankfurt am Main: Johann Wolfgang Goethe Universität, 1963), and Richard J. McGrady's dissertation, "The English Solo Song from William Byrd to Henry Lawes," University of Manchester, 1963. A study by David Greer is in progress.

[2] See the unsigned article by G. E. P. Arkwright, "Early Elizabethan Stage Music," *Musical Antiquary*, I (1909), 30–40, IV (1912), 112–117. A number of these consort songs have been printed from MSS by "Peter Warlock" (Philip Heseltine) in *The First [Second, Third] Book of Elizabethan Songs . . . for one voice to sing and four stringed instruments to accompany* (Oxford, 1926), 3 vols., and more will be included in the forthcoming Vol. XXII of *Musica Britannica*, ed. Philip Brett.

songs are extant in arrangements for voice and tablature—Parsons' "Pandulpho," for one, in King's College Cambridge, Rowe MS 2, for voice and bass lute—and some lute songs were arranged as consort songs (*e.g.*, Do1600. III). All the songs in Byrd's *Psalmes, Sonets, & Songs* (1588) were, as Byrd tells the reader, "orginally made for Instruments to expresse the harmonie, and one voyce to pronounce the dittie," but they "are now framed in all parts for voyces to sing the same." In other words, consort songs are printed as part-songs—but they are not madrigals.[3] Thomas Whythorne, in his *Autobiography* (ed. James M. Osborn, Oxford, 1961) as well as in his music, testifies to the variety of ways one could perform a song. Writing of his life around 1550 he says, "In thes daies I yuzed to sing my songs and sonets sumtym to the liut and sumtyms the virginals" (p. 51). Around 1565, he taught a lady "to sing to liut," and one of the songs she learned was Whythorne's own "If thow that hast A faithfull frend" which he had printed in 1571 as a part-song (pp. 165–166, 309).

Consort songs, part-songs, and lute songs, sharing the common features of a dominant melodic part and a strophic setting of the text, sometimes have their distinctions blurred. But on a spectrum running from the most idiomatic consort songs to the most idiomatic part-songs, the melodic part becomes less distinguishable from the other voices. The lute songs published in the books of airs can move rather far in both directions along this spectrum. The airs printed without an alternative part-song arrangement—some by Cavendish in 1598, Dowland in 1600 and later, Morley in 1600, and John Danyel in 1606—are more closely related to the consort song. The lute accompaniments of some look like transcriptions of polyphonic viol parts, and others that are more in the lute idiom, that are more chordal with fewer voices moving at the same time, were clearly not derived from singing parts. Other airs are sometimes better as part-songs than as instrumentally accompanied solos. All the songs in Dowland's *First Booke* have alternative part-song versions, some of which sound as if that were their original form. Some are more homophonic than anything in Byrd. The ancestors of this kind of air are harder to find in England, mainly because of the scarcity of secular music that can be dated between Whythorne's 1571 collection and the songbooks of Henry VIII's time. But with the help of John Stevens' *Music and Poetry in the Early Tudor Court* (London: Methuen, 1961), it is possible to find a few elements of the air in these early songbooks.

[3] For further comment on Byrd, see Kerman, pp. 101–117.

Many early part-songs, especially those by sophisticated composers like Fayrfax and Cornish, would seem to have little connection with the air. These songs are linear, frequently use points of imitation, and often have long melismas between phrases. Reese (p. 768) even calls them chansons and compares them to the songs of late fifteenth-century composers like Ockeghem. But other songs, many by Henry VIII himself, are simple, chordal, with little or no counterpoint or florid vocalization. This second type of song is essentially harmonized melody, usually in three parts, and in some instances the melody is a popular tune. For example, the tune of "Pastime with good company," attributed to Henry in two MSS, is known in several contemporary continental versions as "De mon triste desplaisir" and is probably of popular origin.[4]

Of more immediate influence on the air as part-song is a later kind of French chanson, which, like the songs of Henry VIII, is usually homophonic and gives a syllabic and strophic setting of the text. Now it is true that the Italian *frottola* and the early madrigal often shared these characteristics. *Frottole* were even arranged as lute-accompanied solos as early as 1509, the date of Franciscus Bossinensis' *Tenori e contrabassi intabulati col sopran in canto figurato per cantar e sonar col lauto*, and some of Verdelot's madrigals were printed in similar arrangements in *Intavolatura de li Madrigali di Verdelotto da cantare et sonare nel Lauto* (Venice, 1540). Moreover, Italian music books were known to be in a few English households by 1552.[5] But other evidence suggests that French influence on the air was stronger and more direct.

First, two of the very few music books printed in England before 1588 contained French chansons: one, *Recuil du Mellange d'Orlande de Lassus*, was printed by the Huguenot immigrant Thomas Vautrollier in 1570; the other, the second English version of Adrian LeRoy's *A briefe and plaine Instruction to set all Musicke of eight divers tunes in Tableture for the Lute* (1574), contained arrangements for solo lute of eleven songs by Lassus (six of which had been included in Vautrollier's collection), thirteen by Nicholas de la Grotte, and a few by Arcadelt, LeRoy, and others.[6] Most are homophonic, with strophic texts set syllabically; thus it is not surprising to find that many of the same songs had been printed in arrangements for solo voice and lute in LeRoy's *Livre d'Airs*

[4] John Ward, "The Lute Music of MS Royal Appendix 58," *JAMS*, XIII (1960), 123.
[5] Walter L. Woodfill cites household accounts in *Musicians in English Society from Elizabeth to Charles I* (Princeton, 1953), pp. 256, 264.
[6] F. W. Sternfeld, "Vautrollier's Printing of Lasso's *Recueil du Mellange*," *Annales Musicologiques*, V (1957), 207.

de Cour miz sur le Luth (1571). LeRoy states in the dedication to this volume that the songs he refers to as *airs de cour* used to be called *voix-de-ville*.[7] The history of the *voix-de-ville* suggests some more specific links between French and English airs, especially the airs of Dowland.

The term *voix-de-ville* was first applied to certain monophonic popular tunes, to which more serious musicians later gave settings in parts.[8] The next step was to arrange these part-songs for accompanied solo, and in 1556 Adrian LeRoy published his *Second Livre de Guiterre, Contenant Plusieurs Chansons en forme de voix de ville: nouvellement remises en tablature.* These songs are simple, strophic, one-note-per-syllable settings of the texts, with simple chordal accompaniments in tablature for the four-stringed guitar or *guiterne*. Significantly, a dance is indicated for most of the songs and others are marked "A Plaisir." A number are *branles*, others are galliards or pavans. Several of Dowland's songs are extant in independent dance versions—"Can shee excuse" (Do1597.V) is "The Earle of Essex Galiard," and "Flow my teares" (Do1600.II) is the famous "Lachrimae" pavan—and in one instance, the similarity of one of Dowland's songs to a *voix-de-ville* is quite striking. Dowland's setting of "Now O now" (Do1597.VI), known separately as the "Frog Galliard," follows the seven-syllable trochaic lines of the text with great exactness, a whole note for a stressed syllable, a half note for an unstressed syllable, in triple time; the accompaniment is plain and chordal. This description also fits one of the *branles* in LeRoy's collection, "Quand j'entens le perdu temps" (sigs. B4v-C1). Dowland's melody in some places seems merely an inversion of the French tune, but the whole is not close enough to suggest direct imitation of this particular song.[9]

Another piece of evidence concerns the song ascribed to "Tesseir" in the collection compiled by Dowland's son Robert. As the note on this

[7] Reprinted in *Chansons au Luth et Airs de Cour Français du XVIe Siècle*, ed. Lionel de la Laurencie, Adrienne Mairy, and G. Thibault (Paris: Société Française de Musicologie, 1934), pp. xxv–xxvi; the songs are on pp. 133–175.

[8] For more on the *voix-de-ville*, see Reese, pp. 389–390; Julien Tiersot, *Histoire de la Chanson Populaire en France* (1889), pp. 229–230; François Lesure, "Éléments Populaires dans la Chanson Français au Début du XVIe Siècle," and Kenneth J. Levy, "Vaudeville, vers mesurés et airs de Cour," both in *Musique et Poésie au XVIe Siècle*, Colloques Internationaux du Centre National de la Recherche Scientifique (Paris, 1954), pp. 169–201; and Howard M. Brown, *Music in the French Secular Theater, 1400–1550* (Cambridge: Harvard University Press, 1963), pp. 105–109, 130, 138.

[9] For another *voix-de-ville* that resembles Dowland's song, see Thurston Dart, "Role de la Danse dans l'Ayre Anglais," *Musique et Poésie* (see note 8), p. 207.

song (RD01610.VII) points out, the music arranged as a lute song was originally printed in Guillaume Tessier's *Premier Livre D'Airs* in a version for four voices. This book was published in 1582, when we know that John Dowland was in Paris,[10] and it is not unreasonable to assume that he studied this and other collections of *airs de cour* then. Like the English airs, many *airs de cour* were published both as part-songs and as accompanied solos, but not in the same volume (see notes to RD01610. XI, XII, and At1622.I).

Nevertheless, it is very difficult to identify exclusively French elements in the English air, or assemble more than circumstantial evidence of influence. Italian influence is much easier to spot, even though its effect on the air is mostly superficial. The first characteristic that comes to mind as being Italianate is the practice of "word-painting," or illustrating the sense of the text by musical conventions. As the madrigalist Thomas Morley instructs in his *Plaine and Easie Introduction to Practicall Musicke* (1597, sig. Aa2v), "You must have a care that when your matter signifieth ascending, high heaven, and such like, you make your musicke ascend: and by the contrarie, where your dittie speaketh of descending loweness, depth, hell, and other such, you must make your musicke descend." The English composers, including the madrigalists, were usually more restrained than the Italians in the use of such conventions, and there is very little of the hyper-subtle "eye music" in which even the best Italians indulged.[11] A number of examples might be cited, but Dowland's "Sorrow stay" (D01600.III) is an obvious choice because of its descending notes on "downe, down, down I fall." (A more extreme device in D01612.XI is explained in the note.) Another indication of Italian influence is the madrigal-like breaking up of lines into short, repeated phrases. This repetition sometimes occurs in through-composed airs, but the strophic form of most of the others prevents the composers from repeating many phrases except in refrains.

Of course madrigals on the model of the elder Ferrabosco's appear in the collections of Cavendish and Greaves, and some of the airs are very close to being four-part madrigals (*e.g.*, D01612.XIIII–XVI). Other Italian forms may have had some effect on the air as well. Morley's description of *balletti* recalls the *voix-de-ville* and Dowland's

---

[10] Letter to Sir Robert Cecil, Cecil Papers 172.91, Hatfield House, printed by the Historical Manuscripts Commission, *Calendar of the Manuscripts of the ... Marquis of Salisbury*, V (1894), 445–447, and by Warlock, *The English Ayre*, pp. 24–27.

[11] See Einstein, I, 234–244.

dance songs when he says they are "songs, which being song to a dittie may likewise be daunced: these and all other kinds of light musicke sauing the *Madrigal* are by a generall name called ayres" (*Introduction*, sig. Aa3v). Morley goes on to discuss a more well-defined kind of *balletto* developed by Gastoldi which has a characteristic structure and a "fa-la" refrain. Many of Morley's most famous "madrigals" are *balletti* from his *First Booke of Balletts* (1595), an edition of which was published at the same time with Italian words.[12] Other composers such as Thomas Weelkes and John Hilton followed Morley in writing *balletti*, and there are even a few clear examples among the airs (Jo1609. VI and Gr1604.XXI). It is interesting to find Morley providing lute accompaniments for the Cantus parts of all but five of his *Canzonets or Little Short Aers* (1597); but critics find only one of these canzonets satisfactory as a lute song.[13] Although Italian canzonets are usually strophic, Morley's are not, and at times only brevity and the characteristic repetition of the first and third strains distinguishes them from light madrigals. The Cantus therefore rarely has the dominant melody found in the air. Perhaps, as Kerman and Greer suggest, Morley was shrewdly competing with Dowland's popular *First Booke*, published the same year, as well as fulfilling his stated purpose of providing lute parts for the solitary amusement of his patron.

Italian influence of another sort is said to have been the main cause of the change in English song between Dowland and Henry Lawes.[14] The presence of four (actually five) Italian songs in Robert Dowland's *A Musicall Banquet* is seen as symptomatic, especially since the songs by Megli and Caccini are monodies of the sort advocated by the Florentine Camerata. The Camerata's efforts to reproduce the legendary effects of ancient music led its members to believe that the music should reproduce the emotional content as well as the natural rhythms and accents of the verse. Only the solo voice with a simple accompaniment should be used, and counterpoint should be abandoned because it would obscure the words.[15] In practice, Caccini's music was declamatory rather

[12] The texts are edited by Obertello, pp. 346–372.

[13] Kerman, pp. 165–167; David Greer, "The Lute Songs of Thomas Morley," *LSJ*, VIII (1966), 26–27.

[14] Pattison, pp. 136–140; McDonald Emslie, "Nicholas Lanier's Innovations in English Song," *M & L*, XLI (1960), 13–27; and Vincent Duckles, "English Song and the Challenge of Italian Monody," in *Words to Music* (Los Angeles: Clark Library, 1967), 3–42.

[15] Pattison, pp. 123–127; see also D. P. Walker, "Musical Humanism in the 16th and Early 17th Centuries," *Music Review*, II (1941), 1–13, 111–121, 220–227, 288–308; III (1942), 55–71; Claude V. Palisca, *Girolamo Mei: Letters on Ancient and Modern Music to Vincenzo Galilei and Giovanni Bardi* (American Institute of Musicology, Studies and

than melodic, and dramatic expressiveness replaced madrigalian word-painting. Trills, runs, and other flourishes were used extensively for expressive purposes. As several writers have noticed, John Dowland's "In darknesse let mee dwell" (RDo1610.X) contains some striking declamatory passages which seem to reflect the examples in Caccini's *Nuove Musiche* (1602). But Marenzio was capable of such declamation (Einstein, II, 682–3), and according to the epistle of Do1597, it was to study with Marenzio that Dowland went to Italy. Nevertheless, Caccini's work seems to have been fairly well known in England in the early 1600's (see the note to RDo1610.XIX), and the presence of declamatory passages in an earlier song like "Sorrow stay" (Do1600. III) may reflect an encounter with Caccini's songs during Dowland's visit to the Florentine court in 1595.

Influence of the Italian monodies is more evident in songs like "Lasso vita mia" (Do1612.XI), or in the two settings of Petrarch by Robert Jones (Jo1609.XX, XXI), the first of which contains some melismatic embellishment of a sort Dowland almost never uses. The expatriate Italian Angelo Notari published his *Prime Musiche Nuoue* in England in 1613, and this collection of monodies, duets, and canzonettas may have had some effect on English composers.[16] Furthermore, Alfonso Ferrabosco the younger, Coprario, Nicholas Lanier, and Robert Johnson are frequently cited as Italianate innovators, and it is true that these composers developed a more declamatory kind of solo song. Yet Ian Spink has convincingly argued that this new style probably grew out of the special requirements of the drama, especially the masque, with Italian influence only secondary. All the composers just named are known to have composed music for plays and masques. According to Spink, the masque demanded a "simple, ceremonial, heroic, rather pretentious type of song," for which the subtleties of lute song were too intimate.[17]

Thus although the English air was not impervious to foreign influences, it remained a basically native form which changed but stayed within a recognizably continuous tradition. The nature of both the changes and the continuity may be clarified by examining the parallel development of the kinds of poems the songwriters chose.

Documents No. 3, 1960); and Palisca's articles in *Musical Quarterly*, XL (1954), 1–20, and XLVI (1960), 344–360.

[16]Ian Spink, "Angelo Notari and his 'Prime Musiche Nuove'," *Monthly Musical Record*, LXXXVII (1957), 168–177.

[17]"English Cavalier Songs, 1620–1660," *PRMA*, LXXXVI (1960), 64 ff.

II

The books of airs, madrigals, and part-songs are second only to the poetical miscellanies as sources of the lyric verse of the period. In a sense, these songbooks are themselves poetical miscellanies, and I would suggest that the poems from the songbooks can be most profitably studied as part of the miscellany tradition. The earliest miscellany, *The Court of Venus*, was probably first printed around 1537, and after that new collections or new editions of old collections followed with shorter and shorter intervals between them until 1602, the date of *A Poetical Rhapsody*. Although new editions or reissues of the *Rhapsody* appeared in 1608, 1611, and 1621, *The Paradise of Dainty Devices* (1576) in 1606, and *England's Helicon* (1600) in 1614, no new miscellany was published between 1602 and 1614, the date of William Browne's *The Shepheard's Pipe*. Moreover, Browne's collection and the few that followed it are quite different from their Elizabethan ancestors. Meanwhile, between 1588 and 1632, over eighty books of secular songs were printed, thirty-three of which appeared between 1602 and 1614 at the rate of at least one new book a year. Twenty-two of these books contained airs. It may be significant that the number of airs, with their greater literary appeal, increased in proportion to the number of madrigals and part-songs printed after the last miscellany. I have excluded from consideration as miscellanies brief collections of memorial or festive verse, which are frequently not even in English; but memorial volumes such as those on Edward Lewkenor (1606) or Prince Henry (1612) have counterparts in the airs of John Coprario, who published *Funeral Teares. For the death of . . . the Earle of Deuonshire* in 1606, and *Songs of Mourning: Bewailing the vntimely death of Prince Henry* in 1613.[1]

If the songbooks can indeed be considered a continuation of the miscellanies, the literary position of the air can be clarified, and what might seem an odd hiatus in the production and consumption of lyrics in a decade full of literary activity can be explained. This idea might also offer some new perspectives from which to view the controversial changes in lyric styles in the late sixteenth and early seventeenth centuries.

The debates over what styles are in the "main line" of English poetry are among the most familiar of modern criticism. They began

---

[1] See Vincent Duckles, "The English Musical Elegy of the Late Renaissance," *Aspects of Medieval and Renaissance Music*, ed. Jan LaRue (New York: W. W. Norton, 1966) pp. 134–153.

with the Donne revival, and have continued on other grounds in the quarrels between C. S. Lewis and Yvor Winters and their disciples over the relative merits of "drab" and "golden" or "plain" and "Petrarchan" or "ornamented" poetry. Winters has made a selection of what, to him, are the best poems from the songbooks, and Lewis has written appreciatively of Campion.[2] But the most recent and detailed study (which follows Winters), Douglas L. Peterson's *The English Lyric from Wyatt to Donne* (Princeton, 1967), says very little about Campion's poems and the other song lyrics, or even about the important subject of metrical developments. Although what follows is not intended to be polemical, I hope it will serve to supplement studies such as Peterson's, for the parallels between the music and poetry should not be overlooked. With a good deal of over-simplification, the case may be stated thus: a "plain" style was dominant in the middle years of the sixteenth century, followed by a period dominated by French- and Italian-inspired "eloquent," "ornamented," or "Petrarchan" poetry, which then merged with the plain style in the work of Greville, Donne, and Jonson; in music, the "plain" style could be that of the psalms and ballads and the native consort song, the "ornamented" style that of the Italianate madrigal, and the merged styles could be found in the airs of Dowland and Campion. Of course the truth of the matter is not so neat, for several styles—not just "plain" and "eloquent"—can be found flourishing at the same time and even in the same poet or composer; besides, there was a good deal of continuity, as a more detailed survey will show.

The Tudor miscellanies contain a great variety of verse. Yet they are mainly repositories of short poems, lyrics or epigrams; they always contain some anonymous poems; and some poems in every volume were either set to music, written to a tune, or are at least suitable for singing. *The Court of Venus* is known to us only in three fragments representing three editions dated roughly 1537–1539, 1547–1549, and 1561–1564. They contain six lyrics usually attributed to Wyatt, plus a few others by unknown contemporaries.[3] Wyatt's verse and that of

[2] Yvor Winters, "The 16th Century Lyric in England," *Poetry*, LIII (1939), 258–272, 320–335; LIV (1939), 35–51. C. S. Lewis, *English Literature in the Sixteenth Century* (Oxford, 1954), pp. 64–65, 222–271, 551–558, and elsewhere. See also John Williams' introduction to *English Renaissance Poetry* (Garden City: Doubleday Anchor, 1963).

[3] Russell A. Fraser, ed., *The Court of Venus* (Durham: Duke University Press, 1955), pp. 11, 33–35; some of Fraser's conclusions are qualified by Charles A. Huttar, "Wyatt and the Several Editions of *The Court of Venus*," *Studies in Bibliography*, XIX (1966), 181–195.

Henry Howard, Earl of Surrey make up the bulk of the next miscellany, the famous *Songes and Sonettes* printed in 1557 by Richard Tottel. Many of the lyrics of Wyatt and Surrey were probably sung, but how they were is just now a subject of controversy. At present, it must suffice to say that Wyatt probably intended his songs to be sung to popular tunes such as those given part-settings in Henry VIII's songbook (BM MS Add. 31922), perhaps with a simple lute accompaniment; or to improvised tunes based on grounds such as the *folía* or the *romanesca*, a practice Wyatt may have brought back from Italy along with the originals of many of his poems. (One of his sources, Serafino d'Aquila, was a famous *improvvisatore*.) Other than references to the lute and singing in the poems themselves, evidence for such musical associations dating from Wyatt's lifetime is almost nil; but by the 1550's, the date of the earliest scraps of musical evidence, it is clear that Wyatt's and Surrey's poems are being sung.[4]

Further evidence that *The Court of Venus* and Tottel's *Songes and Sonettes* served some readers as songbooks is provided indirectly by John Hall's *The Court of Virtue* (1565). The title is obviously a dig at *The Court of Venus*, and the subtitle, which promises "Many holy or spretuall songes Sonettes psalmes ballettes" echoes Tottel's *Songes and Sonettes*. Hall's bias is made clear in his Prologue:

> Suche as in carnall loue reioyce,
> Trim songes of loue they wyll compile,
> And synfully with tune and voyce
> They syng their songes in pleasant stile,
> To Venus that same strompet vyle:
> And make of hir a goddes dere,
> In lecherie that had no pere.
>
> A booke also of songes they haue,
> And Venus court they doe it name.
> No fylthy mynde a songe can craue,
> But therin he may finde the same:
> And in suche songes is all their game.[5]

---

[4] The evidence is presented by the most informed voices in the controversy: Stevens, pp. 27–28, 124–143; John Ward, "Music for *A Handefull of pleasant delites*" and "Lute Music of MS Royal Appendix 58," *JAMS*, X (1957), 151–180, and XIII (1960), 117–125; and Winifred Maynard, "The Lyrics of Wyatt: Poems or Songs?" *RES*, XVI (1965), 1–13.

[5] *The Court of Virtue*, ed. Russell A. Fraser (New Brunswick: Rutgers University Press, 1961), p. 15.

Hall includes moral parodies of two of Wyatt's poems from *The Court of Venus*, "My lute awake" and "My penne take payne." Significantly, Hall provides his verses with thirty-one tunes of a psalm-like flavor, each usually serving for several sets of words. Stevens gives Hall's music for "My lute awake" and the earliest music associated with Wyatt's original, some lute tablature based on the *folía* (p. 137). But the two are not related, except in the ways ballad tunes and psalm tunes are related in general.

Returning for a closer look at the *Songes and Sonettes*, we may note that Tottel himself does not emphasize the musical associations. In his preface, he stresses the "honor of the Englishe tong," and the "profit of the studious of Englishe eloquence."[6] As part of his notorious tidying-up of meter and form, Tottel or his editor omits the refrains in several poems. Of the ninety-seven poems by Wyatt, only about a quarter are "ballets," or the stanzaic poems usually associated with singing. And of the rest, Nicholas Grimald's forty poems seem to have no musical associations at all, and only nine of the poems by Surrey and others are known to have tunes. Yet an examination of those nine poems reveals that ballets are not the only poems we may expect to be sung. One, "Lyke as the lark" (No. 173), is an English sonnet. Music for this poem (a version in five quatrains) appears in Forbes' *Cantus* (1662), sig. L1, along with many songs composed much earlier than the date of publication, and the music is known in a keyboard version dating *c.* 1570.[7] Moreover, it was parodied in *The Court of Virtue* (pp. 233–234; also in quatrains). Perhaps Wyatt's and Surrey's sonnets were sung, as sonnets were in Italy; and possibly the epigrammatic translations of Serafino's *strambotti* (*e.g.*, No. 54), or of poems found in Italian music books (*e.g.*, No. 53), were also sung.[8]

More significantly, four of the poems are in poulter's measure couplets (Nos. 18, 201, 251, 265) and one, Vaux's famous "I lothe that I did loue" (No. 212), is in four-line stanzas which are essentially poulter's measure couplets with internal rhyme. Poulter's and fourteeners are

[6] *Tottel's Miscellany*, ed. Hyder E. Rollins (Cambridge, Mass.: Harvard University Press, rev. ed., 1965), I, 2.

[7] *E.g.*, Tottel No. 265, "If care do cause men cry" (Forbes, sigs. A1–A2). See Ward, "Music for *A Handefull*," p. 179, n. 100. For the keyboard version of "Lyke as the Lark," see *The Dublin Virginal Manuscript*, ed. John Ward (Wellesley, Mass.: Wellesley Editions No. 3, 1954), No. 24 and note.

[8] See Ivy L. Mumford, "Sir Thomas Wyatt's Verse and Italian Musical Sources," *English Miscellany*, XIV (1963), 9–26, and Joel Newman, "An Italian Source for Wyatt's *Madame, withouten many wordes*," *RN*, X (1957), 13–15.

the usual meters of broadside ballads. No. 251 was printed as a ballad, to be sung to "A rich marchant man" or "John come kiss me now," and the first lines of Nos. 16, 18, 211, 212, and 265 became the names of the ballad tunes to which they were sung. According to John Ward, the manner of singing broadside ballads seems to have its origin, not with the vulgar, but with the courtly: "Not until mid-century do ballad tunes begin to be mentioned; most of the early examples are associated with poems of high quality, like those of Tottel's *Songes and Sonettes*, and seem to be products of a court fashion for singing lyric poetry to the lute. This fashion seems, in turn, to have inspired the popular art of singing broadside ballads in England." [9] To follow the broadside ballad from Tottel to the end of the century is to follow the progressive vulgarization of one kind of poetry for singing. By the 1590's its social status had become more or less fixed, and most ballad makers, however briskly they might present news and narratives, made few pretensions to art. In the interim the appeal of the ballad was somewhat broader. The next miscellany to appear after Tottel's was Clement Robinson's *A Handful of Pleasant Delights*, which consists entirely of ballads. This collection was first published in 1566, an edition now lost, and a slightly expanded version was printed in 1584. Rollins has noted that most of the ballads were known in separate broadsides by 1566.[10] Nevertheless, the nature of the poems is so different from expectations based on the later broadsides that Douglas Peterson says (p. 127) that to describe them as "a collection of broadside ballads of the sort hawked on the London streets" is incorrect. It is true that they are not topical, are mostly lyrical and amatory, and that the only two narratives are out of Ovid. Yet they are more "popular" than the verse in Tottel. All but five of the thirty-two poems fit the description on the title page which states that each is "orderly pointed to his proper Tune," and only in the case of the first poem is there no evidence that it was sung (see Ward, p. 155). Of the thirty-two poems, three are in poulter's measure, four are in fourteeners (common or ballad meter), and three are in stanzas combining poulter's measure and fourteener couplets. These are printed, like ballads, in short-line stanzas. Despite a growing preference for these meters and rigidity in other meters and stanza forms, it is still possible to find poems whose tune forces them into

[9] Ward, "Music for *A Handefull*," p. 179; see also Albert B. Friedman, *The Ballad Revival* (Chicago, 1961), pp. 44–45.

[10] *A Handful of Pleasant Delights*, ed. Hyder E. Rollins (Cambridge, Mass.: Harvard University Press, 1924), pp. xiv–xv.

novelty. "Attend thee, go play thee" (pp. 12–14), with its alternating anapestic and iambic lines of varying length, and its feminine rhymes, looks forward to the 1590's—and back to "Alisoun." In the next two miscellanies, broadside ballads continue to be found in company—and at home—with "literary" poetry, as in Tottel. *The Paradise of Dainty Devices* (1576–1606) contains seven poems published as broadsides, and others seem to have been so intended.[11] Four of the broadsides are in fourteeners, and one is in poulter's measure; the other two did not appear until the edition of 1580. Most of these poems would not ordinarily be called "popular." Three (Nos. 7, 52, and 53) are by Richard Edwards, the composer, playwright, and compiler of the miscellany, and are learnedly moral. No. 98, by Francis Kinwelmarsh, was supposedly sung by Walter Devereux, first Earl of Essex, on his death-bed, an entirely appropriate occasion for this poem. No. 103 is "An Epitaph vpon the death of Syr Edward Saunders" by Lodowick Lloyd, and is heavy with classical allusions. *A Gorgeous Gallery of Gallant Inventions* (1578) contains five poems with tunes indicated as in broadsides, parts of which were lifted from poems printed in *A Handful of Pleasant Delights*.[12] There is also a poem with a "willow" refrain like that of Desdemona's song (pp. 83–86). Fifteen of the poems are in poulter's measure, twelve in fourteeners; a few obvious rhetorical devices such as anaphora and alliteration are carried to extremes. Various quatrains and other stanzas in octosyllabic or decasyllabic lines occur, but two of the few poems with stanzas of varying line lengths are written to the tunes of poems from *A Handful*.

After the 1570's, ballads conform more closely to the journalistic stereotype, are generally segregated from other poetry, and develop a miscellany tradition of their own following the precedent of *A Handful of Pleasant Delights*. Anthony Munday published *A Banquet of Daintie Conceits* in 1588, and Thomas Deloney's *Garland of Good Will* was in print by 1596, perhaps earlier.[13] Subsequent collections of ballads came to be known as "garlands." Almost always the balladeer named a popular tune to which the verses could be sung. Skipping ahead to 1620, however, we find history spiraling, if not circling, in the appearance of Richard Johnson's *The Golden Garland of Princely Pleasures and Delicate*

---

[11] *The Paradise of Dainty Devices*, ed. Hyder E. Rollins (Cambridge, Mass.: Harvard University Press, 1927), p. lxviii.

[12] *A Gorgeous Gallery of Gallant Inventions*, ed. Hyder E. Rollins (Cambridge, Mass.: Harvard University Press, 1926), pp. xxi–xxii.

[13] See Deloney's *Works*, ed. F. O. Mann (Oxford, 1912), pp. xii, 562–563.

Delights. The first part of this collection consists of broadsides on elevated historical subjects. The second part is made up of favorite lyrics from the later poetical miscellanies and the songbooks of Dowland and Ford (see the note to Fd1607.VIII).

In this sketchy survey of the early miscellanies, I have so far stressed ballad-singing and certain favorite meters, for I believe them to be important in establishing the general tone of the poetry between Surrey and Sidney. The rigid prosodic notions exemplified by Tottel's editorial changes and the favorite meters of Surrey's followers—poulter's measure, fourteeners, hexameters, or some mild variation or combination of these—seem to have some connection with the prevalence of simple, foursquare tunes that typically consist of four four-measure phrases, with a half-cadence in the middle and a full cadence at the end. The

Duple:	♩ | ♩ ♩ | ♩ ♩ | 𝅝 ♩ | 𝅗𝅥＿
Triple:	♩ | ♩ ♩ | ♩ ♩ | 𝅗𝅥. ♩ | 𝅗𝅥＿

Poulter's:	×	/ ×	/ ×	/ [×	/]			[caesura or silent stress]
Fourteeners:	×	/ ×	/ ×	/ ×	/			
Hexameters:	×	/ ×	/ ×	/ [×	/]			

♩ \| ♩ ♩ \| ♩ ♩ \| o | ＿

♩ \| ♩ ♩ \| ♩ ♩ \| ♩. | ＿   [half cadence]

×	/ ×	/ ×	/ [×	/]
×	/ ×	/ ×	/ [×	/] [strong caesura or silent stress]
×	/ ×	/ ×	/ [×	/]

♩ \| ♩ ♩ \| ♩ ♩ \| 𝅝 ♩ \| 𝅗𝅥＿

♩ \| ♩ ♩ \| ♩ ♩ \| 𝅗𝅥. ♩ \| 𝅗𝅥＿

×	/ ×	/ ×	/ ×	/
×	/ ×	/ ×	/ ×	/
×	/ ×	/ ×	/ [×	/]

♩ \| ♩ ♩ \| ♩ ♩ \| o | ＿

♩ \| ♩ ♩ \| ♩ ♩ \| ♩. | ＿   [full cadence]

×	/ ×	/ ×	/ [×	/]
×	/ ×	/ ×	/ [×	/] [pause at end of line or stanza: silent stress]
×	/ ×	/ ×	/ [×	/]

paradigm below might help explain the isochronous tendencies of these meters. If, indeed, the "medium is the message," and the poets tried— as John Thompson says they did—to make the stresses of the language conform to the abstract metrical pattern with its strong caesuras, then perhaps the reason that some people find both the form and content of these poems "drab" is not far to seek.[14]

For support, we need to look only as far as the parallel and no doubt influential tradition of Protestant psalm-singing. Thomas Sternhold had translated nineteen of the psalms in fourteeners and published them around 1548; in 1549 another edition added more translations by Sternhold and others by John Hopkins. This became the nucleus of the Sternhold and Hopkins psalter, one of the most frequently reprinted books of the period. The Marian exiles took these psalms to Geneva, where they were first printed with music in 1556. After Elizabeth's accession they were sung in the churches. Words and music generally conform more closely to the paradigm given above than do the popular songs. Since the psalms were seen from the first to be in competition with "ungodly Songes and Ballades, which tende only to the norishing of vyce, and corrupting of youth,"[15] it has been thought that Sternhold consciously chose the meter of the ballads. But records of the fourteener or ballad stanza are scarce before the 1540's, and it may well be that Sternhold, adapting a meter from Surrey and the courtly makers, *made* the meter popular through his translations of the psalms. In fact this meter was known as "Sternhold's meter" before it was known as ballad meter. At any rate, the ubiquitousness of the meter and devotional content of these psalms must have contributed to the dominance of the jogging meters and didacticism of the poetry of the early miscellanies.[16] Sternhold was of course only answering to a demand. In the Reformation (and ultimately humanist) insistence on the importance of the word, it was found necessary to make the words of vocal church music intelligible. Words had hitherto been obscured by polyphony and stretching one syllable over many notes. The Royal Injunctions of 1548 for Lincoln Minster stated that anthems were to be sung in English, set to a "plain and distinct note for every syllable one." The Injunctions for York Minister in 1552 required that "there be none other note sung or

[14] *The Founding of English Metre* (New York: Columbia University Press, 1961), pp. 64–75.

[15] *The Whole Booke of Psalmes, collected into Englysh metre by T. Starnhold I. Hopkins & others . . . with apt Notes to synge them with al* (1562), title page.

[16] Hallett Smith, "English Metrical Psalms in the Sixteenth Century and their Literary Significance," *Huntington Library Quarterly*, IX (1946), 251–266. *Cf.* Stevens, p. 93.

used . . . saving square note plain, so that every syllable may be plainly and distinctly pronounced, and without any reports or repeatings which may induce any obscureness to the hearers." In Queen Elizabeth's Injunctions of 1559, church music is to be encouraged, but there is to be "a modest and distinct song, so used in all parts of the Common Prayers in the Church, that the same may be as plainly understood, as if it were read without singing." [17] The psalms fulfilled the requirements of these general injunctions.

Although English singing was affected most directly by such manifestations of the Reformation, similar humanist theories may have had some influence. In the revived Greek literature, scholars found passages describing the almost miraculous psychological effects of ancient music, one of the more familiar being the story of Timotheus. The central concern of the musical humanist became an attempt to recover the qualities of Greek music which produced these effects. [18] We see this concern reflected in Sir Thomas More's description of Utopian music, explicitly unlike contemporary English music:

> For all theire musicke . . . doth so resemble and expresse naturall affections, the sownd & tune is so applied and made agreable to the thynge, that whether it bee a prayer, or els a dytty of gladnes, of patience, of trouble, of mournynge, or of anger: the fassion of the melodye dothe so represent the meaning of the thing, that it doth wonderfullye move, stire, pearce, and enflame the hearers myndes [Robinson's translation, 1551, sig. R5].

In actual music, this concern eventually resulted in songs that emphasized the importance of the words, and generally did not obscure the words with musical complexity, although they never got as simple as the psalms or the broadside ballads. But John Stevens has shown us (p. 65) that what is really new here is the idea of using music to *express* the sense or the emotion of the words. The learned music of Henry VIII's time and before never attempted this effect, and of course the psalm and ballad could not, because the same tune was used for different texts. But after Elizabeth became queen, the learned musicians turned to developing this expressiveness. They could hardly be expected to abandon the richly developed resources of their own art, harmony and counterpoint, and the compromising Elizabethan church found room

[17] *Visitation Articles and Injunctions of the Period of the Reformation*, ed. W. H. Frere and W. M. Kennedy (1910), II, 168, 318; III, 23. See also Stevens, pp. 74–97.

[18] See D. P. Walker's article cited above in section I, n. 15, and John Hollander, *The Untuning of the Sky* (Princeton, 1961), pp. 162–220.

both for simple psalm and learned (but simplified and vernacular) anthem. The development of this expressive potential, in both sacred and secular music, became one of the main contributions of the Renaissance to later music.

All these ideas took part in the development of a kind of song which combined expressive emphasis on words, simple melody, and harmonic and contrapuntal interest. These songs were sometimes performed in parts, sometimes (especially later in the century) as solos with lute accompaniment, but in their early stages most characteristically as solos accompanied by a consort of viols. The connections between the music and the theories may be clarified by this description of a consort song by William Byrd (*e.g.*, No. III of the 1588 set): the text is one of the Sternhold and Hopkins psalms, which is set to a melody almost as simple as a psalm-tune; this melody is floated on a rich, shifting, harmonically and contrapuntally interesting accompaniment provided by four viols. The music is sufficiently solemn to match the text, and the repeated phrase at the end, "be eased of my pain," is set to dissonances easing into resolutions. Nevertheless, expressive devices are not so readily apparent in Byrd as they are in some other consort songs and most later madrigals and airs.

The consort song brings us back, by a rather devious route, to *The Paradise of Dainty Devices*. For besides poems sung as ballads, it also contains poems sung as consort songs, partly justifying the printer's claim in his preface that the poems are "aptly made to be set to any song in .5. partes, or song to instrument." Not counting ballads, eight of the poems have surviving musical settings, two of which, Richard Edwards' "When May is in his prime" (No. 6) and Vaux's "How can the tree" (No. 71), are consort songs, and others which survive in part-song or lute-accompanied solo versions were very likely sung as consort songs (*e.g.*, Nos. 7 and 57).[19] Richard Edwards was Master of the Children of the Chapel Royal from 1561 until his death in 1566 (Rollins, *Paradise*, p. xlviii). Several of the other surviving consort songs are connected with plays performed by the choirboys; some of these, though dating from the 1560's, use music for expressive purposes quite effectively. Perhaps the dramatic context encouraged the development of musical analogues for dramatic expression.

Consort songs provide a link with the first of the Elizabethan printed

[19] See the notes in Rollins' ed., the note to By1596.VII, and John Ward, "*Joan qd John* and Other Fragments at Western Reserve University," in *Aspects of Medieval and Renaissance Music*, pp. 840–841.

songbooks, Thomas Whythorne's *Songes, for three, fower and fiue voyces* (1571). One of Whythorne's songs is clearly a consort song ("By new broom"), and others, though all the parts have words, were no doubt performed as consort songs. We learn from Whythorne's *Autobiography* that he wrote his own song texts, and that he was in his youth a servant of John Heywood, the poet and musician, for whom he copied poems and psalms by Wyatt, Surrey, and Sternhold (p. 14). Whythorne's own poems show these influences clearly: they are very plain, didactic, and often proverbial in the manner of Heywood. His autobiography is ostensibly given as a context for his poems, and its original title, significantly echoing Tottel, is *A book of songs and sonetts.*

III

Among the developments in music that were occurring during the 1570's and 80's were, as we have seen, a simplifying of some aspects of vocal music so that words could be understood when sung, and a growing concern for having music support the expression of the sense and emotions of the words. In poetry we find a preference, after Wyatt, for rigid, heavy meters, especially those that correspond to the simple tunes of the psalms and some of the ballads. This insistence on having language stresses conform to the stresses in the metrical pattern served to fix the pattern firmly in the minds of poets like Sidney and Spenser, who would achieve their effects by varying from the pattern, or opposing the stresses of the pattern to the stresses of speech. John Thompson suggests that Sidney and Spenser learned that metrical pattern and language "could be joined without losing their separate identities" from their humanistic experiments in quantitative meter (pp. 136 ff; 147). Without going too far into this complex subject, we might recall only that quantitative meters and music were always linked in theoretical discussions, and in France (and once in Byrd and Campion) they were linked in practice.[1]

[1] A sample of the extensive literature on this subject would include the works cited by Thompson, pp. 128–137, plus a passage from one of the MSS of Sidney's *Arcadia* (printed in Ringler, pp. 389–90 and elsewhere); Pattison, pp. 122–135; Ing, pp. 96–106; and Miles M. Kastendieck, *England's Musical Poet, Thomas Campion* (New York: Oxford University Press, 1938), pp. 71–102. On *musique mesurée*, see Frances A. Yates, *French Academies of the Sixteenth Century* (London, 1947); the article by D. P. Walker in *Music Review* (cited in section I, n. 15 above); and Walker's articles in *Musica Disciplina*: I (1946), 91–100; II (1948), 141–163; IV (1950), 163–186; and (with François Lesure) III (1949), 151–170. See also Byrd's 1588 set, No. XXIII, and Campion's song in Ros1601.I. XXI.

At any rate, after the 1570's meters became progressively more refined, the use of fourteeners and poulter's measure declined, alliteration became less blatant, and the pause in decasyllabic lines fell less regularly after the fourth syllable. Indeed, if one were to be limited to only two adjectives in describing the changes in style, "stiff" and "supple" might be more accurate—within their implied limitations—than "plain" and "eloquent."

At this point continental influences became more important, but as catalysts to the development of trends already under way rather than as revolutionary forces. Moreover, certain native qualities persisted in both music and poetry, even when foreign influences were most in the ascendant. One of the first publications of the "New Poetry," Spenser's *Shepherd's Calendar* (1579), pits a rustic roundelay against a sestina (*August*), pseudo-medieval four-stress lines (*February, May, September*) against the fluid song-stanzas of *April* and *November*.[2] Fourteeners (*July*) and the old tail-rhyme stanza (*March*) are also present. In music, throughout the vogue of the Italianate madrigal which followed the publication in 1588 of *Musica Transalpina*, composers like Byrd stoutly upheld the native song traditions.

Byrd's collection of 1588 is the first publication of the great phase of English secular song.[3] It shows a characteristic mixture of mostly old and a few new elements. The title will suggest some of its literary affinities: *Psalmes, Sonets, & Songs of Sadnes and Pietie*. The first ten pieces are in fact settings of Sternhold and Hopkins psalms. The next section of sixteen songs, called "Sonets and Pastoralls" includes such didactic dainties as Dyer's "I joy not in no earthly bliss" (No. XI), "My mind to me a kingdom is" (No. XIV) and "Farewell false Love, the

[2] Jane K. Fenyo ("The Rhythmic Basis for the Songs of 'August' 'April' and 'November' of *The Shepherds Calendar*," unpublished M.A. thesis, Queens College, City University of New York, 1964), in the course of some very interesting metrical discussions (in which she explains away some of Thompson's difficulties with these poems by quasi-musical scansion in terms of isochronous "stress-measure") makes a good case for the probability of Spenser having tunes in mind while writing these poems. See pp. 32–35, 154–160. For possible tunes to the *August* roundelay, see Anthony Holborne, *Complete Works*, I, ed. Masakata Kanazawa (Cambridge, Mass.: Harvard University Press, 1967), pp. 122, 141, and 223, n. 36

[3] According to Kerman (pp. 258–263), the date does not reflect an outburst of creativity inspired by the defeat of the Armada, but rather a change in the printer who worked under Byrd's monopoly for music printing; after 1596 when the monopoly expired a number of books, including the first airs, were printed before Thomas Morley received the patent in September, 1598 (see Robert Steele, *The Earliest English Music Printing* [London, 1903], pp. 27–29). Byrd's book is reprinted in EM XIV (revised by Philip Brett).

oracle of lies" (No. XXV). The last group, containing "Songs of sadness and pietie," is softened somewhat by a lullaby carol (No. XXXII, mostly in poulter's measure), and ends with "The funerall Songs of that honorable Gent. Syr Phillip Sidney, knight." Mention of Sidney brings us to what is new: "O you that hear this voice" (No. XVI), the earliest appearance in print of a complete poem known to be by Sidney. I might interject that Sidney's poetry, written mostly before 1582, shows he is in full control of most of the new qualities displayed by poets of the 1590's; yet his influence was limited until after the editions of the *Arcadia* of 1590 and *Astrophil and Stella* of 1591 appeared. One example of this influence may be seen in "Constant Penelope sends to thee, careless Ulysses" (No. XXIII), a poem in quantitative verse, which Byrd sets in a style similar to the French *musique mesurée*. Another poem in Byrd's collection, "Though Amaryllis dance in green" (No. XII), with its light movement and varying line lengths, looks ahead to the verse of *England's Helicon* where it was, in fact, reprinted. Byrd also includes a setting of a favorite text of the Italian madrigalists, a stanza from Ariosto's *Orlando Furioso* beginning "La virginella" (No. XXIV).

Musically, Byrd's book is conservative: all the songs are consort songs in the native tradition. But the growth of interest in the Italian madrigal, testified to later in the same year by the appearance of *Musica Transalpina*, is reflected in Byrd's printing words under what were originally viol parts. *Musica Transalpina* was the first of a series of anthologies of Italian music fitted with English words. These books are very important in helping bring about a new form in English music, the madrigal. But though the English madrigal school flourished, it did not overwhelm the native schools. Byrd's last collection, published in the declining years of the madrigal, is hardly more Italianate either in words or music than his first. Four other composers usually considered madrigalists—Mundy, Carlton, Alison, and Gibbons—are, as Joseph Kerman says (pp. 117–127), really followers of Byrd. Moreover, the air, with its roots in native song, eventually overtook the madrigal in popularity. The madrigal died, but the air was only changed in the work of Lawes and his contemporaries.

The poetical effects of *Musica Transalpina* and its successors are more difficult to evaluate. To begin with, it is doubtful that many people read madrigal books for their poetry alone, as they may have read the collections of airs. Since the madrigalists almost never set poems strophically, the reader has to reconstruct the verse from the musical underlay, where lines are obscured and words and phrases frequently repeated. Yet three of the poems from *Musica Transalpina* were re-printed in *England's Helicon*, and some qualities of these translations seem to have affected later poetry. Perhaps the most marked char-acteristic of the verse of *Musica Transalpina* is the ubiquitousness of feminine rhyme. Of course this is a characteristic of Italian poetry in general, which imitators may or may not choose to adopt. But in trying to fit English words to the Italian music, the translators were *forced* to use it. The same necessity makes the translators more concerned with syllables than with accent; therefore the meter of the poems is sometimes very free. This is by no means unpleasant after the rigidities of *A Gor-geous Gallery*. The *canzone* stanza with its free rhyme scheme and varied line lengths is also a welcome novelty; it has long been recognized as an element in the success of Spenser's marriage poems. Joseph Kerman asks pointedly if "students of Elizabethan poetry have taken enough notice of the effect of the many direct translations of Italian madrigals on English verse structure at this time" (p. 27). But the answer, even after John Thompson and Douglas Peterson, is still no. On the negative side, it must be said that the madrigal is responsible for the kind of verse that J. B. Leishman mocks as mere syllables for singing, "where nymphs and swains on the plains trip at leisure in a measure, view with pleasure Flora's treasure." [4] A ballet from Henry Youll's *Canzonets* (1608, XXIII; Cantus, sig. E4) seems to have been in Leishman's mind:

Where are now those iolly swaines,
That were wont to grace these plaines,
And in their mery mery vaines,
   Sing Fa la la.
Now they haue time and leasure,
They'r gone to take their pleasure,
Each one to dance his measure,
   And sing Fa la la.

In imitation of *Musica Transalpina*, the poet Thomas Watson gathered some Italian madrigals and wrote English words for them in *Italian Madrigalls Englished* (1590). According to the title page, these were written "Not to the sense of the originall dittie, but after the affection of the Noate." Watson uses this freedom to ease some of the strain of finding rhymes, but also to bring in local references, such as allusions in the first song to "Astrophil" and "Stella." This sonnet sequence of Sidney's was not yet in print, but Watson was in a position to know

[4] *The Monarch of Wit* (London: Hutchinson, 6th ed., 1962), p. 16.

about it. Watson himself contributed in a small way to the revival of interest in Petrarchan poetry which was to manifest itself so strongly in the 1590's, for his *Hecatompathia,* a set of one hundred eighteen-line "sonnets" with rather pedantic notes on sources after the manner of E.K., was published in 1582. It is interesting to find one of the early propagandists for continental Petrarchism also pushing the madrigal.

The content of madrigal verse was, of course, pastoral or Petrarchan, and supported the sonneteers in naturalizing the characteristic rhetoric and conceits. Yet the most powerful influence was "our English *Petrarke,*" Sidney, whose immense talent and dramatic technique gave a fresh force to the old conventions. Newman's *Astrophil and Stella* of 1591, however, contains more than Sidney's sonnets; twenty-eight sonnets by Samuel Daniel are included, as well as five poems attributed to Thomas Campion, one by Fulke Greville, and an anonymous poem. In short, the book is a miscellany, in which Daniel, Campion, and Greville are seeing print for the first time. Moreover, two of the Campion poems, those by Greville and Anon., and several of the songs from *Astrophil and Stella* were soon published with music.

Of Sidney's songs, the second, fourth, eighth, ninth, and tenth are in accentual trochees, all but one employing some feminine rhyme as a constant element in the stanza. Sustained trochaic verse, according to Ringler (p. xliii) is an innovation of Sidney's and seems to derive from writing words to a tune. Eight of Sidney's "Certain Sonnets" are written to tunes, five of which have Italian names (see Ringler's notes and the note to Ck1612.IX). "Al my sense thy sweetnesse gained" (see Jo1610.XVII), written "To the tune of Neapolitan Villanell," is trochaic and has feminine rhymes. "No, no, no, no, I cannot hate my foe" is also written "To the tune of a Neapolitan song," has feminine rhymes, and has mixed iambic and trochaic lines of varying lengths. Incidentally, Sidney extended his metrical revolution to translations of the psalms. In his forty-three translations, modeled largely on the French psalter with translations by Clement Marot and Theodore Beza and music by Claude Goudimel, *Les CL. Pseaumes de David* (1562), there is not a single plain fourteener; variety of stanza forms is the rule, there is some feminine rhyme, and Psalms XVI, XXXVIII, XLII, and XLIII are trochaic.[5]

[5] Ringler, pp. 505–508; see also Hallett Smith's article (section II, n. 16 above), and J. C. A. Rathmell's edition of *The Psalms of Sir Philip Sidney and the Countess of Pembroke* (Garden City: Doubleday Anchor, 1963).

In the new miscellanies of the 1590's, several of these characteristics are evident. *Britton's Bowre of Delights* (1591) contains "A pastorall of Phillis and Coridon" which begins (RBBD, p. 23):

> On a hill there growes a flower,
>   Faire befall the daintie sweete:
> By that flower there is a bower
> Where the heauenly *Muses* meete.

This poem was later printed as a broadside, to be sung to the tune of the "Frog Galliard," or John Dowland's "Now O now I needs must part" (Do1597.VI). And in *The Phoenix Nest* (1593) there is a poem by Thomas Lodge, "Now I finde, thy lookes were fained" (RPN, pp. 62–63) set to music later by Thomas Ford (1607.IIII). Another poem by Lodge, "Muses helpe me, sorrow swarmeth" (RPN, pp. 54–55), is trochaic, and several other poems in the collection have interesting stanza forms, especially those by Lodge. "Virginitie resembleth right the Rose" is another translation of the "La Virginella" stanzas of Ariosto which Byrd had set. Rollins notes widespread borrowings from French and Italian poets throughout the miscellany (RPN, pp. xxxviii–xli). But two poems are in poulter's measure, four in fourteeners, and a few (*e.g.*, "These lines I send by waues of woe," p. 73) look like leftovers from *A Gorgeous Gallery*. Many poems tread a sort of middle ground, and as Rollins notes (p. xxxvii), the favorite form in *The Phoenix Nest* is the all-purpose stanza of six ten-syllable lines rhyming *ababcc*. This form proved flexible enough to survive frequent use in the older miscellanies (fourteen poems in *The Paradise*, six in *A Gorgeous Gallery*) and is to be found throughout the songbooks.

Three of the poems in *The Phoenix Nest* were later published as airs with music (Fd1607.IIII, Jo1601.IX, Fer1609.I); and three others appeared in William Barley's *A New Booke of Tabliture* (1596, Nos. III, V, VI). Barley's book is primarily an instruction book for the lute and similar instruments, with exemplary pieces. Among these pieces is music for four songs, the words for two of which (V and VII) are printed together on two leaves separate from the music. Also printed on these two leaves are five other poems; yet these five poems have no connection with any of the music in the book. Apparently these extra poems were included only for their poetical interest, or as filling. Or perhaps Barley was trying, rather clumsily, to make his book something of a miscellany as well as a songbook and instrumental tutor. This is the first hint of something that will soon become more evident, that the audiences for the songbooks and the miscellanies were similar, if not identical.

The songs in Barley's *Booke of Tabliture* are the first printed examples of a new genre, the air. Dowland's *First Booke* followed the next year, and the air soon began to rival the madrigal in numbers of books printed. The air, as noted earlier, is a better vehicle for the humanistic and reformation concern with the text; for in the hands of a man like Dowland, the music in the air does much to express the emotions conveyed by the words without obscuring them. The poems in Dowland's book are anonymous, and the only ones that can be ascribed with certainty are two (Nos. II and XXI) by Fulke Greville, these being printed for the first time; but Dowland hints in his epistle to the reader that the other poets were also courtiers. Ten of the poems are in the popular six-line stanza; the stanza forms and meters of the others are varied, some reflecting the fact that their tunes were known separately as instrumental dances (*e.g.*, Nos. IIII and V). Dowland's book was so popular that it was reprinted four times. That this popularity extended to the verse is suggested by the inclusion of four of the song texts in *England's Helicon* (1600).

At this time the overlapping between the songbooks and the miscellanies becomes quite noticeable. Other songbooks provided verse for *England's Helicon* besides Dowland's. Four poems were taken from William Byrd's *Psalmes, Sonets & Songs* (1588) and *Songs of Sundry Natures* (1589), three from *Musica Transalpina*, and three from Thomas Morley's *Madrigals to Four Voices* (1594). Some fourteen other poems appear in later songbooks. No fewer than forty poems from the last Elizabethan miscellany, Francis Davison's *A Poetical Rhapsody* (1602), have surviving musical settings. Most of these were composed within a few years after the poems were printed in the *Rhapsody*, but at least five of the songs were written earlier. Regardless of whether a given poem was actually set to music or not, it is important to note that many of the poems are highly suitable for music, or seem to have been written with musical forms in mind. Nineteen poems are labelled "Madrigal" (plus three in later editions), and thirty are "Odes," or stanzaic poems of the sort the composers of airs favored. Many of these "Odes" (*e.g.*, Nos. 30, 61, 101) show the careful parallels in sense, phrasing, and meter from stanza to stanza desired by poets like Campion who wish each stanza to fit the music as well as the first.

Although the miscellany petered out in the early 1600's, poetic and musical activity in general increased; and at the same time, publications tended to become more specialized. Instead of publishing a miscellaneous collection of verse, such as Googe's or Gascoigne's, a poet would publish a sonnet sequence, or an Ovidian narrative, or later, a book of epigrams. Between 1602 and 1622, it is difficult to find miscellaneous lyrics in print except in the songbooks or incidentally in plays or romances. I stress *in print*, because it is true that in many ways the poetical miscellany simply returned to its origin, which was the poetical commonplace book or private anthology. The rise of the professional writer may have increased the snob appeal of poetry in manuscript, especially after 1600. Drayton's complaint in *Poly-Olbion* (1613) that "Verses are wholly deduc't to Chambers, and nothing esteem'd in this lunatique Age, but what is kept in Cabinets, and must only passe by Transcription," is well known;[6] but Thomas Campion also noted that some "taste nothing that comes forth in Print, as if *Catullus* or *Martials* Epigrammes were the worse for being published" (1 Camp[1613]; Davis, p. 55). Most of the surviving Renaissance poetical manuscripts are anthologies made by undergraduates and members of the Inns of Court during the middle years of the seventeenth century. Thus the printed songbooks become more important in a careful historical consideration of the lyric.

Yet what are these poems like? Are they all Sidneyan lyrics like those in *England's Helicon*? Do they reflect any of the changes of the sort exemplified by Jonson and Donne? With some notable exceptions, the poems in the books of Byrd and his followers remain old-fashioned; indeed, the poems in Byrd's 1611 collection are in some ways less modern than those he set in 1588. The madrigal texts too, remain generally all of a piece, but as Joseph Kerman has noted, there is some satire of madrigal verse in the later collections (*e.g.*, Weelkes' *Ayeres or Phantasticke Spirites*, 1608), and signs of the urbane, colloquial, witty "cavalier" style as well, as in John Wilbye's *Second Set* (1609), No. XII.

In the verses for the air, one may find both new and old; but generally they reflect current tastes better than the madrigal, and thus provide important evidence in evaluating changes in lyric styles. Changes are perceptible in the first two decades of the century, but they take place in a general atmosphere of continuity. For instance, in John Attey's *First Booke of Ayres* (1622), the last of the genre, one finds balanced couplets like this (No. VII):

Thy skill doth equall *Pallas*, not thy birth,
Shee to the Heauens yeelds Musicke, Thou to the Earth.

---

[6] *Works*, ed. J. W. Hebel (Oxford: Basil Blackwell, 1933), IV, v.

and cavalier drollery (No. X), rubbing shoulders with a poem by Sir Thomas Wyatt (No. XII). The mixture is usually not so extreme, but it does point to the advisability of dating individual poems before generalizing. Moreover, the *Venus and Adonis* stanza, which goes back to Tottel and is abundant in *The Paradise of Dainty Devices* and the miscellanies of the 1590's, is the single most frequently used stanza form, with some eighty poems spread evenly throughout the earliest and latest songbooks. We may note also that Robert Jones's *The Muses Gardin for Delights* (1610)—a fanciful title that recalls the miscellanies—contains poems that raise a cavalier smirk (*e.g.*, Nos. XIII, XV); but we must realize that Jones's *First Booke* (1600) contains similar poems (*e.g.* No. XVI), and conclude that what is being reflected is Jones's taste, not literary history.

Perhaps the best way to determine what the original audiences thought new is to see which poems continued to be popular throughout the century. In some instances, the number of sources may indicate mainly the popularity of the music, as in Do1597.XIII, or interest in the troubles of the great, as in Do1603.XVIII, but "When Phoebus first did Daphne loue" (Do1603.VI), seems to have been genuinely popular as a poem up through the Restoration. It survives in some twenty printed and MS versions. "Sweet stay a while" (Do1612.II) is known in thirty-one versions, mainly because it got into the Donne apocrypha. "Beware faire Maides" (Ck1612.VIII) occurs in fifteen MSS; "Beauty sate bathing by a spring" was set to music three times (Jo1605.II, Pi1605. XVIII, Ck1610.IX) and is found in *England's Helicon* and ten other sources. "Loue is a bable" (Jo1601.XVII) not only has several other versions and settings, but was even put into Latin in 1685. "Like Hermit poore" (Fer1609.I), an old-fashioned poem once attributed to Raleigh, is found in a dozen versions dating from 1591 to 1663. Another poem in Ferrabosco's book, Campion's "Young and simple though I am" (Fer1609.VIII), was set to music by Campion himself and also by Nicholas Lanier; ten other versions exist, one dating as late as 1673.

The only lyrics by Donne printed during his lifetime appeared in the songbooks, "The Expiration" (Fer1609.VII) and "Breake of Day" (Ck1612.IIII). There are of course many MS versions of these poems. But none of the other songbook lyrics are noticeably "metaphysical" in the manner of Donne. It is true that in "The Triple Foole" Donne implies that he expected some of his poems to be set to music; and music is known for at least five other poems from the *Songs and Sonnets*. But it is generally conceded that most of Donne's poems are not suitable for singing because they are too complex. The reasons why this should be so will be discussed in the next section, but for the moment the reader might consider "To aske for all thy loue" (Do1612.III) in conjunction with Donne's "Loves Infiniteness." R. W. Ingram has suggested that Donne's poem has been "translated" for the composer.[7] Despite the differences such a comparison reveals, it is possible that the song lyric influenced Donne in his varied and intricate stanza forms and perhaps—along with dramatic blank verse—in his metrical freedom.

Of the two poets that are generally taken to be the founders of the seventeenth-century styles, it is Ben Jonson who has the closest affinities with the song writers.[8] In 1609, Ferrabosco published seven settings of songs from Jonson's plays and masques, and a number of other settings survive. Jonson could be a "strong-lined" poet like Donne, a poet of the speaking, not the singing voice; but in his lyrics, he could maintain the necessary simplicity and structural requirements of words for singing while imparting his own classical flavor to the verse. Although the later songs are closer to Jonson than to Donne, the only ones that might be mistaken for Jonson's are those by Thomas Campion.

Campion has his own individuality, but he and Jonson were both makers of masques and accomplished classicists. Their development as lyric poets is parallel in that they both move toward an epigrammatic concept of the lyric. Campion, who was a few years older than Jonson, began in the shadow of Sir Philip Sidney—his first published poems appeared in the 1591 *Astrophil and Stella*—and his verse always retained traces of this influence. His experiments in classical meters also derive from Sidney's. But as early as the Campion-Rosseter *Ayres* of 1601, Campion could say to the reader, "What Epigrams are in Poetrie, the same are Ayres in musicke, then in their chiefe perfection when they are short and well seasoned" (Davis, p. 15). He repeats this comparison in the preface to *Two Bookes of Ayres* (c. 1613; Davis, p. 55). These ideas are reflected in Campion's development of what Walter R. Davis calls a "spare and naturalistic mode" (p. xx). This kind of classicism is more like Jonson's: thoroughly at home in the native idiom and meter, but precise, controlled, wise, and witty, like Jonson's beloved

[7] "Words and Music," in *Elizabethan Poetry*, Stratford-upon-Avon Studies No. 2 (London: Edward Arnold, 1960), p. 146.

[8] See Willa McClung Evans, *Ben Jonson and Elizabethan Music* (Lancaster, Pa., 1929; reprinted with a new preface by DaCapo Press, 1965).

Horace. In Campion's *Third Booke* (*c*. 1617, XXVII) we find poems like this:

> Neuer loue vnlesse you can
> Beare with all the faults of man:
> Men sometimes will iealous bee
> Though but little cause they see,
>   And hang the head, as discontent,
>   And speake what straight they will repent.

Campion comes to write a "plain" style without giving up the possibilities of the "eloquent."[9]

With Campion, then, the development of lyric styles as reflected in the songbooks may be summarized briefly as follows: the poems gradually come to display more cleverness and wit, but merely verbal wit and the more artificial rhetorical devices become less apparent; the attitudes of lovers become more sophisticated, and there is more naturalistic sensuousness; religious songs grow somewhat less lugubrious, and there is more melancholy from unspecified causes; sententiousness becomes less proverbial and more epigrammatic. But these changes are gradual and continuous. The novel, highly individual style of Donne could not be readily absorbed—in fact Donne's influence outside the coterie does not begin until after the last book of airs was printed. Even so, one could argue that a "metaphysical" poet like Herbert is as much like Campion as Donne; Herbert was a musician, and shows his ability to use the techniques developed in the air in such poems as "The Dawning."[10]

IV

As might be expected, many of the poems in the songbooks bear marks of their association with music. Bruce Pattison, Catherine Ing, and others have ably described the characteristics of poems written especially to be sung, and it is difficult to say anything new on the

[9] John Irwin's forthcoming article on "Now winter nights enlarge" in *Studies in English Literature* shows how complex Campion can be.

[10] On Herbert and music, see Joseph H. Summers, *George Herbert: his Religion and Art* (Cambridge, Mass.: Harvard University Press, 1954), pp. 156–170; Rosemond Tuve, "Sacred 'Parody' of Love Poetry, and Herbert," *SR*, VIII (1961), 249–290; and Alicia Ostriker, "Song and Speech in the Metrics of George Herbert," *PMLA*, LXXX (1965), 62–68.

subject that would be widely applicable.[1] Nevertheless, a new synthesis may be of some value. Although the generalizations that follow will be true for many of the songbook poems, they cannot apply to all, much less all other lyrics of the period. Pattison's statement that "It is because they were prepared for singing rather than reading that sixteenth- and seventeenth-century lyrics differ from those of later periods" (p. 141) is dangerously broad. The sources of several of the song texts indicate that they were not *intended* for singing. Do1612.X consists of three stanzas taken from a long penitential poem; Do1603.XVIII again takes three stanzas from a longer poem and gives it a musical setting not because it is especially suitable for singing, but because it was famous. A number of other verses in both the lutenists' and madrigalists' books were no doubt set because of their popularity as poems. One must admit that the composers were frequently able to make successful songs out of these poems, although they usually had to make some compromises or sacrifices: in Do1612.X, for instance, it is difficult to sing the second and third stanzas to the music for the first.

But for many of the songs, poets provided texts that show considerable awareness of the composers' problems, and the result was a body of songs that maintain the delicate balance of words and music surprisingly well. One reason for this generally successful union was, as we have seen, that current music and ideas about music disposed the composer to concern himself with the clear presentation of the words and the expression of their meanings and emotions in the music. Another reason was the willingness of some poets to impose severe limits on their verse in order to give the composer more freedom to make his setting musically interesting.

Just what these limitations are and why they were desirable may be demonstrated by the following example. Suppose a composer who has a reputation for treating poems with respect is commissioned to set a poem such as Sir Henry Lee's "Farre from triumphing Court" (RDo1610.VIII) for some ceremonial occasion. The poem consists of

[1] See Pattison, pp. 141–159; Ing, pp. 107–177; Kastendieck, pp. 103–161 and *passim*; V. C. Clinton-Baddeley, *Words for Music* (Cambridge: the University Press, 1941); Ingram, "Words and Music"; Wilfred Mellers, *Harmonious Meeting* (London: Dennis Dobson, 1965), pp. 38–129; C. Day Lewis, *The Lyric Impulse* (Cambridge, Mass.: Harvard University Press, 1965), pp. 1–51; Henry Raynor, "Framed to the Life of the Words," *Music Review*, XIX (1958), 261–271, and "Words for Music," *Monthly Musical Record*, LXXXVIII (1958), 174–182. See also items cited below, and Hoover H. Jordan, "Thomas Moore: Artistry in the Song Lyric," *Studies in English Literature*, II (1962), 403–440.

four stanzas of the common *Venus and Adonis* stanza. The composer can write either a strophic setting or a through-composed setting; the second possibility he immediately rejects as too long and laborious, and likely to become formless. He turns then to a strophic setting. But if the subsequent stanzas are to be sung to the music of the first, other problems arise. How is he to set the first line, "Farre from triumphing Court and wonted glory," so that the corresponding line of the second stanza will fit the music? The stresses in the first two syllables are reversed, and the phrasing is different: "But loe a glorious light from his darke rest." The phrasing looks troublesome in the first lines of the other two stanzas also. The problems multiply line by line. Now music can absorb many textual irregularities, such as extra syllables and feminine endings, and the performer can smooth over many rough places; but irregular phrasing, inverted stresses, and enjambment may cause difficulty unless these irregularities are repeated consistently in each stanza. Accented or important words or syllables are usually given longer note values or pitch-accents (the voice tends to emphasize the higher of two notes). When the stresses are different at the same point in corresponding lines —as with "Farre from" and "But loe"—the careful composer can avoid distortion by giving both syllables equal note values and keeping both on the same pitch. But too much of this sort of compromise results in dull music. Difficulties caused by irregular phrasing and enjambment may be solved by a similar neutralization, that is, by avoiding rests or cadences or repetitions of words or phrases at points where irregularities could cause trouble. Carelessness may have ludicrous consequences, as in Do1603.XIX, where the musical phrase matches the verbal phrase in "Seas haue their source, and so haue shallowe springs," but the corresponding line in the next stanza reads "True hearts haue eyes and ears, no tongues to speake." When this is sung, the meaning seems to be that hearts have eyes, but ears do not have tongues.

The hypothetical composer writing a strophic setting of "Farre from triumphing Court" would also have trouble with his expression. The mood of the first stanza is melancholy, that of the second joy. If the setting is not to sound inappropriate to one mood, it must not be expressive of either. Moreover, if the composer were tempted to indulge in a little "word-painting" by setting "to heau'n is gone" to ascending notes, what happens when "my limbs grow faint" are sung to these same notes?

The conclusion one is forced to draw is that the more variety and contrast a poem contains, the more regular and monotonous—or strained and awkward—a strophic setting of it is likely to be. Under these circumstances, one might expect a composer concerned with his own art to do what Dowland did with "Farre from triumphing Court": do as good a job as possible with the first stanza and leave the performer to handle the others as best he can. Dowland exploits the contrasts in the first stanza between court and country, heaven and earth, joy and melancholy. In the first phrase, he recalls the triumph and glory of court by echoing a trumpet fanfare. The "shadie vnfrequented places" receive a quieter setting, lower in pitch. "That Goddesse whom hee serude" is mentioned with quiet reverence, but she ascends to heaven on a triumphantly rising scale. The contrast with the speaker is emphasized by a downward leap encompassing an octave from "he" to "earth." The final result is a musically interesting song, if not a great one, with considerable variety of note-values and freedom of movement.

The problem for the poet, then, is first a matter of form. Any irregularity of phrasing, meter, or line length is permissible as long as it is repeated with some consistency in succeeding stanzas. The poets' awareness of this problem is reflected in a number of poems in the songbooks, especially those of the poet-composer Thomas Campion. A few less familiar examples that may be cited are Fd1607.VII, Jo1601. VII and XXI, Jo1605.VI and VII, Do1597.IX, and Do1600.XI. Several of these poems also show the fondness of song poets and composers for stanzas made up of lines of varying lengths, a characteristic of song lyrics since Pindar. Pattison has said (p. 146) that this was one of the ways to obtain variety. In spoken verse, notably dramatic blank verse, variety could come from enjambment and shifting the position of the pause within the five-stress line. But poets writing for music tended to conceive of the phrase as the basic unit of rhythm, which is more easily done when the line is shorter than ten syllables or five stresses, for the pause is then not always necessary or noticeable. Therefore instead of varying the length of phrases within a set line length, song poets often vary the line lengths to match the phrases. Short phrases, or lines with internal rhyme, lend themselves naturally to a more intrinsically musical device, the sequence. For example, in Do1603.XII, the fifth and sixth lines of each stanza are set to matching sequential figures, as are the seventh and eighth lines. Short lines also give the composer the option of combining two in a single musical phrase, or giving each a full phrase by using longer note values. Dowland gives emphasis to the lines "One faith one loue" and "New Hopes new ioys" in Do1600. XIII by giving each syllable a half-note, in contrast to the quarter-notes given the syllables of the intervening long lines. Finally, phrases of varied lengths, either within the line or in separate lines, may help establish a rhythm that in itself suggests a tune. Pattison quotes the first four lines of Jo1605.V and says that the poet "has gone half-way towards transforming the poem into a song" (p. 146).

The effect of music on the meter of these poems is a more complex matter, further complicated by Renaissance interests in quantitative meter and modern controversy, inspired by the new linguistics, over just what meter is anyway. A few points must be made, however, in spite of the dangers of saying either too little or too much. Although Dowland had claimed in the dedication to Do1597 that "number" is "the common friend & vniter" of music and poetry, musical and poetical meter are quite different even though they may run parallel at times. Song and poetry share the limits of the sung or spoken phrase and the linguistic features of pitch and juncture; but stress is the main linguistic signal that English verse abstracts and formalizes in meter, while in music (except dance music) stress is not so important as quantity. The musical ictus "on the first beat of the bar" is inapplicable to irregularly barred, slowly flowing airs like "I Saw my Lady weepe" (Do1600.I; also Mo1600.V). As we have seen, however, stressed syllables could be emphasized by length or pitch, or simply by the singer's voice. But although composers can follow the meter of the poem—as in Do1597.VI or in *musique mesurée*—they usually prefer more freedom in using a variety of note values to make the melodies more interesting. Therefore it is often difficult to say, on hearing a song, what the meter of the verse is. Sometimes, as in the case of a poem which depends a great deal upon meter for its effect, a musical setting would result in a net loss; but some poems gain for having their metrical crudities obscured by the music. The jigging poulter's measure of "In darknesse let mee dwell" (RDo1610.X) prejudices the reader against the poem immediately and makes the content seem to be an even worse exercise in trivial melancholia than it is. Dowland's setting is much more flattering to the poem's content, for the new form makes the sentiments not only convincing, but powerfully so.

A poet writing songs can therefore take tremendous liberties with meter, so long as he duplicates them in each stanza. There are not many examples of the poet abandoning ordinary meter altogether (as in Hu1607.I), but a number of poems reflect the metrical freedom that musical setting makes possible. Catherine Ing has analyzed "Weepe you no more sad fountaines" (Do1603.XV) in these terms (pp. 131–138), and Campion is full of examples (*e.g.*, Ros1601.I.X, 4Camp[1617].X). In "Flow my teares" (Do1600.II), apparent metrical freedom is really another and even more severe restraint, for the words were probably written to fit a pre-existent tune, the "Lachrymae" pavan. The music consists of three repeated strains, so the second stanza is sung to the music of the first, the fourth stanza to the music of the third, and the last is simply repeated. Thus ordinary verse form and meter do not appear, but the order imposed by the repeated stanzas is even more exacting than these.

Since discussions of quantitative meters usually involved musical analogies, and since the *musique mesurée* of Baïf's *Académie de Musique et Poésie* embodied the theories in actual songs, one might expect to find traces of these quantitative experiments in the air. Besides, the foremost writer of verse for airs as well as one of the more notable composers, Thomas Campion, had written *Observations in the Art of English Poesie* (1602) advocating classical meters in English and providing some of the best models available. But even Campion published only one quantitative poem with a musical setting, "Come let vs sound" (Ros1601.I.XXI), and other composers show little interest in these experiments. Nevertheless, a case may be made for indirect influence, especially as regards Campion. Unlike many of the enthusiasts for quantitative meter, Campion did not often confuse quantity with stress; perhaps his experience as a neo-Latin poet helped him acquire a genuine feeling for quantity. Therefore it is not surprising to find quantitative subtleties in his airs, when music can give each syllable a definite length and reduce the force of verbal stress by setting unstressed syllables to longer notes. This kind of quantity is not the sort advocated in the *Observations*, but involves a feeling for the weight and speed of words, a sense shared by Milton and Tennyson. One famous example of this effect is "When thou must home" (Ros1601.I.XX).[2] But it is possible that Campion's interest in music and quantitative verse was really only a manifestation of a more basic concern with English versification. As he says in his epistle to the reader of *Two Bookes of Ayres* (*c.* 1613; Davis, pp. 55–56): "I haue chiefly aymed to couple my Words and Notes louingly together, which will be much for him to doe that hath not power ouer both. The light of this will best appeare to him who hath

---

[2] See Ing, pp. 141–142, and Hallett Smith, *Elizabethan Poetry* (Cambridge, Mass.: Harvard University Press, 1952), pp. 280–286.

pays'd our Monasyllables and Syllables combined, both which, are so loaded with Consonants, as that they will hardly keepe company with swift Notes, or giue the Vowell conuenient liberty." Campion wished to make his verse suitable for music, but at times he seems to be mainly concerned with recording a proper reading of his poem in musical notation without considering that the independent interest of music can contribute to the total effect of the song.

But metrical virtuosity is lost upon the person who listens to a song and does not understand what is is all about. A certain degree of clarity and simplicity is necessary in a form that is perceived mainly through the ear; moreover, unlike other oral forms such as drama or oratory, it is removed from speech not only by the artifice of verse, but also by music. This basic requirement of the air naturally had some effect on the structure, rhetoric, diction, and imagery used in the poems written for singing.

Bruce Pattison's statement that "the general quality of sixteenth-century poetic style is very suitable for music" (p. 142) has come in for some criticism, but it is fundamentally true if we exclude the formal demands of the strophic song. In the stimulating work of Marshall McLuhan and Father Ong, the Renaissance is seen to be a period of transition between a predominantly oral culture and a typographical one.[3] Despite a thriving printing industry and growing literacy, oral habits of thinking still led a lively existence, especially in literature, where they were supported by humanistic preoccupation with the works of the ancients. Most of the really vital literary forms of the sixteenth century were written with the possibility of oral performance in mind: sermons, plays, and song lyrics, of course—even romances and long poems were probably read aloud to small groups. The end of rhetoric was good oratory rather than good writing. Common places were still collected and the art of memory was still cultivated.[4] And conversely, audiences were more skilled in listening and comprehending what they heard than we might imagine. Thus although the song lyric had special problems of its own, there were a number of resources available that could be brought in to help solve them. Perhaps the most readily accessible were the poetic conventions. "Conventional" is not usually a favorable adjective, and poetry that is *merely* conventional is rarely interesting in any circumstances. But the conventions are func-

[3] Marshall McLuhan, *The Gutenberg Galaxy* (Toronto, 1962); Walter J. Ong, *Ramus: Method and the Decay of Dialogue* (Cambridge, Mass.: Harvard University Press, 1958).
[4] Frances A. Yates, *The Art of Memory* (London: Routledge and Kegan Paul, 1966).

tional in songs if they provide a familiar, comprehensible base for the listener while he centers his attention on what is novel or artfully expressed. Naturally many songs accept and exploit the Petrarchan love situation; others have pastoral trappings; others conventionally invert or parody the conventions, some amusingly so (*e.g.*, Jo1609.VI). A few manage to convey emotion through the conventions even without the help of music (Jo1609.XI). But there is a considerable variety of conventions as well as of poems within them: there are religious and festive songs as well as love songs and "songs of good life." And the love songs embrace the extremes of Hume's "Tobacco" (Hu1605.3) and Donne's "The Expiration" (Fer1609.VII).

Another resource, formal rhetoric, could be used to order language in such a way that the hearer, recognizing the form, would more easily assimilate the content since it would be partly expected. Some of the figures and schemes that song poets found useful are anaphora (*e.g.*, At1622.III, Bt1606.VII, XII, Ck1610.XII, Jo1610.XI), anadiplosis and climax (Mo1600.XVIII, Do1597.VI), correlative verse (Do1597.VII, Do1600.XI), and exergasia, "when we abide still in one place and yet seeme to speake divers things."[5] This last is not a readily identifiable pattern of words like the others; as Puttenham says, "I doubt whether I may terme it a figure, or rather a masse of many figuratiue speaches, applied to the bewtifying of our tale or argument" and thus "attire it with copious & pleasant amplifications" (p. 247). The copiousness to which those figures lead is not just a product of the textbook Elizabethan's exuberant delight in abundance, but is a means of defining and emphasizing the main point of the poem.[6] Copiousness may not always be to the modern reader's taste, but it is very useful in an oral form.

The strophic form of most of the songs makes exergasia a common feature; the structure of these songs is best described as circular, or spiral, or cumulative. The repeated music discourages the poets from allowing later stanzas to move too far away from the atmosphere and ideas of the first. Walter R. Davis[7] has noticed this structure in poems from Dowland's books (he cites Do1600.II, XIX, Do1612.XIIII–XVI), and it is present in many other poems (*e.g.*, Jo1600. I, III, VII, XI, etc.; Fd1607.II, IIII, V, etc.; Bt1606.V, VI). This tendency of the songs to

---

[5] Henry Peacham the elder, *The Garden of Eloquence* (1577), sig. P4v.

[6] Rosemond Tuve, *Elizabethan and Metaphysical Imagery* (Chicago, 1947), pp. 118–122.

[7] "Melodic and Poetic Structure: the Examples of Campion and Dowland," *Criticism*, IV (1962), 89–107.

hover about a central idea rather than to develop an argument to a conclusion enables singers to omit stanzas of some songs without doing obvious violence to the sense. In a few songs, stanzas have even been transposed without attracting much attention (see the notes to Do1600. II and Do1612.V).

Other kinds of structures such as simple narratives and blazons or other catalogs are fairly common (At1622.I, Bt1606.XIII, Ros1601.I. VIII, Jo1601.V; At1622.V, Bt1606.IIII, Jo1601.XVII). But Davis finds another kind of structure preferred by Campion and other poets which is closer to the later epigrammatic style. Here brevity, selectivity, and a more logical structure are evident. One way the strophic form is used by these poets is in making two stanzas parallel, the first setting forth a situation and the second making an application or drawing an inference. Davis' example is Campion's well-known "When to her lute Corinna sings" (Ros1601.I.VI); Pattison (pp. 152–153) discusses a similar poem from Jones (1600.XVI) and a poem with a reply from Danyel (1606.I). See also Do1603.VI and Cop1606.III.

Poets writing songs are also limited in the ways they can use imagery. These limitations may be illustrated by comparing three poems on a similar subject, Donne's "The Sunne Rising," his "Breake of Day," which was set to music by Corkine (1612.IIII), and "Sweet stay a while" (Do1612.II). The second poem is more suitable for singing than the first, despite the difficulties of fitting the third stanza to the music, if only because the argument is less difficult to follow. The imagery brought to bear is fairly easy to associate with the subject: light and darkness, the sun. The distracting world that calls the lover away is only some unspecified "business." In "The Sunne Rising," however, the reader leaps from "sowre prentices" to "Court-huntsmen," from the lovers' bed to the "India's of spice and Myne." The sun that wakes the lovers and reminds them of the world and daily affairs is chided as a "Busie old foole" and informed in the conclusion of the argument that all the world is rather in the poet's bed. The ideas and images in most of Donne's poetry are complex and interlocked, and depend on what has preceded and what follows for their meaning. These poems are a delight to read, but with the added interest or distraction of music, their progress would be impossible to follow. The third poem, "Sweet stay a while" (Do1612.II; see notes on its connection with Donne), is a more representative song lyric. In this song, as in others, the images may be related to a central theme or conceit, but tend to be isolated from each other; they accumulate rather than develop. Rarely, in fact, do images in songs extend beyond two lines of verse or a corresponding musical period. The phrase or line, as well as being a rhythmic unit, is frequently a unit of sense: the aural memory of the listener is not required to hold too much for too long. Even Donne could use imagery in a manner suited for singing, as in this "Song," which was set to music in Donne's lifetime:

> Goe, and catche a falling starre,
>   Get with child a mandrake roote,
> Tell me, where all past yeares are,
>   Or who cleft the Divels foot,
> Teach me to heare Mermaides singing,
> Or to keep off envies stinging,
>   And finde
>   What winde
> Serves to'advance an honest minde.

Although the rest of the poem gets more complex, the single idea in the stanza, "impossible," is clear because the listener is not required to follow the images consecutively. If he misses the point in the first line, he has it by the fourth line. Although in Do1597.VII the theme is idealistic instead of cynical, the imagery is similar. See also Do1597.V, 1600.IX, 1603.I, and 3Camp[1617]XVIII:

> Thrice tosse these Oaken ashes in the ayre,
> Thrice sit thou mute in this inchanted chayre;
> Then thrice three time tye vp this true loues knot,
> And murmur soft, shee will, or shee will not.

The conditions that affect imagery also apply to diction. I can do no better than quote W. H. Auden's comment:

> The elements of the poetic vocabulary, therefore, which are best adapted for musical setting are those which require the least reflection to comprehend—its most dynamic and its most immediate. For example: interjections, which in one's mother tongue always sound onomatopoeic (fie, O, alas, adieu); imperatives; verbs of physical motion (going, coming, hasting, following, falling) or physical concomitants of emotions (laughing, weeping, frowning, sighing); adjectives denoting elementary qualities (bright, hard, green, sad); nouns denoting states of feeling (joy, love, rage, despair) or objects, the emotional associations of which are common to all, and strong (sea, night, moon, spring).[8]

[8] W. H. Auden, Chester Kallman, and Noah Greenberg, eds., *An Elizabethan Song Book* (Garden City: Doubleday Anchor, 1955), pp. xvi–xvii.

The demand for simplicity in words for music is large, but there is room in a successful song for some of the subtleties that make one return to a work of art with an expectation of finding something new. Dowland's "Weepe you no more sad fountaines" (Do1603.XV) is such a song. It is first a beautiful whole, music and poetry balancing and complementing each other. But it is also an example of a kind of poetic effect that is possible only in the strophic song.

The poem has a conventional subject: the weeping fountains and the melting snow on mountains recall another song in the same book, "Flow not so fast yee fountaines" (Do1603.VIII), and Ben Jonson's "Slow, slow, fresh fount" from *Cynthias Revels* (*Works*, IV, 50). (They may have been in J. B. Leishman's mind when he included the line "where fountains spring from mountains" in his parody in *The Monarch of Wit*, p. 16.) But the refinement of the emotion in "Weepe you no more," while retaining the advantages of the conventions, purges them of dead and facile responses.

This song will bear repeated hearings, not only because of its formal and musical beauty, but also because of the subtleties that gradually reveal themselves. The mood and general meaning of the poem are clear on the first hearing. The lover attempts to stop his weeping by reflecting that his beloved is asleep and cannot see him, and that because "Sleepe is a reconciling," she will look on him with favor when she wakes. The situation and conclusion are understood or inferred; the poem dwells on the moment, the emotions. But in later hearings, the memory juxtaposes the two stanzas because the same melody is used for both; one hears the echo, so to speak, of the first stanza while hearing the second stanza. (Incidentally, the first words of each stanza rhyme.) The two images drawn from nature in the second and third lines of each stanza are at once parallel and contrasting. "Looke how the snowie mountaines,/ heau'ns sunne doth gently waste" is related to the lover's weeping, his melting under the disapproving glare of the sun of his mistress' eye. But "Doth not the sunne rise smiling,/ When faire at eu'n he sets" expresses the hope that after the reconciling sleep the sun-eye will smile on him. The poet is so considerate towards the musician that even though the sentiment has changed, both passages could be sung to the same music without awkwardness, even if the composer wanted to set them pictorially. "Snowie mountaines" corresponds with "rise smiling," and "doth gently waste" with "at eu'n he sets."

Campion frequently exploits these possibilities of the strophic song. In "When thou must home" (Ros1601.I.XX) the last line in the second stanza, "Then tell, O tell, how thou didst murther me," is sung, ironically, to the same music as "From that smoothe toong whose musicke hell can moue." Hallett Smith cites a similar use of repeated musical phrases in Campion's "Blame not my cheeks" (Ros1601.I XIIII; see also Jo1605.IX).[9] Other poets since Campion have used this same device with varying degrees of subtlety. Parodies and burlesques use the memory of the original words and the emotional associations of tunes for comic contrast or irony. One thinks of Lewis Carroll ("Beautiful soup") or perhaps Berthold Brecht, who wrote an anti-Hitler song based on the old chorale: "Nun danket alle Gott/ Der uns den Hitler sandte."

Poetry for music, then, is capable of some unique effects, but it is limited in that much of its content and appeal must be on the surface; richness and density of image and allusion are denied it. Consequently songs as poems are generally minor poems—but we would be poorer without them.

[9] Smith, *Elizabethan Poetry*, p. 284.

The Composers

For more convenient reference, the composers or compilers of the songbooks are listed here with brief biographies. Other facts about their lives may frequently be found in the dedications or prefaces to the songbooks. Sources consulted (unless otherwise noted) are Grove, *MGG*, Warlock, and Jeffery Pulver's *Biographical Dictionary of Old English Music* (London: Kegan Paul, 1927).

ATTEY, John. Attey is said to have died in Ross *c.* 1640, but none of the references give the source of this information.

BARLEY, William (1565–1614). Barley was of course not a composer, but merely the printer and publisher of *A new Booke of Tabliture* (1596). Barley printed a number of music books as the assignee of Thomas Morley, who held the music-printing patent from 1598 until his death in 1603. In 1606, Barley successfully claimed this patent for himself; he printed some music books himself, but more were printed by his assignees. See the introduction to Wilburn W. Newcomb's edition of By1596, *Lute Music of Shakespeare's Time* (University Park: Pennsylvania State University Press, 1966).

BARTLET, John. All that is known of Bartlet is that he took a Bachelor of Music from Oxford in 1610.

CAVENDISH, Michael. (*c.* 1565?–July 5, 1628). Cavendish was the youngest son of William Cavendish of Cavendish Overhall, and was therefore related to the Dukes of Devonshire. In the pedigree of this family (BM MS Add. 19122), Michael Cavendish is listed as "Servant in the Bedchamber to Prince Charles." He contributed to Thomas East's *Whole Book of Psalms* (1592) and to Thomas Morley's *Triumphes of Oriana* (1601; see note to Cav1598.XXIIII).

COPRARIO (or Coperario), John (*c.* 1575?–1626). He was supposedly born in England as John Cooper, but changed his name after a trip to Italy. By about 1605 he was back in England. He wrote some music for an entertainment sponsored by the Merchant Taylor's Company in 1607, and for Campion's *Somerset Masque* in 1614. He had collaborated with Campion in 1613 for their *Songs of Mourning: bewailing the vntimely death of Prince Henry*. He also contributed to Sir William Leighton's *Teares or Lamentacions* (1614). In 1616 and 1617, he again traveled abroad, and sometime before 1625 became composer to the king (he was succeeded by Alfonso Ferrabosco in 1626). He had probably been employed at court earlier as one of the music teachers to the royal family. Other students of his were William and (probably) Henry Lawes. Coprario is perhaps best known for furthering Italian styles in solo song in England, and for his fantasies for viols, a number of which survive in manuscript. See the selections in *Jacobean Consort Music*, ed. Thurston Dart and William Coates (London, 2nd ed., 1962; *MB* IX). He also wrote a treatise called "Rules How to Compose"; see the facsimile edition made from the Huntington manuscript by Manfred Bukofzer (Los Angeles, 1952).

CORKINE, William. Nothing is known of Corkine's life. An anthem of his is in manuscript at Christ Church, Oxford, and a delightful consort song, "What booteth love," was recorded by Alfred Deller ("William Byrd and His Age," Vanguard BG–557).

DANYEL, John (*c.* 1565?–1630?). John Danyel was the son of a music master and was the brother of Samuel Daniel, the poet. He received the Bachelor of Music degree from Oxford in 1604, and was in royal service of one sort and another from about 1612 through 1625. He received warrants for educating the children of the Queen's Revels in 1613 and 1618. He was executor of his brother Samuel's will, and wrote the dedication (to Prince Charles) for his *Works* of 1623.

DOWLAND, John (1563–1626), and Robert (*c.* 1585?–1641). Despite the claims in Grove and elsewhere, Dowland was probably born in England. In about 1580, he went to France in the service of Sir Henry Cobham, the English Ambassador, where he became a convert to Catholicism. Dowland blamed his religion for the failure of his attempt to get a place among the Queen's musicians in 1594, despite his fame (he had taken his Bachelor of Music from Oxford in 1588). He then decided to tour the continent, intending to study with Luca Marenzio in Rome. He visited Brunswick, Cassel, Venice, Padua, Genoa, Ferrara and Florence (where he encountered some English Catholics), but probably did not get to Rome. He returned to Cassel, where he remained in the service of Moritz, Landgrave of Hessen, until late 1596, when he received a summons from his "old Master and Frend," Henry Noel. Noel claimed that a court post was available, but Dowland probably returned early in 1597 to find that his patron, and apparently his hopes, had died. (Dowland composed his "Lamentatio Henrici Noel" at this time.)

Dowland apparently found service with Sir George Carey, Baron Hunsdon, until November 1598, when he was appointed lutenist to Christian IV of Denmark. During a visit to England in 1604, he published his *Lachrimae*. Dowland remained in the Danish service until he was dismissed in 1606. By 1609, he had returned to England and published his translation of Andreas Ornithoparcus' *Micrologus*. Sometime before 1612, he became lutenist to Theophilus Howard, then Lord Walden, who may have helped him to the long-awaited post at the English court, which was granted in October, 1612. After 1621, he is styled "Doctor" Dowland. He remained one of the king's lutenists until his death in February, 1626. He was buried at St. Ann's, Blackfriars.

Robert Dowland succeeded his father at court, after having done some continental traveling of his own (in 1622–23, he had been in the service of the Duke of Wolgast in Pomerania). About eight months after his father's death, Robert married. He served in the King's Musick until his death in 1641.

A more detailed biography of Dowland may be found in Diana Poulton's forthcoming book (Faber); see her articles in *LSJ*, IV (1962), 32; V (1963), 7–17; VII (1965), 32–37; and in *The Consort*, No. 20 (1963), pp. 189–197. My own unpublished dissertation, "Poems from the Songbooks of John Dowland" (Harvard University, 1963), has a long biographical section in the Introduction (pp. 9–86). Dowland's lute music has been collected by Diana Poulton, and will soon be published by Faber.

FERRABOSCO, Alfonso (*c.* 1575–March 1628). Alfonso II was the son of Alfonso I, who was born in Bologna in 1543, son of Domenico Maria Ferrabosco, also a musician. Alfonso I had come to England by 1562, where he established some reputation. He returned to Bologna in 1578, but Alfonso II remained in England to receive an annuity from Queen Elizabeth from 1592 to 1601, and later to serve in the court of James I, both in the royal musicians and as one of Prince Henry's—and later Prince Charles'—music teachers. He participated in and wrote music for several court masques. He was known as a performer on the viol, for which he composed *Lessons for 1. 2. and 3. Viols* (1609). Other vocal instrumental music by Ferrabosco is found in Sir William Leighton's *Teares or Lamentacions of a Sorrowfull Soule* (1614), in continental printed collections, and in manuscript.

FORD, Thomas (*c.* 1580?–November, 1648). Ford became one of Prince Henry's musicians in 1611, and was appointed to King Charles' musicians in 1626. An abstract of his will is given by C. S. Emden in *RES*, II (1926), 419–20. Other music by Ford includes two anthems in Sir William Leighton's *Teares or Lamentacions of a Sorrowfull Soule* (1614), three canons in John Hilton's *Catch that Catch Can* (1652), and several canons, anthems, part-songs and instrumental pieces in manuscript (*e.g.*, Christ Church, Oxford, MSS 736–738).

GREAVES, Thomas. Nothing is known apart from what may be inferred from his songbook.

HANDFORD, George (1582–85?–1647?). It may be that this George Handford is the same as the person of that name who lived in Chancery Lane, was married in 1636 and again in 1641, and was buried in August, 1647, in the church of St. Dunstan's-in-the-West. Handford also composed an anthem, "Long haue I lifted up my voice" (BM MSS Add. 29372, fol. 87; Add. 29427, fol. 67v). See my article in *Anglia*, LXXXII (1964), 474–484.

HUME, Tobias (d. 1645). Hume served as a soldier in Poland and perhaps in Sweden, Germany, and Russia sometime before 1605. Around 1630, he petitioned King Charles for permission to lead 120 men into "Mickle Bury land" (Mecklenburg?) to serve the King of Sweden. By 1642, he was a poor brother at the Charterhouse; in that year was published his insane *True Petition of Colonel Hume as it was presented to the Lords assembled in the High Court of Parliament*, in which he offered to subdue the rebels in Ireland with some instruments of war he had invented, and to raise "twenty millions of gold and silver" in twelve or fourteen weeks.

JONES, Robert (*c.* 1577?–after 1615). Jones took his Bachelor of Music at Oxford in 1597. In 1610, Jones and three partners (including the composer Philip Rosseter) were granted a patent for establishing a school to train children for the Queen's Revels.

Five years later they obtained permission to build a theater for these children on the site of Jones's house in Blackfriars, but this project was opposed by the local authorities and the patent withdrawn. Jones contributed a madrigal to Thomas Morley's *Triumphes of Oriana* (1601), and published his own *First Set of Madrigals* in 1607. Other pieces by Jones may be found in Sir William Leighton's *Teares or Lamentacions of a Sorrow-full Soule* (1614) and in manuscript (*e.g.*, Folger MS V.b.278).

MAYNARD, John (1577–*c.* 1633 ?). Maynard was the son of Ralph Maynard of St. Albans, Hertfordshire. He was probably the "Johan Meinert" brought to Denmark by John Dowland in 1599. Maynard and another English musician fled from Denmark under mysterious circumstances in 1601. But from 1600 to 1610, he was one of the Commissaries of the Musters in Ireland; perhaps this office could be executed by deputy. The Hertfordshire Maynard seems to have lived on the family property from about the time of his father's death in 1614 until 1633. This information comes from the fullest account of Maynard's life, an article by Ian Harwood in *LSJ*, IV (1962), 7–16.

MORLEY, Thomas (1557?–1603 ?). Morley was one of the most important of Elizabethan composers, especially as a naturalizer of Italian vocal forms (madrigal, canzonet, ballet). He received his Bachelor of Music from Oxford in the same year as Dowland, 1588. By 1591 he was organist at St. Paul's, and in 1592 he became one of the Gentlemen of the Chapel Royal. About this time he seems to have been engaged in some sort of anti-Catholic espionage in the Low Countries. In 1598 he received the patent for printing music and music paper, the monopoly once held by his teacher William Byrd. Morley's compositions are numerous. Several volumes of canzonets, ballets, and madrigals, plus a collection of instrumental pieces and the treatise *A Plaine and Easie Introduction to Practical Musicke* (1597) were printed, and a number of services, motets, and anthems survive in manuscript.

PILKINGTON, Francis (*c.* 1565?–1638). As his dedication states, Pilkington's father and brother served the Earl of Derby. He took his Bachelor of Music from Oxford in 1595, and by 1602 was a singer at Chester Cathedral. He later became a minor canon, and was ordained by 1614; he was curate of St. Bridget's, Chester in 1616, and of St. Martin's in 1622. He was a Precentor of Chester Cathedral in 1623, and rector of the church at Aldford, near Chester, in 1633. His other works consist of his *First* and *Second Set of Madrigals* (1614 and 1623), contributions to Sir William Leighton's *Teares and Lamentacions*, 1614, and some lute pieces in manuscript.

Editorial Procedure

An edition of poems taken from music books cannot, strictly speaking, be either a critical edition which attempts to recover the author's original words, or a quasi-facsimile which offers a page-by-page, line-by-line reproduction of an ideal copy of the original book. The authors of most of the poems are anonymous; but when the poet is known and an accurate text established, as with Ben Jonson, no one would wish to see the version of a poem in the Herford and Simpson edition replace the version published with Ferrabosco's music. On the other hand, since the music is excluded, the text cannot be considered even a quasi-facsimile. Therefore the present edition may be described as a conservative critical edition, with the composer's manuscript, not the poet's, as the ideal copy. I therefore give the text as it appears in the original song-book, with changes as described below. When there is more than one voice part, I generally print from the Cantus because it usually has all the words and the fewest purely musical repetitions.

The following changes are made silently:

(1) Music, musical directions, and printing ornaments are omitted.

(2) Long ∫ and *vv* are given as *s* and *w*, and in quotations from manuscripts, initial *I* or *J* is always given as *I*.

(3) Most abbreviations and contractions that do not affect pronunciation are expanded, and the consequent punctuation is altered or omitted;

superior letters are lowered (*e.g.*, *moūt* becomes *mount,* *y^e* becomes *the,* *chariq;* becomes *charique,* but *M^r* becomes *Mr*).

(4) Wrong-fount letters are corrected, and no notice is taken of swash italic capitals except in the bibliographical descriptions.

(5) Spacing is normalized, but changes that result in different words or meanings are recorded in the Variant Readings.

(6) Repetitions of words or phrases brought about by the music are omitted. In a few instances it is difficult to say whether a repetition is primarily musical or rhetorical, but most of the time the pattern established by subsequent stanzas helps to determine the arrangement of the first stanza, which is usually the only one underlying the music.

(7) Line numbers, page numbers, and material in square brackets are editorial.

(8) The original lineation of the prose dedications and epistles is ignored.

All other changes are recorded in the Variant Readings. These changes are usually corrections of obvious misprints, such as turned or transposed letters, or of readings that may be improved from the other voice parts. I permit myself a few conjectural emendations when the original is patently wrong and a good case may be made for a printing-house error or when a correction has strong support from other sources, but most suggested emendations are confined to the notes. The original punctuation has been retained for the most part, but I have found some changes and additions desirable. These are recorded in the Variant Readings.

Besides editorial changes, the Variant Readings include substantive readings from the other voice parts and, in the case of D01597, readings from the later editions (1600–1613). Variants from other sources appear in the Notes, and verbal press-corrections are given in the Textual Introductions to each book. Although musical press-corrections would no doubt be valuable to musicologists and bibliographers, they have no bearing on the poems, and both the labor and practical difficulties involved in recording them are too great for this edition. In all instances, the reading to the left of the bracket is that of the present text.

The Textual Introductions contain bibliographical descriptions of the books on the model of those in Fredson Bowers' *Principles of Bibliographical Description* (Princeton, 1949), with transcriptions of title-pages, collations, descriptions of contents, locations of copies, and notes on printing history. Very few of the books have catchwords, pagination, or running titles. But most have lines of type that are like ordinary running titles in that they were not distributed after printing, but were transferred to the next forme. These usually contain the words indicating the voice part (*e.g.*, CANTVS, ALTVS); I describe them under "Headlines," even though many of these do not occur at the head of the page. Analysis of these headlines can produce the same sort of bibliographical evidence as running titles. (See the essays by Fredson Bowers and Charlton Hinman in the *English Institute Annual: 1941* [New York: Columbia University Press, 1942], pp. 185–222.)

Lyrics from English Airs

William Barley

A New Booke of Tabliture

1596

Barley's book is printed as three separately signed and titled parts. Each part will be described as a separate volume, but the whole will afterwards be considered as one book. For another account (confirming the identifications of the composers) see Howard Mayer Brown, *Instrumental Music Printed before 1600* (Cambridge, Mass.: Harvard University Press, 1965), pp. 407–409. See also the edition by Wilburn W. Newcomb, *Lute Music of Shakespeare's Time* (University Park: Pennsylvania State University Press, 1966), for transcriptions of the music.

Part I:
[Within a border of type ornaments:] A nevv Booke of Tabliture, Containing/ fundrie eaſie and familiar Inſtructions, ſhevving hovve to attaine to the knovvledge, to/ guide and diſpoſe thy hand to play on ſundry Inſtruments, as the *Lute, Orpharion,*/ and *Bandora*: Together vvith diuers nevv Leſſons to each of theſe Inſtruments./ *VVhereunto is added an introduction to Prickeſong, and certaine familliar rules of Deſcant, with other/ neceſſarie Tables plainely ſhewing the true vſe of the Scale or Gamut, and alſo how to ſet any Leſſon/ higher or lower at your pleaſure./* Collected together out of the beſt Authors profeſſing the practiſe of theſe Inſtruments./ [cut of lute on music book between two pillars of type ornaments]/ Printed [r broken] at London for William Barley and are to be ſold at his ſhop in Gratious ſtreet, 1596./

Collation: oblong 4°; A–F⁴G¹ (fully signed except G1; E2 and E4 misprinted as F2 and F4; G1 seems to be A1 of next part); 25 leaves.

Headlines: running title B1v–G1v (recto and verso): AN INSTRVCTION TO THE LVTE. (Two skeletons.)

Contents: A1, title page; A1v blank; A2, dedication; A3, "Certaine Verses"; A3v, epistle; A4, poems I–II; A4v, poems III–IIII; B–D1, "An Instruction to the Lute"; D1v–D3, "A Pauan for the Lute. . . . F[rancis] C[utting]"; D3–D4v, "A Pauan for the Lute. . . . by F. C."; E1–E2v, "Lacrime by I[ohn] D[owland]" (*cf.* D01600.II); E3–F1, "Pipers Pauin By I. D." (D01597.IIII); F1v–F2v, "An Almaine. . . . by F. C."; F3–F3v, "Fortune by I D"; F4–G1, "A Galliard for rhe [*sic*] Lute. . . . by Fr. C."; G1v blank.

Part II:

[Within a border of rules] A nevv Booke of Tabliture for the Orpha-/ rion: Contayning fundrie forts of leffons, collected together out of diuers good Authors, for/ the furtherance and delight of fuch as are defirous to practife on this Inftrument./ *Neuer before Publifhed.*/ [rule/ cut of orpharion with frets lettered/ rule]/ Imprinted at London for VVilliam Barley; and are to be fold at his shop in Gratious/ ftreet neere Leaden-Hall./

Collation: oblong 4°; A⁴ [counting G1 of Part I] B–D⁴ (A1–3 not signed); 16 leaves, counting G1 of Part I.

Headlines: running title, B1–D4v (recto and verso): AN INSTRVCTION TO THE ORPHARION. [B3: *A* inverted. One skeleton.]

Contents: A2 blank; A3, title page; A3v blank; A4, "To the Reader"; A4v blank; B1–B1v, "The Countesse of Sussex Galliard. . . . P[hilip] R[osseter]"; B2–B2v, "Another galliard of the Countesse of Sussex. . . . PP" [Philip Rosseter again? Peter Philips?]; B3, "Another galliard of the Countesse of Sussex . . . P. R."; B3v–B4, "Solus cum Sola made by I. D."; B4v, "A Galliard made by I. D."; C1, "A Galliard made by F. C."; C1v, "A galliard made by Ed[ward] I[ohnson]"; C2, "An Almaine by Frances Cuting"; C2v–C4, "Go from my Windowe made by I. D."; C4v, "Bockingtons Pound by Fr. C."; D1, "Mistris Winters Iumpe made by I. D."; D1v, "Cuttings comfort . . . by Fr. C."; D2–D3, "Walsinggam made by Francis Cutting"; D3v–D4v, "Master Birds Pauan set by Francis Cutting."

Part III:

[Within a border of rules: rule/] A nevv Booke of Tabliture for the Bando-/ ra: Contayning fundrie forts of leffons, collected together out of of diuers good Authors for/ the furtherance and delight of fuch as are defirous to practife on this Inftrument./ *Neuer before Publifhed.*/ [cut of bandora with frets lettered]/ Imprinted at London for VVilliam Barley; and are to be fold at his shop in Gratious/ ftreet neere Leaden-Hall./ [rule]

Collation: oblong 4°, A–D⁴ (all signed except A2); 16 leaves.

Headlines: running title, A4–D3 (recto and verso): AN INSTRVCTION TO THE BAN-DORE. [one skeleton]

Contents: A1 blank except for signature letter A; A1v blank; A2, title page; A2v blank; A3, "Gentle Reader"; A3v blank; A4–B1v, "The Quadron Pauan"; B2–B2v "The Quadron Galliard"; B3, "A Perludium . . . A[nthony] H[olborne]"; B3v–C1,

"The new Hunt sundry waies made by Frances Cutting"; C1v–C2, untitled piece by
"A H."; C2v–C3, "Those eies which set my fancie on a fire"; C3v–C4, "Howe can
the tree but waste and wither away"; C4v–D1, "One ioy of ioyes I only felt"; D1v–
D2, "But this & then no more it is my last of all"; D2v–D3v, "Treschoses"; D4,
poems V–VII; D4v blank.

SR: No entry.

STC: 1433.

Copies: BM (K.1.c.18, the text copy), RCM (Mus.I.F.16), and Huntington (35074;
has Part I only). Howard Mayer Brown notes that another copy was listed in a Sotheby
auction catalogue, *Catalogue of the Famous Musical Library . . . of the Late W. H. Cum-*
mings, Mus. Doc., 1917. I have not seen this copy and do not know of its whereabouts.
Collation of the other copies reveals the following press corrections:

Part I: Outer forme A, uncorrected: BM, RCM (except A1).

A1 (title page, line 9) London . . . 1596.] Londõn . . . 1596 [BM only]

A2v (dedication 45) your Honour] yonr Honour

A4v (IIII.2) haires] heares

Inner forme A, uncorrected: RCM.

A3v (To Reader 3) suf-/ficient] suf-/cient

               promptnes] promptnenes

               19) lost, furthermore] lost. further more

A4 (I.6.) too] to

    (II.21) care] cure

    (II.25) release] heale

          hel] hell

Outer forme F, uncorrected: BM.

F2v, F3: printing blocks containing the tablature inverted.

Inner forme F; uncorrected: BM.

F1v: An Almaine] A Pauin

F4: A galliard for rhe [*sic*] Lute] A Pauin for rhe Lute

Other versions of many of the pieces here, other works by these composers, MS
sources and the like are discussed by Richard Newton, "English Lute Music of the
Golden Age," *PRMA,* LXV (1939), pp. 63 ff., and David Lumsden, "The Sources of
English Lute Music (1540–1620)," unpublished Ph. D. dissertation, Cambridge, 1957.
The instructions for the lute in the first part are, as Howard Mayer Brown has pointed
out, a partial translation of Adrian LeRoy's *Instruction de partir toute musique des huits*
divers tons en tablature de luth (Paris: LeRoy and Ballard, 1557).

The words to the songs on sigs. C2v–D2 of Part III are not printed with the music
(which is printed from wooden blocks), but poems V and VII are the words for the
first two. The text of "But this & then no more it is my last of all," (D1v–D2) is not
found in By1596, but it was written by Sir Arthur Gorges and is included in his *Poems,*
ed. Helen E. Sandison (Oxford: Clarendon Press, 1953), pp. 26–27. The words for
"One ioy of ioyes" (C4v–D1) are not known.

To the Right honorable & vertuous Ladie *Bridgett*
Countesse of Sussex, W. B. wisheth health of bodie, content

of minde, with increase of all Honourable perfection, and eternall happinesse in the *world to come*.

Rıght Honorable and vertuous Ladie: bookes (some of one argument, and some of an other), that are compiled by men of diuers gifts, are published by them to diuers endes: by some in desire of a gainefull reward: some for vaine ostentation, some for good will & affection, and some for common profit which by their workes may be gotten: As the first of these causes doth shew a greedie minde in the Dedicator, 10 so the second cause doth shew foorth the fantasticall spirit of an asspiring minde: Of the two first entents I hold my selfe as cleare, and as for the two latter, I depute them as necessarie to my selfe. First, in regard of the dutifull affection which I beare towards your Honorable Ladyship, whom I haue heard so well reported of, for the noble vertues both of body and minde wherewith God hath graced you. And secondly, for that I my selfe am a publisher & seller of Bookes, whereby I haue my liuing & maintenance: and for these two last reasons I haue caused (to my great cost and charges) sundry sorts of lessons to be collected together out of some of the best Authors professing this excellent science 20 of musique, and haue put them in print: As the Lute Orpharion and Bandora, togeather with an Introduction to pricke song, and the rules of descant. All which I humbly Dedicate vnto your Honorable Ladyship: not doubting but that of your noble & gentle nature you will gentlie accept of them, and take my well meaning in good part, as if it had [A2v] bin a worke of far more excellent perfection. And although to some it may seeme rather presumpteous foolishnes, than any wel aduised discretion, to take in hand the publication of this booke, for that it is very like both the booke published, and the publisher too shall vndergo many censures and reproofes of captious spirits: But neuerthe- 30 lesse I doubt not when the causes that mooued mee to the setting forth of the same shall be indifferent wayed in the ballance of an honest and milde disposition, I hope it will appeare that both my trauell and charges is well imploied: For my desire herein is to expresse my hartes dutifull regarde towardes your Honour; and next to benifit such, as desire to haue a tast of so rauishing a sweet Science as Musique is, beeing the soueraigne salue of a melancholly and troubled minde, and a fitting companion of Princely personages. And further, for that euery one cannot haue a Tutor, this booke will sufficiently serue to be Schoolemaster vnto such that will but spare some of their idle howers, to ob- 40 serue what this booke expresseth vnto them.

And now after long time hauing gotten it finished, such as the worthines or vnworthines of it is, relying on your worthines intermingled with much gentlenes, I come (though much vnworthy) presenting it to the viewe of your Honour, well assuring my selfe that if it will so please you to shrowd it vnder the orient coloured feathers of your heauenly vertues, & the broad spreading wing of your Honour, it will be sure inough from the tallents of the enuious; and remaine safe through your protection, whereby such as loue profitable endeuors, will be ready to embrace your Honour and vertue with it. Which 50 considering, I leaue it with your Ladiship: beseeching the Almightie long to continue your daies, with increase of honour to your harts content, that so when you haue paid a due debt to nature, you may receiue a free gift of God, the framer of nature, euen the Crowne of immortall glorie, amidst the harmonious Quiere of blessed spirits inhabiting the highest heauens.

> *Your Honors in all humble seruice of dutie to*
> *be commanded.   W. B.*

CERTAINE VERSES VPON THE ALPHE-
BET OF HER LADYSHIPS NAME.

B *Bewties chiefe ornament of natures treasure,*
R *Richlie adornes her heauenlie countenance:*
I *In wisdomes schoole she builds her bower of pleasure,*   5
D *Diuine for wit and Godly gouernance.*
G *Garnished with vertue, grace, and modestie,*
E *Euen in her breast true honour is inrold:*
T *To praise her patience, loue, and loyaltie,*
T *The Muses charge it is with pens of gold.*   10

S *She is the starre that giues a golden light*
V *Vnto posterities, for liberall minde:*
S *She puts ambitious couetousnes to flight,*
S *So bountifull she is so meeke and kinde,*
E *Endles her honor, vnspotted is her fame,*   15
X *Xhrist graunt his glorie to this vertuous name.*

To the Reader.

It is not to be doubted but that there are a number of good wits in England, which for their sufficient capacitie and promptnes of spirit, neither Fraunce nor Italie can surpasse, and in respect that they cannot all dwell in or neere the cittie of London where expert Tutors are to be had, by whome they may be trained in the true manner of handling the Lute and other Instruments, I haue here to my great cost and charges, caused sundrie lessons to be collected together for the Lute, Orpharion, Bandora, and out of the best Authors that hath professed the practise of those Instruments, only for the ease and further-ance of such as are desirous to haue a taste of this sweet & commendable practise of musique, and for the more ready attayning thereunto, is added sundrie necessarie rules, plainelie teaching how thou maiest accord or tune these Instru-mentes by Arte or by eare, and the disposing of the hand in handling the necke or bellie of the Lute and the other Instruments, by obseruing of which rules thou maiest in a short time learne by thy self with very small help of a teacher. Thus he who is desirous to haue the vse of those Instruments, and hath not alreadie anie entrance in this Arte for when this booke is perticulerly published, to bestow some certaine houres at thy conuenient leasure to read and marke this little Instruction, and I dare assure thee thy labour will not be lost, furthermore I would request those who hath beene long studious of this Arte and hath attained the perfection thereof, that they would not take my trauaile and cost in ill part, seeing onlie I haue done it for their sakes which be learners in this Art and cannot haue such recourse to teachers as they would.   Vale.

[I.]

THoughts make men sigh, sighes make men sick at hart,
  sicknes consumes, consumption killes at last:
Death is the end of euerie deadlie smart,
  and sweet the ioy where euery paine is past:
But oh the time of death too long delayed,   5
  where tried patience is too ill apayed.

Hope harpes on heauen, but liues in halfe a hell,
  hart thinkes of life but findes a deadly hate:
Eares harke for blis, but heares a dolefull bell,
  Eyes looke for ioy, but see a wofull state: 10
But eyes, and eares, and hart, and hope deceaued,
  tongue tels a truth, how is the minde conceaued.

Conceited thus to thinke but say no more,
  to sigh and sob till sorrow haue an end:

And so to die till death may life restore,   15
  or carefull faith may finde a constant friend:
That patience may yet in her passion proue,
  iust at my death I found my life of loue.

[II.]

Loue is a spirit high presuming,
  that falleth oft ere he sit fast:
Care is a sorrow long consuming,
  which yet doth kill the heart at last:
Death is a wrong to life and loue,   5
  and I the paines of all must proue.

Words are but trifles in regarding,
  and passe away as puffes of winde,
Deedes are too long in their rewardinge,
  and out of sight are out of minde,   10
And those so little fauour feed,
  as findes no fruit in word or deed.

Truth is a thought too long in triall,
  and knowne but coldly entertainde:
Loue is too long in his deniall: 15
  and in the end but hardly gainde:
And in the gaine the sweet so small
  that I must taste the sowre of all.

But oh the death too long enduring,
  where nothing can my paine appease: 20
And oh the care too long in curing,
  where patient hurt hath neuer ease:
And oh that euer Loue should know,
  the ground whereof a greefe doth grow.
But heauens release me from this hel,   25
  or let me die and I am well.

[III.]

Your face	Your tongue	Your wit
So faire	So sweet	So sharpe
First bent	Then drew	So hite
Mine eye	Mine eare	My hart

Mine eye	Mine eare	My hart	5
To like	To learne	To loue	
Your face	Your tongue	Your wit	
Doth lead	Doth teach	Doth moue	

Your face	Your tongue	Your wit	
With beames	With sound	With arte	10
Doth blind	Doth charme	Doth rule	
Mine eye	Mine eare	My hart	

Mine eye	My eare	My hart	
With life	With hope	With skill	
Your face	Your tongue	Your wit	15
Doth feed	Doth feast	Doth fill	

Oh face	O tongue	O wit	
With frownes	With checks	With smart	
Wrong not	Vex not	Wound not	
Mine eye	My eare	My hart	20

This eye	This eare	This hart	
Shall ioy	Shall bend	Shall sweare	
Your face	Your tongue	Your wittes	
To serue	To trust	To feare.	

[Sir Arthur Gorges?]

[IIII.]

FLOW forth abundant teares, bedew this dolefull face,
  disorder now thy haires that liues in such disgrace:
Ah death exceedeth far this life which I endure,
  that still keepes me in warre, who can no peace procure.
I loue whome I should hate, she flyes I follow fast,   5
  such is my bitter state, I wish no life to last:
Alas affection strong, to whom I must obay,
  my reason so doth wrong, as it can beare no sway.
My field of flint I finde my haruest vaine desire,
  for he that sowed wind, now reapeth storme for hire: 10
Alas like flowers of Spaine, thy graces rorie be,
  I pricke these hands of mine for haste to gather thee:
But now shall sorrow slack, I yeeld to mortall strife,
  to die, this for thy sake, shall honour all my life.

FINIS.

[V.]

THose eyes that set my fancie on a fire,
  those crisped haires which hold my hart in chaines,
Those daintie hands which conquered my desire,
  that wit which of my thought doth hold the raines.
Then loue be Iudge what hart may therewith stand,   5
  such eyes, such head, such wit and such a hand:
Those eyes for clearenes doth the starres surpasse,
  those haires obscure the brightnes of the sunne.
Those hands more white than euer Iuorie was,
  that wit euen to the skies hath glory wonne: 10
Oh eyes that pearce our hearts without remorce,
  Oh haires of right that weares a royall crowne:
Oh hands that conquere more than Caesars force,
  Oh wit that turnes huge kingdomes vpside downe.

[VI.]

SHort is my rest whose toyle is ouer long,
  my ioyes are darke but cleare is seene my woe:
In safetie small great wracks I bide through wrong,
  whose time is swift and yet my hope but slow.
Each griefe and wound in my poore soule appeares,   5
  that laugheth houres and weepeth many yeares.
Deedes of the day are fables for the night,
  sighes of desire are smokes of thoughtfull teares:
My steps are false although my path is right,
  disgrace is bold my fauour full of feares.   10
Disquiet sleepe, keepes audite of my life,
  where rare content doth make displeasure rife:
The dolefull clocke which is the voice of time,
  calles on my end before my hap is seene.
Thus falles my hopes whose harmes haue power to clime,   15
  not come to haue which long in wish haue beene,
I trust you loue and feare not others hate,
  be you with me and I haue Caesars fate.

FINIS.

[VII.]

How can the tree but waste and wither away,
that hath not sometime comfort of the sunne:
How can the flower but vade and soone decay,
That alwaies is with darke clouds ouer runne,
  Is this a life? nay death I may it call: 5
  That feeles each paine, and knowes no ioy at all.

What foodles beast, can liue long in good plight,
Or is it life, where sences there be none?
Or what auaileth eyes without their sight,
Or else a tongue to him is alone?   10
  Is this a life? &c.

Whereto serues eares, if that there be no sound,
Or such a head where no deuice doth grow:
But al of plaints, since sorrow is the ground,
Whereby the heart, doth pine in deadlie woe.   15
  Is this a life? nay death I may it call:
  That feeles each paine, and knowes no ioy at all.

[Thomas, Lord Vaux]

FINIS.

John Dowland

The First Booke of Songes or Ayres

1597

First edition

[Within a compartment: McK. & F. No. 99] THE/ FIRST BOOKE/ of Songes or Ayres/ of fowre partes with Ta-/ *bleture for the Lute*:/ So made that all the partes/ together, or either of them feue-/ rally may be fong to the Lute,/ Orpherian or Viol de gambo./ Compofed by *Iohn Dowland* [D swash] Lute-/ nift and Batcheler of muficke in/ both the Vniuerfities./ Alfo an inuention by the fayd/ Author for two to playe vp-/ on one Lute./ [In lower slot:] *Nec profunt domino, quæ profunt omnibus, artes.*/ [rule]/ ¶ Printed by Peter Short, dwelling on/ Bredftreet hill at the fign of the Starre, 1597/

Note: The title page compartment was originally made for William Cuningham's *Cosmographical Glasse*, printed by John Day in 1559. It was also used for Do1603, Jo1600, and Ros1601.

Collation: 2°; π², A–L² (E2 not signed); 24 leaves.

Headlines: Verso, A1v–L1v: I. [–XXI.] CANTVS. Recto, A2–L2: TENOR./ BASSVS./ ALTVS.

Contents: π1, title page; π1v, arms of Sir George Carey; π2, dedication to Carey; π2v, epistle; A1, end of epistle, epigram by Campion, and table of songs; A1v–L2, songs I–XXI, one per opening; L2v, "My Lord Chamberlaine his galliard," for lute.

SR: Entered by Peter Short on "ultimo octobris," 1597, and transferred to Robert Young on December 6, 1630 (Arber, III, 94; IV, 245).

STC: 7091.

Copies: Folger (the text copy); Huntington (59102); Boston Public Library (*G. 400.51); BM (K.2.i.4; lacks D1). Although it is claimed in William W. Bishop's

Checklist of American Copies of STC Books (Ann Arbor: University of Michigan Press, 2nd ed., 1950), p. 49, that a copy is at Yale, this seems to be an error. The copy said to be at Trinity College, Dublin (David Ramage, *A Finding-List of English Books* [Durham, 1958], p. 28), is actually a copy of the 1603 edition (see below). The title page only of a copy of the first edition is in the BM, Ames I.588.

Collation reveals the following press-corrections:

Outer forme π: uncorrected, Boston: π2v, catchword: Not] *omitted*
Inner forme C: uncorrected, Boston, Folger: C2 (V): Bassus part inverted.
Inner forme D: uncorrected Boston, Folger: D1v (VII.1) DEare] DDeare

The signature letter on D2 is lacking in the Boston copy only.

The music for all the songs consists of a Cantus with tablature facing parts for Tenor, Bassus, and Altus, arranged for reading around a table.

Four more editions of this book appeared in Dowland's lifetime; but since they have no textual authority, I have not collated copies of these editions for presss-corrections.

Second edition, 1600

[Within a compartment: McK. & F. No. 99] THE/ FIRST BOOKE/ *of Songes or Ayres* [*A* swash] *of*/ foure partes with Ta-/ *bleture for the Lute.*/ So made that all the partes/ together, or either of them feue-/ rally may be fong to the Lute,/ Orpherian or Viol de gambo./ Compofed by *Iohn Dowland* [*D* swash] Lute-/ nift and Batcheler of Muficke in/ both the Vniuerfities./ Alfo an inuention by the faid Author/ for two to play vpon one Lute./ Newly corrected and amended./ [In lower slot:] *Nec profunt domino, quæ profunt omnibus, artes.*/ [rule]/ ¶ Printed by Peter Short the affigne of/ Th. Morley, and are to be fold at the figne of/ the Starre on Bredftreet hill. 1600./

Note: Thomas Morley received a monopoly for printing music (except psalms) and ruled music paper in September, 1598; the patent is printed in Robert Steele, *The Earliest English Music Printing* (London: The Bibliographical Society, 1903), pp. 27–29. See the Textual Introduction to Do1600.

Collation and contents: same as in 1597.

STC: 7092.

Copies: BM (K.2.i.5.[1]); Liverpool Public Library (not seen); H. L. Bradfer-Lawrence, Ripon, Yorkshire (not seen); and Folger.

Third edition, 1603

[Within a compartment: McK. & F. No. 99] THE/ FIRST BOOK/ *of Songes or Aires of*/ *foure parts with Ta-*/ bleture for the Lute./ So made that all the partes/ *together, or either of them feue-*/ rally may be fung to the Lute,/ *Orpherian or Viol de gambo.*/ Compofed by *Iohn Dowland* Lute-/

niſt and Batcheler of Muſicke in/ both the Vniuerſities./ Alſo an inuention by the ſaide Authour for/ two to play vpon one Lute./ *Newly corrected and amended.*/ [In lower slot:] *Nec proſunt domino, quæ proſunt omnibus, artes.*/ [rule]/ Printed at London by E. Short, and are to be ſold/ by Thomas Adams, at the ſigne of the white/ Lyon in Paules Church-yard. 1603./

Note: Peter Short died in 1603, and his widow, Em or Emma, printed a few books under her name. She soon married Humfrey Lownes. See Arber, III, 703, and R. B. McKerrow, *et al.*, *A Dictionary of Printers and Booksellers . . . 1557–1640* (London: The Bibliographical Society, 1910), p. 244. Morley's name does not appear on this edition because he died in 1603, and William Barley had not yet laid claim to the monopoly (see the Textual Introduction to Jo1609).

Collation and contents: same as in 1597, except πᵢv is blank.

STC: 7092.5.

Copies: Manchester Public Library (BR f410 Ds405), and Trinity College, Dublin (B.7.21; lacks sig. π; not seen).

Fourth edition, 1606

[Within a compartment: McK. & F. No. 99] THE/ FIRST BOOKE/ of Songs or Aires of foure/ parts, with Tableture for/ the Lute./ So made, that all the partes/ *together, or either of them ſeue-*/ rally, may be ſung to the Lute,/ Orpherian or Viol de gambo./ *Compoſed by* IOHN DOWLAND/ Luteniſt & Batcheler of Muſicke/ in both the Vniuerſities./ *Alſo an inuention by the ſaide Author/ for two to play vpon one Lute.*/ [rule]/ Newly Corrected and amended./ [rule]/ [In lower slot:] *Nec proſunt domino, quæ proſunt omnibus artes.*/ [rule]/ Imprinted at *London* by HVMFREY LOWNES,/ *dwelling on Bredſtreet-hill, at the ſigne*/ of the Starre. 1606./

Collation and contents: same as in 1597, except πᵢv is blank, and song XIIII is mis-numbered IX.

STC: 7093.

Copies: BM (K.2.i.6; lacks sig. L) and Fürst Alexander zu Dohna-Schlobitten, Lörrach-Baden, Germany.

Fifth edition, 1613

[Within a compartment: McK. & F. No. 99] THE/ FIRST BOOKE OF/ *SONGS OR AYRES* [*AY* swash] OF/ foure parts, with Table-/ ture for the Lute./ SO MADE, THAT ALL THE/ parts together, or either of them/ feuerally, may be ſung to the Lute,/ Orpherian, or Viol de gambo./ Compoſed by IOHN DOWLAND,/ *Luteniſt and Bacheler of Muſick*/ in both the Vniuerſities./ *Alſo an inuention by the ſaid Author/ for two to play vpon one Lute.*/ [rule]/ Newly corrected and amended./ [rule]/ [In lower slot:] *Nec proſunt domino, quæ proſunt omnibus artes.*/ [rule]/ Imprinted at London by *Humfrey Lownes,*/ dwelling on Bredſtreet-hill, at the ſigne/ of the Starre. 1613./

Collation and contents: same as in 1597, except πιv is blank, and song XIIII is mis-numbered IX.

STC: 7094.

Copies: BM (K.2.i.13); Christ Church College, Oxford, Lincoln Cathedral Library (Aa.2.17); (not seen); St. Michael's College, Tenbury; and Mr. Robert Spencer Woodford Green, Essex (not seen).

Diana Poulton has found some evidence of yet another edition, dated 1608. Three nineteenth-century references mention a 1608 edition, but since they all omit the edition of 1606, the date is probably a mistake. W. C. Hazlitt's *Hand-Book to the Popular, Poetical and Dramatic Literature of Great Britain* (1867), p. 163, lists editions of 1597, 1600, 1603, 1608, and 1613. In A. B. Grosart's commentary on Do1597.III in his edition of Fulke Greville's *Works* (1870), II, 133, he says that E. F. Rimbault had examined editions of 1597, 1600, and 1608. Finally, in William H. Husk's article on Dowland in the first edition of Grove (1879), the editions are listed as 1597, 1600, 1603, 1608, and 1613.

TO THE RIGHT HONOVRABLE SIR GEORGE CAREY, OF THE MOST HONORABLE ORDER OF THE GARTER KNIGHT:

Baron of Hunsdon, Captaine of her Maiesties gentlemen Pensioners, Gouernor of the Isle of Wight, Lieutenant of the countie of Southt. *Lord Chamberlaine of her Maiesties most Royall house, and of* her Highnes most honourable priuie Counsell.

THAT harmony (Right honorable) which is skilfullie exprest by Instruments, albeit, by reason of the variety of number & proportion of it selfe, it easilie stirs vp the minds of the hearers to admiration & delight, yet for higher authoritie and power hath been euer worthily attributed to that kinde of Musicke, which to the sweetnes of instrument applies the liuely voice of man, expressing some worthy sentence or excellent Poeme. Hence (as al antiquitie can witnesse) first grew the heauenly Art of musicke: for Linus Orpheus and the rest, according to the number and time of their Poemes, first framed the numbers and times of musick: So that Plato defines melody to consist of harmony, number & wordes; harmony naked of it selfe: words the ornament of harmony, number the common friend & vniter of them both. This small booke containing the consent of speaking harmony, ioyned with the most musicall instrument the Lute, being my first labour, I haue presumed to dedicate to your

Lordship, who for your vertue & nobility are best able to protect it, and for your honourable fauors towards me, best deseruing my duety and seruice. Besides your noble inclination and loue to all good Artes, and namely the diuine science of musicke, doth challenge the patronage of all learning, then which no greater title can bee added to Nobilitie. Neither in these your honours may I let passe the dutifull remembrance of your vertuous Lady my honourable mistris, whose singular graces towards me haue added spirit to my vnfortunate labours. What time and diligence I haue bestowed in the search of Musicke, what trauel in forren countries, what successe and estimation euen among strangers I haue found, I leaue to the report of others. Yet all this in vaine 30 *were it not that your honorable hands haue vouchsaft to vphold my poore fortunes, which I now wholy recommend to your gratious protection, with these my first endeuors, humbly beseeching you to accept and cherish them with your continued fauours.*

Your Lordships most humble seruant,
Iohn Dowland.

To the courteous Reader.

How hard an enterprise it is in this skilfull and curious age to commit our priuate labours to the publike view, mine owne disabilitie, and others hard successe doe too well assure me: and were it not for that loue I beare to the true louers of musicke, I had concealde these my first fruits, which how they will thriue with your taste I know not, howsoeuer the greater part of them might haue been ripe inough by their age. The Courtly iudgement I hope will not be seuere against them, being it selfe a party, and those sweet springs of humanity (I mean our two famous Vniuersities) wil entertain them for his sake, 10 whome they haue already grac't, and as it were enfranchisd in the ingenuous profession of Musicke, which from my childhoode I haue euer aymed at, sundry times leauing my natiue countrey, the better to attain so excellent a science. About sixteene yeeres past, I trauelled the chiefest parts of France, a nation furnisht with great variety of Musicke: But lately, being of a more confirmed iudgement, I bent my course toward the famous prouinces of Germany, where I founde both excellent masters, and most honorable Patrons of Musicke: Namely, those two miracles of this age for vertue and magnificence, *Henry Iulio* Duke of *Brunswick*, and learned *Maritius Lantzgraue* of *Hessen*, of whose 20 princely vertues and fauors towards me I can neuer speake sufficientlie.

Neither can I forget the kindnes of *Alexandro Horologio*, a right learned master of Musicke, seruant to the royal Prince the *Lantzgraue* of *Hessen*, and *Gregorio Howet* Lutenist to the magnificent Duke of *Brunswick*, both whome I name as well for their loue to me, as also for their excellency in their faculties. Thus hauing spent some moneths in *Germany*, to my great admiration of that worthy country, I past ouer the Alpes into *Italy*, where I founde the Cities furnisht with all good Artes, but especiallie Musicke. What fauour and estimation I had in *Venice, Padua, Genoa, Ferrara, Florence,* & diuers other places I willingly suppresse, least I should any way seeme partiall in mine owne indeuours. Yet can I not dissemble the great content I found in the proferd amity of the most famous *Luca Marenzio*, whose sundry letters I receiued from Rome, and one of them, because it is but short, I haue thought good to set downe, not thinking it any disgrace to be proud of the iudgement of so excellent a man.

Molto Magnifico Signior mio osseruandissimo.

PER *una lettera del Signior Alberigo Maluezi ho inteso quanto con cortese affetto si mostri desideroso di essermi congionto d'amicitia, doue infinitamente la ringratio di questo suo boun' animo, offerendomegli all' incontro se in alcuna cosa la posso seruire, poi che gli meriti delle sue infinite uirtù, & qualità meritano che ogni vno & me l'ammirino & osseruino, & per fine di questo le bascio le mani. Di Roma a' 13. di Luglio.* 1595.

D.V.S. Affettionatissimo seruitore,
Luca Marenzio.

Not to stand to long vpon my trauels, I will onely name that worthy maister *Giouanni Crochio* Vicemaster of the chappel of S. Marks in *Venice*, with whome I had familiar conference. And thus what experience I could gather abroad, I am now ready to practise at home, if I may but find encouragement in my first assaies. There haue bin diuers Lute lessons of mine lately printed without my knowledge, falce and vnperfect, but I purpose shortly my selfe to set forth the choisest of all my Lessons in print, and also an introduction for fingering, with other books of Songs, whereof this is the first: and as this findes fauour with you, so shal I be affected to labor in the rest. *Farewell.*

Iohn Dowland.

Tho. *Campiani Epigramma de*
instituto Authoris.

Famam, posteritas quam dedit Orpheo,
Dolandi melius Musica dat sibi,
Fugaces reprimens archetypis sonos;
Quas & delitias præbuit auribus,
Ipsis conspicuas luminibus facit.

A Table of all the Songs contained
in this Booke.

A Galliard for two to plaie vpon one Lute at the end of the booke.

I.

Vnquiet thoughts your ciuill slaughter stint,
& wrap your wrongs within a pensiue hart:
And you my tongue that maks my mouth a minte,

& stamps my thoughts to coyne them words by arte:
Be still for if you euer doo the like,   5
Ile cut the string that maks the hammer strike.

But what can staie my thoughts they may not start,
Or put my tongue in durance for to dye?
When as these eies the keyes of mouth and harte
Open the locke where all my loue doth lye;   10
Ile seale them vp within their lids for euer,
So thoughts & words and looks shall dye together.

How shall I then gaze on my mistresse eies?
My thoughts must haue some vent els hart wil break,
My tongue would rust as in my mouth it lies   15
If eyes and thoughts were free and that not speake.
Speake then and tell the passions of desire
Which turns mine eies to floods, my thoghts to fire.

II.

WHO euer thinks or hopes of loue for loue,
or who belou'd in *Cupids* lawes doth glorie,
who ioyes in vowes or vowes not to remoue,
who by this light-god hath not ben made sorry:
Let him see me ecclipsed from my son   5
with darke clowdes of an earth Quite ouer runne.

Who thinks that sorrowes felte, desires hidden,
Or humble faith in constant honor arm'd,
Can keepe loue from the friut that is forbidden,
Who thinks that change is by entreatie charm'd,   10
Looking on me let him know loues delights
Are treasures hid in caues, but kept by Sprights.
                                              [Fulke Greville]

III.

MY thoughts are wingde with hopes, my hopes with loue,
mount loue vnto the moone in cleerest night,
and say as she doth in the heauens mooue
in earth so wanes & waxeth my delight:

And whisper this but softly in her eares,   5
  hope oft doth hang the head, and trust shed teares.

And you my thoughts that some mistrust do carry,
If for mistrust my mistrisse do you blame,
Say though you alter, yet you do not varry,
As she doth change, and yet remaine the same: 10
Distrust doth enter harts, but not infect,
  And loue is sweetest seasned with suspect.

If she for this, with cloudes do maske her eies,
And make the heauens darke with her disdaine,
With windie sighes disperse them in the skies,   15
Or with thy teares dissolue them into raine;
Thoughts, hopes, & loue returne to me no more,
  Till *Cynthia* shine as she hath done before.

IIII.

IF my complaints could passions mooue,
  or make loue see wherein I suffer wrong:
my passions weare enough to prooue,
  that my despayrs had gouernd me to long,
O loue I liue and dye in thee   5
thy griefe in my deepe sighes still speakes,
thy wounds do freshly bleed in mee
my hart for thy vnkindnes breakes,
yet thou doest hope when I despaire,
and when I hope thou makst me hope in vaine.   10
Thou saist thou canst my harmes repaire,
yet for redresse thou letst me still complaine.

Can loue be ritch and yet I want,
Is loue my iudge and yet am I condemn'd?
Thou plenty hast, yet me dost scant,   15
Thou made a god, and yet thy power contemn'd.
That I do liue it is thy power,
That I desire it is thy worth,
If loue doth make mens liues too sowre
Let me not loue, nor liue henceforth: 20
Die shall my hopes, but not my faith,

That you that of my fall may hearers be
May here despaire, which truly saith,
I was more true to loue, then loue to me.

V.

CAn shee excuse my wrongs with vertues cloake:
Shall I call her good when she proues vnkind.
Are those cleere fiers which vannish in to smoake:
must I praise the leaues where no fruit I find.

No no where shadowes do for bodies stand,   5
thou maist be abusde if thy sight be dime.
Cold loue is like to words written on sand,
or to bubbles which on the water swim.

Wilt thou be thus abused still,
seeing that she will right thee neuer   10
if thou canst not ore come her will,
thy loue will be thus fruitles euer.

Was I so base that I might not aspire
Vnto those high ioyes which she houlds from me,
As they are high so high is my desire,   15
If she this deny what can granted be.

If she will yeeld to that which reason is,
It is reasons will that loue should be iust,
Deare make me happie still by granting this,
Or cut of delayes if that dye I must.   20

Better a thousand times to dye
Then for to liue thus still tormented,
Deare but remember it was I
Who for thy sake did dye contented.

VI.

Now O now I needs must part,
parting though I absent mourne,
absence can no ioye empart,
ioye once fled can not returne.

While I liue I needs must loue,   5
loue liues not when hope is gone,
now at last despayre doth proue,
loue deuided loueth none:
Sad dispaire doth driue me hence,
this dispaire vnkindes sends.   10
If that parting be offence,
it is she which then offendes.

Deare when I from thee am gone,
Gone are all my ioyes at once,
I loued thee and thee alone   15
In whose loue I ioyed once:
And although your sight I leaue,
Sight wherein my ioyes doo lye
Till that death do sence bereaue,
Neuer shall affection dye.   20
[Sad dispaire, &c.]

Deare if I doe not returne,
Loue and I shall die togither,
For my absence neuer mourne
Whom you might haue ioyed euer: 25
Part we must though now I dye,
Die I doe to part with you,
Him despayre doth cause to lie,
Who both liued and dieth true.
[Sad dispaire, &c.]   30

VII.

Deare if you change ile neuer chuse againe,
sweete if you shrinke Ile neuer thinke of loue,
Fayre if you faile, ile iudge all beauty vaine,
wise if to weake moe wits ile neuer proue.
  Deare, sweete, faire, wise, change shrinke nor be not weake,   5
  and on my faith, my faith shall neuer breake.

Earth with her flowers shall sooner heau'n adorne,
Heauen her bright stars through earths dim globe shall moue,
Fire heate shall loose and frosts of flames be borne,

Ayre made to shine as blacke as hell shall proue: 10
  Earth, heauen, fire, ayre, the world transform'd shall vew,
  E're I proue false to faith, or strange to you.

VIII.

Bvrst forth my teares assist my forward griefe,
And shew what paine imperious loue prouokes:
Kinde tender lambes lament loues scant reliefe,
and pine, since pensiue care my freedome yoaks.
O pine to see me pine my tender flocks.   5

Sad pining care that neuer may haue peace,
At beauties gate in hope of pitty knocks:
But mercy sleeps while deepe disdaine encrease,
And beautie hope in her faire boosome yoaks,
O greiue to heare my griefe, my tender flocks.   10

Like to the windes my sighes haue winged beene,
Yet are my sighes and sutes repaide with mocks,
I pleade, yet she repineth at my teene:
O ruthles rigor harder then the rocks,
That both the Shephard kils, & his poore flocks?   15

IX.

Go christall teares, like to the morning showers,
  & sweetly weepe in to thy Ladies brest,
and as the deawes reuiue the drooping flowers,
so let your drops of pittie be adrest:
  To quicken vp the thoughts of my desert,   5
  which sleeps to sound whilst I from her departe.

Hast haplesse sighs and let your burning breath
Dissolue the Ice of her indurate harte,
Whose frosen rigor like forgetfull death,
Feeles neuer any touch of my desarte: 10
  Yet sighs and teares to her I sacryfise,
  Both from a spotles hart and pacient eyes.

X.

THinkst thou then by thy fayning,
sleepe with a proude disdaining,
Or with thy craftie closing,
thy cruell eyes reposing,
To driue me from thy sight,   5
when sleepe yeelds more delight,
such harmles beauty gracing.
And while sleepe fayned is,
 may not I steale a kisse,
thy quiet armes embracing.   10

O that thy sleepe dissembled,
Were to a trance resembled,
Thy cruell eies deceiuing,
Of liuely sence bereauing:
Then should my loue requite   15
Thy loues vnkind despite,
While fury triumpht bouldly
In beauties sweet disgrace:
 And liu'd in deepe embrace
Of her that lou'de so couldly.   20

Should then my loue aspiring,
Forbidden ioyes desiring:
So farre exceede the duty
That vertue owes to beauty?
No, Loue seeke not thy blisse,   25
Beyond a simple kisse,
For such deceits are harmeles,
Yet kisse a thousand fould,
 For kisses may be bould
When louely sleepe is armlesse.   30

XI.

Come away, come sweet loue,
The goulden morning breakes
All the earth, all the ayre
Of loue and pleasure speakes,

Teach thine armes then to embrace,   5
And sweet rosie lips to kisse,
And mixe our soules in mutuall blisse.
Eies were made for beauties grace,
Vewing ruing Loue long pains,
Procurd by beauties rude disdaine.   10

Come awaie come sweet loue,
The goulden morning wasts,
While the son from his sphere,
His fierie arrows casts:
Making all the shadowes flie,   15
Playing, staying in the groue,
To entertaine the stealth of loue,
Thither sweet loue let vs hie,
Flying, dying, in desire,
Wingd with sweet hopes and heau'nly fire.   20

Come away, come sweet loue,
Doe not in vaine adorne,
Beauties grace that should rise,
Like to the naked morne:
Lillies on the riuers side,   25
And faire Cyprian flowers new blowne,
Desire no beauties but their owne,
Ornament is nurce of pride,
Pleasure, measure, loues delight,
Hast then sweet loue our wished flight.   30

XII.

REst a while you cruell cares,
be not more seuere then loue
beauty kils & beautie spares,
 & sweet smiles sad sighs remoue:
Laura fayre queen, of my delight,   5
Come grant me loue in loues despite,
and if I euer faile to honor thee:
  Let this heauenly light I see,
  be as darke as hel to me.

If I speake my words want waite,   .   10
Am I mute, my hart doth breake,
If I sigh she feares deceit,
Sorrow then for me must speake:
Cruel, vnkind, with fauour view,
The wound that first was made by you: 15
And if my torments fained be,
  Let this heauenly light I see,
  Be as darke as hell to me.

Neuer houre of pleasing rest,
Shall reuiue my dying ghost,   20
Till my soule hath repossest,
The sweet hope which loue hath lost:
Laura redeeme the soule that dies,
By fury of thy murdering eies,
And if it proues vnkind to thee,   25
  Let this heauenly light I see,
  Be as darke as hell to me.

XIII.

Sleep wayward thoughts, and rest you with my loue,
Let not my loue, be with my loue diseasd.
Touch not proud hands, lest you her anger moue,
But pine you with my longings long displeasd.
Thus while she sleeps I sorrow for her sake,   5
So sleeps my loue, and yet my loue doth wake.

But ô the fury of my restles feare,
The hidden anguish of my flesh desires,
The glories and the beauties that appeare,
Between her browes neere *Cupids* closed fires   10
Thus while she sleeps moues sighing for hir sake
So sleepes my loue and yet my loue doth wake.

My loue doth rage, and yet my loue doth rest,
Feare in my loue, and yet my loue secure,
Peace in my loue, and yet loue opprest,   15
Impatient yet of perfect temprature,
Sleepe dainty loue, while I sigh for thy sake,
So sleepes my loue, and yet my loue doth wake.

XIIII.

Al ye whom loue or fortune hath betraide,
All ye that dreame of blisse but liue in greif,
Al ye whose hopes are euermore delaid,
Al ye whose sighes or sicknes wants releife:
Lend eares and teares to me most haples man,   5
that sings my sorrowes like the dying Swanne.

Care that consumes the heart with inward paine,
Paine that presents sad care in outward vew,
Both tyrant like enforce me to complaine,
But still in vaine, for none my plaints will rue,   10
Teares, sighes, and ceaseles cries alone I spend,
My woe wants comfort, and my sorrow end.

XV.

Wilt thou vnkind thus reaue me
  of my harte, of my harte
    and so leaue me: Farewell
but yet or ere I part (O cruell)
kisse me sweete sweete my Iewell.   5

2

Hope by disdayne growes chereles
  feare doth loue, loue doth feare,
    beautie peareles.   Farewell.

3   10

If no delayes can moue thee,
  life shall dye, death shall liue
    stil to loue thee.   Farewell.

4

Yet be thou mindfull euer,   15
  heate from fire, fire from heate
    none can seuer.   Farewell.

5

True loue cannot be chainged,
  though delight from desert 20
    be estranged.   Farewell.

XVI.

Would my conceit that first enforst my woe,
or els mine eyes which still the same encrease,
might be extinct, to end my sorrowes so
which nowe are such as nothing can release:
Whose life is death, whose sweet each change of sowre 5
and eke whose hell renueth euery houre.

Each houre amidst the deepe of hell I frie,
Each houre I wast and wither where I sit,
But that sweet houre wherein I wish to die,
My hope alas may not enioy it yet, 10
Whose hope is such bereaued, of the blisse,
Which vnto all saue me allotted is.

To all saue me is free to liue or die,
To all saue me remaineth hap or hope,
But all perforce, I must abandon I, 15
Sith Fortune still directs my hap a slope,
Wherefore to neither hap nor hope I trust,
But to my thralles I yeeld, for so I must.

XVII.

Come againe: sweet loue doth now enuite,
thy graces that refraine,
to do me due delight,
to see, to heare, to touch, to kisse, to die,
with thee againe in sweetest simphathy. 5

2

Come againe that I may cease to mourne,
Through thy vnkind disdaine,
For now left and forlorne:

I sit, I sigh, I weepe, I faint, I die,   10
In deadly paine, and endles miserie.

                           I

All the day the sun that lends me shine,
By frownes do cause me pine,
And feeds me with delay: 15
Her smiles, my springs, that makes my ioies to grow,
Her frownes the winters of my woe:

                           2

All the night, my sleepes are full of dreames,
My eies are full of streames,   20
My hart takes no delight:
To see the fruits and ioies that some do find,
And marke the stormes are me asignd,

                           3

Out alas, my faith is euer true,   25
Yet will she neuer rue,
Nor yeeld me any grace:
Her eies of fire, her hart of flint is made,
Whom teares nor truth may once inuade.

                           4   30

Gentle loue draw forth thy wounding dart,
Thou canst not pearce her hart,
For I that do approue:
By sighs and teares more hote then are thy shafts:
Did tempt while she for triumps laughs.   35

                        XVIII.

His golden locks time hath to siluer turnde,
O time too swift, O swiftnes neuer ceasing,
his youth gainst time & age hath euer spurnd,
but spurnd in vaine, youth waneth by encreasing:
Beautie, strength, youth are flowers but fading seene,   5
Duty, Faith, Loue are roots and euer greene.

His helmet now shall make a hiue for bees,
And louers sonets turne to holy psalmes:
A man at armes must now serue on his knees,
And feed on prayers which are ages almes,   10
  But though from court to cotage he departe
  His saint is sure of his vnspotted hart.

And when he saddest sits in homely Cell,
Hele teach his swaines this Caroll for a songe,
Blest be the harts that wish my soueraigne well,   15
Curst be the soule that thinke her any wrong:
Goddes allow this aged man his right,
To be your beadsman now that was your knight.
                    [Sir Henry Lee?]

XIX.

Awake sweet loue thou art returnd,
my hart which long in absence mournd
  liues nowe in perfect ioy,
Let loue which neuer absent dies,
now liue for euer in her eyes   5
  whence came my first anoy,
only her selfe hath seemed faire,
  she only I could loue,
she onely draue me to dispaire
  when she vnkind did proue.   10
Dispayer did make me wish to die
  that I my ioyes might end,
she onely which did make me flie
  my state may now amend.

If she esteeme thee now ought worth,   15
She will not grieue thy loue henceforth,
  Which so dispaire hath proued,
Dispaire hath proued now in me,
That loue will not vnconstant be,
  Though long in vaine I loued.   20
If she at last reward thy loue,
  And all thy harmes repaire,

Thy happinesse wil sweeter proue,
  Raisde vp from deepe dispaire.
And if that now thou welcome be,   25
  When thou with her dost meete,
She al this while but plaide with thee:
  To make thy ioies more sweet.

XX.

Come heauy sleepe, the Image of true death:
And close vp these my weary weeping eyes,
whose spring of tears doth stop my vitall breath,
And tears my hart with sorrows sigh swoln crys:
Com & posses my tired thoghts, worne soule,   5
that liuing dies, till thou one me bestoule.

Come shadow of my end: and shape of rest,
Alied to death, child to this black fast night,
Come thou and charme these rebels in my brest,
Whose waking fancies doth my mind affright.   10
O come sweet sleepe, come or I die for euer,
Come ere my last sleepe comes, or come neuer.

XXI.

Away with these selfe louing lads,
whom *Cupids* arrowe neuer glads:
Away poore soules that sigh & weepe
in loue of them that lie & sleepe,
  For *Cupid* is a medooe god,   5
  & forceth none to kisse the rod.

2

God *Cupids* shaft like destinie,
Doth either good or ill decree:
Desert is borne out of his bow,   10
Reward vpon his feet doth go,
  What fooles are they that haue not knowne
  That loue likes no lawes but his owne?

3

My songs they be of *Cynthias* praise,   15
I weare her rings on hollidaies,
On euery tree I write her name,
And euery day I reade the same:
  Where honor, *Cupids* riuall is,
  There miracles are seene of his: 20

4

If *Cinthia* craue her ring of me,
I blot her name out of the tree,
If doubt do darken things held deere,
Then well fare nothing once a yeere: 25
  For many run, but one must win,
  Fooles only hedge the Cuckoo in.

5

The worth that worthinesse should moue
Is loue, which is the bowe of loue,   30
And loue as well the foster can,
As can the mighty Noble-man:
  Sweet Saint, tis true you worthie be,
  Yet without loue nought worth to me.
               [Fulke Greville]

Michael Cavendish

14. Ayres

1598

[Top of leaf of unique copy torn to a depth of about 6 cm. in center; main title, if any, lacking] (I)/ 14. Ayres in Tabletorie to the Lute expreſſed with two/ *voyces and the baſe Violl* [*V* swash] *or the voice & Lute only.*/ 6. more to 4. voyces and in Tabletorie./ And/ 8. *MADRIGALLES* [first *A*, *DR* swash] *to* 5. *Voyces.*/ *By*/ MICHAELL CAVENDISH/ Gentleman./ [device: McKerrow No. 119]/ *AT LONDON* [*A* swash]/ Printed by *Peter Short*, on bredſtreet hill/ at the ſigne of the Starre: 1598./

Collation: 2°; A–M² (10 second leaves signed except C2); 24 leaves.
Headlines: A2v–E1, recto and verso: *CANTVS.* [swash *N*, no period, on B1, B2, C1, C1v, D2, D2v]/ *BASSVS.* [with swash *A* on B2v, C2, C2v, D1, D1v, E1; *BASVS* with swash *A* on B1v; *BASVS.* without swash *A* on D2] Verso, E1v–G2v: *CANTVS.* [all swash but *S*] Verso, H1v–L2v: QVINTVS. / CANTVS. Recto, E2–M1: ALTVS. [*ALT[VS]* on K1]/ BASSVS. / TENOR. [[*T]ENOR* on K1] [The numbers of the songs do not appear on the headline; they are usually in an upper outside corner of the page.]
Contents: A1, title page; A1v blank; A2, dedication; A2v–E1, songs I–XIIII, one per page; E1v–M1, songs XV– XXVIII, one per opening; M1v, complete metrical texts of songs II, IIII, VI, VII, VIII and X; M2, table and shield of the Cavendish family arms (three buck's heads, caboshed); M2v blank.
SR: No entry.
STC: 4878.
Copy: BM (K.2.i.20). The title page and several other leaves are torn, but only on B2 does the damage affect the music or the text—about 10 cm. of the lower outside corner is lacking.
The music for songs I–XIIII consists of a Cantus with lute tablature and a Bassus

(reversed) for voice and/or viol. Only the opening stanzas of Nos. II, IIII, VI, VII, VIII, and X are printed with the music, but the full texts appear on sig. M1v. Songs XV–XX have a Cantus and lute facing parts for Altus, Tenor, and Bassus. Songs XXI–XXVIII are five-part madrigals without tablature. Note: in the original, the first two songs are both numbered I; the corrected numbering is used above.

TO THE HONOVRABLE
protection of the Ladie Arbella.

Notwithstanding your rare perfections in so many knowledges, which haue adorned you and you them, let not, worthie Lady, one sole qualitie of mine seeme the rather insufficiency to your iudgement, or breed lesse acceptance for being offered alone. It commeth out of a profession worthie some grace, and hath in it humors variable for delights sake. I offer them as that whereby I can best expresse my seruice to you, and you may (if it please you) make vse of them at your idlest houres. Manie causes I haue to imbolden mine attempts of dutie to you, and your fauours stande in the top of them: others there are more secrete, and lie in the nature of your owne apprehension. And howsoeuer the policie of times may hold it vnfit to raise men humbled with aduersities to titles of dearnesse, whether to shunne charge, or expresse pride, I rather know not, yet you I hope out of the honour of your nature, will vouchsafe your fauours to a forward seruant so neerely tied to a dutifull deuotion. In what ranke you please to place me, I will not change mine order. It shall be pro-motion to me that you account of me in any place, and all the commendations I seeke to my labors in this woorke, if you will be pleased to heare it at some times, and protect it at all times. Thus your ladiship hauing heard what I can say in this first leafe, you may (if it please you to vouchsafe acceptance) heare what I haue song in the rest that follow. And so I rest:

        10

        20

Yours humbly to be commaunded:

MICHAELL CAVENDISH.

From Cauendish this
   24 of Iuly.

I.

Stay stay stay *Glicia* stay,
And cary not my hart away:
I wil not leaue that Iewell,

to one vnkind & cruell.
But if thereto thou haue a mind,   5
buy it of me by being kind.

II.

WHy should my muse thus restles in her woes,
Summon records of neuer dying feares?
And still reuiue fresh springing in my thoughts,
The true memoriall of my sad dispaires?
  Who forst to loue to those faire eyes am thrall,   5
  Where eyes nor thoughts grant one respect at all?

Endles my grieues since endles is her course,
Still to inflict more torments on my grieues,
Without remorse of poore harts scalding sighes,
When heauen in teares bewailes my no relieues.   10
  A hard regard, where true deuoted loue
  Can merit naught but still these crosses proue:

Cease worlds bright sun, from henceforth once to shine,
But in my death now suffer springs to perish,
Forbeare to grace earths glory with thy beames,   15
her richest treasure now forbid to florish;
  Since that her eies the sun-shine of my life
  Affords no grace but torments death and strife.

III.

Mourne, *Marcus* mourne, and mourning wish to die,
since she is gone on whom my hopes relye:
though *Marcus* faith deserued with the best,
yet of hir loue another is possest
who doth forbid faire *Cleopatra* smyling,   5
on his poore soule for her sweet sake still dying.

IIII.

HAue I vow'd and must not breake it?
Fondly vow'd is wisely broken,
Do I loue and dare not speake it?

Silence doth no loue betoken:
  Thus I bind in this my breaking,   5
  And I am in silence speaking.

Loue is bound though I seeme free,
Wrapt in deepe affections snarė,
Loue I must how so ere it be,
Too late men say doth come beware.   10
  Then vowe no more sith vowes are vaine,
  Wrapt in deepe affections chayne.

V.

Finetta, faire and feat,
star of our towne, a
her bewty bright as Iet,
makes me sing down a
down, down, down a   5
griefe & I both are one,
loue puls me down a.

VI.

Loue is not blind, but I my selfe am so,
  With free consent blindfolded by desire,
  That guides my will along the paths of woe,
  To seeke refreshing for a needeles fire.

Loue is no boy as fooles in fancies faine,   5
  It is my selfe that play the child so right,
  I hope and feare, I weepe and laugh againe,
  And vse no sence against so weake a might.

Loue hath no fire yet is mine only lust,
  Doth raise the flame which makes my thoughts to fry,   10
  Vaine hope and fond conceipts in which I trust,
  Are th'only wings that beare him vp so hie.

Loue hath no bow nor shafts to shoote withall,
  He hath no bands wherewith to tie vs fast,
  He hath no powre, those that be free to thrall,   15
  More than we giue nor can no longer last.

Loue is a Poets Lie, a beggars store,
  A mad mans dreame, an ignorants idoll great,
  In breefe this God whom we so much adore,
  Of maners strange doth find as strange a seat.   20

[after Gaspar Gil Polo]

VII.

Loue the delight of all well thinking minds,
Delight the fruit of vertue dearely lou'd,
Vertue the highest good that reason finds,
Reason the forge on which mens thoughts are prou'd,
  Are from the world by natures power bereft,   5
  And in one creature (for her glory) left.

Beauty hir couer is, the eyes true pleasure,
In honors fame she liues, the eares true musicke,
Excesse of wonder growes from her iust measure,
Her inward parts are passions only phisicke: 10
  From her cleere hart the springs of vertue flow,
  Which (imag'd in her words and deeds) men know.

Time faine would stay that he might neuer leaue her,
Place doth reioice that he must needs containe her,
Death craues of heauen that he may not bereaue her,   15
The heauens know their own and do maintaine her:
  Delight, Loue, Reason, Vertue, let it be,
  To hold all women light but only she.
                                        [Fulke Greville]

VIII.

THe hart to rue the pleasure of the eye,
The eie to wound the hart with his delight,
What may be said that owe them both hereby,
But both two serue vnto his own despite:
  O saue and win them both by one desert,   5
  Please still the eye but pitty on the hart.

The eie beholds as much as much may be,
In beauty grace and honour to require,

The hart conceaues more then the eye can see,
And slaies himselfe to feed his wounds desire: 10
  O saue and wine them both by one desart,
  Please still the eie but pitty on the hart.

IX.

Siluia is faire, yet scorning loue vnseemly,
plaging my soule with torments to vntimely,
Siluia natures perfection, bids me loue her,
but for loues merrit she forbids me moue her,
sweet *Siluia* yet commandris of my thought,   5
reward me so I may not loue for nought.

X.

Cvrst be the time when first mine eies beheld
Those rare perfections all mens thoughts admire,
And iustly may a shepherds swaine bewaile
Those fatall howres which caus'd him first desire;
  Loues sweet consent that makes so deepe impression,   5
  As hart and soule will witnesse in confession.

Why should these eies borne traitors to my rest,
Command my thoughts to yeeld to this presumption,
To loue a nimph whose beauty all surpassing,
In all mens thoughts breeds still a strange confusion;   10
  Heauens forbid that I should dare to moue,
  A face that gods solicite still in loue.

Phillis sweet *Phillis* the shepheards only Queene,
Skornes to admit a swaine into her loue,
He pipes and sings and pleades to her for grace,   15
His songs and Sonnets her can nothing moue:
  He sighes and vowes and praies with true deuotion,
  But vowes and prayers worke in her no motion.

Then *Coridon* must yeeld to this his curse,
Sith that his loue cannot her loue importune,   20
For feare dispaires conuert this ill to worse,

And by disgrace adde more plagues to fortune,
  Poore man sit down powre out thy plaints amaine,
  Phillis thee skornes and holds in high disdaine.

XI.

FAire are those eies whose shine must giue me life,
Sweet is that grace commands my hart to loue,
heauens her thoughts if they once yeeld consent
to that reward affections truth doth moue.
But if my faith can not his merit gaine,   5
Weep eies, breake hart and ende this restles paine.

XII.

WAndring in this place as in a wildernes,
no comfort haue I nor yet assurance,
Desolate of ioy, repleat with sadnesse:
wherefore I may say, O *deus, deus,*
non est dolor, sicut dolor meus.   5

XIII.

Everie bush new springing;
Euery bird now singing,
Merily sate poore *Nico*
chanting tro li lo lo li lo li lo,
Til her he had espide,   5
on whom his hope relide,
Down a down a down,
down, with a frown
oh she puld him down.

XIIII.

Down in a valley,
shady vales are pleasant ports,
for mery lads meet resorts,

Such was our hap to catch a swain
(Oh) happy the valley   5
with flowrs to spangle *Floraes* traine,
Nor did we dalley,
his flowrs we tooke all dyde in graine

(Oh) dyde was the valley,
Shady vales are pleasant ports   10
for mery lads meet resorts.

Of them we made a garland green
(Oh) green was the valley
to crown faire *Lelia* shepheards queen,
Faire as a Lilly,   15
she, sitting in a shade vnseene

(Oh) shadie the valley,
Shady vales are pleasant ports
for mery lads meet resorts.

XV.

WAnton, wanton come hither,
O stay why do you flie me?
my sute though you deny me,
yet let vs walke together,
sweet nymph such hast, why make you,   5
wel could I ouertake you,
But since words wil not moue thee,
farewel, farewell, farwell
I did but this to proue thee,
With that the nymph she staide,   10
& deepely sighing, said
sweet shepheard how I loue thee.

XVI.

SAy shepherds say, where is your iolly swain?
Or what hath bred his anguish,
on idle banke he restles doth remaine,
(O) for loue doth make him languish,

Idle lad,   5
his wit is bad,
there alone
to make such mone
to the weeping fountains,
whilst she plaies   10
sweet roundelayes,
vp & down the mountains.

XVII.

[This song is another version of No. XI.]

XVIII.

FArewel dispaire sith loue hath reconcil'd,
Those strange delaies fond modesty commanded,
And banisht now those idle superstitions,
Feare of offence caus'd her to be enstranged,
Prescribing time this priuiledge affords,   5
Sweet trespasses loue pardons not vaine words.

XIX.

SLie theefe if so you wil beleeue,
it nought or little did me grieue,
that my true hart you had bereft,
til that vnkindly you it left,
leauing you lose, losing you kil   5
that which I may forgo so ill.

XX.

WHat thing more cruell can you do,
then rob a man & kil him to?
wherfore of loue I aske this meed,
to bring you where you did the deed,
That there you may for your amisses,   5
be dammadg'd in a thousand kisses.

XXI.

In flower of April springing,
when pleasant birds to sport them
among the woods consort them,
warbling with cheerful notes and sweetly singing,
for ioy that *Clore* the faire hir song was chaunting,   5
the sweet loues vaunting,
of her and her Elpin, the sweet loues vaunting.

XXII.

Zephirus brings the time that sweetly senteth
with flowres and hearbs and winters frost exileth,
Progne now chirpeth and *Philomel* lamenteth,
Flora the garlands white and red compileth,
fields do reioice the frowning skie relenteth,   5
Ioue to behold his deerest daughter smileth,
the ayre, the water, the earth to ioy consenteth,
each creature now to loue him reconcileth.
                              [after Petrarch]

XXIII.

Mvch it delighted
to see *Phillis* smiling,
But it was her beguiling,
Ah she my faith new plighted,
Scorn'd with disdain reuiling,   5
But sith thy fained lookes faithfull I prou'd not,
false adew, false adew, for I lou'd not.

XXIIII.

Come gentle swains & shepherds dainty daughters,
adorn'd with curtesie & comly duties.
Come sing & ioy & grace with louely laughters
the birth day of the beautist of beauties,
then sang the shepherds & nimphs of *Diana*,   5
Long liue faire *Oriana*.

XXV.

To former ioy now turnes the groue the fountain,
the iolly fresh Aprill now loden with flowres,
the seas are calme, hore frost fals from the mountain,
shepherds & nimphs, they walke to their wanton bowres,
But I all night in teares   5
my pillow steeping,
soone as the sunne appeares
renue my weeping.

                                        [after Petrarch]

XXVI.

Faustina hath the fairer face,
& *Phillida* the feater grace,
both haue mine eie enriched,
This sings full sweetly with her voice,
her fingers make as sweet a noise,   5
both haue mine eare bewitched,
Ay me sith fates haue so prouided
my hart alas, must be deuided.

XXVII.

[This is a five-part version of No. XIII.]

XXVIII.

[This is a five-part version of No. XII.]

A TABLE OF ALL
the Ayres and Madrigals
in this booke.

Loue is not blind, but.	V
Loue the delight of al wel thinking.	VI
The hart to rue the pleasure of the eye.	VII
Siluia is faire, yet scorning loue vnseemly	VIII
Curst be the time when first·mine eyes beheld	IX
Faire are those eyes.	X
Wandring in this place as in a wildernes	XI
Euery bush now springing.	XII
Downe in a valley.	XIII
Wanton wanton come hether wanton.	XIIII
Say shepherd say.	XV
Faire are those eyes whose shine &c.	XVI
Fairewell dispaire.	XVII
Slie theefe if so you will beleeue.	XVIII
What thing more cruell can you doe.	XIX
In flower of Aprill springing.	XX
Zephirus brings the time that &c.	XXI
Much it delighted to see *Phillis* smiling:	XXII
Come gentle Swaines & shepherds.	XXIII
To former ioye now turnes.	XXIIII
Faustina hath the fairer face.	XXV
Euery bush now springing.	XXVI
Wandring in this place:	XXVII

FINIS.

John Dowland

The Second Booke of Songs or Ayres

1600

[Within a compartment: McK. & F. No. 132; in upper oval slot, two lines of music (a canon) with these words:] Pſal. 150./ Praiſe GOD vpon/ the Lute and Vi-oll./ [In center space:] THE/ SECOND BOOKE/ of Songs or Ayres,/ of 2. 4. and 5. parts:/ VVith [first *V* filed] Tableture for the Lute or/ Orpherian, with the Violl/ *de Gamba.* [*G* swash]/ Compoſed by *IOHN DOVVLAND* Batcheler/ of Muſick, and Luteniſt to the King of Den-/ mark: Alſo an excelent leſſon for the Lute/ and Baſe Viol, called/ *Dowlands adew.*/ Publiſhed by George Eaſtland, and are/ to be ſould at his houſe neere the greene Dragon/ and Sword, in Fleetſtreete./ [In lower slot:] LONDON:/ Printed by Thomas Eſte,/ the aſsigne of Thomas/ Morley. 1600./

Note: The title page compartment was used again by East for Piı605 and Danı606, and by Thomas Snodham for Ferı609, RDoı610, Ckı612, Copı613; 1, 2 Camp[ı613]; 3, 4 Camp[ı617]; and George Mason and John Earsden's *Ayres* (ı618).

Collation: 2°; A–M², N¹; 25 leaves.

Headlines: Verso, B1v–M2v: *I.* [–*XXII.* No period after *V*] *CANTO.* [M1v, M2v add: *For a Treble Violl. XXI.* (*XXII.*) *QVINTO.*] Recto, B2–F1: *I.* [–*VIII.*] *BASSO.* [B2 has *CANTO.*] F2–N1: *IX.* [–*XXII.*] *TENORE.*/ *IX.* [–*XXII.*] *BASSO.*/ *IX.* [–*XXII.*] *ALTO.*

Contents: A1, title page; A1v blank; A2, dedication; A2v, Eastland's acrostic and epistle to the reader; B1, table of songs; B1v–N1, songs I–XXII, one per opening; N1v, "Dowlands adew for Master Oliuer Cromwell," for lute and viol.

SR: Entered by Thomas East on July 15, 1600 (Arber, III, 167). Transferred to John Browne by East's widow on December 22, 1610, and entered as the joint copy of Matthew Lownes, John Browne, and Thomas Snodham on September 3, 1611. It was transferred again to William Stansby on February 23, 1625/26 (Arber, III, 450, 465; IV, 152).

STC: 7095.

Copies: Folger (the text copy); Huntington (59101); Boston Public Library (*G. 400.52); BM (K.2.i.5 [2.]); Lincoln Cathedral Library (Aa.2.17; A1 damaged: "and Sword, in Fleetstreete" cut out; lacks sig. E; photocopy seen, but not fully collated); Liverpool Public Library (lacks sigs. A, B, C, L2, M2, and N; not seen); Manchester Public Library (BR f410 406; seen but not fully collated); RCM (II.B.6); St. Michael's College, Tenbury (seen, but not fully collated); and Fürst Alexander zu Dohna-Schlobitten, Lörrach-Baden, Germany.

Litigation over the printing of Do1600 resulted in the recording of important information, some of which may be applicable to the printing of other songbooks. The case is summarized from documents in the Public Records Office by Margaret Dowling in "The Printing of John Dowland's *Second Booke of Songs or Ayres*," *The Library*, 4th series, XII (1932), 365–380. We learn that Dowland sent his MS from Denmark to his wife in London, who sold it to the musician George Eastland for £20 and half of whatever the dedicatee chose to give. Eastland then agreed to pay East £10 for the printing, and £7. 16s. 6d. for paper. The fee paid to the monopolists, Thomas Morley and Christopher Heybourne (who had bought an interest in the original patent), was 6s. a ream, plus 40s. before printing and four of the completed copies. Eastland intended to sell the books for 4s. 6d. a copy, but some copies were sold for as little as 2s.

The printing was completed by August 2, 1600. Since some of the copies were printed surreptitiously, there is some dispute about the total number printed; the best figure is 1056 copies. John Wilbye, the madrigalist, and his fellow musician at Hengrave Hall, Edward Johnson, read proof and acted as Eastland's agents in his absence. After the printing was finished, four errors were discovered and corrected by hand. It is difficult to be sure as to which four errors these were, but one is almost certainly in Eastland's dedicatory acrostic (line 11), where *flowring* has been changed to *floweing* in the Boston, Folger, BM, RCM, and Schlobitten copies. Another may be in V.10, where *thar* is corrected to *that* in the Manchester, Lincoln Cathedral, RCM, BM, Huntington, and Schlobitten copies. The Boston copy has *loue* inserted between *one* and *should* in XIII.22 (H1v), and the Manchester copy corrects the erroneous *CANTO* on B2 to *Basso*. But these last two corrections are not made in other copies.

Ordinary press-corrections are as follows:
Outer forme E: uncorrected, Folger, Boston, RCM, Schlobitten: E1 (VI.1 B) olde] oldc The signature letter reads *Ei* in the Folger, Boston, BM, and RCM copies.
Inner forme H: uncorrected, Folger: H2 (XIII.5 and 7, T) loue, ij./ Ioyes, ij.] *omitted.*

TO THE RIGHT
Honorable the Lady Lucie
Comptesse of BEDFORD.

Excellent Ladie: I send vnto your Ladiship from the Court of a forreine Prince, this volume of my second labours: as to the worthiest Patronesse, of Musicke: which is the Noblest of all Sciences: for the whole frame of Nature, is nothing

*but Harmonie, as wel in soules, as bodies: And because I am now remoued
from your sight, I will speake boldly, that your Ladiship shall be vnthankfull
to Nature hir selfe, if you doe not loue, & defend that Art, by which, she hath
giuen you so well tuned a minde.*

*Your Ladiship hath in your selfe, an excellent agreement of many vertues,
of which: though I admire all, Yet I am bound by my profession, to giue
especiall honor, to your knowledge of Musicke: which in the iudgement of
ancient times, was so proper an excelencie to Wœmen, that the Muses tooke
their name from it, and yet so rare, that the world durst imagin but nine of them.*

*I most humbly beseech your Ladiship to receiue this worke, into your
fauour: and the rather, because it commeth far to beg it, of you. From Helsingnoure in Denmarke the first of Iune.*

1600.

*Your Ladiships
in all humble deuotion:*
Iohn Dowland.

To the right Noble and Vertuous
Ladie, Lucie Comptesse of
BEDFORD.
G. Eastland. To I. Dowlands Lute.

L *Vte arise and charme the aire,*
V *ntill a thousand formes shee beare,*
C *oniure them all that they repaire,*
I *nto the circles of hir eare,*
E *uer to dwell in concord there,*

B *y this thy tunes may haue accesse,*
E *uen to hir spirit whose floweing treasure,*
D *oth sweetest Harmonie expresse,*
F *illing all eares and hearts with pleasure*
O *n earth, obseruing heauenly measure,*
R *ight well can shee Iudge and defend them,*
D *oubt not of that for shee can mend them.*

To the curteous Reader.

GEntlemen, if the consideration of mine owne estate, or the true
worth of mony, had preuailed with me, aboue the desire of pleasuring

you, and shewing my loue to my friend, this second labours of Maister
Dowland, (whose very name is a large preface of commendacions to
the booke,) had for euer laine hid in darknesse, or at the least frozen in a
colde and forreine country. I assure you that both my charge and
paines in publishing it, hath exceeded ordinary, yet thus much I haue
to assure mee of requitall, that neither the work is ordinary, nor are
your iudgements ordinary to whom I present it, so that I haue no   10
reason but to hope for good increase in my labours, especially of your
good fauours toward mee, which of all things I most esteeme. Which
if I finde in this, I meane shortly (God willing) to set at liberty for
your seruice, a prisoner taken at *Cales*, who if hee discouers not something (in matter of Musicke) worthy your knowledge, let the reputation
of my iudgement in Musicke aunswere it. In the meane time, I commend my absent friend to your remembrance, and my selfe to your
fauorable conceits.

George Eastland.
From my house neere the greene   20
Dragon and sword in Fleetstreet.

A TABLE OF ALL
the Songs contained in this
BOOKE.

                        FINIS.

                          I.

To the most famous, Anthony Holborne.

I saw my Lady weepe,
and sorrow proud to bee aduanced so:
in those faire eies, where all perfections keepe,
hir face was full of woe,   5
but such a woe (beleeue me) as wins more hearts,
then mirth can doe, with hir intysing parts.

Sorow was there made faire,
And passion wise, teares a delightfull thing,
Silence beyond all speech a wisdome rare,   10
Shee made hir sighes to sing,
And all things with so sweet a sadnesse moue,
As made my heart at once both grieue and loue.

O fayrer then ought ells,
The world can shew, leaue of in time to grieue,   15
Inough, inough, your ioyfull lookes excells,
Teares kills the heart belieue,
O striue not to bee excellent in woe,
Which onely breeds your beauties ouerthrow.

II.

Lacrime.

FLOW my teares fall from your springs,
Exilde for euer: Let mee morne
where nights black bird hir sad infamy sings,
there let mee liue forlorne.   5

Downe vaine lights shine you no more,
No nights are dark enough for those
that in dispaire their last fortuns deplore,
light doth but shame disclose.

Neuer may my woes be relieued,   10
since pittie is fled,
and teares, and sighes, and grones my wearie dayes,
of all ioyes haue depriued.

From the highest spire of contentment,
my fortune is throwne,   15
and feare, and griefe, and paine for my deserts,
are my hopes since hope is gone.

Harke you shadowes that in darcknesse dwell,
learne to contemne light,
Happie, happie they that in hell   20
feele not the worlds despite.

III.

Sorrow sorrow stay, lend true repentant teares,
to a woefull, woefull wretched wight,
hence, hence dispaire with thy tormenting feares:
doe not, O doe not my heart poore heart affright,
pitty, pitty, pitty, help now or neuer,   5
mark me not to endlesse paine,
alas I am condempne'd, I am condempned euer,
no hope, no help, ther doth remaine,
but downe, down, down, down I fall,
downe and arise I neuer shall.   10

IIII.

Dye not beefore thy day, poore man condemned,
But lift thy low lookes from the humble earth,
Kisse not dispaire & see sweet hope contemned:
The hag hath no delight, but mone for mirth,
O fye poore fondling, fie fie be willing,　　　　　　　　5
to preserue thy self from killing:
Hope thy keeper glad to free thee,
Bids thee goe and will not see thee,
hye thee quickly from thy wrong,
so shee endes hir willing song.　　　　　　　　　　10

V.

Mourne, mourne, day is with darknesse fled,
what heauen then gouernes earth,
ô none, but hell in heauens stead,
choaks with his mistes our mirth.
Mourne mourne, looke now for no more day　　　　　5
nor night, but that from hell,
Then all must as they may
in darkenesse learne to dwell.
But yet this change, must needes change our delight,
that thus the Sunne should harbour with the night.　　10

VI.

Tımes eldest sonne, olde age the heyre of ease,
Strengths foe, loues woe, and foster to deuotion,
bids gallant youths in marshall prowes please,
as for himselfe, hee hath no earthly motion,
But thinks sighes, teares, vowes, praiers, and sacrifices,　5
As good as showes, maskes, iustes, or tilt deuises.

VII.

Second part.

Then sit thee downe, and say thy *Nunc Demittis*,
with *De profundis*, *Credo*, and *Te Deum*,

Chant *Miserere* for what now so fit is,
as that, or this, *Paratum est cor meum,*   5
O that thy Saint would take in worth thy hart,
thou canst not please hir with a better part.

VIII.

Third part.

WHen others sings *Venite exultemus,*
stand by and turne to *Noli emulari,*
For *quare fremuerunt* vse *oremus*
Viuat Eliza, For an *aue mari,*   5
and teach those swains that liues about thy cell,
to say *Amen* when thou dost pray so well.

IX.

PRaise blindnesse eies, for seeing is deceit,
Bee dumbe vaine tongue, words are but flattering windes,
breake hart & bleed for ther is no receit,
to purge inconstancy from most mens mindes.
And if thine eares false Haralds to thy hart,   5
Conuey into thy head hopes to obtaine,
Then tell thy hearing thou art deafe by art,
Now loue is art that wonted to be plaine,
Now none is bald except they see his braines,
Affection is not knowne till one be dead,   10
Reward for loue are labours for his paines,
Loues quiuer made of gold his shafts of leade.
Lenuoy:
  And so I wackt amazd and could not moue,
  I know my dreame was true, and yet I loue.   15

X.

To Maister Hugh Holland.

O Sweet woods the delight of solitarinesse,
O how much doe I loue your solitarinesse.

From fames desire, from loues delight retir'd,
In these sad groues an Hermits life I led,   5
And those false pleasures which I once admir'd,
With sad remembrance of my fall, I dread,
To birds, to trees, to earth, impart I this,
For shee lesse secret, and as sencelesse is.
        [O sweet woods, &c.   10
          O how much, &c.]

Experience which repentance onely brings,
Doth bid mee now my hart from loue estrange,
Loue is disdained when it doth looke at Kings,
And loue loe placed base and apt to change: 15
Ther power doth take from him his liberty,
Hir want of worth makes him in cradell die.
        O sweet woods, &c.
        O how much, &c.

You men that giue false worship vnto Loue,   20
And seeke that which you neuer shall obtaine,
The endlesse worke of Sisiphus you procure,
Whose end is this to know you striue in vaine,
Hope and desire which now your Idols bee,
You needs must loose and feele dispaire with mee.   25
        O sweet woods, &c.
        O how much, &c.

You woods in you the fairest Nimphs haue walked,
Nimphes at whose sight all harts did yeeld to Loue,
You woods in whom deere louers oft haue talked,   30
How doe you now a place of mourning proue,
Wansted my Mistres saith this is the doome,
Thou art loues Childbed, Nursery, and Tombe.
        O sweet woods, &c.
        O how much, &c.

XI.

IF fluds of teares could cleanse my follies past,
And smoakes of sighes might sacrifice for sinne,
If groning cries might salue my fault at last,

Or endles mone, for error pardon win,
Then would I cry, weepe, sigh, and euer mone,   5
mine errors, faults, sins, follies past and gone.

I see my hopes must wither in their bud,
I see my fauours are no lasting flowers,
I see that woords will breede no better good,
Then losse of time and lightening but at houres,   10
Thus when I see then thus I say therefore,
That fauours hopes and words, can blinde no more.

XII.

Fine knacks for ladies, cheape choise braue and new,
Good penniworths but mony cannot moue,
I keepe a faier but for the faier to view,
a begger may bee liberall of loue,
Though all my wares bee trash the hart is true,   5
                        the hart is true,
                        the hart is true.

Great gifts are guiles and looke for gifts againe,
My trifles come, as treasures from my minde,
It is a precious Iewell to bee plaine,   10
Sometimes in shell th'orienst pearles we finde,
Of others take a sheafe, of mee a graine,
                        Of mee a graine,
                        Of mee a graine.

Within this packe pinnes points laces & gloues,   15
And diuers toies fitting a country faier,
But my hart where duety serues and loues,
Turtels & twins, courts brood, a heauenly paier,
Happy the hart that thincks of no remoues,
                        Of no remoues,   20
                        Of no remoues.

XIII.

Now cease my wandring eies,
  Strange beauties to admire,

In change least comfort lies,
  Long ioyes yeeld long desire.
            One faith one loue,   5
Makes our fraile pleasures eternall, And in sweetnesse proue.
            New Hopes new ioyes,
Are still with sorrow declining, Vnto deepe anoies.

One man hath but one soule,
  Which art cannot deuide,   10
If all one soule must loue,
  Two loues most be denide,
            One soule one loue,
By faith and merit vnited cannot remoue,
            Distracted spirits,   15
Are euer changing & haplesse in their delights.

Nature two eyes hath giuen,
  All beautie to impart,
Aswell in earth as heauen,
  But she hath giuen one hart,   20
            That though wee see,
Ten thousand beauties yet in vs one should be,
            One stedfast loue,
Because our harts stand fixt although our eies do moue.

XIIII.

Come yee heauy states of night,
Doe my fathers spirit right,
Soundings balefull let mee borrow,
Burthening my song with sorrow,
Come sorrow come hir eies that sings,   5
By thee are turned into springs.

Come you Virgins of the night,
That in Dirges sad delight,
Quier my Anthems, I doe borrow
Gold nor pearle, but sounds of sorrow: 10
Come sorrow come hir eies that sings,
By thee are tourned into springs.

XV.

WHITE as Lillies was hir face,
   When she smiled,
   She beeguiled,
Quitting faith with foule disgrace,
Vertue seruice thus neglected,   5
Heart with sorrowes hath infected.

2 When I swore my hart hir owne,
   Shee disdained,
   I complained,
Yet shee left mee ouerthrowen,   10
Careles of my bitter groning,
Ruthlesse bent to no relieuing.

3 Vowes and oaths and faith assured,
   Constant euer,
   Changing neuer,   15
Yet shee could not bee procured,
To beleeue my paines exceeding,
From hir scant neglect proceeding.

4 Oh that loue should haue the art,
   By surmises,   20
   And disguises,
To destroy a faithfull hart,
Or that wanton looking women,
Should reward their friends as foemen.

5 All in vaine is Ladies loue,   25
   Quickly choosed,
   Shortly loosed,
For their pride is to remoue,
Out alas their looks first won vs,
And their pride hath straight vndone vs.   30

6 To thy selfe the sweetest faier,
   Thou hast wounded,
   And confounded,
Changles faith with foule dispaier,
And my seruice hath enuied,   35
And my succours hath denied.

7 By thine error thou hast lost,
        Hart vnfained,
        Truth vnstained,
And the swaine that loued most,   40
More assured in loue then many,
More dispised in loue then any.

8 For my hart though set at nought,
        Since you will it,
        Spoile and kill it,   45
I will neuer change my thoughts,
But grieue that beautie ere was borne.

XVI.

Wofull hart with griefe oppressed,
Since my fortunes most distressed,
  From my ioyes hath mee remoued,
Follow those sweet eies adored,
Those sweet eyes wherein are stored,   5
  All my pleasures best beeloued.

Fly my breast, leaue mee forsaken,
Wherein Griefe his seate hath taken,
  All his arrowes through mee darting,
Thou maist liue by hir Sunne-shining,   10
I shall suffer no more pining,
  By thy losse, then by hir parting.

XVII.

A Shepheard in a shade, his plaining made,
  Of loue and louers wrong,
Vnto the fairest lasse, That trode on grasse,
  And thus beegan his song.
Restore, restore my hart againe,   5
  Which loue by thy sweet lookes hath slaine,
Least that inforst by your disdaine, I sing,
  Fye fye on loue, it is a foolish thing.

Since loue and Fortune will, I honour still,
  your faire and louely eye,   10

What conquest will it bee, Sweet Nimph for thee,
  If I for sorrow dye.
[Restore, restore, &c.]

My hart where haue you laid O cruell maide,
  To kill when you might saue,   15
Why haue yee cast it forth as nothing worth,
  Without a tombe or graue.
O let it bee intombed and lye,
  In your sweet minde and memorie,
Least I resound on euery warbling string,   20
  Fye fye on loue that is a foolish thing.

XVIII.

  FAction that euer dwels,
  In court where wits excells,
    hath set defiance,
  Fortune and loue hath sworne,
  That they were neuer borne,   5
    of one aliance.

1 Fortune sweares, weakest harts
  The booke of *Cupids* arts
    Turne with hir wheele,
  Sences themselues shall proue   10
  Venture hir place in loue
    Aske them that feele.

2 This discord it begot
  Atheists that honour not
    Nature thought good,   15
  Fortune should euer dwell
  In court where wits excell
    Loue keepe the wood.

3 So to the wood went I
  With loue to liue and die   20
    Fortunes forlorne,
  Experience of my youth
  Made mee thinke humble truth
    In desert borne.

4 My saint is deere to mee,   25
   And Ione hir selfe is shee
    Ione faier and true,
   Ione that doth euer moue,
   Passions of loue with loue
    Fortune adiew.   30
         [Fulke Greville]

XIX.

Sнall I sue shall I seeke for grace?
   Shall I pray shall I proue?
Shall I striue to a heauenly Ioy,
   with an earthly loue?
Shall I think that a bleeding hart   5
   or a wounded eie,
Or a sigh can ascend the cloudes
   to attaine so hie.

2 Silly wretch forsake these dreames,
   of a vaine desire,   10
O bethinke what hie regard,
   holy hopes doe require.
Fauour is as faire as things are,
   treasure is not bought,
Fauour is not wonne with words,   15
   nor the wish of a thought.

3 Pittie is but a poore defence,
   for a dying hart,
Ladies eies respect no mone,
   in a meane desert.   20
Shee is to worthie far,
   for a worth so base,
Cruell and but iust is shee,
   in my iust disgrace.

Iustice giues each man his owne   25
   though my loue bee iust,
Yet will not shee pittie my griefe,
   therefore die I must,

Silly hart then yeeld to die,
   perish in dispaire,   30
Witnesse yet how faine I die,
   When I die for the faire.

XX.

     for
Finding in fields:
  ye shall finde a
  better dittie.

Tosse not my soule, O loue twixt hope and feare,   5
Shew mee some ground where I may firmely stand
or surely fall, I care not which apeare,
So one will close mee in a certaine band.

Take mee *Assurance* to thy blisfull holde,
Or thou *Despaire* vnto thy darkest Cell,   10
Each hath full rest, the one in ioyes enrolde,
Th'other, in that hee feares no more, is well:
Lenuoy:
  When once of ill the vttermost is knowen,
  The strength of sorrow quite is ouer throwne.   15

XXI.

Cleare or cloudie sweet as Aprill showring,
Smoth or frowning so is hir face to mee,
Pleasd or smiling like milde May all flowring,
When skies blew silke and medowes carpets bee,
Hir speeches notes of that night bird that singeth,   5
Who thought all sweet yet Iarring notes out-ringeth.

Hir grace like Iune, when earth and trees bee trimde,
In best attire of compleat beauties height,
Hir loue againe like sommers daies bee dimde,
With little cloudes of doubtfull constant faith,   10
Hir trust hir doubt, like raine and heat in Skies,
Gently thundring, she lightning to mine eies.

Sweet sommer spring that breatheth life and growing,
In weedes as into hearbs and flowers,
And sees of seruice diuers sorts in sowing,   15
Some haply seeming and some being yours,
Raine on your hearbs and flowers that truely serue,
And let your weeds lack dew and duely sterue.

XXII.

A Dialogue.
[1] Hvmor say what mak'st thou heere,
      In the presence of a Queene,
[2] Princes hould conceit most deere,
      all conceit in humor seene: 5
[1] Thou art a heauy leaden moode,
[2] Humor is inuencions foode:
Chorus:
      But neuer Humor yet was true,
      but that which onely pleaseth you.   10

1 O, I am as heauy as earth,
      Say then who is Humor now.
2 I am now inclind to mirth,
      humor I as well as thou.
1 Why then tis I am drownde in woe,   15
2 No no wit is cherisht so,
[Chorus:] But neuer Humor, &c.

1 Mirth then is drownde in sorrowes brim,
      Oh, in sorrow all things sleepe.
2 No no foole the light's things swim,   20
      heauie things sinck to the deepe:
1 In hir presence all things smile,
2 Humor frolike then a while.
[Chorus:] But neuer Humor, &c.

Robert Jones

The First Booke of Songes or Ayres

1600

[Within a compartment: McK. & F. No. 99] THE/ FIRST BOOKE/ *of Songes or Ayres of* [*A* swash]/ foure parts with Ta-/ *bleture for the Lute.*/ So made that all the/ parts together, or either of/ them feuerally may be fong/ to the Lute, Orpherian/ or Viol de gambo./ Compofed by Robert Iones./ [rule]/ *Quæ profunt fingula multa iuuant* [*Q* swash]/ [rule]/ [In lower slot:] ¶ Printed by Peter Short with the affent/ of Thomas Morley, and are to be fold at the/ figne of the Starre on Bredftreet hill./ 1600./

Collation: 2° in fours; A²B–F⁴G² (A1, G2 not signed); 24 leaves. Since one of the two surviving copies lacks A1–2, and the other lacks G1–2, it is impossible to say for certain whether or not A and G are contiguous; however, the Folger copy has stubs for four leaves before A1 and after F4.

Headlines: Verso, B1v–G1v: Robert Iones. I. [–XXI.] CANTVS Recto, B2–G2: TENOR./ BASSVS./ ALTVS.

Contents: A1, title page; A1v blank; A2, dedication; A2v, epistle to the reader; B1, table; B1v–G2, songs I–XXI, one per opening; G2v blank.

SR: No entry.

STC: 14732.

Copies: BM (K.9.a.17.[1], the text copy) lacks A1, A2; the Folger copy lacks D2, D4, G1, G2, and is generally worn and tattered. There are no verbal press corrections.

All the songs have parts for Cantus and lute facing Tenor, Bassus, and Altus as in Do1597.

TO THE HONORABLE AND VERTV-
OVS GENTLEMAN SIR ROBERT SIDNEY, KNIGHT
Gouernour vnder her Maiestie of the towne of *Vlushing,* and
the Castle of the *Ramekins* in the Low Countries, and of
the forts of the same appendant, with the garrison there-
in placed as well of horse as foote.

Your great loue and fauour Honorable Syr, euer manifested to all worthy Sciences, hath imboldened me to offer vppe at your Lordships Shryne, these the vnworthie labours of my musicall trauels. And though in respect of their weakenes, they may perhaps seeme vntimely brought forth, and therefore the vnlikelier to prosper; yet doubt I not but if tenderd by you, they shall happelie find gentle cherishing, which may be a meane to make them more stronger, or else miscarrying, to encourage my endeuours to beget a better: for as no arts wincks at fewer errors than musicke: so none greater enimies to their owne profession then Musicians; who whilst in their own singularitie, they condemne euery mans workes, as some waie faulty, they are the cause, the art is the lesse esteemed, and they themselues reputed as selfe-commenders, and men most fantasticall. Wherefore if this one censuring infirmitie were remoued, these my ayres (free I dare say from grosse errours) would finde euery where more gratious entertainment. But since euen those, who are best seene in this art, cannot vaunt themselues free from such detractours, I the lesse regard it being so well accompanied. Howsoeuer if herein I may gaine your Honors good allowance, I shall thinke I haue attained to the better ende of my labours (which with my selfe, and the best of my seruice) restes euer more at your Lordships imploiment.

Your Lordships deuoted in
all dutifull seruice.
Robert Iones.

TO THE READER.

GEntlemen, since my desire is your eares shoulde be my indifferent iudges, I cannot thinke it necessary to make my trauels, or my bringing vp arguments to perswade you that I haue a good opinion of my selfe, only thus much I will saie: that I may preuent the rash iudgements of such as know me not. Euer since I practised speaking, I haue practised singing; hauing had noe other qualitie to hinder me from the perfect knowledge of this faculty, I haue been incouraged by the warrant of diuers good iudgments, that my paines herein shall at the least procure good liking, if not delight, which yet for mine owne part I must needes feare as much as I desire, especially when I consider the 10 *ripenes of this industrious age, wherein all men endeuour to knowe all thinges, I confesse I was not vnwilling to embrace the conceits of such gentlemen as were earnest to haue me apparell these ditties for them; which though they intended for their priuate recreation, neuer meaning they should come into the light, were yet content vpon intreaty to make the incouragements of this my first aduenture, whereuppon I was almost glad to make my small skill knowne to the world: presuming that if my cunning failed me in the Musicke: yet the words might speake for themselues, howsoeuer it pleaseth them to account better of that, then of these. Of purpose (as it should seeme) to make me beleeue I can do something; my only hope is, that seeing neither my cold ayres, nor* 20 *their idle ditties (as they will needes haue me call them) haue hitherto beene sounded in the eares of manie: they maie chance to finde such entertainment, as commonlie newes doth in the world: which if I may be so happie to heare, I will not saie my next shall be better, but I will promise to take more paines to shew more points of musicke, which now I could not do, because my chiefest care was to fit the Note to the Word, till when, I must be as well content with each mans lawfull censure, as I shall be glad of some mens vndeserued fauours.*

R. I.

A Table of all the Songs contained

in this Booke.

I.

A Womans looks
are barbed hooks,
that catch by art
the strongest hart,
when yet they spend no breath,   5
but let them speake
& sighing break,
forth into teares,
their words are speares,
that wound our souls to death.   10

2

The rarest wit
Is made forget,
And like a child
Is oft beguild,
With loues sweete seeming baite: 15
Loue with his rod
So like a God,
Commands the mind
We cannot find,   20
Faire shewes hide fowle deceit.

3

Time that all thinges
In order bringes,
Hath taught me now   25
To be more slow,
In giuing faith to speech:

Since womens wordes
No truth affordes,
And when they kisse   30
They thinke by this,
Vs men to ouer-reach.

II.

Fond wanton youths make loue a God,
which after proueth ages rod,
their youth, their time, their wit, their arte,
they spend in seeking of their smarte,
  and which of follies is the chiefe,   5
  they wooe their woe, they wedde their griefe.

2 All finde it so who wedded are,
Loues sweetes they finde enfold sowre care:
His pleasures pleasingst in the eie,
Which tasted once, with lothing die: 10
  They find of follies tis the chiefe,
  Their woe to wooe to wedde their griefe:

3 If for their owne content they choose,
Forthwith their kindreds loue they loose:
And if their kindred they content,   15
For euer after they repent.
  O tis of all our follies chiefe,
  Our woe to wooe to wedde our griefe.

4 In bed what strifes are bred by day,
Our puling wiues doe open lay: 20
None friendes none foes we must esteeme,
But whome they so vouchsafe to deeme:
  O tis of all our follies chiefe,
  Our woe to wooe to wedde our griefe.

5 Their smiles we want if ought they want,   25
And either we their wils must grant,
Or die they will or are with child,
Their laughings must not be beguild:
  O tis of all our follies chiefe,
  Our woe to woo to wedde our griefe.   30

6 Foule wiues are iealous, faire wiues false,
  Mariage to either bindes vs thrall:
  Wherefore being bound we must obey,
  And forced be perforce to say:
    Of all our blisse it is the chiefe,   35
    Our woe to wooe to wed our griefe.

III.

SHE whose matchles beauty stayneth,
what best iudgment fairst maintaineth,
shee O shee my loue disdaineth.

2

Can a creature so excelling,   5
Harbour scorne in beauties dwelling,
All kinde pitty thence expelling?

3

Pitty beauty much commendeth,
And th'imbracer oft befriendeth,   10
When all eie-contentment endeth.

4

Time proues beauty transitory;
Scorne, the staine of beauties glory,
In time makes the scorner sorie.   15

5

None adores the sunne declining,
Loue all loue fals to resigning,
When the sunne of loue leaues shining.

6   20

So when flowre of beauty failes thee,
And age stealing on assailes thee,
Then marke what this scorne auailes thee.

7

Then those hearts which now complaining,   25
Feele the wounds of thy disdaining,
Shall contemne thy beauty waining.

8

Yea thine owne hart now deere prized,
Shall with spite and griefe surprised,   30
Burst to finde it selfe despised.

9

When like harmes haue them requited,
Who in others harmes delighted,
Pleasingly the wrong'd are righted.   35

10

Such reuenge my wronges attending,
Hope still liues on time depending,
By thy plagues my torments ending.

IIII.

ONce did I loue and yet I liue,
though loue & truth be now forgotten.
Then did I ioy nowe doe I grieue,
that holy vows must needs be broken.

2   5

Hers be the blame that causd it so,
Mine be the griefe though it be little,
Shee shall haue shame, I cause to know
What tis to loue a dame so fickle.

3   10

Loue her that list I am content,
For that Camelion like shee changeth,
Yeelding such mistes as may preuent
My sight to view her when she rangeth.

4   15

Let him not vaunt that gaines my losse,
For when that he and time hath prou'd her,
Shee may him bring to weeping crosse:
I say no more because I lou'd her.

V.

Lᴇᴅ by a strong desire
  to haue a thing vnseene,
nothing could make mee tire
  to bee where I had been,
I got her sight which made me think,   5
my thirst was gone because I saw my drinke.

2

Kept by the carefull watch
  Of more then hundred eies,
I sought but could not catch   10
  The thing she not denies:
Tis better to be blind and fast,
Then hungrie see thy loue and cannot tast.

3

But louers eies doe wake
  When others are at rest,   15
And in the night they slake
  The fire of daies vnrest:
Mee thinkes that ioy is of most worth,
Which painful time & passed fears brings forth.   20

4

Yet husbands doe suppose
  To keepe their wiues by art,
And parents will disclose
  By lookes their childrens hart: 25
As if they which haue will to doe,
Had not the wit to blind such keepers to.

5

Peace then yee aged fooles
That know your selues so wise,   30
That from experience schooles
Doe thinke wit must arise:
Giue young men leaue to thinke and say,
Your senses with your bodies doe decay.

6   35

Loue ruleth like a God
Whom earth keepes not in awe,
Nor feare of smarting rod
Denounc'd by reasons law:
Giue graue aduise but rest you there,   40
Youth hath his cours, & wil, & you youths wer.

7

Thinke not by prying care
To picke loues secrets out,
If you suspitious are   45
 Your selues resolue your doubt,
Who seekes to know such deede once done,
Findes periury before confession.

VI.

Lie downe poore heart and die a while for griefe,
thinke not this world will euer do thee good,
fortune forewarnes thou looke to thy reliefe,
and sorrow sucks vpon thy liuing bloud,
 then this is all can helpe thee of this hell,   5
 lie downe and die, and then thou shalt doe well.

2

Day giues his light but to thy labours toyle,
And night her rest but to thy weary bones,
Thy fairest fortune followes with a foyle: 10
And laughing endes but with their after grones.
 And this is all can helpe thee of thy hell,
 Lie downe and die and then thou shalt doe well.

3

Patience doth pine and pitty ease no paine,   15
Time weares the thoughts but nothing helps the mind,
Dead and aliue aliue and dead againe:
These are the fits that thou art like to finde.
  And this is all can helpe thee of thy hell,
  Lie downe and die and then thou shalt doe well.   20

VII.

WHere lingring feare doth once posses the hart,
        there is the toong
        forst to prolong,
& smother vp his suite, while that his smart,
like fire supprest, flames more in euery part.   5

2

Who dares not speake deserues not his desire,
        The Boldest face,
        Findeth most grace:
Though women loue that men should them admire,   10
They slily laugh at him dares come no higher.

3

Some thinke a glaunce expressed by a sigh,
        Winning the field,
        Maketh them yeeld: 15
But while these glauncing fooles do rowle the eie,
They beate the bush, away the bird doth flie.

4

A gentle hart in vertuous breast doth stay,
        Pitty doth dwell,   20
        In beauties cell:
A womans hart doth not thogh tong say nay
Repentance taught me this the other day.

5

Which had I wist I presently had got,   25
    The pleasing fruite,
    Of my long suite:
But time hath now beguild me of this lot,
For that by his foretop I tooke him not.

VIII.

HEro care not though they prie,
I will loue thee till I die,
Ielousie is but a smart,
that tormentes a ielous hart:
  Crowes are blacke that were white,   5
  for betraying loues delight.

2

They that loue to finde a fault,
May repent what they haue sought,
What the fond eie hath not view'd,   10
Neuer wretched hart hath rew'd:
  Vulcan then, prou'd a scorne,
  When he saw he wore a horne.

3

Doth it then by might behoue,   15
To shut vp the gates of loue,
Women are not kept by force,
But by natures owne remorse.
  If they list, they will stray,
  Who can hold that will away.   20

4

Ioue in golden shower obtain'd,
His loue in a towre restrain'd,
So perhaps if I could doe,
I might hold my sweete loue to: 25
  Gold keepe out at the doore,
  I haue loue that conquers more.

5

Wherefore did they not suspect,
When it was to some effect,   30
Euery little glimmering sparke,
Is perceiued in the darke:
  This is right, howlets kinde,
  See by night, by day be blinde.

IX.

WHen loue on time and measure makes his ground,
time that must end though loue can neuer die,
tis loue betwixt a shadow and a sound,
a loue not in the hart but in the eie,
  A loue that ebbes and flowes now vp now downe,   5
  a mornings fauor and an euenings frowne.

2

Sweete lookes shew loue, yet they are but as beames,
Faire wordes seeme true, yet they are but as wind,
Eies shed their teares yet are but outward streames: 10
Sighes paint a sadnes in the falsest minde.
  Lookes, wordes, teares, sighes, shew loue when loue they leaue,
  False harts can weepe, sigh, sweare, and yet deceiue.
                              [John Lilliat?]

X.

Sweet come away my darling,
and sweetly let me heare thee sing,
come away, come away, come away and bring
my hart thou hast so fast in keeping.

2   5

Oh fie vpon this long stay,
That thus my louing hopes delay:
Come againe, come againe, come againe and say,
Sweet hart ile neuer more say thee nay.

3   10

Deere be not such a tryant,
Still to reioice thee in my want:
Come and doe, come and doe, come and doe not scant
Me of thy sight, so faire and pleasant.

4   15

Why hearst thou not his sighing,
Whose voice all hoarce is with crying:
Come and doe, come and doe, come and doe something,
That may reuiue thy true loue dying.

5   20

This is the pride of women,
That they make beggers of all men:
We must sigh, we must crie, we must die, and then
Forsooth it may be they will hearken.

XI.

Women, what are they, changing weather-cocks,
that smallest puffes of lust haue power to turne,
women what are they, vertues stumbling blockes,
whereat weake fooles doe fall, the wiser spurne,
  wee men, what are wee, fooles and idle boies,   5
  to spend our time in sporting with such toies.

2

Women what are they? trees whose outward rinde,
Makes shew for faire when inward hart is hallow:
Women what are they? beasts of Hiænaes kinde,   10
That speak those fairst, whom most they mean to swallow:
  We men what are wee? fooles and idle boies,
  To spend our time in sporting with such toies.

3

Women what are they? rocks vpon the coast,   15
Where on we suffer shipwracke at our landing:
Women what are they? patient creatures most,
That rather yeld then striue gainst ought withstanding.

We men what are wee? fooles and idle boies,
To spend our time in sporting with such toies.   20

XII.

FArewel dear loue since thou wilt needs be gon,
mine eies do shew my life is almost done,
    nay I will neuer die,
    so long as I can spie,
    there be many mo   5
    though that she do go,
there be many mo I feare not,
why then let her goe I care not.

2

Farewell, farewell, since this I finde is true,   10
I will not spend more time in wooing you:
    But I will seeke elswhere,
    If I may find her there,
    Shall I bid her goe,
    What and if I doe?   15
Shall I bid her go and spare not,
O no no no no I dare not.

3

Ten thousand times farewell, yet stay a while,
Sweet kisse me once, sweet kisses time beguile: 20
    I haue no power to moue,
    How now, am I in loue?
    Wilt thou needs be gone?
    Go then, all is one,
Wilt thou needs be gone? oh hie thee,   25
Nay, stay and doe no more denie mee.

4

Once more farewell, I see loth to depart,
Bids oft adew to her that holdes my hart:
    But seeing I must loose,   30
    Thy loue which I did chuse:

Go thy waies for me,
   Since it may not be,
Go thy waies for me, but whither?
Go, oh but where I may come thither.   35

5

What shall I doe? my loue is now departed,
Shee is as faire as shee is cruell harted:
   Shee would not be intreated,
   With praiers oft repeated: 40
   If shee come no more,
   Shall I die therefore,
If shee come no more, what care I?
Faith, let her go, or come, or tarry.

XIII.

O My poore eies that sun whose shine
late gaue you light doth now decline
  and set to you to others riseth,
she who would sooner die then change,
not fearing death delights to range,   5
  and now O now my soule despiseth.

2

Yet O my hart thy state is blest,
To finde out rest in thy vnrest:
  Since thou her slaue no more remainest,   10
For shee that bound thee sets thee free,
Then when shee first forsaketh thee:
  Such O such right by wrong thou gainest.

3

Eies gaze no more, heart learne to hate,   15
Experience tels you all too late:
  Fond womans loue with faith still warreth,
While true desert speakes, writes and giues,
Some groome the bargaine neerer driues:
  And he, O he the market marreth.   20

XIIII.

Iꜰ fathers knew but how to leaue
their children wit as they do wealth,
& could constraine them to receiue
that physicke which brings perfect health,
  the world would not admiring stand,   5
  a womans face, and womans hand.

2

Women confesse they must obey,
We men will needes be seruants still:
We kisse their hands and what they say,   10
We must commend bee't neuer so ill.
  Thus we like fooles admiring stand,
  Her pretty foote and pretty hand.

3

We blame their pride which we increase,   15
By making mountaines of a mouse:
We praise because we know we please,
Poore women are too credulous.
  To thinke that we admiring stand,
  Or foote, or face, or foolish hand.   20

XV.

  Lɪfe is a Poets fable,
  & al her daies are lies
  stolne from deaths reckoning table,
for I die, for I die as I speake,
death times the notes that I doe breake.   5

2

  Childhood doth die in youth,
  And youth in old age dies,
  I thought I liu'd in truth:
But I die, but I die, now I see,   10
Each age of death makes one degree.

3

Farewell the doting score,
Of worlds arithmeticke,
Life, ile trust thee no more,   15
Till I die, till I die for thy sake,
Ile go by deaths new almanacke.

4

This instant of my song,
A thousand men lie sicke,   20
A thousand knels are rong:
And I die, and I die as they sing,
They are but dead and I dying.

5

Death is but lifes decay,   25
Life time, time wastes away,
Then reason bids me say,
That I die, that I die, though my breath
Prolongs this space of lingring death.

XVI.

Sweet Philomell in groaues and desarts haunting,
oft glads my hart and eares with her sweet chaunting,
  but then her tunes delight me best,
  when pearcht with prick against her breast,
shee sings fie fie as if shee suffred wrong   5
till seeming pleas'd sweete sweete concludes her song.

2

Sweete Iinny singes and talkes and sweetly smileth,
And with her wanton mirth my griefes beguileth:
  But then me thinkes shee pleaseth best,   10
  When, while my hands moue loues request,
Shee cries phy, phy, and seeming loath gainsaies,
Till better pleas'd sweete sweete content bewraies.

XVII.

THat hart wherein all sorrowes doth abound,
lies in this breast, and cries alowd for death,
O blame not her when I am vnder ground,
that scorning wisht t'outliue my panting breath,
  O doe not her despise,   5
  but let my death suffice,
  to make all young men wise.

2

My louing hopes prolongd my lothed life,
Till that my life grew lothsome to my lou'd,   10
Then death and I were at no longer strife:
And I was glad my death her wish approu'd.
  O let not her be shent,
  Yet let my president,
  Make womans harts relent.   15

XVIII.

WHat if I seeke for loue of thee,
shall I find beauty kind
to desert that still shall dwell in mee.
But if I sue and liue forlorne,
then alasse neuer was   5
any wretch to more misfortune borne.
Though thy lookes haue charmd mine eies,
I can forbeare to loue,
but if euer sweete desire
set my wofull hart on fire   10
then can I neuer remoue.

2

Frowne not on me vnlesse thou hate,
For thy frowne cast me downe
To despaire of my most haplesse state: 15
Smile not on me vnlesse thou loue,
For thy smile, will beguile
My desires if thou vnsteedfast proue:

If thou needs wilt bend thy browes,
A while refraine my deare,   20
But if thou wilt smile on me,
Let it not delayed be,
Comfort is neuer too neare.

XIX.

My Mistris sings no other song
but stil complains I did her wrong,
beleeue her not it was not so,
I did but kis her and let her goe.

2   5

And now she sweares I did, but what,
Nay, nay, I must not tell you that:
And yet I will it is so sweete,
As teehee tahha when louers meete.

3   10

But womens words they are heedlesse,
To tell you more it is needlesse:
I ranne and caught her by the arme,
And then I kist her, this was no harme.

4   15

But shee alas is angrie still,
Which sheweth but a womans will:
She bites the lippe and cries fie fie,
And kissing sweetly away shee doth flie.

5   20

Yet sure her lookes bewraies content,
And cunningly her brales are meant:
As louers vse to play and sport,
When time and leisure is too too short.

XX.

Perplexed sore am I,
thine eies fair loue like Phebus brightest beames
doth set my hart on fire and daze my sight,
yet doe I liue by vertue of those beames,
for when thy face is hid comes fearefull night   5
  and I am like to die,
then since my eies can not indure so heauenly sparke,
sweet grant that I may stil feele out my loue by darke.

2

So Shall I ioyfull bee,   10
Each thing on earth that liueth by the sunne
Would die if he in glorie still appeare,
Then let some cloudes of pitty ouerrunne
That glorious face, that I with liuely cheere,
  May stand vp before thee.   15
Or, Since mine eies cannot endure so heauenly sparke,
Sweet grant that I may still feele out my loue by darke.

XXI.

Can modest plaine desire
to the ioies of loue aspire?
Can worthinesse procure
more then hardinesse assure?
  no no no where feare of each frowne,   5
  takes hopes height downe a downe downe.

2

Granting is so eschew'd,
Least the grant lie vnpursued:
Least sutors brag they might,   10
And account the grantors light:
  No no no is a weake defence growne,
  Till force beare downe downe a downe.

3

Yet who would staine loues seate,   15
With a blot of such a feate:
Or for so vile a toy,
Ioine repentance with his ioy.
  No no no her vertue well knowne,
  Beates vaine thoughts downe downe a downe.   20

FINIS.

Thomas Morley

The First Booke of Ayres

1600

[Within a frame of rules (25.4 × 15.1 cm), a border of fleuron type orna-
ments, and another frame of rules] THE/ FIRST BOOKE/ OF AYRES./
OR [R swash]/ LITTLE SHORT/ SONGS, TO SING AND/ *PLAY TO
THE LVTE*, [PY, *T*'s swash]/ WITH THE BASE/ VIOLE./ NEWLY
PVBLISHED/ BY [swash]/ *THOMAS MORLEY* [T, M's, ARY swash]/
Bachiler [B swash] *of Muſicke, and one of*/ the Gent. of her Maieſties Royall/
CHAPPEL./ [device with motto "DEVS. IN. ÆTERNVM.", McKerrow
No. 322]/ *Imprinted at London in litle S. Helen's by VVilliam Barley*, [B swash]/
the aſsigne of Thomas Morley, and are to be ſold at/ his houſe in Gracious
ſtreete. 1600./ *Cum Priuilegio.*/

Note: McKerrow says that the device on the title page is probably the arms of John
Bossewell, the author of *Workes of Armorie* (1572), in which the device is first used.
H. Ballard used it in the 1597 edition of Bossewell, and McKerrow wonders why
Barley got it to use in Anthony Holborne's *Pavans* (1599). Mo1600 was unavailable
to McKerrow; perhaps it is of some significance that Morley dedicated his book to
a kinsman of Bossewell's, Sir Ralph Bosville. Barley may have acquired the device
to use in Mo1600, but used it incidentally in Holborne.

Collation: 2° in fours: A–F⁴G²(?). The unique copy lacks all after D4 (16 leaves
extant). It is possible that the collation runs only through F4 if the last two instrumental
pieces were printed together on F4v instead of on a full opening apiece. C1 is not signed,
and the whole gathering is hinged, but the watermarks do not suggest a cancel.

Headlines: Verso, A3v–D4v: *CANTVS. I.* [*–XIIII.*] *THO. MORLEY.* Recto,
A4–D4: *FOR THE BASE VIOLE. I.* [*–XIII.*] *THO. MORLEY.*

Contents: A1, title page; A1v blank; A2, dedication; A2v, epistle to the reader; A3,
table; A4v–D4v, songs I–XIIII, one per opening. For the remainder of the contents,
see the table.

SR: No entry.

STC: 18115.5.

Copy: Folger (U-18116a), lacking all after D4. The only other known copy, presumably complete, was destroyed when the Birmingham Public Library burned in 1878. The present copy was once in the Halliwell-Phillips collection, and was eventually acquired by Henry Clay Folger. Folger kept the book out of sight until the Folger Library was built after his death, much to the frustration of scholars (see Warlock, pp. 117–118; EMV, p. xiii; and ELS, series I, XVI, ii).

The music for the songs consists of a voice part with lute tablature facing an inverted bass viol part.

TO THE WORTHIE AND VERTVOVS
LOVER OF MVSICKE, RALPH
BOSVILE ESQVIRE.

Sir, the loue which you do beare to my qualitie, proceedeth (no doubt) of an excellent knowledge you haue therein. (For vncouth vnkist saith venerable Chaucer:) But that which (among so many professors thereof) you beare to my selfe in particular, must simply flowe from the bountie of a generous spirit, there being no other meanes in me to deserue the same, but onely desire. In recompence therefore of my priuate fauours, I thought it the part of an honest minde, to make some one publique testimonie and acknowledgement thereof. And that, by consecrating vnto your protection these few light Ayres for the Lute voice and Violl onely. Which as they were made this vacation time, you may vse likewise at your vacant howers. But see the folly of me, who whilst I look for a Patrone, haue lighted on a iudge. This must be the comfort that, as they must endure the censure of your iudicious eare: so shall they bee sure of the protection of your good word. And herewith once more I humbly commend them and me to your good opinion.

10

At your deuotion now and euer.

THO. MORLEY.

TO THE READER.

LEt it not seeme straunge (courteous Reader) that I thus farre presume to take vpon me, in publishing this volume of Lute Ayres, being no professor thereof, but like a blind man groping for my way, haue at length happened vpon a method: which when I found, my heart burning loue to my freinds would not consent I might conceale. Two causes mooued me heereunto, the first to satisfie the world of my no idle howers (though both Gods visitation in sicknesse, and troubles in the world, by sutes in Law haue kept me busied.) The other cause was to make tryall of my first fruites, which being effected, I will commend to indifferent and no partiall iudges. If *Momus* doe euer carpe, let him doe it with iudgement least my booke in silence flout his little iudgement. If he would faine scoffe, yet feareth to doe it through his wits defect, let him shew iudgement in his tongues restraint, in the allowance of that which I doubt not, but more iudiciall eares shall applaude. Too many there are, who are sillily indewde with an humour of reprehension, and those are they that euer want true knowledge of apprehension. I know that *Scientia non habet inimicum praeter ignorantem*: but I shall not feare their barking questes. This booke exspects the fauourable censure of the exquisite iudiciall eares, scorning the wel-come of any *Mydas*, if therefore the more worthie receiue it into their fauour, it is as much as euer I wished, or can expect. In lue whereof, I shall by this encouragement promise and produce sundrie fruites of this kind, which verie shortly I will commend vnto you. In the meane time I commend and commit both this and my selfe, to your euer good opinion. And salute you with a hartie. *Adieu.*

Yours in all loue.
THO. MORLEY.

A TABLE CONTAINING
ALL THE SONGS IN
THIS BOOKE.

FINIS.

I.

A Painted tale by Poets skill deuised,
where words well plast great store of loue profest,
In loues attyre can neuer Maske disguysde,
For looks and sighs true loue can best expresse,
And he whose wordes his passions might can tell   5
Dooth more in wordes then in true loue excell.

II.

The first part.

THirsis and *Milla*, arme in arme together,
In meri may to the greene garden walked,
Where all the way they wanton ridles talked,
The youthfull boye, kissing her cheekes all rosie   5
Beseecht her there to gather him a posye.

III.

The second part.

SHee straight hir light greene silken cotes vp tucked
and May for Mill and Time for *Thersis* plucked,
which when she broght hee clasp't her by the middle,

And kist her sweete but could not read her riddle,   5
Ah foole, with that the Nimph set vp a laughter,
And blusht, and ran away And he ran after.

IIII.

With my loue my life was nestled,
In the some of happines,
From my loue my life was wrested,
To a world of heauines,
O let loue my life remoue,   5
Sith I liue not wher I loue.

2 Where the truth once was and is not,
Shadowes are but vanities,
Shewing want that helpe they cannot,
Signes not slaues of miseries,   10
Painted meate no hunger feedes,
Dying life each death exceedes.

3 O true loue since thou hast left me,
Mortall life is tedious,
Death it is to liue without thee,   15
Death of all most odious,
Turne againe and take me with thee,
Let me die, or liue thou in me.
                    [Robert Southwell]

V.

I Saw my Ladye weeping,
And sorrowe proud to bee aduaunced so,
In those fayre eyes Where all perfection kept
her face was full of woe,
But such a woe, Beeleeue mee as winnes mennes hearts,   5
Then myrth can doo with her intising partes.

VI.

It was a louer and his lasse,
With a haye, with a hoe and a haye nonie no,

That o're the green corne fields did passe
in spring time the only preti ring time
when birds do sing, hay ding a ding a ding   5
sweete louers loue the springe.

2 Betweene the Akers of the rie,
   With a hay, with a ho and a hay nonie no,
   These prettie Countrie fooles would lie,
   In spring time, the onely prettie ring time,   10
   When Birds doe sing, hay ding a ding a ding,
   Sweete louers loue the spring.

3 This Carrell they began that houre,
   With a hay, with a ho and a hay nonie no,
   How that a life was but a flower,   15
   In spring time, the onely prettie ring time,
   When Birds doe sing, hay ding a ding a ding,
   Sweete louers loue the spring.

4 Then prettie louers take the time,
   With a hay, with a ho and a hay nonie no.   20
   For loue is crowned with the prime,
   In spring time, the onely prettie ring time,
   When Birds doe sing, hay ding a ding a ding,
   Sweete louers loue the spring.
               [William Shakespeare]

VII.

Who is it that this darke night,
Vnder my window playneth,
It is one that from thy sighte
beeing ah exilde disdaineth
euerie other vulgar light.   5

2 Why alas and are you he,
   Be not those fond fancies chaunged,
   Deare when you find change in me,
   Though from me you be estranged,
   Let my change to ruine be.   10

3 Well in absence this will die,
   Leaue to see, and leaue to wonder,
   Absence sure will helpe if I,
   Can learne how my selfe to sunder,
   From what in my heart doth lie.   15

4 But time will these thoughts remoue,
   Time doth worke what no man knoweth:
   Time doth as the subiect proue.
   With time still the affection groweth,
   In the faithfull turtle Doue.   20

5 What if you new beauties see,
   Will not they stirre new affection,
   I will thinke they pictures bee:
   Image like of Saints perfection,
   Poorely counterfeiting thee.   25

6 But the reasons purest light,
   Bids you leaue such minds to nourish,
   Deare doe reason no such spite.
   Neuer doth thy beautie flourish,
   More then in my reasons sight.   30

7 But the wrongs loue beares will make
   Loue at length leaue vndertaking,
   No the more fooles it doe shake,
   In a ground of so firme making,
   Deeper still they driue the stake.   35

8 Peace I thinke that some giue eare,
   Come no more least I get anger,
   Blisse I will my blisse forbeare,
   Fearing sweete you to endaunger,
   But my soule shall harber there,   40

9 Well be gon, be gon I say,
   Least that Argues eyes perceiue you,
   O vniustest fortunes sway,
   Which can make me thus to leaue [you],
   And from Loutes to runne away.   45
                        [Sir Philip Sidney]

VIII.

Mᴀsteresse mine well may you fare,
Kind be your thoughts and void of care,
Sweete Saint Venus bee your speede,
That you may in loue proceede,
Coll mee and clip and kisse me to,   5
So so so so so true loue should doo.

2 This faire morning Sunnie bright,
   That giues life to loues delight:
   Euerie hart with heate inflames,
   And our cold affection blames.   10
   Coll me and clip and kisse me to,
   So so so so so true loue should do.

3 In these woods are none but birds,
   They can speake but silent words:
   They are prettie harmelesse things,   15
   They will shade vs with their wings.
   Coll me and clip and kisse me to,
   So so so so so true loue should do.

4 Neuer striue nor make no noyes,
   Tis for foolish girles and boyes,   20
   Euerie childish thing can say,
   Goe to, how now, pray away.
   Coll me and clip and kisse me to,
   So so so so so true loue should do.

IX.

Cᴀn I forget what reasons force, Imprinted in my heart,
Can I vnthinke these restlesse thoughtes when first I felt loues
                                                        dart,
Shall tongue recall what thoughts & loue by reason once did
                                                        speake.
No, no all thinges saue death wantes force that faithfull band
                                                        to breake.

2 For now I proue no life to loue, where fancie breeds content,　5
　True loues reward with wise regard, is neuer to repent,
　It yeelds delight that feedes the sight, whilst distance doe
　　　　　　　　　　　　　　　　　　　them part,
　Such foode fedd me when I did see, in mine another hart,

3 Another hart I spied, combin'd within my brest so fast,
　As to a straunger I seemde straunge, but loue forc'd loue at
　　　　　　　　　　　　　　　　　　　last,　10
　Yet was I not as then I seem'd, but rather wish to see,
　If in so full of harbour loue, might constant lodged bee.

4 So *Cupid* playes oft now a dayes, and makes the foole seeme
　　　　　　　　　　　　　　　　　　　faire,
　He dims the sight breeding delight, where we seeme to dispaire,
　So in our hart he makes them sport, and laughes at them that
　　　　　　　　　　　　　　　　　　　loue,　15
　Who for their paine gets this againe, their loue no liking
　　　　　　　　　　　　　　　　　　　moue.

X.

　Loue wingd my hopes and taught them how to flie,
　Farre from base earth, But not to mount to hie.
　　　　For true pleasure liues in measure
　　　　which if men forsake,
　Blinded they into follie run, And griefe for pleasure take.　5

2 But my vaine hopes proud of their new taught light,
　Enamard sought to woe the Sunnes faire light,
　　　　Whose rich brightnesse, moued their lightnesse,
　　　　To aspire so high:
　That all scorcht & consumd with fire, now drownd in woe
　　　　　　　　　　　　　　　　　　　they lie.　10

3 And none but loue their wofull hap doth rue,
　For loue doth know that their desires were true:
　　　　Though fates frowned and now drowned,
　　　　They in sorrow dwell,
　It was the purest light of heauen, for whose faire loue they
　　　　　　　　　　　　　　　　　　　fell.　15

XI.

Wнат if my mistresse now will needs vnconstant be,
Wilt thou be then so false in loue as well as shee,
No no such fals-hood flee, though women faithlesse be.

2 My mistresse frownes and sweares that now I loue her not,
The change shee finds, is that which my dispaire begot,   5
Dispaire which is my loue, since shee all faith forgot.

3 Shee blames my truth and causelesly accuseth me,
I must not let mine eyes report what they doe see,
My thoughts restraind must be, and yet shee will goe free,

4 If shee doth change shee must not be in constancie,   10
For why shee doth professe to take such libertie,
Her selfe shee will vntie, and yet fast bound am I.

5 If shee at once doe please to fauour more then one,
I agreed in humble sort to make my mone,
I spake not to a stone, where sence of loue is none.   15

6 But now let loue in time redresse all these my wrongs,
And let my loue receiue the due to her belongs,
Els thus ile frame my song or chaunge my mistresse longs.

7 Which if I find my hart some other where shall dwell,
For louing not to be beloued it is a hell,   20
Since so my hap befell, I bid my loue farre well.

XII.

Come sorrow come sit downe and morne with me,
Hange downe thy head vppon thy balefull brest,
That God and man and all the world may see,
Our heauie heartes doo liue in quiet rest,
  Enfold thine armes and wring thy wretched hands,   5
  To shewe the state wherein poore sorrowe standes.

2 Crie not out-right for that were childrens guise,
But let thy teares fall trickling downe thy face,
And weepe so long vntill thy blubbered eyes,
May see (in Sunne) the depth of thy disgrace.   10
  Oh shake thy head, but not a word but mumme.
  The heart once dead, the tongue is stroken dumme.

3 And let our fare be dishes of dispight,
   To breake our hearts and not our fastes withall,
   Then let vs sup, with sorrow sops at night,   15
   And bitter sawce, all of a broken gall,
     Thus, let vs liue, till heauens may rue to see,
     The dolefull doome ordained for thee and mee.

XIII.

FAire in a morne oh fairest morne was euer morne so faire,
When as the sun but not the same that shined in the ayre,
And on a hill, oh fairest hill was neuer hill so blessed,
Ther stood a man was neuer man for no man so distressed.

2 But of the earth no earthly Sunne, and yet no earthly creature,   5
   There stoode a face was neuer face, that carried such a feature,
   This man had hap O happie man, no man so hapt as he,
   For none had hap to see the hap, that he had hapt to see.

3 And as he behold this man beheld, he saw so faire a face,
   The which would daunt the fairest here, and staine the brauest
                                                     grace,   10
   Pittie he cried, and pittie came, and pittied for his paine,
   That dying would not let him die, but gaue him life againe.

4 For ioy where of he made such mirth, that all the world did
                                                     ring,
   And *Pan* for all his *Nimphes* came forth, to heare the
                                                     Shepherds sing.
   But such a song song neuer was, nor nere will be againe,   15
   Of *Philida* the shepheards Queene, and *Coridon* the swaine.
                                        [Nicholas Breton]

XIIII.

ABsence heere thou my protestation,
       Against thy strength,
       distaunce and length,
doo what you dare, For alteration,
   For hartes of truest mettall,   5
Absence dooth ioyne, And time dooth settle.

[All after D4 missing. Continued from *A Poetical Rhapsody*, 1602:]

Who loues a Mistris of such qualitie,
    Hee soone hath found
    Affections ground
Beyond time, place, and all mortality.   10
  To harts that cannot vary,
Absence is present, Time doth tarry.

My Sences want their outward motions,
    Which now within
    Reason doth win,   15
Redoubled in her secret notions:
  Like rich men that take pleasure,
In hiding, more then handling Treasure.

By Absence, this good meanes I gaine,
    That I can catch her,   20
    Where none can watch her,
In some close corner of my braine,
  There I embrace and kisse her,
And so I both enioy and misse her.
            [John Hoskins?]

XV.

["White as Lillies" missing. See Notes.]

XVI.

["What lack ye Sir" missing.]

XVII.
[From Christ Church, Oxford, MS 439, pp. 80–81:]

Will you buy a fine dogg with a hole in his head,
with a dildo with a dildo dildo,
muffes cuffes rebatoes and fine Sisters thred,
with a dildo dildo with a dildo dildo.
I stand not one poyntes pinnes periwigges combes glasses   5
gloues garters girdles buskes, for the briske lasses,
but I haue other dainty daintie trickes:
sleeke stones and potinge stickes,
with a dilldo dildo dildo didle didle dildo,

and for a need my pretty pretty pretty pods,   10
Amber Civett and muskecods,
with a dildo with a didle didle dildo.

XVIII.

[From Christ Church, Oxford, MS 439, pp. 1–2:]

Sleepe slumbringe eyes give rest vnto my cares,
my cares the Infants of my troubled braine,
my cares surprisde, surprisde with Blacke dispaire
doth the assention of my hopes restraine.
Sleepe then my eyes ô sleepe & take your Reste   5
To banishe sorrow from a free borne Breste.

2 My freborne brest borne Free to sorrowes Smarte
brought in subiection by my wandringe Eye
Whose traytrus sighte conceavd that to my harte,
For which I waile, I sob, I sighe, I Dye.   10
Sleepe then my eyes, disturbed of quiet reste,
To banishe sorrow From my captive breste.

3 My captive brest stounge by these glistringe starres:
these glistringe starres: the bewty of the skye:
that bright blacke skye which doth the soone beames baine: 15
From Her sweete comforte on my harts sad eye:
Wake then my eyes trewe partners of vnreste:
For Sorrow still must harboure in my breste.

XIX.

["Much haue I loued" missing.]

XX.

["Fantasticke loue, the first part" missing.]

XXI.

["Poore soule, the second part" missing.]

XXII.

["Pauane" missing.]

XXIII.

["Galliard" missing.]

Robert Jones

The Second Booke of Songs and Ayres

1601

[Within a border: McK. & F. No. 140] THE SECOND/ BOOKE OF SONGS/ AND AYRES,/ Set out to the Lute, the bafe Violl/ *the playne way, or the Bafe by*/ tableture after the leero/ *fafhion:*/ *Compofed by* Robert Iones./ Printed by *P. S.* for *Mathew Selman* by the/ *affent of Thomas Morley, and are to be*/ fold at the Inner temple/ gate, 1601./

> *Note:* "P. S." on the title page stands for Peter Short. According to McK. & F., the compartment had been used in the same year by A. Hatfield for J. Norton, and was subsequently used by the Eliots Court Press for J. Bill in 1614.
>
> *Collation:* 2°; A–M² [A1, M2 not signed]; 24 leaves.
>
> *Headlines:* Verso, B1v–M1v: CANTVS I. [III.–XXI.] Robert Iones. [B2v: Robert Iones. CANTVS] Recto, B2–M2: BASSVS / The tableture Base [no period after *Base* only on B2, C2, E2, G2, H2, L1, M2]
>
> *Contents:* A1, title page; A1v, arms of Sir Henry Leonard; A2, dedication; A2v, epistle to the reader; B1, table; B1v–M2, songs I–XXI, one per opening; M2v blank.
>
> *SR:* No entry.
>
> *STC:* 14733.
>
> *Copies:* The only complete copy is in the BM (K.9.a.17.[2]), the copy text; the Manchester copy (BR f410 Jt302) lacks sig. I. There are no verbal press corrections.
>
> All of the songs have a Cantus with lute tablature facing a lyra-viol part in tablature and a mensural Bassus with words for the first stanza.

TO THE RIGHT VERTVOVS
AND WORTHY KNIGHT, SIR
HENRY LEONARD.

WORTHY Sir, and my Honourable friend: I giue you this *Child*, I praie you bring it vp, because I am a poore man and cannot maintaine it: it may suffer much aduersitie in my name: your Fortune maie alter his starres and make him happie. Though his Father be aliue, I maie call him an *Orphane*, for poore mens *Children* are *Orphanes* borne, and more to be pittied then they that haue changed their fathers for their lands; such maie raise themselues in due time: we haue no waie to heighten our being, but by another power. As Gentlewomen peece themselues with Tires and Coronets, to appeare more personable and tall: so must we adde vnto our littlenes (if we will not be scorned for dwarfes) the crowne of gentle persons more eminent and high. Our statures are not set aboue danger; wee lie lowe, fit for euerie foote to treade vpon: our place is the ground, there is nothing beneath vs, and yet detraction will pull vs lower, if wee haue not good aspects. They will find meanes to digge and let vs downe into the earth, and burie vs before our time: This is the cause of patronage, and this is the persecution of them that would ingrosse all Glorie into their owne hands. But see the rage of these men, they bite the fruites themselues should feede vpon. Vertue would bring forth manie *Children* but they hold them in the wombe that they dare not come out. As the couetous man besiegeth all the land about him, with statutes, fines, and bands, and other such like ciuill warre: so doth the ambitious intrap the little portion of anie commenda-tions that maie fall besides him. And like the mercilesse Souldiers; the Castles they cannot take, they blow vp. They are as sparing of euerie small remnant of credit, as if it were laide vp in common-banke; and the more were giuen awaie, the lesse would come to their shares. They are miserable men, I will only brand them with this marke, and let them goe. They were Eagles, if they did not catch flyes, as they are; they are great things, much lesse then nothing. For my part, I will not contend with them, I desire no applause or commendations: let them haue the fame of Ecchoes and sounds, and let me be a Bird in your Cage, to sing to my selfe and you. This is my content, and this is my ambition: if I haue this, I faile not in my expectation, if more for your sake, that is my aduantage, and I will owe you duetie for it: in the meane time I rest,

At your Worships seruice,
ROBERT IONES.

TO THE READER.

READER, *I haue once more aduentured to aske thy counsell, whether I haue doone well, or no; in taking thus much paines to please thee. All that I will say for my selfe, is: My intent towards thee was good, yet because perhaps I know thee not; and I as yet am not growne so confident to warrant my endeuours against all men: I hold it no shame to craue vprightnesse in thy censure, as I meane not to accuse my selfe of negligence by begging thy fauour; wherein I chuse rather to deserue thy commendations, then by my owne praises, to set my labours out to sale. The trueth is, although I was not so idle when I composed these Ayres, that I dare not stand to the hazard of their examination:* 10 *Yet I would be glad (if it might be) that thy friendly approbation might giue me incouragement, to sound my thankefulnes more sweetely in thine eares hereafter. If the Ditties dislike thee, 'tis my fault that was so bold to publish the priuate contentments of diuers Gentlemen without their consents, though (I hope) not against their wils: wherein if thou find anie thing to meete with thy desire, thank me; for they were neuer meant thee. I know not how the vulgar esteeme of trauell, but me thinkes there should be no Gentleman (when he may buy so much paines, for so little money) that will not conclude, he can at least be no looser by the bargaine. If anie Musicion will out of the pride of his cunning disdaine me and these my beginnings, as things not worth his enuie,* 20 *these are to desire him (if he be not growne past all charitie,) that he would accept the subscription of my Name, as a sufficient Testimonie, that I am not ashamed of instruction, wherein soeuer I may appeare to haue out-run my Iustification. As for the rest that would faine informe men, they know some thing by their generall dislike of euerie thing; I will not so much as desire them to be silent, least I should hereby teach them at least how they might seeme wise. For the Booke I will saie onely thus much; there hath not yet beene anie extant of this fashion, which if thou shalt pronounce to be but worth thy hearing, I rest satisfied, if not thy debtor.   Farewell.*

Least anie man should seeme to accuse me of singularitie for expressing 30
the time of my songes, by pricke-song Notes neuer heretofore vsed:
I haue for his better instruction hereunto indeuoured to satisfie him.

A Semibreefe, Minnum, Chrochet, Quauer.

A Table of all the Songs contained
in this Booke.

I.

Loue wing'd my hopes and taught me howe to flie
farre from base earth but not to mount too hie,
    for true pleasure
    liues in measure
    which if men forsake,   5
blinded they into follie runne, and griefe for pleasure take.

2

But my vaine hopes proude of their new taught flight,
Enamour'd sought to woo the Sunnes fayre light,
    whose rich brightnesse   10
    mooued their lightnesse
    to aspire so hye,
That all scorch't and consum'd with fire, now drowned in woe
               they lye.

3

And none but loue their wofull hap did rue,   15
For loue did know that their desires were true,
    though fate frowned,
    and now drowned,
    they in sorrow dwell,
It was the purest light of heauen, for whose fayre loue they fell.   20

II.

My loue bound me with a kisse
that I should no longer stay,
when I felt so sweete a blisse,
I had lesse power to part away,
alas that women doth not know   5
kisses makes men loath to goe.

2

Yes she knowes it but too well,
For I heard when Venus doue
In her eare did softlie tell,   10
That kisses were the seales of loue,
Oh muse not then though it be so,
Kisses makes men loth to goe.

3

Wherefore did she thus inflame   15
My desires, heat my bloud,
Instantlie to quench the same,
And starue whome she had giuen food.
I I, the common sence can show,
Kisses make men loath to go.   20

4

Had she bid me go at first
It would nere haue greeued my hart,
Hope delaide had beene the worst,
But ah to kisse and then to part,   25
How deepe it strucke, speake Gods you know
Kisses make men loth to goe.
             [Thomas Campion?]

III.

O how my thoughts do beate mee,
which by deepe sighs intreat thee,
hey ho, fie fie, what a thing is this
thus to lie still when we might kisse
    and play and foole   5
    heere in the coole
of the stillest cleerest sweetest euening,
Philomell did euer choose for singing.

2

See how my lips complaine them,   10
Thy lips should thus detaine them,
Aye me harke how the Nightingales,
In the darke each to other cals,
    Whil'st thou, O thou,
    Dar'st not avow,   15
The enioying of the truest pleasure,
Loue did euer hoord vp in his treasure.

IIII.

DReames and Imaginations
are all the recreations
  absence can gaine me:
dreames when I wake confound me,
thoghts for her sake doth wound me   5
  least she disdaine me,
then sinking let me lie,
or thinking let me die,
  since loue hath slaine me.

2   10

Dreames are but coward and doe,
Much good they dare not stand too,
  Asham'd of the morrow,
Thoughts like a child that winketh,
Hee's not beguild that thinketh,   15
  Hath peir'st me thorow,

Both filling me with blisses,
Both killing me with kisses,
  dying in sorrow.

               3   20

Dreames with their false pretences,
And thoughts confounds my senses,
  In the conclusion,
Which like a glasse did shew mee,
What came to passe and threw mee,   25
  Into confusion,
Shee made mee leaue all other,
Yet had she got another,
This was abusion.

                     V.

MY thought this other night
I sawe a pretie sight
  that pleasd me much,
A faire and comly maid
not squemish nor afraid   5
  to let me tuch,
Our lips most sweetly kissing
each other neuer missing,
her smiling lookes did shew content
and that shee did but what she meant.   10

               2

And as her lips did moue,
The eccho still was loue,
  loue loue me sweete,
Then with a maiden blush,   15
Instead of crying pish
  Our lips did meete,
With Musicke sweetely sounding,
With pleasures all abounding,
We kept the burden of the song,   20
Which was that loue should take no wrong.

3

And yet as maidens vse,
She seemed to refuse,
  The name of loue,   25
Vntill I did protest,
That I did loue her best,
  And so will proue.
With that as both amazed,
Each at the other gazed,   30
My eyes did see, my hands did feele,
Her eyes of fire, her brest of steele.

4

Oh when I felt her brest,
Where loue it selfe did rest,   35
  My loue was such,
I could haue beene content,
My best bloud to haue spent,
  In that sweete tutch.
But now comes that which vext vs,   40
There was a bar betwixt vs,
A bar that bard me from that part,
Where nature did contend with art.

5

If euer loue had power,   45
To send one happie houre,
  Then shew thy might,
And take such bars away,
Which are the onely stay
  Of loues delight.   50
All this was but a dreaming,
Although another meaning,
Dreames may proue true, as thoughts are free,
I will loue you, you may loue mee.

VI.

Who so is tide must needs be bound,
and he thats bound cannot bee free,

who so is lost is hardly found
& he thats blind is bard to see,
  who so is watcht with iealous eies   5
  must sit vp late, and early rise.

2

He may well write that cannot come,
And send his eyes to plead his case,
He may well looke that must be dum,   10
Vntill he find both time and place,
  He that is tyde to houres and times,
  Though not himselfe may send his rimes.

3

What hap haue they who doth abound,   15
With all things that the earth doth beare,
And yet for want some time doth sound,
Breathing a life twixt hope and feare,
  Alas poore soule my case is such,
  I want my will, yet haue too much.   20

4

I would, but dare not what I would,
I dare, but cannot what I dare,
I can, but must not if I could,
I can, I must, I will not spare,   25
  I write no more, but shall I come,
  I saie no more, but closely mume.

VII.

Fie fie fie what a coile is heere,
why striue you so to get a kisse,
doe doe doe what you will,
you shall be nere the neere,
had I been willing   5
so to be billing
you had preuailed long ere this,
sweete stand away let me alone,
or els in faith Ile get me gone.

2   10

Come come come doe you not perceiue,
I am not yet dispos'd to yeeld,
Staie staie staie but a while,
My loue will giue you leaue,
This my denyall,   15
Is but a tryall,
If faint desire will flie the field,
Whoop looke you now, I pray be still,
Naie then in faith doe what you will.

VIII.

Beautie stand further,
repine not at my blaming,
  Is it not murther,
to set my hart on flaming,
  Thus hopelesse to take   5
bare sight of such a glorie
  doth tempt me to make
my death beget a storie,
Then pitie me, least some worst thing ensue it,
My deaths true cause, will force thy gilt to rue it.   10

2

  Is it not better,
To loue thy friend in good sort,
  Then to be debter,
For kindnesse name to report,   15
  If you had the lesse,
For this rich mercie lending,
  Then should I confesse,
No thrift were in such spending.
Oh pittie me, the gaine shall be thine owne all,   20
I would but liue, to make thy vertues knowne all.

IX.

Now what is loue I pray thee tell,
it is that fountaine and that well
where pleasures and repentance dwell,

it is perhaps that sancesing bell
that towles all in to heau'n or hell,   5
and this is loue as I heare tell.

2

Now what is loue I praie thee saie,
It is a worke on holy daie,
It is December match't with Maie,   10
When lustie blood in fresh arraie,
Heare ten monethes after of their plaie,
And this is loue as I heare saie.

3

Now what is loue I praie thee faine,   15
It is a Sunne-shine mixt with raine,
It is a gentle pleasing paine,
A flower that dyes and springs againe,
It is a noe that would full faine,
And this is loue as I heare saine.   20

4

Yet what is loue I praie thee saie,
It is a pretie shadie waie,
As well found out by night as daie,
It is a thing will soone decaie,   25
Then take the vantage whilst you maie,
And this is loue as I heare saie.

5

Now what is loue I praie thee show,
A thing that creepes it cannot goe,   30
A prize that passeth to and fro,
A thing for one a thing for moe,
And he that proues shall find it so,
And this is loue as I well know.

X.

Loues god is a boy
none but cowards regard him,
his dart is a toy
great opinion hath mard him,

        the feare of the wagg   5
        hath made him so bragg,
        chide him, heele flie thee
        and not come nie thee,
little boy, prety knaue shoote not at randome,
for if you hit mee, slaue Ile tell your grandome.   10

                        2

        Fond loue is a child,
        And his compasse is narrow,
        Yoong fooles are beguild
        With the fame of his arrow,   15
        He dareth not strike,
        If his stroke do mislike,
        Cupid doe you heare mee?
        Come not too neere mee,
Little boy, pretie knaue, hence I beseech you,   20
For if you hit me slaue, in faith Ile breech you.

                        3

        Th'ape loues to meddle,
        When he finds a man idle,
        Else is he a flurting,   25
        Where his marke is a courting,
        When women grow true,
        Come teach mee to sue,
        Then Ile come to thee,
        Pray thee, and woo thee,   30
Little boy, pretie knaue, make me not stagger,
For if you hit me slaue, Ile call thee begger.

                        XI.

Over these brookes trusting to ease mine eies,
mine eies euen great in labour with her teares,
I laid my face, my face wherein there lies
clusters of clowdes, which no sunne euer cleeres,
in watry glasse, my watry eies I see   5
sorrowes ill eased, where sorrowes painted be.

2

My thoughts imprisoned in my secret woes,
With flamie breathes, doe issue oft in sound,
The sound to this strange aire no sooner goes,   10
But that it doth with Ecchoes force rebound,
And make me heare the plaints I would refraine,
Thus outward helpes my inward griefes maintaine.

3

Now in this sand I would discharge my mind,   15
And cast from me part of my burdnous cares,
But in the sand my tales foretold I find,
And see therein how well the waters fares,
Since streames, ayre, sand, mine eyes and eares conspire,
What hope to quench, where each thing blowes the fire.   20
                    [Sir Philip Sidney]

XII.

Whither runneth my sweet hart,
        stay a while pree thee,
        not too fast,
        too much haste
        maketh waste,   5
but if thou wilt needes be gone,
        take my loue with thee,
thy minde doth binde me to no vile condition,
so doth thy truth preuent me of suspition.

2   10

Go thy wayes then where thou please,
        So I by thee
        Daie and night
        I delight
        In thy sight,   15
Neuer griefe on me did seaze
        When thou wast nie mee.
My strength at length, that scorn'd thy faire commandings
Hath not forgot the prise of rash withstandings.

3

20

Now my thoughts are free from strife,
    Sweete let me kisse thee,
    Now can I
    Willingly
    Wish to die,

25

For I doe but loath my life,
    When I doe misse thee,
Come proue my loue, my hart is not disguised,
Loue showne and knowne ought not to be despised.

XIII.

Once did I loue where now I haue no liking,
  like can I not for shee was neuer louing.
Once did I proue, but then put by my striking,
  strike nill I now though shee were euer prouing,
       to proue or strike it now rests at my will,

5

       to make me loue or like tis past her skill.

2

Rest in vnrest, was once my chiefest pleasure,
  Please will I now my selfe in her disquiet,
Bad for the best I chose at wanton leasure,

10

  Ease bids me now to brooke a better dyet,
      Rich in content I rest to see her plaining,
      Whose best at best is bad, not worth the gaining.

XIIII.

Faire women like faire iewels are,
whose worth lies in opinion,
to praise them al must be his care
that goes about to win one,
& when he hath her once obtain'd,

5

to her face he must her flatter,
but not to others least he moue
their eies to leuell at her.

2

The way to purchase truth in loue,   10
If such way there be anie,
Must be to giue her leaue to roue,
And hinder one by manie,
Beleeue thou must that she is fayre,
When poysoned tongues doe sting her,   15
Rich Iewels beare the selfe same hew,
Put vpon anie finger.

3

The perfectest of mind and shape,
Must looke for defamations.   20
Liue how they will they cannot scape,
Their persons are temptations,
Then let the world condemne my choyse,
As laughing at my follie,
If she be kind the selfe same voyce,   25
Is spred of the most hollie.

XV.

DAinty darling kinde and free
fairest maide I euer see,
deare vouchsafe to looke on mee,
listen when I sing to thee,
     what I will doe   5
     with a dildoe,
     sing doe with a dildoe.

2

Sweete now goe not yet I praie,
Let no doubt thy minde dismaie,   10
Here with mee thou shalt but staie,
Onelie till I can displaie,
     What I will doe
     With a dildo,
     Sing doe with a dildo.   15

3

Quicklie prithee now be still,
Naie you shall not haue your will,
Trow you men will maidens kill,
Tarrie but to learne the skill,   20
        What I will doe
        With a dildo,
        Sing doe with a dildo.

4

Prettie, wittie, sit mee by,   25
Feare no cast of anie eye,
Wee will plaie so priuilie,
None shall see but you and I,
        What I will doe
        With a dildo,   30
        Sing doe with a dildo.

XVI.

My loue is neither yoong nor olde,
not fiery hot nor frozen colde,
but fresh and faire as springing brier,
blooming the fruit of loues desire,
not snowy white nor rosie red,   5
but faire enough for sheepheards bed,
and such a loue was neuer seene,
on hill or dale or countrey greene.

XVII.

Loue is a bable,
  no man is able
to say tis this or tis that,
  tis full of passions
  of sundry fashions,   5
tis like I cannot tell what.

2

Loues fayre i'th Cradle,
  Foule in the sadle,
Tis eyther too cold or too hot,   10
  An arrand lyar,
  Fed by desire,
It is, and yet it is not.

3

Loue is a fellowe,   15
  clad oft in yellowe,
The canker-worme of the mind,
  A priuie mischiefe,
  And such a slye thiefe,
No man knowes which waie to find.   20

4

Loue is a woonder,
  That's here and yonder,
As common to one as to moe,
  A monstrous cheater,   25
  Euerie mans debter,
Hang him, and so let him goe.

XVIII.

ARise my thoughts & mount you with the sunne,
call all the windes, to make you speedy winges,
and to my fayrest Maya see you runne
and weepe your last, while wantonly shee singes,
  then if you cannot moue her hart to pittie,   5
  let oh alas ayh me be all your dittie.

2

Arise my thoughts no more if you returne,
Denyed of grace, which onely you desire,
But let the Sunne your winges to ashes burne,   10
And melte your passions in his quenchles fire,
  Yet if you moue faire Mayes heart to pittie,
  Let smiles, and loue, and kisses, be your dittie.

3

Arise my thoughts beyond the highest star,   15
And gently rest you in faire Mayes eye,
For that is fairer then the brightest ar,
But if she frowne to see you climbe so hye,
  Couch in her lap, and with a mouing dittie,
  Of smiles, and loue, and kisses, beg for pittie.   20

XIX.

Dɪd euer man thus loue as I,
        I thinke I was made
        for no other trade,
my minde doth it so hard apply,
and all fond courses else doth flie.   5

2

Vndooing were a pettie care,
        Loosing my best hopes,
        In their largest scopes,
Two louing when I doe compare,   10
Me thinks I could as trifles spare.

3

All my sad thoughts, though wide begunne,
        In her still doe meete,
        Who makes thinking sweete,   15
And then to me againe they runne,
To tell me all that they haue doone.

4

Thus doe I spend my dayes and houres,
        In a pleasant round,
        Where true ioyes are found,   20
And there alone my soule deuours,
All loues deare foode with longing powers.

5

A heau'n on earth is loue well met,   25
    There is more content,
    Then can well be spent,
When in two fruitfull hearts 'tis set,
Which will not bee in eithers debt.

XX.

To sigh and to bee sad,
to weepe and wish to die,
is it not to be madd
if not hypocrisie,
    men of this sort   5
    are womens sport,
beauties alluring lookes rob wise men of their reason,
that they speake nought at all, or speake all out of season.

2

Haue all men eyes to see?   10
And haue none wit to know?
Blossomes commend no tree,
Where neuer fruit did growe,
    Disire doth blind
    A louers mind.   15
He sees and doth allow that vice in his beloued,
From which no woman can be free or be remoued.

3

Let euerie thought of loue,
Mixt with a world of feares,   20
At last themselues remoue,
Oh let consuming teares,
    Life blood distil'd
    No more be spil'd,
Since all that scape the fall of womanish reiecting,   25
Must yet be subiect to the pride of their neglecting.

XXI.

Come sorrow, come sweet scayle,
by the which we ascend to the heauenlie place
where vertue sitteth smyling,
to see how some looke pale
with feare to beholde thy ill fauoured face,   5
vaine shewes their sence beguiling,
for mirth hath no assurance
nor warrantie of durance.

Hence pleasures, flie, sweete baite,
On the which they may iustly be said to be fooles,   10
That surfet by much tasting;
Like theeues you lie in waite,
Most subtillie how to prepare sillie soules,
For sorrowes euerlasting.
Wise griefes haue ioyfull turnings,   15
Nice pleasures ende in mournings.

FINIS.

John Dowland

The Third and Last Booke of Songs or Aires

1603

[Within a compartment: McK. & F. No. 99] THE/ THIRD AND/ LAST BOOKE/ OF SONGS OR/ AIRES./ Newly compofed to fing to the/ *Lute, Orpharion, or viols, and a dia-*/ logue for a bafe and meane/ Lute with fiue voices to/ fing thereto./ *By* IOHN DOWLAND, *Bacheler* [B's swash]/ *in Muficke, and Lutenift to the moft*/ *high and mightie* CHRISTIAN/ *the fourth by the grace of God*/ *king of Denmark* [D swash] *and*/ *Norwey, &c.*/ [In lower slot:] *Bona* [B swash] *quò communiora eò meliora.*/ [rule]/ Printed at London by P. S. for Thomas Adams,/ *and are to be fold at the figne of the white Lion in*/ Paules Churchyard, by the affignement of a Pa-/ tent granted to T. Morley. 1603./

Collation: 2°; A–M² (A1, B2 not signed); 24 leaves.

Headlines: Verso, B1v–N2v: I. [–XX.] CANTVS. [No period after CANTVS on D1v; M1v has: CANTVS PRIMA XXI Dialogue/ Dialogue. QVINTVS.] Recto, B2–D1: BASSVS. D2–M1: TENOR./ BASVS. [E1–F1, G1–M1: BASSVS.]/ ALTVS. [M2 has: Dialogue. SECVNDA PARS./ Dialogue. BASSVS./ Dialogue. TENOR.]

Contents: A1, title page; A1v, arms of John Souch; A2, dedication; A2v, epistle; B1, table of songs; B1v–M2, songs I–XXI, one per opening; M2v blank.

SR: Entered by Thomas Adams on February 21, 1602/3 (Arber, III, 228).

STC: 7096.

Copies: Folger (the text copy); Huntington (34002); BM (K.2.i.5 [3]); RCM (I.G. 21); Lincoln Cathedral Library (Aa.2.17; lacks A1; not seen); Manchester Public Library (BR f410 407; seen but not fully collated); Fürst Alexander zu Dohna-Schlobitten, Lörrach-Baden, Germany; and Mr. H. L. Bradfer-Lawrence, Ripon, Yorkshire (not seen). The title page only of one copy is in the BM Harleian collection, 5936 (309).

The music for songs I–IIII consists of a Cantus with tablature facing a Bassus without words. Songs V–XX have the usual Cantus and tablature facing parts for Altus, Tenor, and Bassus. No. XXI is a dialogue, with Cantus and lute plus a Quintus (with words for the chorus only) facing a Secunda Pars with bass lute and a Bassus and Tenor (with words for the chorus only).

TO MY HONORABLE GOOD FRIEND

Iohn Souch Esquire, for many curtesies for which I imbol-
den my selfe, presuming of his good fauour, to present this
simple worke, as a token of my thankefulnes.

THE estimation and kindnes which I haue euer bountifully receiued from your fauour, haue mooued me to present this nouelty of musick to you, who of al others are fittest to iudge of it, and worthiest out of your loue to protect it. If I gaue life to these, you gaue spirit to me; for it is alwaies the worthy respect of others that makes arte prosper in it selfe. That I may therefore professe, and make manifest to the world both your singular affection to me, and my gratefull minde in my weake ability to you, I haue here prefixt your honourable name, as a bulwark of safetie, and a title of grace, thinking my selfe no way able to deserue your fauours more, then by farther engaging my selfe to you for this your noble presumed patronage. He that hath acknowledged a fauour, they say, hath halfe repaide it: and if such payment may passe for currant, I shal be euer readie to grow the one halfe out of your debt, though how that should be I knowe not, since I owe my selfe (and more, if it were possible) vnto you. Accept me wholy then I beseech you, in what tearmes you please, being euer in my vttermost seruice

Deuoted to your Honours kindnesse,
IOHN DOWLAND.

The Epistle to the Reader.

THE *applause of them that iudge, is the incouragement of those that write: My first two bookes of aires speed so well that they haue produced a third, which they haue fetcht far from home, and brought euen through the most perilous seas, where hauing escapt so many sharpe rocks, I hope they shall not be wrackt on land by curious and biting censures. As in a hiue of bees al labour alike to lay vp honny opposing them selues against none but fruitles drones;*

so in the house of learning and fame, all good indeuourers should striue to ad
somewhat that is good, not malicing one an other, but altogether bandying
against the idle and malicious ignorant. My labours for my part I freely offer   10
to euerie mans iudgement, presuming, that fauour once attayned, is more
easily encreased then lost.

IOHN DOWLAND.

A Table of all the songs contained in
this Booke.

I.

FArewell too faire, too chast but too too cruell,
discretion neuer quenched fire with swords:
Why hast thou made my heart thine angers fuell,
and now would kill my passions with thy words.
This is prowd beauties true anatamy,   5
if that secure seuere in secresie,
farewell, farewell.

Farewell too deare, and too too much desired,
Vnlesse compassion dwelt more neere thy heart:
Loue by neglect (though constant) oft is tired,   10
And forc't from blisse vnwillingly to part.
This is prowd beauties, &c.

II.

Time stands still with gazing on her face,
stand still and gaze for minutes, houres and yeares,
                        to her giue place:
All other things shall change, but shee remaines the same,
till heauens changed haue their course & time hath lost his name.
Cupid doth houer vp and downe blinded with her faire eyes,   5
and fortune captiue at her feete contem'd and conquerd lies.

When fortune, loue, and time attend on
Her with my fortunes, loue and time, I honour will alone,
If bloudlesse enuie say, dutie hath no desert.
Dutie replies that enuie knowes her selfe his faithfull heart,   10
My setled vowes and spotlesse faith no fortune can remoue,
Courage shall shew my inward faith, and faith shall trie my loue.

III.

Behold a wonder here
Loue hath receiu'd his sight
which manie hundred yeares,
hath not beheld the light.

2 Such beames infused be   5
By *Cinthia* in his eyes,
As first haue made him see,
And then haue made him wise.

3 Loue now no more will weepe
For them that laugh the while,   10
Nor wake for them that sleepe,
Nor sigh for them that smile.

4 So powrefull is the beautie
That Loue doth now behold,
As loue is turn'd to dutie,   15
That's neither blind nor bold.

5 This Beautie shewes her might,
To be of double kind,
In guing loue his sight
And striking folly blind.   20

[Robert Devereux, Earl of Essex ?]

IIII.

DAphne was not so chaste as she was changing,
Soon begun Loue with hate estranging:
  he that to day triumphs with fauors graced,
  fals before night with scornes defaced:
Yet is thy beautie fainde, and eu'rie one desires,   5
still the false light of thy traiterous fires.

Beautie can want no grace by true loue viewed,
Fancie by lookes is still renued:
  Like to a fruitfull tree it euer groweth,
  Or the fresh-spring that endlesse floweth.   10
But if that beautie were of one consent with loue,
Loue should liue free, and true pleasure proue.

V.

ME me and none but me,
  dart home O gentle death
and quicklie, for
  I draw too long this idle breath:
O howe I long till I   5
  may fly to heauen aboue,
vnto my faithfull and
  beloued turtle doue.

Like to the siluer Swanne,
  before my death I sing: 10
And yet aliue
  my fatall knell I helpe to ring.
Still I desire from earth
  and earthly ioyes to flie,
He neuer happie liu'd,   15
  that cannot loue to die.

VI.

WHen *Phoebus* first did *Daphne* loue,
and no meanes might her fauour moue,
he crau'd the cause, the cause quoth she
is, I haue vow'd virginitie.
Then in a rage he sware, and said,   5
past fifteene none none but one should liue a maid.

If maidens then shal chance be sped
Ere they can scarsly dresse their head,
Yet pardon them, for they be loth
To make good *Phoebus* breake his oth.   10
And better twere a child were borne,
Then that a god should be forsworne.

VII.

SAy loue if euer thou didst find,
a woman with a constant mind,
                none but one,
and what should that rare mirror be,
some Goddesse or some Queen is she   5
shee shee shee and onelie she
she onely Queene of loue and beautie.

But could thy firy poysned dart
At no time touch her spotlesse hart,
                Nor come neare,   10
She is not subiect to Loues bow,
Her eye commaunds, her heart saith no,
No, no, no, and only no,
One no another still doth follow.

How might I that faire wonder know,   15
That mockes desire with endlesse no
                See the Moone
That euer in one change doth grow,
Yet still the same, and she is so;
So, so, so, and onely so,   20
From heauen her vertues she doth borrow.

To her then yeeld thy shafts and bowe,
That can command affections so:
Loue is free,
So are her thoughts that vanquish thee,   25
There is no queene of loue but she,
She, she, she, and only she,
She onely queene of loue and beautie.

VIII.

FLOW not so fast yee fountaines,
what needeth all this haste,
Swell not aboue your mountaines,
nor spend your time in waste,
  Gentle springs, freshly your salt teares   5
   must still fall dropping from their spheares.

Weepe they apace whom Reason,
Or lingring time can ease:
My sorow can no season,
Nor ought besides appease   10
  Gentle springs, &c.

Time can abate the terrour
Of euerie common paine,
But common griefe is errour,
True griefe will still remaine.   15
  Gentle springs, &c.

IX.

WHat if I neuer speede,
  shall I straight yeeld to dispaire,
and still on sorow feede
  that can no losse repaire.
or shal I change my loue,   5
  for I find power to depart,
and in my reason proue
  I can command my hart.
But if she will pittie my desire,
  and my loue requite,   10
then euer shall shee liue my deare delight.

Come, come, come,
while I haue a heart to desire thee.
  Come, come, come,
for either I will loue or admire thee.   15

Oft haue I dream'd of ioy,
  yet I neuer felt the sweete,
But tired with annoy,
  my griefs each other greete.
Oft haue I left my hope,   20
  as a wretch by fate forlorne.
But Loue aimes at one scope,
  and lost wil stil returne:
He that once loues with a true desire
  neuer can depart,   25
For *Cupid* is the king of euery hart.
  Come, come, &c.

X.

Loue stood amaz'd at sweet beauties paine:
Loue would haue said that all was but vaine,
                  and Gods but halfe diuine,
But when Loue saw that beautie would die:
hee all agast, to heau'ns did crie,   5
                  O gods what wrong is mine.

2 Then his teares bred in thoughts of salt brine,
Fel from his eyes, like raine in sun shine
                  expeld by rage of fire:
Yet in such wise as anguish affords,   10
He did expresse in these his last words
                  his infinite desire.

3 Are you fled faire? where are now those eies
Eyes but too faire, enui'd by the skies,
                  you angrie gods do know,   15
With guiltles bloud your scepters you stain,
On poore true hearts like tyrants you raine:
                  vniust why do you so?

4 Are you false gods? why then do you raine?
Are you iust gods? why then haue you slaine   20
        the life of loue on earth.
Beautie, now thy face liues in the skies,
Beautie, now let me liue in thine eyes,
        where blisse felt neuer death.

5 Then from high rock, the rocke of dispaire,   25
He fals, in hope to smother in the aire,
        or els on stones to burst,
Or on cold waues to spend his last breath,
Or his strange life to end by strange death,
        but fate forbid the worst.   30

6 With pity mou'd the gods then change loue
To Phenix shape, yet cannot remoue
        his wonted propertie,
He loues the sunne because it is faire,
Sleepe he neglects, he liues but by aire,   35
        and would, but cannot die.

XI.

LEnd your eares to my sorrow
good people that haue any pitie:
  for no eyes wil I borow
mine own shal grace my doleful ditty:
  Chant then my voice though rude like to my riming,   5
and tell foorth my griefe which here in sad despaire
  can find no ease of tormenting.

Once I liu'd, once I knew delight,
No griefe did shadowe then my pleasure:
  Grac'd with loue, cheer'd with beauties sight,   10
I ioyed alone true heau'nly treasure,
  O what a heau'n is loue firmely embraced,
Such power alone can fixe delight
  In Fortunes bosome euer placed.

Cold as Ice frozen is that hart,   15
Where thought of loue could no time enter:
  Such of life reape the poorest part
Whose weight cleaues to this earthly center,

Mutuall ioies in hearts truly vnited
Doe earth to heauenly state conuert   20
  Like heau'n still in it selfe delighted.

XII.

By a fountaine where I lay,
al blessed bee that blessed day
by the glimring of the sun,
ô neuer bee her shining done
  when I might see alone   5
  my true loues fairest one,
        loues deer light,
        loues cleare sight
No worlds eyes can clearer see
a fairer sight none none can be.   10

2 Faire with garlands all addrest,
Was neuer Nymph more fairely blest,
Blessed in the highest degree,
So may she euer blessed be,
  Came to this fountaine neere,   15
  With such a smiling cheere,
        Such a face,
        Such a grace,
Happie, happie eyes that see
Such a heauenly sight as she.   20

3 Then I forthwith tooke my pipe
Which I all faire and cleane did wipe,
And vpon a heau'nly ground,
All in the grace of beautie found,
  Plaid this roundelay,   25
  Welcome faire Queene of May,
        Sing sweete aire,
        Welcome faire.
Welcome be the shepheards Queene,
The glorie of all our greene.   30

XIII.

Oʜ what hath ouerwrought
my all amazed thought
or whereto am I brought,
that thus in vaine haue sought,
Till time and truth hath taught,   5
I labor all for nought.
The day I see is cleare,
but I am nere the neere,
For griefe doth stil appeare,
to crosse our merie cheere,   10
while I can nothing heare,
but winter all the yeare.
Cold, hold, the sun wil shine warme,
therefore now feare no harme.
O blessed beames,   15
where beautie streames
happie happie light to loues dreames.

XIIII.

Fᴀrewell vnkind farewell,
  to mee no more a father,
since my heart my heart
  holdes my loue most deare:
The wealth which thou doest reape,   5
  anothers hand must gather,
Though thy heart thy heart
  still lies buried there,
Then farewell, then farewell, O farewell,
welcome my loue, welcome my ioy for euer.   10

Tis not the vaine desire
  of humane fleeting beautie,
Makes my mind to liue,
  though my meanes do die.
Nor do I Nature wrong,   15
  though I forget my dutie:
Loue, not in the bloud,
  but in the spirit doth lie.
Then farewell, &c.

XV.

WEepe you no more sad fountaines,
  what need you flowe so fast,
looke how the snowie mountaines,
  heau'ns sunne doth gently waste.
But my sunnes heau'nly eyes   5
  view not your weeping,
    That nowe lies sleeping
softly now softly lies sleeping.

Sleepe is a reconciling,
  A rest that peace begets: 10
Doth not the sunne rise smiling,
  When faire at eu'n he sets,
Rest you, then rest sad eyes,
  Melt not in weeping,
    While she lies sleeping   15
Softly now softly lies sleeping.

XVI.

Fie on this faining,
is loue without desire,
heat still remaining
& yet no sparke of fire?
Thou art vntrue, nor wert with fancie moued,   5
for desire hath powre on all that euer loued.

2 Shew some relenting,
Or graunt thou doest now loue,
Two hearts consenting
Shall they no comforts proue?   10
Yeeld, or confesse that loue is without pleasure,
And that womens bounties rob men of their treasure,

3 Truth is not placed
In words and forced smiles,
Loue is not graced   15
With that which still beguiles,
Loue or dislike, yeeld fire, or giue no fuell,
So maist thou proue kind, or at the least lesse cruell.

XVII.

I must complaine, yet do enioy my loue,
she is too faire, too rich in beauties parts:
Thence is my griefe for nature while she stroue
with all her graces and deuinest artes,
To forme her too too beautifull of hue,   5
she had no leisure left to make her true.

Should I agrieu'd then wish she were lesse faire,
That were repugnant to my owne desires,
She is admir'd, new suters still repaire,
That kindles dayly loues forgetfull fires,   10
Rest iealous thoughts, and thus resolue at last,
She hath more beautie then becomes the chast.
                              [Thomas Campion]

XVIII.

It was a time when silly Bees could speake,
and in that time I was a sillie Bee,
who fed on Time vntil my heart gan break,
yet neuer found the time would fauour mee.
Of all the swarme I onely did not thriue,   5
yet brought I waxe & honey to the hiue.

2 Then thus I buzd, when time no sap would giue,
Why should this blessed time to me be drie,
Sith by this Time the lazie drone doth liue,
The waspe, the worme, the gnat, the butterflie,   10
Mated with griefe, I kneeled on my knees,
And thus complaind vnto the king of Bees.

3 My liege, Gods graunt thy time may neuer end,
And yet vouchsafe to heare my plaint of Time,
Which fruitlesse Flies haue found to haue a friend,   15
And I cast downe when Atomies do clime.
The king replied but thus, Peace peeuish Bee,
Th'art bound to serue the time, the time not thee.
                    [Robert Devereux, Earl of Essex]

XIX.

Th e lowest trees haue tops, the Ant her gall,
the flie her spleene, the little sparke his heate,
and slender haires cast shadowes though but small,
and Bees haue stings although they be not great.
Seas haue their source, and so haue shallowe springs,   5
and loue is loue in beggers and in kings.

Where waters smoothest run, deep are the foords,
The diall stirres, yet none perceiues it moue:
The firmest faith is in the fewest words,
The Turtles cannot sing, and yet they loue,   10
True hearts haue eyes and eares, no tongues to speake:
They heare, and see, and sigh, and then they breake.

[Sir Edward Dyer?]

XX.

Wh at poore Astronomers are they,
take womens eies for stars
and set their thoughts in battell ray
to fight such idle warres,
when in the end they shal approue,   5
Tis but a iest drawne out of loue.

2 And loue it selfe is but a ieast,
Deuisde by idle heads,
To catch yong fancies in the neast,
And lay it in fooles beds.   10
That being hatcht in beauties eyes,
They may be flidge ere they be wise.

3 But yet it is a sport to see
How wit will run on wheeles,
While wit cannot perswaded be   15
With that which reason feeles:
That womens eyes and starres are odde,
And loue is but a fained god.

4 But such as will run mad with will,
I cannot cleare their sight: 20
But leaue them to their studie still,
To looke where is no light.
Till time too late we make them trie,
They study false Astronomie.

XXI   Dialogue

CANTVS PRIMA
    Come when I cal, or tarie til I come,
    if you bee deafe I must proue dumb.
SECVNDA PARS.   5
    Stay a while my heau'nly ioy,
    I come with wings of loue,
    when enuious eyes time shal remoue.
[1] If thy desire euer knew
    the griefe of delay,   10
    no danger could stand in thy way.
[2] O die not, ad this sorrow to my griefe
    that languish here, wanting relief.
[1] What need wee languish?
    can loue quickly quickly flie: 15
    feare euer hurts more then iealousie.
[Chorus:]
    Then securely enuie scorning,
    let vs end with ioy our mourning,
    iealousie still defie,   20
    and loue till we die.

Thomas Greaves

Songes of sundrie kindes

1604

[Within a compartment: McK. & F. No. 232] SONGES/ of ſundrie kindes:/ FIRST,/ AIRES TO BE SVNG TO/ the Lute, and Baſe Violl./ NEXT, [*T* swash]/ Songes of ſadneſſe, for the Viols/ *and Voyce.*/ LASTLY,/ *Madrigalles, for fiue voyces.*/ Newly Compoſed and publiſhed, by/ THOMAS GREAVES, *Luteniſt to Sir*/ Henrie Pierrepont,/ *Knight.*/ [device: McK. No. 282]/ LONDON/ Imprinted by *Iohn Windet* dwelling at Powles wharfe,/ *at the Signe of the Croſſe Keyes, and are there*/ *to be ſolde.* 1604./

Note: This is Windet's first use of the title page compartment, which was first used by Adam Islip in 1602 and subsequently used for Hu1605, Bt1606, Cop1606, Fd1607, and Hu1607 (see McK. & F.).

Collation: 2°; A–K²L¹ (A1, D2 not signed); 21 leaves.

Headlines: B1v–D1v, verso and recto; D2v–K2v, verso only: CANTVS [Period follows on B2–D1v; MEDIVS. D2v; MEANE. E1v, E2v; TRIPLEX. F1v, F2v; TRIPLEX, G1v; ALTVS. H1v, H2v, I2v, K2v, no period on I1v, K1v] I [–XXI. Periods after III, IIII, VI, VIII–XXI.] Thomas Greaues [Period follows on B2, B2v, C1v–G2v, I1v, K1v; Greues G1v; Greaue I2v]/ BASSVS [Period follows on B2, B2v, C1v–D1v; TRIPLEX. D2v–E2v; MEANE. F1v, F2v, G2v; MEDIVS. G1v; CANTVS. H1v–K2v] Recto, E1–K2: TENOR [Period follows on F1, G1; MEDIVS. H2, L1; MEANE. I1, K1, K2] X [–XXI Periods after XII–XV, XVII–XXI; XIX misprinted as XV.] Thomas Greaues [Period follows on F1, F2, G1, G2, H2, L1]/ BASSVS. [No period on F2; turned wrong on G1]/ CONTRATENOR [Period follows on F1, F2, G2; CANTVS. G1; TENOR H2, L1, with period on I1, K1, K2; MEANE. I2]

Contents: A1, title page; A1v blank; A2, dedication; A2v, commendatory verses; B1, table; B1v–D1v, songs I–IX, one per page; D2 blank; D2v–K1, songs X–XX, one per opening; K1v–L1, song XXI; L1v, verses of songs X and XI.

SR: Entered by John Windet on April 2, 1604; it was transferred to William Stansby on September 11, 1611 (Arber III, 259, 467).

STC: 12210.

Copy: BM (K.9.a.18, the text copy).

The music for songs I–IX consists of a Cantus with lute and viol accompaniment; X–XV, solo voice with four viols; XVI–XXI, *a capella* madrigals for five voices. All but X and XI are through-composed. The texts of I–IX, XVII–XIX, XXI are taken from the Cantus; X and XI from the metrical versions on L1; XII from the Meane; XIII–XVI from the Triplex; and XX from the Altus.

TO THE MOST WORTHY
GENTLEMAN AND BEST AF-
fected Patron of Musicke, and all Learning,
Sir HENRIE PIERREPONT
Knight.

SIR the zeale of that dutie, which long since arrested at your suite, vpon an Action of debt, hath hetherto remained close prisoner in my heart, vnder a double barre of modesty & want; I know not now by what boldnes corrupted, her Keepers haue suffered to make a wilfull escape. Yet such is the weakenes of her poore estate, and such the shame   10 to deceiue so louing a Creditor, that shee dare not aduenture to shew her face in the world, till she hath first entreated your protection. For which cause (to procure her selfe the more easie admission) knowing how the excellencie of your owne skill, hath made you generally kinde to all of that profession, she comes disguised to your presence, in the habite of Musicke, most humbly desiring your accustomed gentlenes, (not to release her of that bond, which can neuer bee cancelled) but to accept in good part, what presently she is able to pay, and giue day for the rest, till her ability be bettered: which if you grant, as she vnfainedly professeth, that what is currant in this payment, was wholy receiued   20 from you; so doe I vow on her behalfe, that if any her owne industrie, may enrich her estate; her best endeuors, shall bee deuoted to your seruice.

Your most humble deuoted seruant,
THOMAS GREAVES.

Ad Greauum suum.

Qvis furor aethereas mouit te scandere sphaeras
  mira vt prodires Musicus arte novus?
Non nouus es, tenerum lauro te cinxit Apollo:
  ortus vt in lucem, concipis vsqué modos.   5
Perge senescentem sic instaurare camaenam,
  hoc tu maior eris, quo viget illa magis.
                          I. T. Μουσόφιλος

Ad Authorem.

IF that the Shepheards God did merit prayse,
Who rurall musicke forth of reedes could raise,
Why should the feare of base detraction
Bury thy Arte in blacke obliuion?   5
The sweet resounding of whose pleasing straines,
Delightes the sences, captiuates the braines;
Wrapping the soule in contemplation,
With sweetest musickes delectation.
  Produce them therefore, let them come to light,   10
  Thy musicke is a charme against despight.
                          W. W.

IN home-bred springs thy muse hath dipt her quill,
Yet like the eare inchaunting Philomel,
In Countrey groues obscurde, displaies her skill,
With various tunes, her feruent zeale to tell.
  Nor on the steame of terrene prayse doth dwell,   5
But sometimes mounts her cloud aspiring wing;
To pierce the walles of heauen, the gates of hell,
While she doth sweete contritions story sing.
Such are the layes that please the heauenly King.
  Should enuious mortals do thy labours wrong,   10
  Celestiall spirits will attend thy song.
                          W. A.

As once *Appelles* the craftes man controlde,
For passing his lasts limit all too bolde,
Disliking what his skill could neuer mend:
So I could wish to each man (as a friend)

That neuer got his gammut yet by hart, 5
Forbeare to censure so diuine an arte,
  Least with the Cobler he be set to learne
  To speake of nought, but what he doth discerne.
But you sence-rauishers of mortall men,
That ioies all louers, comforts in distresse, 10
With fauour looke vpon all faults, and then
What is amisse, I pray in loue redresse:
For should he bide the storme of enuies blast,
These same vntimely fruites might proue the last,
  And he neglect his after comming time, 15
  Because his hopes were nipt before their prime.
                              W. T.

Said *Pithagor* true, that each mans seuered soule
Must be a Pilgrime? then if ere thou dye,
Thy spirit must not drinke of *Lethes* boule,
But into a siluer plumed Swanne shall flye:
  That though thou diest, it may inshrined be 5
  In her that is th'embleme of Harmony.
                           P. B. [?]

A TABLE CONTAI-
ning all the Songes in
this Booke.

  The first are Ayres, to be sung to the Lute and Base-Violl.

The second are Songs of sadnes, for the Viols and Voice

The Third, Madrigals, for fiue voices.

I

Shaded with Oliue trees sate Celestina singing
then the warbling birdes more sweet harmony ringing,
with curious cost
that gold embost
her fingers duelie placed   5
whiles voice & hand
both at command
each other truely graced.
Thus vsing time
not loosing time   10
right well apaide
shee closd her ditty
with oh tis pretty
to liue a maide.

II

Flora sweete wanton bee not ouer coy:
Nay, then in faith if you wil needs be gon
Farewell sweet Flora, sweete fancy adue,
farewel, till Flora her fancy renue.

III.

Yᴇ bubling springs that gentle musick makes
to louers plaints with hart sore throbs immixt,
when as my deare this way her pleasure takes,
tell her with teares how firme my loue is fixt:
And Philomel report my timerous feares   5
and eccho sound my heighoes in her eares:
But if she aske if I for loue will dye,
tell her good faith, good faith, good faith not I.

IIII.

I wil not force my thoughts to yeeld to such desire
where light affection onely fewelleth the fire:
thogh Cupid's a god
I feare not his rod
Cupid may hit,   5
but I do not feare it:
Cupids arrow hurts, but doth not kill:
Cupid allures me,
but cannot procure me:
Cupid hath his might and I my will.   10

V

The first part.

I pray thee sweet Iohn away,
I cannot tell how to loue thee,
pish, phew, in faith all this will not moue me,
O mee, O mee, I dare not before our marriage day: 5
if this will not moue thee, gentle Iohn
come quickly kisse mee, and let me bee gone.

VI.

The second part.

Nᴀʏ will ye faith, this is more then needs,
this fooling, I cannot abide:
leaue of or in faith I must chide,
see now faith here are proper deedes,   5

haue done then I now bewaile my hap,
repentance followes with an after clap:
aye me my ioyes are murdered with a frowne
and sorrow puls vntimely pleasure down a down.

VII

WHat is beauty but a breath?
fancies twin at birth & death
the colour of a damaske rose,
that fadeth when the northwind blowes:
Tis such that though all sorts do craue it,   5
they know not what it is that haue it:
a thing that som time stoops not to a king
and yet most open to the commonst thing:
for she that is most fair,
is open to the aire.   10

VIII.

The first part.

STay Laura stay, doe not so soon depart
from him whom thou hast robbed of a heart,
heare my laments view but my brinish teares,
one wil moue pity the other deafe thine eares: 5
flye me not then I know thou dost but iest,
and wilt returne thy theft with interest.

IX.

The second part.

INconstant Laura makes mee death to craue:
for wanting her I must embrace my graue:
a little graue will ease my malady
and set me free from loues fell tyranny:
Intombe me then, & shew her where I lye   5
and say I dide, throgh hir inconstancy.

X.

1 When I behold my former wandring way,
And diue into the bottome of my thought,
And thinke how I haue led that soule astray,
Whose safetie with so precious bloud was bought:
  With teares I cry vnto the God of truth,   5
  Forgiue O Lord, the errours of my youth.

2 A blessed Sauiour left his heauenly throne,
To seeke my straying soule, and bring it backe:
Himselfe the way, the way, I should haue gone,
The way I left, and sought eternall wracke,   10
  Which makes me crye in depth of bitter ruth,
  Forgiue O Lord, the errours of my youth.

3 Inestimable gaine he did propose
T'allure my erring fancy to retire:
But idle fancy would haue none of those,   15
Delighting still to wallowe in the mire,
  Wherefore I crye, vnto the God of truth,
  Forgiue O Lord, the errours of my youth.

4 I saw the way, the way it selfe did cleare it,
I knew the way, the way it selfe did shew it,   20
I markt the way, but fondly did forbeare it,
I left the way, because I would not know it:
  But now I cry vnto the God of truth;
  Forgiue O Lord, the errours of my youth.

5 Iesu the onely way, most perfect true,   25
Iesu the onely truth of heauenly life,
Iesue the onely life, that doth renue
My sinne-sicke soule, halfe slaine by Sathans strife.
  With teares I beg, teach me the way of truth;
  Forgiue O Lord, the errours of my youth.   30

XI.

1 MAn first created was in single life,
To serue his God in fruitfull Paradise,
Till heauenly wisedome saw he lackt a wife

To comfort him, and giue him good aduise:
  And from mans side a rib he did remoue,   5
  And woman made, which wo to man did proue.

2 With tender flesh the hollow place did fill,
Neare to his heart, which made his heart relenting.
The stubborne rib makes woman ful of will,
Hard bone, soft flesh, she rash, but he repenting: 10
  Thus gainst poore man his owne flesh did rebell,
  And woman (wo to man) brought man to hell.

3 Yet from the flesh, which to this bone did cleaue,
A second came, from whence a branch did spring,
Not wo to man, but woing man to leaue   15
An earthly state, to serue the heauenly King.
  Though woman (wo to man) made man to fall,
  This Sauiours bloud hath made amends for all.

XII.

Who keepes in compasse his desires,
and calmes his minde with sweet content,
needes not to feare those furious fires,
whose force will all in smoke bee spent,
whiles proud ambition blowes the coales,   5
that yeeldes no warm'th to humble soules.

XIII.

The first part.

Let dread of pain for sinne in after time,
let shame to see thy selfe ensnared so:
let griefe conceiu'd for fowle accursed crime,
let hate of sinne the worker of thy woe,   5
with dread, with shame, with griefe, with hate, enforce
to deaw thy cheeks with tears of deep remorse.

XIIII.

The second part.

So hate of sin shall cause Gods loue to grow:
so griefe shall harbor hope within thy hart,

so dred shal cause the floud of ioy to flow,
so shame shall send sweete solace to thy smart,   5
so loue, so hope, so ioy, so solace sweet,
shall make thy soule in heauenly blisse to fleete.

XV.

The third part.

Woe where such hate, doth no such loue allure:
wo where such grief doth make no hope proceede:
woe, where such dread doth no such ioy procure:
wo where such shame doth no such solace breed: 5
wo wher no hate, no grief, no dread, no shame,
doth neither loue, hope, ioy, or solace frame.

XVI.

ENgland receiue the rightfull king with chearefull hart & hand,
the present Ioy, the future hope of this his loyall land,
his birth makes chalenge to his right, his vertues to our loue,
both are his due both are our debt, which nothing can remoue,
long haue he life, long haue he health, long haue hee happie
                                                        raigne,   5
his seede possesse his realmes in peace, till Christ shall come
                                                        againe.

XVII.

The first part.

Sweet Nimphes that trippe along the English lands
go meet faire Oriana beauties Queene,
vertue inuites, & chastitie commands
your golden tresses trim with garlands greene,   5
for such a sight hath not before beene seene:
then sing in honour of her and Diana:
Long liue in ioy, the faire chaste Oriana.

XVIII.

The second part.

Long haue the Shepheards sung this song before,
as prophecying what shuld com to passe:
then gentle Nimphes, henceforth lament no more,
the times are chang'd, it is not as it was,   5
·Dian shall flowre and Venus fade like grasse:
then sing in honour of her, and Diana:
Long liue in ioy the faire chaste Oriana.

XIX.

LΛdy the melting Christall of your eye,
like frozen drops vpon your cheekes did lye,
mine eye was dauncing on them with delight,
and saw loues flames within them burning bright,
which did mine eye intice   5
to play with burning ice,
but O, my hart, my hart thus sporting with desire,
my carelesse eye did set my heart on fire.

XX.

The second part.

O that a drop from such a sweet fount flying,
should flame like fire, & leaue my hart a dying,
I burn, I burn my teares can neuer drench it,
till in your eyes I bath my hart and quench it,   5
but there alas loue with his fire lyes sleeping,
and all conspire to burne my hart with weeping.

XXI.

Come away sweet loue & play thee,
least griefe & care betray thee,
fa la la,
leaue off this sad lamenting,
and take thy harts contenting,   5
the Nimphs to sporte inuite thee,
& running in and out delights thee,
fa la la.

Tobias Hume

The First Part of Ayres

1605

[Within a compartment: McK. & F. No. 232. See Gr1604] THE/ FIRST PART/ of Ayres, French, Pollifh, and others/ *together, fome in Tabliture, and fome in* [*T* swash]/ Pricke-Song: With Pauines, Galliards, and Almaines/ for the Viole De Gambo alone, and other Muficall Con-/ ceites for two Bafe Viols, exprefsing fiue partes, with plea-/ fant reportes one from the other, and for two Leero/ *Viols, and alfo for the Leero Viole with two* [*V* of *Viole* swash]/ *Treble Viols, or two with one* [*TV* swash]/ *Treble.* [*T* swash]/ Laftly for the Leero Viole to play a-/ *lone, and fome Songes to bee fung*/ to the Viole, with the Lute, or better/ *with the Viole alone.* [*V* swash]/ Alfo an Inuention for two to play vp-/ on one Viole./ Compofed by TOBIAS HVME Gentleman./ [ornament]/ LONDON/ Printed by *Iohn Windet*, dwelling at the Signe of the Croffe Keyes at Powles/ Wharfe. 1605./

Collation: 2°; B–R^2; 32 leaves.

Headlines: Running title, C1: Captaine Humes Musicall Humors. C1v–R2v: Captaine Humes [verso]/ Musicall Humors. [recto] Note: N2 and O2 are inverted, and P1 turned sideways for convenience in playing two- and three-part pieces.

Contents: B1, title page; B1v, table; B2, dedication; B2v, epistle to the reader; C1–1v, (1) The Souldiers Song; C1v, (2) The Earl of Pembrooke his Galliard; C2 (3) Tobacco; C2v–I2v, Nos. 4–49 for the lyra viol; K1–M1v, Nos. 50–88, for bass viol; M2–P2v, Nos. 89–111, for lyra viol(s); Q1, (112) Fain would I change; Q1v, (113) What greater griefe; Q2–R1, (114) Alas poore men; R1–R2, (115) Captain Humes Lamentations (two viols); R2v, (116) The olde humor (lyra viol).

SR: No entry.

STC: 13958.

Copies: BM (K.2.g.10, the text copy) and Manchester (RF 410 Hx 15).

The music for all the songs consists of a voice part and a part in tablature for the lyra viol, which can be played on the lute.

A Table containing all the Songes in this Booke.

My Mistresse hath a prettie thing. 31
She loues it well. 32
Hit it in the middle. 33
Tickell, tickell. 34
Rosamond. 35
I am falling. 36
Tickle me quickly. 37
Touch me lightly. 38
Duke Iohn of Polland his Galliard. 39
A Carelesse humor. 40
An English Frenchman. 41
A Pauin. 42
A humorous pauin. 43
A Pauin. 44
A Pauin. 45
Captaine Humes Pauin. 46
Loues farewell. 47
A Souldiers Galliard. 48
Loues Galliard. 49
Captaine Humes Galliard. 50
A Preludum. 51
A Toy. 52
Maister Crasse his Almaine. 53
A merry meeting. 54
A toy for a Gallant. 55
The second part. 56
The third part. 57
My Mistresse Maske. 58
A Caueleiroes humor. 59
The second part. 60
A French ayre. 61
Tsa ala mod du' france. 62
A French Iigge. 63
A toy. 64
Ha couragie. 65
A Souldiers Maske. 66
The new Knightes humor. 67
The Lord Beccus Almaine, 68
Captaine Humes Almaine. 69
Galliards. 70. 71. 72. 73. 74

FINIS.

TO THE MOST
NOBLE AND WORTHY LORD
WILLIAM Earle of Pembrooke, L. Herbert of
Cardyf, L. Par and Rosse of Kendall, Lord Marmion,
and S. *Quintin, Lord Warden of the Stannaries, and
Knight of the most Noble Order of
the Garter.*

SIR, Art and the loue of Art continually are leagude together, It
shall be no dishoner therefore for your height to imbrace the humblest
endeuors of those that seeke not you but your vertues: For mine own   10
side I haue beene traind vp without the verge of Complement, nor can
I phrase the zeale I beare you in swelling discourses. My Life hath beene
a Souldier, and my idlenes addicted to Musicke, of both which I here
doe offer the seruice to your best worthy selfe. The Acceptance I feare
not, since I know great heartes are as farre from contempt, as from
basenes. I rest the seruant of your vertues.

TOBIAS HVME.

To the vnderstanding Reader.

*I Doe not studie Eloquence, or professe Musicke, although I doe loue Sence,
and affect Harmony: My Profession being, as my Education hath beene, Armes,
the onely effeminate part of me, hath beene Musicke; which in mee hath beene
alwayes Generous, because neuer Mercenarie. To prayse Musicke, were to
say, the Sunne is bright. To extoll my selfe, would name my labors vaine
glorious. Onely this, my studies are far from seruile imitations, I robbe no
others inuentions, I take no Italian Note to an English dittie, or filch fragments
of Songs to stuffe out my volumes. These are mine own Phansies expressed
by my proper* Genius, *which if thou dost dislike, let me see thine,* Carpere vel   10
noli nostra, vel ede tua, *Now to vse a modest shortnes, and a briefe expression
of my selfe to all noble spirities, thus, My Title expresseth my Bookes Contents, which (if my Hopes faile me not) shall not deceiue their expectation, in
whose approuement the crowne of my labors resteth. And from henceforth, the
statefull instrument* Gambo Violl, *shall with ease yeelde full various and as*

deuicefull Musicke as the Lute. For here I protest the Trinitie of Musicke, parts, Passion and Diuision, to be as gracefully vnited in the Gambo Violl, as in the most receiued Instrument that is, which here with a Souldiers Resolution, I giue vp to the acceptance of al noble dispositions.

The friend of his friend,

TOBIAS HVME.

If you will heare the Viol de Gambo in his true Maiestie, to play parts, and singing thereto, then string him with nine stringes, your three Basses double as the Lute, which is to be plaide on with as much ease as your Violl of sixe stringes.

1

The Souldiers Song.

I Sing the praise of honor'd wars,
the glory of wel gotten skars,
the brauery of glittring shields,
of lusty harts & famous fields: 5
For that is Musicke worth the eare of Ioue,
a sight for kings, & stil the Soldiers loue:
Look, ô me thinks I see
the grace of chiualry,
the colours are displaid,   10
the captaines bright araid:
See now the battels rang'd
bullets now thick are chang'd:
Harke, harke, shootes and wounds abound,
the drums allarum sound: 15
the Captaines crye za za za, za, za
the Trumpets sound tar ra ra ra ra ra.
O this is musicke worth the eare of Ioue,
a sight for Kinges, and stil the Soldiers loue.

3

Tobacco, Tobacco
sing sweetly for Tobacco,
Tobacco is like loue,
     O loue it
for you see I wil proue it.   5

Loue maketh leane the fatte mens tumor,
so doth Tobacco,
Loue still dries vppe the wanton humor
so doth Tobacco,
loue makes men sayle from shore to shore   10
so doth Tobacco
Tis fond loue often makes men poor
so doth Tobacco,
Loue makes men scorne al Coward feares
so doth Tobacco,   15
Loue often sets men by the eares
so doth Tobacco.

Tobaccoe, Tobaccoe
Sing sweetely for Tobaccoe,
Tobaccoe is like Loue,   20
    O loue it,
For you see I haue proude it.

112

FAin would I change that note
to which fond loue hath charmd me,
long, long to sing by roate,
fancying that that harmde me,
 yet when this thought doth come   5
 Loue is the perfect summe
    of all delight.
 I haue no other choice
 either for pen or voyce,
    to sing or write: 10

O Loue they wrong thee much,
That say thy sweete is bitter.
When thy ripe fruit is such,
As nothing can be sweeter,
 Faire house of ioy and blisse,   15
 Where truest pleasure is,
    I doe adore thee:
 I know thee what thou art,
 I serue thee with my hart,
    And fall before thee.   20

113

WHat greater griefe then no reliefe in deepest woe
death is no friend that will not end such harts sorrow
helpe I do crie, no helpe is nie, but winde and ayre
which to and fro do tosse & blow all to dispayre
  sith then dispaire I must yet may not dye   5
  no man vnhapier liues on earth then I.

Tis I that feele the scornfull heele of dismall hate,
My gaine is lost, my losse deere cost repentance late
So I must mone be monde of none O bitter gal,
Death be my friend with speed to end and quiet all   10
  But if thou linger in dispaire to leaue me,
  Ile kill dispaire with hope and so deceiue thee.

114

ALas poore men, why striue you to liue long
to haue more time & space to suffer wrong, O wrong?

Our birth is blind and creeping,
our life all woe and weeping
Our death all paine and terror   5
birth, life, death; what all but error,
Alas poore men

O world nurse of desires,
Fostresse of vaine attires
What reason canst thou render   10
why man should hold thee tender.
Alas poore men

Thou pinst the pale cheekt Muses
and Souldier that refuses
no woundes for countries safetie,   15
he onely thriues thats craftie.
Alas poore men

On crutches vertue halts,
Whilest men most great in faultes
suffers best worth distrest   20
with empty pride opprest.
Alas poore men.

O vertue yet at length
rouze thy diuiner strength
& make no musicke more   25
our sadde state thats deplore
Then las poore men why [etc.]

Robert Jones

Vltimum Vale

1605

[Within a compartment: McK. & F. No. 212] *VLTIMVM VALE*, [*T* swash]/ with a triplicity of Muficke,/ WHEREOF/ *The firft part is for the Lute, the*/ Voyce, and the Viole Degambo, The/ 2. *part is for the Lute, the Viole, and foure*/ partes to fing, The third part is for/ two Trebles, to fing either to/ *the Lute, or the Viole or to*/ *both, if any pleafe.*/ Compofed by ROBERT IONES./ *Quæ profunt fingula, multa inuant.* [sic; Q swash]/ Printed at London by *Iohn Windet,* and/ are to be fold by *Simon Waterfon,* in/ *Powles Churchyeard, at the Signe* [*C* swash]/ *of the Crowne* 1605./ [wide ornament below compartment]

Note: Windet and Waterson's use of the compartment is not recorded in McK. & F. It was first used by T. Creede and W. Ponsonby for the 1593 edition of Sir Philip Sidney's *Arcadia*: and in 1611 it was used by Humphrey Lownes and Matthew Lownes.

Collation: 2°; *A–M*²; 24 leaves.

Headlines: Verso, B1v–M1v: CANTVS. [I2v–M1v: PRIMVS CANTVS.] I. [–XXI.] Robert Iones. [No period after Iones on K2v.] Recto, B2–E1: BASSVS. E2–I2: TENOR. [No period on H2, I1.]/ BASSVS./ ALTVS. K1–M2: SECVNDVS CANTVS.

Contents: A1, title page; A1v, blank; A2, dedication; A2v, epistle; B1, table; B1v–M2, songs I–XXI, one per opening; M2v, blank.

SR: No entry.

STC: 14738.

Copies: RCM (I.G.23), which lacks the title page and the upper outside corner of A2 (including part of the first three lines of the dedication). The only complete copy (the text copy) is owned by Fürst Alexander zu Dohna-Schlobitten, of Lörrach-Baden, Germany; it is bound with several copies of books by John and Robert Dowland.

See the Textual Introduction to Do1597. The absence of the title page in the RCM copy has allowed the erroneous date found in most reference books, 1608, to go uncorrected until Otto H. Mies published the date from the Schlobitten copy in *Musica Disciplina*, III (1949), 171. There are no verbal press-corrections, but inner forme L is inverted in the Schlobitten copy.

The music of songs I–VI is for voice and tablature facing a bass viol part which has only the opening words. Songs VII–XV have the usual Cantus with tablature facing parts for alto, tenor, and bass. Songs XVI–XXI have a Primus Cantus and tablature facing a reversed Secundus Cantus; all these songs except XIX have complete sets of words for both parts.

TO THE GREAT IOY AND
HOPE OF PRESENT AND FVTVRE
Times, Henrie Prince of *Wales*, Duke of *Cornwall*.
Earle of the *Countie Palatine of Chester*, Knight *of the Honourable Order of the Garter*, Heyre Apparant to the Realmes of *England*, Scotland, France and Ireland.

Most Excellent Prince, The strength of our Art, (I should say, the weakenes,)
cannot endure the force of Soueraigne Vertue come neare it, we may, as near
as to you, your Eares will yet beare to deale with soundes, though not to dwell
there, yet to passe by them, and by them to learn to tune senses in a riper age. 10
Almost all our knowledge is drawne through the senses, they are the Soules
Intelligencers, whereby she passeth into the world, and the world into her, and
amongst all of them, there is none so learned, as the eare, none hath obtained
so excellent an Art, so delicate, so abstruse, so spirituall, that it catcheth vp
wilde soundes in the Aire, and bringes them vnder a gouernement not to be
expressed, but done, and done by no skill but it owne. There is Musicke in
all thinges, but euery man cannot finde it out, because of his owne iarring, hee
must haue a harmony in himselfe, that shold goe about it, and then he is in a
good way, as he that hath a good eare, is in a good forwardnes to our facultie.
Conceite is but a well tunde fancy, done in time and place. An excellent 20
sentence, is but a well tunde reason well knit together, Politie or the subject
therof, a Common wealth, is but a well tunde Song where all partes doe agree,
and meete together, with full consent and harmony one seruing other, and euery
one themselues in the same labour. But now I intrude into your Art, in which
all pray (and see hopes) that God will giue you a godly and prosperous know-
ledge, and then all other Artes shal prosper vnder it. Our gracious Soueraign
(Your Highnes dear Father) hath warmed and comforted some great professions
already, such little ones as this, looke for it, and beg it of you, your princely

nature promiseth it, which makes my boldnes hope for pardon; Vouchsafe me (*most excellent Prince*) *your Protection; whome you allow, all others will commend, their censures wait vpon your liking, that otherwise wold despise me. Euen your name in the forefront is a charme for malitious tongus. Thus praying, that your Highnes may alwayes haue an eare able to endure and distinguish, the sound of truth, I kneele at your Highnes feet.*

Your Highnes in all humble
dutie and seruice
ROBERT
IONES

To the silent Hearer.

THE kinde Applause wherewith I haue beene rewarded in my former Ayres, by such Gentlemen aś can iudge, by the eare, & are not other mens Echoes; hath now this third time giuen me heart from them to hope for the like in these which I haue composed, euen to shew my gratitude towardes them, I know euery Father is partiall ouer the issue of his body, and hauing his iudgement corrupted by his affection, is wont to speake his Childrens prayses, according to his own desires, rather then their deserts. It may be, I haue thus ouerlooked this issue of my braine, wherefore, I will onely commend my purpose, to make this last my best, expecting to reade the truth of my selfe out of thy report. And because I am not ignorant enough, to bee grossely taxed by any of our cunning Maisters, nor bigge enough to be flattered or enuyed, I hope I shall not be driuen to enquire out my enemies, to heare of my faults, nor to bespeake my friendes fauours. For howsoeuer I am set in an vnderfortune, that hath need of friendship, yet if my workes cannot iustifie me, my wordes shall not, I had rather dye a begger, then liue a boaster: what skill, time, and my continuall practice hath giuen me, here I gladly impart to euery wel-willer, that grauntes me but acceptance for my paines, And so I commit my selfe to thy censure, Farewell.

Robert Iones.

A TABLE CONTAI-
ning all the Songs in this
BOOKE.

3   *Goe to bed sweete Muze, take thy rest.*
4   *Shall I looke to ease my griefe.*
5   *What If I sped where I least expected.*
6   *Sweete if you like and loue me still.*
7   *Sease troubled thoughts to sigh.*
8   *Scinthia Queene of Seas and Lands.*
9   *Blame not my cheekes.*
10 *There is a Garden in her face.*
11 *Sweete Loue my onely Treasure.*
12 *Thinkst thou Kate to put me downe.*
13 *When will the fountaine of my teares be drye.*
14 *Flye from the world.*
15 *Happy he who to sweete home retirde.*

These following are for 2. Trebles.

16 *Disdaine that so doth fill me.*
17 *Now let her change and spare not.*
18 *Since iust disdaine began to rise.*
19 *At her fayre hands how haue I grace intreated.*
20 *Oft haue I muzde the cause to finde.*
21 *Now haue I learnd with much adoo at last.*

I.

Doe not, O doe not prize thy beauty at too high a rate,
Loue to be lou'd whilst thou art louely, least thou loue too late,
    Frownes print wrincles in thy browes,
    at which spightfull age doth smile,
    women in their froward vowes,   5
    glorying to beguile.

2

Wert thou the onely worlds admired, thou canst loue but one,
And many haue before beene lou'd, thou art not lou'd alone.
    Couldst thou speake with heauenly grace,   10
    Sapho might with thee compare:
    Blush the Roses in thy face,
    Rozamond was as faire.

3

Pride is the canker that consumeth beautie in her prime,   15
They that delight in long debating feele the curse of time,
    All things with the time do change,
    That will not the time obey,
    Some euen to themselues seeme strange,
    Thorowe their owne delay.   20

II.

Beauty sate bathing by a spring
where fairest shades did hide her,
the windes blew calme, the birds did sing,
The coole streames ranne beside her,
    My wanton thoughtes intiste my eye   5
    to see what was forbidden,
    but better memory cride fie,
    so vaine delights were chidden.

2 Into a slumber then I fell,
  But fond imagination   10
Seemed to see, but could not tell
Her feature or her fashion.
    But euen as babes in dreames do smile
    And sometime fall aweeping:
    So I awakt as wise the while   15
    As when I fell asleeping.
            [Anthony Munday]

III.

Goe to bed sweete Muze take thy rest,
Let not thy soule bee so opprest
    Though shee deny thee,
    shee doth but trie thee,
    whether thy mind   5
  will euer proue vnkinde:
O loue is but a bitter-sweete Iest.

2

Muze not vpon her smiling lookes,
Thinke that they are but baited hookes,   10
  Loue is a fancy,
  Loue is a Franzy,
  Let not a toy,
 Then breed thee such annoy,
 But leaue to looke vppon such fond bookes.   15

3

Learne to forget such idle toyes,
Fitter for youthes, and youthfull boyes,
  Let not one sweete smile
  Thy true loue beguile,   20
  Let not a frowne
 For euer cast thee downe,
 Then sleepe and go to bed in these ioyes.

IIII.

Sнall I looke to ease my griefe,
no my sight is lost with eying,
Shall I speake and begge reliefe,
no, my voyce is hoarse with crying:
 what remaines, but onely dying.   5

2

Loue and I of late did part,
But the boy my peace enuying,
Like a Parthian threw his dart
Backward, and did wound me flying: 10
 What remaines but onely dying.

3

She whome then I looked on,
My remembrance beautifying
Stayes with me, though I am gone,   15
Gone, and at her mercy lying.
 What remaines but onely dying.

4

Shall I trye her thoughts and write,
No, I haue no meanes of trying: 20
If I should yet at first sight
She would answere with denying.
  What remaines but onely dying.

5

Thus my vitall breath doth waste,   25
And my bloud with sorrow drying,
Sighes and teares, make life to last
For a while, their place supplying,
  What remaines but onely dying.

V.

Wнat if I sped where I least expected, what shall I say?
                                        shall I lye?
What if I mist where I most affected, what shall I do,
                                        shall I dy?
                No, no, Ile haue at all,
                tis as my game doth fall,
                If I keepe my meaning close,   5
                I may hit how ere it goes,
                For time & I
                do meane to try
                what hope doth lye in youth, Fa la la.
                The minds that doubt   10
                are in & out,
                & women flout at truth: Fa la la.

2 She whome aboue the skies I renowned, she whome I loued,
                                        shee,
Can she leaue all in Leathe drowned, can she be coy to me?
                Her passions are but cold: 15
                She stands and doth beholde,
                She retaines her lookes estrangde,
                As if heauen and earth were changde.
                I speake she heares,
                I touch, she feares,   20
                Herein appeares her wit, fa la la:

> I catch, she flies,
> I hold, she cries,
> And still denies, and yet fa la la.

3 May not a wanton looke like a woman, tell me the reason
why? 25

And if a blinde man chance of a birdes nest, must he
be pratling? fye:

> What mortall strength can keepe,
> That's got as in a sleepe?
> The felony is his
> That brags of a stolne kis: 30
> For when we met,
> Both in a net,
> That *Vulcan* set, were hid, fa, la, la la:
> And so god wot
> We did it not,   35
> Or else forgot we did. Fa la la la.

VI.

Sweet if you like & loue me stil,
And yeeld me loue for my good wil,
And do not from your promise start,
when your fair hand gaue me your hart.
  If dear to you I be,   5
    As you are dear to me,
then yours I am, & wil be euer,
no time nor place my loue shall seuer,
but faithfull still I will perseuer,
  Like constant Marble stone,   10
  Louing but you alone.

2

But if you fauour moe then one,
(Who loues thee still, and none but thee,)
If others do the haruest gaine,   15
That's due to me for all my paine:
  Yet that you loue to range,
  And oft to chop and change.

Then get you some new fangled mate:
My doting loue shall turne to hate,   20
Esteeming you (though too too late)
  Not worth a peble stone,
  Louing not me alone.
                    [Francis Davison]

VII.

CEase troubled thoughtes to sigh, or sigh your selues to death,
or kindle not my griefe, or coole it with your breath:
  Let not that spirit which made me liue
  seeke thus vntimely to depriue
        mee of my life   5
        vnequall strife,
  that breath which gaue mee beeing
  should hasten mee to dying.

                            2

Cease melting tears to streame, stop your vncessant course,   10
Which to my sorrowes childe are like a fruitfull Nurse,
  From whence death liuing, comfort drawes,
  And I my selfe appeare the cause
        Of all my woe,
        But tis not so: 15
  For she whose beautie won mee,
  By falshood hath vndone mee.

VIII.

Scinthia Queene of seas and lands,
that fortune euery where commands,
sent forth fortune to the sea,
to trye her fortune euery way:
ther did I Fortune meete,   5
which makes mee now to sing,
there is no fishing to the Sea,
nor seruice to a King.

All the Nimphes of *Theatis* traine
Did *Scinthias* fortune entertaine: 10
Many a Iewell, many a Iem
was to her fortune brought by them:
Her fortune sped so well,
Which makes me now to sing,
There is no fishing to the Sea,   15
Nor seruice to a King.

Fortune that it might be seene,
That she did serue a royall Queene,
A franke and royall hand did beare,
And cast her fauoures euery where: 20
Such toyes fell to my lot,
Which makes me now to sing,
There is no fishing to the Sea,
Nor seruice to a King.
                    [Sir John Davies?]

IX.

BLame not my cheekes, though pale with loue they be,
the kindly heate into my heart is flowne
To cherish it that is dismaide by thee,
who art so cruell and vnstedfast growne:
  For nature cald for by distressed heartes,   5
  neglects, & quite forsakes the outward partes.

2

But they whose cheekes with carelesse bloud are staind,
Nurse not one sparke of loue within their hearts,
And when they wooe, they speake with passion faind,   10
For their fat loue lies in their outward parts:
  But in their brest, where loue his Court should holde,
  Poore *Cupid* sits, and blowes his nayles for colde.
                    [Thomas Campion]

X.

THere is a Garden in her face,
where Roses and white Lillies grow,
a heauenly paradise is that place
wherein these pleasant fruits do flow,
There cheries grow which none can buy   5
till chery ripe themselues do crye.

2 These cheries fairely do inclose
Of Orient Pearle a double rowe,
Which when her louely laughter showes,
They looke like Rose buds fild with snowe: 10
Yet them no Peere nor Prince may buy,
Till chery ripe themselues do crye.

3 Her eyes like Angels watch them still,
Her browes like bended bowes do stand
Threatning with piercing shaftes to kill   15
All that presume with eye or hand
Those sacred cheries to come nie,
Till chery ripe themselues do crye.
                    [Thomas Campion]

XI.

Sweete loue my onely treasure,
for seruice long vnfained
wherein I nought haue gained,
vouchsafe this little pleasure,
  to tell mee in what part   5
  my Lady keepes my heart.

              2

If in her haire so slender,
Like golden nets vntwined,
Which fire and arte haue fined: 10
Her thrall my hart I render
  For euer to abide,
  With lockes so daintie tide.

3

If in her eyes she bind it,   15
Wherein that fire was framed,
By which it is inflamed,
I dare not looke to finde it,
 I onely wish it sight,
 To see that pleasant light.   20

4

But if her brest haue dained
With kindnesse to receiue it,
I am content to leaue it,
Though death thereby were gained: 25
 Then Lady take your owne,
 That liues for you alone.

XII.

Tнinkst thou Kate to put me downe
with a no, or with a frowne,
since loue holds my hart in bandes,
I must do as loue commands.

2   5

Loue commaundes the hands to dare,
When the tongue of speech is spare:
Chiefest lesson in loues Schoole
Put it in aduenture foole.

3   10

Fooles are they that fainting flinch
For a squeake, a scratch, a pinch,
Womens words haue double sence:
Stand away, a simple fence.

4   15

If thy Mistresse sweare sheele crye,
Feare her not, sheele sweare and lye,
Such sweet oathes no sorrowe bring
Till the pricke of conscience sting.

XIII.

WHen wil the fountain of my teares be dry,
   when will my sighs be spent:
When wil desire agree to let me dye,
   when will thy heart relent:
  It is not for my life I plead,   5
  since death the way to rest doth leade:
    but stay for thy consent
    least thou bee discontent.

2

For if my selfe without thy leaue I kill,   10
   My Ghost will neuer rest,
So hath it sworne to worke thine onely will,
   And holdes it euer best:
  For since it onely liues by thee,
  Good reason thou the ruler be:
    Then giue me leaue to dye,   15
    And shew thy power thereby.

XIIII.

FLye from the world O fly thou poor distrest,
where thy diseased sence infectes thy soule
and wher thy thoghts do multiply vnrest,
trobling with wishes what they straight controule
O worlde, O worlde betrayers of the mind   5
O thoughts O thoughts that guide vs being blinde.

Come therefore Care Conduct me to my end,
And steere this shipwracke Carcase to the graue:
My sighes a strong and stedfast wind will lende,
Teares wet the sayles, repentance from rockes saue,   10
Haile death, hayle death, the land I do descry,
Strike sayle, go soule, rest followes them that dye.

XV.

    HAppy he
who to sweet home retirde
shuns glory so admirde,
    and to him selfe liues free,

whilst he who striues with pride to clime the skies   5
fals down with foule disgrace, before he rise.

2   Let who will,
  The Actiue life commend,
  And all his trauels bend,
     Earth with his fame to fill.   10
Such fame so forst, at last dyes with his death,
Which life maintainde by others idle breath.

3   My delightes
  To dearest home confinde,
  Shall there make good my mind: 15
     Not Awde with fortunes spights.
High trees heauen blastes, windes shake, and honors fel,
When lowly plantes, long time in safetie dwell.

4   All I can
  My worldly strife shall be   20
  They one day, say of me,
     He dyde a good old man:
On his sad soule, a heauy burden lies,
Who knowne to all, vnknowne to himselfe dyes.

XVI.

Dısdaine that so doth fil me,
hath surely sworne to kill mee,
  and I must dye:
Desire that still doth burne me,
to life againe wil turne me,   5
  and liue must I:
O kill me then disdain,
that I may liue againe.

     2

Thy lookes are life vnto me,   10
And yet thy lookes vndoo me:
  O death and life:

Thy smiles some rest do shew me,
Thy frownes with warre orethrow me:
  O peace and strife: 15
Nor life, nor death is either,
Then giue me both or neither.

3

Life onely cannot ease me,
Death onely cannot please me,   20
  Change is delight:
I liue, that death may kill me,
I dye, that life may fill me,
  Both day and night,
If once despaire decay,   25
Desire will weare away.

XVII.

Now let her change & spare not,
since shee proues strange I care not,
Fained loue so bewitcht my delight,
that still I doted on her sight,
but she is gone, new desires embrasing,   5
  and my desertes disgracing.

2 When did I erre in blindnesse,
Or vexe her with vnkindnesse?
If my heart did attend her alone,
Why is she thus vntimely gone?   10
True loue abides to the day of dying,
  False loue is euer flying.

3 Thou false farewell for euer,
Once false proues faithfull neuer:
He that now so triumphes in thy loue,   15
Shall soone my present fortunes proue:
Were he as fayre as Adonis,
  Faith is not had where none is.
                              [Thomas Campion]

XVIII.

Since iust disdaine beganne to rise
and crye reuenge for spightfull wrong
what erst I praisde I now despise,
and thinke my loue was to too long.
    I treade in durt that scornefull pride   5
    which in thy looks I haue discride
    thy beautie is a painted skinne
    for fools to see their faces in.

Thine eyes that some as stars esteeme,
From whence themselues, they say take light,   10
Like to the foolish fire I deeme,
That leades men to their death by night.
    Thy words and oathes as light as wind,
    And yet far lighter is thy mind:
    Thy friendship is a broken reed: 15
    That fales thy friends in greatest need.

XIX.

At her faire hands how haue I grace entreated
    with prayers oft repeated,
    yet still my loue is thwarted,
heart let her goe for sheele not be conuerted.
    say shall she go?   5
    O no, no, no, no, no,
shee is most faire though she be marble hearted.

2 How often haue my sighes declarde my anguish,
    Wherein I daily languish,
    yet doth she still procure it,   10
Hart, let her go, for I cannot endure it,
    Say, shall shee go,
    O, no, no, no, no, no.
Shee gaue the wound, and shee alone must cure it.

3 The trickling tears, that down my cheeks haue flowed   15
    my loue hath often shewed:

yet still vnkind I proue her,
Hart let her goe, for nought I do can moue her
   Say, shall she go,
    O no, no, no, no, no,   20
Though me she hate, I cannot chuse but loue her.

4 But shall I still a true affection beare her,
Which prayers, sighes, teares do shew her?
   And shall she still disdaine me?
Heart let her goe, if they no grace can gaine me,   25
    Say, shall she goe?
    O no, no, no, no, no:
She made me hers, and hers she will retaine me.

5 But if the loue that hath, and still doth burne me
  No loue at length returne me: 30
  Out of my thoughts Ile set her:
Hart let her goe, O, heart I pray thee let her,
    Say, shall she goe?
    O no, no, no, no, no:
Fixt in the heart, how can the heart forget her.   35

6 But if I weepe and sigh, and often wayle me,
  Till teares, sighes, prayers faile me,
  Shall yet my loue perseuer?
Heart let her goe, if she will right thee neuer:
    Say, shall she goe?   40
    O no, no, no, no, no:
Teares, sighes, prayers faile, but true loue lasteth euer.
                  [Walter Davison]

XX.

Oft haue I muz'd the cause to finde,
why loue in Ladies eyes shuld dwel,
I thought because him selfe was blinde
hee lookt that they shuld guide him wel,
  And sure his hope but seldome failes,   5
  for loue by Ladies eyes preuailes.

2 But time at last hath taught me wit,
Although I bought my wit full deare:
For by her eyes my heart is hit,
Deepe is the wound, though none appeare,   10
  Their glancing beames, as dartes he throwes,
  And sure he hath no shaftes but those.

3 I muz'd to see their eyes so bright,
And little thought they had beene fire.
I gaz'd vpon them with delight,   15
But that delight hath bred desire:
  What better place can loue require,
  Then that where growe both shaftes and fire?

XXI.

Now haue I learnd with much adoo at last
    by true disdaine to kill desire:
this was the marke at which I shot so fast,
    vnto this height I did aspire,
proud loue now do thy worst & spare not: 5
for thee & all thy shaftes I care not.

2 What has thou left wherewith to moue my minde?
    What life to quicken dead desire?
I count thy words and oathes as light as winde,
    I feele no heate in all thy fire.   10
Go change thy bow and get a stronger,
Go breake thy shaftes and buy thee longer.

3 In vaine thou baitst thy hooke with beauties blaze,
    In vaine thy wanton eyes allure,
These are but toyes for them that loue to gaze,   15
    I know what harme thy lookes procure:
Some strange conceit must be deuis'd,
Or thou and all thy skill despis'd.

FINIS.

Francis Pilkington

The First Booke of Songs or Ayres

1605

[Within a compartment: McK. & F. No. 132 (see Textual Introduction to D01600); in upper oval slot, two lines of music (a canon in the bass clef) with this under the first line:] 4. parts in .1. reſt 2. [At the end of the second line:] I. M. [Boyd, p. 121, conjectures that these initials stand for John Mundy. Within the main opening:] THE/ FIRST BOOKE OF/ Songs or Ayres of 4. parts:/ vvith Tableture for the/ Lute or Orpherian, vvith/ the Violl de/ Gamba./ *Newly compoſed by Francis Pilkington,* [*NP* swash]/ Batcheler of Muſick, and Luteniſt: and one/ of the Cathedrall Church of Chriſt,/ in the Citie of Cheſter./ [in lower slot:] LONDON:/ Printed by T. Eſte, dwelling in/ Alderſgate-ſtreete, and are/ ther to be ſould. 1605./

Collation: 2°; *A*–M²; 24 leaves.
Headlines: Verso, B1v–M1v: I. [–XXI.] CANTO. Recto, B2–M2: I. [–XXI.] TENORE. [No period on I2, M2]/ I. [–XXI.] BASSO. / I. [–XXI.] ALTO.
*Contents: A*1, title page; *A*1v blank; *A*2, dedication; *A*2v blank; B1, table; B1v–M2, songs I–XXI, one per opening; M2v, XXII, "A Pauin for the Lute and Base Violl."
SR: Entered by Thomas East on August 23, 1604. It was not among the books transferred after his death (Arber, III, 268, 450, 465).
STC: 19922.
Copies: BM (K.2.i.11, the text copy); Glasgow (R.x.12); Folger; and Huntington (13569). Collation reveals the following verbal press corrections (the Glasgow copy was not fully collated, but the librarian confirmed the corrections listed):
Inner forme A: corrected on cancel slips in BM and Glasgow, uncorrected in Huntington and Folger:
  A2 8 not that] But that
     numbers] Bumbees

Inner forme F: uncorrected, Huntington:
  F1v (IX.5) leauy] leavy
Inner forme M: uncorrected, BM, Glasgow:
  M1v (XXI.1) Elegie] Elogie
  M2 (XXI.1 ATB) Elegie] Elogie
    (XXI.1 A) Worshipfull] Worshiptfull
    (XXI.9 ATB) too cruell] to Cruell
    (XXI.10 ATB) too timely] to timely
All of the songs have the usual Cantus and tablature facing parts for alto, tenor, and
bass, as in Do1597, except XVI, where ATB seem to be intended for instruments, since
words are given only for the chorus.

To the Right honourable William Earle
of Darby, Lord Stanly, Lord Strange, of Knocking
and of the Isle of Man, and Knight of the most noble
Order of the Garter. *Francis Pilkington* wisheth health,
with increase of Honour in this life, and Eternitie
heereafter.

ARistoxenus (*thrice noble Lord*) *held that the Soule of man was Musicke:
not that the being thereof was framed of numbers, as the Pithagorians affirme:
But for that it is the subiect and obiect of all harmonicall concents: Intimating
heereby the dignitie and high renowne of that Art, which descended from so*   10
*noble a stemme, seeketh by all meanes possible to nobilitate the same, and that
man to bee vnfit for the society and commerce of men, that honoureth not so
worthy a Iewell for the life of man. Which opinion verely is worthy* Aristoxenus, *that is to say, a noble Philosopher, yet how litle squaring with the
time, experience a perfect Mistresse of truth hath a long time taught. For who
regardeth the melodius charmes of* Orpheus, *or enchanting melodie of* Arion?
surely but a few, Quos æquus amauit Iupiter dijs geniti, aut ardeus euexit
ad æthera virtus. *Of which rancke seeing your Lordship hath giuen vn-
doubted testimonies of your honour to bee one: Musitions should commit an
vndiscreet part of ingratitude not to acknowledge so great a fauour. For mine*   20
*owne part (who am meanest of many which professe this diuine skill, though
not meanest in good will & humble affection to your Honor) I must confesse
my selfe many waies obliged to your Lordships familie, not onely, for that my
Father and Brother receiued many graces of your Honours noble Father, whom
they followed, but that my self had the like of your most honorable Brother,
euen from the first notice he chanced to take of mee. And therfore (most*

honourable Lord) *I haue heere presented this oblation, howsoeuer meane, a token of mine affectionate good will and Loue, yea onely deuoted to your Lordship, which if it may gaine your gracious acceptation, will feare neither* Zoilus *nor* Momus *his reprehension.*

Your Honours in all dutie
Francis Pilkington.

THE TABLE.

FINIS.

I.

Now peep, boe peep, thrise happie blest mine eies,
For I haue found faire *Phillis* where she lies,
Vpon her bed, with armes vnspred, all fast asleepe,
Vnmaskt her face, thrise happie grace, farewell my Sheepe,
Looke to your selues, new charge I must approue,   5
Phillis doth sleepe, And I must guard my Loue.

2 Now peep boe peep, mine eyes to see your blisse,
Phillis closd eyes atrackts you, hers to kisse:
Oh may I now performe my vow, loues ioy t'impart,
Assay the while, how to be-guile, farewell faint hart.   10
Taken she is, new ioyes I must approue,
Phillis doth sleep, and I will kisse my Loue.

3 Now peep, boe peep, be not too bould my hand,
Wake not thy *Phillis*, feare shee doe with-stand:
Shee stirs alas, alas, alas I faint in spright,   15
Shee opes her eie, vnhappie I, farewell delight.
Awakt shee is, new woes I must approue,
Phillis awakes, and I must leaue my Loue.

II.

My choice is made and I desire no change,
My wandring thoughts in limits now are bound:
The deserts wilde wherin my wits did range,
Are now made easie walks and pleasant ground:
Let him that list sooth humors that be vaine,   5
Till vanitie all meane exceeds,
Let passions stil possesse the idle braine,
And care consume whom folly feeds.
I rest resolu'd no fancies fits can mee estrange,
My choice is made, and I desire no more to change.   10

2 Change they their choice, to whose delicious sence,
The strangest obiects are of most esteeme:
Inconstant likeing may find excellence,
In things which (being not good) yet best doe seeme.

Let gallant blouds still crowne their sports with ioy,   15
Whom honor, wealth, and pleasure fils:
Let sweet contentment neuer find annoy,
While *Fortune* frames things to their wills.
This stirs not mee, I am the same, I was before,
My choice is made, and I desire to change no more.   20

3 Be my choice blamde, or be I thought vnwise,
To hold my choice, by others not approued,
I say, that to my selfe I fall or rise,
By feare, or force I cannot be remoued.
Let friends in pittie doubt of my successe,   25
Their pittie gets no thanks at all:
Let foes be glad to see my hopes grow lesse,
I scorne the worst that wish they shall:
Still stand I firme, my hart is set, and shall remaine,
My choice is made, and neuer will I change againe.   30

III.

CAn she disdaine, can I persist to loue,
can she be cruell, I subiected still.
Time will my truth, compassion hers aproue,
release the thrald, and conquer froward will.
I loue not lust, Oh therfore let her daigne,   5
to equal my desires with like againe.

Am I not pleasing in her prouder eies,
Oh that she knew Loues power as well as I,
Wittie she is, but Loues more wittie wise,
She breathes on earth, he Raignes in heauen on high.   10
I loue not lust, oh therefore let her daigne,
To equall my desires with like againe.

Loue scornes the abiect earth, his sacred fires
Vnites diuided mindes disseuers none,
Contempt springs out of fleshly base desires,   15
Setting debate twixt loue and vnion.
I loue not lust, oh therefore let her daigne,
To equall my desires, with like againe.

IIII.

ALas faire face why doth that smoothed brow:
those speaking eies ros'd lips, and blushing beautie,
All in them selues confirme a scornfull vow:
to spoile my hopes of loue, my loue of dutie.
The time hath bin, when I was better grast: 5
I now the same, and yet that time is past.

Is it because that thou art onely faire,
Oh no such gracefull lookes banish disdaine,
How then, to feede my passions with dispaire,
Feede on sweet loue, so I be loued againe.   10
Well may thy publike scorne, and outward pride,
Inward affections, and best likings hide.

Breath but a gentle aire, and I shall liue,
Smyle in a clowde, so shall my hopes renue,
One kind regard, and second seing giue,   15
One rising Morne, and my blacke woes subdue.
If not, yet looke vpon the friendly Sunne,
That by his beames, my beames to thine may runne.

V.

WHether so fast, see how the kindly flowres,
perfumes the aire, and all to make thee stay,
The climing woodbind clipping al these bowrs,
clips thee likewise, for feare thou passe away,
Fortune our friend, our foe will not gainesay.   5
Stay but a while, *Phoebe* no teltale is,
She her *Endimion*, Ile my *Phoebe* kisse.

Feare not, the ground seekes but to kisse thy feete
Harke, harke how *Philomela* sweetly sings,
Whilst water wanton fishes as they meete,   10
Strike crochet time amid'st these christall springs,
And *Zephirus* mongst the leaues sweet murmure rings,
Stay but a while, *Phoebe* no teltale is,
She her *Endimion*, Ile my *Phoebe* kisse.

See how the *Helitrope* hearbe of the Sunne   15
Though he himselfe long since be gon to bed,
Is not of force thine eies bright beames to shun,
But with their warmth his gouldy leaues vnspred,
And on my knee inuites thee rest thy head.
Stay but a while, *Phoebe* no teltale is,   20
She her *Endimion*, Ile my *Phoebe* kisse.

VI.

REst sweet Nimphs let goulden sleepe,
charme your star brighter eies,
Whiles my Lute the watch doth keep
with pleasing simpathies,
Lulla lullaby, Lulla Lullaby,   5
sleepe sweetly, sleep sweetly, let nothing affright ye,
in calme contentments lie.

Dreame faire virgins of delight,
And blest Elizian groues:
Whiles the wandring shades of night,   10
Resemble your true loues:
Lulla lullaby, Lulla lullaby
Your kisses your blisses send them by your wishes,
Although they be not nigh.

Thus deare damzells I do giue   15
Good night and so am gone:
With your hartes desires long liue
still ioy, and neuer mone.
Lulla lullaby, Lulla lullaby
Hath pleasd you and easd you, & sweet slumber sezd you,   20
And now to bed I hie.

VII.

AYE mee, she frownes, my Mistresse is offended,
Oh pardon deare, my misse shall be amended:
My fault from loue proceeded, It merits grace the rather,
If I no danger dreaded, it was to win your fauour.
Then cleere those clouds, then smile on mee, And let vs bee
                                            good friends.   5
Come walke, come talke, come kisse, come see, how soone
                                            our quarrell ends.

Why low'rs my loue, and blots so sweete a beautie,
Oh be apeasd with vowes, with faith and duetie:
Giue ouer to be cruell, sith kindnesse seemes you better,
You haue but changd a Iuell, and loue is not your detter.　　10
Then welcome mirth, and banish mone, shew pittie on your
　　　　　　　　　　　　　　　　　　　louer,
Come play, come sport, the thing thats gon no sorrow can
　　　　　　　　　　　　　　　　recouer.

Still are you angry, and is there no relenting?
Oh wiegh my woes, be mou'd with my lamenting:
Alas my hart is grieued, myne inward soule doth sorrow,　　15
Vnles I be releeud, I dye before to morrow.
The coast is cleard, her countnance cheard, I am againe in grace,
Then farewell feare, then come my deare, lets dallie and embrace.

VIII.

Now let her change and spare not,
since she proues false I care not,
Fained loue so bewitched my delight,
That still I doated on her sight,
But she is gon, New desires imbracing,　　　　　　　　　5
And my deserts disgracing.

When did I erre in blindnesse,
Or vex her with vnkindnesse,
If my care did attend her alone,
Why is she thus vntimely gone?　　　　　　　　　　10
True loue abides till the day of dying,
False loue is euer flying.

Then false fare-well for euer,
Once false proue faithfull neuer,
He that now so triumphes in thy loue,　　　　　　　　15
Shall soone my present fortunes proue.
Were I as faire as diuine *Adonis*,
Loue is not had where none is.
　　　　　　　[Thomas Campion]

IX.

Vɴderneath a *Cypris* shade, the Queene of Loue sat mourning,
Casting downe the Rosie wreaths, Her heauenly brow adorning:
Quenching fiery sighes with teares, But yet her hart still
                                                    burning.

2 For within the shady mourne, the cause of her complaining,
Mirrhas Sonne the leauy bowres did haunt, her loue disdaining,   5
Counting all her true desires, in his fond thoughts but faining.

3 Why is youth with beauty grast, vnfeeleing Iudge of
                                                    vnkindnesse,
Spotting loue with the foule report, of crueltie and blindnesse,
Forceing to vnkind complaints, the Queene of all diuinenesse.

4 Stint thy teares faire Seaborne Queene, & greife in vaine
                                                    lamented,   10
When desire hath burnt his hart, that thee hath discontented,
Then to late the scorne of youth, by age shall be repented.

X.

For his vnfortunate friend William Harwood.

   Sound wofull plaints in hils and woods,
Fly my cries, to the skies, Melt mine eies, and hart languish,
   Not for the want of friends, or goods,
make I moane, though alone, thus I groane, by soules anguish.   5
   Time, friends, chance, goods, might againe recouer,
   Black woes, sad griefes, ore my life doe houer,
Since my losse is with dispaire, No blest Star to me shine faire,
   All my mirth turne to mourning,
Hart lament, for hope is gon, Musicke leaue, Ile learne to
                                                    moane,   10
   Sorrowes the sads adorning.

   Aye mee my daies of blisse are done,
Sorrowing must I sing, nothing can relieue mee:
   Eclipsed is my glorious Sunne,
And mischance doth aduance horrors lance, still to greiue mee.   15
   Poore hart, ill happ hath all ioy bereft thee:
   Gon's the sole good, which the Fates had left mee.

Whose estate is like to mine? Fortune doth my weale repine,
   Enuying my one pleasure,
Patience must mee assure, other plaster can not cure,   20
   Therefore in this my treasure.

XI.

You that pine in long desire,
     helpe to cry.
Come Loue, come Loue, quench this burning fire,
     Least through thy wound I die.

2 Hope that tyres with vaine delay,   5
     euer cryes
Come loue, come loue, howers and yeares decay,
     In time loues treasure lyes.

3 All the day, and all the night
     still I call   10
Come loue, come loue, but my deare delight,
     yealds no releefe at all.

4 Her vnkindnesse scornes my moane,
     that still shrykes
Come loue, come loue, beauty pent alone   15
     dyes in her owne dislikes.

XII.

Looke Mistresse mine within this hollow brest,
See heere inclosd a tombe of tender skin,
wherin fast lockt is framd a *Phenix* nest,
That saue your selfe, there is no passage in.
Witnesse the wound that through your dart doth bleed,   5
And craues your cure since you haue done the deed.

Wherefore most rare and *Phenix* rarely fine,
Behould once more the harmes I do possesse:
Regard the hart that through your fault doth pine,
Attending rest yet findeth no redresse.   10
For end, waue wings and set your nest on fire,
Or pittie mee, and grant my sweet desire.

XIII.

To his louing friend M. Holder, M. of Arts.

CLime O hart, clime to thy rest,
Climing yet take heed of falling,
Climers oft euen at their best,
catch loue, down fal th'hart appaling.   5

2 Mounting yet if she do call,
And desire to know thy arrant:
Feare not stay, and tell her all,
Falling shee will be thy warrant.

3 Rise, oh rise, but rising tell,   10
When her beautie brauely wins thee,
T'sore vp where that she doth dwell,
Downe againe thy basenesse brings thee.

4 If she aske what makes thee loue her,
Say her vertue, not her face: 15
For though beauty doth approue her,
Mildnesse giues her greater grace.

5 Rise then rise if she bid rise,
Rising say thou risest for her:
Fall if she do thee dispise,   20
Falling still do thou adore her.

6 If thy plaint do pittie gaine,
Loue and liue to her honor:
If thy seruice she disdaine,
Dying yet complaine not on her.   25

XIIII.

THanks gentle Moone for thy obscured light,
My Loue and I betraid thou set vs free,
And *Zephirus* as many vnto thee,
Whose blasts conceald, the pleasures of the night,
Resolue to her thou gaue, content to mee.   5
But be those bowers still fild with Serpents hisses,
That sought by treason, to betray our kisses.

And thou false Arbor with thy bed of Rose,
Wherein, wheron toucht equall with loues fyer,
We reapt of eyther other loues desire,   10
Wither the twining plants that thee enclose.
Oh be thy bowers still fild with serpents hisses,
That sought by treason, to betray our kisses.

Torne be the frame, for thou didst thankles hide,
A trayterous spy, her brother, and my foe,   15
Who sought by death, our ioyes to vnder goe,
And by that death, our passions to deuide,
Leauing to our great vows, eternall woe.
Oh be thy bowers still fild with serpents hisses,
That sought by treason, to betray our kisses.   20

XV.

I Sigh as sure to weare the fruit of the Willow tree,
I sigh as sure to lose my sute, for it may not bee.
I sigh as one that loues in vaine, I sigh as one that liues in paine,
very sorie, very weary of my miserie.

2 I hate my thoughts which like the Flie, flutter in the flame,   5
I hate my teares which drop, and dry, quench and frid the same:
I hate the hart which frozen burnes, I hate the hart which
                                                    chosen turnes,
Too and from mee, making of mee nothing but a game.

3 My thoughts are fuell to desire, which may hart doth moue,
My teares are oyle to feed the fire, smart whereof I proue: 10
She laughes at sighes that come from mee, I sigh at laughes in
                                                    her so free,
Who doth glory, in the storie of my sorie loue.

4 Her louely lookes, and louelesse mind doe not well agree,
Her quick conceipt, and iudgement blind, as ill suted bee:
Her forward wit, and froward hart, that like to knit, this glad
                                                    to part,   15
Makes so prettie, and so wittie, not to pittie mee.

5 The more I seeke, the lesse I find what to trust vnto,
The more I hold, the lesse I bind, she doth still vndoe:
I weaue the web of idle loue, which endles will, and frutles

                                                        proue,
If the pleasure for the measure of my treasure goe.   20

XVI.

Chorus.

Down a down, Thus *Phillis* sung,
by Fancie once oppressed,
Who so by foolish Loue are stong,
Are worthely distressed,   5
and so sing I, with a down,
with a down a down a down.

1 Verse.

WHen Loue was first begot, and by the mothers will,
Did fall to humane lot, his solace to fulfill,   10
Deuoid of all deceit, a chast and holy fire,
Did quicken mans conceit, and womens brest inspire.
The Gods that saw the good, that mortals did approue,
With kinde and holy moode, began to talke of loue.
            Chorus.   Downe a downe.   15

2 But during this accord, a wonder strange to heare
Whilst loue in deed and word, most faithfull did appeare:
False semblance came in place, by Ielocie attended,
And with a double face, both loue and fancie blended,   20
Which made the gods forsake, and men from fancie flie,
And maidens scorne a mate, forsooth and so will I.
            Chorus.   Downe a downe, &c.
                                      [Thomas Lodge]

XVII.

Diaphenia like the Dafdowndillie,
White as the Sunne, faire as the Lillie,
   Heigh ho, how I doe loue thee:

I doe loue thee as my Lambs,
Are beloued of their dambs,   5
  How blest were I if thou wouldst proue mee.

2 *Diaphenia* like the spreading Roses,
That in thy sweetes, all sweetes incloses,
  Faire sweete how I doe loue thee?
I doe loue thee as each flower,   10
Loues the Sunnes life giuing power,
  For dead, thy breath to life might moue mee.

3 *Diaphenia* like to all things blessed,
When all thy praises are expressed,
  Deare ioy, how I doe loue thee?   15
As the birds doe loue the spring,
Or the Bees their carefull king,
  Then in requite, sweete virgin loue mee.

[Henry Chettle?]

XVIII.

Beautie sat bathing by a spring,
Where fairest shades did hide her:
The winds blew calme, the birds did sing,
The coole streames ranne beside her.
My wanton thoughts entic'd mine eie,   5
To see what was forbidden:
But better memory said fie,
So vaine desire was chidden.
  Hey nony, hey nony, hey nony no nony nony.

Into a slumber then I fell,   10
When fond imagination,
Seemed to see, but could not tell,
Her feature, or her fashion.
But euen as Babes in dreames doe smile,
And sometime fall a-weeping: 15
So I a-wakt, as wise this while,
As when I fell a sleeping.
  Hey nonnie, nonnie. &c.

[Anthony Munday]

XIX.

Mvsick deare sollace, to my thoughts neglected,
Musick time sporter, to my most respected,
Sound on, sound on, thy golden harmony is such,
That whilst she doth vouchsafe her *Ebon* Lute to tuch,
By descant numbers I doe nimbly clime, from Loues secluse,   5
Vnto his Courts wher I in fresh attire, attire my Muse.

2 I doe compare her fingers swift resounding,
Vnto the heauens Sphaericall rebounding:
Harke, harke, she sings no forst, but breathing sound I heare,
And such the concord *Diapasons* shee doth reare,   10
As when th'immortall god of nature from his seate aboue,
First formd words all, & fairely it combind, combind by loue.

3 Diuine *Appollo* bee not thou offended,
That by her better skill thy skils amended,
Schollers doe oft more lore, then maisters theirs attaine,   15
Though thine the ground, all parts in one though she contain,
Yet maist thou triumph, that thou hast a Scholler onely one,
That can her Lute to thine, and to thy voice, her voice attone.

XX.

With fragrant flowers we strew the way,
And make this our chiefe holy day,
For though this Clime were blest of yore,
Yet was it neuer proud before:
O gracious King, of second *Troy*,   5
Accept of our vnfained ioy.

2 Now th'Aire is sweeter then sweet Balme,
And Satires daunce about the Palme:
Now earth with verdure newly dight,
Giues perfect signes of her delight.   10
O gracious King of second *Troy*,
Accept of our vnfained ioy.

3 Now Birds record new harmonie,
And trees doe whistle melodie:
Now euery thing that Nature breeds   15
Doth clad it selfe in pleasant weeds.
O gracious King of second *Troy*,
Accept of our vnfained ioy.
           [Thomas Watson]

XXI.

An Elegie in remembrance of his Worshipfull friend *Thomas Leighton* Esquier.

Come come all you that draw heauens purest breath,
Come Angell brested sonnes of harmonie,
Let vs condole in tragicke Eligie,
Condole with me our deerest *Leightons* death,   5
Leighton in whose deere losse death blemisheth
Ioues beautie and the soule of true delight,
Leighton heauens fauorite and the Muses Iewell,
Muses and heauens onely heerein too cruell,
Leighton to heauen, hath tane too timely flight.   10

Come then sith Seas of teares, sith sighes and grones,
Sith mournefull plaints, lowd cries, and deepe laments,
Haue all in vaine deplord these drerements,
And fate in-explorable scornes our mones,
Let vs in accents graue, and saddest tones,   15
Offer vp *Musicks* dolefull sacrifice:
Let these accords which notes distinguist frame,
Serue for memoriall to sweet Leightons name,
In whose sad death *Musicks* delight now dies.

John Bartlet

A Booke of Ayres

1606

[Within a border: McK. & F. No. 232 (see Textual Introduction to Gr1604)] A/ BOOKE/ OF AYRES/ VVith a Triplicitie of/ Mᴠsɪᴄᴋᴇ,/ *WHEREOF THE FIRST* [*RRTTI* and *E* in *THE* swash]/ Part is for the Lute or Orphanion,/ *and the Viole de Gambo, and 4. Partes* [*VP* swash]/ to ſing, The ſecond part is for 2. Trebles to ſing/ *to the Lute and Viole, the third part is for*/ the Lute and one Voyce, and the/ Viole de Gambo./ Compoſde by Iᴏʜɴ Bᴀʀᴛʟᴇᴛ/ Gentleman and praƈtitioner in this Arte./ [ornament]/ Lᴏɴᴅᴏɴ/ Printed by Iᴏʜɴ VVɪɴᴅᴇᴛ, for *Iohn Browne* and [*B* swash]/ are to bee ſolde at his ſhoppe in Saint *Dun-*/ ſtones Churchyeard in Fleet ſtreet./ 1606./

Collation: 2°: A–M²; 24 leaves.

Headlines: A2v–M1v, verso: I. [–XXI.] CANTO [H2v–K1v: PRIMVS CANTO] B1–H2, recto: I [–XIIII. Periods after VI, VIII–X, XII, XIIII] TENOR/ I. [–XIIII. II. repeated in error for III.] BASSO/ I [–XIIII. Periods after VI–XIIII.] ALTO/ I1–K2, recto: XV [–XVIII. Periods after XVI–XVIII.] SECVNDVS CANTO [I2: CANT] L1, M2, recto: XIX. [XXI.] BASSO L2, recto: XX. CANTO M1, recto: CANTO XX./ BASSO

Contents: A1, title page; A1v blank; A2, dedication; A2v–L1, songs I–XIX, one per opening; L1v–M1, song XX ("The 2. part"); M1v–M2, song XXI ("The third part"); M2v, table of songs.

SR: Entered on March 29, 1606 by John Browne as "A Booke of Ayres with A triplicitie of musicke . . . to singe to or as you please . . . by John Hartlet [*sic*] gent." (Arber III, 317.)

STC: 1539.

Copies: BM (K. 8. h. 3, the text copy), and Huntington (13567). In the Huntington copy, some lines of songs II, VIII, and X have been trimmed off the bottom of the page in the process of binding.

Sig. I was entirely reset, but since both formes were involved, it was probably not because of pieing. Perhaps some other accident ruined enough of the perfected sheets to make resetting necessary. The changes are mostly in spelling and punctuation, and not all are corrections. The second state seems to be represented by the Huntington copy, the reading to the left of the bracket.

Outer forme I: I1 (No. XV)
    CANT] CANTO
    (XV.5) flight, in rage] flight in rage,
I2v (XVII.1) part]=.
    XVII]=.
    2 hart,]=
    3 stay, stay, stay, stay,] stay stay stay stay
      mee] me
    5 see me] seeme
    8 a prety thing] *placed under the tablature in BM*
Inner forme I: I1v (XVI)
    XVI]=.
    4 cō]=–
    10 compell:]=,
    12 still]=,
I2 (XVI)
    Iz] I2
    2 Power] power
    4 be] bee
Songs I–XIIII have the usual CATB arrangement with lute tablature under C. Songs XV–XVIII have a Primus Canto with tablature facing a Secundus Canto with a bass viol part. Songs XIX–XXI have a Cantus with lute and a Basso (with words).

To the right honorable his singular
good Lord and Maister Sir Edward Seymoore.
Knight, Baron Beacham, Earle of Hartfoord, and Lieftenant
of his Maiesties Counties of Somerset and Wiltes.

It is a question hardly to be determined (my most honorable Lord) whether Musicke may esteeme her selfe more graced by the singular skil & exquisite knowledge wherwith your Lordship is indued, both in the speculation and practise thereof: or by the many benefites, and infinite fauours your Honourable bountie hath conferred on the professors of that faculty: in both are the muses greatly honoured, and we   10 (their seruants) highly blest; whose vertuous endeuours and studious labours, not in this onely, but in many other kindes of Learning, haue receiued their life; growth, and perfection, chereshed and enabled by the warmth your beames haue cast vpon them. Amongst many, that on the Muses behalfe doe owe your Lordshippe the tribute of their pennes, I must profes my self to stand deepliest engaged in the debt of dutie, in that the poornes of my merit holds least proportion with the largenes of your grace, and that my vtmost desert can reach no further, then humbly to acknowledge, that what delight or sweetenes soeuer these my simple trauels may bring to such generous and well composed spirits as beare affection to this quality, was inspired me by no other power then the influence of your fauour. And though the error of conceite cannot make me so far ouervalew them, as to esteem them worthy your Lordships iudicious hearing, yet I will confesse their want of worth (wherewith my selfe as an impartial censurer, haue already iustly taxte them) could not diuert my purpose from publishing to the world the zeale I beare to thankefulnesse: wherin I am ambitious of nothing but your Lordshippes fauourable acceptance and protection, which if it may please you to vouchsafe to this first birth of my Muse, I shall then be as farre from fearing detraction and censure, as I am free from affecting glory and prayse.

Your Lordships most humble deuoted seruant,
IOHN BARTLET.

I.

O Lord thy faithfulnes and prayse
I will with viole sing
my harpe shal sound thy laud and prayse
O Israels holy King:
my mouth wil ioy with pleasant voyce   5
when I shall sing to thee,
and eke my soule will much reioyce,
for thou hast made me free.

[Psalm 71]

II.

IF euer haples woman had a cause
to breath her plaintes into the open ayre,
and neuer suffer inward griefe to pause
or seeke her sorrow shaken soules repayre

then I for I haue lost my onelie brother   5
whose like this age can scarsly yeeld another.

2 Come therefore mournefull Muses and lament,
Forsake all wanton pleasing motions,
Bedew your cheekes, stil shal my teares be spent:
Yet still increast with inundations,   10
For I must weepe, since I haue lost my brother.
Whose like, &c.

3 The cruell hand of murther cloyde with bloud,
Lewdly depriude him of his mortall life:
Woe the death attended blades that stoode,   15
In opposition gainst him in the strife,
Wherein he fell, and where I lost a brother,
Whose like &c.

4 Then vnto griefe let me a Temple make,
And mourning dayly, enter sorrowes portes,
Knocke on my breast, sweete brother for thy sake,
Nature and loue will both be my consorts,
And helpe me aye to wayle my onely brother,
Whose like this age can scarsely yeeld another.

III.

WHen from my loue I lookte for loue and kind affections due,
to wel I found her vowes to proue most faithles and vntrue
for when I did aske her why
most sharpely she did reply
that shee with mee did neere agree   5
to loue but iestingly.

Marke but the subtle policies that female louers finde,
Who loues to fixe their constancies, like fethers in the wind
Though they sweare, vow and protest,
That they loue you chiefly best,   10
Yet by and by theyle all denie,
And say twas but in iest.

IIII.

WHO doth behold my mistres face
and seeth not good hap hath he
who hears her speake & marks her grace
shal think none euer spake but she
In short for to resound her praise   5
she is the fayrest of her dayes.

2 Who knowes her wit and not admires:
shal show himselfe deuoide of skil,
Her vertues kindle strange desires,
In those that thinke vpon her stil.   10
In short &c.

3 Her red is like vnto the rose,
When from a bud vnto the sunne,
Her tender leaues she doth disclose,
The first degree of ripenes wonne,   15
In short, &c.

4 And with her red mixt is a white,
Like to that same of faire moone shine,
That doth vpon the water light,
And makes the colour seeme deuine.   20
In short &c.

V.

IF there bee any one whome loue hath wounded
& of the hurt is neere his death,
If there bee any one in grief confounded
& stil with sighes doth fetch his breath,
such is my case let him com sit with me & mourn   5
whome griefe doth gripe and Cupid blind doth ouerturne.

2 If there be any one which hath beene racked,
And ioynt from ioynt is al to torne,
If there be any one these pangs haue smacked,
And in his heart with loue doth burne,   10
Such is my case, come let him sit with me and mourne,
For I am rackte and scorcht with loue & left forlorne.

3 If there be any one in shippe oppressed,
   at pinch of wracke to drowned be:
   If there be any one with waues betossed,   15
   Or blinded that he cannot see,
   Such is my case, let him come sit with me and mourne,
   Whom shipwracke spoiles & eyes put out, as louers scorn.

4 If there be any one that fraude hath perplext,
   Or burst his heart at loues commaund,   20
   If there be any one, whome al greefes haue vext,
   Or in hels paines do dayly stand,
   Such is my case, let him com sit with me and mourne,
   That feeles hels paine and louers griefe with loues greate scorn.

VI.

I heard of late that loue was falne asleepe
to late alas I finde it was not so
me thoght I saw the little villain weepe,
but theefe he laughs at them that waile in woe,
I dreamt his bow was brok & he was slain   5
but loe awakte I see all whole againe.

His blinking eyes will euer be awake,
His idle head is ful of laughing toyes,
His bow and shafts are tickle thinges to take,
It is no medling with such apish boyes,   10
For they shal finde that in his fetters fall,
Loue is a deadly thing to deale withal.

Yet where the wretch doth take a happy vaine,
It is the kindest worme that euer was,
But let him catch a coy conceite againe,   15
In frantike fits, he doth a fury passe,
So that in sum who hopes of happy ioy,
Take heede of loue, it is a perlous boy.

VII

Al my wits hath will inwrapped,
all my sence desire intrapped.

Al my faith to fancy fixed,
all my ioyes to loue a mixed.
All my loue I offer thee,   5
once for all yet looke on me.

2 Let me see thy heauenly feature,
Oh heauens what a heauenly Creature,
All the powers of heauen preserue thee,
Loue himselfe is sworne to serue thee,   10
Princesse in a Goddes place,
Blessed be that Angels face.

3 Looke how loue thy seruant dyeth,
Harke how hope for comfort crieth,
Take some pitty on poore fancy,   15
Let not fancie proue a franzie;
Comfort this poore hart of mine,
Loue and I and all are thine.

VIII

Goe wailing verse the issue of thy sire
begot on sighes which vent from my torne heart,
tel thou thy parents neuer quenchd desire,
tel of his griefes & of his endles smart,
 tel of his passions and his sad laments   5
 how stil he sues hard she yet neere relents.

2 Deepe sobs the silent Orators of loue,
Sad sighes the muttering ecchoes of my pain,
Heart renting groanes the agent which would moue,
Compassion with that cheeke bedewed raine.   10
 Raine which doth trickle from my watrie eyes,
 Hoping at length sheele heare my doleful cries.

3 But Oh would that sweete faire had been the butte
For Cupid to haue aymde at with his shaftes,
Then had not these my pations boulted out,   15
Blasing my follies vnto wise mens hates,
 Then could not I disciphering my harmes,
 Sought to haue gaind that faire with my rude charms.

4 But why wish I to Cupid so much good,
  When he hath broke his shafts and siluer bow,   20
  And finds a flame inkindled in my bloud,
  Which neither ise can quench nor mountain snow
    And sure no maruaile if he conquere men,
    when gods so faire a saint, haue neuer seene.

5 Her eyes like globes contain a thousand orbs,   25
  Her ruby lips her perled teeth in number,
  with that sweet tong such harmony affordes,
  As with applause makes all the world to wonder
    To wonder at her onely and no other,
    Since Cupid did mistake her for his mother.   30

IX.

A prety ducke there was that said,
to whome shall I make mone
I haue beene long a pretie maid
and yet I lie alone.

Alone I lie in deepe dispaire,   5
Which kils my louely heart,
For none wil my sweete ioyes repaire,
Or play a louers part.

A tickling part that maidens loue,
But I can neuer get,   10
Yet long haue sought, and stil do craue,
At rest my hart to set.

X.

Of all the birds that I doe know
Philip my sparrow hath no peer,
for sit she high or sit shee lowe,
be she far off or bee she neere
there is no birde so fayre so fine   5
nor yet so fresh as this of mine,
for when she once hath felt a fitte,
Philip will crie still yet yet yet yet,
yet yet yet yet yet yet yet yet yet yet.

2 Come in a morning merily,   10
   When Philip hath beene latelie fed,
   Or in an Euening soberlie,
   When Philip list to go to bed,
   It is a heauen to heare my Phippe,
   How she can chirpe with merry lippe,   15
   For when

3 She neuer wanders far abroad,
   But is at home when I do call,
   If I commaund she laies on loade,
   With lips, with teeth, with tong and all,   20
   She chaunts, she cherpes, she makes such cheare,
   That I beleeue she hath no peere.
   For when

4 And yet besides all this good sport,
   My Philip can both sing and daunce,   25
   with new found toyes of sundrie sort,
   My Philip can both pricke and praunce.
   And if you say but fend cut phippe,
   Lord how the peate wil turne and skippe,
   For when   30

5 And to tel truth he were to blame,
   Hauing so fine a bird as she,
   To make him all this goodly game,
   Without suspect or ielousie,
   He were a churle, and knew no good,   35
   Would see her faint for lacke of food.
   For when

                              [George Gascoigne]

                              XI.

   THe Queen of Paphos Ericine
   in hart did rose checkte Adone loue
   he mortal was but she deuine,
   and oft with kisses did him moue
   with great giftes stil she did him woo,   5
   but he would neuer yeeld thereto.

2 Then since the Queene of loue by loue,
   To loue was once a subiect made,
   And could thereof no pleasure proue,
   By day by night, by light or shade,   10
   Why being mortall should I grieue,
   Since she her selfe could not relieue.

3 She was a Goddesse heauenly,
   And loude a faire facde earthly boy,
   Who did contemne her deity,   15
   And would not grant her hope of ioy,
   For loue doth gouerne by a fate,
   That heare plants will, and their leaues hate.

4 But I a haples mortall wight,
   To an immortall beautie sue,   20
   No maruaile then she loaths my sight,
   Since Adone Venus would not woo,
   Hence groning sighes, mirth be my friend
   Before my life, my loue shall end.

XII.

I would thou wert not fayre or I were wise,
I wold thou hadst no face or I no eyes,
I would thou wert not wise or I not fond,
or thou not free or I not so in bond.

2 But thou art fayre and I cannot be wise.   5
   Thy sun-like face hath blinded both mine eyes,
   Thou canst not but be wise, nor I but fond,
   Nor thou but free, nor I but still in bond.

3 Yet am I wise to thinke that thou art faire,
   Mine eyes their purenes in thy face repaire,   10
   Nor am I fond that do thy wisedome see,
   Nor yet in bond because that thou art free.

4 Then in thy beauty onely make me wise,
   And in thy face, the grace, guide both mine eyes,
   And in thy wisedom onely see me fond,   15
   And in thy freedome keepe me still in bond,

5 So shalt thou still be faire, and I be wise,
  Thy face shines still vpon my clered eyes,
  Thy wisedome onely see how I am fond,
  Thy fredome onely keepe me still in bond.   20

6 So would I thou were faire, and I were wise,
  So would I thou hadst thy face, and I mine eyes,
  So would I thou wert wise, and I were fond,
  And thou wert free and I were still in bond.
                                      [Nicholas Breton]

XIII.

VNto a flie tranceformd from humain kind
me thought I ranged on a sunshine day,
when for to ease my sadde afflicted mind
vpon my mistres robe I gan to play
at length I mounted vppe her dainetie breast   5
from whence I soght my solace and my rest.

2 Yet not content with these aspiring toyes
  Changing my seate into her curled heyre,
  By seeking to encrease my new found ioyes,
  I turnde my sweete applause to sudden feares,   10
  For chauncing on her eyes of flame and fire,
  I burnt my winges whereby I did aspire.

3 Thus falling to the ground in my decay,
  With mourneful bussings crauing her reliefe,
  Me thought she moude with ruth my heauy lay,   15
  And crusht me with her foot to end my griefe,
  And said lo where the silly wretch doth lie,
  Whose end was such because he flue so hie.

XIIII

WHat thing is loue, I pray thee tel,
it is a prickle it is a sting,
it is a prety prety thing,

it is a fire it is a coale
whose flame creeps in at euery hole,   5
and as my wits can best deuise,
loues darling lies in Ladies eyes.
                    [George Peele]

XV.

Fortune loue & time hath made me happy
happy I was by Fortune loue & time,
my hap at highest the gods began to vary
and threw me down that causde me first to clime,
they proude their wings and tooke their flight in rage,   5
fortune to fooles, loue to youth, time to age.

XVI.

Poets to loue such power ascribes
as no power else can circumscribe,
true loue by true desire refinde
can neuer be by bowns confinde.

2 It first did kindle in mine eye,   5
  And thence stole inward presently,
  Possest my breast, my heart and soule,
  And doth my better parts controll.

3 The more I seeke it to expell,
  The more it doth my thoughts compell: 10
  Since then it hath such power within,
  To let it burne still were a sinne.

XVII.

The first part.

WHether runeth my sweet hart,
stay and take me with thee,
merily Ile play my part,
stay, and thou shalt see me,   5
O haue I ketcht thee,
hay ding a ding a ding
this ketching is a pretty thing.

XVIII.

The second part.

Tʌrrie are you gone againe
what no longer liking,
I wil ketch thee once againe
stay while I am rising,   5
do you tarry then
prety little one I thought
I shold please thee ere we did part.

XIX.

The first part.

Svrchargd with discontent
to Siluanes boure I went
to ease my heuy grief oppressed hart,
and trie what comfort winged creatures   5
coulde yeelde vnto my inwarde troubled smarte
by modulating their delightfull mesurs,
mesurs delightful to my eares pleasing euer,
of straines so sweet sweete birdes depriue vs neuer.

XX.

The 2. part.

Tʜe thrush did pipe ful cleare,
and eke with very mery chere
the Lenit lifted vppe her pleasant voice,
the Goldfinch chirpid & the Pie did chatter,   5
the black bird whistled and bedde mee reioyce,
the stock doue mormerd with a solemne flat,
the little daw ka ka ka ka he cride,
the hic-quaile he beside
tickled his part, in a partie coloured coate,   10
The Iay did blow his howboy gallantly
the wren did treble many a pretty note,
the woodpecker did hammer melowdie.

the kite tiw whiw ful ofte
cride soring vp aloft   15
and downe againe returned presently,
to whom the heralde of Cornutoes all sung coockoo
euer whilst poor Margery cride who who
did ring nights larum bell,
withall all did do wel   20
O might I heare them euer
of straines so sweet sweete birds depriue vs neuer.

XXI.

The third part.

Then Hesperus on high
brought cloudy night in skie,
when loe the thicket keeping company
of fethered singers left their madrigal   5
sonets and elegies, and presently
shut them within their mossie seuerals,
and I came home and vowde to loue them euer,
of straines so sweet sweet birdes depriue vs neuer.

FINIS.

The Table of all the Songes contained in this Booke.

Songes with two Trebles.

Fortune loue and time, hath made me happy,		XV
Poets to Loue such power ascribes		XVI
Whether runneth my sweet hart,	The first part	XVII
Tarry tarry are you gone againe,	The second part	XVIII

Songs for the Lute, Viole de Gambo and Voyce.

Sur-chargde with discontent,	The first part	XIX
The Thrush did pipe full cleare,	The 2. part	XX
Then Hesperus on hie brought	The third part.	XXI

John Coprario

Funeral Teares

1606

[Within a border: McK. & F. No. 232 (see Textual Introduction to Gr1604)] FVNERAL/ *TEARES.* [*TERE* swash]/ For the death of the Right Hono-/ rable the Earle of Deuonſhire. [*D* swash]/ FIGVRED/ In ſeauen ſonges, whereof ſixe are ſo ſet/ *forth that the wordes may be expreſt by a/* treble voice alone to the Lute and Baſe Viole, or elſe/ *that the meane part may bee added, if any ſhall/ affect more fulneſſe of parts.*/ THE SEAVENTH/ *Is made in forme of a Dialogue,* [*D* swash] *and can/* not be ſung without two voyces./ Inuented by IOHN COPRARIO. *Pius piè.*/ [device: McK. No. 282]/ *AT LONDON* [*ATD* swash]/ Printed by *Iohn VVindet* the Aſſigne of *William Barley,* for/ *Iohn Browne,* [*B* swash] and are to be ſold at his ſhop in S. Dunſtons/ *Churchyeard in Fleet ſtreet.* 1606./

Collation: 2°: A–E²; 10 leaves.

Catchword: A2v–B1 *But*

Headlines: Bv–E1, verso: CANTO I. [–VII.] recto: ALTO I. [–VII.]/ BASSO. I. [–VII.]

Contents: A1, title page; A1v, "Vno Sol Mountioie," etc.; A2, "To the Ayre"; A2v, "In honorable memory," etc., ll. 1–47; B1, ll. 48–87; B1v–E2, songs I–VII, one per opening; E2v, "Tis true," etc., table of songs, and "Quid mortuous," etc.

SR: No entry.

STC: 5679.

Copies: BM (K. 2. g. 7, the text copy); Folger; Huntington (13574); and another copy (not seen), bound with the Campion-Coprario *Songs of Mourning* (1613), is in the possession of H. P. Kraus of New York.

Collation reveals two minor press corrections:

Outer forme B: uncorrected, Huntington

B1 (l. 75 of "In honorable memory") mortalitie] mortaliie

Outer forme D: uncorrected, Huntington
 D2v (VI. 11) harte] hatte
 As the title-page indicates, the songs have two voice parts, a Canto with lute tablature facing an Alto and bass-viol part. The text is based on metrical versions of the poems printed on the same openings as the musical settings.

Vno Sol Mountioie tuus contentus ocello est,
Cuncta tamen cernit, nihil est oculatius illo.
Omnia qui vt videat magnus quae continet orbis,
Cernere te potuit toto nil pulchrius orbe.

Iam tuus ah periit pulcher Sol, dulcis ocellus   5
 Penelope, periit nec tamen ille tibi.
Qui Mortalis inexplendo te amplexus amore est,
 Quid ni Coelestis te quoque factus amet?

To the Ayre

 Ev'n to thy sweetnesse pure benigne, kind Ayre
That first embrac't these teares, these I present.
 Know them, though now transform'd from Christall faire
Th'appeare to thee in Musicall ornament: 5
 Free passage to melodious pearcing sounds
Thine open bosome yeelds: greefe owes to thee
 Her groanes, and sighes: through thy swift-healed wounds
Her shrikes are shot, and thine her clamours be.
 Receiue then chearefull Ayre these sad laments,   10
Though thou art but one Element, and she
 That owes them, of all foure the quintessence,
The Starre of honor, and the sphere of beautie.
 Goe, heare her sing these farewels, thou wilt weepe,
 And mouelesse euer in thy regions sleepe.   15

 Sing Lady, sing thy Deu'nshires funerals,
And charme the Ayre with thy delightfull voyce,
 Let lighter spirits grace their Madrigals,
Sorrow doth in the saddest notes reioyce.
 Fairest of Ladies since these Songs are thine,   20
 Now make them as thou art thy selfe, deuine.

The deuoted seruant of
true noblenesse.

Iohn Coprario.

In honorable memory of the Right
noble the Earle of Deuonshire
late deceased.

Noe sooner had the Fates pale Minister
  At th' high commaund of sterne Necessitie   5
Seazd the terrestriall part of Deuonshire,
  And rendred his free Soule t' Eternitie:
But loe th' imperfect broode of fruitfull Fame
  (That swarming thicke as atomes buze in th' ayre)
Light winged Rumours in right of their Dame   10
  Claimed great Mountioyes name, with swift repaire
Heauing it vp to Fames high Consistorie,
  Where she with doome impartiall register
All names t' Eternall fame, or infamie,
  And in her finall iudgement neuer errs.   15
You sacred seede of Mnemosine pardon me
  If in this suddaine rapture I reueale
Mist'ries which only rauisht sprights can see,
  And enuious time did till this houre conceale.
In Christal chaire when starre-like shining Fame   20
  Her state had plac't, strait with confused noyse
The thronging miscreates brought in Deu'nshires name,
  Some figuring lamentations, others ioyes:
Some wept, some sobd, some howld, some laught, some smild,
  And as their passions strange, and different were,   25
So were their shapes, such heapes were neuer pil'd
  Of Monstrous heades as now consorted here.
For some like Apes peere out, like foxes some,
  Many like Asses, Wolfes, and Oxen seem'd,
Like hissing Serpents, and fell Hydras some,   30
  Rhinoceroes some by their arm'd snowtes I deem'd,
Others like Crocodiles hang their slie heads downe:
  But infinite of humane forme appeare
Whose simple lookes were voide of smile or frowne,
  Yet somewhat sad they shewd like skies vncleare: 35
In this confusion the great Registresse
  Commaunding silence seu'rallie gaue leaue
To all reportes, and with milde sobernesse
  Both partiall, and impartiall did receiue.

First as accusers spake the busie Ape,   40
  The enuious bould Wolfe, and the spitefull snake,
And diuers in the braying Asses shape,
  But all their malice did one period make.
Deu'nshire did loue, loue was his errour made,
  That only gainst his vertues was oppos'd,   45
As if for that his honoured name should fade,
  Whose brest both vertue, and true loue enclos'd.
But now rise high my spright, while I vnfould
  What th' humane speakers in defence replyed:
To latter ages let this tale be told   50
  Which is by fame for euer verified.
Did Montioy loue? and did not Hercules
  Feele beauties flame, and couch him vnderneath
The winges of Cupid? or did ere the lesse
  His sacred browes deserue a victours wreath?   55
Did not he free the trembling world from feare,
  And dire confusion? who else could subdue
Monsters that innocents did spoyle, and teare,
  Or Saturnes auncient goulden peace renue?
Did Mountioy loue? and did not Mountioyes sword   60
  When he marcht arm'd with pallace dreadfull helme
The rough vnquiet Irish rebels curbe?
  And the inuading Spaniard ouerwhelme?
Lou'd he? and did not he nathlesse assist
  Great Brittaines counsils, and in secret cells   65
The Muses visite? and alone vntwist
  The riddles of deepe Philosophick spels?
Did Deu'nshire loue? and lou'd not Deu'nshire so
  As if all beautie had for him beene fram'd?
For beautie more adorn'd no age shall know   70
  Then hers whom he his owne for euer nam'd.
Let then base enuie breake, fond rumour sleepe,
  Blacke malice turne to doue-white charitie,
Let Deu'nshire triumph, and his honor keepe
  Immune, and cleare from darke mortalitie.   75
This spoken, Fame charg'd Zepherus to sound
  His goulden trumpet, after whose smooth blast
These words she made from earth to heau'n rebound,
  Braue Mountioyes glory shall for euer last.

Then forth was brought a boss't booke destined 80
  For Kings, and Heroes, where with liquid gould
Deceased Deu'nshires name she registred
  In charmed letters that can nere grow old.

Omnia vincit Amor, & nos cedamus Amori,
  Scripsit; cuius erant nescia scripta mori. 85
Annuit huic fortis Mountioius, victus Amori
  Cessit; cuius erunt nescia facta mori.

I.

Oft thou hast with greedy eare,
Drunke my notes and wordes of pleasure;
In affections equall measure,
  Now my songs of sorrow heare.
  Since from thee my griefes doe grow 5
  Whome aliue I pris'd so deare:
  The more my ioy, the more my woe.

2 Musicke though it sweetens paine
Yet no whit empaires lamenting:
But in passions like consenting 10
  Makes them constant that complaine:
  And enchantes their fancies so,
  That all comforts they disdaine,
  And flie from ioy to dwell with woe.

II.

O sweete flower too quicklie fading,
  Like a Winter sunshine day:
Poore pilgrim tir'd in the midway,
  Like the Earth it selfe halfe shading.
    So thy picture shewes to mee, 5
    But onely the one halfe of thee.

2 O deare Ioy too swiftly flying
  From thy loues enchanted eyes:
Proud glorie spread through the vast skies,
  Earth of more then earth enuying. 10
    O how wondrous hadst thou been,
    Had but the world thy whole life seene.

III.

O th'unsure hopes of men! the brittle state!
The vaine contentions that vnluckilie,
Oft in midst of the race fall ruinate,
And in their course long ouerwhelmed be,
And swallow'd vp ere they the port could see.   5

2 O womens fruitlesse loue! vnquiet state!
Too deare affections, that despightfully,
Ev'n in their height of blisse proue desolate!
And often fall farre from all hope of ioy.
Ere thy haue time to dreame on their annoy.   10

IIII.

In darknesse let me dwell, the ground shall sorrow be,
The roofe despaire to barre all chearefull light from me,
The walles of marble black that moistned stil shall weepe,
My musicke hellish iarring sounds to banish frendly sleepe.
  Thus wedded to my woes, and bedded in my tombe,   5
  O let me dying liue till death doth come.

My dainties griefe shall be, and teares my poisned wine,
My sighes the aire, throgh which my panting hart shall pine:
My robes my mind shall sute exceeding blackest night,
My study shall be tragicke thoughtes sad fancy to delight.   10
  Pale Ghosts and frightful shades shal my acquaintance be:
  O thus my haples ioy I haste to thee.

V.

My ioy is dead, and cannot be reuiu'de,
Fled is my ioy, and neuer may returne:
Both of my ioy, and of my selfe depriu'de
Far from all ioy I sing, and singing mourne.
  O let no tender hart, or gentle eare   5
  Partake my passions, or my plainings heare.

2 Rude flintie breastes that neuer felt remorse,
Hard craggy rocks that death and ruine loue,
Those onely those my passions shall enforce,
Beyond their kind, and to compassion moue.   10
  My griefe shall wonders worke, for he did so
  That causde my sorrowes, and these teares doth owe.

VI.

Deceitfull fancy why deludst thou me,
  The dead aliue presenting?
My ioyes faire image caru'd in shades I see,
  O false! yet sweet contenting?
    Why art not thou a substance like to mee?   5
    Or I a shade to vanish hence with thee?

2 Stay gentle obiect, my sence still deceiue,
  With this thy kind elusion:
I die throgh madnes if my thoughts you leaue
  O strange? yet sweet confusion?   10
    Poore blisselesse harte that feeles such deepe annoy,
    Only to loose the shadowe of thy ioy.

VII.

A Dialogue.

Canto. Foe of mankind why murderest thou my loue?
Alto.   Forebeare he liues.
C.   Oh where?
A.   In heauen aboue.   5
C.   Poore wretched life that onely liues in name.
A.   Man is not flesh, but soule, all life is fame:
C.   That is true fame which liuing men enioy.
A.   That is true life, which death cannot destroy.
Chorus. Liue euer through thy merited renowne,   10
          Faire spirit shining in thy starry crowne.

  Tis true, that whom the Italian ★Spider stinges ★Tarantula
He sings, or laughs, or daunces till he dies,
  Or spends his short time in such idle things
As the seuerer sort call vanities:

Musicke alone this fury can release,   5
This venomous rancour that the flesh doth eate
 Like enuie which in death doth seldome cease
To feede vpon the honours of the great.
 Well haue we toyld in prosperous harmonie
If we the enuy-poysned wounds doe cure   10
 Of spitefull adder-toongd hypocrisie
That speakes washt wordes, but works darke deeds impure.
 If such proue past recure, suffice it then
 We song not to brute beasts, but humane men.

A Table of the Songs contained in
this Booke.

Quid mortuos mordes canis? nihil retro
Cernis, neque vides manticae quod in tergo est.

The dead why bit'st thou dogge? th'art backward blinde,
And doest not see the bagge thou bear'st behind.

John Danyel

Songs for the Lute Viol and Voice

1606

[Within a compartment: McK. & F. No. 132 (see Textual Introduction to D01600), with printer's ornament in upper oval slot] SONGS/ FOR THE LVTE VIOL/ and Voice:/ Compoſed by I. Danyel,/ *Batchelar in Muſicke.* [*B* swash]/ 1606./ To Mᵣⁱˢ *Anne Grene.* [*AG* swash]/ [ornament]/ [in lower slot:] LONDON/ Printed by T. E. for Thomas Adams,/ At the ſigne [*sic*] of the white Lyon, in Paules Church-yard./

Collation: 2°; *A–L²*; 22 leaves.

Headlines: Verso, *A*2v–I1v: I. [–XVII.] CANTO. [O broken on G2v] I2v–L1v: XIX. [XX.] CANTO Primo. On B1v, C2v, and I1v, also: II. [V., XVII.] BASSO. [XX. TENORE. on K1v and K2v]
Recto, B1–L1: I. [–XX.] BASSO. On B2, C1, D1, and I2, also: III. [IIII., VI., XVIII.] CANTO. On K1, also: XIX. ALTO. / XIX. CANTO Secundo. On K2 and L1, also: XX. CANTO Secundo.

*Contents: A*1, title page; *A*1v blank; *A*2, dedication; *A*2v–B1, song I; B1v–B2, songs II and III, one per page; B2v–C2, song IIII; C2v–D1, songs V and VI, one per page; D1v–I1, songs VII–XVI, one per opening; I1v–I2, songs XVII and XVIII, one per page; I2v–K1, song XIX; K1v–L1, song XX; L1v–L2v, No. XXI, "Mrs *Anne Grene* her leaues bee greene," for lute; L2v, table.

SR: Entered April 9, 1606, by Thomas Adams (Arber, III, 319). "T.E.," the printer, is Thomas East (or Este).

STC: 6268.

Copies: BM (K.2.g.9, the text copy), Folger, and Huntington (34971; lacks sig. G, restored in facsimile from the BM copy).

There are two minor press-corrections:
Outer forme B: uncorrected, BM, Huntington: B1 (I.3) mute;]=,

Outer forme D: uncorrected, BM, Huntington: D2v (VIII.3) shee] sche
   The music for songs I–XVIII is for voice, lute, and viol; song XIX has parts for a
Canto Secundo, Alto, and Basso facing the Canto Primo and lute; song XX has a
Canto Primo with one lute and tenor voice facing a Canto Secundo with a bass lute
and bass voice. In addition to the words under the music, all the songs except XX have
complete metrical versions of the poems printed separately on the same opening; the
text is based on these.

To Mrs Anne Grene
the worthy Daughter to
Sir *William Grene* of Milton
Knight.

Tʜat which was onely priuately compos'd,
For your delight, Faire Ornament of Worth,
Is here, come, to bee publikely disclos'd:
And to an vniuersall view put forth.
Which hauing beene but yours and mine before,
(Or but of few besides) is made hereby   10
To bee the worlds: and yours and mine no more.
So that in this sort giuing it to you,
I giue it from you, and therein doe wrong,
To make that, which in priuate was your due:
Thus to the world in common to belong.
And thereby may debase the estimate,
Of what perhaps did beare some price before:
For oft we see how things of slender rate,
Being vndiuulg'd, are choisely held in store:
And rarer compositions once expos'd,   20
Are (as vnworthy of the world) condemn'd:
For what, but by their hauing beene disclos'd
To all, hath made all misteries contemn'd.
   And therefore why had it not beene ynow,
That Milton onely heard our melodie?
Where *Baucis* and *Philoemon* onely show,
To Gods and men their hospitalitie:
And thereunto a ioyfull eare afford,
In mid'st of their well welcom'd company:
Where wee (as Birds doe to themselues record)   30
Might entertaine our priuate harmonie.

But fearing least that time might haue beguild
You of your owne, and me of what was mine,
I did desire to haue it knowne my Child:
And for his right, to others I resigne
Though I might haue beene warn'd by him, who is
Both neare and deare to mee, that what we giue
Vnto these times, we giue t'vnthankfulnesse,
And so without vnconstant censures, liue.
  But yet these humours will no warning take,   40
    Wee still must blame the fortune that wee make.
And yet herein wee doe aduenture now,
But Ayre for Ayre, no danger can accrew,
They are but our refusalls wee bestow,
And wee thus cast the old t'haue roome for new:
Which I must still addresse t'your learned hand,
Who mee and all I am, shall still command.

Iohn Danyel.

I.

Coy *Daphne* fled from *Phaebus* hot pursuite,
Carelesse of Passion, sencelesse of Remorse:
Whil'st hee complain'd his griefes shee rested mute,
He beg'd her stay, shee still kept on her course.
  But what reward shee had for this you see,   5
  She rests transform'd a winter beaten tree.

The Answere.

Chast *Daphne* fled from *Phaebus* hot pursuit,
Knowing mens passions Idle and of course:
And though he plain'd twas fit shee should be mute,   10
And honour would shee should keepe on her course.
  For which faire deede her Glory still wee see,
  Shee rests still *Greene*, and so wish I to bee.

II.

Thou prety Bird how doe I see,
Thy silly state and mine agree:
For thou a prisoner art,
  So is my hart.

Thou sing'st to her and so doe I addresse,   5
My Musicke to her eare that's mercilesse:
But heerein doth the difference lie,
That thou art grac'd so am not I,
Thou singing liu'st, and I must singing die.
                         [after G. B. Guarini]

III.

He whose desires are still abroad I see,
Hath neuer any peace at home the while:
And therefore now come back my hart to mee,
It is but for superfluous things we toile.
  Rest alone with thy selfe be all within,   5
For what without thou get'st thou dost not win.
Honour, wealth, glory, fame, are no such things,
But that which from Imagination springs.
  High reaching power that seemes to ouer grow,
  Doth creepe but on the earth, lies base and low.   10

IIII.

  Like as the Lute delights or else dislikes,
As is his art that playes vpon the same:
So sounds my Muse according as shee strikes
On my hart strings, high tun'd vnto her fame.
  Her touch doth cause the warble of the sound,   5
Which here I yeeld in lamentable wise:
A wayling descant on the sweetest ground,
Whose due reports giues honour to her eyes.
  If any pleasing relish here I vse,
Then Iudge the world her beautie giues the same: 10
Else harsh my stile vntunable my Muse,
Hoarse sounds the voice that praiseth not her name.
  For no ground else could make the Musicke such,
  Nor other hand could giue so sweet a touch.
                         [Samuel Daniel]

V.

Dost thou withdraw thy grace,
For that I should not loue:
And think'st thou to remoue,
M'affections with thy face?

As if that loue did hould no part,   5
But where thy beautie lies:
And were not in my hart,
Greater then in thy faire eyes?

Ah yes tis more, more is desire,
There where it wounds and pines: 10
As fire is farre more fire,
Where it burnes then where it shines?

VI.

Why canst thou not as others doe?
Looke on mee with vnwounding eyes:
And yet looke sweet but yet not so,
Smile but not in killing wise.
  Arme not thy graces to confound,   5
  Onely looke but doe not wound.

Why should mine eyes see more in you,
Then they can see in all the rest:
For I can others beauties view,
And not finde my hart opprest.   10
  O bee as others are to mee,
  Or let mee, bee more to thee.

VII.

Stay Cruell stay,
Pittie myne anguish,
And if I languish
For that which you do beare away,
Ah, how can you be so vnkind,   5
As not to greeue for that you leaue behind,
And if you'l goe, yet let your pittie stay,
But will you goe and shew that you neglect mee?
Yet say farewell, and seeme but to respect mee.

VIII.

Tyme cruell tyme canst thou subdue that brow,
That conquers all but thee, and thee too stayes:
As if shee were exempt from scyeth or bow,
From Loue and yeares vnsubiect to decayes.
  Or art thou growne in league with those faire eyes,   5
That they might help thee to consume our dayes,
Or dost thou loue her for her cruelties,
Being mercilesse lyke thee that no man wayes?
  Then doe so still although shee makes no steeme,
Of dayes nor yeares, but lets them run in vaine: 10
Hould still thy swift wing'd hours that wondring seeme
To gase on her, euen to turne back againe.
  And doe so still although she nothing cares,
Doe as I doe, loue her although vnkinde,
Hould still, yet O I feare at vnawares,   15
Thou wilt beguile her though thou seem'st so kinde.
[Samuel Daniel]

IX.

Mrs. M. E. her Funerall teares for the death of her husband.
The first part.

Gʀeefe keep within and scorne to shew but teares,
Since Ioy can weepe as well as thou:
Disdaine to sigh for so can slender cares,   5
  Which but from Idle causes grow.
Doe not looke forth vnlesse thou didst know how
To looke with thine owne face, and as thou art,
And onely let my hart,
That knowes more reason why,   10
Pyne, fret, consume, swell, burst and dye.

X.

The second part.

Dʀop not myne eyes nor Trickle downe so fast,
For so you could doe oft before,
In our sad farewells and sweet meetings past,
And shall his death now haue no more?   5

Can niggard sorrow yeld no other store:
To shew the plentie of afflictions smart,
Then onely thou poore hart,
That knowst more reason why,
Pyne, Fret, Consume, Swell, Burst and Dye.   10

XI.

The third part.

Haue all our passions certaine proper vents,
And sorow none that is her owne?
But she must borow others complements,
To make her inward feelings knowne?   5
Are Ioyes delights and deathes compassion showne,
With one lyke face and one lamenting part?
Then onely thou poore hart that know'st more reason why,
Pine, Fret, Consume, Swell, Burst, and Dye.

XII.

Let not *Cloris* think because
She hath invassaild mee,
That her bewtie can giue lawes,
To others that are free.
  I was made to be the pray,   5
And bootie of her eyes:
In my bosome she may say,
Her greatest kingdome lyes.

  Though others may her brow adore,
Yet more must I that therein see far more,   10
Then any others eyes haue powre to see,
Shee is to mee
More then to any others she can bee.
  I can decerne more secret notes,
That in the margine of her cheekes Loue quotes: 15
Then any else besides haue art to read,
No lookes proceed,
From those fayre eyes but to mee wonder breed.

O then why,
Should shee fly,   20
From him to whom her sight,
Doth ad so much aboue her might:
Why should not shee,
Still Ioy to raigne in mee?

XIII.

The first part.

Can dolefull Notes to measur'd accents set,
Expresse vnmeasur'd griefes that tyme forget?

XIIII.

The second part.

No, let Chromatique Tunes harsh without ground,
Be sullayne Musique for a Tunelesse hart:
Chromatique Tunes most lyke my passions sound,
As if combynd to beare their falling part.   5

XV.

The third part.

Vncertaine certaine turnes, of thoughts forecast,
Bring backe the same, then dye and dying last.

XVI.

Eyes looke no more, for what hath all the earth that's worth
                                                   the sight?
Eares heare no more, for what can breath the voyce of true
                                                   Delight?
Cloath thee my hart, with darke black thoughts, and think
                                                   but of dispaire,
Silence lock vp my words, and scorne these Idle sounds of Ayre.

Thinke Glory, Honour, Ioyes, Delights, Contents,   5
Are but the emptie reports
Of vnappropried termes that breath inuents,
Not knowing what it imports.
  But Sorrow, Griefe, Affliction, and Dispaire,
These are the things that are sure,   10
And these wee feele not as conceyts in th'ayre,
But as the same wee endure.

  Ioyes, delights, and pleasures in vs hould such a doubtfull part,
As if they were but thrall,
And those were all in all,   15
For Griefes, Distrusts, Remorce, I see must domineere the hart.
  Ioyes, Delights, and Pleasures, makes griefe to tiranize vs worse,
Our mirth brings but distastes:
For nought delights and lastes,
Griefe then take all my hart, for where none striue there needs
                                        lesse force. 20

XVII.

If I could shut the gate against my thoughts,
And keepe out sorrow from this roome with-in:
Or memory could cancell all the notes,
Of my misdeeds and I vnthink my sinne,
  How free, how cleare, how cleane my soule should lye,   5
  Discharg'd of such a lothsome company.

Or were there other roomes with-out my hart,
That dyd not to my conscience ioyne so neare,
Where I might lodge the thoughts of sin a-part,
That I might not their claim'rous crying heare.   10
  What peace, what Ioy, what ease should I possesse,
  Free'd from their horrors that my soule oppresse.

But O my Sauiour, who my refuge art,
Let thy deare mercies stand twixt them and mee:
And be the wall to seperate my hart,   15
So that I may at length repose mee free:
  That peace, and Ioy, and rest may be within,
  And I remaine deuided from my sinne.

XVIII.

I Dye when as I doe not see
Her that is lyfe and all to mee:
And when I see her yet I dye,
In seeing of her crueltie:
  So that to mee like miserie is wrought,   5
  Both when I see and when I see her not.

Or shall I speake or silent greeue,
Yet who will silencie releeue:
And if I speake I may offend,
And speaking not, my hart will rend: 10
  So that I see to mee it is all one,
  Speake I or speake I not, I am vndone.
                    [after G. B. Guarini]

XIX.

Wнat delight can they enioy,
Whose harts are not their owne?
But are gon abroade astray,
And to others bosomes flowne.
Seely comforts, seely Ioy,   5
Which fall and ryse as others moue,
Who seldome vse to turne our way,
And therefore *Cloris* will not loue:
For well I see,
How false men bee,   10
And let them pyne that Louers proue.

XX.

Now the earth, the skies, the Aire,
All things faire,
Seemes new borne thoughts t'infuse,
Whil'st the returning spring,
Ioyes each thing,   5
And blasted hopes renewes.

When onely I alone,
Left no mone,
Finde no times borne for mee,
No flowres, no Medow springs,   10
No Bird sings,
But notes of miserie.

XXI.

Mʳˢ *Anne Grene* her leaues bee greene.
        [Solo for lute]

THE TABLE.

Coy *Daphne* fled:		I.
Thou pretie Bird:		II.
Hee whose desires:		III.
Lyke as the Lute:		IIII.
Stay cruell stay:		V.
Dost thou withdraw:		VI.
Why canst thou not:		VII.
Tyme cruell tyme:		VIII.
Griefe keepe within:	First part.	IX.
Drop not mine Eies:	Second part.	X.
Haue all our passions:	Third part.	XI.
Let not *Cloris* think:		XII.
Can dolefull notes:	First part.	XIII.
No, let Chromatique tunes:	Second part.	XIIII.
Vncertaine certaine turnes:	Third part.	XV.
Eies looke no more:		XVI.
If I could shut the gate:		XVII.
I dye when as I doe not see:		XVIII.
What delight can they enioy:		XIX.
Now the Earth, the Skies, the Ayre:		XX.
Mrs *Anne Grene* her leaues bee greene.		XXI.

FINIS.

Thomas Ford

Musicke of Sundrie Kindes

1607

[Within a compartment: McK. & F. No. 232—see Textual Introduction to Gr1604] MVSICKE/ OF/ SVNDRIE/ *KINDES*, [*KNDE* swash]/ Set forth in two Bookes./ *THE FIRST WHEREOF ARE*, [*TE* in *THE*, *RT* in *FIRST*, the first *E* and *R* in *WHEREOF*, and *R* in *ARE* swash]/ *Aries* [sic] *for 4. Voices to the Lute, Orphorion,*/ or Baffe=Viol, with a Dialogue for two/ Voices, and two Baffe Viols in parts,/ tunde the Lute way·/ *THE SECOND ARE* [*TE*, *ECND*, and *A* swash]/ *Pauens, Galiards, Almaines, Toies,* [*P, A, T* swash]/ *Iigges, Thumpes* and fuch like, for two/ Baffe-Viols, the Liera way, fo made as the/ *greateft number may ferue to play alone, very*/ eafie to be performde./ Compofed by THOMAS FORD./ [ornament]/ Imprinted at London by IOHN WINDET at the Affignes/ of WILLIAM BARLEY and are to be fold by IOHN BROVVNE/ in Saint Dunftons churchyard in Fleetftreet 1607,/

Collation: 2°; A–M²; 24 leaves.
Headlines: Part I: Verso, A2v–F1v: CANTVS I. [–X.] [period after CANTVS on B1v–F1v] Recto, B1–F2: TENOR. I. [–X.] [No periods on B2, CDE1, F2]/ BASSVS. I. [–X.] [No period after BASSVS on CDE2, F1]/ ALTVS. I [–X.] [Period after number on B2, CDE1, F2]
Part II: Verso, G2v–M1v: PRIMA PARS. I. [–XVI.] Recto, H1–M2: SECVNDA PARS I. [–XVI.] [No period after II, IIII, V, VII, VIII] M2v: PRIMA PARS. XVII. SECVNDA PARS. XVII. [Numbers III, VI, IX, XI, XIII, XV, XVIII are not on the headline since they are on the same opening as the number preceding.]
Contents: A1, title page; A1v, table of songs; A2, dedication to Sir Richard Weston; A2v–G1, songs I–XI, one per opening; G1v, table of pieces for viols; G2, dedication to Sir Richard Tichborne; G2v–M2v, duets for lyra viols as follows: G2v–H1, "M.

Southcotes Pauen"; H1v–H2, "The Galiard" and "An Almaine" ("M. Westouers farewell"); H2v–I1, "A Pauin" ("M. Mayes Choice"); I1v–I2, "The Galiard" and "Forget me not"; I2v–K1, "A Pauen" ("Sir Richard Westons delight"); K1v–K2, "An Almaine" ("Mounsieur Lullere his choice") and "The wild goose chase" ("Sir Iohn Philpots delight"); K2v–L1, "What you will" and "And if you do touch ile crie" ("Sir Richard Tichbornes toy"); L1v–L2, "The Baggepipes" ("Sir Charles Howards delight") and "Why not here"("M. Crosse his choice"); L2v–M1, "Change of Ayre" and "Whipit and Tripit" ("M. Southcotes Iig"); M1v–M2, "Cate of Bardie" ("The Queenes Iig"); M2v, "A Snatch and away" ("Sir Iohn Paulets toy") and "A Pill to purge Melancholie" ("M. Richard Martins Thumpe").

SR: Entered by John Browne on March 11, 1606/7, with this note: "Yt is agreed 13 *marcij Anno supradicto,* that this copye shall neuer hereafter be printed agayne without the consent of master fford the Aucthour [signed] John Browne" (Arber III, 344).

STC: 11166.

Copies: BM (K.9.a.19, the text copy), Glasgow (R.x.5), Folger, and Harvard (Mus. 680.5.45F*). I have seen all these, but have not collated the Glasgow copy fully.

There appears to be only one press correction, probably a letter pulled out in printing. Outer forme C: C2v (V.4): encreasing] increasing *Harvard.*

The music for songs I–X is arranged in the usual manner: Cantus and lute facing the Tenor, Bassus, and Altus. Song XI has one voice with tablature for lyra viol facing a second voice with a second lyra viol part.

A Table of the Songs contained
in this booke.

1 Not full twelue yeares
2 What then is loue
3 Vnto the temple.
4 Now I see thy lookes were fained.
5 Goe passions.
6 Come phillis.
7 Faire, sweet, cruell.
8 Since first I saw your face.
9 There is a Ladie.
10 How shall I then.
11 A Dialogue.

When you sing alone to the Basse, such notes as are broken
   or deuided by reason of the words, must be sung or
      plaide in one stroke according to this Direction
[Here follow a half-note bracketed with two eighth notes, and a whole note, all on bass G.]

TO THE WORTHIE
and vertuuos Knight,
SIR Richard Weston.

Sir albeit musicke may iustly chalenge an interest in the best parte of my education, I could be content for manie reasons to conceale my defects from the censure of sharper iudgementes, but the perswasion of some priuate friendes, together with the general good of such as take delight therein, hath encouragde me to vndergoe this hazard, which stands vpon the tickle point of liking, being in nothing more variable then in musicke: I shall not neede to make an Apologie in defence of these musickes, since none are so much in request nor more generally receiued then of these kindes, which with all hartie affection I offer to your fauorable iudgement not as a worke whose merit or worth deserues so iudicious a patron, but a manifestation of my worthlesse affection bound vnto you by many particular fauours: nor dare I vpon mine owne iudgement make expectation great with fair promises, yet thus much I dare presume, you shal find variety, and sith some of them hath beene gracd with your speciall fauour and liking, I doubt not they may also giue contentment to those that seekes delight, more then fautes, to whose kind acceptance vnder your worthie protection, I commend these first fruites of my studies.

Your Worships humbly deuoted
Thomas Forde.

I.

Not full twelue yeeres twice tolde A wearie breath
I haue exchangde for A wished death,
my course was short the longer is my rest,
God takes them soonest whom he loueth best
for he thats borne to day and dies to morrow   5
loseth some dayes of mirth but months of sorrow.
Why feare we deth that cures our sicknesses
Author of rest and ende of all distresses.
O there misfortunes often come to grieue vs
deth strikes but once and that stroke doth relieue vs.   10
[Henry Morrice]

II.

WHAT then is loue sings Coridon
since Phillida is growne so coy.
A flattring glasse to gaze vppon
a busie iest A serious toy.
A flowre stil budding neuer blown,   5
A scantie dearth in fullest store
yeelding least fruite where most is sowne,
  my dalie note shal be therefore
  heigh ho heigh ho chill loue no more.

Tis like a morning dewie rose   10
Spread fairely to the suns arise,
But when his beames he doth disclose,
That which then flourisht quickly dies,
It is a selfe fed dying hope
A promisde blisse, a saluelesse sore,   15
An aimelesse marke, an erring scope,
  My dailie note shall be therefore,
       Heigh ho, &c,

Tis like a Lampe shining to all,
Whilst in it selfe it doth decay,   20
It seemes to free, whome it doth thrall,
And leades our pathles thoughts astray,
It is the spring of wintred harts,
Parcht by the summers heate before,
Faint hope to kindly warmth conuerts,   25
  My daily note shall be therefore
       Heigh ho.

III.

VNTO the temple of thy beauty
  & to the tombe where pittie lies
I pilgrime clad with zeale & deuty
  do offer vppe my hart mine eyes,
my hart loe in the quenchlesse fire   5
  on loues burning alter lies
conducted thither by desire
  to be beauties sacrifice.

But pity on thy sable herse,
  mine eyes the teares of sorrow shed   10
What though teares cannot fate reuerse,
  Yet are they duties to the dead,
O mistresse in thy sanctuarie,
  why wouldst thou suffer cold disdaine,
To vse his frozen crueltie,   15
  and gentle pitty to be slaine.

Pittie that to thy beautie fled,
  and with thy beautie should haue liu'de,
Ah in thy hart lies buried,
  and neuer more may be reuiu'de,   20
Yet this last fauour deare extend,
    to accept these vowes, these teares I shed
Duties which I thy pilgrime send,
  to beauty liuing pitty dead.

IIII.

Now I see thy lookes were fained
quickly lost and quickly gained
soft thy skin like wooll of wethers
hart vnconstant light as feathers,
tongue vntrusty subtle sighted   5
wanton will with change delighted,
  Syren pleasant foe to reason,
  Cupid plague thee for thy treason.

Of thine eye I made my mirror,
From thy beauty came my error,   10
All thy words I counted witty,
All thy sighes I deemed pitty,
Thy false teares that me agreeued,
First of all my trust deceaued,
         Syren,   15

Fain'de acceptance when I asked,
Louely words with cunning masked,
Holy vowes but hart vnholy,
Wretched man my trust was folly,

Lilly white, and prety winking,   20
Sollemne vowes, but sorrie thinking,
        Syren.

Now I see O seemely cruell,
Others warme them at my fuell,
Wit shall guide me in this durance   25
Since in loue is no assurance,
Change thy pasture, take thy pleasure,
Beauty is a fading treasure.
        Syren.

Prime youth lasts not age will follow,   30
And make white those tresses yellow,
Wrinckled face for lookes delightfull,
Shall acquaint the dame despitefull,
And when time shall date thy glorie
Then to late thou wilt be sorry,   35
        Syren.
           [Thomas Lodge]

V.

Goe passions to the cruell faire,
pleade my sorrowes neuer ceasing,
Tell her those smiles are emptie ayre
growing hopes but not encreasing,
  hasting wasting with swift pace,   5
  date of ioy in dull disgrace.

Vrge her (but gently I request)
With breach of faith and wracke of vowes,
Say that my griefe, and minds vnrest,
Liues in the shadow of her browes,   10
  plying, flying, there to die,
  In sad woe and miserie.

Importune pittie at the last
(pittie in those eyes should houer,)
Recount my sighes and torments past,   15
As Annals of a constant louer
  Spending, ending many dayes,
  Of blasted hopes and slacke delayes.

VI.

Come Phillis come into these bowers,
here shelter is from sharpest showers,
Coole gales of winds breaths in these shades,
daunger none this place enuades,
  here sit and note the chirping birdes,   5
  pleading my loue in silent wordes.

Come Phillis, come bright heauens eye,
Cannot vpon thy beautie prie,
Glad Eccho in distinguisht voyce,
Naming thee will here reioyce,   10
  Then come and heare her merry layes
  Crowning thy name with lasting prayse.

VII.

Faire, sweet cruell, why doest thou flie mee,
go not, goe not, oh goe not from thy deerest,
though thou doest hasten I am nie thee,
when thou seem'st farre then am I neerest,
  Tarrie then Tarrie then Oh tarrie,   5
  Oh tarrie then and take me with you.

Fie, fie, sweetest here is no danger,
Flie not, flie not, oh flie not loue pursues thee,
I am no foe, nor forraine stranger,
Thy scornes with fresher hope renewes me,   10
        Tarrie then, &c.

VIII.

Since first I saw your face I resolude to honour & renowne yee,
If now I be disdayned I wishe my hart had neuer knowne yee,
What I that lou'de and you that likte shal wee beginne to
                           wrangle,
No, No, no, my hart is fast and cannot disentangle.

If I admire or prayse you too much, that fault you may forgiue
mee, 5
Or if my hands had stray'd but a touch, then iustly might you
leaue me,
I askt you leaue, you bad me loue, ist now a time to chide me?
No, no, no, ile loue you still, what fortune ere betide me.

The Sunne whose beames most glorious are, reiecteth no
beholder,
And your sweet beautie past compare, made my poore eyes the
boulder, 10
Where beautie moues, and wit delights, and signes of kindnes
bind me
There, O there where ere I go, ile leaue my hart behinde me.

IX.

THere is a Ladie sweet & kind,
was neuer face so pleasde my mind,
I did but see her passing by,
and yet I loue her till I die.

Her iesture, motion and her smiles,   5
Her wit, her voyce, my hart beguiles,
Beguiles my hart, I know not why,
And yet I loue her till I die.

Her free behauiour winning lookes,
Will make a Lawyer burne his bookes   10
I toucht her not, alas not I,
And yet I loue her till I die.

Had I her fast betwixt mine armes,
Iudge you that thinke such sports were harmes,
Wert any harm? no, no, fie, fie,   15
For I will loue her till I die.

Should I remaine confined there,
So long as Phebus in his spher,
I to request shee to denie,
Yet would I loue her till I die.   20

Cupid is winged and doth range,
Her countrie so my loue doth change,
But change she earth, or change she skie,
Yet will I loue her till I die.

X.

How shall I then discribe my loue, when all mens skilfull arte
is Far inferior to her worth, to prayse th'unworthiest parte,
shee's chaste in looks mild in her speech in actions all discreet,
of nature louing pleasing most in vertue all compleate,

And for her voyce a Philome, her lip may all lips skorne,   5
No sunne more cleare then is her eye, in brightest Summer

morne

A mind wherein all vertues rest, and takes delight to be
And where all vertues graft themselues in that most fruitfull

tree.

A tree that India doth not yeeld, nor euer yet was seene,
Where buds of vertue alwaies springes, and all the yeere growes

greene, 10

That countries blest wherein she growes, and happie is that

rocke,

From whence she springes, but happiest he that grafts in such a

stocke.

XI.

A Dialogue

[Altus]   Shut not sweet brest to see me all of fire,
[Cantus] Flie not deer hart to find me all of snow,
[A]   Thy snow inflames these flames of my desire,
[C]   and I desire desires sweet flames to know.   5
[A]   Thy snow ni'll hurt me
[C]   Nor thy fire will harm me
[A]   This cold wil coole me
[C]   and this heate will warm me,
[A]   Take this chast fire to that pure virgin snow.   10
[C]   being now thus warmd ile neuer seeke other fire.

[A]   Thou giust more blisse than mortall harts may know,
[C]   more blisse I take then Angels can desire.
 Chorus Let one griefe harme vs
            and one ioy fill vs,   15
            let one loue warm vs
            & one death kill vs.

                                        [Francis Davison]

                    A Table of the Lessons
                    contained in this booke.

 1 A Pauen.
 2 The Galliard.
 3 An Almaine.
 4 A Pauen.
 5 The Galliard.
 6 Forget me not.
 7 A Pauen.
 8 An Almaine.
 9 The wild goose chase.
10 What you will
11 And if you do touch me Ile crie.
12 The Bag-pipes.
13 Why not here.
14 Chang of Aire
15 Whip it and Trip it.
16 Cate of Bardie
17 A snatch and away.
18 A pill to purge Malancholie.

                    TO THE WORTHY
                  and vertuous knight Sir
                  RICHARD TICHBORNE

   Sir hauing so contriued these Musickes as their seuerall natures
requires a diuision I could not amongst manie friendes thinke vpon two
more worthy to bee ioynde in this Dedication then your selues, aswell
for your neere alliance in blood, loue and fauour to Musicke, which
neuer goes vnaccompanied with other vertues, as also the many

particular fauours I haue receiued from you both, hauing no gratifica-
tion or token of my loue and thankefulnes, but these issues of my   I
braine, which I intreate you to accept & take in good part, my cheifest
labor in setting them forth hath bin to expresse my inuention with as
much facility and ease as possibly I could to the end (since it is a Musicke
so generally pleasing) they who best affect it, may with little labour be
actors of their owne delightes. If you find in them any matter of worth
I haue my rewarde, if any matter of content I haue my end, which is
nothing else then by some agreeable testimony, to leaue in you both,
an impression of my thankefull remembrance of your loue and fauors.

Your Worships humbly deuoted
THO. FORDE.

Tobias Hume

Captaine Humes Poeticall Musicke

1607

[Within a compartment: McK. & F. No. 232 (see the Textual Introduction to Gr1604)] CAPTAINE/ HVMES/ Poeticall Muſicke./ *Principally made for two Baſſe-Viols,* [*PBV* swash]/ yet ſo contriued, that it may be plaied 8. ſeuerall/ *waies vpon ſundry Inſtruments with/ mnch* [sic] *facilitie.*/ 1 The firſt way or muſicke is for one Baſſ-Viole to play alone in parts, which/ ſtandeth alwaies on the right ſide of this Booke./ 2 The ſecond muſicke is for two Baſſe-Viols to play together./ 3 The third muſicke, for three Baſſe-Viols to play together./ 4 The fourth muſicke, for two Tenor Viols and a Baſſe-Viole./ 5 The fift muſicke, for two Lutes and a Baſſe-Viole./ 6 The ſixt muſicke, for two Orpherions and a Baſſe-Viole./ 7 The ſeuenth muſicke, to vſe the voyce to ſome of theſe muſicks, but eſpe-/ cially to the three Baſse-Viols, or to the two Orpherions with one/ Baſſe-Viole to play the ground./ 8 The eight and laſt muſicke, is conſorting all theſe Inſtruments together/ with the Virginals, or rather with a winde Inſtrument and the voice/ Compoſed by *Tobias Hume* Gentleman./ [ornament]/ LONDON/ Printed by Iohn VVindet. [limb of first *V* filed]/ 1607./

Collation: 2°; A–N² (A1, G1 not signed); 26 leaves.

Headlines: Running titles: B1, F2v, G2v, H1: Captaine Humes Poeticall Musicke. [Inverted on B1 without a period or *si* ligature; with period but without ligature on F2v; F2v inverted has Poetical Musicke with ligature, but without period; G2v has Poeticall Musickc. [sic] with ligature and period.] Verso, B1v–F1v, H1v–M2v: Captaine Humes Recto, B2–F2, H2–N1: Poeticall Musicke. [No period or *si* ligature on C2, E1, F2; Poetical Musicke—one *l*, no period, but with ligature on I2, L1, M1, and N1.]

SR: No entry.

STC: 13957.

Copies: BM (K.2.g.11, the text copy; this was the presentation copy to Queen Anne); Folger (Part II only; lacking before G1); Glasgow (R.x.35); and Manchester Public Library (RF 410 Hx16; G1–N2 bound before A1–F2). Only two of the surviving copies are alike, as will be seen from the contents.

Contents: A1, title page; A1v blank (table of songs in Manchester copy only); A2, dedication to Queen Anne; A2v–B1, "The Queenes New-yeeres gift"; B1v–F2, the following instrumental pieces, one per opening: "The King of Denmarkes delight"; "A Mery Conceit" ("The Q. delight"); "My hope is reuiued" ("The Lady of Suffolkes delight") and in the same opening, "My ioyes are comming" ("The Lady of Bedfords delight"); "Musicke and Mirth" ("The Lady Hatton's delight"); "The Earle of Mountgomeries delight"; "Start" ("The Lady of Sussex delight"); "An Almaine" ("The Lady Caues delight") and in the same opening, "The Dukes Almaine" ("The Duke of Halstones delight"); "A Maske" ("The Duke of Lenox delight"); and F2v, "An Almaine" ("M. S. Georges delight").

Part II begins with G1, which is blank in BM and Glasgow, but has the same title page as A1 in Folger and Manchester. G1v has "Alwaies thus to the Reader" (in Manchester, a head ornament is omitted, and a "Table of the Songs . . . in this Second Booke" is added after the epistle). G2 is blank in BM and Glasgow, has a dedication to the Earl of Arundel in Folger, and a dedication to the Lords and Sir Christopher Hatton in Manchester. G2v–N1 have the following pieces, one per opening: "Graue Musickes for three Bass-Viols, with the Voice" (No. XIIII); "Sweete musicke"("The Earle of Salisburies delight"); "The state of Gambo" ("The Earle of Worcesters fauoret"); "The virgins muse" ("The Lady Arbellaes fauoret"); "Sweet ayre" ("The Earle of Arundels fauoret"); "Musickes delight" ("The Earle of Southamptons fauoret"); "The Earle of Pembrookes Galiard"; "A Spanish humor" ("The Lord Hayes fauoret"); "The Spirit of Gambo" ("The Lord Derrys fauoret"); "The pashion of Musicke" ("Sir Christopher Hattons choice"); "The King of Denmarks health"; and N1v–N2v, "The Hunting Song."

Other press-corrections, besides those variants described in the Contents, are as follows:

Outer forme A: uncorrected, BM, Glasgow: A2v (l.30) ioyes.] = :

Inner forme G: uncorrected, BM, Folger, Glasgow: G1v, "Alwaies thus to the Reader":

> *dost*] *doest*
> Carpere] Capere

Also head ornament omitted, table added. See variant dedication on G2.

Several of these pieces are versions of pieces first printed in Hu1605; for example, "The Earle of Pembrookes Galiard" is No. 2 in 1605, "The Spirit of Gambo" is No. 4b in 1605, and "The Dukes Almaine" is No. 99 in 1605. The musical arrangement of each song is described in the notes.

A transcription of Hu1607 by Sidney Beck was printed from the BM copy by the New York Public Library in 1934. The New York Public has lost its copy, and I have not been able to trace another. Mr. Beck informs me that it contains no editorial matter.

The table of the songs
contained in this first booke.

TO THE SACRED
MAIESTIE OF
QVEENE *ANNE.*

Thrice-Royall Princes,

Since to commend Musique were but to reach the Sunne a paire of spectacles; or to extol my own indeauors, would prooue but super-fluous gyldings, since I hope they shal instantly come to the touch of your quicke discouering iudgement. I will only presume in most deuoted zeale, to offer vp this last hope of my labours, to your most princely acceptance, humbly imploring, that it would please your thrice-royall spirit, not to esteeme my Songs vnmusicall, because my Fortune is out of tune; or to grant me little grace, because my deserts may be valued nothing: but be once pleasd (Right excellent Princes) as the onely and last refuge of my long expecting hopes, to patronize and second the modest ends of the Author of these vncommon Musiques, not for any thing he yet can claime of iust merit, but for what the ample gracings of the King & my excited affection to do your Maiesty seruice, may happily expect.

I cease to offend your delicate eare with my harsh style, and therefore kissing the ground that sustaineth your Sacred person. I euer rest

The humblest of your subiects,
TOBIAS HVME.

[I.]
A new Musicke made for the Queenes
most Excellent Maiestie, and my
New-yeeres Gift to her
HIGHNES.

Three Base Viols and the Voice, with the Meane Lute   5
to play the Ground if you please.

Cease leaden slumber dreaming,
my Genius presents
the cause of sweet musickes meaning,
now which breedes my soules content,   10
and bids my Muse awake, awake,
to heare sweete musickes note,
that cherefully glads me so cherefully:

Me thought as I lay sleeping
dreames did enchaunt me   15
with the prayse of musicke and her worth
and her eternisht fame,
but now I finde indeed
my leaden windowes open,
that cherefully comforts full cherefully.   20

Night gloomy vaile to the morn,
dreames affright, no more no more,
where sweet musicke is now still appearing,
leaue passions to perplexe,
for now my soule delights   25
in musicks harmony,
whose heauenly noyse,
glads soules with tongue and voice,
for now my soule delights in heauenly noyse
of musickes sweetest ioyes.   30

Alwaies thus to the Reader.

I Doe not studie Eloquence, or professe Musicke, although I doe loue Sence,
and affect Harmony. My Profession beeing, as my Education hath beene,
Armes, the onely effeminate part of mee, hath beene Musicke; which in me

hath beene alwaies Generous, because neuer Mercenarie. To praise Musicke, were to say, the Sunne is bright. To extoll my selfe, would name my labours vaine-glorious. Onely this, my studies are farre from seruile imitations, I rob no others inuentions, I take no Italian Note to an English Dittie, or filch fragments of Songs to stuffe out my volumes. These are mine owne Phansies expressed by my proper Genius, which if thou dost dislike, let me see thine, 10 Carpere vel noli nostra, vel ede tua, *Now to vse a modest shortnes, and a briefe expression of my selfe to all noble spirits, thus, My Title expresseth my bookes Contents, which (if my hopes faile me not) shall not deceiue their expectation, in whose approuement, the crowne of my labours resteth. And from henceforth, the statefull instrument* Gambo Violl, *shall with ease yield full various and deuicefull Musicke as any other instrument. For here I protest the Trinitie of Musicke, parts, Passion and Diuision, to be as gracefully vnited in the* Gambo Violl, *as in the most receiued Instrument that is, which here with a Souldiers Resolution, I giue vp to the acceptance of all noble dis-positions.* 20

The friend of his friend,
Tobias Hume.

Your Viols must be tuned as the Lute, beeing the best Set that euer was inuented, for these kind of Musickes, which may bee compared with the highest and curious musicke in the world.

The table of the Songes contained in this second booke

TO ALL WORTHY
AND RIGHT HONORABLE
Lordes, Louers of Musicke and fauourers of all liberall
Artes and Learning.

And to the truly noble knight of the high
Esteemed order of the BATH.
Sir CHRISTOPHER HATTON.

As great men haue many cares to hinder their delights, so haue they much choice of delights to sweeten their cares. Among which more elected and almost diuine pleasures, Humanity must needs giue Musicke a supreame worth: which euer allowed trueth giues mee heart to hope that your right noble spirits will esteeme it no il-fitting complement, to receiue these fewe musicall Essaies from him who euer deuotes his vtmost indeauors to the deseruing of your happy-making fauours, which I protest I persue not for any second ends, or euer shal desire to receiue more of then I might giue a iust account how I came by. I confesse I loue Benefits but feare to loose my liberty with them, since he that receiues greater rewards then his vertue may requite sels his freedome. I shall therfore in these onely protest my willingnes to doe your Lordships the readiest and choicest seruice my studies can affoord: which humblest tender, if it obtaine acceptance, my labours are happy, and my selfe in my largest hopes amply satisfied. Of which, I cannot dispaire, since I know Heroicke spirits are as farre from contempt as from basenesse.

The seruant of your noble vertues,
TOBIAS HVME.

TO THE RIGHT WOR
thely innobled, PHILIP Earle of
Arundel, &c.

As great men haue many cares to hinder their delights, so haue they much choice of delights to sweeten their cares. Among which more elected and almost diuine pleasures, Humanity must needes giue Musicke a supreame worth: which euer allowed trueth giues mee heart to hope that your right noble spirit will esteeme it no il-fitting complement, to receiue these fewe musicall Essaies from him who euer deuotes his vtmost indeauors to the deseruing of your happy-making fauour. I shall therefore in these onely protest my willingnes to doe your Honor the readiest and choicest seruice my studies can affoard: which humblest tender, if it may obtaine acceptance, my labours are happy, and my selfe in my largest hopes amply satisfied. Of which, I cannot dispaire, since I knowe Heroicke spirits are as farre from contempt as from basenesse.

The seruant of your noble vertues,
Tobias Hume.

[XIV.]

Graue Musickes for three Bass-Viols,
with the Voice.

WHat greater griefe then no reliefe in deepest woe,
death is no friend that will not end such harts sorrow,
helpe I do crie, no helpe is nie, but winde and aire,   5
which to and fro do tosse and blow all to dispaire,
  sith then dispaire I must yet may not die
  no man vnhapier liues on earth then I.

Tis I that feele the scornefull heele of dismall hate,
My gaine is lost, my losse cleere cost repentance late,   10
So I must mone bemonde of none, O bitter gal!
Death be my friend with speed to end and quiet all.
  But if thou linger in dispaire to leaue mee,
  Ile kill dispaire with hope, and so deceiue thee.

[XXV.]

The Hunting Song
to be sung to the Bass-Viol.

  [The call in the Morning.
  All these seuerall tunes must
  bee drawne together in one Bow.   5
  the Hounds do yorne
Come come my hearts a hunting let vs wende,
that echoing cries the hills and heauens may rend
with shoutes and soundes
of hornes and houndes.   10
    [Blow the vncoupling

Why then my lads vncouple, Kill Bucke, keene
Ringwood and Roler,
Chaunter and Ioler,
Trounser and Drummer,   15
Bowman and Gunner,
Acteons hounds were nere like these I weene.
          [Blow the seeke
          the hounds are now a hunting
The stagge is now rowzde the game is on foote,   20
          [The Hounds hunt still
Harke, harke, harke Beuty Dainty prates
          [the Hounds hunt
the crie is full
          [the hounds hunt   25
harke how they holde the crie
          [the hounds hunt
          The huntsman rates
but soft the Huntsman rates
          [the hunt fals   30
Clowder hunts Counter
and so doth Mounter
there all at fault
Harke Ringwood spends
and makes amends.   35
          [Play lowde for Ioler is in.
List of Ioler, a Ioler, a Ioler.
          [the crie is full
Thats he, thats he, ho, ho, ho,
          [the halow   40
          Al the standers by must halow twise
          the hornes
          the hunt still
Ioler crost it,
else we had lost it,   45
the Bucke is quite spent,
since to soile hee went.
Why heauenlier sport then this there cannot be.
          [hounds do hunt againe
See Plowman hath pincht,   50
and Ioler nere flincht,
now with full crie,
they all come trowling, trowling, trowling to the fall.

Winde the morte.
  [winde the death of the Buck with horns   55
  [the hounds do yorne
Oh well done there boyes,
all other sports to these are but toyes.

  Here endeth the hunting Song, which was sung before
    two Kings, to the admiring of all braue
        Huntsmen.

Alfonso Ferrabosco

Ayres

1609

[Within a compartment: McK. & F. No. 132 (see Textual Introduction to D01600); in upper oval slot, cut with musical instruments and the motto:] MVSICA LÆTIFICAT COR:. [In center space:] AYRES:/ BY/ *Alfonſo* [*A* swash] *Ferraboſco.*/ [ornament]/ LONDON:/ Printed by T. SNODHAM, for IOHN BROVVNE,/ and are to be ſould at his ſhoppe in S./ Dunſtones Church-yard/ in Fleetſtreet./ [in lower slot:] 1609./

Collation: 2°; A–I², K¹; 19 leaves.

Headlines: None; only song numbers.

Contents: A1, title page; A1v blank; A2, dedication; A2v, commendatory verses; B1–C1, songs I–V, one per page; C1v–C2, song VI; C2v–D1, songs VII and VIII; D1v–D2, song IX; D2v–H2, songs X–XXV, one per page; H2v–K1, songs XXVI–XXVIII, one per opening; K1v, table of songs.

SR: Entered by John Browne on February 1, 1608–9 (Arber, III, 401).

STC: 10827.

Copies: BM (K.8.h.2, the text copy); Folger (lacking after H2, replaced in facsimile); Huntington (59751); and the Newberry Library in Chicago (Case VM 1620 F36a; upper inside corners of I1, I2 repaired, pen facsimile; K1 lacking, replaced in facsimile). Collation reveals only one press correction: Outer forme K, uncorrected, Huntington: K1 (XXVIII.10) that] thar

All of Ferrabosco's songs except the dialogues (XXVI–XXVIII) have only one voice part with lute and bass viol accompaniment.

TO THE MOST EQVALL
TO HIS BIRTH, AND ABOVE
all Titles, but his owne Vertue:
Heroique *Prince Henry.*

Excellent Prince:

    THat which was wont to accompany all Sacrifices, is now become a
Sacrifice, *MVSIQVE*: And to a Composition so full of *Harmony* as
yours, what could bee a fitter Offring? The rather, since they are the
Offerers *first fruits*, and that he giues them with *pure hands.* J could, now,
with that solemne industry of many in *Epistles*, enforce all that hath   10
beene said in praise of the *Faculty*, and make that commend the worke,
but J desire more, the work should commend the *Faculty*: And therefore suffer these few *Ayres* to owe their Grace rather to your *Highnesse*
iudgement, then any others testimonie. J am not made of much speach.
Onely J know them worthy of my Name: And, therein, J tooke paynes
to make them worthy of Yours.

Your Highnesse
most humble Seruant
Alfonso Ferrabosco.

TO MY EXCELLENT FRIEND
ALFONSO FERRABOSCO.

To vrge, my lou'd *Alfonso*, that bold fame
  Of building Townes, and making wilde Beasts tame,
Which *Musique* had; or speake her knowne effects,   5
  That she remoueth cares, sadnesse eiects,
Declineth anger, perswades clemency,
  Doth sweeten mirth, and heighten pietie,
And is to'a body, often, ill inclinde
  No lesse a soueraigne cure, then to the minde;   10
To'alledge, that greatest men were not asham'd
  Of old, euen by her practise, to be fam'd;
To say, indeed, she were the *Soule* of *Heauen*,
  That the eight *Spheare*, no lesse then *Planets* seauen
Mou'd, by her order; And the ninth, more high,   15
  Including all, were thence call'd *Harmony*:

I, yet, had vtter'd nothing, on thy part,
  When these were but the praises of the *Art*.
But when I'haue saide, The proofes of all these be
  Shed in thy *Songs*; Tis true: But short of thee.   20
                                        Ben: Ionson.

TO THE WORTHY AVTHOR.

Mvsicks maister, and the offspring
  Of rich *Musicks* Father,
Old *Alfonso's* Image liuing,
  These faire flowers you gather   5
Scatter through the *Brittish* soile;
  Giue thy fame free wing,
And gaine the merit of thy toyle:
  Wee whose loues affect to praise thee,
  Beyond thine owne deserts, can neuer raise thee.   10
                          By *T. Campion*, Doctor
                                    in Physicke.

AMICISSIMO ET PRÆSTANTISSIMO IN RE
MVSICA, ALFONSO FERRABOSCO.

          Percellissimo oro, mitte animam meam
            O diue Syren, vinculaque auribus
              Iniecta soluas, nec potenti   5
                Perpetuò moriar camœná.
            Ardore rapta mens furit entheo,
            Scanditque Lunam, & circuit æthera,
              Ter millies cœlo repôsta,
              Et totiès relocata terris.   10
            O Musicœ artis quanta potentia,
Ferra-bosco *Non in ferarum sola vagum nemus,*
              Sed in virorum plus cateruas
                Participes melioris aurœ!
            Alfonse, dux & rex Lyrici gregis;   15
            Pulsare dignus cœlicolûm lyram,
              Excellis omnes sic canendo
                Sempèr vt ipse sies canendus.
                              N. Tomkins.

I.

Like Hermit poore, in place obscure,
I meane to spend my dayes of endlesse doubt,
To waile such woes as time cannot recure,
Where none but Loue shall finde mee out,
And at my gates dispaire shal linger still,   5
To let in death when Loue and Fortune will.
      [Sir Walter Raleigh? after Desportes]

II.

Come home my troubled thoughts, stay and retire,
Call home your erring fellowes make a stand,
Follow not still the coulours of desire,
False are her wishes cruel her command,
Come then obay this summons come away,   5
For here vaine hopes must serue you for your pay.

III

Come away, come away,
we grow ielous of your stay,
If you doe not stoppe your eare,
We shall haue more cause to feare,
Sirens of the land then they,   5
to doubt the Sirens of the Sea.
      [Ben Jonson]

IIII.

Deere when to thee my sad complaint I make,
And shew how oft Loue doth my death renue,
And how afresh I suffer for thy sake,
I euer feare this answere to insue,
  Who would bewaile the Bird that scapes the snare,   5
  And euer caught and neuer can beware?

But my reply is iust, that if the eye
That sees the danger, yet obayes the hart
That leades the sence, for his delight to dye,
In that this pray preferres the better part,   10
  The gayner should haue mercy to forgiue,
  If Beautie be a Tyrant who can liue?

V.

FAine I would but O I dare not,
Speake my thoughts at full to praise her,
Speake the best cryes Loue, and spare not,
Thy speech can no higher raise her,
Thy speach then thy thoughts are lower,   5
Yet thy thoughts doth not halfe know her.

VI.

Come my *Celia*, let vs proue,
while wee may the sweets of loue,
Time wil not be ours for euer,
he at length our good wil seuer,
Spend not then his gifts in vaine,   5
Sunnes that set may rise again,
But if we once loose this light,
tis with vs perpetuall night,
Why should wee deferre our ioyes,
fame and rumour are but toyes?   10
Cannot we delude the eyes
of a few poore houshold spyes,
Or his easier eares beguile,
Thus remoued by our wile.
T'is no sinne loues fruits to steale,   15
But the sweet theft to reueale,
To be taken, to be seene,
These haue crimes accounted beene.
                        [Ben Jonson]

VII.

So, so, leaue off, this last lamenting kisse,
which sucks two soules and vapours both away,
Turne thou ghost that way, And let me turne this,
and let our selues benight our happy day,
  we aske none leaue to loue, nor will we owe   5
  any so cheape a death as saying goe.

Goe, goe, and if that word haue not quite kild thee,
Ease me with death by bidding me goe to:
O, if it haue let my word worke on me,
And a iust office on a murderer doe.   10
  Except it be too late to kill me so,
  Being double dead, going and bidding goe.
                              [John Donne]

VIII.

Young and simple though I am, I haue heard of *Cupids* name,
Guesse I can what thing it is, Men desire when they doe kisse,
Smoake can neuer burne they say, But the flames that follow
                                        may.

2 I am not so foule or faire, to be proud or to dispaire,
Yet my lips haue oft obseru'd, men that kisse them presse them
                                        hard,   5
As glad louers vse to doe, when their new met loues they wooe.

3 Faith tis but a foolish minde, yet me thinkes a heat I finde,
Like thirst longing that doth bide euer one my weaker side,
Where they say my hart doth moue, *Venus* graunt it be not
                                        Loue.

4 If it be alas what then, were not Women made for Men?   10
As good tis a thing were past, that must needes bee done at last,
Roses that are ouer-blowne, grow lesse sweet then fall alone.

5 Yet nor Churle, nor silken Gull, shall my maiden blossome
                                        pull,
Who shall not I soone can tell, who shall would I could as well,
This I know who ere hee be, loue hee must or flatter mee.   15
                              [Thomas Campion]

IX.

Drowne not with teares my deerest Loue,
Those eyes which my affections moue,
Doe not with weeping those lights blinde,
Which me in thy subiection binde,
Time that hath made vs two of one,   5
And forst thee now to liue alone,

Will once againe vs revnite,
To shew how shee can Fortune spight,
Then will we our time redeeme,
And hould our howres in more esteeme,   10
Turning all our sweetest nights,
Into millions of delights,
And striue with many thousand kisses,
To multiply exchange of blisses.

X.

I Am a louer yet was neuer lou'd,
well haue I lou'd and wil though hated euer,
Troubles I passe yet neuer any mou'd,
sighs haue I giuen and yet she heard me neuer,
I would complaine, and she would neuer heare me,   5
and flie from loue, but it is euer neare me,
Obliuion onely blamelesse doth beset mee,
for that remembreth neuer to forget me.
              [Bartholomew Yong after Montemayor]

XI.

WHY stayes the bridegroome to inuade
her, that would be a matron made,
Good night whilst yet we may,
good night to you a virgin say,
To morrow rise, the same   5
your mother is, and vse a nobler name,
Speed well in hymens war,
that what you are,
by your perfections wee
and all may see.   10
                        [Ben Jonson]

XII.

First part.

SIng wee then heroyque grace,
So with louely light adorning,
that faire heauen of his face,
As the Starre that leads the morning,   5

body braue for part and whole,
purest seate of purer soule,
Where reposed lodge by nature,
Princely strength and comely stature.

XIII.

Second part.

Sing the riches of his skill,
Long by studious toyle prouided,
Wit that neuer guideth ill,
Will that neuer ill is guided,   5
Iudgement that can best discerne,
Memory that needs not learne,
Courage where such thoughts assemble,
Iustly may his haters tremble.

XIIII

Third part.

Sing the nobles of his race,
Sing his power, his wealth, his glory,
Breaking all the bounds of place,
endlesse ages, agelesse storry,   5
Peace that maketh one of two,
more then euer warre could doe,
Terror chased, Iustice fixed,
Mercy still with Iustice mixed.

XV.

With what new thoughts should I now entertaine
my minde, if I my sadnesse should forgoe,
What pleasing hopes haue I not proued vaine,
or what false shew of ioy doe I not know?
O partiall loue there is no power in thee,   5
to make her loue or else to set me free.

XVI.

Fly from the world O flye thou poore distrest,
where thy diseased soule infects thy soule,
And where thy thoughts doe multiply vnrest,
Tiring with wishes what they straight controule,
  O world, O world betrayer of the minde,   5
  O thoughts, O thoughts that guide vs being blinde.

2 Come therefore care, conduct me to my end,
And steere this shipwrackt carkasse to the graue:
My sighes a strange and stedfast winde shall lend,
Teares wet the sailes, Repentance from rocks saue.   10
  Haile death, haile death, the land I doe discry,
  Strike saile, goe soule, rest followes them that dye.

XVII.

Shall I seeke to ease my griefe?
No my sight is lost with eying,
Shall I speak and beg reliefe?
No my voyce is hoarse with crying,
  What remaines but onely dying?   5

2 Loue and I of late did part,
But the Boy my peace enuying,
Like a Parthian threw his dart,
Backward and did wound me flying.
  What remaines but onely dying?   10

3 She whom then I looked one,
My remembrance beautifying
Stayes with me, though I am gone,
Gone, and at her mercy lying.
  What remaynes, but onely dying?   15

4 Thus my vitall breath doth wast,
And my blood with sorrow drying,
Sighes and teares make life to last,
For a while his place supplying.
  What remaynes but onely dying?   20

XVIII.

First part.

If all these *Cupids* now were blinde,
as is their wanton brother,
Or play should put it in their mindes,
to shoot at one another,   5
What prety battaile they would make
if they their obiects should mistake,
and each one wound his mother.

XIX.

Second part.

It was no pollicie of court,
although the place be charmed,
To let in earnest or in sport,
so many loues in armed,   5
For say the dames should with their eyes
vpon the hearts here meane surprise,
Were not the men like harmed.

XX.

Third part.

Yes were the loues or false or straying,
or beautie not their beautie waying,
But here no such deceipt is mixt,
their flames are pure their eyes are fixt,   5
They doe not warre with diffrent darts,
but strike a musicke of like hearts.
                              [Ben Jonson]

XXI.

So beautie on the waters stood,
when Loue had seuer'd earth from floud,
So when hee parted ayre from fire,
hee did with concord all inspire,

And then a motion hee them taught,   5
that elder then himselfe was thought,
which thought was yet the childe of earth,
for loue is elder then his birth.

[Ben Jonson]

XXII.

HAd those that dwell in error foule
and hold that women haue no soule,
But seene those moue, they would haue then
said, women were the soules of men,
so they doe moue each heart and eye,   5
with the worlds soule their harmonie.

[Ben Jonson]

XXIII.

IF all the ages of the earth
were crown'd but in this famous birth,
and when that they would boast their store
of worthy Queenes they knew no more,
how happier is that age can giue,   5
a Queene in whom they all doe liue?

[Ben Jonson]

XXIIII.

VNconstant loue why should I make my moane,
or send sad sighes vnto thy carelesse eare?
Since thy affection and thy faith is gone,
and all those vertues which I once held deare,
Farewell, farewell, most false of all to mee,   5
that with affection deerely loued thee.

XXV.

O Eyes, O mortall starres,
the authors of my harmes,
that in slumbring wage wars,
to kill me with sweet charmes,
If closed you annoy me,   5
be'ng open you'ld destroy me.

[after G. B. Guarini]

XXVI.

A Dialogue betweene a Shepheard and a Nimph.

[Shepheard]	Fᴀyre cruell Nimph why thus in griefe & anguish,
	Mak'st thou him that adores thee pine and languish?
[Nimph]	Wʜy Shepheard dost thou mee condemne as cruell,
	Since thine owne fancies are thy passions fuell?
[S.]	O but these fancies from thy beautie flow,
[N.]	Then shall reliefe to thee from bountie grow,
[Both]	O how I ioy in thee my happy choise,
	As thou in me, so I in thee reioyce:
	Then let vs still together liue and loue,
	and sing the ioyes that happy louers proue.

5

10

XXVII.

A Dialogue.

[First voice]	Wʜᴀt shall I wish?
	what shall I flye?
[Second voice]	Tʀue Loue I seeke,
[1st]	False I defie,
[2nd]	Wordes haue their truth,
[1st]	Such euer speake,
[2nd]	Deeds haue their faith,
[1st]	Such neuer breake,
[Both]	Flattery yeelds pleasure,
[1st]	Onely truth yeelds waight,
[Both]	Happy are they that neuer knew deceit.

5

10

XXVIII.

A Dialogue betweene a Shepheard and a Nimph.

[Shepheard]	Tᴇll me O Loue, when shall it be
	that thy faire eyes shall shine on me?
	Whom nothing now reuiueth,
[Nimph]	I Pray thee Shepheard leaue thy feares,
	Drowne not thy heart and eyes with teares,
	Such sighes my sence depriueth,
[S.]	Alas sweet Nymph, I cannot chuse
	since thou estranged liues from me,

5

[N.]	O doe not me for that accuse,	10
	My Loue, my life doth liue in thee,	
[Both]	Alas, what ioy is in such loue	
[S.]	that euer liues apart?	
[N.]	and neuer other comforts proue,	
	but cares that kill the hart?	15
[S.]	O, let me die,	
[N.]	And so will I,	
[Both]	yet stay sweet Loue, and sing this song with me,	
	time brings to passe, what loue thinks could not be.	

FINIS.

A Table of all the Songs contained
in this Booke.

George Handford

Ayres

1609

The present text is based on the unique MS now at Trinity College, Cambridge, bearing the shelf-mark R.16.29. It was first published with a biographical note on Handford, and without the music, in my article in *Anglia*, LXXXII (1964), 474–484. That transcription is corrected here (with thanks to David Greer) and modified according to the editorial procedures described in the Introduction. Almost all the punctuation is editorial.

The MS originally consisted of 28 leaves in folio, one of which (the 21st) is now lacking. The text is in a neat italic hand, perhaps that of a professional scribe, but probably not Handford's. It is bound in vellum with gold tooling, and was to all appearances prepared for presentation to the dedicatee, Prince Henry, and not (as Warlock says, p. 125) for the press. The provenance of the MS seems to support this idea. Sir Henry Newton, afterwards Puckering (1618–1701) presented the MS to Trinity College, probably along with the large donation of books he made in 1691. In 1654, Newton had inherited the estates of his uncle, Sir Thomas Puckering, and had assumed his name. Sir Thomas had been a companion of Prince Henry between 1605 and 1610; therefore it seems that Handford presented his work to the Prince, who passed it on to Puckering, who in turn left it to Newton (*DNB*, s.v. "Newton, Sir Henry" and "Puckering, Sir John").

Title, fol. 2: Ayres/ To be ſunge to yᵉ Lute and Baſe Vyole,/ Newly com-poſed by George Handford. [Arms of Trinity College stamped below this.]

Contents: fol. 1 blank; fol. 2, title; fols. 2v–3 blank; fol. 3v, dedication; fol. 4 blank; fol. 4v, table of songs; fol. 5 blank; fols. 5v–25, songs 1–20 (fol. 21, song 17 lacking), one per opening; fols. 25v–28v blank.

The voice part and lute accompaniment begin on the verso of each leaf, and on the facing recto is the bass viol part (inverted), extra stanzas of text, and in some songs, voice and lute parts running over from the facing verso. Therefore the missing leaf contains the bass and possibly further stanzas of song 16 as well as the voice and lute for song 17; but the bass for song 17 survives on fol. 22.

To the high and mighty Prince, Henry, Prince of Wales.

Most excellent Prince giue leaue to an humble vassall to prostrate the best of his labours at the foote of your transplendent greatnesse. I bringe no wax nor hony to the hiue of which the Almighty hath maide your highness the hopefull Stay and comfort. I onely make an vnprofit-able murmur, living like an idle bee of others labours, whilst they laborious are a litle refreshed with the Ecchoes of my harmony and musicall endevours. The best of which I haue selected in humble con-secration vnto your highnes yet fearing my harshnes will not arride   10 the eare acquainted with nothing but supereminence on the bowed knee of lowest humilitye I craue of your excellence that the submissiue devotion of my vttermost endevours may not be distastefull. The Lord Almighty preserue your highnes grace to his glory and the eternall good of the comon wealth. From Cambridge the 17th of December *1609*.

Your highnes most humbly devoted.

George Handford.

A Table of the songes contained in this Booke.

Come sullen night.   9.
Say ye gods that powers haue.   10.
Hide not from me those eyes.   11.
Now ech creature ioyes the other   12.
Yow watry yssue of a mourning minde.   13.
Breath out my sighs.   14.
flow flow my teares   15.
Come teares and sighs. Mall Newberris Repentance   16.
Ah now I fall: the first part.   17.
But now I rise. the second part.   18.
see o see sweet Amyntas, A Dyalogue betwene
    Amyntas and Pastorella.   19.
Daphny stay o stay. Another Dyalogue betweene
    Phyllis, Daphny, and Thirsis.   20.

1.

Come come sweete fyre why stayest thou?
alas come quickly come
consume me all at once and giue me leaue to try
yf lyfe be sweeter then a louers martyrdome
or dyeinge soe to liue in loue then liueing dye: 5
come come sweete fyre why stayest? nay then I see
that thou wilt yet alas in pitty cruell be.

Come come away ô sweete why doe you stay?
O come away sweete fyre
And let me proue yf rest to loue my death can giue   10
Or yf my luke warme ashes haue not still desyre
To kindly heate of loue wherin I dyeing liue.
Then come sweete fyre why stayst? nay then I see
That thou wilt yet alas in pitty cruell be.

2.

My mournefull thoughts I safely may disclose
here all alone yf stones can silence keepe,
yf not then doth the calme ayre call me forth
and bids me to these woods bewray my griefe:
to mourne with me things sencles doth consent   5
and stones and trees will help me to lament.

Witnes you trees how oft I doe lament
And help to number yf you can how oft
I doe let fall a teare and tare my haire
And wring my hands vnder your shady bowes,   10
O deare woods, and let my Cinthia see
That Cinthias name is grauen in euery tree.

Tell her yf this you tell her fayned be
A firmer loue she shall not liue to see,
Echo say she hates me and euer euer will   15
But that vnles she leaue to hate me still
feare of her loue at my last obsequie
All ready is a present death to me.

3.

Florella lay a sleepeinge,
her Clorus sate by weepeinge;
Ay me
quoth he
canst thou sleepe soe secure   5
while I these paines for want of loue endure?
but rest thee still and sleepeinge lye,
the while I weepe and weepinge dye.

With that florella waked
And Clorus wepein slaked: 10
Aye me
Quoth she
I dreamt I was in loue
But heauens forbid it shold in earnest proue,
Which made poore Clorus hart soe bleed   15
He wept a fresh and dyed in deed.

4.

Two Cinthias did at once appeere
the one far of the other nere,
one on the earth and very nye
the other fixed in the skie.

The heauenly Cinthia blusht to see   5
This one on earth more fayre then she
Then she on earth lookt pale for feare
To see bright Cinthias blushinge cheare.

Feare not fayre star then Cinthia spake
But let those rayes thy wonder make   10
Though thou on earth yet sure deuine
Thy beauty is that equalls myne.

5.

Griefe presse my soule, that I may neuer find reliefe
since weary'd lyfe is still prolong'd by vtterd griefe:
my fruitles teares distill noe more from your sad eye,
but let that passion back retourne that I may dye,
and as my singinge is a mournefull swanlike cryeinge   5
soe let my liuing be A senceles life a dying.

6.

Goe weepe sad soule and to thy loue complayne thee
and begge with teares that she will not disdayne thee:
yf still her flinty hart doth grace deny,
goe weep sad soule and sighe and dye.

7.

Grone weary soule too too much opprest,
weary of life yet neuer death procuringe:
grone tyr'd soule restles in thine vnrest
tyr'd with griefe yet euer griefe indureinge:
grone grone my soule with such a pittyous sound   5
as may thine owne amazed self confound.

8.

If the tongue durst one word speake
or the hart durst one thought breake
true vertue from her seate t'expell
tongue and hart be damn'd in hell.

But tongue now thy thoughts then hidden 5
Speake more freely more forbidden
And yf by noe meanes words can moue
Then speake eyes dreames sighes and loue.

Say those sacred eyes and face
Vertue doth thy vertue grace 10
In them the graces all are found
And in them sits vertue cround.

Cinthia there herself enshrineth
And in all her glory shineth
Now then since they are both deuine 15
I adore both Saynt and shrine.

9.

Come sullen night that in thy sylent couer
like ruthfull birds my swarmeinge cares may houer,
come sullen night let could dispayre assay
the restles fludgate of my eyes to stay,
but come what will ahlas noontyde or morrow 5
all seemeth darke in this my night of sorrow.

Yet come sweete morne though you my ysce feares
canst not dissolue, or keepe truce with my teares,
Nor that thy pleasure can my payne redeeme
But that all change of payne doth pleasure seeme. 10
Then come what will alas noonetyde or morrow
All seemeth darke in this my night of sorrow.

10.

Say ye gods that power haue,
louers to destroy or saue,
what offerrings might your alters please
a wofull louer to release,
say where your temples placed are, 5
that to them I may make repaire.

Cupid sweete shall I deuine
Where thy mother hath her shrine,
Yf that on earth her temple bee,
But ô sweete Venus pardon me   10
For beinge soe prophane to tell
The world where all thy graces dwell.

Sure my loue that temple is
Heauenly modell of all blis
Whose face a sweete consorted quire   15
Whose eyes the lamp light of loues fyre
Whose lips your Alters where wold I
In offering kisses liue and dye.

11.

Hide not from me those eyes in whose bright flame
my hart doth like the Salamander burne,
hide them but now and then least by the same
my heate ore come thou me to ashes turne,
soe shalt thou cherish not surcharge desyre   5
and keepe me liueinge in a double fyre.

O gently gently come but not to fast
And lett me feele those kindly burneing rayes,
Now come away away ô sweete make hast,
Alas why make you longer longer stay?   10
Make hast or stay and feede me with desyre
And keepe me liueing in a double fyre.

12.

Now each creature ioyes the other,
passing happy dayes and howers,
one bird reports vnto another
in the fall of siluer showers,
whilst the earth our common mother   5
hath her bosome deckt with flowers.

Whilst the greatest torch of heauen
With bright rayes warmes floras lap
Now makeing nights and dayes both even
Cheereing the plants with fresher sap,   10
My field of flowers quite bereuen
Wants refresh of better hap.

Echo daughter of the ayre
Babling guest of rocks and hills
Doth knowe the name of my fierce fayre   15
And sounds the accents of my ills:
Each thing pittyes my dispayre
Whilst that she her louer kills.

Whilst that she ô cruell mayde
Doth me and my loue despise   20
My lyfes florish is decayd
The which depended on her eyes:
But her will must be obay'd
And well he ends for loue who dyes.
                    [Samuel Daniel]

                    13.

You watry yssue of a mourneing mynd,
ye teares true picterers of discontent,
the only help where help is none to find,
helpe me my sadde misfortune to lament:
flow flowe my teares noe other help I know,   5
no other help but teares and therefore flow.

                    14.

Breath out my sighes and sigh my lauish breath
and like a earthquake shall my pantinge breast:
that which giues others lyfe shall cause my death,
breathing by too much breathing being supprest,
and thus my breath my breathles hart shall pyne: 5
her breath did murther me then why not myne.

15.

Flow flow my teares as flouds and fountaynes flow,
distill my soule out of my watry eyes:
weepe weepe my eyes created euen for woe,
let a full sea of trickling streames arise:
since she hath turnd our sweete to bitter sowers 5
turne ye your Aprill smiles to Aprill showers.

Flow flow my teares till all my vaynes ye straine,
Flow till your cunduite pipes be quite drawn drye
And being dry'd gush out a fresh agayne
Till ouer whelm'd in waues of woe I ly, 10
That by too much of teares that flow along
Myne eyes washt out may not behold theyr wronge.

16.

Mall Newberry her Repentance.

Come teares and sighes, woes constant wofull mates,
and cloude the luster of lasciuious eyes:
and tare this yelding hart that oped the gate
to sin and shame to endles mysery: 5
my teares exhaust, and all my sighes be spent,
teares, sighs, doe fayle me when I shold lament.

17.

["Ah now I fall: the first part." All but the bass is lacking.]

18.

The second part.

But now I rise and riseing liue agayne,
and liueing loue ritch guerdon for my paine,
her words did rayse me vp, her smiles gaue breath,
her letters wrote of loue then farwell death: 5
then farwell death, can kindest Clara loue?
then wellcome lyfe from my turtledoue.

19.

Pastorella. [Amyntas.]

[P.] See ô see sweete Amyntas with what bashfull grace
    blushing Aurora viewes the rosye tincture in thy face.
[A.] See Pastorella fayre how Phebus feares to rise,
    seeinge the heauen borne light darted from both thine eyes.   5
[P.] ô come then ô come deare fyre
    let thy eyes my eyes couer
    and shade this ardor of desyre
    that they haue to theyre louer.
[A.] soe shall those starry rayes expell   10
    life from my hart light from my eyes.
[Both.] soe shall Aurora cease to blushe
       and fearfull Phebus hast to rise.

20.

Phillis. Daphne. Thirsis

[P.] Daphnie stay o stay and doe not still deny me.
[D.] No no I cannot loue.
[P.]   yet doe not fly me,
    sweete ô sweetest daphnie doe but heare.   5
[D.] myne eares are deafe to loue leaue of my deare.
[T.] Aye me
[D.]   harke
[P.]   harke
[T.] aye me, hath she bid me adieue?   10
    Ah cruell fayre.
[P.]   ô see my Thirsis true.
[D.] calst thou him thine, and seest to fly him still?
[P.] call thou me thine and me with kindnes kill.
[T.] Ah my Phillis canst not pitty me?   15
[D.] she sues to me yet cannot pitty thee.
[P.] he pleads for thee yet cannot pitty me.
[T. & P.] ô loueing hate disdainefull pitty,
        pitty ye powers deuine,
          we both for pitty plead and both   20
          alas for pitty pine.

[All.] then let vs take hands,
          daunce round and sing
          disdaine and pitty
          with hate and loue all in a ringe.   25

Robert Jones

A Musicall Dreame

1609

A/ MVSICALL/ *DREAME.* [First three lines xylographic with many flourishes, lines 1 and 3 swash]/ [rule]/ OR THE FOVRTH BOOKE OF AYRES. [Period may be comma with bent tail]/ The Firſt part is for the Lute, two Voyces, and the Viole de Gambo; The/ *Second part is for the Lute, the Viole and foure Voices to Sing*: *The Third part* [*VVTT* swash]/ is for one Voyce alone, or to the Lute, the Baſſe Viole, or to both if you pleaſe,/ *VVhereof, two are Italian Ayres.*/ Compoſed by ROBERT IONES./ *Quæ proſunt ſingula, multa iuuant.* [Q swash; ſ in *ſingula* has bent descender]/ [Device: McK. No. 282, used by Windet 1592–1609]/ LONDON/ Imprinted by IOHN WINDET, and are to be ſolde by SIMON WATERSON, in Powles/ *Church-yeard, at the Signe of the Crowne.* 1609./

[Thus the Huntington copy. The book was reissued with the following changes on the title-page: the device is moved slightly, then]/ LONDON/ Imprinted by the Aſſignes of WILLIAM BARLEY, and are to be ſolde in Powles/ *Church-yeard, at the Signe of the Crowne.* 1609./

Note: The reissue was probably demanded by William Barley, who had claimed the patent on music printing after Thomas Morley's death. Barley's claim was upheld by the Stationers' Company in disputes with Thomas East in 1606 and with Thomas Adams in 1609. See W. A. Jackson, ed., *Records of the Court of the Stationers' Company 1602–1640* (London: The Bibliographical Society, 1957), pp. 19–20, 39.

Collation: 2°; A–M² (A1, M2 not signed), 24 leaves.

Headlines: B1v–M1v, verso: CANTVS. I. [–XXI.] ROBERT IONES [period lacking after CANTVS on verso of B2, DFHI1–2; period after IONES on verso of CKL1–2, M1] B2–F1, recto: BASSVS./ ALTVS. [BSASVS. on C1]; F2–L1: BASSVS./ ALTVS./ TENOR. [BSASVS. on K1–2, L1]; L2–M2: BASSVS.

Contents: A1, title page; A1v blank; A2, dedication; A2v, epistle; B1, table of songs; B1v–M2, songs I–XXI, one per opening; M2v blank.

SR: No entry.

STC: 14734–5.

Copies: BM (K.2.g.2, the text copy), Glasgow (R.x.7), and Huntington (62106; first issue; sig. M rearranged in binding in this order: M2v, M2, M1v, M1).

The music for songs I–VIII consists of a Cantus with lute tablature facing an Altus with a bass-viol part; songs IX–XVIII have the usual Cantus and lute with alternate four-part setting; and songs XIX–XXI have parts for one voice and lute facing a bass-viol part.

Collation reveals the following press-corrections:

Outer forme H: uncorrected, Huntington:

> H1 (T, XII.1) aye] nye

Inner forme H: uncorrected, Huntington:

> H2 (A, XIII.2) it] ii
> (B, XIII.4) though] rhough

Inner forme I: uncorrected, BM:

> I1v (XV.5) requium] requeum
> (XV.9) giues] gines
> (XV.11) requium] requeum
> I2 (XV.5AT, 5B) requium] requeum

Outer forme L: uncorrected, BM: L1, signature omitted.

TO THE RIGHT
WORSHIPFVLL AND WOR-
thy Gentleman, Sir IOHN LEVINTHORPE Knight
perpetuall Happinesse and Content.

IT is not vnknowne vnto your wel deseruing selfe, Right Worship-full, that not long since I tooke my *Vltimum vale*, with a resoluing in my selfe, neuer to publish any workes of the same Nature and Fashion, whereupon I betooke me to the ease of my Pillow, where *Somnus* hauing taken possession of my eyes, and *Morpheus* the charge of my senses; it happened mee to fall into a Musical dreame, wherein I chanced to haue many opinions and extrauagant humors of diuers Natures and Conditions, some of modest mirth, some of amorous Loue, and some of most diuine contemplation; all these I hope, shall not giue any distaste to the eares, or dislike to the mind, eyther in their words, or

in their seuerall sounds, although it is not necessarie to relate or diuulge all Dreames or Phantasies that Opinion begets in sleepe, or happeneth to the mindes apparition. And continuing long in this my dreaming slumber, I began to awake, and vpon my eyes vnclosing, I bethought my selfe, being full awaked, aduising in my mind, whome to elect and chuse as a Patrone for the same, I was easily inuited to make choice of   20
your Worship, as one to whome I necessarily ought both loue and duety, And howsoeuer I might feare that you wil not acknowledge it, yet in that Nature hath inriched you with more then ordinarie know-ledge in this Art, beeing a witnes of that Loue which you haue alwayes afforded to Musicke, I emboldened my selfe the rather to present it vnto you. Accept it then (good Sir) as a Token of vnfained Loue, and a debt worthily due vnto you for your many fauours done to him that is

At your Worships commaund.
ROBERT IONES.

To all Musicall Murmurers,
This Greeting.

THou, whose eare itches with the varietie of opinion, hearing thine owne sound, as the Ecchoe reuerberating others substance, and vnprofitable in it selfe, shewes to the World comfortable noyse, though to thy owne vse little pleasure, by reason of vncharitable censure. I speake to thee musicall Momus, *thou from whose nicetie, numbers as easily passe, as drops fall in the showre, but with lesse profite. I compare thee to the hie way dust that flies into mens eyes, and will not thence without much trouble, for thou in thy dispersed iudgement, not onely art offensiue to seeing knowledge, but most faulty false to deseruing*   10
industry, picking moates out of the most pure Bisse, and smoothing the plainest veluet, when onely thine owne opinion is more wrinckled and more vitious in it selfe, then grosser soyle, so that as a brush infected with filth, thou rather soylest then makest perfect any way. I haue stood at thine elbow, and heard thee prophane euen Musickes best Note, and with thy vntunde rellish Sol Fade most ignobly. I am assured, and I care not greatly, that thou wilt lay to my charge, my whilome vow, Neuer againe, because I promised as much: but vnderstand me thou vnskilfull descanter, deriue from that Note of Plaine Song charitable numbers, and thou shalt find harsh voices are often a Note aboue Ela reduced by truer iudgement, which I bereaue thee of, knowing thy Rules,   20
are as our new come Lutes, being of many stringes, not easily vsed, vnlesse in aduenture, till practise put forward into deseruing Diuision. This my aduenture

is no deed but a dreame, and what are dreames, but airie possessions, and seuerall ayres, breathing harmonious whisperings, though to thee discord, yet to others indifferent, I will not say excellent, because it is an others office not mine, but let them be as they are, others profites and my paines, set forth for pleasure, not for purposed poyson to infect imagination, no, but as a showre falling in a needfull season, so I flatter my selfe at least, and will say so euer by any other, whose labour shall vplift Musicall meditation, the onely wing of true courage, being the most pleasing voice of man, whose sweetenes reacheth vnto heauen it selfe. It is hard if al this paines reape not good com-mendations, and it is water wrung out of a Flint in thee, sith thou neuer thinkst well of any, and wert in thy selfe so vnskilfull euer, as thy Tutor from the first howre could neuer make thee sing in Tune; be as thou art a lumpe of deformity without fashion, bredde in the bowels of disdaine, and brought forth by bewitcht Megæra, *the fatall* Midwife *to all true merite.*

Giue me leaue to depart, or if not, without it I am gone, carelesse of thy censuring, and fully perswaded thou canst not thinke well, and therefore art curst in thy Cradle, neuer to be but cruell, and being borne with teeth in thy head, bitst euery one harmeles in this or what else honest industry, makes thy eare gossip too.

Farwell if thou wilt in kindnesse, or hold thy selfe from further carping.

A TABLE CON-
taining all the Songes in
this Booke.

Griefe of my best loues absenting   14
If in this flesh where thou indrencht dost lie,   15
O thred of life when thou art spent   16
When I sit reading all alone.   17
Faine would I speake, but feare to giue offence   18
In Sherwood liude stout Robin Hood,   19

Ite Caldi sospiri,   20
S'amor non è che dunque.   21

I.

THough your strangenes frets my heart,
  yet must I not complaine,
You perswade me tis but Art
  which secret loue must faine,
If another you affect,   5
  tis but a toy to auoide suspect,
Is this faire excusing,
  O no all is abusing.

2 When your wisht sight I desire,
  Suspition you pretend,   10
Causlesse you your selfe retire,
  Whilst I in vaine attend,
Thus a louer as you say,
  Still made more eager by delay,
Is this faire excusing,   15
  O no, all is abusing.

3 When another holds your hand,
  Youle sweare I hold your heart,
Whilst my riuall close doth stand,
  And I sit farre apart,   20
I am neerer yet then they,
  Hid in your bosome as you say,
Is this faire excusing,
  O no all is abusing.

4 Would a riuall then I were,   25
  Some else your secret friend,
So much lesser should I feare,
  And not so much attend,

They enioy you euery one,
  Yet must I seeme your friend alone,   30
Is this faire excusing,
  O no all is abusing.
          [Thomas Campion]

II.

     Sweete Kate
      of late
ran away and left me playning.
     Abide
     I cride   5
or I die with thy disdayning.
     Te hee hee quoth shee
     gladly would I see
any man to die with louing
     Neuer any yet   10
     died of such a fitte:
Neither haue I feare of prouing.

   2   Vnkind,
      I find,
Thy delight is in tormenting,   15
     Abide,
     I cride,
Or I die with thy consenting.
     Te hee hee quoth she,
     Make no foole of me,   20
Men I know haue oathes at pleasure,
     But their hopes attaind,
     They bewray they faind,
And their oathes are kept at leasure.

   3   Her words   25
     Like swords,
Cut my sorry heart in sunder,
     Her floutes,
     With doubts,
Kept my heart affections vnder.   30

Te hee hee quoth shee,
    What a foole is he,
Stands in awe of once denying,
    Cause I had inough,
    To become more rough,   35
So I did, O happy trying.

III.

ONce did I serue a cruell hart
with faith vnfainde I still importune
her piersing lookes that wrought my smart,
she laughes and smiles at my misfortune
and sayes perhaps you may at last   5
by true desart, loues fauour taste.

IIII.

Will saide to his mammy
  that hee woulde goe woo,
faine would he wed but he wot not who
  Soft a while my lammy
stay, and yet abide,   5
  hee like a foole as he was replide,
In faith chil haue a wife, a wife, a wife,
  O what a life do I lead
for a wife in my bed
  I may not tell you,   10
O there to haue a wife, a wife, a wife,
  O tis a smart to my hart,
tis a racke to my backe
  and to my belly.

2

Scarcely was hee wedded,   15
  Full a fortnights space,
But that he was in a heauie case,
  Largely was he headded,
And his cheekes lookt thinne: 20
  And to repent he did thus beginne:

A figge for such a wife, a wife, a wife,
  O what a life doe I lead,
With a wife in my bedde,
  I may not tell you?   25
There to haue a wife, a wife, a wife,
  O tis a smart to my heart,
Tis a racke to my backe,
  And to my belly.

                        3   30

All you that are Batchelers,
  Be learnd by crying will,
When you are well to remaine so still,
  Better for to tarry,
And alone to lie,   35
  Then like a foole with a foole to crie.
A figge for such a wife, a wife, a wife,
  O what a life doe I leade,
With a wife in my bed,
I may not tell you,   40
  There to haue a wife, a wife, a wife,
O tis a smart to my heart,
Tis a racke to my backe,
  And to my belly.

                        V.

Harke wot yee what nay faith and shall I tell
  I am afraide to die a maid and then lead Apes in hell,
O it makes me sigh & sob with inward griefe,
  but if I can but get a man hele yeeld me some reliefe.

2 O it is strange how nature works with me,   5
  My body is spent and I lament mine owne great folly,
O it makes me sigh and powre forth flouds of teares,
  Alas poore elfe none but thy selfe would liue, hauing such
                                                         cares.

3 O now I see that fortune frownes on me
  By this good light I haue beene ripe,   10
O it makes me sigh and sure it will me kill,
  When I should sleepe I lie and weepe, feeding on sorrowes still.

4 I must confesse as maides haue vertue store,
  Liue honest still against our wils, more fooles we are therefore:
O it makes me sigh, yet hope doth still me good,   15
  For if I can but get a man, with him ile spend my blood.

VI.

MY complayning is but faining,
  all my loue is but in iest,   fa, la, la,
And my Courting is but sporting
  in most shewing meaning, least   fa la la.

2   5

Outward sadnesse inward gladnesse,
  Representeth in my mind,   fa la la,
In most faining most obtaining,
  Such good faith in loue I find.   fa la la.

3   10

Towards Ladies this my trade is,
  Two minds in one breast I were, fa la la,
And my measure at my pleasure,
  Ice and flame my face doth beare. Fa la la.

VII.

ON a time in summer season,
  Iocky late with Ienny walking
like a lout made loue with talking,
  when he should be doing, Reason
still he cries, when he should dally,   5
  Ienny sweet, sweet shall I, shall I.

2 Ienny as most women vse it,
  Who say nay when they would haue it,
With a bolde face seemed to craue it,
  With a faint looke did refuse it,   10
Iocky lost his time to dally,
  Still he cries, sweete shall I, shall I.

3 She who knew that backward dealing
  was a foe to forward longing,
To auoide her owne hearts wronging,   15
  with a sigh loues sute reuealing,
Said Iocky sweet when you would dally,
  Doe you cry sweet, shall I shal I.

4 Iocky knew by her replying,
  That a no is I in wooing,
That an asking without doing,   20
  Is the way to loues denying.
Now he knowes when he would dally
  How to spare sweet shall I shall I.

VIII.

FArewell fond youth, if thou hadst not bin blind
  out of my eye thou mightst haue read my minde,
but now I plainely see how thou wouldst faine leaue me;
  sure I was acurst,
not to goe at first,   5
  sure I was acurst, O fie no,
sweete stay & I will tell thee why no.

2

Once more farewell, since first I heard thee speake,
  And had but sung farewell, my heart would breake,   10
But now since I doe find thy loue is like the wind,
  What a foole was I
To be like to die.
  What a foole was I, I was not,
Yet say I was a foole I passe not.   15

3

Woes me alasse, why did I let him goe,
  These be the fruites of idle saying no,
Now that he can disproue me, how shall he euer loue me,
  Nay but is he gone,   20
Then I am vndone,
  Nay but is he gone, O hold him,
Fie, forty things are yet vntold him.

IX.

How should I shew my loue vnto my loue
  but hide it from all eyes saue my loues eyes:
The way by pen or tong I dare not proue
  their drifts are oft discouered by the wise,
Lookes are more safe, yet ouer them are spies,   5
  Then whats the way to cosen iealousie
which martyrs loue, by marking narrowly.

2 By all these wayes may thy affections walke,
  Without suspition of the iealous guarde:
Thy whispering tong to her closde eare shall talke,   10
  And be importunate till it be harde,
Papers shall passe lookes shall not be debarde,
  To looke for loues young infants in her eyes,
Be franke and bold as she is kind and wise.

3 O who can be so francke as she is kind,   15
  Whose kindnesse merites more then Monarchies,
Boldnesse with her milde grace, grace cannot find,
  Onely her wit ouer that doth tyrannize,
Then let her worth and thy loue simpathize,
  Sith her worth to thy loue cannot be knowne,   20
Nor thy loue to her worthinesse be showne.

X.

O He is gone and I am here
  aye me why are wee thus deuided,
My sight in his eyes did appeare
  my soule by his soules thought was guided,
then come againe my all my life, my being,   5
  soules zeale, harts ioy, eares guest, eyes onely seeing.

2 Come sable care sease on my heart,
  Take vp the roomes that ioyes once filled,
Natures sweet blisse is slaine by Art,
  Absence black frost liues spring hath killed,   10
Then come againe, my loue, my deere, my treasure,
  My blisse, my fate, my end, my hopes full measure.

XI.

ANd is it night, are they thine eyes that shine,
　are we alone and here and here alone
may I come neere, may I but touch thy shrine,
　is Ielousie asleepe, and is he gone,
O Gods no more, silence my lippes with thine,　　　　　　5
　lippes, kisses, Ioyes, happe, blessings most diuine.

2

O come my deare our griefes are turnde to night,
　And night to ioyes, night blinds pale enuies eyes,
Silence and sleepe prepare vs our delight,　　　　　　10
　O cease we then our woes, our griefes our cries,
O vanish words, words doe but passions moue,
　O deerest life, ioyes sweet, O sweetest loue.

XII.

SHe hath an eye ah me, ah me
shee hath an eye, an eye to see
　ah me that shee hath two
which makes me sigh as louers doe, hey hoe, hey hoe,
　hey hoe, ah me that an eye　　　　　　5
　should make her liue and mee to die,
wise mens eyes are in their mind
but louers eyes are euer blind.

2 She hath a lippe, ah, ah alas,
Two lippes which doe themselues surpasse,　　　　　　10
　Alasse two lips for kisses,
Of earthly loue the heauenly blisses, hey hoe, hey hoe
　Alasse, oh woe that a heauen,
　Should make vs ods that make all euen,
Ladies kisses are a charme,　　　　　　15
That kill vs were they doe vs harme.

3 She hath a heart ah me, ah me,
A heart she hath which none can see,
　Ah me that I haue none,
Which makes me sigh, yea sighing grone, hey hoe, hey hoe　　　　　20

Hey hoe aye me that I part,
　And liue, yet leaue with her my heart.
Hartlesse men may liue by loue.
This she doth know, and this I proue.

XIII.

I Know not what yet that I feele is much,
　it came I know not when, it was not euer,
it hurtes I know not how, yet is it such
　as I am pleasd though it be cured neuer,
It is a wound that wasteth still in woe　　　　　　　　5
　and yet I would not, that it were not so.

2 Pleasde with a thought that endeth with a sigh,
　Sometimes I smile when teares stand in my eyes,
Yet then and there such sweet contentment lieth,
　Both when and where my sweet sower torment lies,　　　10
O out alas, I cannot long endure it,
　And yet alasse I care not when I cure it.

3 But well away, me thinks I am not shee,
　That wonted was these fits as foule to scorne.
One and the same, euen so I seeme to be,　　　　　　15
　As lost I liue, yet of my selfe forlorne,
What may this be that thus my mind doth moue,
　Alasse I feare, God shield it be not loue.

XIIII.

Griefe of my best loues absenting:
　Now O now wilt thou assayle mee,
　I had rather life should fayle mee
then endure thy slow tormenting,
　life our griefes and vs doe seuer　　　　　　　5
　　　　once for euer,
absence, griefe haue no relenting.

2

Well, be it foule absence spights me,
　So far of it cannot send her,　　　　　　　10
　As my heart should not attend her.

O how this thoughts thought delights me
  Absence doe thy worst and spare not,
     Know I care not
When thou wrongst me, my thoughts right me.   15

3

O but such thoughts proue illusions,
  Shadowes of a substance banisht,
  Dreames of pleasure too soone vanisht,
Reasons maimde of their conclusions,   20
  Then since thoughts and all deceiue me,
     O life leaue me,
End of life ends loues confusions.

XV.

IF in this flesh where thou indrencht dost lie
  poore soule thou canst reare vp thy limed wings,
carry my thoughts vp to the sacred skie
  and wash them in those heauenly hallowed springs,
where ioy and requiem The holy Angels sings   5
  whilst all heauens vault with blessed Echoes rings.

2 Awaked with this harmony diuine,
  O how my soule mounts vp her throned head,
And giues again with natiue glory shine,
  Wash with repentance then thy dayes misled,   10
Then ioyes with requiem mayest thou with Angels sing,
  Whilest all heauens vault with blessed Ecchoes ring.

XVI.

O Thred of life when thou art spent how are my sorrowes eased.
  O vaile of flesh when thou art rent how shal my soule be
                                        pleased:
O earth why tremblest thou at death
  that did receiue both heate and breath
by bargain of a second birth,   5
  that done again to be cold earth,
Come death deere midwife to my life,
  see sin and vertue holde at strife,

Make hast away
    lest thy delay   10
    bee my decay,
 world of inanity,
 schoolhouse of vanity,
        minion of hell
        farewell farewell.   15

2 O coward life whose feare doth tie me in distasting sences,
  Infused part mount vp on hie, life gets on life offences,
O flie immortall flie away,
  Be not immurde in finite clay,
Where true loue doth with selfe loue fight,   20
  Begetting thoughts that doe affright,
Courage faint heart, sound trumpet death,
  Ile find it wind with all my breath.
        O case of glasse,
        Confusions mase,   25
        A flouring grasse,
     Temple of treachery,
     Soule yoake to misery,
        Store-house of hell
        Farewell, farewell.   30

XVII.

Wнen I sit reading all alone that secret booke
    wherein I sigh to looke
    how many spots there bee,
    I wish I could not see,
    or from my selfe might flee.   5

                2

Mine eyes for refuge then with zeale befixe the skies,
    My teares doe cloude those eyes,
    My sighes doe blow them drie,
    And yet I liue to die,   10
    My selfe I cannot flie,

3

Heauens I implore, that knowes my fault, what shall I doe,
  To hell I dare not goe,
  The world first made me rue,   15
  My selfe my griefes renew,
  To whome then shall I sue.

4

Alasse; my soule doth faint to draw this doubtfull breath,
  Is there no hope in death,   20
  O yes, death ends my woes:
  Death me from me will lose,
  My selfe am all my foes.

XVIII.

Faine would I speake but feare to giue offence,
makes mee retire: and in amasement stand,
still breathing forth my woes in fruitlesse silence,
whilst my poore hart is slaine by her faire hand:
faire hands indeed the guiders of the dart   5
that from her eyes were leueld at my heart.

2

Those eyes two pointed Diamonds did engraue,
Within my heart the true and liuely forme,
Of that sweet Saint whose pitty most I craue,   10
Whose absence makes me comfortlesse to mourne,
And sighing say (Sweet) would she knew my loue,
My plaints perhaps her mind may somewhat moue.

3

But if she knew, what if she did reiect,   15
Yet better twere by her sweet doome to die,
That she might know my deare loues true effect,
Then thus to liue in vnknowne misery,
Yet after death it may be she would say,
His too much loue did worke his liues decay.   20

XIX.

IN Sherwood liude stout Robin Hood
  an Archer great none greater.
His bow & shafts were sure & good,
  yet Cupids were much beter:
Robin could shoot at many a Hart and misse,   5
  Cupid at first could hit a hart of his,
      hey iolly Robin
      hoe iolly Robin
      hey iolly Robin Hood,
      loue finds out me   10
      as well as thee
      to follow me to the green wood.

2

A noble thiefe was Robin Hoode,
  Wise was he could deceiue him,   15
Yet Marrian in his brauest mood,
  Could of his heart bereaue him,
No greater thiefe lies hidden vnder skies
  then beauty closely lodgde in womens eyes.
      Hey iolly Robin.   20

3

An Out-law was this Robin Hood,
  His life free and vnruly,
Yet to faire Marrian bound he stood
  And loues debt payed her duely.   25
Whom curbe of stricktest law could not hold in,
  Loue with obeyednes and a winke could winne.
      Hey iolly Robin.

4

Now wend we home stout Robin Hood   30
  Leaue we the woods behind vs,
Loue passions must not be withstood,
  Loue euery where will find vs,
I liude in field and towne, and so did he,
  I got me to the woods, loue followed me.   35
      Hey iolly Robin.

XX.

*I*TE *caldi sospiri all freddo core,*
Rompete il ghiaccio che pieta coontente
e se prego mortale al ciel s'intende
morte O mercè sia fine al mio dolore.
                              [Petrarch]

XXI.

S' Amor non è che dunque è quel ch'io sento?
Ma s'egli è amor, per dio che cosa è quale?
Se buona, onde è effetto aspro mortale?
Se ria, onde è si dolce ogni tormento?
Sa' mia voglia ardo onde è il pianto el lamento   5
Sa' mal mio grado, il lamentar che vala
O viua morte O dilettose male
come puoi tanto in me s'io no'l consento.
                              [Petrarch]

FINIS.

William Corkine

Ayres

1610

[Within a frame made up of six pieces: four side pieces (Mars, over Venus with Cupid at her feet, on each side) linked at top and bottom with head-piece ornaments as in Plomer No. 48] AYRES,/ TO [*T* swash]/ SING AND PLAY/ TO THE LVTE AND/ Basse Violl./ VVith [first V trimmed] Pauins, Galliards, Almaines, and/ Corantos for the Lyra/ *VIOLL.*/ By *William Corkine.*/ [device: McK. No. 292]/ *LONDON* [final *N* swash]/ Printed by *W. Stansby* for *Iohn Browne*, and are to be fold at his/ Shop in Saint *Dunſtanes* Church-yard in Fleete-ftreete./ 1610./

Collation: 2°; A–F², G¹ (A, second leaves not signed). 13 leaves.

Headlines: A2–D2v: *CANTVS.* I. [–XII.]/ *BASSVS.* [On each page, except for B1v and C2v which have only *CANTVS.* IIII. [IX.], and B2 and D1 which have only *BASSVS.*] E1–G1: *Lessons for the Lyra Viall.* [On each page.]

Contents: A1, title page; A1v, dedication; A2–B1, songs I–III, one per page; B1v–B2, song IIII; B2v–C2, songs V–VIII, one per page; C2v–D1, song IX; D1v–D2v, songs X–XII, one per page; E1–G1, "Lessons for the Lyra Viall," in tablature, as follows: E1, "Almaine"; E1v, "Pauin" and "Coranto"; E2, "Almaine" and "Coranto"; E2v, "Pauin" and "Coranto"; F1, two Galliards; F1v–F2, "Whoope doe me no harme good man" (see Simpson, pp. 777–780); F2, "Galliard"; F2v–G1, "Fortune"; G1, table of songs; G1v blank.

SR: No entry.

STC: 5768.

Copies: BM (K.8.h.4, the text copy); Glasgow (R.x.66; lacking after D2); RCM (I.G.38; seen, but not fully collated); and Mr. Robert S. Pirie of Hamilton, Mass. I have not seen this last copy, but Mr. Pirie has kindly informed me that sig. C of his copy is in an uncorrected state, thus:

Outer forme: C2v, headline omitted (*CANTVS.* IX.)

Inner forme: C1v: VII.] VIII.
      C2: VIII.] VII.
The music for Corkine's songs consists of a Cantus with lute tablature and a bass viol part in mensural notation with only the opening words.

TO THE TWO HONOVRA-
BLE KNIGHTS, SIR Edward
Herbert, *OF THE NOBLE*
ORDER OF THE BATH, AND SIR
WILLIAM HARDY.

It was long before the vse of Notes and Tableture came in to our English Presse, but hauing found the way, there are few Nations yeeld more Impressions in that kind then ours. Euery Musition according to his abilitie increasing the number. Among so many, I haue now made one, yeelding my priuate inuentions subiect to publicke censure: To which aduenture I was drawen by two reasons. First, that I might shew my humble duetie, and gratefull minde to you my two Honourable Masters, whose bountie bestowed on me that knowledge (whatsoeuer it is) that I haue attain'd in Musicke; Next for that I am assured, that both the worthinesse of your Names, as also your loues to Musicke, and extraordinary skils therein, either to expresse, or Masterly to compose, will bee such a protection to my deuoted labours, that I shall not need to feare the blacke breath of any enuious detractor. All my desire is, that your fauourable acceptance will better them, for I shall esteeme them as you receiue them. So, as my duetie requires; I will dayly pray for you both, as my bountifull Masters, and worthiest Patrons.

Your humble seruant,
William Corkine.

I.

1

Sinke downe proud thoughts, your mounting hopes must now descend,
Come griefe and care, hence ioyes your triumph now must end,
Heauens now will smile no more my light is shaded,
I pine without redresse, my life my spirits like flowers are faded. 5

2

O time conceale my woe, in mine owne teares drowne my distresse,
Griefes none should know, when none their anguish can redresse,
Pale Death hath pierst my blood, and forth it streameth,
I sleepe, and in my trance, my head my heart of sorrow dreameth.　　　　10

II.

Some can flatter, some can faine,
simple trueth shall pleade for mee
Let not beautie trueth disdaine,
Trueth is euen as faire as shee.

2　　　　　　　　　　　　　　　　5

But since Paires must equall proue,
Let my strength her youth oppose,
Loue her beautie, faith her loue,
On eu'n termes so may we close.

3　　　　　　　　　　　　　　　10

Corke or Leade, in equall waight,
Both one iust proportion yeeld,
So may breadth be pays'd with height,
Steepest mount with plainest field.

4　　　　　　　　　　　　　　　15

Vertues haue not all one kind,
Yet all vertues merits bee:
Diuers vertues are combind,
Diff'ring so Deserts agree.

5　　　　　　　　　　　　　　　20

Let then loue and beautie meete,
Making one diuine concent,
Constant as the sounds, and sweete,
That enchant the firmament.
　　　　　　　[Thomas Campion?]

III.

1

Sweete restraine these showers of kindnesse,
  From distrust proceeding,
Nurse not wrong conceiued blindnesse,
  By too much sigh breeding.   5
Loue by error seemes astray,
  But dies if once suspected,
Women most beleeue when they,
  most by men are neglected.

2   10

Some, forg'd flatteries onely venture,
  Yet returne true fauours,
Iust affection like a Center,
  Once fixt neuer wauers:
Easily as the day from night,   15
  May womens eyes discouer,
If they frame their minds aright,
  From the false the true louer.

IIII.

If streames of teares, Could lessen extreame griefe,
or cause a minutes truce to woe,
If deepest sighes, Sad plaints might yeeld reliefe,
these sorrowes to forgoe,
Myne eyes my heart, my tongue should neare refraine   5
to weepe, to sigh and to complaine,
But sorrowe such impression left,
of sight of speech, it mee bereft,
onely to sigh is left to mee,
in this my greatest miserie.   10

V.

Sweete sweete sweete Let me goe,
What doe you meane to vexe mee so,
cease cease cease Your Pleading force
doe you thinke thus, To extort remorce,
now, now, now no more. Alas you ouer beare me,   5
And I would crie, But some would heare I feare mee.

VI.

HEe that hath no mistresse, must not weare a fauor,
he that wooes a mistris, must serue before he haue her,
he that hath no bedfellow, must lie alone,
and he that hath no Lady, must be content with Ione,
and so must I, for why alas my loue and I am parted,   5
False Cupid I will haue thee whipt, and haue thy mother carted.

VII.

1

Sweete Cupid ripen her desire,
Thy ioyfull haruest may begin,
If age approch a little nyer,
Twill be too late to get it in.   5

2

Cold Winter stormes lay standing Corne,
Which once too ripe will neuer rise,
And louers wish themselues vnborne,
When all their ioyes lie in their eyes.   10

3

Then sweete let vs imbrace and kisse,
Shall beautie shale vpon the ground,
If age bereaue vs of this blisse,
Then will no more such sport be found.   15

VIII.

VAine is all this worlds contention,
Fortunes fraile, and hopes deceiuing,
Chance layes ambush of preuention,
Our atempts of end bereuing,
future things are plast   5
beyond our weake conceiuing,
minds in euery age
new thoughts engender
till all to fate wee render.

IX.

BEautie sate bathing by a Spring,
where fairest shades did hide her,
the windes blewe calme, the Birds did Sing,
the coole streames ranne beside her,
my wanton thoughts intis't mine eye   5
to see what was forbidden,
but better memorie said, Fie,
So vaine desire was chidden.

2

Into a slumber then I fell,   10
But fond imagination
Seem'd to see, but could not tell,
Her feature or her fashion.
But euen as babes in dreames doe smile,
And sometime fall a weeping: 15
So I awakt as wise the while,
As when I fell a sleeping.

[Anthony Munday]

X.

Now would chwore hong'd, zis but thou most ma wrong,
gods bors I crie God mercy to zweare,
hast not my Rings and things, and geare with vaith and troth,
among
and wout vorzake ma now, nay masse ware that, vor if thou doo,
chil take a knife & honge my zelfe vor one of thow,   5
yea I woll, so I woll, that I woll, I vaith la.

Hadds voote zweete zis what aild tha woo ma now,
I cham as like to zarue thy turne,
As yer I wos zince chos I borne, and sha not I haue thow,
Lets zee who dare I chould but zee huds lid I zweare,   10
Chill take a zweard & make a yend of I or hee,
Yea I would, &c.

Ha not I bought my Kerzie wedding briche,
Hudds hate cham angrie thou makes ma vret,
And is not my bond redie zet, woold zarue ma zuch a twich,   15
Chill breake his brow, I vaith, I chill that shall loue thou,
Then take a rop and drown thy zelf vor mere good will,
Yea I would, &c.

XI.

1

Thinke you to seduce me so with words that haue no meaning,
Parets can learne so to speake our voice by peeces gleaning,
Nurses teach their Children so about the time of weaning.

2   5

Learne to speake first, then to woe, to woeing much pertaineth,
He that hath not Art to hide, soone falters when he faineth,
And as one that wants his wits, he smiles when he complaineth.

3

If with wit we be deceiued, our fals may be excused,   10
Seeming good with flatterie grac't, is but of few refused,
But of all accurst are they that are by fooles abused.
                                    [Thomas Campion]

XII.

1

Shall a frowne or angrie eye,
Shall a word vnfitly placed?
Shall a shadow make me flie,
As I were with Tygers chaced?   5
Loue must not be so disgraced.

2

Shall I woe her in dispight?
Shall I turne her from her flying?
Shall I tempt her with delight,   10
Shall I laugh out her denying?
Noe, beware of louers crying.

3

Shall I then with patient mind,
Still attend her wayward pleasure,   15
Time will make her proue more kind,
Let her coynesse then take leasure,
Paines are worthy such a treasure.

A Table of all the Songs contained in
this Booke.

                              FINIS.

Robert Dowland

A Musicall Banquet

1610

[Within a compartment: McK. & F. No. 132; in upper oval slot, a cut with musical instruments, and the motto:] MVSICA LÆTIFICAT COR:. [In center space:] A/ MVSICALL/ BANQVET./ Furnifhed with varietie of delicious/ Ayres, Collected our of the beft Authors in/ Englifh, French, Spanifh and Italian./ By *Robert Douland*. [*RD* swash]/ [In lower slot:] LONDON:/ Printed for *Thomas Adams*. [*A* swash] 1610./

Note: For the title page compartment, see the Textual Introduction to Do1600. Thomas Snodham, who used the compartment for Fer1609, and who printed John Dowland's translation of Ornithoparcus' *Micrologus* (1609) for Adams, is no doubt the printer of RDo1610.

Collation: 2°; *A–L*², M¹; 23 leaves.

Headlines: I note only the constant items, although the names of the authors of the words and music, when given, are printed on the headline, verso for the poet, recto for the composer. Verso, B1v–F2v: I. [–X.] CANTVS. G1v–L2v: *XI.* [*–XX.*] *CANTO.* [G2v: *CANTVS.*] Recto, B2–G1: I. [–X.] BASSVS. G2–M1: *XI.* [*–XX.*] *BASSO.*

Contents: A1, title page; A1v blank; A2 dedication; A2v, epistle and verses by Peacham; B1, "The Right Honourable the Lord Viscount *Lisle*, Lord Chamberlaine to the Queenes most excellent Maiestie, his Galliard" for the lute, by "*Iohn Douland*, Batchelar of Musick"; B1v–M1, songs I–XX, one per opening; M1v, table of songs.

SR: No entry.

STC: 7099.

Copies: BM (K.2.i.9, the text copy); Bod. (B.5.12 Art.; seen but not fully collated); RCM (I.G.22; lacks all after H2); Huntington (13570; lacks M1); Library of Congress, Washington (M 1490. D75 M8); and Fürst Alexander zu Dohna-Schlobitten, Lörrach-Baden, Germany.

Collation reveals the following press-correction:
Inner forme A: uncorrected, Library of Congress:
A2 (dedication) these my first labours] these few, and my first labours
The music for the songs consists of a voice part with lute tablature facing a bass part. The bass parts for songs I, VIII, X, XV–XX have only the opening words.

TO THE RIGHT HO-
NORABLE SYR ROBERT
SYDNEY, KNIGHT: Lord Gouernour of
Vlissingen, and the Castle of Ramekins, Lord
SYDNEY of Penshurst, Viscount *Lisle*, and Lord
Chamberlaine to the Queenes most excellent
Maiestie.

RIGHT Honourable Lord: Since my best abilitie is not able in the least manner to counteruaile that dutie J owe vnto your Lordship, for two great respects; the one in regard (your Lordship vndertaking for mee) J was made a member of the Church of Christ, and withall receiued from you my name: the other the loue that you beare to all excellency and good learning, (which seemeth haereditarie aboue others to the Noble Familie of the *Sydneys*,) and especially to this excellent Science of Musicke, a skill from all antiquity entertayned with the most Noble & generous dispositions. May it please your Honour therefore to accept these my first labours, as a poore pledge of that zeale and dutie which J shall euer owe vnto your Honour, vntill time shall enable me to effect something more worthy of your Lordships view, hauing no other thing saue these few sheetes of Paper to present the same withall.

To your Honour
in all dutie most deuoted,
Robert Douland.

TO THE READER.

GENTLEMEN: Finding my selfe not deceiued in the hope I had of your kinde entertayning my collected Lute-lessons which I lately set foorth, I am further encouraged to publish vnto your censures these AYRES, being collected and gathered out of the labours of the rarest and most iudicious Maisters of Musick that either now are or haue lately liued in Christendome, whereof some I haue purposely sorted to the capacitie of young practioners, the rest by degrees are of greater depth and skill, so that like a carefull Confectionary, as neere as might be I haue fitted my Banquet for all tastes; if happily I shall be distasted by any, let them   10 know what is brought vnto them is drest after the English, French, Spanish and Italian manner: the assay is taken before, they shall not need to feare poysoning. You Gentlemen and friends that come in good-will, and not as Promooters into a country Market, to call our viands into question, whatsoeuer here is, much good may it doe you, I would it were better for you: for the rest I wish their lips such Lettuce as *Silenus* Asse, or their owne harts would desire.

Thine, *Robert Douland.*

Ad Robertum Doulandum Ioannis
filium de Musico suo conuiuio.

Ergonè *diuini genitoris plectra resumis,*
Reddat vt attonitos iterum tua Musa Britannos?
Vt nimia totum rapias dulcedine mundum,   5
DOVLANDI & resonet nomen nemus omne, superbam
Quà mundi dominam vaga TIBRIDIS alluit vnda;
Littora quà rutilis verrit Pactolus arenis,
Aut sese immiscet glaciali Vistula ponto,
Vincere quem nequeat LINVS, nec Thracius ORPHEVS,   10
Credo equidem, vt nostras demulceat Entheus aures.
Somnio Threicidum voces, & murmura cœli
Antiquosque modos, rediuiuaque Dorica castra,
Illius vt vario cantillet gutture Musa,
Macte animo ROBERTE tuo, charique parentis   15
Pergito candorem, moresque imitarier artes
Auspicijsque bonis celebret te fama per orbem
Funera post Patris Phœnixque renascitor alter.

Henricus Peachamus.

I.

The Right Honourable *George* Earle of Cumberland.

My heauie sprite opprest with sorrowes might,
Of wearied limbs the burthen soare sustaines,
With silent grones and harts teares still complaines,
Yet I breath still and liue in lifes despight.   5

Haue I lost thee? All fortunes I accurse,
bids thee farewell, with thee all ioyes farewell,
And for thy sake this world becomes my hell.
[Music by] *Anthony Holborne.*

II.

The Right Honourable *Robert* Earle of Essex: Earle Marshall of
England.

Change thy minde since she doth change,
Let not Fancy still abuse thee:
Thy vntruth cannot seeme strange,
When her falshood doth excuse thee.   5
  Loue is dead and thou art free,
  She doth liue but dead to thee.

2 Whilst she lou'd thee best a while,
See how she hath still delaid thee:
Vsing shewes for to beguile,   10
Those vaine hopes that haue deceiu'd thee.
  Now thou seest although too late,
  Loue loues truth which women hate.

3 Loue no more since she is gone,
Shee is gone and loues another: 15
Being once deceiu'd by one,
Leaue her loue but loue none other.
  She was false bid her adew,
  She was best but yet vntrue.

4 Loue farewell more deere to mee   20
Then my life which thou preseruest:
Life all ioyes are gone from thee,
Others haue what thou deseruest.
  Oh my death doth spring from hence
  I must dye for her offence.   25

5 Dye, but yet before thou dye
Make her know what she hath gotten:
She in whom my hopes did lye,
Now is chang'd, I quite forgotten.
  She is chang'd, but changed base,   30
  Baser in so vilde a place.
[Music by] *Richard Martin.*

III.

O Eyes leaue off your weeping,
Loue hath the thoughts in keeping,
   That may content you:
Let not this misconceiuing,
Where comforts are receiuing,   5
   Causles torment you.

2 Cloudes threaten but a shower,
Hope hath his happy houre,
   Though long in lasting.
Time needs must be attended,   10
Loue must not be offended
   With too much hasting.

3 But O the painfull pleasure,
Where Loue attends the leasure
   Of liues wretchednesse: 15
Where Hope is but illusion,
And Feare is but confusion
   Of Loues happinesse.

4 But happy Hope that seeth
How Hope and Hap agreeth,   20
   Of life depriue me,
Or let me be assured,
When life hath death endured,
   Loue will reuiue me.

[Music by] *Robert Hales*,
Groome of her Maiesties Priuie
Chamber.

IIII.

Sir *Phillip Sidney*.

GOE my Flocke, goe get you hence,
Seeke some other place of feeding,
Where you may haue some defence,
Fro the stormes in my breast breeding,   5
And showers from mine eyes proceeding.

2 Leaue a wretch in whom all woe
Can abide to keepe no measure.
Merry flocke such one forgoe,
Vnto whom Myrth is displeasure,   10
Onely rich in measures treasure.

3 Yet alas before you goe
Heare your wofull Maisters story,
Which to stones I else would shew,
Sorrow onely then hath glory   15
When tis excellently sorry.

4 *Stella*, fayrest Shepherdesse,
Fayrest but yet cruelst euer.
Stella, whom the heau'ns still blesse,
Though against me she perseuer,   20
Though I blisse inherit neuer.

5 *Stella*, hath refused mee:
Stella, who more Loue hath proued
In this Catiffe hart to be
Then can in good to vs be moued   25
Towards Lambe-kins best beloued.

6 *Stella* hath refused mee
Astrophel, that so well serued,
In this pleasant spring (*Muse*) see
While in pride Flowers be preseru'd   30
Himselfe onely Winter-starued.

7 Why alas then doth she sweare
That she loueth mee so deerely,
Seeing mee so long to beare
Coales of Loue that burne so cleerely,   35
And yet leaue me hopelesse meerely.

8 Is that Loue? forsooth I trow
If I saw my good Dogge grieued
And a help for him did know
My Loue should not be belieued   40
But hee were by mee relieued.

9 No she hates mee (*well away*)
Fayning Loue, somewhat to please mee,
Knowing, if she should display
All her hate, Death soone would seize me,   45
And of hideous torments ease me.

10 Then my flocke now adew,
But alas, if in your straying
Heauenly *Stella* meet with you,
Tell her in your pittious blaying,   50
Her poore slaues iust decaying.
                          [Music:] *D'incerto.*

V.

Sir *Phillip Sidney.*

O Deere life when shall it be,
That mine eyes thine eyes may see,
  And in them thy minde discouer,
Whether absence hath had force,   5
Thy remembrance to diuorce,
  From the Image of thy Louer?

2 O if I my selfe finde not,
By thine absence oft forgot,
  Nor debarde from *Beauties* treasure: 10
Let no Tongue aspire to tell
In what high [ioyes] I shall dwell,
  Onely Thought aymes at the pleasure.

3 Thought therefore will I send thee,
To take vp the place for mee,   15
  Long I will not after tarry:
There vnseene thou mayst be bolde
Those fayre wonders to behold,
  Which in them my hopes doe carry.

4 Thought, see thou no place forbeare,   20
Enter brauely euery where,
  Seize on all to her belonging:
But if thou wouldest guarded be,
Fearing her beames, take with thee,
  Strength of liking, rage of longing.   25

5 O my Thoughts, my thoughts, surcease,
Your delights my woes increase,
  My life fleetes with too much thinking:
Thinke no more, but dye in mee
Till thou shalt receiued be   30
  At her lips my *Nectar* drinking.
                          [Music:] *D'incerto*.

VI.

The Right Honourable *Robert*, Earle of Essex: Earle Marshall of England.

To plead my faith where faith hath no reward,
To moue remorse where fauour is not borne:
To heape complaints wher she doth not regard,
Were fruitlesse, bootelesse, vaine and yeeld but scorne.   5
I loued her whom all the world admir'de.
I was refus'de of her that can loue none:
And my vaine hopes which far too high asspir'de
Is dead and buri'd and for euer gone.
Forget my name since you haue scornde my Loue,   10
And woman-like doe not too late lament:
Since for your sake I doe all mischiefe proue,
I none accuse nor nothing doe repent.
I was as fonde as euer she was faire,
Yet lou'd I not more then I now dispaire.   15
            [Music by] M. *Daniell Batchelar*, Groome of
                her Maiesties Priuie Chamber.

VII.

Sir *Phillip Sidney*.

  IN a groue most rich of shade,
Where Birds wanton musicke made,
May then in his pide weeds shewing,
New perfumes with flowers fresh growing.   5

  2 *Astrophell* with *Stella* sweet
Did for mutuall comfort meet,
Both within themselues oppressed,
But either in each other blessed.

3 Him great harmes had taught much care   10
Her faire necke a foule yoke bare,
But her sight his care did banish,
In his sight her yoke did vanish.

4 Wept they had, alas the while,
But now teares themselues did smile,   15
While their eyes by Loue directed,
Interchangeably, reiected.

5 Sigh'd they had: but now betwixt
Sighs of woe were glad sighs mixt,
With Armes crost, yet testifying   20
Restlesse rest, and liuing dying.

6 Their eares hungry of each word
Which the deare tongue would afford:
But their tongues restrain'd from walking,
Till their harts had ended talking.   25

7 But when their tongues could not speake,
Loue it selfe did silence breake:
Loue did see his lips asunder,
Thus to speake in Loue and wonder.

8 *Stella*, soueraigne of my Ioy,   30
Faire Triumphres in annoy:
Stella, starre of heauenly fire,
Stella, load-starre of desire.

9 *Stella*, in whose shining eyes,
Are the lights of Cupids skyes,   35
Whose beames when they are once darted,
Loue therewith is straight imparted.

10 *Stella*, whose voice when it speakes,
Senses all asunder breake:
Stella, whose voyce when it singeth,   40
Angels to acquaintance bringeth.

11 *Stella*, in whose body is,
Writ the Caracters of blisse:
Whose sweet face all beautie passeth,
Saue the minde which it surpasseth.   45

12 Graunt, O graunt, but speach (alas)
Failes me, fearing on to passe:
Graunt to me, what am I saying?
But no fault there is in praying.

13 Graunt (O deere) on knees I pray,   50
(Knees on ground hee then did stay)
That not I but since I proue you,
Time and place from mee nere moue you.

14 Neuer season was more fit,
Neuer roome [more] apt for it: 55
Smiling ayre allowes my reason,
These Birds sing, now vse the season.

15 This small winde which so sweet is,
See how it leaues leaues doth kisse,
Each tree in his best attyring,   60
Sence of Loue to Loue inspyring.

16 Loue makes earth the water drinke,
Loue to earth makes water sincke,
And if dumbe things be so wittie,
Shall a heauenly Grace want pittie?   65

17 There his hands in their speech faine
Would haue made tongues language plaine
But her hands his hands compelling,
Gaue repulse, all Grace expelling.

18 Therewithall, away she went   70
Leauing him with passion rent
With what she had done and spoken,
That therewith my song is broken.
         [Music by Guillaume] *Tesseir.*

VIII.

Sir *Henry Lea.*   For one Voice only to sing.

FArre from triumphing Court and wonted glory,
He dwelt in shadie vnfrequented places,
Times prisoner now he made his pastime story,
Gladly forgets Courts erst afforded graces,   5
That Goddesse whom hee serude to heau'n is gone,
And hee on earth, In darknesse left to moane.

2 But loe a glorious light from his darke rest
Shone from the place where erst this Goddesse dwelt
A light whose beames the world with fruit hath blest   10
Blest was the Knight while hee that light beheld:
Since then a starre fixed on his head hath shinde,
And a Saints Image in his hart is shrinde.

3 Rauisht with ioy so grac't by such a Saint,
He quite forgat his Cell and selfe denaid,   15
He thought it shame in thankfulnesse to faint,
Debts due to Princes must be duely paid:
Nothing so hatefull to a noble minde,
As finding kindnesse for to proue vnkinde.

4 But ah poore Knight though thus in dreame he ranged,   20
Hoping to serue this Saint in sort most meete,
Tyme with his golden locks to siluer changed
Hath with age-fetters bound him hands and feete,
Aye mee, hee cryes, Goddesse my limbs grow faint,
Though I times prisoner be, be you my Saint.   25
        [Music by] M. *Iohn Douland* Batchelar of Musicke.

IX.

LAdy if you so spight me,
Wherefore do you so oft kisse and delight mee?
Sure that my hart opprest and ouer-cloyed,
May breake thus ouer-ioyed,
If you seeke to spill mee,   5
Come Kisse me sweet and kill mee,
So shal your hart be eased,
And I shall rest content and dye well pleased.
        [Music by] M. *Iohn Douland* Batchelar of Musicke.
                [poem after Cesare Rinaldi]

X.

In darknesse let mee dwell, The ground shall sorrow be,
The roofe Dispaire to barre all cheerfull light from mee,
The wals of marble blacke that moistned still shall weepe,
My musicke hellish iarring sounds to banish friendly sleepe.

Thus wedded to my woes, And bedded to my Tombe,   5
O Let me liuing die, Till death doe come,
In darknesse let mee dwell.
> [Music by] M. *Iohn Douland* Batchelar of Musicke.

XI.

Airs du Court.

Si le parler & le silence
Nuit à nostre heur esgalement,
Parlons donc ma chere esperance
Du coeur & des yeux seulement: 5
   Amour ce petit dieu volage
   Nous apprend ce muet langage.

Que le regard vole & reuole
Messager des nos passions,
Et serue au lieu de la parole   10
Pour dire nos intentions.
   Amour.

Mais si quelque ame est offencée
De nous voir discourir des yeux,
Nous parlerons de la pensée   15
Comme les Anges dans les cieux.
   Amour.

Ainsi par vn doux artifice
Nous tromperons les courtisans,
Et nous rirons de la malice   20
De mile facheux mesdisans,
   Qui n'en scauront pas d'auantage
   Ignorant ce muet langage.
> [Music:] D'incerto

XII.

Airs du Court.

Ce penser qui sans fin tirannise ma vie,
Se montre tellement contre moy coniuré,
Que tant plus ie m'efforce à dompter son enuie,
Et tant moins à mon bien ie le voy preparé.   5

I'ay quitté la beauté dont il a pris naissance,
Esperant par l'oubly ses charmes deceuoir
Mais ie trouue à la fin que la veue & l'absence
Sont tous deux differends, & d'vn mesme pouuoir.

I'ay maintefois iuré du change faire espreuue   10
Pour faire qu'vn dessein fust par l'autre deffait,
Mais à toutes les fois, aussi tost ie me treuue
Infidelle en parole, & fidelle en effect.

I'ay des plus fiers dedains la puissance empruntée
Pour repousser le trait dont i'ay le coeur attaint,   15
Mais plus ie recognois par leur force domptée
Ma douleur veritable & mon remede feint.

Ainsi donc combatant le mal qui me possede
Sans voir par ces moyens ses tempestes calmer,
Ie me vay consommant dans mon propre remede   20
Comme vn Vaisseau qui brusle au milieu de la Mer.

Voilà comme en viuant en toute seruitude
Ie nourris vn penser dont l'impiteux effort,
Se monstre en mon endroit si plain d'ingratitude,
Qu'en luy donnant la vie il me donne la mort.   25
                    [Music:] D'incerto.

XIII.

Airs du Court.

Vous que le bon heur r'appelle
A vn seruage ancien,
Mourez aux peids de la belle
Qui vous daigne faire sien.   5

Glorieuse en vostre perte
Honorez vostre vainqueur,
Qui vous a la porte ouuerte
De la prison de son coeur.

Heureux venez vous donc rendre   10
A celle qui vous a pris,
C'est honneur de ce voir prendre
A qui tient tout à mespris.

Ainsi vostre ame reprise,
Finis toute liberté: 15
Glorieuse est l'enterprise
Qui guide à l'eternité.
              [Music:] *D'incerto.*

XIIII.

Espagnol.

PAssaua amor su arco dessarmado,
Los oios baxos blando y muy modesto,
Dexaua m'ya atras muy descuidado.

Quam poco espacio pude gozar esto,   5
Fortuna deembidiosa dixo luego:
Teneos amor porque vays tam presto.

Boluio de presto ami el nigno ciego,
Muy enoiado enuersé reprehendido
Que no ay reprehension do sta su fuego.   10

Ay prados, bosques, seluas, que criastes,
Tan libre coracon como ero el mio
Porque tan graue mal no te estoruastes.
              [Jorge de Montemayor]

XV.

Espagnol.

STa note mien yaua,
Call inferno mesctana my nandaua,
Non per ly mei pecate,
Ma per uider chi fanno lyny.   5

Standola mi pareua
Chi nel medso Plutone ses sedeua
Tra qui Spiriti infernali
Chi donno l'alma tanti stragi mali.

XVI.

VEstros oios tienen d'Amor no se que,
Que me yelan me roban me hieren me matan,
Que me matan, me matan a fè,
Porque me mirays con ta asticion,
y al mi coracon me aprisionays,   5
Que si vos me mirays yo os acusare.

XVII.

Italien. Dominico Maria Megli.

SE di farmi morire,
Con crudeltà pensate,
Certo che u'inganate.
Che da la crudeltà nascono lire,   5
E da lire lo sdegno,
Che scaccia Amor,
Dal suo superbo regno.

XVIII.

Giulio Caccini detto Romano.

Dourò dunque morire?
Pria che di nuouo io miri,
Voi bramata cagion de miei martiri
mio perduto tesoro   5
non potrò dirui
pria ch'io mora io moro?
O', miseria inaudita,
Non poter dir a voi moro mia vita.

XIX.

Giulio Caccini detto Romano.

AMarilli mia bella,
Non credi ò del mio cor dolce desio,
D'esser tu l'amor mio,
Credilo pur, è se timor t'assale,   5
Prendi questo mio strale
Aprimi'il petto, è vedrai scritto il core,
Amarilli e'l mio amore.

XX.

Italien.

O Bella piu che la stella Diana,
Chi par inansi de la mia patrona,
mi regina, dolce mi amore,
pieta, cor mia pieta, non piu dolore   5
bene mio caro, Core mio
bella, bella, tu se la mala morte mio
la fretsa chi mi pas il core.

THE TABLE.

Italian.

Se di farmi morire.	*Dom. Maria Megli.*	XVII.
Dourò dunque morire?	*Gui. Caccini det. Ro.*	XVIII
Amarilli mia bella.	*Gui. Caccini detto Ro.*	XIX.
O bella pipiu.	*D'incerto.*	XX.

FINIS.

Robert Jones

The Muses Gardin for Delights

1610

[First three lines xylographic; capitals are swash, and the tail of the *g* in *Delights* forms a flourish] THE/ *Muſes Gardin for/ Delights,/* [the following in type:] Or the fift Booke of Ayres, onely for the Lute, the/ Baſe-vyoll, and the Voyce./ [rule]/ *Compoſed* [C swash] *by* ROBERT IONES./ *Quæ* [Q swash] *proſuntſingula, multa iuuant./* [rule]/ [cut of garden, arbor, and two gardeners]/ *LONDON* [second *N* swash]/ Printed by the Aſsignes of *William Barley.* [*B* swash] 1610./

Note: The cut on the title page first appeared on sig. D1 of Thomas Hill's *The Gardeners Labyrinth*, first printed by Henry Bynneman in 1577. Subsequent editions by Bynneman (1578), John Wolfe (1586), and Adam Islip (1594) also have the cut on D1, but it is missing from H. Ballard's edition (1608). The type used in Jones's book indicates that the printer was John Windet (as for Jo1609); Windet no doubt got the cut from Islip, from whom he also got the title page compartment used in Gr1604, Bt1606 and others, McK. & F. No. 232.

Collation: 2°; π², A–G² (second leaves not signed); 16 leaves.

Headlines: Recto and verso, A1v–G1v (no headline on C1): *CANTVS. [ANTVS* D1] I. [–XXI Periods after all but XXI] *ROBERT IONES. | BASSVS. [BASSVS* on facing recto for XII (D2), XIII (E1), XX (G1), and XXI (G2)]

Contents: π1, title page; π1v blank; π2, dedication; π2v, epistle; A1, table; A1v–B2, songs I–VI, one per page; B2v–C1, song VII; C1v–D1, songs VIII–XI, one per page; D1v–D2, song XII; D2v–E1, song XIII; E1v–F2, songs XIIII–XIX, one per page; F2v–G2, songs XX–XXI, one per opening; G2v blank.

SR: No entry.

STC: 14736.

Copy: Huntington (62107).

The music for all the songs consists of a Cantus with lute tablature and a bass viol part either inverted on the same page or on the facing page.

TO THE TRVE HONOVRABLE,
AND ESTEEMED WORTHIE, THE
RIGHT WORSHIPFVLL THE
LADY Wroth.

Most Honoured Lady, my eldest and first issue, hauing thriu'd so well vnder the protection of your Right Honourable Father, blame not this my yongest and last Babe, if it desirously seeke Sanctuarie with your selfe, as being a most worthy branch from so Noble and renowned a stocke: It is hereditarie to your whole house, not onely to be truely Honourable in your selues, but to be the fauourers and furtherers of all honest and vertuous endeuours in others. And that makes me so farre daring, as to presume to offer this Dedication to your faire acceptance; And howsoeuer my defects therein may happily (or rather vnhappily) be many: Yet am I most confident (and that growes from the worthinesse of your owne nature) that your Honourable minde will be pleased (since it casts it selfe most humbly in your armes) to giue it willing entertainement, and to countenance it with the faire Liuerie of your noble Name, It may bee slighted in respect of its owne valew, but your fauourable acceptance, will both grace it, and my selfe, as a poore Table hung vp, euen in Princes Gallories, not for the Wood, but for the Picture, And so (Noble Lady) not daring to bee iealous of your Honourable entertainement, I rest

Your Ladyship deuoted in all dutie,
ROBERT IONES.

To the friendly Censurers.

DEare friends, for so I call you, if you please to accept my good meaning, I presented you last with a Dreame, in which I doubt not but your fantasies haue receiued some reasonable contentment, and now if you please to bee awaked out of that Dreame, I shall for your recreation and refreshing, guide you to the MVSES GARDEN, *where you shall find such varietie of delights, that questionlesse you will willingly spend some time in the view thereof. In your first entrance into which Garden, you shall meete with Loue, Loue, and nought but Loue, set foorth at large in his colours, by way of decyphering him in his nature. In the midst of it, you shall find Loue reiected, vpon inconstancie* 1 *and hard measure of ingratitude: Touching them that are louers, I leaue them to their owne censure in Loues description. And now for the end, it is variable in another maner, for the delight of the eare to satisfie opinion. I am not so arrogant to commend mine owne gifts, neither yet so degenerate, as to beg your tolleration. If these delights of Flowers, or varietie of Fruites, may any wayes be pleasing to your senses, I shall be glad. Otherwise I will vow neuer to set, sow, plant or graft, and my labours henceforth shall cease to trouble you, if you will needs mislike, I care not. I will preuent your censures, and defie your malice, if you despise me, I am resolute, if you vse me with respect, I bid you most heartily* 2

Farewell.
R. I.

THE TABLE.

I.

Loue Is a prettie Frencie,
a melancholy fire,
begot by lookes, maintain'd with hopes,
and heythen'd, by desire.

2

5

Loue is a pretie Tyrant,
By our affections armed,
Take them away, none liues this day,
The Coward boy hath harmed.

3

10

Loue is a pretie Idole,
Opinion did deuise him,
His votaries is slouth and lies,
The Robes that doe disguise him.

4

15

Loue is a pretie Painter,
And counterfeiteth passion,
His shadow'd lies, makes fansies rise,
To set beliefe in fashion.

5

20

Loue is a pretie Pedler,
Whose Packe is fraught with sorrowes,
With doubts with feares, with sighs with teares,
Some ioyes, but those he borrowes.

6

25

Loue is a pretie nothing,
Yet what a quoile it keepes,
With thousand eyes of iealousies,
Yet no one euer sleepes.

II.

Soft Cupid soft, There is no haste,
For all vnkindnesse gone and past.
Since thou wilt needs forsake me so,
let vs parte friendes, before thou goe.

2

5

Still shalt thou haue my heart to vse,
When I cannot otherwise chuse,
My life thou mayst command Saunce doubt,
Command I say and goe with out.

3

10

And if that I doe euer proue,
False and vnkind to gentle Loue,
Ile not desire to liue a day,
Nor any longer then I may.

4

15

Ile dayly blesse the little God,
But not without a smarting rod,
Wilt thou still vnkindly leaue mee,
Now I pray God all ill goe with thee.

III.

As I the silly Fish deceiue,
so Fortune playes with me,
whose baites my heart of ioyes bereaue,
and Angels taketh mee,
I still doe fish, yet am I caught,
and taken am, their taking taught.

5

2

The Riuer wherein I doe swimme,
Of streames of hope is made,
Where ioyes as flowers dresse the brimme,
And frownes doe make my shade.
Whence smiles as sun-shine giues me heat,
And shadow frownes from showers beat.

10

3

Thus taken like an enuious one,
Who glads for others care,
Since he himselfe must feele such mone,
Delights, all, so should fare,
And striue to make them know like smart,
So make I this to beare a part.

15

20

IIII.

THe fountaines smoake, And yet no flames they shewe,
Starres shine all night Though vndesern'd by day,
and trees doe spring, yet are not seene to growe,
And shadowes mooue, Although they seeme to stay,
  in Winters woe, Is buried Summers blisse,   5
  and Loue loues most, when loue most secret is.

2 *The stillest streames descries the greatest deepe,*
  The clearest skie is subiect to a shower,
  Conceit's most sweete, when as it seemes to sleepe,
  And fairest dayes doe in the morning lower,   10
    The silent Groues sweete Nimphs they cannot misse,
    For loue loues most, where loue most secret is.

3 *The rarest Iewels, hidden vertue yeeld,*
  The sweete of traffique, is a secret gaine,
  The yeere once old doth shew a barren field,   15
  And Plants seeme dead, and yet they spring againe,
    Cupid is blind, the reason why, is this,
    Loue loueth most, where loue most secret is.

V.

WAlking by a Riuer side,
in prime of Summers morning,
viewing Phœbus in his pride,
the siluer streames adorning,
  And passing on my selfe alone,   5
  Me thought I heard a wofull grone.

2

Still I stood as one amaz'd
To heare this wofull crying,
Round about me then I gaz'd,   10
In euery Meddow prying.
  Yet could I not this wight surprise,
  Although the voice did pierce the skies.

3

Venus thou hast kild my heart,   15
And quite my soule confounded,
Thy sonne Cupid with his dart,
My vitall parts hath wounded,
  Shoote home proud boy, and doe thy worst,
  That shee may die that liues accurst.   20

4

Draw thy shaft vnto the head,
And strongly it deliuer,
Draw that thou mayst strike her dead,
That liues a hopelesse Louer,   25
  Let come blind boy to satisfie,
  His mind that most desires to die.

VI.

I Cannot chuse but giue a smile,
To see how Loue doeth all beguile,
Except it bee my frozen heart,
That yeeldes not to his fierie Dart.

2   5

Belike I was Achillis like,
Drencht in that fatall hardning flood,
My flesh it feares no push of pike,
The speare against me doth no good.

3   10

Onely my heele may Cupid hit,
And yet I care not much for it,
Because the hurt I cannot feele,
Vnlesse my heart were in my heele.

The Answere.   15

I

I cannot chuse but needes must smile,
To see how Loue doth thee beguile,
Which did of purpose frieze thy heart,
To thaw it to thy greater smart.   20

2

Suppose thou wert Achillis like,
Drencht in that fatall hardning flood,
That might auaile gainst push of pike,
But gainst his dart t'will doe no good. 25

3

For if thy heele he doe but hit,
His venom'd shaft will rancle it,
The force whereof the heart must feele,
Conuaide by Arteryes from thy heele. 30

VII.

Ioye in thy hope, the earnest of thy Loue,
For so thou mayst Enioye thy hearts desire
True hopes, things absent doe as present prooue,
And keepe aliue Loues still renewing fire.

2 5

But of thy hope let silence be thy tongue,
And secresie the heart of louing fire,
For hopes reuealed may thy hopes prolong,
Or cut them off in prime-time of desire.

3 10

Sweete are those hopes that doe them selues enioy,
As vowed to them selues to liue and Dye,
Sweetest those ioyes and freest from annoy,
That waken not the eye of iealousie.

L'ENVOY. 15

Thy loue is not thy loue, if not thine owne,
And so it is not, if it once be knowne.

VIII.

How many new yeres haue grow'n old,
Since first your seruant old was new,
How many long howers haue I told,
Since first my loue was vow'd to you,
  And yet alas, Shee doeth not know 5
  whether her seruant loue or no.

2

How many wals as white as Snow,
And windowes cleere as any glasse,
Haue I coniur'd to tell you so,   10
Which faithfully performed was,
  And yet you'l sweare you do not know,
  Whether your seruant loue or no.

3

How often hath my pale leane face,   15
With true Characters of my loue,
Petitioned to you for grace,
Whom neither sighs nor teares can moue,
  O cruell yet doe you not know,
  Whether your seruant loue or no?   20

4

And wanting oft a better token,
I haue beene faine to send my heart,
Which now your cold disdaine hath broken,
Nor can you healt by any art,   25
  O looke vpon't and you shall know,
  Whether your seruant loue or no.

IX.

THere was a Shepheard that did liue,
  And helde his thoughtes as hie
As were the Mounts, whereon his flockes
  did hourely feede him by.
He from his youth, his tender youth,   5
  which was vnapt to keepe,
Or hopes, or feares, or loues, or cares,
  or thoughts but of his sheepe

2

Did with his dogge as Shepheards doe,   10
  For Shepheards wanting wit,
Deuise some sports, though foolish sports,
  Yet sports for Shepheards fit,

The boy that (yet) was but a boy,
  And so desir's were hid,   15
Did grow a man, and men must loue,
  And loue this Shepheard did,

3

He loued much, none can too much.
  Loue one so high diuine,   20
As but her selfe, none but her selfe,
  So faire, so fresh, so fine,
He vowed by his Shepheards weede,
  An Oath which Shepheards keepe,
That he would follow Phillyday,   25
  Before a flocke of sheepe.

X.

THe Sea hath many thousand sands,
  The Sunne hath motes as many,
The skie is full of starres, And loue
  as full of woes as anny,
Beleeue me that doe knowe the elfe,   5
  and make no tryall by thy selfe.

2

It is in trueth a prettie toye,
  For babes to play withall,
But O the honies of our youth,   10
  Are oft our ages gall,
Selfe proofe in time will make thee know,
  He was a Prophet told thee so.

3

A Prophet that Cassandra like,   15
  Tels trueth without beliefe,
For head-strong youth will runne his race,
  Although his Goale be griefe,
Loues Martyr when his heate is past,
  Prooues cares Confessor at the last.   20

XI.

Once did my thoughts both ebbe and flowe,
  As passion did them mooue,
Once did I hope, straight feare againe,
  And then I was in Loue.

2

                        5

Once did I waking spend the night,
  And told how many minutes mooue,
Once did I wishing waste the day,
  And then I was in loue.

3

                       10

Once by my caruing true loues knot,
  The weeping trees did proue,
That wounds and teares were both our lots,
  And then I was in loue.

4

                       15

Once did I breath an others breath,
  And in my mistris moue,
Once was I not mine owne at all,
  And then I was in loue.

5

                       20

Once woare I bracelets made of hayre,
  And collers did aproue,
Once were my clothes made out of waxe,
  And then I was in loue.

6

                       25

Once did I Sonnet to my Saint,
  My soule in number mou'd,
Once did I tell a thousand lies,
  And then in trueth I lou'd.

7

                       30

Once in my eare did dangling hang,
  A little turtle Doue,
Once in a word I was a foole,
  And then I was in loue.

XII.

I Am so farre from pittying thee,
That wear'st a branch of Willow tree,
That I doe enuie thee and all,
that once was high & got a fall,
  O willow willow willo tree   5
  I would thou didst belong to mee.

2

Thy wearing Willow doth imply,
That thou art happier farre then I,
For once thou wert where thou wouldst be,   10
Though now thou wear'st the Willow tree,
  O Willow willow sweete willow,
  Let me once lie vpon her pillow.

3

I doe defie both bough and roote,   15
And all the friends of hell to boote,
One houre of Paradised ioye,
Makes Purgatorie seeme a toye,
  O willow willow doe thy worst,
  Thou canst not make me more accurst.   20

4

I haue spent all my golden time,
In writing many a louing rime,
I haue consumed all my youth,
In vowing of my faith and trueth.   25
  O willow willow willow tree,
  Yet can I not beleeued bee.

5

And now alas it is too late,
Gray hayres the messenger of fate,   30
Bids me to set my heart at rest,
For beautie loueth yong men best,
  O willow willo I must die,
  Thy seruants happier farre then I.

XIII.

As I lay lately in a dreame,
me thought I saw a wonderous thing,
a woman faire transformed was
into a Fidle without a string,
A Metamorphosis so rare,   5
as all most made mee wake for feare,
  O this is rare,
  yea verie rare,
  A wonderous thing
  so faire a Fidle   10
  Didle, didle didle,
  So faire a Fidle
  should want a string.

2

Till honest neighbours dwelling nigh,
Said they would all her wants supply,
And said that they haue strings in store,   15
For such a Fidle and fortie more,
For loue they beare vnto the sport,
Theyle make her fit for the consort.
  O this is rare,
  Yea, very rare.   20

3

Theyle send her first to some that can,
Put in the peg, and peg her than,
If that her bridge be broken so,
As that the Fidle cannot go,   25
Theyle soone deuise some other way,
To make her sound the round-delay.
  O this is rare,
  Yea very rare.

4   30

When they haue set her in the keye,
You must not straine her strings so high,

For feare the Fidle chance to crake,
Nor let the strings be too too slacke,
The Diapason is her sound, 35
The lowest note is most profound.
 O this is rare,
 Yea very rare.

                    5

But note a discord in Musicke, 40
To sound some Note without the pricke,
And then for keeping of your moode,
Sing three to one thats passing good,
Of all the Notes in Gamuet scale,
The Long is that which must not faile. 45
 O this is rare.
 Yea very rare.

                XIIII.

THere was a wyly ladde, met with a bonny lasse,
much pretie sport they had, but I wot not what it was,
hee woed her for a kisse, She plainely said him no,
  I pray quoth he, nay nay quoth Shee,
  I pray you let mee goe. 5

                2

Full many louely tearms did passe in merrie glee,
He cold her in his armes, and daunc't her on his knee,
And faine he would haue paide such debts as he did owe,
  I pray quoth he, nay nay quoth shee, 10
  I pray you let me goe.

                3

Sweete be you not so nice to gratifie a friend,
If kissing be a vice, my sute is at an end,
Noe noe it is the rule, to learne a man to woe, 15
  I pray quoth he, nay nay quoth shee,
  I pray you let me goe.

4

For Cupid hath an eye, to play a louers part,
And swift his arrowes flie to leauell at the heart,   20
Thy beautie was my bane, that brought me to his bowe,
 I pray quoth he, nay nay quoth shee,
 I pray you let me goe.

5

Good Sir alas you feede, your fancie with conceit,   25
Sweete sweet how should we speede, if louers could not speake.
I speake but what I wish, the spirit wils me so,
 I pray quoth he, nay nay quoth shee,
 I pray you let me goe.

6   30

With that shee swore an Oath, and loth she was to breake it,
And so to please them both, he gaue and shee did take it,
There was no labour lost, true amitie to show,
 Adew quoth he, nay, stay quoth shee,
 Let's kisse before you goe.   35

XV.

My father faine would haue mee take
a man that hath a beard,
my mother shee cries out alacke,
and makes mee much afraide,
forsooth I am not olde enough,   5
nowe surely this is goodly stuffe,
Faith let my mother marrie mee,
or let some young man burie mee.

2

For I haue liu'd these fourteene yeeres,   10
My mother knowes it well,
What neede shee then to cast such feares,
Can any body tell?
As though yong women doe not know,
That custome will not let them wo,   15
I would bee glad if I might chuse,
But I were madde if I refuse.

3

My mother bids me goe to Schoole,
And learne to doe some good,   20
T'were well if shee would let the foole,
Come home and sucke a dugge,
As if my father knew not yet,
That maidens are for yong men fit,
Giue me my mind and let me wed,   25
Or you shall quickly find me dead.

4

How soone my mother hath forgot,
That euer shee was yong,
And how that shee denyed not,   30
But sung another song,
I must not speake what I doe thinke,
When I am drie I may not drinke.
Though her desire be now growen old,
She must haue fier when shee is cold.   35

5

You see the mother loues the sonne,
The father loues the maide,
What would shee haue me be a Nun?
I will not be delaide,   40
I will not liue thus idle still,
My mother shall not haue her will,
My father speaketh like a man,
I will be married doe what shee can.

XVI.

My loue hath her true loue betraide,
Why tis a fault that is to common
yet shall it not be euer saide,
my faith depended on a woman,
  If shee did, to prooue vntrue,   5
  I shall doe worse, to change for new.

2

She hath some vertues followe them,
Take not example by her lightnesse,
Be not amongst the vulgar men.   10
Though she be clouded, keepe thy brightnesse:
  Perhaps her selfe in time may prooue,
  What tis to wrong a constant loue.

3

The many vowes giuen by my faire,   15
Were none of hers: the wind did owe them,
Then weare they breath, now are they ayre.
Whence first they came, there she bestowes them.
  Then maruell not thou women alter,
  When all things turne to their first matter.   20

XVII.

ALL my sense thy sweetenesse gained,
Thy faire hayre my heart enchained.
My poore reason thy wordes mooued,
So that thee like heauen I loued.
  Fa, la, la, lire deridan,   5
  Fa, la, la, leridan,
  Fa, la, la, lerideridane,
  lerideridan leridan dei,
while to my minde the outside stoode,
for messenger of inward good.   10

2

Now thy sweetnesse sowre is deemed,
Thy hayre not worth a hayre esteemed,
While to my minde the outside stood,
Finding that, but words they proou'd,   15
        Fa, la, la,
        Dan, dan, dan.
For no faire Signe can credit winne,
If that the substance faile within.

3   20

No more in thy sweetenesse glorie,
For thy knitting hayre be sorie,
Vse thy words but to bewaile thee,
That no more thy beames auaile thee,
    Fa, la, la,   25
    Dan, dan, dan:
Lay not thy colours more to viewe,
Without the Picture be found true.

4

Woe to me, alas shee weepeth,   30
Foole in me, what folly creepeth.
Was I to blasphemie enraged,
Where my soule I haue engaged,
    Fa, la, la,
    Dan, dan, dan,   35
And wretched I must yeeld to this
The fault I blame her chastnesse is.

5

Sweetnesse sweetely pardon folly,
Tye my hayre your captiue solly,   40
Words O words of heauenly knowledge,
Know my words their faults acknowledge,
    Fa, la, la,
    Dan, dan, dan,
And all my life I will confesse,   45
The lesse I loue, I liue the lesse.
        [Sir Philip Sidney]

XVIII.

To the deafe Aspe with dying voice,
Sadly I Sing this heauie charme,
that if thy heart doe ere reioyce,
and set at nought my grieuous harme,
this verse writ with a dead mans arme,   5
  may haunt thy senselesse eyes and eares,
  turne ioyes to Cares, and hopes to feares.

By thy Creators pietie,
By her that brought thee to this light,
By thy deare Nurses loue to thee, 10
By Loue it selfe, Heauens, Day, and Night,
By all that can thy sense delight,
  When I am cold, and wrapt in Lead,
  Remember oft thy seruant dead.

So shall my shadow thee attend, 15
Like calmest breath of Westerne wind,
If not: with grones it shall ascend,
Like Rauen, Owle, Beare, or hellish feind,
Ratling the chaines which doe it bind,
  And where thou art by silent night, 20
  It shall thy guiltie soule affright.

Yet Sea-men tost with stormie Wind,
Voide of all hope, resolu'd to die,
From powerfull heauens oft mercie find,
And so may I find grace with thee, 25
No, no, thou canst not pitie me,
  Aspes cannot heare, nor liue can I,
  Thou hearest not, vnheard I die.

XIX.

Behold her locks like wyers of beaten gold,
her eyes like stars that twinkle in the skie,
Her heauenly face, not fram'd of earthly mold,
her voice that sounds the heauens melody,
  the miracles of time, the worldes storie, 5
  Fortunes Queene, Loues treasure, Natures glorie.

No flattering hopes shee likes, blind Fortunes baite,
Nor shadowes of delight, fond fancies glasse,
Nor charmes that doe inchant, false Arts deceipt,
Nor fading ioyes, which time makes swiftly passe, 10
  But chast desires, which beateth all these downe,
  A Goddesse looke is worth a Monarches Crowne.

XX.

Aᴌthough the wings of my desires bee clipte,
and my Loue thoughtes, from mounting lowlye bounded,
though slie suspect my ioyes with frost hath nipt,
So as my hopes with feares are still surrounded,
yet will I liue to loue, although through loue I die,   5
and Cumbers still do grow, and comforts from mee flie,
No iealous thoughts shall force mee to retyre,
but I will hope to enioye my hearts desire.

Which likes to Loue, and yet the same conceale,
Remembrance chiefly working my relieuing,   10
Though times of ioye be short, yet will I steale
Such times, to keepe my heart from further grieuing,
Force may remooue my lookes, but not expell my ioy,
Though Cupids shaft giue curelesse wounds, tis no annoy,
Whilest life endures, Ile loue though seeme to shunne   15
That Port of rest, from whence my comforts come.

XXI.

Mɪght I redeeme myne errours with mine eyes,
and shed but for each seuerall sinne a teare,
The summe to such a great account should rise,
that I should neuer make mine Audit cleare,
  The totall is too bigge to paye the score,   5
  I am so rich in sinne, in teares so poore.

2.

O wretched wealth that doth procure such want,
Vnhappy soule to bee so rich in sin,
The store whereof doth make all graces scant,   10
And stops thy teares, ere they doe scarce begin,
  What once a famous Poet sung be fore,
  I finde too true my plenty makes me poore.

3.

O might I prooue in this a prodigall,   15
And bate my meanes by less'ning of my stocke,
I should in grace grow great, in sinnes but small,

If I could euery day from forth the shocke
  But pull one eare, O ten-times happy want,
    When teares increase and sinnes doe grow more scant.   20

4.

O that my God with such sweete strokes would strike,
And by his grace so bank-rout mine estate,
That growing poore in sinne I Lazar like,
Might dayly beg for mercy at his gate,   25
  And craue (though not admittance to his feast)
  Some crums of grace to feede my soule at least.

FINIS.

John Maynard

The XII. Wonders of the World

1611

[Row of fleuron ornaments; cf. Plomer No. 66] THE/ XII. WONDERS/ OF THE VVORLD. [first *V* filed to make *W*]/ [rule]/ Set and compofed for the Violl de/ Gambo, the Lute, and the Voyce to Sing the/ Verfe, all three ioyntly, and none feuerall: alfo Leffons for/ the Lute and Bafe Violl to play alone: with fome Leffons to play/ *Lyra-wayes alone, or if you will, to fill vp the parts,/* with another Violl fet Lute-way./ Newly compofed by *Iohn Maynard,* [IM swash] Lutenift at the moft/ famous Schoole of St. *Iulians* [*I* swash] in Hartfordfhire./ [woodcut circular music staff with music, numerals 1–8 under the staff, and these words over it:] Oh followe me Tom Iohn and Wilcok three knaues in A knott followe mee hooe then [Printed at the left of the circle:] Eight parts in one vp-/ on one Plaine-fong,/ begin and end where/ you will, fo as you do/ come in a Semibriefe/ one after another./ [Below circle:] LONDON:/ Printed by *Thomas Snodham* for *Iohn Browne*, and are to be folde at his Shop/ in Saint *Dunftones* Church-yard in Fleetftreete. 1611./

Collation: 2°, *A–M*²; 24 leaves.

Headlines: A2v–G1v, verso: A Wonder. [C1v: A Wonder,] The Courtier. [–The Maide.] I [–XII. Periods after all but I] CANTVS. B1–G2, recto: A Wonder. [C1: A wonder.] The Courtier. [–The Maide.] I. [–XII.] BASSVS. G2v–I2v, verso: XIII. [–XVII.] Lute Lessons. H1–K1, recto: XIII. [–XVII. XVI misprinted for XV] BASSVS. K1v–L1, verso and recto: XVIII. [–XXI.] Lessons forthe [for the *after* K1v] Lyra Violl./ XVIII. [–XXI.] BASSVS. L1v–M1v, verso: XXII. [–XXIIII.] Lessons for the Lyra Violl. L2–M2, recto: XXII. [–XXIIII.] BASSVS.

Contents: A1, title page; A1v blank; A2, dedication; A2v–G2, songs I–XII, one per opening; G2v–K1, pieces for lute and viol, XIII–XVII, one per opening; K1v–L1, pieces for lyra and bass viols, XVIII–XXI, one per page; L1v–M2, pieces for lyra and bass viols, XXII–XXIIII, one per opening; M2v, table of songs and pieces.

SR: No entry.

STC: 17759.

Copies: BM (K.8.h.6, the text copy) and Bodleian (B.5.12 Art.).

Songs I–XII have a voice and lute accompaniment facing a bass viol part. Nos. XIII–XXIIII have tablature for lute or (after XVII) lyra viol facing a bass viol part (except XVIII–XXI, in which the bass is on the same page, inverted).

TO HIS EVER-HONOV-
RED LADY AND MISTRIS
the Lady *Ioane Thynne*, of Cause-Castle in
Shropshire, *Nestors* yeeres on earth, and Angels
happinesse in Heauen.

Madame.

W‍Hat at first priuately was entended for you, is at last publickely commended to you. This poore play-worke of mine, had its prime originall and birth-wrights in your own house, when by nearer seruice I was obliged yours. I am humbly-bould to present it to your Ladiships view and protection (if you will daigne to make happy by your Patronage so meane a worke) both for your well knowne loue to the Science, and your many many fauours conferred vpon my vndeseruing selfe, the louer and admirer of your Vertues. The powrefull perswasion of that nobly-disposed Gentlewoman Mris. *Dorothy Thynne*, your vertuous Daughter, whose breast is possest with an admirable hereditary loue of Musicke, and who once laboured mee to that effect, hath not a little emboldned mee herevnto. If there liue any good thing in mee, onely your *Onely-Selfe* is firstly interessed in the same, I being doubly bound, by your bountie on the one side, and my dutie on the other. Accept then, Gracious Lady, with vnwrinkled brow, the affectionate, though weake deuoyre of him that strongly desires to doe you seruice. I know it is not able Eagle-like to looke with an vndaunted eye against the brightfull Sunne of your matchlesse iudgement; wherein notwithstanding, if your Clemencie shall allowe it fauourable roome, I feare not the vnequallest front of the sowrest Criticke.

Thus lowly-laying both it and my selfe, the worthlesse Authour at your Worships seruice, I beseech *Him* that is the *Giuer of all things*, to

graunt vnto you, and your vertuous Daughters, a full confluence of
vnited Happinesse heere, and glory eternall hereafter.   30

Your Ladiships
in all humble
seruice
Iohn Maynard.

I

A Wonder.   The Courtier.

Long haue I liude in Court, yet learn'd not all this while,
To sell poore suters smoake, nor where I hate to smile:
Superiours to adore, Inferiours to despise:
To flie from such as fall, to follow such as rise,   5
To cloake a poore desire vnder a rich aray,
Nor to aspire by vice though t'were the quicker way.

[Sir John Davies]

II.

A Wonder.   The Deuine.

My calling is diuine, and I from God am sent,
I will no chop Church be, nor pay my Patron rent,
nor yeeld to sacriledge, but like the kinde true mother,
rather will loose all the Childe, then part it with another: 5
Much wealth I will not seeke, nor worldly Masters serue,
so to grow rich and fat while my poore flocke doth starue.

[Sir John Davies]

III.

A Wonder.   The Souldiour.

My Occupation is the Noble trade of Kings,
the tryall that decides the highest right of things.
Though *Mars* my Maister be I doe not *Venus* loue,
nor honour *Bacchus* oft, nor often sweare by *Ioue*,   5
Of speaking of my selfe I all occasion shunne,
and rather loue to doe, then boast what I haue done.

[Sir John Davies]

IIII.

A Wonder.   The Lawyer.

THE Law my Calling is, my robe, my tongue, my pen,
wealth and opinion gaine, and make me Iudge of men,
The knowne dishonest cause I neuer did defend,
nor spunne out sutes in length, but wisht and sought an end,   5
nor counsaile did bewray, nor of both parties take,
nor euer tooke I fee, for which I neuer spake.

[Sir John Davies]

V.

A Wonder.   The Phisition.

I Studie to vphold the slippery state of Man,
who dies when wee haue done the best, and all wee can,
From practise and from bookes I draw my learned skill,
not from the knowne receipt or Pothecaries bill.   5
The earth my faults doth hide, The world my Cures doth see,
What youth and time effects is oft ascrib'd to mee.

[Sir John Davies]

VI.

A Wonder.   The Marchant.

MY trade doth euery thing to euery land supply,
Discouers vnknowne coasts, strange countryes doth allye:
I neuer did forestall, I neuer did ingrose,
Nor custome did withdraw though I return'd with losse,   5
I thriue by faire exchange, By selling and by buying,
And not by Iewish vse, Reprisall fraud or lying.

[Sir John Davies]

VII.

A Wonder.   The Country Gentleman.

THough strange out landish spirits praise Townes, and
                                         Countries scorne,
The Country is my home, I dwell where I was borne:

There profit and command with pleasure I pertake,
yet doe not Haukes and Dogs my soul companions make.   5
I rule but not oppresse, End quarrels not maintaine,
See Townes but dwell not there to abridge my charge or traine.

[Sir John Davies]

VIII.

A Wonder.   The Batchelar.

How many things as yet are deare alike to mee?
The field, the horse, the Dog, Loue, Armes, or liberty.
I haue no Wife as yet, which I may call mine owne,
I haue no children yet that by my name are knowne,   5
Yet if I marryed were, I would not wish to thriue,
if that I could not tame, the veriest shrew aliue.

[Sir John Davies]

IX.

A Wonder.   The Marryed man.

I Onely am the man among all married men,
that doe not wish the Priest to be vnlinck'd agen,
And though my shoe did wring, I would not make my mone,
Nor thinke my neighbours chance more happy then mine owne,   5
Yet court I not my Wife, but yeeld obseruance due,
Being neither fond, nor crosse, nor iealous, nor vntrue.

[Sir John Davies]

X.

A Wonder.   The Wife.

The first of all our sexe came from the side of Man,
I thither am return'd from whence our sexe began.
I doe not visit oft, nor many when I doe,
I tell my minde to few, and that in counsaile too,   5
I seeme not sicke in health, Nor sullen but in sorrow,
I care for some what else then what to weare to morrow.

[Sir John Davies]

XI.

A Wonder.   The Widdow.

Mʏ dying Husband knew how much his death would grieue
mee,
and therefore left me wealth to comfort and relieue mee,
Though I no more will haue, I must not loue disdaine,
Penelope her selfe did Sutors entertaine,   5
And yet to draw on such as are of best esteeme,
nor younger then I am nor richer will I seeme.
[Sir John Davies]

XII.

A Wonder.   The Maide.

I Marriage would forsweare, but that I heare men tell,
that shee that dyes a mayde must lead an Ape in hell,
Therefore if fortune come I will not mocke and play,
nor driue the bargaine on, till it be driuen away,   5
Titles and lands I like, yet rather fancy can,
A man that wanteth gould, then gould that wants a man.
[Sir John Davies]

Here endeth the twelue Wonders of the world.

THE TABLE.

A Pauin.	XIII
A Galliard to the Pauin.	XIIII
A Pauin.	XV
A Galliard to the Pauin before.	XVI
Adew.	XVII
A Pauin.	XVIII
A Pauin.	XIX
A Pauin.	XX
A Pauin.	XXI
A Pauin.	XXII
A pauin.	XXIII
A Pauin.	XXIIII

FINIS.

William Corkine

The Second Booke of Ayres

1612

[Within a compartment: McK. & F. No. 132 (see Textual Introduction to D01600); in upper oval slot, cut with musical instruments and the motto:] MVSICA LÆTIFICAT COR:. [In center space:] THE/ SECOND BOOKE/ OF/ AYRES,/ Some, to Sing and Play to the/ Bafe-Violl alone:/ Others, to be fung to the Lute and/ Bafe Violl./ VVith new Corantoes, Pauins, Almaines;/ as also diuers new Defcants vpon old Grounds,/ *fet to the Lyra-Violl.*/ By *William Corkine.* [C swash]/ [in lower slot:] *LONDON*: [*N*'s swash]/ Printed for *M. L. I. B.* and *T. S.* [*BT* swash]/ Affigned by *W. Barley.*/ 1612./

Note: The publishers were Matthew Lownes, John Browne, and Thomas Snodham. See the Textual Introduction to D01612.

Collation: 2°; A–I² (A1, C2 not signed); 18 leaves.

Headlines: A2–F2v: I. [–XVIII.] CANTVS. BASSVS. [On each page except for C2v and F1v, which have only: IX. [XVII.] CANTVS. D1 has only IX BASSVS. and F2 has BASSVS Primus. and BASSVS secundus. F2v omits BASSVS.] G1v–I2v, on each page: *Lessons for the Lyra Violl.*

Contents: A1, title page; A1v, dedication 1 (to Dymmocke); A2–C1v, songs I–VIII, one per page; C2, dedication 2 (to Rich brothers); C2v–D1, song IX; D1v–E2, songs X–XV, one per page; E2v, dedication 3 (to Misses Stapleton and Cope); F1, song XVI; F1v–F2, song XVII; F2v, song XVIII; G1, "A Lesson for two Lyra Viols"; G1v, "If my Complaints" (for lyra viol); G2, "Perlude"; G2v–H1, "Come liue with me, and be my Loue" and (H1) "Perlude"; H1v–H2, "Walsingham" and (H2) "Coranto"; H2v–I1, "Mounsiers Almaine" and (I1) "Coranto"; I1v, "The Punckes delight"; I2, "Pauin"; I2v, "Almaine" and table.

SR: No entry.

STC: 5769.

TO THE VALEROVS AND
TRVELY MAGNANIMOVS KNIGHT
SYR *EDWARD DYMMOCKE*, THE KINGS
CHAMPION.

SYR

As a poore man, indebted to *many*, and desirous to pay what hee can, deuides that *little* hee hath among *many*, to giue contentment, at least, to *some*: so, I (right Worthy *SYR*) am constrayned to make the like distribution of this poore *Mite* of mine; being all I haue, for the present, to content you my Worthiest *Creditors.* But first, for that I   10
stand most obliged to you, euen *Conscience* moues mee to shew my *willingnesse* to satisfie you first. Your approued and generally-beloued Noble-*Nature* (resembling that *Diuine*) will (I hope) take my *Will* for *Deed*, who in *both* euer will be

Yours intirely to dispose,
William Corkine.

I.

EAch louely grace my Lady doth possesse,
Let all men view, and in their view admire,
In whose sweet breast all vertuous thoughts doe rest,
Zealous to pitty, Chast in her owne desire,
And to make vp a rare and worthy creature,   5
Both wise, and chast, and faire in forme and feature,
Enter but in to thought of her perfection,
Thou wilt confesse, and in confessing proue,
How none deserues like praise, nor yet like loue.

II.

Truth-trying Time shall cause my Mistresse say,
My Loue was perfect, constant as the Day:
And as the day when Euening doth appeare,
Doth suffer doome to be or foule or cleere,
  So, shall my last bequeast make knowne to all,   5
  My Loue in her did rise, did liue, did fall.

2 You Gods of Loue, who oft heard my desires
Prepare her hart by your Loue-charming fires,
To thinke on those sweet reuels, peacefull fights,
Nere-changing Custome, taught at Nuptiall rites.   10
  O guerdonize my prayers but with this,
  That I may taste of that long wisht-for blisse.

III.

Two Louers sat lamenting,
hard by a Christall brooke,
Each others hart tormenting,
Exchanging looke for looke,
  With sighes and teares bewraying,   5
  Their silent thoughts delaying,
    At last coth one,
    shall wee alone,
sit here our thoughts bewraying?
    Fie, fie, fie, fie,   10
Oh fie, it may not be,
    Set looking by,
let speaking set vs free.

2 Then thus their silence breaking
Their thoughts too long estranged   15
They doe bewray by speaking,
And words with words exchanged:
  Then one of them replyed
  Great pitty we had dyed,
    Thus all alone   20
    in silent moane
And not our thoughts descryed.

Fie, fie, oh fie,
Oh fie, that had beene ill
   that inwardly   25
Sylence the hart should kill.

3 From lookes and words to kisses
They made their next proceeding,
And as their onely blisses
They therein were exceeding.   30
 Oh what a ioy is this,
  To looke, to talke, to kisse?
   But thus begunne
   is all now done?
Ah: all then nothing is.   35
 Fie, fie, oh fie,
Oh fie, it is a Hell
  And better dye
Then kisse, and not end well.

IIII.

Tɪs true, t'is day, what though it be?
and will you therefore rise from me?
What will you rise because tis light?
Did we lye downe because twas Night?
 Loue that in spight of darknesse brought vs hether,   5
 In spight of Light should keepe vs still together.

2 Light hath no tongue, but is all Eye,
If it could speake as well as spye,
This were the worst that it could say,
That being well I faine would stay.   10
 And that I loue my hart and honor so
 That I would not from him that hath them goe.

Ist businesse that doth you remoue?
Oh, that's the worst disease of Loue,
The poore, the foule, the false, loue can   15
Admit, but not the busied man:
 He that hath businesse, and makes loue doth doe,
 Such wrong as if a marryed man should woe.
               [John Donne]

V.

Deere, though your minde stand so auerse,
That no assaulting words can pierce,
Your swift and angry flight forbeare,
What neede you doubt, what neede you feare?
  In vaine I striue your thoughts to moue,   5
  But yet, stay, and heare me sweet loue.

2 Words may entreat you, not enforce,
Speake though I might till I were hoarse,
Already you resolue I know
No gentle looke or Grace to show.   10
  My passions all must haplesse roue,
  But stay and heare me yet sweet loue.

3 Sith here no help nor hope remaines,
To ease my griefe, or end my paines,
Ile seeke in lowest shades to finde   15
Rest for my heart, peace for my minde.
  Goe thou more cruell farre then faire,
  And now, leaue me to my despaire.

VI.

Shall I be with ioyes deceiued?
Can Loues bands be sealed with kisses?
Cupid of his eyes bereaued,
Yet in darknesse seldome misses,
  Let not dallying lose these blisses.   5

2 Sleepe hath sealed their eyes and eares
That our loues so long haue guarded:
Himen hides your mayden feares,
Now my loue may be rewarded,
  Let my suite be now regarded.   10

VII.

Downe, downe proud minde, thou soarest farre aboue thy
                                                    might,
Aspiring heart, wilt thou not cease to breed my woe?

High thoughts, meete with disdaine, Peace and Loue fight,
Peace thou hast wone the field, and Loue shall hence in
> bondage goe.

This fall from Pride my rising is from griefes great deepe   5
That bottome wants, vp to the toppe of happy blisse:
In peace and rest I shall securely sleepe,
Where neither scorne, disdaine, Loues torment, griefe, or
> anguish is.

Or this:

Stoope, stoope, proud heart, and mounting *hopes* downe,
> downe descend,   10
Rise *Spleene* and burst, hence *Ioyes*; for, *Griefe* must now
> ascend:
My *Starres* conspire my spoile; which is effected:
I dye, yet liue in death; of *Loue* and *Life* (at once) reiected.

Then, O descend; and from the height of *Hope* come downe:
My *Loue* and *Fates* on mee (aye mee) doe ioyntly frowne,   15
Then Death (if euer) now come doe thy duty;
And martir him (alas) that martir'd is by *Loue* and *Beauty*.

VIII.

Beware faire Maides of Musky Courtiers oathes,
Take heede what gifts and fauours you receiue,
Let not the fading glosse of Silken Clothes,
Dazell your vertues, or your fame bereaue.
  For loose but once the hould you haue of Grace,   5
  Who will regard your fortune, or your face?

2 Each greedy hand will striue to catch the Flower,
When none regards the stalke it growes vpon:
Each nature seekes the Fruit still to deuoure,
And leaue the Tree to fall or stand alone.   10
  Yet this aduise (faire Creatures) take of mee,
  Let none take Fruit vnlesse he take the Tree.

3 Beleeue no othes, nor much protesting men,
Credit no vowes, nor their bewayling songs:
Let Courtiers sweare, forsweare, and sweare againe,   15
Their hearts doe liue tenne regions from their tongues.
  For, when with othes they make thy heart to tremble,
  Beleeue them least, for then they most dissemble.

4 Beware least *Caesar* doe corrupt thy minde,
And fond Ambition sell thy modestie: 20
Say though a King thou euer courteous finde,
He cannot pardon thine impuritie.
  Beginne with King, to Subiect thou wilt fall,
  From Lord to Lackey, and at last to all.

TO THE MOST NOBLE
AND WORTHY BRETHREN,
Sir *ROBERT*, AND Sir *HENRY RICH*:
Knights of the Honourable Order of the
BATH.

IN your truely Noble affections *there is an heau'nly* harmonie, *by the operation of* Grace; *in your* corporall constitutions, *an* harmony *of the* Elements, *by the highest* art *of* Nature; *in your* heroicall carriage *and* actions, *an* harmonie *by the worke of* wel-discerning Iudgement; *and, in all, such an highly-commended* symphonie *each with other, that to no* two   1
(*as* One) *could I more properly consecrate these ensuing* Accents, *comming* from, *and tending* to Harmonie, *then to you. If then they like you, it argues them most* harmonious, *sith* like loues the like. *But howsoeuer, I humbly referre both* my selfe *and* them, *to your* fauour *and* good opinion; *which with my* harts-ioy *makes such* harmonie, *as* Amphions *sweetest* straines *cannot halfe so much glad mee; Euer remayning, the humble honourer and admirer of your heroicall* perfections.

William Corkine.

IX.

THE Fire to see my woes for anger burneth,
The Aire in raine for my affliction weepeth,
The Sea to Ebbe for griefe his flowing turneth,
The Earth with pitty dull his Center turneth.

Fame is with wonder blased,   5
Time runnes away for sorrow,
Place standeth still amased,
To see my night of ils which hath no morrow.
    Alas, all onely she no pittie taketh
    to know my miseries, But Chast and cruell,   10
    My fall her glory maketh,
Yet still her eyes giue to my flames their fuell.

Fire, burne mee quite, till sense of burning leaue mee:
Aire, let me draw thy breath no more in anguish:
Sea, drown'd in thee, of tedious life bereaue me: 15
Earth, take this earth, wherein my spirits languish.
    Fame, say I was not borne,
    Time, haste my dying houre,
    Place, see my graue vptorne.
Fire, Aire, Sea, Earth, Fame, Time, Place, show your power.   20
    Alas, from all their helps I am exiled:
    For hers am I, and death feares her displeasure,
    Fye death thou art beguilde.
Though I be hers, she sets by me no treasure.
                    [Sir Philip Sidney]

X.

  Goe heauy thoughts downe to the place of woe,
Tell Griefe, tell Paine, and torments how they vsde mee,
Say vnto Sorrow who is now my foe,
And fretfulnes which long time hath abusde mee,
Mauger them all, in time they shall excuse mee,   5
  Till then my hart shall beare my wrongs so hie,
  Vntill the strings doe burst, and then I dye.

  2 For being dead, what griefe can mee offend?
All paines doe cease, all sorrowes haue their end,
Vexation cannot vexe my flesh no more,   10
Nor any torments wrong my soule so sore;
All liuing will my liuelesse corps abhorre.
  Yet thus Ile say, that death doth make conclusion,
  But yet with righteous soules there's no confusion.

XI.

My deerest Mistrisse, let vs liue and loue,
And care not what old doting fooles reproue,
Let vs not feare their sensures, nor esteeme,
What they of vs and of our loues shall deeme,
Old ages critticke and sensorious brow,   5
Cannot of youthfull dalliance alow,
Nor neuer could endure that wee should tast,
Of those delights which they themselues are past.

XII.

Man like a Prophet of ensuing yeeres,
Beginnes his life with cryes, hee ends with paine,
The rest is so distract twixt hopes and feares,
That life seemes but a losse and death a gaine,
  My hopelesse loue is like my haplesse life,   5
  Begun in paine, and ends it selfe in griefe.

Yet death in one's an end of paine and feares,
But cruell Loue though euer liuing dyes:
And shee that giues me death when death appeares
Reuiues my dying hopes, and death denyes.   10
  My hopelesse loue is like my haplesse life,
  Begun in paine, and ends it selfe in griefe.

XIII.

As by a fountaine chast *Diana* sate,
Viewing of Natures pride, her beauteous face,
The waters boild with loue, she boyles with hate,
Chastning their pride with exile from their place;
They murmuring ranne to Sea and being there;   5
Each liquid drop turn'd to a brinish teare.

XIIII.

Away, away, call backe what you haue said,
When you did vow to liue and dye a Maid,
O if you knew what shame to them befell,
That dance about with bobtaile Apes in hell,

You'd breake your oath, and for a world of gaine,   5
From *Hymens* pleasing sports no more abstaine.
Your selfe, your Virgin girdle would diuide,
And put aside the Maiden vaile that hides
the chiefest Iemme of Nature, And would lye,
Prostrate to eu'ry Peasant that goes by,   10
Rather then vndergoe such shame, No tongue can tell,
what iniury is done to Maids in hell.

XV.

WHen I was borne, *Lucina* crosse-legg'd sate,
The angry starres with omminous aspects,
frownd on my birth, And the foredooming Fate,
ordain'd to brand me with their dire effects,
The Sunne did hide his face, and left the night   5
to bring me to this worlds accursed light.

TO THE TWO TRVELY VER-
TVOVS AND DISCREET GENTLE-
WOMEN, Mis. *VRSVLA STAPLETON*, AND Mis.
ELIZABETH COPE, DAVGHTERS TO
the Right Worthy Knights, Sir *Robert Stapleton*,
and Sir *Walter Cope*.

   How quickly the Art of Musicke may be abolished, or at leastwise
fall to decay (worthie Ladies) may easily be conceiued, if it were not
guarded vnder your Patronaging fauours, or rather shrouded vnder
such Eagles wings as Yours, to preuent all future malignant reproaches,   10
or by your commanding powers (as who knowes not what your beauties
may commaund?) able to make all tongues silent at any crimes by me
committed. To your vertues haue I Dedicated these few Songs and
Lyra Lessons, and the rather because you are both welwishers and well-
affected to Musicke, and are ledde away with a more then ordinarie
delight in the same. Onely let me be bould to entreate your fauourable
acceptance of them, and that you will not let this Booke be made an
Orphant in his birth, but that it may be a Childe of your fostering, and
liue vnder your protections. Then shall I thinke my selfe happy, and

hereafter be encouraged in more ample sort to publish my poore
labours. Thus hoping for no lesse then I haue formerly entreated, I
euer rest

Yours in all loue, dutie and seruice
William Corkine.

XVI.

SHall a smile, or guilefull glance,
Or a sigh, that is but fayned,
Shall but teares that come by chance,
make mee dote that was disdayned?
  No, I will no more be chayned.   5

2 Shall I sell my freedome so,
Being now from Loue remised?
Shall I learne (what I doe know
To my cost) that Loue's disguised?
  No, I will be more aduised.   10

3 Must she fall? and I must stand?
Must she flye? and I pursue her?
Must I giue her hart, and land,
And, for nought, with them endue her?
  No, first I will finde her truer.   15

XVII.

WEe yet agree, but shall be straight wayes out,
Thy Passions are so harsh and strange to mee,
That when the concord's perfect I may doubt,
The time is lost which I haue spent for thee,
Yet one the ground must be, which you shall proue,   5
Can beare all parts that descant on my loue.

XVIII.

FLy swift my thoughts, possesse my Mistris heart,
And as you finde her loue plead my desert,
If she be somewhat wayward happy my desires,
A little coynesse doth but blow mens fires,
But will she needs forbid the baines I craue,   5
Retire, and be buri'd in your Masters graue.

A Table of all the Songs contained in this Booke.

FINIS.

John Dowland

A Pilgrimes Solace

1612

[Within a compartment: McK. & F. No. 249] A Pilgrimes Solace./ [rule]/ VVherein is contained Muſicall/ Harmonie of 3. 4. and 5. parts, to be/ ſung and plaid with the Lute/ and Viols./ By *Iohn* [*I* swash] *Douland*, Batchelor of Muſicke in/ both the Vniuerſities: and Luteniſt to the/ Right Honourable the/ Lord Walden./ [date within a small factotum:]· 1612/ *LONDON:*/ Printed for *M. L. I. B.* [*I* swash] and *T. S.*/ by the Aſſignment of/ *William Barley.* [*B* swash]/

Collation: 2°; *A–M²*; 24 leaves.
Headlines: Verso, Bɪv–Mɪv: CANTVS. [ALTVS. on Fɪv, Gɪv; TENOR. on Lɪv; CANTVS secundus./ CANTVS [CNTVS] primus. on N2v, Mɪv] I. [–XXI. No period after X] Recto, B2–M2: TENOR. [Not on F2–G2; CANTVS. on L2] I. [–XXI. Not on F2–G2.]/ BASSVS. I. [–XXI.]/ ALTVS. [CANTVS. on F2–G2; QVINTVS. on Mɪ, M2] I. [–XXI.]
Contents: Aɪ, title page; Aɪv blank; A2, dedication; A2v, epistle; Bɪ, table; Bɪv–M2, songs I–XXI, one per opening; M2v, No. XXII, "A Galliard to *Lachrimae*" for the lute.
SR: Entered by "Matthue" Lownes, John Browne, and Thomas Snodham, "by assignemente from William Barley and with consent of master H[umfrey] Lownes warden," on October 28, 1611 (Arber, III, 470). Snodham was the printer; his share was transferred to William Stansby on February 23, 1625/26, and Lownes's share to Thomas Lownes on April 10, 1627 (Arber, IV, 153, 176).
STC: 7098.
Copies: Folger (the text copy); Huntington (59103); BM (K.2.i.10); and Lincoln Cathedral Library (Aa.2.17; lacks Aɪ; not seen). There seem to be no press corrections.
The music for songs I–VII and XII–XVIII consists of the usual Cantus and tablature facing parts for alto, tenor, and bass. Songs VIII and XIX–XXI are similar, except that

the two inner parts (and the bass of XX) have words and music only for the last lines or chorus. No. XIX is a dialogue between the tenor and bass, with Cantus and alto joining in on the last lines and conclusion. Nos. IX–XI have a solo voice with tablature facing parts for bass and treble viols.

TO THE RIGHT HONORABLE
THEOPHILVS, LORD WALDEN, SONNE AND HEIRE TO THE MOST NOBLE, *THOMAS*, BARON OF WALDEN, EARLE OF SVFFOLKE, LORD CHAMBERLAINE OF HIS MAIESTIES HOVSEHOLD, KNIGHT OF THE MOST Noble Order of the Garter, and one of his Maiesties most Honourable *Priuie Counsell.*

Most Honoured Lord:

As to exell in any qualitie is very rare, so is it a hard thing to finde out those that fauour Vertue and Learning; but such being found, men of Iudgment are drawne (I know not by what Sympathie) to loue and Honor them, as the 10 *Saints and Soueraignes of their affections and deuices: wherefore (most Worthy Lord) your Honor being of all men noted (as natural borne heire of your most Renowned father and mother) to be the onely and alone Supporter of goodnes and excellencie, knowne to none better (vnles I should be the most vngratefull of all others) then my selfe, who am held vp onely by your gratious hand; for which I can shew no other meanes of thankfulnes then these simple fruits of my poore endeauors which I most humbly present as a publike pledge from a true and deuoted heart, hoping hereafter to performe something, wherein I shall shew my selfe more worthy of your Honorable seruice. In the meane time you shall haue a poore mans praiers for your Lordships continuall* 20 *health and dayly increase of Honor.*

Your Honours
humble seruant
IOHN DOVLAND.

TO THE READER.

Worthy Gentlemen, and my louing Countrymen; mooued by your many and fore-tasted courtesies, I am constrained to appeare againe vnto you. True it is, I haue lien long obscured from your sight, because I receiued a Kingly entertainment in a forraine climate, which could not attaine to any (though neuer so meane) place at home, yet haue I held vp my head within this Horizon, and not altogether been vn-affected elsewhere. Since some part of my poore labours haue found fauour in the greatest part of Europes, and beene printed in eight most famous Cities beyond the Seas, *viz*: *Paris, Antwerpe, Collein, Nuren-burge, Franckfort, Liepsig, Amsterdam*, and *Hamburge*: (yea and some of them also authorized vnder the Emperours royall priuiledge,) yet I must tell you, as I haue beene a stranger; so haue I againe found strange entertainment since my returne; especially by the opposition of two sorts of people that shroude themselues vnder the title of Musitians. The first are some simple Cantors, or vocall singers, who though they seeme excellent in their blinde Diuision-making, are meerely ignorant, euen in the first elements of Musicke, and also in the true order of the mutation of the *Hexachord* in the *Systeme*, (which hath been approued by all the learned and skilfull men of Christendome, this 800 yeeres,) yet doe these fellowes giue their verdict of me behinde my backe, and say, what I doe is after the old manner: but I will speake openly to them, and would haue them know that the proudest Cantor of them, dares not oppose himselfe face to face against me. The second are young-men, professors of the Lute, who vaunt themselues, to the dis-paragement of such as haue beene before their time, (wherein I my selfe am a party) that there neuer was the like of them. To these men I say little, because of my loue and hope to see some deedes ensue their braue wordes, and also being that here vnder their owne noses hath beene published a Booke in defence of the Viol de Gamba, wherein not onely all other the best and principall Instruments haue beene abased, but especially the Lute by name, the words, to satisfie thee Reader I haue here thought good to insert, and are as followeth: *From henceforth, the statefull Instrument Gambo Violl, shall with ease yeeld full various, and deuicefull Musicke as the Lute: for here I protest the Trinitie of Musicke, Parts, Passion, and Deuision, to be as gracefully vnited in the Gambo Viol, as in the most receiued Instrument that is, &c.* Which Imputation, me thinkes, the learneder sort of Musitians ought not to let passe vn-answered. Moreouer that here are and daily doth come into our most famous kingdome, diuers strangers from beyond the seas, which auerre before our owne faces, that we haue no true methode of application or fingering of the Lute. Now if these gallant yong Lutenists be such as they would haue the world beleeue, and of which I make no doubt, let them remember that their skill lyeth not in their fingers endes: *Cucullus non facit Monachum.* I wish for the Honor therfore and generall benefit

of our Countrie, that they vndertake the defence of their Lute profession, seeing that some of them aboue other, haue most large meanes,
conuenient time, and such encouragement as I neuer knew any haue,
beleeue me if any of these obiections had beene made when those famous
men liued which now are thought worthy of no fame, not derogating   50
from these skillfull men present; I dare affirme that these obiections had
beene answered to the full, and I make no doubt but that those few of
the former time which liue yet, being that some of them are Batchelors
of Musicke, and others which assume vnto themselues to be no lesse
worthy, wilbe as forward to preserue their reputation. Perhaps you
will aske me, why I that haue trauailed many countries, and ought to
haue some experience, doth not vnder goe this busines my selfe? I
answere that I want abilitie, being I am now entered into the fiftieth
yeare of mine age: secondly because I want both meanes, leasure, and
encouragement. But (Gentle Reader to conclude, although abruptly)   60
this worke of mine, which I here haue published, containeth such things
as I my selfe haue thought well of, as being in mine opinion furnished
with varietie of matter both of Iudgement and delight, which willingly I
referre to the friendly censure, and approbation of the skilfull: hoping
it will be no lesse delightfull to all in generall, then it was pleasing to me
in the composition. *Farewell.*

Your friend
Iohn Douland.

THE TABLE.

FINIS.

I.

Dɪsdaine me still, that I may euer loue,
  For who his Loue inioyes, can loue no more.
The warre once past with ease men cowards proue:
  And ships returnde, doe rot vppon the shore.
    And though thou frowne, Ile say thou art most faire: 5
    And still Ile loue, though still I must despayre.

As heate to life so is desire to loue,
  and these once quencht both life and loue are gone.
Let not my sighes nor teares thy vertue moue,
  like baser mettals doe not melt too soone.   10
    Laugh at my woes although I euer mourne,
    Loue surfets with reward, his nurse is scorne.

II.

To my worthy friend Mr. *William Iewel* of Exceter Colledge in Oxford.

Sweet stay a while, why will you rise?
The light you see comes from your eyes:
The day breakes not, it is my heart,
To thinke that you and I must part.
O stay, or else my ioyes must dye,   5
And perish in their infancie.

Deare let me dye in this faire breast,
Farre sweeter then the Phoenix nest.
Loue raise desire by his sweete charmes   10
Within this circle of thine armes:
And let thy blissefull kisses cherish
Mine infant ioyes, that else must perish.

III.

To aske for all thy loue, and thy whole heart
                    t'were madnesse,
  I doe not sue,
    nor can admit
  (fairest) from you   5
    to haue all, yet
who giueth all hath nothing to impart,
                but sadnesse.

He that receiueth all, can haue no more
                then seeing.   10
  My Loue by length
    of euery houre,
  Gathers new strength,
    new growth, new flower.
You must haue daily new rewards in store,   15
                still being.

You cannot euery day giue me your heart
                for merit:
  Yet if you will,
    when yours doth goe,   20
  You shall haue still
    one to bestow:
For you shall mine when yours doth part
                inherit.

Yet if you please, Ile finde a better way,   25
              then change them:
  For so alone
    dearest we shall

  Be one and one,
    anothers all.   30
Let vs so ioyne our hearts that nothing may
                              estrange them.

IIII.

Loue those beames that breede, all day long breed, and feed,
                                   this burning:
Loue I quench with flouds, flouds of teares, nightly
                            teares and mourning.
But alas teares coole this fire in vaine,
The more I quench, the more there doth remaine.

Ile goe to the woods, and alone, make my moane, oh cruell: 5
For I am deceiu'd and bereau'd of my life, my iewell,
O but in the woods, though Loue be blinde,
Hee hath his spies, my secret haunts to finde.

Loue then I must yeeld to thy might, might and spight
                                   oppressed,
Since I see my wrongs, woe is me, cannot be redressed.   10
Come at last, be friendly Loue to me,
And let me not, endure this miserie.

V.

Sʜall I striue with wordes to moue,
when deedes receiue not due regard?
Shall I speake, and neyther please,
nor be freely heard?

Griefe alas though all in vaine,   5
her restlesse anguish must reueale:
Shee alone my wound shall know,
though shee will not heale.

All woes haue end, though a while delaid,
our patience prouing.   10
O that times strange effects
could but make her louing.

Stormes calme at last, and why may not shee
leaue off her frowning?
O sweet Loue, help her hands   15
my affection crowning.

I woo'd her, I lou'd her,
and none but her admire.
O come deare ioy,
and answere my desire.   20

VI.

WEre euery thought an eye,
and all those eyes could see,
Her subtill wiles their sights would beguile,
and mocke their ielousie.

Her fires doe inward burne,   5
they make no outward show.
And her delights amid the dark shades,
which none discouer, grow.

Desire liues in her heart,
Diana in her eyes.   10
T'were vaine to wish women true, t'is well,
if they proue wise.

The flowers growth is vnseene,
yet euery day it growes.
So where her fancy is set it thriues,   15
but how none knowes.

Such a Loue deserues more grace,
Then a truer heart that hath no conceit,
To make vse both of time and place,
When a wit hath need of all his sleight.   20

VII.

STay time a while thy flying,
Stay and pittie me dying.
For fates and friends haue left mee,
And of comfort bereft mee.
  Come, come close mine eyes, better to dye blessed,   5
  Then to liue thus distressed.

To whom shall I complaine me,
When thus friends doe disdaine mee?
T'is time that must befriend me,
Drown'd in sorrow to end mee.   10
  Come, come close mine eyes, better to dye blessed,
  Then to liue thus distressed.

Teares but augment this fewell,
I feede by night, (oh cruell)
Light griefes can speake their pleasure,   15
Mine are dumbe passing measure.
  Quicke, quicke, close mine eyes, better to dye blessed,
  Then here to liue distressed.

VIII.

TEll me true Loue where shall I seeke thy being,
  In thoughts or words, in vowes or promise making,
In reasons, lookes, or passions neuer seeing,
  In men on earth, or womens minds partaking.
    Thou canst not dye, and therefore liuing tell me   5
    where is thy seate, Why doth this age expell thee?

2 When thoughts are still vnseene and words disguised;
  vowes are not sacred held, nor promise debt:
By passion reasons glory is surprised,
  in neyther sexe is true loue firmely set.   10
    Thoughts fainde, words false, vowes and promise broken
    Made true Loue flye from earth, this is the token.

3 Mount then my thoughts, here is for thee no dwelling,
  since truth and falshood liue like twins together:
Beleeue not sense, eyes, eares, touch, taste, or smelling,
  both Art and Nature's forc'd: put trust in neyther.   15
    One onely shee doth true Loue captiue binde
    In fairest brest, but in a fairer minde.

O fairest minde, enrich'd with Loues residing,
  retaine the best; in hearts let some seede fall,
In stead of weeds Loues fruits may haue abiding;   20
  at Haruest you shall reape encrease of all.
    O happy Loue, more happy man that findes thee,
    Most happy Saint, that keepes, restores, vnbindes thee.

IX.

Goe nightly cares, the enemy to rest,
　Forbeare a while to vexe my grieued sprite,
So long your weight hath lyne vpon my breast,
　that loue I liue, of life bereaued quite,
O giue me time to draw my weary breath,　　　　　　5
　Or let my dye, as I desire the death.
Welcome sweete death, Oh life, no life, A hell,
　Then thus, and thus I bid the world farewell.

False world farewell the enemy to rest,
　now doe thy worst, I doe not weigh thy spight:　　10
Free from thy cares I liue for euer blest,
　Enioying peace and heauenly true delight.
Delight, whom woes nor sorrowes shall amate,
　nor feares or teares disturbe her happy state.
And thus I leaue thy hopes, thy ioyes vntrue,　　　15
　and thus, and thus vaine world againe adue.

X.

To my louing Country-man Mr. *Iohn Forster* the younger, Merchant
of Dublin in Ireland.

FROM silent night, true register of moanes,
　From saddest Soule consumde with deepest sinnes,
From hart quite rent with sighes and heauie groanes,
　My wayling Muse her wofull worke beginnes.　　　5
　　And to the world brings tunes of sad despaire,
　　Sounding nought else but sorrow, griefe and care.

2 Sorrow to see my sorrowes cause augmented,
　and yet lesse sorrowfull were my sorrowes more:
Griefe that my griefe with griefe is not preuented,　　10
　for griefe it is must ease my grieued sore.
　　Thus griefe and sorrow cares but how to grieue,
　　For griefe and sorrow must my cares relieue.

3 If any eye therefore can spare a teare
　to fill the well-spring that must wet my cheekes,　　15
O let that eye to this sad feast draw neere,
　refuse me not my humble soule beseekes:

For all the teares mine eyes haue euer wept
Were now too little had they all beene kept.
                [Robert Devereux, Earl of Essex]

XI.

LASSO vita mia, mi fa morire,
Crudel amor mio cor consume,
Da mille ferite,
Che mi fa morir,
Ahi me, Deh, che non mi fa morire,   5
Crudel amor mi fa sofrir mille martire.

XII.

IN this trembling shadow, cast
  from those boughes which thy wings shake,
Farre from humane troubles plac'd:
  Songs to the Lord would I make,
  Darknesse from my minde then take,   5
    For thy rites none may begin,
    Till they feele thy light within.

As I sing, sweete flowers Ile strow,
  from the fruitfull vallies brought:
Praising him by whom they grow,   10
  him that heauen and earth hath wrought,
  him that all things framde of nought,
    Him that all for man did make,
    But made man for his owne sake.

Musicke all thy sweetnesse lend,   15
  while of his high power I speake,
On whom all powers else depend,
  but my brest is now too weake,
  trumpets shrill the ayre should breake,
    All in vaine my sounds I raise,   20
    Boundlesse power askes boundlesse praise.

XIII.

IF that a sinners sighes be Angels foode,
Or that repentant teares be Angels wine,
Accept O Lord in this most pensiue moode,
These hearty sighes and dolefull plaints of mine,
That went with *Peter* forth most sinfully: 5
But not as *Peter* did, weepe bitterly.

XIIII.

The first Part.

THOU mightie God, that rightest euery wrong,
Listen to patience in a dying song.
When *Iob* had lost his Children, Lands, and goods,
Patience asswaged his excessiue paine,   5
And when his sorrowes came as fast as flouds,
hope kept his hart, till comfort came againe.

XV.

The second Part.

WHEN *Dauids* life by *Saul* was often sought,
And worlds of woes did compasse him about,
On dire reuenge he neuer had a thought,
But in his griefes, Hope still did help him out.   5

XVI.

The third Part.

WHEN the poore Criple by the Poole did lye,
Full many yeeres in misery and paine,
No sooner hee on Christ had set his eye,
But hee was well, and comfort came againe.   5
No *Dauid*, *Iob*, nor Criple in more griefe,
Christ giue mee patience, and my Hopes reliefe.
                              [Nicholas Breton]

XVII.

Where Sinne sore wounding, daily doth oppresse me,
There Grace abounding freely doth redresse mee:
So that resounding still I shall confesse thee,
                    Father of mercy.

Though Sinne offending daily doth torment mee,   5
Yet Grace amending, since I doe repent mee,
At my liues ending will I hope present mee
                    cleare to thy mercy.

The wound Sinne gaue me was of Death assured,
Did not Grace saue mee, whereby it is cured: 10
So thou wilt haue mee to thy loue invred,
                    free without merit.

Sinnes stripe is healed, and his sting abated,
Deaths mouth is sealed, and the Graue amated,
Thy Loue reuealed, and thy Grace related   15
                    giues me this spirit.

XVIII.

My heart and tongue were twinnes, at once conceiued,
   Th'eldest was my heart, borne dumbe by destinie,
The last my tongue, of all sweet thoughts bereaued:
   Yet strung and tunde to play hearts harmonie.
Both knit in one, and yet a sunder placed: 5
   what heart would speake the tongue doth still discouer.
What tongue doth speake is of the heart embraced,
   and both are one to make a new found Louer.
New found, and onely found in Gods and Kings,
   whose wordes are deedes, but wordes, nor deedes regarded.   10
Chaste thoughts doe mount and flye with swiftest wings,
   my loue with paine, my paine with losse rewarded.
                    Conclusion.
   Then this be sure, since it is true perfection,
   That neyther men nor Gods can force affection.   15

XIX.

Vp merry mates, to *Neptunes* prayse,
  Your voyces high aduance:
  The watrie Nymphs shall dance,
and *Eolus* shall whistle to your layes.
[*Master*:] Stereman, how stands the winde?   5
  [*Stereman*:] Fvll North, North-east,
  [*M.*] What course?
  [*S.*] Full South South-west.
  [*M.*] no worse,
    and blow so faire,   10
    Then sincke despayre,
Come solace to the minde,
ere night we shall the hauen finde.
[*Chorus*:] O happy dayes,
      who may containe,   15
      but swell with proud disdaine,
when seas are smooth, sailes full, and all things please?

Stay merry mates, proud *Neptune* lowres,
  Your voyces all deplore you,
  The Nymphes stand weeping o're you: 20
And *Eolus* and *Iris* bandy showres.
Mr. Boates man hale in the Boate.
  S. Harke, harke the ratlings,
  M. Tis haile.
  S. Make fast the tacklings.   25
  M. Strike saile.
  Make quicke dispatches,
  Shut close the hatches.
Hold sterne, cast Ancour out,
This night we shall at randome floate.   30
[*Chorus*:] O dismall houres,
      Who can forbeare,
      But sinke with sad despaire.
When seas are rough, sailes rent, and each thing lowres.
                Conclusion: 35
The golden meane that constant spirit beares,
in such extreams that nor presumes nor feares.

XX.

WElcome black night *Hymens* faire day,
help *Hymen* Loues due debt to pay,
Loues due debt is chaste delight,
which if the turtles want to night,
Hymen forfets his Dietie,   5
and night in loue her dignitie,
Help, help black night *Hymens* faire day,
Help *Hymen* Loues due debt to pay.
Chorus.
  Hymen, O *Hymen* myne   10
  of treasures more diuine,
  what dietie is like to thee
  that freest from mortalitie.

Stay (happie paire) stay but a while,
Hymen comes not, loue to beguile,   15
These sports are alluring baites,
And sawce are to Loues sweetest Cates:
Longing hope doth no hurt but this,
It heightens Loues attained blisse.
Then stay (most happie) stay a while,   20
Hymen comes not, Loue to beguile.
[*Chorus.*
  Hymen, &c.]

XXI.

CEase these false sports. Hast away,
Loue's made a trewant by your stay,
Good night, yet virgin Bride;
but looke ere day be spide,
You change that fruitlesse name,   5
least you your sex defame,
Fear not *Hymens* peaceful war,
you'le conquer, thogh you subdued are,
good night, And ere the day be old,
rise to the sun a Marigold.   10
  Chorus.
Hymen, O *Hymen*, blesse this night,
that Loues darke workes may come to light.

John Attey

The First Booke of Ayres

1622

[Within a compartment: McK. & F. No. 76; motto at foot of original border, "ARISE, FOR IT IS DAY," cut out by 1574] THE/ FIRST BOOKE/ *OF*/ AYRES/ OF FOVRE PARTS,/ With Tabletvre for the/ *LVTE*: [*T* swash]/ So made, that all the parts/ may be plaide together with the/ *Lute*, or one voyce with the *Lute*/ and *Bafe-Vyoll*. [*V* swash]/ [rule]/ Compofed by Iohn Attey/ Gentleman, and Practitioner in/ Mvsicke./ [rule]/ *LONDON*: [*D* swash]/ Printed by *Thomas Snodham*./ 1622./ [rule]/ *Cum Priuilegio*./

Collation: 2°; *A–G²*, H¹; 15 leaves.

Headlines: Verso A2v–G2v: CANTVS. I. [–XII.] There are actually 14 songs but because III is on the same opening as II, III was not numbered; VII appears on both D2v and E1v. The same skeleton is used throughout except on D1v (see below). Recto B1–H1: TENOR./ BASSVS./ ALTVS. The same skeleton is used throughout except on D1 and 2, where the music crowded out the usual furniture of the skeleton.

Contents: A1, title page; A1v blank; A2, dedication; A2v–B1, song I; B1v–B2, songs II and III; B2v–H1, songs IIII–XIIII, one per opening; H1v, table of songs.

SR: No entry.

STC: 901.

Copies: BM (K.8.h.8, the text copy); Huntington (83690); and Folger. There are no verbal press corrections.

The music is the usual arrangement of Cantus and lute tablature facing alternate Tenor, Bassus, and Altus.

TO THE RIGHT
HONOVRABLE, *IOHN*, EARLE
of *Bridge-water*, Viscount *Brackley*, and
Baron of *Ellesmere*:
AND
THE TRVELY NOBLE, AND
VERTVOVS Lady, *FRANCES*,
Covntesse of *Bridge-water*, &c.
His singular good Lord, and Lady.

Right Honovrable: 1

It is no disparagement to the glorious Sunne, that it discends to
fructifie and illustrate the low and humble Vallies; neither can it bee
so to your Eminence if you vouchsafe to bow so low, as to Patronize
these my vnworthy Essaies; wherein your *Honours* haue so much the
more interest, because the best part thereof were composed vnder your
roofe, while I had the happinesse to attend the Seruice of those worthy
and incomparable young Ladies your Daughters, who (by Gods
fauour) shall one day repay vnto you a plentifull Haruest, of that Noble
and Vertuous education you now bestow vpon them.

For me to vndertake the due prayses of diuine Mvsicke, before your   2
Honours, who are no strangers, either to the *Theory* or *Practicke* thereof,
were but to heare one read old *Phormio's* Lecture of Warre, before the
heroicke *Hanniball*: And therefore contenting my selfe, with this in-
dubitable Assertion, *That there is no Creature (rightly Composed) either*
Animall or Rationall, but beares an innated loue and propension to this excel-
lent faculty; And that many great Princes haue not disdayned to make their
Maister-peece thereof, as may appeare by those heauenly Hymnes and raptures
of that Kingly Prophet, with some others, recommended by Historie; or to tran-
scend them, by the delicious Musicke of the harmonious Spheares; or aboue all,
by the sweet Songs of the holy Angels, with their Gloria in Excelsis; The   3
consideration whereof, leaues me rather to admiration then expression.
Right Honorable, I shall esteeme my selfe abundantly graced, is vnder
the Noble protection of your Honours, I may by this meanes but vindi-
cate my selfe from being held a Drone in the mellifluous garden of the
Mvses, and contribute but the smallest drop to the immense Ocean of
this diuine knowledge. Beseeching that Sacred power who first made
you great, and vertuous, to retaine you so to the end, and that after a

long life, crowned with all your worthy desires, you may leaue a sweet
memorie behinde you, for Posteritie to emulate; Which is, and euer
shall be, the Prayer of   40

YOUR HONOVRS
most humble and deuoted Seruant,
IOHN ATTEY.

I.

ON a time, the amorous Siluy,
said to her Shepheard, Sweet how doe you?
Kisse mee this once, And then God b'wee you,
            My sweetest deare,
Kisse me this once, And then God b'wee you,   5
For now the morning draweth neare.

With that her fairest bosome shewing,
Opening her lips, rich perfumes blowing;
She said, now kisse me and be going,
            My sweetest deare.   10
Kisse me this once and then be going,
For now the morning draweth neare.

With that the Shepheard wak'd from sleeping,
And spying where the day was peeping,
He said now take my soule in keeping: 15
            My sweetest deare.
Kisse me, and take my soule in keeping,
Since I must goe now, day is neare.

II.

THe gordian knot which *Alexander* great,
Did whilome cut, with his all-conquering sword;
Was nothing like thy Busk-point pretty peat,
Nor could so faire an Augury afford:
Which if I chance to cut or else vntye,   5
Thy little world Ile conquer presently.
                        [Thomas Tomkis]

III.

WHat is all this world but vaine?
What are all our ioyes but paine?
What our pleasures but a dreame,
Passing swiftly like a streame?

2 Like a flower now we grow,   5
Like the Sea we ebbe and flow:
Still vncertaine is our change,
Like the winde so doe we range.

3 No contented ioy wee haue,
Till within the silent graue   10
Our fraile flesh be laid to sleepe;
Then we cease to mourne, to weepe.

4 Who would trust to worldly things,
Which beguile the greatest Kings?
I will set my heart on high,   15
And contented so will dye.

IIII.

IN a groue of Trees of Mirtle,
Venus met faire *Mirrhas* childe;
Kisse quoth she my pretty Turtle,
But her hopes hee did beguile.
With no no no, with no no no,   5
no no no no no no no no,
with no no no no no.

2 Come, oh come my dearest treasure,
And looke Babies in my eyes:
Coll, and kisse, inioy thy pleasure;   10
But her kindnesse he denyes,
With no &c.

3 Lowtish Lad come learne to venture,
On the Iuory brest of loue:
I dare stay thy worst encounter;   15
But her words as winde did proue,
With no &c.

4 Shall then loue be thus abused,
By the beauty of a Boy?
Shall my Temple be refused,   20
Will *Adonis* still be coy?
With no, &c.

5 Then I vow that beauty euer,
Shall neglected be of loue:
Let the foolish Boy perseuer,   25
He the folly now shall proue,
Of no no.

V.

SHall I tell you whom I loue?
Hearken then a while to me,
And if such a Woman moue,
As I now shall versifie,
  Be assur'd tis Shee or none,   5
  That I loue and loue alone.

2 Nature did her so much right,
As she scornes the helpe of Art:
In as many vertues dight,
As ere yet imbrac'd a heart.   10
  So much good so truely try'd
  Some for lesse were Deify'd.

3 Wit she hath without desire,
To make knowne how much shee hath;
And her anger flames no higher,
Then may fitly sweeten wrath.   15
  Full of pitty as may be,
  Though perhaps not so to me.

4 Reason masters euery Sence,
And her vertues grace her birth;   20
Louely as all Excellence:
Modest in her most of myrth.
  Likelyhood enough to proue,
  Onely worth could kindle loue.

5 Such She is, and if you know,   25
Such a one as I haue sung,
Be she browne or faire, or so,
That Shee be but somewhat young.
  Be assur'd tis shee or none,
  That I loue and loue alone.   30
                    [William Browne]

VI.

My dearest and deuinest loue,
Imagine my distresse,
When thou retir'st from my desires,
And sorrowes me oppresse.
For my sence sees no other Sunne,   5
But that within thine eyes,
That in another Spheare doth runne,
And clowds thy natiue skyes.
Then come againe, then come againe,
Display thy pleasing Beames,   10
Else all my pleasures are but paine,
My comforts are but dreames.

VII.

Bright Starre of beauty, on whose Temples sit,
Appolloes wisdome, and Dame *Pallas* wit:
O what faire garland, worthy is to fit,
Thy faire blest brows that compasse in all merrit?
Thou shalt not Crowned be with vulgar Bayes,   5
Because for thee it is a Crowne too base:
Appolloes Tree can yeeld thee but small praise,
It is too stale a Vesture for that place.
The Birds, the Beasts, their Goddesse doe thee call,
Thou art their Keeper, Thou preseru'st them all.   10
Thy skill doth equall *Pallas*, not thy birth,
Shee to the Heauens yeelds Musicke, Thou to the Earth.

VIII.

THinke not tis I alone that sing her praise,
No, all regard her whom my Muse respects,
Each sweetly singing Syren in her layes,
Deserued Trophes of her worth erects,
And *Philomela* on her thorny perch,   5
Her neatest notes to note her praise doth search.

IX.

Ioy my Muse, since there is one,
Deserues best admiration,
Of all that ere did heede her,
Let all the deities yeeld their places,
To her still well-deseruing graces,   5
Since none of them Exceeds her.

X.

My dayes, my moneths, my yeares I spend
  About a moments gaine.
A ioy that in th'inioying ends,
  A fury quickly slaine.

2 A fraile delight, like that Waspes life,   5
  Which now both friskes and flies:
And in a moments wanton strife,
  It faints, it pants, it dyes.

3 And when I charge my Lance in rest,
  I triumph in delight: 10
And when I haue the ring transperst,
  I languish in despite.

4 Or like one in a luke-warme Bath,
  Light wounded in a vaine:
Sperts out the spirits of his life,   15
  And fainteth without paine.

XI.

MAdame, for you I little grieue to dye,
In, and to whom I liue, because I loue.
For if my ill doe please your dainty eye,
It cannot me displease, nor greatly moue.
  Vnlesse a minde in you so cruell be,   5
  To kill your selfe, To make an end of mee.

2 Onely I grieue that all my life is you,
Who by my death must needs in danger be:
For if I dye it cannot be but true,
The sweetest of my life must die with mee;   10
  If that a minde in you so cruell be,
  To kill your selfe, to make an end of mee.

3 Wherefore, if of my life you haue no care,
Which I esteeme but onely for your sake:
Yet of your owne, which death it selfe would spare,   15
I am in hope you will some pitty take;
  Vnlesse a minde in you so cruell be,
  To kill your selfe, to make an end of mee.

XII.

REsound my voyce, yee woods that heare me playne,
Both Hils and Dales causing reflection,
And Riuers eke record, yee of my paine,
that oft hath forc'd you to compassion,
  Mongst whom pitty I finde, doth yet remaine,   5
  But where I seeke, alas there is disdaine.

2 Ye wandring Riuers oft to heare me sound,
Haue stopt your course, and plainly to expresse
Your griefes, haue cast teares on the wayling ground:
The Earth hath mourn'd to heare my heauinesse,   10
  Whose dull and sencelesse nature I doe finde,
  Farre more relenting then a Womans minde.

3 When that my woes I doe re-iterate,
The mighty Okes haue roared in the winde;
And in the view of this my wretched state,   15
Each liuing thing bemones me in their kinde,
  Saue onely shee that most my plaints should rue,
  Vpon my ore-charg'd heart doth griefes renew.
                          [Sir Thomas Wyatt]

XIII.

VAine hope adue, Thou life-consuming moath,
Which frets my soule in peeces with delay.
My well-spun threads, Will make no cloath,
To shrowd me from the tempest of decay.
For stormes of fortune drench me like a floud,   5
Whilst rancors frost, nips Merit in her bud.

XIIII.

Sweet was the song the Virgin sung,
when she to *Bethelem* was come,
And was deliuered of her Son,
That blessed IESVS hath to name,
Lullaby,   5
Lullaby sweet Babe quoth she,
My Son, and eke a Sauiour borne,
Who hath vouchsafed from on high,
To visit vs that were forlorne,
Lulla, Lulla,   10
Lullaby, sweet Babe sang she,
And sweetly rockt him on her knee.

THE TABLE.

Bright Starre of Beauty, on whose Temples sit.   VII
Thinke not tis I alone that sing her praise.   VIII
Ioy my Muse, since there is one.   IX
My dayes, my moneths, my yeares.   X
Madame, for you I little grieue to dye.   XI
Resound my voyce.   XII
Vaine hope adue.   XIII
Sweet was the song the Virgin sung.   XIIII

FINIS.

Variant Readings
Notes
Glossarial Index
Index of First Lines

Variant Readings

The following list contains: (1) All editorial departures from the original songbooks (the Cantus parts, C, unless stated otherwise), except for those changes to be made silently as described in the Editorial Procedure. The original reading is to the right of the bracket. For variants caused by press-correction, see the Textual Introductions. When changes are made in the original punctuation, the word preceding the punctuation (or lack thereof) is represented on the right of the bracket by an equal sign (=).

(2) All verbal variants from other voice parts, Altus (A), Tenor (T), Bassus (B), and sometimes Countertenor (Ct), Quintus (Q), Medius or Meane (M), Triplex (Tx), or Cantus Secundus (C2), or from the metrical text (Mt) when present. See the Textual Introductions for the number of parts in a given song. Variants in punctuation, spelling, or omissions or repetitions occasioned by the music are not usually recorded.

(3) Substantive variants from later editions. This applies only to Do1597.

By1596
The numbers of all the songs in this book are editorial.
    I.6 patience is] patienceis
    II.11 those so] though so
    III.24 feare.] =
    IIII.4 procure.] =
    VII.12 there be] therebe

DO1597

All references are to the first edition, unless followed by *b*, *c*, *d*, or *e*, indicating the editions of 1600, 1603, 1606, or 1613 respectively. When the first edition must be distinguished, it is indicated by *a*.

Dedication
  .29 successe] snccesse *c*
     among] amongst *e*
To the Reader
  .6 fruits, which] fruites. Which *de*
  .17 toward] towards *d*
  .21 towards] toward *cde*
  .31-2 indeuours. Yet] indeuours: yet *e*
  .43 *Luglio*] *Iuglio c*, *Giuglio de*
  .47 *Crochio*] *Croce de*
     S. Marks] St. Markes *e*
  .48 conference] couference *d*
  .52 vnperfect] imperfect *e*
  .56 *Iohn Dowland*] omitted *cde*
I.1 slaughter] slaughters B
  .12 together.] =,
  .18 fire.] =
II.4 light-god] light, God A*ab*; light god A*c*, C*d*
  .5 son] sunne *cde*
  .9 fruit] fruit *bcde*
  .10 charm'd,] *comma seems to be a stray italic s in* a
III.1 hopes . . . hopes] hops . . . hops C*a*
  .12 seasned] seasoned *de*
IIII.8 vnkindnes] vnkinde vnkindenes AT*a-e musical repetition*
  .9 doest] dost *de*, AT *abc*
  .11 Thou] thou
  .12 complaine] complaline T*a*
  .14 am I] I am *cde*
  .23 here] heere *e*
V.3 Are] are
   fiers] fires *e*
   smoake ATB] smoakc C*a*
  .6 sight] light A*a*
  .7 written] writ . . . writen A*a-e musical repetition*
  .20 dye I] I die *d*
VI.1 NOw] NNow C*a*
  .2 absent] obsent C*a*, absence B*a*
  .5 While ATB] while C*a*
  .22 togither] together *b-e*
VII.7 heau'n] heauen *cde*
  .9 loose] lose *e*
VIII.14 then *b-e*] the *a*
  .15 That] Thath *e*

IX.1 showers] showrs *de*
   .3 drooping T*a*, *b–e*] dropping CAB*a*
   .7 haplesse] restlesse *b–e*
X.3–4 Or . . . eyes] *omitted* C*e*
  .7 such] sueh B*a*
  .8 And] and
  .11 thy] me *e*
  .19 deepe] sweet *cde*
   embrace] = :
XI.5 embrace] embracc A*a*
  .9 Vewing] Vewind T*a*
   Loue long pains] loues long pains *de*
  .10 beauties] beouties B*a*
  .13 son] Sun *cde*
  .25 riuers side] riuer side *bc*
  .26 flowers] flowres *de*
XII.8 heauenly] heau'nly TB*a–e*
   light ATB*ab*; *cde*] sight C*ab*
  .25 proues] proue *e*
   vnkind] vnking *b*
XIII.3 lest] least ATB*a*
   anger] auger B*a*
  .4 pine] piue B*a*
   you ATB*a*; *b–e*] yon C*a*
   longings] lougings T*a*; longing A*a*
  .5 while ATB*a*; *b–e*] wile C*a*
  .16 temprature] temperature *cde*
  .17 thy] thv *a* (*brcken* y ?)
XIIII.] IX. *de*
  .2 greif] grief ATB*a*; *b–e*
  .6 sorrowes ATB*a*; *b–e*] sorrewes C*a*
XV.2 of my harte, of my harte] of my harte, ii. *a–e*
  .9 peareles] peereless *cde*
XVI.2 mine eyes] the same T*a–e*
  .5 sweet] sweer A*a*
  .16 a slope] aslope *cde*
XVII.5 simphathy] simpathie TB*a*; sympathy *cde*
  .10 faint *b–e*] faind *a*
  .14 do] doth *e*
  .17 frownes *b–e*] frowes *a*
  .35 triumps] triumphs *cd*; triumph *e*
XVIII.14 Hele] Hee'l *d*
  .16 thinke] thinks *cde*
   her] him *de*
  .17 Goddes] Gods *c*; Yee Gods *de*
XIX.6 whence ATB*a*; *b–e*] when C*a*
  .11 Dispayer ATB*a*;] dispayer C*a*

.12 might ATB*a*; *b–e*] migyt C*a*

.15 ought] aught *de*

.16 grieue] greiue *d*

.21 loue,]=.

.26 dost] doest *b–e*

XX.2 eyes] eics A*a*

.8 this] his *b–e*

　　fast] fac'd *c*, fac't *de*

.10 doth] doe *e*

.12 sleepe comes, *b–e*] sleepe, coms *a*

XXI.4 them] those ATB*a–e*

.5 medooe] medow ATB*a*; *b–e*

.11 feet] foote *b–e*

.15 songs *b–e*] song *a*

　　Cynthias *b–e*] Cyntihas *a*

.16 hollidaies] holie dayes *cde*

.25 well fare] welfare *cde*

.26 one] owne *d*

Cav1598

The numbers of songs I, II, III, VII, X, XII, XXII, and XXVII are torn or trimmed off. The songs are misnumbered in the original (III for IIII, etc.); the corrected numbers are used here. The texts of II, IIII, VI, VII, VIII, and X are taken from the metrical versions (Mt) printed on M1v, but are put in the order of the musical versions.

I.] *No number*

I.1 stay stay B] ij. ii. C

II.] *No number*

II.17 life]=. Mt

III.] *No number*

III.2 my] thy B

　　relye B] relyes C

.3 though] Sith B

.6 dying. B]= C

IIII.] III

IIII.2 vow'd Mt] wo'd C

V.] IIII

V.3 bewty] beanty B *in repetition*

VI.] V

VI.2 blindfolded] blindfould did B

VII.] *No number*

VII.1 LOue Mt] FOue C

.4 prou'd, C]= : Mt

.5 power bereft Mt] prouerb rest C

VIII.] VII

VIII.4 two C] tow Mt, to B

IX.] VIII

IX.4 merrit] mirrit B

.6 nought.]=, *before repeat*

X.] *No number*

X.2 admire Mt] admires C

  .6 As] (O) as B *in repetition*

  .13 *Phillis sweet*] *Phlllis sweet* Mt

  .16 songs] sons Mt (*see Note*)

  .21 this] *h broken* Mt

XI.] X *See* XVII *below.*

XI.1 life, B]= C

XII.] *No number. See* XXVIII *below.*

XII.3 Desolate] desolute B, disolate B *in repetition*

  .5 *sicut* B *and* C *in repetition*] *scicut* C

XIII.] XII *See* XXVII *below.*

XIII.1 new] now B

  .5 Til] Tel B

  .8 down] d CB

  .9 oh] *omitted* B

XIIII.] XIII

XIIII.6 flowrs] flowers B

XV.] XIIII

XV.1 WAnton] WVanton T

    hither] hether AT

  .4 together] togither ATB

  .12 how] (Oh) how AT

XVI.] XV

XVI.4 (O)] *omitted* ATB

  .9 to] (O) to A

  .12 vp] (O) vp AT *in repetition*

XVII.] XVI *This is an alternate arrangement of* XI,

      containing this variant: 1 life XI] light XVII CATB

XVIII.] XVII

XVIII.2 fond] (that) fond T

    commanded] commands ATB

XIX.] XVIII

XIX.3 that] (O) that A, thar T

  .4 til] tell B

    vnkindly] vnkind, vnkindly A *in repetition*

  .5 lose, ATB]= C

XX.] XVIIII

XXI.] XX

XXI.4 sweetly] sweet CATBQ *in repetition*

  .5 hir] (then) her T *in repetition*

  .7 the sweet] (O) the sweet AT *in repetition*

XXII.] *No number*

XXII.1 senteth] sents C *in repetition*

  .2 frost C *in repetition*, ATB] frosts CQ

  .4 red compileth, ATBQ] red, compileth C

.7 ioy ATBQ]=, C
.8 loue A]=, C, *and* TBQ *before repeat*
XXIII.] XXII
XXIII.6 not, ATQ]= CB
XXIIII.] XXIII
XXIIII.2 comly] (with) comly C *in repetition,*
comliness A *first time*
XXV.] XXIIII
XXV.4 they] *omitted* TB
.6 steeping, ATB]= CQ
.8 weeping. ATBQ]= C
XXVI.] XXIIIII (verso), XXV (recto)
XXVI.2 the ATBQ] (hath) the C
grace, A]= CQ
.6 both] (Oh) both A
eare] eie A
bewitched ATBQ] bewtiched C
XXVII.] *No number. This is a five-part version*
of XIII, *from which it varies thus:*
.3 Merily] Merely ATBQ, (and) merely C *in*
repetition
Nico] Nicho CATQ
.4 chanting] chaunting QC
.9 oh] *omitted* TBQ
XXVIII.] XXVII *This is a five-part version of* XII,
with no variants.
Table
I II . . . XXVIII] I I . . . XXVII

Do1600

Dedication
.16 humbly] humby
"Lute arise," etc.
.11 floweing] flowring *The* r *is changed to* e *by*
hand in several copies (*Folger, BM,*
Boston, Dohna); *see the* "*faults*"
mentioned in the Textual Introduction.
To the Reader
.11 increase] inerease
II.7 nights are] night is B
.8 last] *omitted* B
IIII.1 condemned] condemn'd B
.2 the humble] t'humble B
.7 glad to free] is glad for to free B
.8 Bids] and bids B
V.1 day is] daies B
.9 needes change our] change B

VIII.7 say] sing B
      dost] doest B
XI. 6 faults TB] fault CA
XII.7 is ATB] =. C
XV.4 faith] fath B
      with] wirh T
  .41 many,] =.
  .42 any.] =,
XVI.5 sweet] faier A
XVIII.4 Fortune] Forrune T
  .6 one] oue B
  .13 begot EMV] beget
  .14 Atheists EMV] Atheist
  .21 Fortunes EMV] Fortune
XX.14 of ill . . . knowen] the vttermost of ill is knowne Mt
XXI.5 singeth] sings A
XXII.23 2] *omitted; this line placed with words for*
        first voice

Jo1600

III.13 transitory;] =
  .14 Scorne,] = ;
IIII.8 shame, . . . know] shame . . . know:
  .13 preuent] = :
V.4 where ATB] where as C
VI.5 helpe] rid BA
  .20 well.] = :
VII.4 suite] smart A
      smart] suit A
  .5 part] place T
IX.1 on ATB] and C
X.3 come . . . away] come away, ii. come away
  .8 Come . . . againe] Come againe, come againe, ii.
  .13 Come . . . doe] Come and doe, come and doe, ii.
  .18 Come . . . doe] Come and doe, ii. come and doe
XI.2 haue] hath B
  .6 to] that ATB
  .18 withstanding.] =
XII.2 mine] my ATB
  .3 nay] yet ATB
  .6 go, ATB] = C
XIII.6 soule] loue ATB
XV.4 die, T] = C
  .5 that] which ATB
  .10 But . . . die] But I die, ii.
  .16 Till . . . die] Till I die, ii.
  .22 And . . . die] And I die

.28 That . . . die] That I die,
XVI.11 request,]=.
    .12 phy, phy] phy, phy, ii.
XVIII.7 mine] my T
    .10 set . . . fire] burne my wofull hart A
    .11 can I] I can TB
XX.1 sore am I] *omitted* ATB
    .3 doth] do B
    .6 and . . . die] *omitted* ATB
    .7 my] thine T, mine AB
    .11 sunne] = :
XXI.5 where . . . frowne] is a weake defence T, is a
                    weake defence growne AB
    .6 takes . . . downe] till force beare downe downe
                    a downe ATB

M01600

To the Reader
    .4–5 at length] atlength
I.2 profest,]=.
    .5 might] night
II.3 meri may] merimerimay
III.6 foole,]=.
VI.2 haye,] *comma conjectural*
    .4 preti ring] pretiring
VII.24 perfection,]=.
    .30 sight.] *may be comma*
    .31 make]=,
    .32 at length] atlength
    .44 you *Sidney*] *omitted; see note.*
IX.9 combin'd] combi'nd
X.8 lightnesse,]=.
XIII.16 the shepheards] ths shepheards
        Queen,]=.
XIIII.3 length,]=
XVII. *All punctuation editorial except line 6 (buskes,).*
XVIII.1 cares,]=
    .2 braine,]=
    .3 surprisde,]=
    .4 restraine.]=
    .6 Breste.]=
    .9 harte,]=.
    .11 reste,]=.
    .18 breste.]= :

Jo1601

Dedication
    .35 selfe] felfe

To the Reader
  .20 enuie, these] enuie. These
I.9 Sunnes] Suunes
II.] *Number omitted; see Textual Introduction.*
II.2 stay,]=
  .15 inflame]=,
  .16 desires,]=
III.13 other cals] other to cals
IIII.3 me:]=
V.5 squemish] sqnemish B
VIII.10 deaths] death B
      thy B] the C
IX.19 would] l *broken, or perhaps* wou'd
X.2 cowards B] cowherds C
  .6 bragg, B]= C
  .21 if you] if I you
  .23 loues] lones
XI.3 face,]=
  .4 cleeres, B]= C
XII.4 too B] to C
  .19 forgot] sorgot
XIII.4 were] bee B
XIIII.19 perfectest] perfectefl
XVII.9 sadle] sable *See note.*
    .13 It is] Is is
XVIII.4 singes,]=
    .11 melte EMV] meete
XX.2 die, B]= C
  .6 sport B] sports C
  .13 neuer] nener
XXI.8 warrantie] *thus repeated in* C *and in* B; *first*
              time in C *reads* warrantly
  .9 pleasures,]=
  .11 tasting;]=,
  .12 waite,]=.

DO1603
VI.2 moue, TB]= CA
IX.12 Come, come, come AT] Come, :/: :/: CB
X.24 death.]=
XI.5 then] it ATB
XII.14 blessed] bessed
  .16 cheere,]=. (?)
XIII.5 hath] haue AT
XIIII.1 FArewell ATB] FAarewell C
  .8 still lies] lies still B, lies T
XV.3 snowie] sowie A
  .4 doth] doeth AB

.6 weeping, ATB]=. C
.7 lies B] lie CAT
.8 lies] ly T
.15 sleeping] sleeping ://:
.16 Softly] Softly ://:
XVII.2 parts: AB]=. T, = C
.4 artes, TB]=. C, = : A
.5 forme] frame T
XX.7 ieast,]=.
XXI.4 dumb.]=
.8 remoue.]=

Gr1604

See the Textual Introduction for the sources of the texts.
Dedication
.9 corrupted, her Keepers] corrupted her Keepers,
.25 GREAVES] GREAVES
Ad Authorem
.4 blacke] *final* e *may be a smudge*
Said *Pithagor* true
.7 P. B.] *blurred; see note*
I.2 ringing,]=
.8 graced.]=
.13 with] wirh
II.4 Flora] Flota
V.7 quickly] quick *in repetition*
VI.2–3 needs, /this] needsthis
.3 abide:]=
.4 chide,]=
.6 hap,]=
.7 clap:]=
.8 ay me] ay em e
VII] II
VIII.2 soon depart] soondepart
IX.3 embrace] r *inverted*
X.1 former Mt] fortmer M
.2 thought M] thoughts Mt
XII.3 not *in repetition*] no *first time*
XV.4 procure] procnre Tx
.7 frame] r *inverted* Tx
XVI.1 hand, TCtB]= MTx
XVIII.5 chang'd, ATMB]= C
.6 Venus] Venns A
XIX.] XV T
XIX.3 mine] my T
.8 on fire] osie B

XX.4 I burn, I burn] I burn, .ii. CAMTB
   .6 alas] *first* a *looks like inverted* e *in* A
   .7 hart] rt *blurred in* A

Hu1605

Table
  62 france] franec
  110 second] seeond
3.5 it.] =
  .15 Tobacco,] =
  .22 proude] prowde
112.4 me,] =
  .7 delight.] =
113.12 thee.] =
114.1 men,] = .
  .2 wrong?] =
  .14 Souldier] = .

Jo1605

IIII.4 with] wirh
V.14 Leathe] leathe
  .15 cold:] = : ,
VIII.2 where] way B
  .3 sent] send B
  .4 fortune] seruice A, fottune B
     way] where T
  .14 Which] Whicn
  .21 lot,] = , .
IX. 3 it that] that whieh T, that which AB
XI.1 my] mine ATB
XII.3 loue] lone T
XIII.1 WHen] WWhen T
    fountain] fountaines B
  .5 life] llfe B
XIIII.5 O worlde] O wotld B
  .6 guide] guides C *in repetition*
    blinde] dead B *in repetition*
    blinde. AT] = , C
  .12 dye.] = :
XV.1 HAppy] most happy B *in repetition*
  .4 free, ATB] = C
  .5 striues . . . clime ATB] strius . . . clim C
  .6 rise. ATB] = , (rise *omitted in repetition*) C
XVI.1 that] thar C2
  .6 I: C2] = C1
  .26 away.] = : C1C2
XVII.1 not, C2] = C1

.2 care C1] eare C2
.5 desires C2] desire C1, C2 *in repetition*;
           delights C1
.10 vntimely C2] vnrimely C1
.16 fortunes C1] fottunes C2
XVIII.1 iust C2] first C1
   .4 to too C1] all to C2
XIX.3 thwarted, C2]= C1
   .4 conuerted.]=
   .5 go? C2]= C1
   .13 O, no,]= ;
   .34 O . . . no:] O no, no, no, no:
XX.12 And C2] Aud C1
XXI.1 learnd C2] leaarnd C1
   .3 shot C2]=, C1
      fast,]=
   .7 2 C1] *omitted* C2
      my C1] thy C2
   .13 3 C1] *omitted* C2
      baitst C1] baitest C2

                              Pi1605

I.2 faire] my T
II.2 wandring] mandring B
  .6 exceeds] exceede B
  .9 resolu'd] resoln'd A
III.3 my] in T
   .13 earth,]=
      fires]=,
IIII.2 beautie,]=. CATB
   .6 that] the B
V.2 perfumes] perfume A
  .3 climing] clipping T
VI.4 pleasing] pleasant A
VII.2 shall be] shalbe TB
   .4 your] thy ATB
IX.2 adorning] adoring TB
X.10 lament] la: T
XI.3 come Loue] *omitted* T
XII.6 cure] care A
  .   deed] dead T
XIII.3 falling] salling A
   .5 fal th'hart] falth, hart C, falt'h hart TA,
                  falth hart B
XV.2 may] will ATB
XVI.18 faithfull] faihfull
XIX.4 tuch, A]=. CTB

Bt1606

Dedication
  .19 sweetenes] = *followed by smudge, perhaps comma*
  .21 spirits as] spiritsas
    me by] meby
I.7–8 reioyce, for TB] reioycefor C
V.1,3 IF] *The initial I serves for both lines in CA*
  .2 death,] = .
  .4 breath] creath T *in repetition*
    breath,] = .
  .18 scorn.] =
VI.3 saw] heard A
  .6 awakte] awake A
  .8 ful] sul
VIII.1 sire] fire T
  .2 heart, ATB] = C
  .3 desire] *first* e *blotted* C
  .4 griefes] greeues TB
    of his] *omitted* B
    smart, AT] = CB
  .24 saint,] = ;
IX.1 prety] very prety CB *in repetition*
  .2 mone] my mone ATB
  .3 pretie] very prety CATB *in repetition*
X.31 5] 4
XI.2 checkte] checckt T, cheeckt B
  .6 thereto. ATB] = C
  .7 Queene] Que cne
  .23 friend] sriend
XII.2 eyes, ATB] = C
  .3 fond, ATB] = C
  .8 bond] band
XIII.1 tranceformd] trance formd C, transformd ATB
XIIII.1 tel, TB] = CA
  .2 sting, ATB] = C
  .3 thing, T] = CAB
XV.2 time, C2] = C1
  .4 clime, C2] = C1
  .5 rage, C2] = C1
  .6 fooles, C2] = C1
    youth, C2] = C1
XVII.3 thee C1] thce C2
XVIII.1 part C2] parr C1
  .8 ere we C1] ere that we C2 *in repetition*
XIX.3 Siluanes] Siluars B
  .7 mesurs, B] = C
  .8 euer, B] = C

XX.2 cleare, B] = C
  .4 voice, B] = C
  .5 chatter, B] = C
  .6 reioyce, B] = C
  .7 flat, B] = C
  .8 cride, B] = C
  .10 coate, B] = C
  .11 howboy] hoboy B
  .12 note, B] = C
  .14 ofte B] of C
  .16 presently, B] = C
XXI.1 part B] parr C
  .4 the B] *omitted* C
  .9 neuer. B] = : C
Table
  X birdes] b rdes
  XIII transformde] f *broken, looks like* st

Cop1606

In honorable memory
  .9 atomes] *at om es*
  .12 *Consistorie*] Cousistorie
  .40 *the*] ths (*foul case*)
  .57 *subdue*] d *broken?*
I.6 pris'd] *apostrophe faint* Mt
IIII.6 come CA] comc Mt
  .12 thee] thēe
VI.1 Deceitfull CA] Deceitfnll Mt
VII.2 murderest] *first* e *inverted* Mt, murdrest C
  .5 heauen] heau'n A
  .9 which death] that death A

Dan1606

I.1 *Phœbus* Mt] *Phœbus* C
II.5 sing'st C] fing'st Mt
III.9 power] powre C
IIII.3 according] it sounds according C
  .10 Then Iudge] Iudge then C
     giues] *omitted* C
V.1 Dost] O dost C *in repetition*
 .2 For that] Because C
VII.7 you'l] you will C *in repetition*
  .8 But . . . goe] But will you goe? say will you?
        O will you goe C
  .9 mee. C] = – Mt
VIII.6 help] aide C
X.2 Drop] O drop C *in repetition*

.5 And shall] ah shall C *in repetition*
XII.2 invassaild C] vnvassald Mt
XIII.3 that] which C
      tyme forget] time euen all time forget C
              in repetition
XVI.3 darke black] blacke darke C
XIX.7 seldome . . . turne] doe seldome turne A *in repetition*
   .11 And let them] And they must CTB, then A
      proue] bee AB
XX.1 earth . . . Aire] Skies, Earth and Aire, the Earth,
               Skies, Aire C1 *in repetition*; the
               Earth, Skies, Aire C2 *in repetition*
  .2 All] and all C1, *in repetition* C2; the
      Skies and all B
  .5 Ioyes] that ioyes C2 *in repetition*
  .7 When . . . alone] *see note*
  .8 Left] Left all alone T
  .11 Bird] birds C2, bird C2 *in repetition*

Fd1607

Table
  11 A Dialogue.] *period raised*
Dedication to Weston
  .4 iustly] instly
I.6 of mirth ATB] oi mirth C
  months] moneths B
 .7 feare ATB] seare C
  sicknesses ATB] sicknesse C
 .9 O] *omitted* A
  often] oft B, *first time in* A
  come] comes ATB
 .10 but ATB] bnt C
II.5 blown, AT] = CB
 .7 least] lest AB
  sowne, ATB] = C
III.4 mine] my T
IIII.5A vntrustie] i *inverted* A
      sighted] sighred T
  .6 delighted, ATB] = C
V.1 faire, ATB] = C
 .2 pleade] and pleade T
 .4 encreasing, ATB] = C
 .5 pace, ATB] = C
VI.1 bowers] bowres ATB
  .2 showers] showres ATB
  .3 shades, AB] = CT
  .4 enuades, ATB] = C

VII.1 doest] dost ATB, C *in repetition*
  .2 oh] *omitted* T
  .3 doest] dost TB
    thee, ATB] = C
  .4 seem'st] see'mst C, seemst TB, seemest A
  .7 danger,] danger, .ii,
VIII.3 wrangle, ATB] = C
  .9 beholder] heholder
IX.1 kind, ATB] = C
  .2 mind, ATB] = C
  .3 by, ATB] = C
X.2 th'unworthiest] thu'n worthiest CT, thunworthiest B,
                      the vnworthiest A
  .3 looks] looke B
    discreet, ATB] = C
  .12 springes,] = .
XI.3 Flie] FFlie
  .5 desire desires] desire desire
  .10 this] ths
  .12 blisse] blisle (?)
Table of the Lessons
  booke.] = ,
Dedication to Tichborne
  .12 forth] forh
  .18 remembrance] rememrance

Hu1607

I.11 my] m *broken*
  .21 morn,] =
  .22 dreames] dramees
    more,] =
Alwaies thus to the Reader
  .6 *selfe] sefe*
To All . . . Lordes . . . And . . . Hatton
  .14 happy-making fauours,] = .
XIV.1 woe,] =
  .2 sorrow,] =
XXV.10 houndes.] =
    .25 hounds] honnds
    .32 Mounter] Mountet
    .37 List] list
    .39 Thats] thats
    .41 twise] e *inverted*
    .53 come trowling] come frowling (*broken* f)
    .54 Winde] winde
      morte.] =

Fer1609

IIII.10 pray] = ,
  part,] =
VI.14 wile.] =
XIII.2 skill,] = ; (?)
XXVI.8 thee *1st voice*] this *2nd voice*
XXVIII.19 brings *2nd voice*] bring *1st voice, first time*

Han1609

1.1 thou?] =
.5 dye:] =
.6,13 stayest?] =
.7,14 be.] =
.8 stay?] =
.12 liue.] =
2.2 keepe,] =
.4 grief:] =
.10 bowes,] =
.11 woods,] =
.12 tree.] =
.14 see,] =
.18 me.] =
3.1 Florella] florella
.6 endure?] =
.8 dye.] =
.10 slaked:] =
.14 proue,] =
16. deed.] =
4.4 skie.] =
.8 cheare.] =
.12 myne.] =
5.2 griefe:] =
.4 dye,] =
.5 mournefull] mounefull
.6 dying.] =
6.2 thee:] =
.4 dye.] =
7.1 opprest,] =
.2 procuringe:] =
.4 indureinge:] =
.6 confound.] =
8.2 durst] dust
.4 hell.] =
.8 loue.] =
.12 cround.] =
.16 shrine.] =
9.2 houer,] =

.4 stay,]=
.6 sorrow.]=
.8 teares,]=
.10 seeme.]=
.12 sorrow.]=
10.4 louer] louell *with* r *above caret after* e
.6 repaire.]=
.8 shrine,]=
.9 bee,]=
.12 dwell.]=
.18 dye.]=
11.2 the] th
.4 turne,]=
.6 fyre.]=
.8 rayes,]=
.9 hast,]=
.10 stay ?]=
.12 me] *omitted*
12.6 flowers.]=
.10 sap,]=
.12 hap.]=
.15 knowe] kowe
.16 ills:]=
.18 kills.]=
.22 eyes:]=
.24 dyes.]=
13.1 mynd,]=
.2 discontent,]=
.4 lament:]=
.5 know,]=
.6 flow.]=
14.2 breast:]=
.3 death,]=
.4 supprest,]=
.5 pyne:]=
.6 myne.]=
15.1 Flow] flow
.2 eyes:]=
.3 woe,]=
.4 arise:]=
.6 showers.]=
.7 Flow] flow
    straine,]=
.8 Flow] flow
.10 ly,]=
.12 wronge.]=
16.2 sighes,]=

   mates,]=
 .4 and] an
 .5 mysery:]=
 .7 me] *inserted above a caret*
   lament.]=
18.5 death:]=
 .6 loue?]=
 .7 turtledoue.]=
19.1 Amyntas.] Daphne. *erroneously taken from 20*
 .3 face.]=
 .5 eyes.]=
 .9 louer.]=
 .11 eyes.]=
 .13 rise.]=
20.2 me.]=
 .3 loue.]=
 .4 me,]=
 .5 heare.]=
 .6 deare.]=
 .10 adieue?]=
 .11 fayre.]=
 .12 true.]=
 .13 still?]=
 .14 kill.]=
 .15 me?]=
 .16 thee.]=
 .17 me.]=
 .18 pitty,]=
 .19 deuine,]=
 .21 pine.]=
 .23 round] round a round *Phyllis' part*
 .25 hate] a hate *Daphne's part*
   all] both *Phyllis' part*
   ringe.]=

Jo1609

To all Musicall Murmurers
 .36 *Midwife*] *Widwife*
Table
 21 S'amor] Samor
I.6 but] bnt A
 .32 abusing.]=,
II.1 Sweet] SSweet C
 .7 Te] He A
 .12 Neither] Neuer A
 .31 quoth] qnoth
III.3 piersing] smiling A

.6 loues] loue A *first time*
IIII.1 mammy A] manmmy C
  .6 wife . . . wife] .ii. .ii. A, .ii. .ti. C
  .11 wife . . . wife] .ii. .ii. CA
  .37 such] snch
V.2 die] dle A *in repetition*
  then] so A
  hell, A] = C
 .4 can] cau A
  reliefe] teliefe A *in repetition*
 .8 none] *first* n *broken*
  but] bnt
  cares.] =
VII.1 summer] summers A
  .6 Ienny . . . I] Ienny sweet Ienny sweet shal I .ii.
               sweet Ienny sweet shall I, shall I,
               shall I. C; Ienny sweet .ii. sweet
               sweet sweet Ienny, sweet shall I,
               shall I Ienny .ii. shall I. A
  .13 dealing] = .
  .16 reuealing,] = .
VIII.2 my eye] mine eyes A
  .5 first, A] = C
  .6 acurst, A] = C
  .23 vntold] vnt old
    him.] =
IX.3 tong] tongbe T
  dare not] daren B
  .4 wise ATB] wisee C
  .6 iealousie] iealonsie B
X.2 aye] ah AT
 .3 My sight . . . appeare] my sight by his soules thought
                  was gnided did appeare T
 .4 guided, AB] = CT
 .6 soules] = , CTAB; soule TA
  guest ATB] gester C
 .10 Absence] Asence
  killed,] =
XI.1 thine] thy B
  .3 neere, AT] = CB
  touch] touch and touch T, toueh B
  shrine, AB] = CT
  .5 lippes] Iips A
  .6 lippes . . . happe, ATB] lippes kisses Ioyes haue C
  blessings] blessing AT, O blessing B
  .9 ioyes,] = .
XII.2 hath an eye TB] .ii. CA

.3 two T] too CAB
.4 hey hoe, hey hoe, A] = C; with hey hoe, with
                 hey hoe TB
.5 hoe, AB] = CT
  ah me] O B, alasse T, aye me A
.7–8 wise . . . blind] Ladies kisses are a charme
              that kill vs ere they doe vs harme AB
.7 their] the T
.12 earthly] earrhly
.19 none,] = .
.22 with] wieh
XIII.1 what] with T
  .2 euer, T] = CB
  .3 it TB] yet C
    not] now T
    yet is it such] it is, it such yet is it, such T
  .4 neuer, B] = CAT
XIIII.2 mee, ATB] = C
   .5 griefes] griefe A
   .6 euer, AT] = CB
   .7 absence, T] = CAB
    griefe] griefes A
XV.1 this] the A
  .2 soule] sonle B
   thou] shou A
   canst] caust T
   thy . . . wings] *omitted* T
  .5 ioy] ioyes A
   sings] sing A
  .6 Echoes] Ecchoe A *first time*, TB
   rings] Ring AT
XVI.6 to . . . earth] *omitted* A
  .7 midwife AB] widwife CT
  .11 decay, AT] = CB
  .12 inanity, ATB] = C
  .13 vanity, ATB] = C
  .14 minion] O minion B
XVII.4 could] conld A
  .7 for] f *or* s?
XVIII.2 retire ATB] tetire C
   .3 forth TB] = , CA *before repeat mark*
   my . . . silence] *omitted* A
  .4 hand ATB] hands C
  .5 hands] hand B
   guiders] guider B *in repetition*
XIX.4 beter:] =
  .11 as well] aswell

.18 skies] =.
.26 could] eould
XX.4 *sia*] *sie* in repetition
XXI.1 *S' Amor* B] *S Amor* C
  .4 *si*] *fi*
      tormento] *tormentk*
  .5 *voglia*] =.
      pianto] *piauto*
  .7 *male*] *m* inverted
  .8 *consento*] *cousento*

Ck1610

III.2 *restraine* C] *restraiue* Mt
 .8 *most* C] *must* Mt
IIII.3 plaints] plants
V.1 Sweete sweete sweete] Sweete sweete .ij.
 .3 cease cease cease] cease .ij. .ij.
 .5 Alas] alas
VII.5 *to* C] *too* Mt
 .15 *found.*] =,
VIII.5 things] thing
 .6 conceiuing,] =
 .8 new] =,
XII.5 *were*] weare C

RD01610

III.20 agreeth,] =.
V.12 ioyes *Sidney*] omitted; *see note*
VI.12 proue, B] =. C
VII.5 flowers C] flowres B
 .9 blessed] bIessed C
 .55 more *Sidney*] omitted; *see note*
IX.4 ouer-ioyed CB *in repetition*] ouerioyde CB *first time*
 .8 pleased] pleas'd B
XX.2 O *Bella piu*] O *Bella pipiu* (first time)

Jo1610

Dedication
 .9 renowned] renowmed
I.4 heythen'd] hey th'end
 .27 *keepes*] *kcepes*
II.1 Soft] SSoft
III.20 *a part*] *apart*
IIII.4 stay,] =
V.27 *desires to die*] *desire to dies*
VI.12 *And*] *Aud*
 .22 *like,*] =.

.27 *heele*] *hecle* (?)
VII.4 keepe] keeepe
  .12 *Dye*] *Dey*
  .17 *knowne*] knowen C
VIII.6 seruant] =.
IX.20 *diuine*] *diuiue*
  .26 *sheepe*] *sheepc* (?)
XI.1 ONce] LNce
XIII.47 *rare.*] =,
XIIII.15 *rule*] *rulc*
  .28 *nay nay*] *nay ny*
XVI.8 *She*] *Che*
  .13 *loue.*] =
  .17 *breath,*] =.
  .20 *matter.*] =,
XVII.4 like] like like
  .14 *While . . . stood*] (*sic*; see note)

Ma1611

III.2 trade of] trade, the trade of C
IIII.2 is, B] = C
VII.2 praise Townes,] praise, Townes C *also RPR*
X.4 oft,] =. C
XII.5 till] t *broken*

Ck1612

V.18 now, leaue] now, ://: leaue
VIII.17 tremble] bremble
Dedication to Stapleton and Cope
  .7 HOW] HOH
XVII.3 That . . . doubt B] *omitted* C
  .6 Can . . . parts B] *omitted* C

Do1612

Dedication
  .1 RIGHT] RIHGT
To the Reader
  .10 Seas,] =.
III.1 loue ATB] lone C
IIII.2 mourning] morning ATB
  .6 iewell,] *comma inverted*
V.6 must ATB] umst C
VI.3 sights] sight TB
VIII.19 residing,] =. (?)
XII.2 wings] wirdes ATB
XVIII.3 thoughts] ioyes B
      bereaued] bereaude AB

XIX.37 that nor] that not A
XX.3 delight,]=.
    .8 pay.]=

At1622

Dedication
    .14 vnworthy] vnwrothy
    .28 *Historie*;]=, (*perhaps*)
II.5 chance ATB]=, C
III.] *no number*
IIII.] III.
IIII.2 *Mirrhas* ATB] *Mirrahs* C
    .10 Coll] *possibly* Cull *in BM copy*?
V.] IIII.
V.4 now] *omitted* A
VI.] V.
VI.6 within AB] which in CT
    .7 That] Which A (That *in repetition*)
VII.] VI.
VIII.] VII.
IX.] VII.
IX.4 deities AB]=, CT
    .6 them AB]=, CT
X.] VIII.
XI.] IX.
XII.] X.
XIII.] XI.
XIIII.] XII.

Notes

William Barley, *A New Booke of Tabliture*, 1596

Dedication

Bridgett Countesse of Sussex. The daughter of Sir Charles Morison of Hertfordshire, she married Robert Radcliffe, 5th Earl of Sussex while he was still Viscount Fitzwalter. Robert Greene subtitled his *Philomela* (1592) *The Lady Fitzwater's Nightingale*; two other books were dedicated to her. She died in 1623 (DNB, Williams).

To the Reader

16–18 *Thus he who is desirous . . . to bestow*. There seem to be two sources of corruption in this sentence: *for when* should be *for which* or perhaps *for whom*; *I urge him* (or *thee*) before *to bestow* would also help, but the sentence still remains an awkward tangle.

I.

7–12 Correlative verse.

8 *life*. EMV, p. 726, speculates that this should read *love*, which would continue the antithesis of *heaven–hell*.

II.

7–8 *Words . . . winde*. *Cf*. Tilley W833, "Words are but wind."

10 *out of sight are out of minde*. Tilley S438.

11 *those so*. The original reading, *though so*, is clearly the result of a misplaced juncture.

22 *hurt*. Collier (p. 35) suggests *hart*.

III.

Rollins calls this "the most worthless poem in *The Phoenix Nest*, though it was one of the most popular," and notes as possible authors Nicholas Breton, Sir Walter Raleigh, and his own conjecture, Thomas Lodge (RPN, pp. 173–178). Agnes M.C.

Latham, in her edition of *The Poems of Sir Walter Raleigh* (Cambridge, Mass.: Harvard University Press, 1951), prints the version from *The Phoenix Nest* among other poems from that book (*e.g.*, By1596.V; see note) conjectured to be Raleigh's (p. 80), and discusses the authorship and other versions on pp. xlvii–l and 159–161. She regards the authorship as uncertain, or perhaps a joint effort by Raleigh and his cousin Sir Arthur Gorges. See also her earlier edition (London: Constable, 1929, pp. 38, 143–145). Helen E. Sandison, the editor of Gorges' *Poems* (Oxford: Clarendon Press, 1953), is inclined to accept Gorges' authorship, although she also thinks joint authorship with Raleigh possible (pp. xxxix–xl).

For details and collations of the following versions, see Rollins' note in RPN, pp. 173–178: *Brittons Bowre of Delights* (1591, 1597), RBBD, pp. 51–53; Francis Davison's *A Poetical Rhapsody* (1602–1621), RPR, I, 223; BM MS Add. 15227, fols. 84v–85; Bod. MS Rawlinson Poet. 117, fols. 161, 168v; BM MS Add. 22118, fol. 34; *Wits Recreations* (1641), sig. T1v; John Cotgrave's *Wits Interpreter, The English Parnassus* (1655), sigs. G7v–G8; and *Le Prince d'Amour* (1660, 1669), pp. 131–132 (initialed "W. R.").

Miss Sandison (pp. 77–78) prints what may be the original version from BM MS Egerton 3165, fol. 61, a collection called "The Vanytes of Sir Arthur Georges Youthe" (D). In her notes (pp. 209–212), she gives the texts for versions listed but not collated by Rollins: (E) from John Moulton's commonplace book, one stanza printed in Colbeck, Radford and Company's Catalogue No. 9, 1930, lot 192 (the company's records were destroyed during World War II, and the location of the MS is not known); and (F) BM MS Harleian 7392, fol. 66v (RPR, II, 184–185) to which the signature "Raley" was, apparently, added later. Miss Sandison also gives the texts for (G) one stanza printed in *The Card of Courtship...*, by "Musophilus" (1653), p. 146; and (H) Cambridge MS Dd.v.75, fol. 36. H differs so greatly as to make collation impractical; see Sandison, p. 211, for the full text. A copy of the first stanza is in (I) John Rylands Library MS 410 (after 1641), fol. 21. Variants from DEFGI are:

  1 Your ... Your ... Your] Her ... Her ... Her DFGI
  2 sweet] smooth I
  3 First] Hath E
    bent] drew GI
    Then drew] hath drawne E, then bent G, first cut I
    So hite] then hitt DF, hath hit E, last knit G, first knit I
  4 Mine eye Mine eare] My eyes, my eares E, My ey, my eare I
  7 Your ... Your ... Your] her ... her ... her D
  9 Your ... Your ... Your] Her ... Her ... Her DF
  11 rule] knitt D
  13 My eare] Myne eare DF
  15 Your ... Your ... Your] her ... her ... her D
  20 My eare] myne eare DF
  22 bend] yeald D (*Gorges' revision of* bend), bynd F
  23 Your ... Your ... Your] her ... her ... her D
    wittes] witt DF
  24 trust] Loue F

The closest to Barley of all versions, except for the substitution of *her* for *your*, is D; then F, then *Wits Interpreter*, then *Brittons Bowre of Delights*.

Rollins lists a number of analogous "reporting verses" in RPN, pp. 176–178. One example from which he quotes six lines, beginning "The luck—The life—the loue," may also be found in Folger MS V.a.345, p. 281. In RPR, II, 185, Rollins cites four lines from a longer poem in Bartholomew Yong's translation, not of Montemayor's *Diana*, but of Gil Polo's *Diana Enamorada*, included in the Montemayor volume (1598), sig. Ss2v. To Rollins' examples one might add the fifth of Sir John Davies' "Gulling Sonnets," which begins, "Myne Eye, mine eare, my will, my witt, my harte" (*Poems*, ed. Clare Howard [New York: Columbia University Press, 1941], pp. 225–226). See also HAH, I, 292, and the examples in Abraham Fraunce, *The Arcadian Rhetoricke* (1588), ed. Ethel Seaton (Oxford: Basil Blackwell for the Luttrell Society, 1950), pp. 56–63.

13, 20 *My eare.* EMV, p. 350, emends to *mine ear.*
23 *wittes.* EMV, p. 351, emends to *wit.*

IIII.

10 *he that sowed wind &c.* Cf. Tilley W437, who cites this line and Hosea 8:7.
11 *flowers of Spaine . . . rorie.* EMV emends *Spaine* to *spine* and *rorie* to *rosy* (p. 351). *Rorie* means *dewy,* and should be retained; but I can find no appropriate "flower of Spain," and the sense of line 12, rhyme, and (incidentally) the name of a character in Ariosto's *Orlando Furioso* (Book XXV), Fiordispina, point to the reading *spine.*

V.

Another version—perhaps the source—of this poem may be found in (D) *The Phoenix Nest* (RPN, pp. 76–77), and a much later one in (E) *Cupids Master-Piece. Or, The Free-School of Witty and Delightful Complements* (*c.* 1650), sig. B4v, quoted by Rollins, RPN, p. 166. The latter is headed "This Song in her praise," referring to one of the speakers, Rebecca. A third version (F) is in John Cotgrave's *Wits Interpreter* (1655; not in 1662 ed.), sig. H1v–H2, entitled "In praise of his Mistress." The variants follow:

1 that] which DEF
  set] sets F
  fancie] fancies EF
  on a] all on E
2 which] that F
3 Those . . . conquered] That dainty Hand that conquers EF
4 thought] thoughts D, heart EF
5–6 *These lines come at the end in DEF. See note below.*
5 may] can EF
  therewith stand] thee withstand DEF
6 head] haire DE, haires F
7–10 *Omitted* E
7 doth] doe DF
8 brightnes] brighthess F
9 Those hands] That hand F
10 euen . . . wonne] ev'ns with the godds hath won renown F
11 hearts] eyes E
12 Oh . . . weares] O Heart, of worth to wear EF

13 hands] Head E, hand F
   conquere] conquers EF
14 turnes huge kingdomes] turns the world even E, turneth the World F

Bond, without evidence, attributed the *Phoenix Nest* version to Lyly (III, 474). Agnes M.C. Latham, following Hoyt H. Hudson's account of the "Raleigh group" of poems in *The Phoenix Nest* (*MLN*, XLVI [1931], 386–389), includes it among the conjectural pieces in her edition of Raleigh's *Poems* (Cambridge, Mass.: Harvard University Press, 1951), p. 78. Queen Elizabeth may be intended by lines 12–14. *Cf.* Walter Okeshott, *The Queen and the Poet* (London: Faber and Faber, 1960), pp. 150–152.

As Rollins notes (RPN, p. 166), the poem is a translation of a sonnet by Philippe Desportes, "Du bel oeil de Diane est ma flamme empruntee" (*Les Amours de Diane*, I.11, ed. Victor E. Graham [Paris: Librairie Minard, and Geneva: Librairie Droz, 1959], p. 42). What seems to be a freer version of Desportes, "Those eies that holds the hand of euery hart," may also be found in RPN, pp. 82–83, as well as in Latham's Raleigh, p. 83; RBBD, pp. 22–23; RAAD, pp. 42–43; BM MS Add. 34064, fol. 7v; and Bod. MS Rawlinson Poet. 85, fol. 24v.

5 *therewith stand.* This should probably read *thee withstand* as in DEF; Collier (p. 37) suggested *these withstand.*

5–6 In all other versions, these lines are the final couplet. Rollins, RPN, p. 165, suggests that Barley may have intended them as a refrain. The music (Part III, sig. C2v–C3, melody in mensural notation over tablature accompaniment) is clearly for six lines of verse, and the last phrase has an ascending sequence which is most suitable for line 6. It is probable that the MS Barley used had the words of lines 1–6 underlying the music, with lines 7–14 written out below, and that a performer, seeing the repeat signs in the music after line 4, would then sing the other two quatrains before proceeding to lines 5–6. This seems to have been a common method of setting a sonnet: see Do1600.IX, and Do1612.XVIII. A less musical publisher or typesetter could easily misread the music and set the poem up as it is here. The music, incidentally, would also fit "Those eies that holds the hand of euery hart" if the repeat were *not* taken.

VI.

This poem is also found in BM MS Harleian 6910 (*c.* 1596), fol. 148–148v; Bod. MS Rawlinson Poet. 85, fol. 50v, signed "A.H."; *The Phoenix Nest* (1593), sig. N2v–N3 (RPN, pp. 100–101; Rollins collates the copies so far listed, including By1596 and BM MS Add. 28635, a 19th century transcript of the Arundel Harington MS, on p. 197); BM MS Harleian 7392, fol. 73, signed "R all"; and HAH, I, 240 (Hughey collates all copies on II, 213). Hughey's collation is the most nearly complete, but these variants from By1596 in the HAH text should be added:

14 my end] myne ende
17 you] your

The "R all" of MS Harleian 7392 is Robert Allot (see H. H. Hudson, *MLN*, XLVI, 386–389). As Hughey says (HAH, II, 313), the ascription to Allot, the compiler of *England's Parnassus* (1600), possibly means only that the poem was taken from his collection, and that he was not necessarily the poet.

17 *you.* EMV, p. 352, follows the other texts in reading *your.*

18 *Caesars fate.* The reading in RPN, p. 101, "Caesars state," seems more appropriate.

VII.

This poem was first printed in (D) the highly popular *Paradise of Dainty Devices* (1576–1606) where it is ascribed to "L. Vaux" (Thomas, Lord Vaux); see the edition by Hyder E. Rollins (Cambridge, Mass.: Harvard University Press, 1927), pp. 72–73. Rollins gives variant readings from the other editions of the *Paradise* on pp. 160–161, and lists modern reprints of the version in By1596 on pp. 236–237. Other versions of the poem are found in (E) BM MS Harleian 6910 (*c.* 1596), fol. 168v; (F) BM MS Add. 24665 ("Giles Earle his booke," 1615–1626), fols. 27v–28, with notes for the melody and bass, the tune being the same as By1596, Part 3, sigs. C3v–C4; (G) NLS Advocates' MS 5.2.14 (William Stirling's Cantus partbook, *c.* 1639), fol. 14v, also with the same tune; another copy of the poem is in (H) a two-page MS in the Chetham Library, Manchester; J. O. Halliwell-Phillipps reprinted the first stanza in his *Catalogue of Proclamations, Broadsides, Ballads, and Poems* (1851), p. 157, No. 1200, the version collated here. The tune with the title, but no other words, is in (I) BM MS Add. 4388 (an early leaf in a miscellaneous collection), fol. 105. According to Rubsamen (p. 274), the Taitt MS (J) at U.C.L.A. has the music and one stanza of the text (No. 39, Cantus, fol. 62); and (K) Christ Church, Oxford, MSS 984–8, No. 113, has a version for voice and four viols. Other sources for the music alone are noted by Simpson, pp. 315–316.

Variants from all but IJK are:

1 the] that G
2 sometime] alwayes G
3 the] that DG
   vade] fade DEFGH *Three editions of D have* vade.
5 this] that I
   nay] no G
   I] you D–G
6 feeles] feele H
   knowes] knoweth D *Four editions of D have* knowes.
7–18 *omitted* H
8 is it] what's the F
   be] is E, ar G
9 auaileth] auaile the F
   sight] light DG
10 a] the F
11 D,E,G *repeat their versions of lines* 5 *and* 6 *here*; F *reads only* "Is this &c"; D *reads* knowes *in the last line of the stanza.*
12 serues] serue DF
14 al of] of all E
   plaints] paine G
16 nay] no G
   I] you D–G

The tune of "How can the tree" is named by Thomas Deloney as a suitable alternative to the notes he provides for singing "Of King Edward the second, being poysoned," a ballad in his *Strange Histories* (1602); see Deloney's *Works*, ed. F. O. Mann (Oxford: Clarendon Press, 1912), p. 405.

Similar verses are spoken by the character Neronis in *Clyomon and Clamydes* (1599), sometimes attributed to George Peele; see Rollins, *Paradise*, p. 237, and *Clyomon and Clamydes*, ed. W. W. Greg (Oxford: Malone Society, 1913), sigs. D4v–E1. The lines begin: "How can that tree but withered be/ That wanteth sap to moist the roote?"

John Dowland, *The First Booke of Songes or Ayres*, 1597

Dedication

Sir George Carey (1547–1603) second Baron Hunsdon, had several other books dedicated to him, including Thomas Morley's *Canzonets or Little Short Aers to Fiue and Six Voices* (1597) (Williams). One of Dowland's lute pieces is called "My Lady Hunsdon's Puffe" (BM MS Add. 6402, fol. 2).

16 *Plato defines melody*. See the *Republic*, III.398. Dowland probably found this in a theoretical work such as Gioseffe Zarlino's *Istitutioni harmoniche* (1558, reprinted in 1562 and 1573; see II.12, sig. k4v and IV.32, sig. V2). We know from Robert Dowland's *Varietie of Lute-lessons* (1610, sig. D2) that John Dowland knew Heinrich Glarean's *Dodecachordon* (Basle, 1547), which contains a similar statement but does not cite Plato (sig. A1).

To the courteous Reader

Dowland's account of his travels is confirmed by the remarkable letter he wrote Sir Robert Cecil in 1595 (Cecil Papers 172.91, Hatfield House, printed by the Historical Manuscripts Commission, *Calendar of the Manuscripts of the . . . Marquis of Salisbury*, V (1894), 445–447, and by Warlock, pp. 24–27). Although Dowland never makes it clear, he probably did not get to Rome.

10 *our two famous Vniuersities*. Dowland took his Bachelor of Music at Oxford in July, 1588, with Thomas Morley (Anthony à Wood, *Fasti Oxonienses*, ed. Philip Bliss [1815], pp. 241–242). There is no record of his Cambridge degree.

19–20 *Henry Iulio Duke of Brunswick*. Heinrich Julius, Duke of Braunschweig, often entertained English acting troupes at Wolfenbüttel. See E. K. Chambers, *The Elizabethan Stage* (London, 1923), III, 275.

Maritius Lantzgraue of Hessen. Moritz "der Gelehrte" seemed especially fond of Dowland's music, for he later wrote to Dowland in England asking him to return to Cassel (Folger MS V.a.321, fol. 53). The Landgrave was also a composer: a pavan of his in Robert Dowland's *Varietie of Lute-lessons* (1610), sig. H2v, is inscribed "in honorem Ioanni Doulandi Anglorum Orphei." See also Henry Peacham's comment in *Minerva Britanna* (c. 1611), sig. P4v.

22 *Alexander Horologio*. Alessandro Orologio (d. 1633) was composer and organist at the Dresden Court Chapel and in Wolfenbüttel. He published several volumes of madrigals and canzonets, one of which was printed with English words in Thomas Morley's collection of Italian *Madrigals to fiue voyces* (1598, No. XII); see Obertello, pp. 322, 482.

24 *Gregorio Howet*. Robert Dowland's *Varietie of Lute-lessons* (1610) contains a fantasy for the lute by "Gregorio Huwet of Antwerpe" (sig. G2).

33 *Luca Marenzio* (1553–1599) perhaps the most famous of the Italian madrigalists. See Einstein, II, 608–688. Most of the madrigals in Thomas Watson's *Italian Madri- galls Englished* (1590) are by Marenzio.

47 *Giouanni Crochio.* Croce (1557?–1609) was also a madrigalist of some reputation in England: some of his madrigals were included in Nicholas Yonge's second *Musica Transalpina* (1597), and Morley mentions him in his *Plaine and Easie Introduction.* His *Sette Sonetti Penitentiali* (1603) were printed with English words as *Musica Sacra* (1608).

57 *Tho. Campiani.* Campion included another Latin poem in praise of Dowland in his *Poemata* (1595). See Vivian, pp. 346–347; Davis gives translations of both poems, pp. 195, 441–443.

I.

This song, with Dowland's music, is found in (D) William Stirling's MS, NLS Advocates' MS 5.2.14 (*c.* 1639), fol. 19 (treble only); in (E) Bod. MS Mus. f. 7–10 (*c.* 1630–40), Cantus (of four part-books), fols. 3v–4, without variants; and without music in (F) Bod. MS Don. d. 58 (*c.* 1647), fol. 22v. Variants, except for Scotticisms in D, are

1 ciuill] cruell D
3 you] thou F
6 string] strings F
9 these] those D, their F
15 would] will D
16 that] could D, yett F

16 *that.* This refers to *tongue* (line 15), but the reading in F, *yet,* is a possibility.

II.

This is Sonnet V of Fulke Greville's *Caelica* cycle. See Bullough's edition, I, 75 and 232. Bullough's text is taken from *Certaine Learned and Elegant Workes of the Right Honorable Fulke Lord Brooke* (1633) sig. Aa2 (D); on p. 232 he records the variants from the Warwick Castle MS (E). Bullough thinks Dowland's version is earlier than D or E. The variants from Bullough's edition are:

1 euer thinks] trusts for trust DE
4 light-god] light God DE
5 son] Sunne DE
6 darke clowdes] shadowes DE
8 in constant] with constant DE
   arm'd] armed DE
9 friut] fruit DE
10 Who . . . charm'd] Change I doe meane by no faith to be charmed DE
12 by] with DE
   Sprights] sprites E, sp'rits D

The poem was also set to music by Martin Peerson, *Mottects Or Grave Chamber Musique*, 1630, Nos. 17–18. Peerson's text is the same as the 1633 edition, except that line 5 reads *Sonne.* Dowland's version was copied without variants into the four part-books of Bod. MS Mus. f. 7–10 (*c.* 1630–40); only the Cantus part has both stanzas (fols. 2v–3). Dowland set to music two other poems by Greville, 1597.XXI and 1600.XVIII.

4 *light-god.* The meaning of *light* here is *wanton.* Although Cupid is not known as a god of light, the possible pun may be an ironical reference to his blindness.

6 *darke clowdes . . . ouer runne. Cf.* By1596.VII.4.

12 *treasures . . . Sprights.* Bullough, I, 232, notes: "Spirits (*e.g.* the Bucca of Cornish legend) were said to guard mines and attack miners. *Cf.* refs. in J. D. Wilson *Hamlet*, pp. 164, 165. The imagery of 11–12 recalls the saying of Democritus 'That the truth of nature lies hid in certain deep mines and caves' (cited by Bacon, *De Augm. Scient.*, iii.3). *Cf.* Drayton, *Idea* (1605), LVIII, based on the same notion." *Cf.* also Greville's *Treatie of Humane Learning*, stanza 119 (Bullough, I, 183), "like treasures with strange spirits guarded."

III.

The music to this song was printed in an instrumental version in Dowland's *Lachrimae* (1604, No. 13), called "Sir John Souch his Galiard." The subject matter suggests that the poem may have been addressed to Queen Elizabeth, and has led Walter Oakeshott to attribute it to Sir Walter Raleigh on internal evidence (*The Queen and the Poet* [1960], pp. 157–158). W.J. Linton, *Rare Poems* (1883), p. 255, also suggests Raleigh. It was printed with the title "Another to his Cinthia" in *England's Helicon* (1600; REH, I, 160–161) along with VIII, XI, and XXI, where it is followed by a note reading: "These three ditties were taken out of Maister Iohn Dowlands booke of tableture for the Lute, the Authours names not there set downe, & therefore left to their owners." But Francis Davison's MS list of the contents of *England's Helicon* (BM MS Harl. 280, fols. 99–101) ascribes the poem to the "Earle of Cumberland" (REH, II, 39, 176). Edmund Malone noted in his copy of *England's Helicon*, now in the Bodleian, that the poem was by "M. F. G.", which Rollins (II, 176) takes to be "Master Fulke Greville." Malone may have made this guess because it follows a poem by Greville (Do1597.XXI). Rollins also notes that J. P. Collier, in *A Bibliographical and Critical Account of the Rarest Books in the English Language* (1865), I, 73, "incorrectly said that Dowland assigned it to Greville;" and that "A.B. Grosart reprinted it in his edition (1870, II, 139–140 [*Fuller Worthies' Library*]) of Greville, without, however, accepting that poet's claim." Bond (III, 478) attributed the poem to Lyly without evidence. A. H. Bullen, *Lyrics from the Song-Books of the Elizabethan Age* (1887), p. 190, said that in a MS commonplace book at Hamburg, the poem is signed "W. S." Rollins says this may be William Smith, but wisely concludes: "The author is entirely uncertain."

The copy in *England's Helicon* contains the following variants:

4 in] On
  waxeth] wexeth
12 seasned] seasoned

Bod. MS Mus. f. 7–10 (*c.* 1630–40, Cantus, fol. 9) contains Dowland's music in parts and the first stanza of the text, without variants.

The music for this song may have been the "Dowlands Galliard" to which Anthony Munday wrote verses published in *A Banquet of Daintie Conceits* (1588; entered 1584), sigs. G4v–H1. As Diana Poulton has suggested, this seems to be the only one of Dowland's surviving galliards to which Munday's words can be fitted. In an interesting preface (sig. A3), Munday admits that he has no knowledge of music, but works by ear; nevertheless, the songs "haue beene tryed by them of iudgment." Munday's verses (six stanzas) begin:

> It chaunced on a time, that a lewde Theefe:
> Did enter in a mans house for some releefe.
> Where seeking busilie what he might finde:
> At length he found such things as pleasde his minde.
> Sorting them earnestly what he did lacke:
> At last of all the best he made a packe.

It is possible, then, that the music to No. III had been composed before 1584, that it was known as a galliard, and that "My thoughts are wingde" was written to the previously composed tune, as Munday's verses had been.

IIII.

This song was known in an instrumental version as "Captaine Digorie Piper his Galiard" (*Lachrimae*, 1604, No. 18). Words and music to the song, complete and in fragments, appear in seven manuscripts. All are later than Do1597, and were probably copied from it or a later edition; hence the few textual variants they show are of little importance. The MSS are: (D) BM Add. 15117 (after 1614), fol. 15v, for voice and lute; (E) BM Add. 24665 (1615–1626), fols. 12v–13 (Giles Earle's MS), for treble and bass; (F) BM Add. 29481 (*c.* 1630), fol. 14, for treble and bass, first stanza only; (G) BM Add. 36526 A (after 1597), fol. 7v, first stanza only, copied from the bass part, with the music on fols. 2, 8, and no variants from Do1597.IIII.B; (H) Christ Church, Oxford, MS 439 (*c.* 1620), pp. 52–53, for treble and bass, has the first stanza only; (I) Bod. Mus. f. 7–10 (*c.* 1630–40, Bassus, fols. 8v–9); and (J) Brussels MS Fetis 3095 (II.4.109), pp. 2–3 (4 partbooks, words in Cantus only, *c.* 1620). Two other sources have the words only: (K) Folger MS V.a.345 (*c.* 1630), pp. 65–66 (six four-line stanzas headed "A Song"); and (L) Sir Benjamin Rudyerd's *Le Prince d'Amour* (1660), sig. L6, headed "The Expostulation." The variants are:

1 complaints] complaint H
 could] myght HL, should K
 passions] passion KL
2 or] and F
3 passions] Patience L
4 despayrs] dispaire HIL
6 thy ... my] My ... me L
 deepe] great K
7 thy] My L
8 for] with L
9 doest] dost DEHKL
10 makst] makest D
11 harmes] hopes L
 repaire] redresse J
12 letst] letts H
13 yet I] I in K
14 am I] I am JL
18 worth] wroth L

19 doth] do L
    too sowre] so lower L
20 loue, nor liue] live, nor love L
21 hopes] hope L
22 hearers] heirs L
23 here] heare DKL
24 then] the I

17–18 *That . . . worth.* I.e., "I live because of your power, I desire because of your worth."
    23 *here.* Read *hear.*

V.

The music for this song was first printed as a galliard for the orpharion in By1596, part II, sig. B4v; a version for instrumental consort in *Lachrimae* (No. 12) is called "The Earle of Essex Galiard." Since the music is in a dance form, and the verse follows the irregular musical phrases so closely, it may be that the text was written to fit the previously composed tune. The music incorporates a popular tune, "Shall I go walk in the woods so wild," in the setting of lines 9–12, 21–24; see W. Chappell, *Popular Music of the Olden Time* (1859), I, 66, and Stevens, pp. 286, 433.

Diana Poulton has speculated that Robert Devereux, Earl of Essex (for whom the galliard was named) might have provided the words. To support this conjecture, Mrs. Poulton recalls other songs with which Dowland and Essex are associated (Do1603.III and XVIII, Do1612.X, RDo1610.II and VI), and cites Sir Henry Wotton's *A Parallel betweene Robert late Earle of Essex, and George late Duke of Buckingham* (1641), sig. A3. According to Wotton, on at least one occasion of difficulty with Queen Elizabeth,

> my Lord of Essex chose to evaporate his thoughts in a Sonnet (beeing his common way), to be sung before the Queene, (as it was) by one Hales, in whose voyce shee tooke some pleasure; whereof the complot me thinkes, had asmuch of the Hermit as of the Poet:
>
> > And if thou shouldst by Her be now forsaken,
> > She made thy Heart too strong for to be shaken.
>
> As if hee had beene casting one eye backe at the least to his former retirednesse.

The rest of the poem which Wotton quotes here is lost, but he implies that Essex had his verses sung to the Queen more than once. Hales was no doubt Robert Hales; see the note to XVIII below and RDo1610.III. "To plead my faith" (RDo1610.VI) has some interesting, if inconclusive, similarities to "Can shee excuse," for one is tempted to see both as addresses to the Queen. Finally, Mrs. Poulton suggests that the allusion to "Shall I go walk in the woods so wild" may refer to Essex's habit of retreating to his "retirednesse" at Wanstead when out of favor with the Queen (see Do1600.X and notes).

A copy of the poem is preserved among the papers of the actor Edward Alleyn at Dulwich College, which he founded. (Alleyn Papers, III, fol. 12; printed in *The Alleyn Papers*, ed. J.P. Collier for the Shakespeare Society [1843], p. 21.) The poem is written in a neat imitation of blackletter print, and concludes "Finis 1596." Variants are as follows:

1 vertues] vertious
2 proues] proues so
3 Are . . . vannish] shall those cleare fires vannisht
4 must] shall
  leaues] leafes
6 maist be abusde] mayes be deseued
  sight] site (*Collier*: lite)
7 on] in
8 on] uppon
  swim] swimd
9 abused] deluded
12 thus] but
14 houlds] holds so
15 they] the
16 can] may
17 If . . . yeeld] or yf that she will graunt
18 loue] trwe loue
19 still] then
  this] thus
20 delayes] my dayes
  that dye] so be dy
24 Who] that
  sake] loue

The poem was copied into six other manuscripts, all of which date after 1597: (D) BM Add. 24665 (1615–1626, Giles Earle's MS), fols. 42v–43, with Dowland's music for the treble and bass; some of the original words of lines 6–12 have been deleted, and changed from the second to the first person, but I do not list these changes in the variants; (E) BM Add. 36526 A (after 1597), fol. 7v, contains the words (the first twelve lines) to the music on fols. 2 and 8; (F) Bod. Douce 280 (John Ramsey's MS, before 1633), fol. 67v, contains the first twelve lines (no music), with a note indicating the source, "Mr Jno: Dowland."; (G) Bod. Mus. f. 7–10 (*c.* 1630–40, Tenor of four partbooks, fols. 7v–8); (H) King's College Cambridge, Rowe MS 2 (Turpyn's Book; *c.* 1610–15), fols. Iv–2, for voice and lute, with only the first twelve lines; and (I) Brussels MS Fetis 3095. II.4.109, pp. 4–5 (four parts, words in Cantus only, *c.* 1620). The variants are:

1 wrongs] wrong H
6 abusde] abused F
8 water] waters EH
14 high] hight G
16 can] may D
20 dye I] I die I
22 thus] this *deleted* thus D

Dowland's tune appears in Dirck R. Camphuysen, *Stichtelycke Rymen* (Amsterdam,

1647), sigs. I1v–I2v, where it is entitled "Galliarde Essex" and provided with Dutch words beginning "Wanneer de groote dag."

VI.

The music to this song was known in many instrumental versions as the "Frog Galliard" (*e.g.*, the lute solo in Folger MS 1610.1, fol. 12v). A poem attributed to Nicholas Breton, "On a hill there growes a flower," printed in *England's Helicon* (REH, I, 34–35) was also printed as a broadside, "The Shepherd's Delight," to be sung to the tune of the "Frog Galliard" (*The Roxburghe Ballads*, ed. William Chappell [1874], II, 526–529). See also Simpson, pp. 242–244, and John M. Ward, "Apropos *The British Broadside Ballad and Its Music*," *JAMS*, XX (1967), 44, who list other sources for the music. Ward asks if there might not be some allusion to the Duke of Alençon, whom Queen Elizabeth had nicknamed "grenouille." According to Ward, "The sentiments expressed in the text of Dowland's song were appropriate to any one of the Duke's departures from the English court."

Obertello, pp. 136, 452–53, calls attention to similarities between this poem and one set to music by Luca Marenzio, "Parto da voi mio sole," which was in turn printed with English translation in Yonge's *Musica Transalpina*, I (1588), No. 51, "Now must I part, my Darling" (Obertello, p. 249). These similarities are, however, very slight, and certainly do not suggest that VI is a translation.

The words and music of this song may be found in Bod. MS Mus. f. 7–10 (*c.* 1630–40, all three stanzas in bass part only, fols. 6v–7); the Turpyn MS (Rowe MS 2, King's College, Cambridge, *c.* 1610–15), for voice and lute, fol. 2v (first 12 lines only); Christ Church, Oxford, MS 439 (*c.* 1620), p. 45, for treble and bass (first 12 lines only); and BM MS Add. 36526 A (after 1597), fol. 7v, in which the words to the music on fols. 2v and 8v are copied from the bass part. Of these MSS, only Bod. Mus. f. 7–10 varies from the original in that *ioyed* in lines 16 and 25 becomes *ioyned*. The part-song version also appears in BM MS Add. 29291 (18th century), fol. 22. Other sources are in (D) Forbes's *Cantus* (1622), sig. T2v–V1, with Dowland's tune; (E) Brussels MS Fetis 3095 (II.4.109), pp. 6–7 (Dowland's music, words in Cantus of four partbooks, *c.* 1620); (F) Folger MS V.a.399 (after 1603), fol. 16v, without music, headed "A newe conceite to the tune of the frogge"; and (G) Bod. MS Ashmole 38 (*c.* 1630), p. 128 (no music, written in quatrains). Variants are:

  1 I . . . part] I must departe F
  2 absent] absence FG
  3 ioye] ioyes EG
  4 ioye . . . not] Ioyes once fleed will ner G
  5–8 While . . . none] *omitted* G
  6 liues] leaves D
 10 this] Such G
 12 which] that G
 13–16 Deare . . . ioyed once] *omitted* G
 13 I . . . am] I am from thee D
 17 And] Deare *deleted* And *added* G
 18 Sight] sith F
      doo] did G
 19 do] dothe FG

22 I] you F
    not] ner G
23 shall] will G
24 my] his G
25 ioyed] enioyed F
26 we] I G
    though now] allthough G
27 doe] must F
28 doth . . . lie] ner Caused to dye G
29 dieth] died DEFG

The first two lines of the song are quoted (inaccurately) by Quicksilver in Marston, Chapman, and Jonson's *Eastward Hoe* (1605), III.ii (Jonson, *Works*, IV, 562), and line 9 is quoted by Philautus in *Euerie Woman in her Humor* (1609), sig. B2v.

Dowland's tune is printed with the title "Forgs Gaillarde" (*sic*) in Dirck Raphaels Camphuysen's *Stichtelycke Rymen* (Amsterdam, 1647), sig. C4v, with Dutch words beginning "Van te strijden wil ik singen."

VII.

Both stanzas with the music of the bass part were copied into BM MS Add. 36526 A (after 1597), fol. 9v, without variants. The words and Dowland's music for four voices appear in Bod. MS Mus. f. 7–10 (*c*. 1630–40), also without variants (Cantus, fol. 9v). The version in Brussels MS Fetis 3095 (II.4.109; *c*. 1620), pp. 18–19, with music in four parts, words under the Cantus, varies thus:

4 moe] more
    proue] trie
6 on] of
8 dim] *omitted*
11 vew] see

Both stanzas are good examples of correlative verse. For other poems using the four elements in a similar fashion, see Jo1601.XI and Ck1612.IX.

9 *Fire . . . borne. Cf.* Tilley F261, "The fire is never without heat," and F284, "To force fire from snow." (For *loose*, read *lose*.)

VIII.

The poem was reprinted in *England's Helicon* (1600; REH I, 158) with the title, "To his Flocks." Although a note in *England's Helicon* says that only three poems were taken from Dowland (see note to III), this poem makes a fourth. It immediately precedes the other three (III, XI, XXI). The compiler made one change: line 8 reads *disdaines*.

Words and music were copied into Bod. MS Mus. f. 7–10 (*c*. 1630–40, Cantus, fol. 11v), without variants. Brussels MS Fetis 3095 (II.4.109), pp. 10–11 (Cantus of four parts), reads *greife* for *greiue* in line 10.

9 *yoaks.* The emendation in EMV, p. 737, of *yoaks* to *locks* is probably correct, even though the word is not changed in later editions. Apparently the printer repeated line 4.

IX.

Compare Petrarch's Sonnet CXX, "Ite caldi sospiri, al freddo core," especially with lines 7–12.

Words and music occur in Bod. MS Mus. f. 7–10 (*c.* 1630–40), fol. 10 (Cantus); line 3 reads *dropping*, as in CAB of the first edition.

X.

The music and part of the words of this song were copied into Bod. MS Mus. f. 7–10 (*c.* 1630–40). Only the Altus part book (fol. 5) has the second stanza; it has no variants.

XI.

This poem (along with III, VIII and XXI) was reprinted from Dowland in *England's Helicon* (REH, I, 158–159) with the title "To his Loue." The following changes were made:

     9 Loue long pains] Loues long paine
    13 son] Sunne
    20 heau'nly] heauenly
    22 adorne] adiorne

Dowland's music (in four parts) and the first two stanzas of the text were copied into Bod. MS Mus. f. 7–10 (Tenor, fol. 5v). Another MS version is in BM Add. 29409, fol. 265–265v. This part of Peter Buchan's nineteenth-century collection of Scotch ballads and songs was copied from the commonplace book of Lady Robertson of Lude (*c.* 1630) (REH, II, 173–174, cites the British Museum catalogue of manuscripts). The variants from Buchan's MS are:

     4 pleasure] fauour
     5 Teach] Reach
     6 rosie] your
     7 soules] soule *the order of lines is 6, 8, 9, 7*
     8 were made] warm and
     9 Vewing . . . pains] During vowing loves long pains
    10 Procurd] Procured
    13 While] Quhill
        sphere] speir
    16 groue] ground
    17 stealth] flech
    18 hie] flie
    19 in] into
    27 beauties] bewtie
        their] his

9 *pains.* EMV, p. 460, emends to *pain.*

XII.

The four-part version of Dowland's song was copied into Bod MS Mus. f. 7–10 (*c.* 1630–40; Altus, fols. 7v–8); and a copy for one voice and tablature is in Rowe MS 2, the Turpyn MS, at King's College, Cambridge (after 1610; fols. 3v–4). The latter is subscribed, "Mr John Dowlande," and its single stanza retains from C of the first edition the misprint *sight* in line 8. The poem appears without music in two MSS. One copy occurs in Bod. MS Rawl. Poet. 152, a miscellany volume, on a leaf (fol. 34) which also contains a copy of Shakespeare's Sonnet 128. This fact may suggest a date for the leaf after 1609. The MS has only the first stanza; line 6 reads "gaine (?) of loues despite." Another version is found in (D) Buchan's nineteenth-century collection of Scotch ballads, BM MS Add. 29409, fol. 264–264v (see notes to XI). The transcriber retained the Scotch spelling (*sie, sueit, sche,* etc.) but wrote the thorn as a *y*, without superscripts. (See the note to XIII, MS D.) Another copy, with the treble and bass of Dowland's music, in (E) the New York Public Library Drexel MS 4175 (*c.* 1620), fol. 8, No. XL. Variants from DE are as follows:

2 not] no D
6 Come . . . me] grant mee thy E
  despite] dispute (?) D
7 and] which E
  euer] *omitted* E
  thee] ye D
8 this] yis D
10 want waite] went weat (want weight) *sic* D
12 sigh] sight D
13 must] most D
14 view] nou (? vou) D
15 wound that] wone (?) yat D
16 fained] samed (?) D
17 this] yis D
19 pleasing] quiet E
21 soul hath] sauell haue D
22 which] that E
26 this] yis D

7 *and . . . thee.* There seems to be an extra foot in this line, although the music requires it; compare lines 16 and 25.

XIII.

This song appears, with Dowland's music, in a number of other versions. BM MS Add. 29481 (*c.* 1630), fol. 2, has the first stanza only (without variants) and music for treble and bass; and BM MS Add. 15118 (*c.* 1633), fol. 4v, has the music for the treble and bass, but only the opening few words. Other copies are in (D) Forbes's *Cantus* (1662), sigs. H2v–I1 (with Dowland's tune), (E) BM MS Add. 15117 (after 1614), fol. 7, with Dowland's treble and lute part; (F) BM MS Add. 24665 (1615–1626), fols. 28v–29, with Dowland's treble and bass; (G) Christ Church, Oxford, MS 439 (*c.* 1620), p. 46, one stanza only, with Dowland's treble and bass; (H) Bod. MS Mus. f. 7–10 (*c.* 1630–40), four part books (Tenor fols. 6v–7); (I) Brussels, Fetis MS 3095. II.4.109 (*c.* 1620), pp. 12–13, four parts with words under the Cantus; and (J) John Playford, *A Brief Introduction to the skill of Musick* (3rd ed., 1660), sig. D5, treble and bass ascribed to "Mr. Dowland." It appears without music in (K) Richard Johnson, *The Golden Garland of Princely Pleasures* (3rd ed., 1620), sig. F5, entitled "The Shepheards Pipe"; (L) Bod. MS Douce 280 (before 1633) fol. 67v, headed "Jno Dowland"

and lacking stanza 2; (M) BM MS Harl. 3511 (after 1642), fol. 1; and (N) BM MS Add. 29409 (19th century transcript of a collection of Scotch ballads, *c.* 1630), fols. 264–265. The variants are:

   1 wayward] way word M
   2 diseasd] displeas'd FIJM
   3 proud] proud *deleted* her F
      hands] hand N
      lest] least M
      you] ye N
   4 my] the J
      longings] longest G, longing IJN
      long] longest G
      displeasd] diseas'd FIJM, Loue G
   5 while] quhile N, whyles E, whiles L
  6, 12, 18 my loue *repeated* D
   7 fury . . . my] fate of these my K
      feare] feares EKN
   8 my] *omitted* H
      desires] desyre N
   9 that] yet M
      appeare] appeares EKN
  10 Between] Betwixt DM
      neere] where M
      Cupids closed] closit Cupides N
      fires] fyre N, eise M
  11 Thus] So I
      moues sighing] more sighing F, moue sighing I, I sorrow M
      hir] thy K
  12 sleepes] sleep N
      loue doth] loues does N
  13 doth . . . doth] doe . . . doe N
  14 Feare in] Fear's in F
  17 while] why E

This song is quoted by Girtred in Marston, Chapman, and Jonson's *Eastward Hoe*, I.ii (Jonson's *Works*, IV, 530), who says "Thus whilst shee sleepes I sorrow, for her sake, &c." Philautus, in *Euerie Woman in her Humor* (1609) sig. B1v, quotes the first line when he says, "Boy, sleepe wayward thoughts."

2 *diseasd.* That is, *dis-eased*, made uneasy. The position of *diseasd* over *displeasd* in the songbook is such that they may have been reversed. Four copies (collated above) also reverse the original reading. But the original makes sense as it stands, and in spite of the unfortunate implications of line 2, is not changed here.

XIIII.

Bond (III, 492) ascribes this poem to John Lyly without evidence.

6 *the dying Swanne.* The comparison is commonplace (Tilley S1028), but see Robert Dowland's *Varietie of Lute-lessons* (1610), sig. A2v, referring to his father as "like the Swan, but singing towards his end." *Cf.* Do1603.V.9–10.

XV.

The music requires the repetition of lines 4 and 5 with each stanza.

The song also appears in (D) Bod. MS Mus. f. 7–10 (*c.* 1630–40), with Dowland's music for four voices (Cantus, fol. 12); and in (E) BM MS Add. 15118 (*c.* 1633), fol. 5v, with Dowland's treble and bass. Stanzas 3 and 4 are reversed in E; other variants are:

> 4 or] *omitted* D
> 11 can] will E
> 20 delight] delights D

16–17 *heate . . . seuer. Cf.* Tilley F261.

XVII.

The last line of each of the last four stanzas seems to be short two syllables. Should the fact that they are numbered 1–4 instead of 3–6 suggest that they constitute a separate poem? As Pattison has pointed out (p. 154), a poem by T[homas] L[odge] in *The Phoenix Nest* (1593; RPN, p. 57), "Strive no more," has the same stanza form. In Lodge's poem, the last line of each stanza has the same number of syllables as the same lines in the last four stanzas of XVII. The two poems are remarkably similar: one could be attached to either end of the other and make a reasonably coherent single poem. Although it is barely possible that these poems have a common author, the stanza form, unusual as it is, cannot be considered very meaningful evidence, for a highly moral song by Jones (1605.XV), "Happy he," also employs this stanza. In this last poem, however, the last lines have the same number of syllables as the first two stanzas of XVII. It is conceivable that some of these verses may have been written to Dowland's tune, which seems to have been popular. An anonymous solo lute version called "Come away" survives in Cambridge MS Nn. 6, fol. 21v. Diana Poulton has shown me a version in the Landesbibliothek, Kassel, from MS Mus. 108 [1–8, fol. 32v. The music is corrupt, and the words are in Italian:

> In me non é piu vita
> che per se giur'amor e gia finita
> E pur mi sento gran martire
> Che non si puo soffrire.

Other copies of this song appear in (D) Forbes's *Cantus* (1662), sig. Aa2–2v, with Dowland's tune; (E) Bod. MS Mus. f. 7–10 (*c.* 1630–40), four parts copied (including misprints) from Do1597, omitting the last stanza (Altus, fol. 10); (F) BM MS 36526 A (after 1597), fol. 9, first stanza only with music for Dowland's bass; (G) BM MS Add. 24665 (1615–1626), fols. 26v–27, with Dowland's treble and bass; (H) Brussels MS Fetis 3095. II.4.109 (*c.* 1620), pp. 14–15, with Dowland's music in four parts, omitting the last two stanzas; the part song version is also in BM MS Add. 29291 (18th century), fol. 11v. The poem appears without music in (I) Bod. MS Douce 280 (before 1633), fol. 67–67v, with this note: "Mr Jno: Dowland. first booke. For tableture & pricke song," and with the last stanza omitted. (J) Bod. MS Don. d. 58 (*c.* 1647), fol. 24v, is headed "Cant 12." Variants from DFGHIJ are:

> 1 now] thee D
> 2 thy] the G, Her I

4 to kisse, to die] to dy to dy F
9 now left] now I am left J
13 that lends] doth lend H
14 By] thy H
    do] doth GJ
16 makes] make G
17 Her . . . the] and her frownes are the H
    winters] winter GJ
19 night] nightes J
    sleepes are] sleepe is G
20 My] mine GJ
22 fruits and ioies] ioyes & fruites G
23 stormes are me] cares that are to me G, stormes are me by her H
24–35 *omitted* H
25 Out] But D
    is] was G
26 will she neuer] neuer will shee G
29 truth] trueth DG
    may once] can once herself G
30–35 *omitted* I
35 for] for mightie G
    triumps] triumphe J

28 *her hart of flint. Cf.* Tilley H311.

XVIII.

This song was performed in a pageant staged by Sir Henry Lee for the accession tilt of 1590, when he retired from his post as the Queen's champion to be succeeded by the Earl of Cumberland. It is likely that Dowland's setting was used, especially since he set to music two other poems connected with Lee (Do1600.VI–VIII and RDo1610. VIII). William Segar describes the occasion in his *Honor, Military and Civill* (1602), sigs. R3–4v:

> On the 17 day of Nouember, *Anno 1590.* this honourable Gentleman [Lee] together with the Earl of *Cumberland,* hauing first performed their seruice in Armes, presented themselues vnto her Highnesse, at the foot of the staires vnder her Gallery window in the Tilt yard at *Westminster.* . . . Her Maiesty beholding these armed Knights comming toward her, did suddenly heare a musicke so sweete and secret, as euery one thereat greatly marueiled. And hearkening to that excellent melodie, the earth as it were opening, there appeared a Pauilion, made of white Taffata, containing eight score elles, being in proportion like vnto the sacred Temple of the Virgins Vestall. . . . The musicke aforesayd, was accompanied with these verses, pronounced and sung by M. *Hales* her Maiesties seruant, a Gentleman in that Arte excellent, and for his voice both commendable and admirable.

Segar's version of the poem (in the first person) follows. Hales is no doubt Robert Hales, the composer of RDo1610.III; see also the note to No. V above. Hales seems to have been primarily a singer, and although it is conjectured in EMV, p. 738, that he may have composed the setting used, it is not likely that an occasional poem would be set to music more than once. For further comment on the tilts, see Frances A. Yates, "Elizabethan Chivalry: The Romance of the Accession Day Tilts," *Journal of the Warburg and Courtauld Institutes*, XX (1957), 4–25.

The poem entitled "A Sonet," appeared on the last page (sig. B4v) of George Peele's *Polyhymnia* (1590), a poem describing the tilt, and has consequently been attributed to Peele. But David H. Horne, *Life and Minor Works of George Peele* (New Haven: Yale University Press, 1952), pp. 169–173, following Thorlief Larsen ("The Canon of Peele's Works," *MP*, XXVI [1928], 195–199), doubts that Peele was the author. There is no evidence that Peele had anything to do with this pageant except to describe it after the event in *Polyhymnia*. The song is not mentioned in Peele's description, which would be the appropriate place to insert it, but after the "Finis" on B4—a position suggesting that it was only a filler. Nor does the "Sonet" appear in the MS of *Polyhymnia* at St. John's College, Oxford. Larsen says that the poem shows none of Peele's mannerisms, and is, moreover, "far too good for Peele" (p. 198). Variants from *Polyhymnia* are as follows (Horne, p. 244):

    8 turne] turn'd
    10 ages] Age his
    16 soule] soules

Although Segar's version differs greatly from Dowland's and from that in *Polyhymnia*, the last two may be closer to the version used in the pageant. As Horne notes (p. 173), the third person would have been more appropriate since Hales, not Lee, sang the song; besides, Segar's book was published several years after the event.

Bond (I, 410) also denies Peele's authorship, but tries to attribute the poem to Lyly on the evidence of parallel phrases and images. But these were fairly commonplace; even the striking image of the helmet and the beehive may be found (as Horne, p. 172 n., points out) in Geffrey Whitney's *A Choice of Emblemes* (1586), p. 138. See Edgar Wind, *Pagan Mysteries in the Renaissance* (London: Faber and Faber, 1958), p. 86 n., for further examples.

These scholars agree that Peele was probably not the author of the "Sonet," and their best guess is that Lee himself wrote it. E. K. Chambers (*Sir Henry Lee* [1936], pp. 142–144) says that Lee is known to have written verse; he also calls attention to the manuscript versions which ascribe this poem to Lee (described below), and to the fact that Lee's name was printed in RD01610 as the author of "Farre from triumphing Court" (No. VIII). These two poems and D01600.VI–VIII are all in the same form and show marked similarities. Horne (pp. 170–173) agrees that the three may have a common author, who might be Lee, but suggests that Richard Edes, who wrote verses for Lee's Ditchley entertainment (Chambers, pp. 276–297), may have had a hand in the songs.

The poem appears in several manuscripts. Hughey (HAH, II, 323–324) collates the following versions with the Arundel Harington copy (headed "Sir H. lea," HAH, I, 243): Dowland, Segar, Peele's *Polyhymnia*; BM MS Stowe 276, fol. 2, headed "Sir Henrye Lee" and subscribed "O St John," *i.e.* Oliver St John, first Earl of Bolingbroke (born *c.* 1580); BM MS Add. 33963, fol. 109, on paper pasted on a leaf bearing a note saying that it was cut from the flyleaf of a copy of Sidney and Golding's translation of Philippe de Mornay, *A Woorke Concerning the Trewnesse of the Christian Religion*

(1587); Folger MS V.a.103 (early 17th century; formerly MS I. 28), fol. 52, headed "Sir Henry Lea his Farewell to the Court"; and BM MS Add. 36526 A (after 1597), fol. 9–9v, first stanza only, with the bass part of Dowland's music. Hughey does not record the following versions:(D) Brussels MS Fetis 3095. II.4.109 (*c.* 1620), pp. 16–17, with Dowland's music for four voices; (E) Bod. MS Mus. f. 7–10 (*c.* 1630–40), four partbooks with Dowland's music (Cantus fol. 11); and (F) Bod. MS Rawl. Poet. 148, fol. 75v, third stanza only (as fourth stanza of Do1600.VI–VIII), copied between poems dated 1597 and 1598, and headed "In yeeldinge vp his Tilt staff: sayd," and subscribed, "quod Sir Henry Leigh." Variants from DEF are:

> 13 he saddest sits] thow sadly sitst F
>   homely] homily E
> 14 Hele . . . his] Then . . . thy F
> 16 soule] soules F
>   thinke her] thinkes him D
> 17 Goddes] Ye gods D, Good God F

D was probably copied from the 1606 or 1613 edition; see the Variant Readings. The changes seem to have been made in lines 16 and 17 to fit King James.

    The first ten lines of the poem were quoted in Thackeray's *The Newcomes* (Chapter 76), where they are called "those noble lines of the old poet."

XIX.

    The music for this song appears as an instrumental galliard in three manuscripts in the Cambridge University Library, Add. 3056, Dd. 2.11., and Dd. 5.78.III (Diana Poulton, "Dowland's Songs and their Instrumental Forms," *Monthly Musical Record*, LXXXI [1951], 177). One stanza of the text was copied under the music of the bass part of Dowland's song in BM MS Add. 36526 A, fol. 9v, without variants. The part-song version was copied in BM MS Add. 29291 (18th century), fol. 11. The song also appears in Forbes's *Cantus* (1662), sigs. K1v–K2, with the following variants:

> 9 draue] drew
> 13 flie] flee
> 21, 22 thy] my

XX.

    Bond (III, 492) ascribes this poem to Lyly without evidence.

    Another setting, attributed to Robert Johnson, is found in New York Public Library Drexel MS 4041 (*c.* 1650), No. 39. This version was printed in ELS, 2nd series, XVII (ed. Ian Spink, 1961), pp. 4–5. Variants are as follows:

> 3 spring] springes
> 4 sigh] sighes
> 5 thoghts, worne] thought worne
> 6 bestoule] bee stolen
> 7–12 *omitted*

> 1 *sleepe . . . death.* Tilley S527.
> 5 *thoghts, worne.* Johnson's version (above) lends support to the emendation in

EMV, p. 466, *thought-worn*. One might stretch a point, however, and read *worne soule* in apposition to *tired thoghts*.

8 *fast.* I.e., *faced.*

XXI.

This poem by Fulke Greville is also found in: *Certaine Learned and Elegant Workes of the Right Honorable Fulke Lord Brooke* (1633), sig. Ee3-3v, "Sonnet LI" of the *Caelica* cycle, printed by Bullough, I, 104 (correcting the number to LII), with variants from the Warwick Castle MS on I, 255; the Arundel Harington MS (HAH, I, 242–243); and *Englands Helicon* (1600; REH, I, 159–160). Variants from all these sources and Do1597 are given by Hughey (HAH, II, 321–322). Hughey, Rollins, and Bullough do not record the following versions: (D) Bod. MS. Mus. f. 7–10 (*c.* 1630–40), four partbooks with Dowland's music (Cantus, fol. 12v), first two stanzas only; (E) Brussels MS Fetis 3095. II.4.109 (*c.* 1620), pp. 8–9, four-part version of Dowland's music; BM MS Add. 29291 (18th century), fol. 12, the part-song version; and (not seen), Edinburgh University MS La III, 488, with Dowland's tune. Variants from (F) Bullough's text, D, and E are:

2 arrowe] arrows D
4 them . . . sleepe] those that lye asleepe F
8 God] Young E, Sweet F
　shaft] shafts DEF
9 Doth either] Doe causelesse F
11 feet] fate D, wing F
13 likes] like D
14-34 *omitted* D
16 rings] ring E
　hollidaies] Holy dayes F
17 On] In F
30 bowe] boone E
31 the] thee F

13 *loue likes no lawes but his owne.* Rollins (REH, II, 175–176) cites Apperson's *Proverbs*, pp. 385, 387; H. C., *The Forrest of Fancy* (1579), sig. Q2; and T.H., *Oenone and Paris* (1594), sig. D4v. See Tilley L508, "Love is lawless."

25 *well fare . . . yeere.* Tilley N335.

27 *Fooles only hedge the Cuckoo in.* As Collier suggested (p. 62), the tale in the popular sixteenth-century jestbook, *Merie Tales of the Mad Men of Gotam*, by "A.B." (n.d.; STC 1020.5), sigs. A3v-4, is probably the origin of this line: "On a time the men of Gotam, wold haue pynned the Cockow, that she should sing all the yeare and in the myddest of the towne they did make a hedge. . . . The Cocow as soone as shee was set wyth in the hedge, flew her waye. A vengeaunce on her sayde they, we made not our hedge high ynough." This tale is illustrated on the title page of later editions of the book.

30 *bowe of loue.* That is, love (Cupid's bow?) is the instrument of producing love. See Tilley L515, "Love is the reward of love."

31-32 *loue . . . Noble-man.* Cf. Do1603.XIX.6. Rollins (REH, II, 176) cites Thomas Lodge, *Rosalynde*, sig. F4. See Tilley L519, "Love lives in cottages as well as courts."

Michael Cavendish, *14. Ayres*, 1598

Dedication

Lady Arbella or Arabella Stuart (1575–1615), once considered as a possible successor to Elizabeth, was Cavendish's second cousin. She was the employer of a lutenist named Cutting, probably Thomas Cutting, who, however, left her service in 1607/8 to replace John Dowland at the court of Christian IV of Denmark; on this occasion she declared that she was "sorry, to haue lost the contentment of a good Lute" (see the letters in BM MS Harleian 6986, fols. 74–79v). All or part of seven other books were dedicated to her. (Warlock, p. 111, Williams, DNB.)

II.

The copy on M1v is headed "*This is the ditty of the second song.*"

IIII.

The version printed on M1v is headed, "*This is the ditty of the third song.*"
2 *vow'd.* The reading from the Cantus, *wo'd*, used in EMV, p. 420, destroys the proverbial quality of the line. *Cf.* Tilley O7, "An unlawful oath is better broken than kept."

VI.

The copy on M1v is headed, "*This is the Ditty of the fift song.*"
This poem is based on a sonnet from Gaspar Gil Polo's *Diana Enamorada* (Valencia, 1564), sig. A7:

> No es ciego Amor, mas yo lo soy, que guio
> mi voluntad camino del tormento:
> no es niño amor, mas yo que en vn momento
> espero y tengo miedo, lloro y rio.
> Nombrar llamas de Amor es desuario,
> su fuego es el ardiente y biuo intento:
> sus alas son mi altiuo pensamiento
> y la esperança vana en que me fio.
> No tiene Amor cadenas ni saetas,
> para prender y herir, libres y sanos:
> que en el no hay mas poder del que le damos
> Por qu'es Amor mentira de Poetas,
> sueño de locos, idolo de vanos:
> mirad que negro Dios el que adoramos.

Bartholomew Yong's version (1598) begins: "Love is not blinde, but I which fondly guide/ My will to tread the path of amorous paine." See *A Critical Edition of Yong's Translation of George of Montemayor's Diana and Gil Polo's Enamoured Diana*, by Judith M. Kennedy (Oxford: Clarendon Press, 1968), p. 251. Kennedy quotes another translation on p. 441 from BM MS Add. 23229, fol. 122v.

1 *Loue is not blinde. Cf.* Tilley L506.
9 *yet.* EMV, p. 421, emends to *it.*

VII.

The copy on M1v is headed, "*This is the ditty of the sixt song.*"
This poem is No. I of Fulke Greville's *Caelica*. See Bullough, I, 73; on p. 231, Bullough gives variants from Cav1598 (which he says may be from an earlier version),

the Warwick Castle MS of Greville's poems, and a version set to music in Martin Peerson's *Mottects or Graue Chamber Musique* (1630), Nos. I–III (Cantus, sigs. B1–B2). Bullough's text is based on Greville's *Certaine Learned and Elegant Workes* (1633), and varies thus:

4 forge on which] fire wherein
  are] bee
8 true] sweet
9 iust] true
10 Her . . . only] Her worth is passions wound, and passions
11 cleere] true
  the . . . vertue] cleare . . . wisdome
13, 14, 15 he] she
18 hold] set

Note the rhetorical organization in lines 1–4, using the figure *climax* (Puttenham, p. 208), and the correlative summary in line 17.

18 *but only.* I.e., *except.*

VIII.

Headed "*This is the ditty of the seuenth song*" on M1v.

3–4 *What . . . despite.* The sense seems to be, "What may be said about this by one that owns both heart and eye, but that both contribute to his own despite?"

IX.

2 *to.* Read *too.*

X.

Headed "*This is the ditty of the ninth song*" on M1v.

16 *songs.* EMV, p. 423, retains the *sons* of the original, and explains (p. 733) that it had appeared earlier as a Scottish form. But since the phrase "songs and sonnets" is so common, and the Scottish *sone* (sound, tone, voice) so rare, I see no reason not to regard this as a simple misprint.

22 *fortune.* Perhaps this should be *misfortune*; the line lacks a syllable.

XI.

This song also appears as a five-part madrigal (No. XVII). See the Variant Readings. Obertello (p. 133) notes its similarity to Italian madrigal verse, but offers no specific source.

XII.

Also arranged as a madrigal for five voices (No. XXVIII). See the Variant Readings.

5–6 *Cf.* Lamentations 1:12 (Vulgate): "Videte, si est dolor sicut dolor meus."

XIII.

Also arranged as a five-part madrigal (No. XXVII). See the Variant Readings. Cavendish's treble and bass were copied into Christ Church, Oxford, MS 439 (*c.* 1620), pp. 70–71, without variants (*Nico* in line 3 is spelled *Nicho* as in XXVII).

XIIII.

Cf. D01603. XII.

This song might be regarded as a carol, for it consists of an initial three-line burden which is then repeated after each of the two five-line stanzas.

XIX–XX.

These two songs are apparently settings of two stanzas of one poem, and would normally have been marked "First part" and "Second part." Such is the case in Michael East's setting of these stanzas in his *Madrigales to 3. 4. and 5. parts* (1604), Nos. XXI–XXII (Cantus, sigs. D3–D3v). Except for slight variants produced by musical repetition, and "this deede" for "the deede" (XX.4), East's version is identical.

A single eight-line stanza in Thomas Vautor's *The First Set: Being Songs of diuers Ayres and Natures* (1619), No. XI (Cantus, sig. C2), is clearly derived from the present text, but has a number of changes:

> Sweet theefe, when me of heart you reft,
> You did a murther and a theft,
> And could you oft more cruell doe,
> Then rob a man and kill him too?
> Wherefore of loue I craue this meede,
> To bring you where you did the deede,
> That there you may for him disgracing,
> Suffer in chaines of my imbracing.

XXI.

These verses were taken from Nicholas Yonge's *Musica Transalpina . . . The Second Booke* (1597), No. X (Cantus, sig. C1v), without significant variants (Yonge has *Clori* in line 5). The music in Yonge is by Alfonso Ferrabosco the elder, from his *Secondo Libro de Madrigali* (Venice, 1587), No. XX; the original words (Canto, sig. C3v–4) are as follows:

> Nel piu fiorito Aprile
> All'hor che vaghi augelli
> Di soura gl'arboscelli
> Cantano in vario soun [i.e., *suon*] dolc'e gentile
> A garra anco con lor cantaua Clori
> Di lei e del suo Elpin i dolci amori.

See Obertello, pp. 297, 473.

XXII.

These verses were taken from (D) Nicholas Yonge's *Musica Transalpina . . . The Second Booke* (1597), No. II (Cantus, sig. B1v), where they were printed with music by Alfonso Ferrabosco the elder. These lines make up the octave of a translation of Petrarch's Sonnet CCCX, "Zefiro torna e'l bel tempo rimena." Yonge had printed a translation of the whole poem with a madrigal in two parts by Gironimo Conversi in (E) the first part of *Musica Transalpina* (1588), Nos. LII–LIII (Cantus, sigs. G4v–H1). But Cavendish uses only the first eight lines, as does Ferrabosco, and his music shows Ferrabosco's influence. See Joseph Kerman, *The Elizabethan Madrigal* (New York: American Musicological Society, Studies and Documents No. 4, 1962), pp. 94–96, and Obertello, pp. 250–251, 290, 453–455. As Obertello and Kerman point out, Cavendish uses the sestet of another translation of this same sonnet for the text of No. XXV.

The version in the 1588 *Musica Transalpina* was reprinted in (F) *Englands Helicon* (1600), REH, I, 179; and the 1597 version was copied (with Ferrabosco's music) in (G) BM MSS Add. 29372–7 (Cantus, fols. 89v–90). Obertello (p. 290) cites (H) BM

MS 36484, fol. 30v (a 17th century MS, not seen). The variants are as follows (NB: *cf.* Variant Readings):

1 brings] bringis H
2 and] which F
3 and *Philomel*] Philomel F
7 the ayre] Th'ayre DEGH

Many poets have imitated or borrowed from this sonnet. Obertello (pp. 453–454) names some English versions and quotes from several Italian analogues. Thomas Watson translated the octave for a madrigal of Luca Marenzio published in his *The first sett Of Italian Madrigalls Englished* (1590), No. IIII (Obertello, p. 266). Richard Carlton set still another translation in his *Madrigals to Fiue voyces* (1601), Nos. IV–V (EMV, p. 78). *Cf.* also Dan1605.XX.

3 *Progne . . . Philomel.* The swallow and the nightingale. See Ovid, *Metamorphoses*, VI, 424–674.

6 *his deerest daughter.* Venus. See the translation of Petrarch by Morris Bishop in *Renaissance and Baroque Lyrics*, ed. Harold M. Priest (Chicago: Northwestern University Press, 1962), p. 19.

XXIIII.

This is the first madrigal by an English composer containing the refrain, "Long liue faire *Oriana*," but the idea no doubt arose from the English words to a madrigal by Giovanni Croce in Nicholas Yonge's *Musica Transalpina . . . The Second Booke* (1597), No. XXIIII, "Hard by a Cristal fountaine." Both poems were based on Italian madrigals from the famous anthology *Il Trionfo di Dori* (Venice, 1592, plus other eds.). Cavendish's text is based on No. VI of the *Trionfo*; the verses were attributed there to Lorenzo Guicciardi, and the music is by Luca Marenzio (Obertello, p. 513). The Italian original is given by Obertello, p. 401:

> Leggiadre Ninfe e Pastorelli amanti
> Che con lieti sembianti
> In queste ombrose valli all'onde chiare
> Di viuo font'hoggi vi trasse Amore
> Per tesser ghirlandette & coronare
> La mia Ninfa gentile
> Mentre vezzosi Satiri e Siluani
> Ne i lor'habiti strani
> Danzan con mod'humile
> Voi cantate spargend'e rose e fiori
> Viua viua la bella Dori.

In 1601 Thomas Morley published an English imitation of the *Trionfo*, in honor of Queen Elizabeth, *The Triumphes of Oriana, to 5. and 6. voices*, and included a revised version of Cavendish's madrigal as No. XI (Cantus, sig. C3v). The music shows considerable revision, but the text varies only in line 4: beautist] beauties. For further discussion of the *Oriana* madrigals, see Joseph Kerman, *The Elizabethan Madrigal* (New York: American Musicological Society, 1962), pp. 194–209, and Roy C. Strong, "Queen Elizabeth I as Oriana," *SR*, VI (1959), 251–260.

Compare Gr1604.XVII–XVIII and note.

XXV.

This poem is a paraphrase of the last six lines of Petrarch's Sonnet CCX, "Zefiro torna." See the note to No. XXII.

XXVI.

This poem was printed, probably from Cav1598, in Francis Davison's *A Poetical Rhapsody* (1602; RPR, I, 220), with the title "Madrigal." There are no variants (but see the Variant Readings to the present volume).

XXVII.

A five-part version of No. XIII.

XXVIII.

A five-part version of No. XII.

John Dowland, *The Second Booke of Songs or Ayres*, 1600

Dedication

Lucy Russell, Countess of Bedford (1581?–1627) was the friend and patron of a number of authors; Jonson and Donne both addressed several poems to her. Many other books were dedicated to her, but no other music (DNB, Williams).

4 *a forreine Prince*. Dowland was lutenist to Christian IV of Denmark from 1598 until he was dismissed under rather mysterious circumstances in 1606. See Angul Hammerich, *Musiken ved Christian den Fjerdes Hof* (Copenhagen, 1892), pp. 22–23.

17 *Helsingnoure*. I.e., Elsinore.

To the right Noble, etc.

4 *G. Eastland*. Little is known of George Eastland besides what can be gathered from this book and the lawsuit described in the Textual Introduction.

To the curteous Reader

14 *a prisoner taken at Cales*. As Diana Poulton has suggested, this probably refers to some book stolen on Essex's 1596 raid on Cadiz, perhaps from the bishop's library at Faro. See K.P.M., "A Grand Inquisitor and his Library," *Bodleian Quarterly Record*, III (1922), 239–244. A copy of Victoria's Motets (1585) at Christ Church, Oxford, is inscribed, "ex domo Episcopali Faronesi, 1596."

I.

See also Mo1600.V.

Bond (III, 471) attributes this poem to Lyly, and suggests that it is the missing song of the Shepherds in his *Woman in the Moone* (1597), I.i.224 (Bond, III, 248). This is an interesting guess, but there is no evidence for it.

As Obertello suggests (pp. 440–441), the poem may possibly be based on a sonnet by Alessandro Lionardi, printed in his *Secondo Libro de le Rime* (1550), sig. B7:

> Vidi pianger Madonna, & seco Amore
> Et del lor pianto farsi un tal concento
> Che non fu mai il piu dolce lamento
> Formato di pietate, o di dolore.

Lasciando i fiumi'l lor soaue errore
Stauan' ad ascoltar & ciascun uento,
Et parea mitigato insieme et spento
L'usato orgoglio, & uinto il duro core.

Come da ciel seren rugiada suole
Cader, & hor quel fior, hora quest' herba
Rinfrescando nudrir al tempo estiuo;
Cosi bagnar le rose & le uiole
Che fiorian nel bel uiso, onde superba
N'andaua primauera & ogni riuo.

Alfonso Ferrabosco the elder wrote a madrigal to this text, which was printed as Nos. 23 and 24 in Nicholas Yonge's *Musica Transalpina* (1588), Cantus, sig. C4–C4v, with the following translation:

I Saw my Lady weeping, & loue did languish,
& of their plaint ensued so rare consenting,
that neuer yet was heard more sweet lamenting,
made all of tender pittie & mournfull anguish,
the flouds forsaking their delightfull swelling,
stayd to attend their plaint, the windes enraged,
still & content to quiet calme asswaged,
their wonted storming, & euery blast rebelling.

Like as from heauen the dew full softly showring,
doeth fall, & so refresh both fields and closes,
filling the parched flowers with sappe & sauour?
so while she bath'd the violets & the roses,
vpon hir louely cheekes so freshly flowring,
the spring reneued his force with hir sweete fauour.

It will readily be seen that only the first line of Dowland's text could be called anything like a translation.

   1 *Anthony Holborne.* The lutenist and composer, author of *The Citharne Schoole* (1597), *Pauans, Galliards, Almains* (1599), and several lute pieces in manuscript. He contributed a pavan for the lute to Robert Dowland's *Varietie of Lute-lessons* (1610, sig. I1v), where he is described as "Gentleman Vsher to the most Sacred *Elizabeth*, late Queene of England, &c." See also RDo1610.I.

   15 *leaue . . . grieue.* I.e., cease grieving after a time.

II.

The music of this song was one of the most famous melodies of the period. It became Dowland's trademark: he signed himself "Jo: dolande de Lachrimae" in Johann Cellarius' *album amicorum* (BM MS Add. 27579, fol. 88). "To sing Lachrymae" became proverbial (see Tilley L15). The tune is mentioned in a number of sources, especially plays: the Citizen's Wife calls for it in Beaumont and Fletcher's *The Knight of the Burning Pestle* (1613; *Works*, ed. A. R. Waller, 1908, VI, 193); it is also referred to in Fletcher's *The Bloody Brother* (c. 1617; II.ii; *Works*, IV, 262); in Ben Jonson's masque, *Time Vindicated* (1622; *Works*, VII, 662); in John Webster's *The Devil's Law-Case* (1623; IV.ii.537; *Works*, ed. F. L. Lucas, 1927, II. 303); in Philip Massinger's *The Picture* (1630) and *The Maid of Honour* (1632; *Plays*, ed. W. Gifford, 3rd ed., 1856, pp. 281 and 226); and in Thomas Middleton's *No Wit, No Help, Like a Woman's* (1657; I.i.227; *Works*, ed. A. H. Bullen, 1885, IV, 293). It is also mentioned in one of *The Roxburghe Ballads* (ed. William Chappell, 1875, III, part I, 68) and in *Sir Thomas Overbury his Wife with . . . divers more characters* ("tenth impression," 1618, sigs. M8v–N1).

Dowland's music was first published as a pavan for the lute in By1596, part I, sigs. E1–E2v. This fact, together with the unusual verse form, suggest the possibility that the words were written later to fit the tune. Since this song seems to epitomize a characteristic emotional attitude, it may not be unreasonable to speculate that this was one occasion for which Dowland provided his own words. (He is known to have written commendatory poems for some of his friends' publications: see Pattison, pp. 72–73.)

Many copies of Dowland's music survive in MS and in print, and several composers used his theme as a basis for their own variations. Dowland himself published a set of seven instrumental variations in his *Lachrimae, or Seauen Teares* (n.d., *c.* 1604). The melody appears in Dirck Raphaels Camphuysen's *Stichtelycke Rymen* (Amsterdam, 1647), sig. G4, with the title "Doulants Lacrymae" and with Dutch words beginning "Traen, oogen, traen, en word fonteynen." The music is given in four parts on sigs. F2v–G3. A full account of other musical sources is given in Diana Poulton's forthcoming edition of the *Collected Lute Music* (Faber).

The words also appear in the following sources: (D) Forbes's *Cantus* (1662), sig. Bb1–1v, with Dowland's tune; (E) Sir Benjamin Rudyerd's *Le Prince d'Amour* (1660), sig. L5–5v, headed "Farewell to Content"; (F) BM MS Add. 24665 (1615–1626), fols. 11v–12, with Dowland's music for treble and bass; (G) Tenbury MS 1018 (first half of 17th century), fol. 30v, with the music for treble and bass of the first strain only, and with incomplete words; (H) Christ Church, Oxford, MS 439 (*c.* 1620), pp. 6–7, with the music for treble and bass. The first, third, and fifth quatrains of this last version are set as one stanza, with the second and fourth quatrains copied separately as a second stanza (to be followed by the fifth as a refrain). John P. Cutts prints this version in his *Seventeenth Century Songs and Lyrics* (Columbia: University of Missouri Press, 1959), pp. 114–115, and claims (p. 441), that this arrangement is preferable. But the music of the song demands that each of the three sections be repeated, not played through twice (as in H); see Thomas Morley's definition of a pavan in *A Plaine and Easie Introduction* (1597), sig. Aa4. A final copy, with music for the treble, is in Edinburgh University MS La. III.483 (not seen). Variants from D–H are:

2 my] forth my E
3 Exilde] Exile E
  morne] moan E
4 infamy] infamies F, Inchantment E
6 lights] delights EF
  you] your E, yee F, *omitted* G
7 nights are] night is E
8 their] there H
  last] lost EF
9 light . . . disclose] There let me live forlorne E
  but] *omitted* H

shame] sinne F
10 may] shall E
   relieued] released E
11 is] it is E
12 and . . . dayes] And sighs, and sobs, and tears,
                    For my deserts, for my deserts E
13 haue depriued] are bereaved E, haue depri- G
14 spire] Spheare DE
15 fortune is] fortunes are E
   throwne] thy owne H, thrown down E
16 and . . . deserts] And griefs, and groans, and cares,
                       My wearied dayes, my wearied dayes E
   griefe] greefes H
17 are my hopes] are my hope H, Of all hope E, *omitted* F
   hopes . . . gone] *omitted* G
18-21 *omitted* G
18 dwell] dwelles H
20 that in hell] that are in Heaven D
21 feele] ffeeles H

8 *last.* EMV, p. 468, emends to *lost.*

III.

Some of the repetitions in this poem may be musical rather than poetic; but it is perhaps better to err on the side of completeness here. The poem seems to be connected in theme with Nos. IIII and V, and the form of all three is roughly similar. Perhaps they were used in a masque or play.

This song appears in the following manuscripts: (D) BM Add. 24665 (1615–1626), fols. 31v–32, with Dowland's music for the treble and bass parts, and with no verbal variants; (E) Christ Church, Oxford, MS 439 (*c.* 1620), p. 70, which has only a fragment of the first two lines of the text, with one line of the music for treble and bass; (F) Bod. Douce 280 (before 1633), fol. 68v, without music, and headed: "Mr Jno Dowlan. 2d. Booke./ For tableture & pricke songe./" (this version copies most of the repetitions or repeat marks); (G) BM Add. 17790 (Sextus book of Add. 17786–17791, early 17th century), fols. 4v–5v, a version for solo voice with a consort of viols headed: "Dowlands sorrow. 5. william wigthorpe"—Wigthorpe was no doubt the arranger; and (H) BM Add. 37402 (treble book of Add. 37402–37406, after 1601), fols. 58v–59, another (different) arrangement for voice and viols. The variants are:

1 stay] come G
   lend] send H
   repentant] repentance H
2 woefull] wooful G
3 thy] sad G
5 pitty . . . neuer] *alternative in* G: pittie sweet Jesu://:
                                    help now and ever
6 mark me not to] oh make me not H
   mark . . . paine] Make me not endless in paine F

7 alas] alacke G
 alas . . . condempned] *alternative in* G: alas that I haue synd
 euer] for euer H, *omitted* G
8 no hope] noe helpe H
 no help] nor help G
 no . . . ther] *alternative in* G: I hope I hope helpe
9 but downe, down] *alternative in* G: though that downe
10 down and arise] *alternative in* G: yet I shall rise
 I neuer shall] shall I neuer H, *alternative in* G: & never fall

9–10 *but downe, &c.* Compare these lines with the end of No. 33 of John Wilbye's *Second Set of Madrigales* (1609), EM, VII, 224–235.

IIII.

This enigmatic poem must have come from a masque or play; perhaps it was sung by a comforting spirit. See Do1600.III.
 1 *Dye not beefore thy day.* Cf. the first line of No. XXV in John Ward's *First Set of English Madrigals* (1613; EMV, p. 271).
 4 *The hag.* That is, Despair (line 3).

V.

This poem, like Nos. III and IIII, may have come from a masque or play.
 8 *in . . . dwell.* Cf. RDo1610.X.1.

VI.–VIII.

This poem is probably about Sir Henry Lee, and may have been written by him. See Do1597.XVIII and note. A copy of the poem is found in Bod. MS Rawl. Poet. 148, fol. 75v, between poems dated 1597 and 1598, headed: "In yeeldinge vp his Tilt staff: sayd." and subscribed: "Qd Sir Henry Leigh." This MS version has been printed by David H. Horne, *Life and Minor Works of George Peele* (New Haven: Yale, 1952) pp. 171–72. Variants from the MS are:

VI.3 youths] youth
 .5 thinks] thankes
 and] *omitted*
VII.5 as that] That
VIII.2 sings] singe
 .4 *fremuerunt*] frementum
 oremus] oramus
 .5 *in left margin of MS*: Regina:
 .7 dost] doest

The MS has a fourth stanza which is really the third stanza of Do1597.XVIII.
 The poem may be related to the occasion in which Lee yielded up his tilt staff, but it may also have been used in some connection with Lee's installation as a Knight of the Garter, May 23, 1597 (E. K. Chambers, *Sir Henry Lee* [1936], p. 172.) For other comment, see Frances A. Yates, "Queen Elizabeth as Astraea," *Journal of the Warburg and Courtauld Institutes*, X (1947), 27–82.
 A note under No. VIII reads, "*Heere endeth the Songes of two parts.*"

VII.2 *Nunc Demittis.* The opening words of the *Canticum Simeonis* (Luke 2:29–32), "Lord, now lettest thou thy servant depart in peace," are especially appropriate to Lee.

.3 *De profundis.* Psalm 129 (Vulgate); Psalm 130 (King James), "Out of the depths have I cried unto thee, O Lord."

Te Deum. "Te Deum laudamus" is a hymn of thanksgiving often sung after victory in battle.

.4 *Miserere.* This usually refers to Psalm 50 (Vulgate; King James, Psalm 51).

.5 *Paratum est cor meum.* Psalm 56:8 (Vulgate) "Paratum cor meum, Deus, paratum cor meum"; Psalm 57:7 (King James), "My heart is fixed."

VIII.2 *Venite exultemus.* Psalm 94 (Vulgate); Psalm 95 (King James), "O come, let us sing unto the Lord."

.3 *Noli emulari.* The opening words of Psalm 36 (Vulgate); Psalm 37 (King James) "Fret not thyself."

.4 *quare fremuerunt.* Psalm 2 (Vulgate); "Why do the heathen rage" (King James). The opening of this psalm represents the active life, to be contrasted to the contemplative life (*oremus*, "let us pray").

IX.

In the songbook, the first quatrain is followed by "Lenvoy" and lines 5–12 are printed at the bottom of the page, followed by "And so I wackt, &c." The music has a repeat sign before "Lenvoy", so it is fairly clear that the three quatrains are sung before the last couplet and that the poem is a sonnet (as in EMV) instead of three six-line stanzas. *Cf.* By1596.V, Do1600.XX, Jo1610.VII, and Do1612.XVIII.

Bond (III, 484) ascribes the poem to Lyly without evidence.

The first quatrain and the concluding couplet were written as one stanza on fol. 2 of Bod. MS Tanner 221, a leaf bound up with some printed books by Nicholas Breton (1600–1614). The lines are placed as a third stanza of a copy of Do1600.XI (see note). Both poems were probably copied from the songbook; there are no variants in No. IX. Another copy of Dowland's song, with music in four parts, is in Brussels MS Fetis 3095 II.4.109 (*c.* 1620), pp. 28–29; it reads *eare* for *eares* in line 5.

2 *words . . . windes.* Tilley W833.

9 *Now . . . braines.* Bond (III, 484) calls attention to this passage from *Euphues and his England* (1580): "I haue oftentimes sworne that I am as farre from loue as he, yet will he not beleeue me, as incredulous as those, who thinke none balde, till they see his braynes" (Bond, II, 48). But *cf.* the many entries in Tilley B597.

X.

The first two lines of this poem are the opening lines of a poem by Sir Philip Sidney from the *Old Arcadia*, Second Eclogues, No. 34. The text given by Ringler, (pp. 68–69) reads "I do like" in line 2. The rest of Sidney's piece is different from Dowland's text, and is in quantitative verse. "Wanstead" (line 32) provides another link with Sidney. In May 1578 or 1579, an entertainment written by Sidney (printed at the end of the 1598 *Arcadia*, sigs. Bbb3v–6v, and subsequently called *The Lady of May*) was performed before Queen Elizabeth during a visit to Wanstead Manor (Ringler, p. 361). The Earl of Leicester owned Wanstead at this time; his stepson, Robert Devereux, second Earl of Essex, lived there from time to time in the later years of the century. After receiving his famous box on the ear from the Queen in 1598, Essex retired to Wanstead until he was returned to favor (E. P. Cheyney, *A History of England from the Defeat of the Armada to the Death of Elizabeth* [1926], II, 77). Diana Poulton has suggested that Essex may possibly have written this poem; see Do1597.V and notes. But the dedication to Hugh Holland may suggest that the poem is his. Collier (p. 90) thinks that this mention of Wanstead indicates that the song was performed there.

1 *Hugh Holland*. A minor poet who specialized in prefatory verses. He wrote a sonnet for the 1623 folio of Shakespeare, and verses commending Jonson's *Sejanus* (1605), Giles Farnaby's *Canzonets* (1598), and other works. Dowland also wrote a poem for Farnaby's work. Holland died in 1633. See Herbert Berry, "Some Notes about Hugh Holland," *N & Q*, CCIX (1964), 149–151.

2–3 *O Sweet woods, &c.* These two lines are printed as a refrain to the second, third and fourth stanzas; it was probably sung both before and after the first stanza, and after the others; therefore I have inserted lines 10 and 11 as a reminder. Ringler (p. 404) notes that Mona Wilson (*Sir Philip Sidney* [1931], p. 314) says the first line is a translation of Giovanni della Casa's "O dolce selva solitaria, amica," but that the idea is commonplace. Obertello (p. 136) suggests Bembo's sonnet "Lieta e chiusa contrada ov'io m'involo" as a source.

22 *procure*. The emendation in EMV, p. 470, *prove*, is probably correct because of the ryhme with *Loue*.

XI.

The verses of this song first appeared in Thomas Newman's edition of Sir Philip Sidney's *Astrophel and Stella* (1591), sig. L4v, among the "other rare Sonnets of divers Noblemen and Gentlemen," as the title-page says. This volume (or a later edition, STC 22538, sig. K4v) may have been Dowland's source.

Bond, III, 484, ascribed the poem to Lyly without evidence. J. P. Collier assigned it to Thomas Nashe because it appeared anonymously in the 1591 *Astrophel and Stella*, for which Nashe had written a preface (see Collier's ed. of Nashe's *Pierce Penniless's Supplication to the Devil* [Shakespeare Society, 1842], pp. xxi–xxii). R. B. McKerrow, ed., *Works of Thomas Nashe*, III (1905), 396, included the poem among Nashe's "Doubtful Works," but notes (V, 139–140) that it is probably not by him. *Cf.* Ck1610.IIII; the opening of Elegie III from Giles Fletcher's *Licia* (n.d.; 1593), sig. K4, "If sadde complaint would shewe a lovers payne"; and Sir Arthur Gorges' "Yf teares avayle to ease the gryved mynde," printed in his *Poems*, ed. Helen E. Sandison (Oxford, 1953), p. 55. Sandison notes (p. 200) that Gorges' poem is based on a sonnet by Joachim du Bellay (*Regrets*, LII; *Oeuvres Poetiques*, ed. Henri Chamard [Paris, 1910], II. 92), which begins:

> Si les larmes servoient de remede au malheur,
> Et le pleurer pouvoit la tristesse arrester,

The rest of the poem does not seem to be very close to Dowland's.

Besides the 1591 *Astrophel and Stella* (D), the words of No. XI appear in the following sources: (E) Thomas Bateson's *Second Set of Madrigales to 3. 4. 5. and 6. Parts: Apt for Viols and Voyces* (1618), No. XII (Cantus, sig. C2v), which contains the first stanza set for solo voice and viol accompaniment; (F) Forbes's *Cantus* (1662), sigs. E2v–F, set to the tune of "Sleep wayward thoughts," (Do1597.XIII); this version was copied into the Taitt MS at U.C.L.A. (see Rubsamen, pp. 259–284); (G) BM MS Harl. 6910 (*c*. 1601), fol. 156–156v; (H) Bod. MS Tanner 221, fol. 2, on a leaf bound up in a collection of printed books by Nicholas Breton, (the stanzas here are reversed, and the first quatrain and final couplet of "Praise blindnesse eies" [Do1600.IX] are included as a third stanza); (I) Brussels, Fetis MS 3095. II.4.109 (*c.* 1620), pp. 24–25, with Dowland's music for four voices; and (J) Tenbury MS 1019 (early 17th century), fol. 1, with music for voice and lute not by Dowland or Bateson. Other versions (not seen) are in the Wode partbooks (BM MS Add. 33933, fol. 85; Edinburgh University MS La. III.483, pp. 184, 200) and in NLS Advocates' MS. 5.2.15 (*c.* 1625), p. 114. Variants from D–J are as follows:

1 cleanse] change F
2 And] Or EFHJ
  sighes] sights G, sythes H
  might] could F
3 might salue] could free F
  fault] faults EI
4 error] ever F
5 cry . . . mone] weep sigh cry and ever groan F
  sigh] sight D, syth E
6 mine . . . gone] for follies faults faults for sinnes and errors gone F
  errors] error DGH
  faults] fault DGH
  follies] folly H
7 hopes] hope F
  their] the GH
8 I . . . flowers] I find mens favors are not lasting flowrs F
9 I see] I find F
  will] can J
  breede] breath DGJ
10 Then] But FJ
   at] an I
11 Thus] Then DJ, Which G
   when] since F
   thus] this DG
12 can] shall G
   blinde] binde F

Forbes adds a third stanza:

> Since man is nothing but a masse of clay,
> Our days not else but shaddowes on the wall,
> Trust in the Lord, who lives and lasts for ay,
> Whose favour found will neither fade nor faile
> My God to thee I resigne my mouth & minde
> No trust in youth, in youth, no faith in Age I finde

Tenbury 1019 adds a third and fourth stanza:

> These hands shall beate vpon my pensiue brest
> And sad to death, for sorrow rent my hayre
> my Voyce to call on thee shall neuer rest
> Thy grace I seeke, thy Judgment I do feare
> Vpon the ground all groueling non [on?] my face
> Lord I beseech thy fauor & thy grace

Thy mercy greater is then any sinne
thy greatnes none could euer comprehend
wherefore good lord let me thy mercy winne
whose glorious name no tyme can euer ende
Then shall I sing with thyne elect in heauen
Thy prayse & power world without ende Amen/

2 *smoakes of sighes.* R. B. McKerrow (Nashe's *Works*, IV, 480) compares Lyly's *Love's Metamorphosis*, IV.i.11–12 (Bond, II, 317), "my sighes couer thy Temple with a darke smoake," but says that the source is probably Pettie's *Petite Palace of Pleasure* (1576), sig. T3, "For if plaintes may proue my paine, I haue still continued in carefull cries: if sighes may shew my sorrow, the smoake of them hath reached to the skies: if teares may trie my truth, the water hath flowen as a floud from my eyes." *Smoke* could mean steam or vapor.

10 *lightening but at houres.* That is, making light or alleviating sorrow only temporarily.

XII.

Variations on the theme of the peddler's song were popular, but most were less didactic than this, and many employed actual street-cries (*e.g.* Campion's poem in Jo1605.X). Other examples are Mo1600.XVII, and the analogues to Autolycus' "Lawne as white as driven Snow" in *The Winter's Tale* listed by Seng (pp. 240–242): a round by John Jenkins beginning "Come, pretty maidens, what is't you buy"; a song from the "Masque of Mountebanks" (1618; BM MS Add. 29481, fols. 17v–19), beginning "What is't you lack, what would you buy?"; and a passage in Anthony Munday's *The Downfall of Robert, Earle of Huntington* (1601), sig. F4v, beginning "What lack ye? what lack ye? what ist ye wil buy?" See also the "Broom Song" in Fletcher's *The Loyal Subject* (*c.* 1618), III.v.303 ff.; "New broomes, greene broomes, will you by any," from Robert Wilson's *The Three Ladies of London* (1584), sig. D4; and four songs published by Thomas Ravenscroft: two beginning "New Oysters" in *Pammelia* (1609), sigs. B2 and B3; and "Broomes for old Shooes" and "Where are you faire maides" in *Melismata* (1611), sigs. D1 and D2v–D3.

4 *begger . . . loue.* Cf. Do1603.XIX.6.

10 *Iewell . . . plaine.* See Tilley P381, "Plain dealing is a jewel," and *cf.* P382.

11 *th'orienst.* EMV, p. 740, suggests *th'orient's,* but since *orient* became a common adjective applied to pearls denoting superior value or brilliancy rather than origin, *orienst* could be a contracted superlative.

17 *But my.* The emendation in EMV, p. 472, to *But in my* is probably correct.

18 *Turtles . . . paier.* I.e., within his heart are symbols of true love: a pair of turtle-doves and the heavenly twins, Castor and Pollux. Since the latter were born from Leda's egg, they are also perhaps the "courts brood," which is in contrast to the country toys of line 16. See Diana Poulton's note in *LSJ*, VII (1965), 45.

XIII.

The first and third stanzas were copied into BM MS Add. 28009, fol. 94, among a group of poems sent by Henry Oxinden of Barham to his wife, in the time of Charles I. Another item of Oxinden's (fol. 83) is dated 1641. The only variant occurs in line 4: the MS reads *desires.*

12 *most.* I.e., *must.*

15 *spirits.* As the rhyme with *delights* suggests, this word was sometimes pronounced as its monosyllabic variant, *sprites.* See Kökeritz, p. 213.

XIIII.

Collier (p. 87) speculates that this song came from a masque or play. The music for the treble and bass parts and the first stanza of the text are found in Christ Church, Oxford, MS 439 (*c.* 1620), p. 47; someone has since written "Dowland" in pencil by the song. Variants are as follows:

1 states] Stars
2 right] *omitted*
3 Soundings balefull] sound imball full
4 Burthening] both your kinge

9 *Quier. I.e., choir,* as in EMV.

XV.

This song was reprinted with Dowland's tune in Forbes's *Cantus* (1662), sigs. R1v–R2, with the following variants:

4 Quitting] quiteing
10 ouerthrowen] overthrown
18 From] Erom
27 loosed] lossed
29 won] win
37 hast] hath
39 Truth] trueth
40 swaine] Swan
41 many] they
46 thoughts] thought

Forbes supplies this line needed to complete the last stanza: "To banish love with froward scorne." The copy of Do1600 at St. Michael's College, Tenbury, contains a line added in a seventeenth-century hand, "and so I'le live as one forlorne," which EMV, p. 474, prints as line 48. The version from Forbes may possibly have more authority, however, as will be seen from the following. Mo1600.XV, unfortunately lacking in the unique copy of Morley's book, is, according to the Table of Contents, "White as Lillies." Since Morley used another text also set by Dowland, "I Saw my Lady weepe" (Do1600.I), the two poems beginning "White as Lillies" are probably identical. Since Forbes had seen a copy of Morley (he reprints Morley's No. IIII) it is possible that he got his line 48 from Morley's setting of the poem.

Michael East published a setting of what is apparently this poem in his *Fift Set of Bookes* (1618), No. XI, but only the opening words are printed with the music.

11 *groning.* The emendation in EMV, p. 473, to *grieving* makes a better rhyme.

XVI.

12 *thy losse. Thy* refers to the "Wofull hart" of line 1.

XVII.

The arrangement of this poem is somewhat confusing in the songbook, for lines 9–12 are printed under the music with lines 1–4. It is almost certain that lines 5–8 were intended to be repeated after line 12.

The first stanza was copied into Bod. MS Douce 280 (before 1633), fol. 69, without variants; it is headed, "Mr: Jno: Dowland./" Another copy is in (D) Brussels MS Fetis 3095 II.4.109 (*c.* 1620), pp. 22–23, with Dowland's music in four parts. The song was reprinted in (E) Forbes's *Cantus* (1662), sig. Z1–Z1v. Variants are:

1 plaining] playing E
3 trode] tread E
8 Fye fye on] Fye vpon D
10 eye] eyes E
11 conquest] conpuest E

XVIII.

This poem is No. XXIX of Fulke Greville's *Caelica* cycle, which was printed in *Certaine Learned and Elegant Workes of the Right Honorable Fulke Lord Brooke* (1633), sig. Cc2. It also appears among the miscellaneous poems of the 1591 *Astrophel and Stella* (sig. L4), where it is titled "Meglior aspero" and subscribed "E.O." I give the variants from the 1633 edition (D) and the Warwick Castle MS (E) from Bullough's edition, I, 88–89, and 244, and from *Astrophel and Stella* (F). See the other poems by Greville which Dowland set, Do1597.II and XXI.

2 court] Courts DE
  wits] Wit DEF
4 hath] haue DEF
6 *In* DEF *this stanza follows:*

> *Cupid*, that doth aspire
> To be God of desire,
>   Sweares he giues lawes:
> That where his arrowes hit,
> Some ioy, some sorrow it,
>   Fortune no cause.

8 booke] books DEF
9 Turne] turnd F
10 Sences] Sensles F
11 Venture hir] Venture hath D, hazard hath E *revision,* venter hir F
17 court] Courts DE
19 So] Thus DE
23 Made mee thinke humble] Thus makes me thinke the DE
24 desert] desart DE, desarts F
25 is deere to me] I keepe to mee F
26 And Ione] Myra DE
27 Ione] She DE
28 Ione that doth euer] Myra that knowes to DE, Shee that doth onely F

3 *defiance.* Bullough (I, 244) explains this as "a quarrel, with the idea here of formal combat as in chivalric battles preceded by defiant speeches."

10–11 *Sences . . . loue.* That is, the senses shall attest to Venture's (hazard's or risk's) place in love.

13, 14, 21 *begot . . . Atheists . . . Fortunes.* See Variant Readings.

XIX.

A copy of this song with Dowland's music in four parts is in Brussels MS Fetis 3095 II.4.109 (*c.* 1620), pp. 30–31; it has the first stanza only, and reads *earthly* for *heauenly* in line 3. Another copy with Dowland's treble part (not seen) is in Edinburgh University MS La. III.488.

XX.

The Table lists "Finding in fields my *Siluia* all alone" as No. XX. If the "better dittie" was inserted so late in the printing of the work as to prevent a correction in the Table, the change cannot have been made with Dowland's knowledge, for he was in Denmark. This is probably the work of the publisher, George Eastland. Should we assume then, that Eastland or someone else wrote this poem to fit Dowland's music for "Finding in fields"? Or are the songs entirely different? A copy of "Finding in fields" would be very useful at this point.

The arrangement of the words in the songbook is rather confusing. Lines 5–8 and 13–15 are printed with the music, while lines 9–12 and another version of lines 14–15 are printed below (see Variant Readings). In other instances, "Lenuoy" indicates a conclusion rather than a refrain (see the note to Do1600.IX).

A copy of this song with Dowland's music for four voices and without verbal variants is in Brussels MS Fetis 3095 II.4.109 (*c.* 1620), pp. 26–27.

A note at the end of the song in Do1600 reads "*The end of the foure parts.*"

14–15 *When once, &c.* Compare Tilley W915, "To know the worst is good."

XXI.

Obertello (pp. 514–516) cites this poem in comparison with Thomas Morley's madrigal, "Aprill is in my Mistris face," (*Madrigalls to Foure Voyces* [1594], No. I), which is a version of the first stanza of a poem by Livio Celiano, "Porta nel viso Aprile" (*Rime di diversi celebri poeti* [1587], sig. G8). Although there are parallels between Dowland's song and the Italian poem, they are not very close or significant. Compare these lines from a poem in Robert Greene's *Perimedes the Blacke-Smith* (1588), sig. H2v:

> Faire is my loue for *Aprill* in her face,
> Hir louely brests *September* claimes his part,
> And Lordly *Iuly* in her eyes takes place,
> But colde *December* dwelleth in her heart.

As other Italian poems quoted by Obertello demonstrate, the basic conceit is fairly commonplace.

8 *height.* Pronounced to rhyme with *faith.* See E. J. Dobson, *English Pronunciation 1500–1700* (Oxford, 1957), II, 666, 954.

XXII.

This dialogue, apparently from a masque, was copied with Dowland's music into BM MS Add. 15117 (*c.* 1614), fol. 12. It contains only one stanza, with the words altered thus:

A Dialogue
1] Saye fonde love what seekes thowe heere
in the sylence of the night,
2] heere I seeke those Ioyes my deere,
that in silent most delight,

> 1] nightes heavy humor Calls to sleep
> 2] But loves humor watch doth keepe
> Both] let never humor hapie prove,
>   but that which onelye pleasethe love.

Another copy with Dowland's music for four voices is in Brussels MS Fetis 3095 II.4.109 (*c.* 1620), pp. 20–21; it reads *light'st* in line 20.

For other dialogues, see Do1603.XXI, Cop1606.VII, Fd1607.XI, Fer1609.XXVI, XXVII, XXVIII, Han1609.19, 20 and Do1612.XIX.

2 *Queene.* This may or may not refer to Queen Elizabeth. It could be merely the character of a queen in the masque.

Robert Jones, *The First Booke of Songes or Ayres*, 1600

Dedication

Sir Robert Sidney (1563–1626), younger brother of Sir Philip, later had the Earldom of Leicester revived for him. Ben Jonson praised his hospitality in his poem "To Penshurst" (*Works*, VIII, 93–96), and a number of books were dedicated to him, including one by his godson, Robert Dowland (RD01610). See also the dedication to Jo1610. (DNB, Williams.)

To the Reader

3 *my trauels.* Probably an allusion to Dowland's epistle in Do1597.

I.

Bond (III, 485–6) suggests without evidence that John Lyly was the author of these verses.

21 *Faire shewes. Cf.* Tilley F3 and F29.

21 *deceit.* Rhymes with *bait* (line 16). Shakespeare rhymes *deceit* and *conceit* with *state, straight* and *waite.* See Kökeritz, pp. 407, 421, 475.

23–24 *Time . . . bringes. Cf.* Tilley T333.

II.

This poem also appears in (D) Richard Johnson's collection, *The Golden Garland of Princely Pleasures* (1620), sigs. F7–F8, with the title, "Of the inconueniences by Marriage. To the tune of When Troy town." (See the discussion of this tune in Simpson, pp. 587–590.) Another copy occurs in (E) BM MS Add. 22603 (mid 17th century), fol. 58–58v, headed "A Songe against Marriage." The variants are as follows:

> 1 youths make] youth makes DE
> 3 their arte] and art D
> 7 finde] know E
>   so] *omitted* E
>   who] that D, which haue E
>   are] bin E
> 8 sweetes . . . sowre] sweet-sharpe sowres inclosed in E
> 9 pleasures . . . in] pleasing'st pleasures are in E

11 They . . . chiefe] And which of follyes &c E
13 content] delight E
   choose] chose E
15 And . . . content] If they theyr kindred will content E
17 O . . . chiefe] So that of follyes is &c E
19 strifes . . . bred] greifes . . . wrought E
23 O . . . chiefe] Of follyes all it is the &c E
25 smiles] smile D
26 And . . . grant] If what they craue, we doe not graunt E
27 Or] Then
28 laughings] laughing D, longinges E
29 O . . . chiefe] Of follyes &c E
31 false] fall D
32 bindes vs thrall] makes vs thralls E
33 Wherefore] And E
34 be] are E
35 blisse it is] follies tis D

A poem by Robert Greene from *Ciceronis Amor. Tullies Loue* (1589; 5th ed. 1609, sig. D3), has a similar opening line: "Fond faining Poets makes of loue a god." The rest of the poem is different, however. Bond (III, 486) ascribes Jones's text to John Lyly without evidence.

7 *are.* Rhymes with *care* (line 8). See Kökeritz, p. 405.
28 *laughings.* The reading from E above, *longings,* may be preferred.
31 *Foule wiues . . . false.* This sounds proverbial, but is not in Tilley. *Cf.* Chaucer, *Wife of Baths Tale,* 1213–1226 (*Works,* ed. F. N. Robinson [Boston: Houghton Mifflin, 2nd ed., 1957], p. 88), and Thomas Deloney, *Jack of Newberry* in *The Novels,* ed. Merritt E. Lawlis (Bloomington; University of Indiana Press, 1961), pp. 9–11: "As young maides are fickle, so are old women iealous."

III.

9–11 *Pitty . . . endeth. I.e.,* Pity adorns or graces beauty, and the beautiful woman who has embraced Pity finds it a friend when her beauty is gone.

IIII.

Bond (III, 487) ascribes this poem to Lyly without evidence. Other copies of the poem may be found in (D) Bod. MS Ashmole 38 (mid-17th century), p. 118, where it is "Song the 14th," and in (E) Bod. MS Douce 280 (before 1633, poems probably before 1603), fol. 68–68v, with "Tho: Say:" in the margin. E begins with this stanza:

> In Prime of youth when loue was younge,
> My restless ranginge minde regarded,
> A louinge harte yet false her tounge,
> Whose wilye witts he he hath obserued.

In the margin after each stanza, E has "Againe." The variants continue:

1 and yet] yet still DE
2 though] Since E
   loue . . . now] faith and troath be quite D, faith & troth is quite E

3 Then] Once E
nowe . . . grieue] yet now I proue E
4 vows . . . be] oathes & vowes are E
6 Hers . . . it] Curst be the chance that chanced E
7 griefe] fault E
8 Shee . . . cause] ere long you may haue cause D, In tyme thou mayest haue
cause E
9 tis] i'st D *first time*
loue] trust E
10–15 *omitted* D
11 Loue] Take E
that] whoe E
12 For . . . changeth] Like the Camelion still shee changes E
13 Yeelding] Castinge E
14 My . . . rangeth] Her selfe vnto me wheare shee ranges E
16 Let . . . vaunt] Ioye to the man E, Let noe man boast D
gaines] getts D
17 For . . . time] Vntill such tyme that he E
that . . . time] as tyme and hee D
18 Shee . . . bring] He may bringe her E
19 I] Ile DE

12 *Camelion . . . changeth.* Tilley C221.
18 *weeping crosse.* Tilley W248.

V.

9 *hundred eyes.* The usual allusion to Argus in connection with watchful jealousy;
Cf. Mo1600.VII.42, and Tilley E254.

VI.

Bond (III, 501) ascribes these verses to Lyly without evidence.
5 *this hell.* EMV, p. 550, emends to *thy hell.*

VII.

Bond (III, 487) ascribes these verses to Lyly without evidence.
5 *like fire supprest.* Tilley F265; *cf.* Shakespeare, *Venus and Adonis*, 331–332.
7–11 *Cf.* Tilley H302, "Faint heart ne'er won fair lady," and F601.
17 *beat . . . flie.* Tilley B740.
22 *A womans . . . say nay. Cf.* Tilley W66.
28–29 *time . . . foretop. Cf.* Tilley T331.

VIII.

Bond (III, 488) ascribes to Lyly without evidence. This poem may have been one
of the many inspired by Marlowe's *Hero and Leander.*
5–6 *Crowes . . . white. Cf.* Chaucer's *Manciple's Tale* and its source in Ovid,
Metamorphoses, II, 531–632.
23 *His loue in a towre.* I.e., Danaë.

IX.

This poem may be by John Lilliat, for it appears in a MS which contains a number of poems in his autograph, Bod. MS Rawlinson Poet. 148. On fols. 112v–113, the first stanza is given with music for two voices (not Jones's), and headed "Uni, soli, semper. J.L." A note on fol. 113 says, "The residue of this ditie in fol. 8 before." This leaf (fol. 8) is now missing, and the words on fols. 112v–113 are not in Lilliat's hand. But since Lilliat is usually careful to sign his own poems or ascribe other poems to their authors, it is probable that the poem is his, despite Bond's suggestion (III, 489) that the initials stand for John Lyly. The missing fol. 8 would have been between poems dated 1592 and 1596; and since enough dates occur to show that the MS was kept chronologically, the poem was probably composed between those years. The only variant in the first stanza is *or measure* for *and measure* in line 1.

The poem is found with another musical setting (voice and lute, not Jones's or Lilliat's) in (D) Tenbury MS 1019 (early 17th century), fol. 1. Another copy of the poem is in (E) BM MS Harleian 2127, fol. 41 (mid-17th century). The variants are:

2 though . . . die] and loue that neuer dies D
3 tis] its D
4 eie] eies D
6 an] a E
   euenings] euening D
8 yet they are] yet are they E (*E puts 8–10 between 4–5, but has a correcting arrow*)
12 teares, sighes] sighes and teares D

8–13 Correlative verse.
9 *Faire wordes . . . wind.* Tilley W833.

XI.

Bond (III, 489) ascribes this to Lyly without evidence (except, perhaps, for lines 10–11; see note below).

This poem occurs in two MSS: (D) BM MS Harleian 6057 (mid-17th century), fol. 7v, headed "An Invective against weomen"; and (E) Rosenbach MS 1083/16 (formerly Phillipps 9549; *c.* 1630), pp. 39–40, poem No. 53. The variants are:

2 that] which E
   puffes] proffes D
5 idle] silly E
6 sporting with] courtinge of D
8–11 *follow 20 in* E
8 rinde] rine E
9 Makes] Make E
   for] of E
   hallow] hollowe DE
10 Hiænaes kinde] hainous kind [*or* kine?] E
11 That] Who E
   fairst] faire D
   most they] least they E, they moste D
   swallow] followe DE
12–13 *omitted* E

13 sporting with] courtinge of D
15 rocks . . . coast] like to a quicksand coast E
17 creatures] weathers E
18 rather . . . ought] yeelds it selfe to euery thing E
19 idle] silly E
20 sporting with] courting of D

E contains "The Reply" (No. 54):

> O men what are you? but vnconstant creatures
> Whom Smallest puffe of wind hath power to change.
> You men what are you but faire Virtues creatures
> Deeming [Damning?] women when you lust to change,
>   Women what are we, but euen worse then them
>   To spend our times in trusting to these men:
>
> You men what are you? flowers whose outward show
> Doth promise sweetnes, but indeed are sowre
> You men what are you? Crocodiles that shew
> And weepe to them you soonest would deuoure.
>   Women what are we, but euen worse then them
>   To spend our times in trusting to those men,
>
> You men what are you Rockes neere to the shore
> Which swallow vp when least we thinke the same
> You men what are you? false Ile say noe more
> Yet on our trouth you still lay all the blame
>   women what are wee but eene worse &c.

1, 5 *Women . . . wee men.* A.H. Bullen, *Lyrics from the Songbooks of the Elizabethan Age* (New York, 3rd ed., 1892), p. 224, notes this play on words in George Peele's *Edward I*; see the ed. by Frank S. Hook in Peele's *Dramatic Works*, II (New Haven, 1961), p. 134.

10–11 *Hiænaes kinde.* This vulgar error probably originated in Pliny's *Natural History* VIII.xliv, and was repeated by (among others) John Lyly in *Euphues* (ed. Bond, I, 250).

XII.

As various scholars have noted, Shakespeare parodies the words (and probably used the tune) of the first two stanzas of this song in *Twelfth Night*, II.iii.110–121. See the summary of comments in Seng, pp. 105–108. The tune must have been popular, because other verses were written to fit it. Alexander Montgomerie wrote a religious poem beginning "Auay! vane world bewitcher of my hairt" "To the Toon of— 'Sall I let hir go,' &c." This text is printed from one of Drummond of Hawthornden's MSS in the Scottish Text Society edition of Montgomerie's *Poems*, ed. James Cranstoun (Edinburgh, 1887, Nos. 9–11), pp. 237–238. Montgomerie's poem also appears as "A Comfortabill Song" at the end of Lady Elizabeth Malvill's *Ane Godlie Dreame* (Edinburgh, 1603; see *The Poems of Alexander Hume*, ed. Alexander Lawson [Edinburgh, 1902, Scottish Text Society No. 48], pp. 197–198), and was printed again with Jones's tune in Forbes's *Cantus* (1662), sigs. Q2v–P1. A copy with the music in four parts is in the Taitt MS at U.C.L.A. (Cantus, fol. 75; see Rubsamen, p. 272). This MS has still another poem written to Jones's tune; it begins, "Farewell fond fancies of my former joyes" (Cantus, fol. 50). A third poem written to this tune, beginning "O sillie soul alace," is in NLS Advocates' MS 5.2.15, pp. 6–7. Rubsamen notes other sources of the music in Thomas Robinson's *New Citharen Lessons* (1609), p. 40; in the Quintus part of the Wode partbooks, Trinity College, Dublin MS F.5.13, pp. 108–109; and in NLS Panmure MS 11 (*c*. 1630–1665), fol. 7. The tune is also used in Dirck Raphaels Camphuysen's *Stichtelycke Rymen* (Amsterdam, 1647), sig. A2v. Music for Jones's melody is given, with the title, "Sang: Shal I bed her go; Of: O slaep o soete slaep." The Dutch words begin, "Heylgierig mensch."

Jones himself alludes to the song in Jo1609.VIII, which seems to be the lady's answer. It is in the same stanza form, and the tune is reminiscent of No. XII. Jones later set a poem (Jo1605.XIX) from *A Poetical Rhapsody* (RPR, I, 110–111) which uses as a refrain lines similar to lines 15 and 16 of the present poem.

Other copies of the original poem occur in (D) NLS Advocates' MS 5.2.14, fol. 8 (with music for Jones's tune), and in (E) Richard Johnson's *The Golden Garland of Princely Pleasures* (1620), sig. F5 and F5v, with the title, "*Coridons* farewell to *Phillis*." Bishop Percy prints this version in his *Reliques* (1765), I, 187–189. Variants from D and E are:

13 her] loue DE
17 E *has* 5 no's.
19 Ten] then D
28 farewell] adieu E
32 waies] way E
33 it] that E
38 is as] is als D
39 Shee] we E
40 repeated] repea E *page cut off here*

28–29 *I see loth to depart, Bids.* "Loth to depart," the title of a song, became a commonplace phrase (see OED, sv. *loath*). The tune is given in Simpson, p. 456, from Cambridge MS Dd.2.11. The whole phrase may have been intended as an epithet for the speaker referring to himself in the third person. Or the passage may have originally read, "I seem loth to depart, Bid. . . ."

XIIII.
Bond (III, 490) ascribes this poem to Lyly without evidence.
16 *mountains of a mouse.* Cf. Tilley M1035, "Of a molehill he makes a mountain," and Tilley M1215, "The mountain was in labor and brought forth a mouse."

XV.
Bond (III, 501) ascribes this poem to Lyly without evidence.
1–3 *Life . . . table.* David Greer compares William Byrd's *Psalmes, Songs, and Sonnets* (1611), No. XVII, lines 5–6 (EMV, p. 749).

XVI.
These words were set to music for four parts later in the century by Henry Bowman in his *Songs* (1677), pp. 45–46, with the following variants:

1 in] the
2 hart . . . chaunting] Soul, with her melodious Chanting

3 her . . . me] me thinks shee pleases
4 when . . . prick] when prickt with thorns
5 sings] cry's
7–13 *omitted*

Cf. a song from John Marston's *The Dutch Courtezan* (1605), sig. B2v, here from
the copy with music in BM MS Add. 24665, fols. 58v–59:

> The darke is my delight,
> soe tis the Nightingalls.
> My musick's in the nighte,
> soe is the Nightingalls.
> My bodie is but little
> soe is the Nightingalls.
> I loue to sleepe against the prickle,
> soe doth the Nightingale.

4 *prick . . . breast.* Tilley N183.

XVIII.

Another copy of this song occurs in BM MS 15117, (after 1614), fol. 22v, with
music for voice and lute which differs from Jones's at some points. There is only one
stanza of text, which varies as follows:

3 to . . . dwell] with desert that shall still lyve
4–6 *omitted in MS*
7 haue charmd] doe Charme
9 sweete] fond
11 can I] I cann
12–23 *omitted in MS*

XIX.

These verses also appear in (D) Folger MS V.a.399 (after *c.* 1630), fol. 13v, and in
(E) Rosenbach MS 240/2 (*c.* 1640–1650; this poem seems to be in an even later hand),
p. 137. The variants are:

3 it . . . not] 'twas nothing E
  was] is D
6 what] that E
7 must] maye D
9 louers] ere we E
12 it is] it were D, it's but E
16 is angrie] in anger
18 bites . . . cries] kickt she winst shee cryed D
19 kissing sweetly] sweetly kissinge D
  shee doth flie] shee flyes E
21 Yet] If E
22 brales] brawles D, browes E
  are meant] her bent E
24 too too] too E

A fragment of this song is sung—in a nondescript foreign accent—by Franceschina in Marston's *The Dutch Courtezan* (1605), sig. C3:

> Aunt *Mary*, Mettre *Faugh*, stooles, stooles for des gallantes: mine Mettre sing non oder song, frolique, frolique Sir, but still complaine me doe her wrong, lighten your heart Sir, for me did but kisse her, for me did but kis her, and so let go.

Lines 1–2 and 4 were also sung by Philautus in *Everie Woman in her Humor* (1609) on sigs. H2 and D3v respectively, changing the first to "My loue can sing" and adding "For" to the beginning of the second. Line 4 is also quoted in James Shirley's *Love's Cruelty* (*c.* 1631), IV.i, *Dramatic Works*, ed. A. Dyce (London, 1833), II, 239: "For he did but kiss her, for he did but kiss her, and so let her go." See John P. Cutts, "*Everie Woman in her Humor*," *RN*, XVIII (1965), 210–212. *Cf.* also Thomas Coryat, *Coryats Crudities* (1611), sig. A3, a distich explaining a picture on the title page:

> A Punke here pelts him with egs. How so?
> For he did but kisse her, and so let her go.

As David Greer informs me, the tune to this song is to be used for singing a poem printed in J. Starter's *Boertigheden* or *Friesche Lusthof* (1621), sig. B1v. The poem is headed, "*Stemme:* My Mistris sings no other song, &c." and begins "Ick weet niet wat myn Vryster schort."

XX.

12 *die . . . glorie. Cf.* Semele (Ovid, *Metamorphoses*, III, 259–315).

Thomas Morley, *The First Booke of Ayres*, 1600

Dedication
Ralph Bosville of Bradbourne, Kent, a militia officer, was knighted by James at Whitehall, July 23, 1603 (Nichols, *Progresses of James I*, I, 209). He later shared the dedication of William Barriffe's *Military Discipline* (1635), STC 1506. (Williams.)

5 *vncouth . . . Chaucer.* Proverbial: Tilley U14; but see *Troilus & Creseyde*, I, 809: "Unknowe, unkist, and lost, that is unsought" (*Works*, ed. F. N. Robinson [Boston: Houghton Mifflin, 2nd ed., 1957], p. 398).

12 *vacation time.* As Ernest Brennecke, Jr., has shown, this vacation lasted from June 29 to September 29. (Shakespeare's Musical Collaboration with Morley," *PMLA*, LIV [1939], 143.) Morley was a member of the Chapel Royal, whose vacation was from St. Peter's day to Michaelmas, according to E. F. Rimbault, *The Old Cheque Book of the Chapel Royal* (London: Camden Society, 1872), pp. 73, 123. Of course Morley could have meant the vacation of 1599 as well as that of 1600.

To the Reader
4 *no professor thereof.* Morley wrote mainly vocal music, and his instrument was the organ. His lute accompaniments are frequently difficult to play.

18 *Scientia . . . ignorantem.* Tilley S142.

I.

2 *profest.* EMV, p. 623, emends to *profess.*

5 *might.* Fellowes (ELS, series I, XVI, 4) and EMV emend the original *night* to *right*, but *might* is more probable; if the source of the error is in foul case or a misreading of the MS, *n* for *m* is more likely than *n* for *r*.

II.–III.

These two parts make up a single poem, which is related to another poem found in several MSS: (D) BM MS Add. 29481 (*c.* 1630), fol. 23, with music for treble and bass (not Morley's); (E) BM MS Add. 10309 (*c.* 1625), fol. 59v; (F) New York Public Library Drexel MS 4175 (*c.* 1620), fol. 2v, also with music for treble and bass (not Morley's); and (G) Folger MS V.a.345, p. 92. F was printed by J. P. Cutts, *Seventeenth Century Songs and Lyrics* (Columbia, Mo.: University of Missouri Press, 1959), p. 226. I give the D version, despite its errors:

> Milla the glorie of whose bewties raise
> gaind heavn her wonder and the earthes best praise
> whom thirsis met was faire and loulie to
> he likt her well but knew not how to wooe
>
> Thay arme in arme into the garden walked
> wheare all the daye thaie endles riddles talked
> her speech, & actions wiselie had an end
> yet wist he not wherto she did intend
>
> Shee greeud to see his youthe no better taught
> to gather him a posie he her besought
> with that her light greene goune she then vp tucked
> & may for time & him for her shee plucked
>
> Which when shee brought he took her by the middle
> he kist her oft but could not reade her riddle
> Ah foole quoth shee with that burst forth in laughter
> blusht rann a waie & scornd him euer after

If it were not for the relative stability of the rhyme words and similarity of phrasing, one might think that the poems were two different translations of a foreign original.

III. 3, 5. *May . . . Time . . . riddle.* May is hawthorn and Time is thyme; the riddle seems to be in the language of flowers which may be interpreted with the help of "A Nosegaie" from *A Handful of Pleasant Delights* (1584), ed. Hyder E. Rollins (Cambridge, Mass.: Harvard University Press, 1924), sig. A3:

> *Time* is to trie me,
>   as ech be tried must,
> [Le]tting you know while life doth last,
>   I wil not be vniust.

(*Cf.* Tilley T336.) See also *The Paradise of Dainty Devices* (1576–1606), ed. Hyder E. Rollins (Cambridge, Mass.: Harvard University Press, 1927), p. 9: "Take *May* in time, when *May* is gone, the pleasant time is past." And on p. 61: "The Hauthorne so is had in prise"; *cf.* p. 101: "May is much of price," *i.e.*, is much esteemed.

IIII.

This poem consists of stanzas 5, 4, and 3 (in that order) of Robert Southwell's "Marie Magdalens complaynt at Christes death." This identification was made by

Louis L. Martz in *The Poetry of Meditation* (New Haven: Yale University Press, 2nd ed., 1962), p. 192, and independently by the present editor in *LSJ*, IV (1962), 28–30. Morley's selection and rearrangement results in a secularization of what was originally a religious parody on the secular theme of the lost lover. Southwell's poem, which begins "Sith my life from life is parted" and continues for seven stanzas, is printed from the first edition of *Saint Peters Complaint, With other Poemes* (1595) in James H. McDonald and Nancy P. Brown's edition of the *Poems* (Oxford, 1967), pp. 45–46, with variants from the second edition (also 1595) and from the following MSS: Stonyhurst College Library MS A.v.27; Virtue and Cahill Library, Portsmouth, MS 8635; BM MS Add. 10422; BM MS Harl. 6921; and MS corrections made in the Folger copy of the first edition of *Saint Peters Complaint.* Excluding the omitted stanzas, Morley's text varies from that in McDonald and Brown as follows:

2 some] sonne (*four MSS read* somme)
3 was] is
8 vanities] vanitie
10 slaues] salves
13 loue] life
    since] sith (*thus MSS; 1st ed. reads* since)
17 and] or
    with] to

Miss Brown (p. xcvii) quotes a passage from a sermon by Southwell on Mary Magdalen which parallels the poem at several points:

> She had lost her master whome she so singulerlye loved that besyde him she could love nothynge she could hope nothynge She had lost the lyfe of her soule and now she thought it better to dye then to lyve for peradventure she myght fynd dyynge whome she could not fynd lyvynge and without whome lyve she could not. (Stonyhurst College MS A.v.4, fol. 56v.)

Versions of the poem which derive from Morley's are found in (D) Christ Church, Oxford, MS 439 (*c.* 1620), p. 37, with Morley's melody and bass; (E) Bod. MS Don. d. 58 (*c.* 1647), fol. 23, headed "Cant 8"; (F) BM MS Add. 27879 (Bishop Percy's folio, late 17th century), fol. 144, entitled, "I liue where: I loue"; (G) John Forbes's *Cantus, Songs and Fancies* (1662), sig. T1v, with Morley's tune; (H) Trinity College, Dublin, MS F.5.13, p. 37 (according to Vincent Duckles, "Florid Embellishment in English Song," *Annales Musicologiques*, V [1957], 343–344); and (I) Edinburgh University MS La. III.-483, p. 188 (according to Rubsamen, p. 276). H and I are the quintus and bassus of the Wode partbooks. Variants from DEFG are:

1 loue] hart F
    nestled] nested G
2 In] into F
    some] seeme E, Sun G
4 To] into F
5 let] lett my F
6 Sith . . . loue] since I loue not where I wold F
7–18 *omitted in* F, *and replaced by five new stanzas.* (See *Bishop Percy's Folio Manuscript*, ed. J. W. Hales and F. J. Furnivall [London: N. Trübner, 1868], II, 325–326.)

   9 that] yet D, which E
  10 Signes not] sinnes or D
     miseries] miserie D
  15 thee] mee D
  18 thou in] you with G

Note the attempts in D to correct the corruption of *salues* in line 10. The 1666 ed. of G. reads "Are but slaves."

   Morley's tune may have served later as a ballad tune. Simpson prints the tune from Forbes's *Cantus*, and discusses the ballads related to it on pp. 336–339, but does not identify the tune as Morley's. The tune was also used with verses beginning "My sweet love is fair to see" in the Taitt MS at U.C.L.A., No. 20 (according to Rubsamen, p. 276). A moralized version of this text is also in the Taitt MS and is printed from Edinburgh University MS La. III. 490, pp. 48–49, by John P. Cutts in *Seventeenth Century Songs and Lyrics* (Columbia: University of Missouri Press, 1959), pp. 236–237. See David Greer, "The Lute Songs of Thomas Morley," *LSJ*, VIII (1966), 36.

V.

   See D01600.I and notes. Dowland's text seems superior.
   5 *mennes.* EMV, p. 624, emends to *more.*

VI.

   These words are also found in Shakespeare's *As You Like It* (V.iii.17–34). The play was entered "to be staied" in the Stationers' Register on August 4, 1600 (Arber, III, 37), and was not printed until the 1623 Folio. The variants from the Folio (sig. S1) are as follows:

   2 with a hoe] and a ho
   3 fields] feild
   4 in] In the
     ring] rang
   6 F *has lines 19–22 after this line*
   9 fooles] folks
   10–12, 16–18 In . . . the spring] In spring time, &c.
   19 Then . . . time] And therefore take the present time
   22–24 In . . . the spring] In spring time, &c.

One other copy of the song exists in NLS, Advocates' MS 5.2.14 (*c.* 1640), fol. 18 and 18v, with Morley's tune. It was probably copied from the printed text, for it has only these variants:

   3 fields] field
   9 would] did
   15 but] bot

   The exact relationship of this song to Shakespeare's play has been the subject of much discussion. One can say at the outset that none of the available evidence warrants conclusions of any certainty, but it is probable that the words are Shakespeare's and that Morley's music was sung in the play. The mere existence of the music and the presence of the words in the Folio demand that this possibility be considered first. Yet there is no need to go so far in speculations about collaboration between Morley and Shakespeare as Ernest Brennecke (*PMLA*, LIV [1939], 139–149). On the other hand, E. H. Fellowes' disintegrationist position is made plausible because of the late printing of the play and the lack of connection between the play and the scene in which the song appears (ELS, series I, XVI, p. iii; see also "A Reply and Symposium" following Brennecke's article, pp. 149–152).

Arguing against interpolation, Brennecke and others have pointed out that the source of *As You Like It*, Lodge's *Rosalynde*, contains a similar song which might have suggested "It was a lover." Nevertheless, the similarity of Lodge's "A Blithe and bonny Country-Lasse" to "It was a lover" is not so significant as its relationship to "It fell vpon a holly eue" from the August eclogue of Spenser's *Shepheard's Calendar*, and "Fie on the sleights that men deuise" from *England's Helicon* (REH, I, 165–166), for all three are modelled on the "Hey ho holiday" roundelay (see Pattison, p. 174).

Brennecke and Fellowes both try to support their positions by citing the difference between the Folio ordering of the stanzas of "It was a lover" and Morley's text, but to little purpose. A possible explanation of the order in the Folio may be that stage experience showed that the song needed to be shortened, and that the first and last stanzas could make an acceptable unit. Then someone may have made a note or drawn an arrow in the prompt copy to remind the performers to sing the last stanza after the first, and the typesetter simply followed the direction meant for the singers.

One final possibility to be considered in the relationship between Shakespeare's words and Morley's music is that a different setting was used in the play, and that Morley heard it and made his own setting. Morley may have picked up the words to "I saw my Ladie weeping" (V) from Dowland's version (1600.I), and perhaps "White as Lillies" (XV) as well (*cf.* Do1600.XV), so using words from another man's song would not have been unusual for him. Yet Morley's text of "It was a lover" is good, while that of "I saw my Ladie weeping" is incomplete and corrupt.

For a recent survey of other commentary on the Morley-Shakespeare relationship, see Seng, pp. 87–90, 97–100.

15 *life . . . a flower.* Tilley B165.
19 *take the time.* Tilley T312.

VII.

This is the "Eleventh Song" from Sir Philip Sidney's *Astrophil and Stella*. The first two lines of each stanza are understood to be spoken by Stella, the last three by Astrophil. Morley's text is probably derived from that printed in *The Countesse of Pembrokes Arcadia . . . with sundry new additions* (1598); see Ringler's edition, p. 566. Ringler gives the text and the variants from other substantive texts on pp. 233–235, and lists the derivative texts on p. 447; he notes (p. 490) that Morley conjecturally corrected three of the obvious errors in the 1598 *Arcadia* (line 23: they] thy; 40; there] thee; 43: vniustest] vniust). Variants from Ringler's text are as follows:

2 Vnder] Underneath
3 that] who
7 those fond] yet those
26 the] your
42 Argues] Argus
44 leaue] leaue you

(Sidney's reading in line 44 is adopted in the present text.)

16 *time . . . remoue. Cf.* Tilley T340.

18 *Time . . . proue.* Ringler (p. 490), explains: "Things change in time in accordance with their own natures."

33 *doe.* EMV, p. 626, reads *doth.*

33–35 Ringler (p. 490) notes the recurrence of this image in *The New Arcadia* (i.115).

42 *Argues. I.e., Argus',* as in Sidney and EMV.

VIII.

This song, with the melody and bass of Morley's music, is found in (D) BM MS Add. 24665 (*c.* 1615–1626), fols. 43v–44; the words alone are in (E) Bod. MS Don. d. 58 (*c.* 1647), fol. 25v (headed "Cant 14"). The tune and first few words are found in BM MS Add. 33933 (altus of the Wode partbooks), fol. 84, and a keyboard version of the tune is in Paris Conservatory MS Rés. 1186, fol. 54. See Greer's article cited in the note to IV above. Variants from DE are:

3 speede] guide E

4 you . . . loue] in loue you may E

5 clip and] clipp me E

8 That] which D
　life] light D
　loues] coole E

10 affection] affections DE

11–12 Coll . . . do] Coll me D, coll me and clip &c. E

17–18 Coll . . . do] Coll &c. D, coll me and clip &c. E

19 no noyes] an oyes D

20 Tis] It's D

22 pray] prithee D

23–24 Coll . . . do] Coll &c. D

The first line of the refrain is sung by Philautus in *Euerie Woman in her Humor* (1609), sigs. D3v–D4, as "Coll her and clip her & kisse her too, &c." There is, however, another poem with this same refrain and the same meter, perhaps written to the same tune, in Bod. MS Add. B. 97 (after 1609), fol. 17v, headed "A songe":

1 Kisse me sweete now we are heere,
　All is hush't, nay neuer feare,
　The whole House doth soundlie sleepe,
　Come lett vs our Loues- watch Keepe.
　　Come cole me & clipp me & Kisse me to
　　So, so, so should Louers doe.

2 Twentie dayes are past & gonn
　Since our two Harts were made one
　Twentie pleasaunt Nights are spente
　Since my Loue did giue consente.
　　To cole me &c.

3 Blessed be that happie Tyme
　Which did first our Harts combine,
　Maye this night be ended neuer
　That thus ioynes our Lipps togeather,
　　O cole me &c.

5 Out, alas the daye appeeres,
  And my voyce my mother heeres,
  Soone when Night shall showe her face
  Sweete, then meete me in this place
  And cole me &c.

4 [*sic*] Last longe Night & bannish Daye,
  Which will all our Ioyes betraye,
  When Night comes, Come Turtle trewe
  That we maye our Loves renewe.
  Then will I cole the &c.

The following variants are given in the margin, in the same hand:

1 now] since
2 nay neuer] you neede not
6 So, so, so should] So should wanton
8 two Harts were made] our hartes were both
23 betraye] bewraye
25 Loves] sports

10 *our*. EMV, p. 755, claims the original has *out*, but it actually reads *our*.

IX.

The punctuation of many lines in this poem serves to indicate the metrical pause in the fourteener line rather than normal phrasing; I retain the original, but note that no comma is needed after *force* (line 1), *see* (line 8), and in line 12, it should come before *loue*.

12 *full of harbour*. The *of* should no doubt be *a* or *an*, as Fellowes notes (ELS, series I, XVI, iii). EMV, p. 627, reads *a*.

13 *foole*. Probably this should be understood as *foul*, the usual combination with *faire*. The northern pronunciation of *foul* sounds like *fool* (Kökeritz, p. 247).

X.

Also in Jo1601.I with a better text (line 6: *flight* for *light*).

The main conceit is of course taken from the story of Icarus (Ovid, *Metamorphoses*, VIII, 183–235).

2 *to hie*. Read *too high*.

XI.

18 *or chaunge my mistress longs*. EMV, p. 628, makes *mistress* possessive, making *longs*, I suppose, mean "long notes." But the relation to the next stanza would be clearer if *or* were emended to *for*, and the line understood thus: "I'll sing this song: 'My mistress longs for change.'"

XII.

Another copy of this poem is found in Cambridge MS Dd.v.75, fol. 26 (a poem on fol. 20 is dated 1612). It has the following variants:

4 liue in quiet] lie at little
7 were] is
10 May see (in Sunne)] do shew in somme
16 And . . . gall] a dish for death to make an end withall

Fellowes (ELS, series I, XVI, iii) compares this poem to Nicholas Breton's "An Epitaph on the death of a noble Gentleman" (RAAD, p. 45), but only the first line is similar: "Sorrow come sit thee downe, and sigh and sob thy fill." See also a song in New York Public Library Drexel MS 4175, fol. 13, which begins, "Come sorrowe sitt downe by this tree."

The signs of melancholy described here should be compared to those compiled by Lawrence Babb, *The Elizabethan Malady* (East Lansing: Michigan State College Press, 1951), pp. 135–136.

10 *in Sunne.* The MS reading *in somme* (in sum) is probably right. Fellowes reads "in sum" in ELS, p. 54.

11 *not a word but mumme.* Tilley W767.

XIII.

This poem is attributed to Nicholas Breton in *England's Helicon* (1600); see REH, I, 53–55. ("*N. Breton*" is on a cancel-slip covering "*S. Phil. Sidney.*") As Rollins notes (II, 110), the attribution to Breton is also made by Francis Davison (BM MS Harleian 280, fol. 99v), and by the compiler of Bod. MS Rawlinson Poet. 85, fols. 1v–2. *Cf.* D01603.XII.

Morley's version of the poem differs so radically from all the others that ordinary collation is impractical. The reader should consult *England's Helicon* and Rollins' lists of variants from the sources described below (REH, II, 110–114). Briefly, Morley's version transposes lines 3–4 with lines 5–6, omits the seventh and eighth lines of the *England's Helicon* text, and alters the eleventh and twelfth beyond recognition. Morley, like the transcribers of versions E and H listed below, omits the second part of the poem (REH, I, 54–55, lines 16ff.). There are many smaller variations.

Other copies of the poem, all closer to *England's Helicon* than to Morley, are: (D) Bod. MS Rawlinson Poet. 85 (late 16th century), fols. 1v–2, signed "Britton" (divided into two poems, the first ending where Morley's does); (E) BM MS Harleian 6910 (c. 1596), fol. 140 (18 lines); (F) BM MS Add. 34064 (c. 1596), fol. 17v, among other poems by Breton (18 lines, with a space before continuing the rest of the poem); (G) John Cotgrave, *Wits Interpreter* (1655), sig. H1–1v (no break in the poem); (H) Folger MS V.a.339 (formerly 2071.7; Joseph Hall's MS; mid-17th century), fol. 183v. Since Rollins does not collate this version, it is given here:

> Faire in a mornine oh fariest morne, was never morne so faire
> there shone a sunne yet not the sunne that shineth in the aire
> for of the earth & from the earth, yet not an earthly creature
> did come this face oh never face that caried such a feature
> now on a hill, oh blessed hill was never hill so blessed
> there stoode a man was never man, for on man more distressed.
> This man [had] happ oh happy man, more happy none then hee
> for none had hap to see the happ that he had hap to see
> this silly swaine, & silly swaines, are men of meanest grace
> had yet the grace oh gracious happ to hap on such a face
> he pitty cried & pitty came & pittied so his paine
> as dyinge would not let him die but gaue him life againe
> For Ioy whereof he made such myrth, as all the woods did ringe
> & Pan with all his swaines came foorth to heere the shepheard singe
> but such a songe sunge never was, nor will be sung againe
> of Phillida the shepheards queene & Corydon the Swaine.

Another version is found in a MS compiled by Thomas Smith, later bishop of Carlisle, and dated 1637. This MS was described by its former owner, James W. Brown, in *The Cornhill Magazine*, LI (1921), 285–296; although Brown wrote that he intended to give the MS to the Bodleian, the two part-books are now in the library at Carlisle Cathedral. The first stanza of the song, with Morley's treble and bass, is on p. 90 of the Bassus part-book, and varies thus: 1 euer] neuer; 2 same . . . shined] sun . . . shineth.

Fellowes (ELS, series I, XVI, 59), EMV, p. 629, and Noah Greenberg, *et al.*, *An Elizabethan Song Book* (Garden City: Doubleday Anchor, 1955), pp. xx–xxii and 210, exchange lines 3–4 with 5–6; Greenberg omits *And* in line 9, and Fellowes and EMV make these further changes:

2 shined] shineth
6 stoode] shone
9 he behold] he beheld
14 for] with

XIIII.

Since the rest of this poem after the first stanza would probably have been printed on E1 (which is missing from the unique copy), it is here completed from the next earliest version, that of *A Poetical Rhapsody* (1602), where it is entitled "Ode" (RPR, I, 225). The only variant in the first stanza is *thou canst* for *you dare* in line 4.

This poem was attributed to John Donne in *The Grove* (1721), pp. 37–39, but H. J. C. Grierson thinks that it is probably by John Hoskins. Louise Brown Osborne agrees; see *The Life, Letters, & Writings of John Hoskyns* (New Haven: Yale Studies in English, No. 87, 1937), p. 285. Grierson bases his ascription on a copy initialed "J. H." transcribed by William Drummond (Edinburgh, Society of Antiquaries, Hawthornden MS XV, fols. 65–66) from a collection of poems "belonging to John Don." Another poem in the MS initialed J. H. is elsewhere ascribed to Hoskins (Grierson, II, cl–clii). The poem is not mentioned in Helen Gardner's edition of *The Elegies and the Songs and Sonnets* (Oxford: Clarendon Press, 1965). Grierson prints the poem (I, 428) from BM MS Stowe 961, fol. 80v, and gives variants from the Hawthornden MS; BM MS Lansdown 740, fol. 107; the Ellesmere MS (now Huntington MS EL 6893); the Phillips MS (now Bod. MS Eng. Poet. f. 9, p. 43); Harvard MS Eng. 966.5 (the O'Flaherty MS), p. 309; Harvard MS Eng. 966.1 (the Carnaby MS), pp. 65–66, signed "J. D."; Harvard MS Eng. 966.6 (the Stevens MS), p. 236; *Wit Restor'd* (1658), sigs. H6v–H7 (whose reading of l. 7, "Who loves but where the Graces be," he omits); *The Grove*; and *A Poetical Rhapsody*. Grierson had not seen (D) Rosenbach MS 243/4 (formerly the Wischart MS; after 1662), p. 44, signed "John Donne"; and (E) Huntington MS HM 198, Part II (mid-17th century), fol. 34–34v. Variants from DE are:

4 you dare] thou canst D, thou darest E
7 Who loues a Mistris] Whose Mistress is D
  such] such a D
8 Hee soone] His minde DE
10 all] his D
13 motions] motion D
16 in] by D
  her] theire D, the E

notions] notion DE
17 that] which E
18 hiding] hoarding E
22 my] my silent D
23 kisse] there kisse D
24 I both enioy and] enioy her and so DE

XV.

"White as Lillies," the song listed in the Table but lacking in the Folger copy, probably had the same words as Do1600.XV.

XVI.

Lacking in Folger. Probably a peddler's song like XVII.

XVII.–XVIII.

From Christ Church, Oxford, MS 439 (*c.* 1620), pp. 80–81 and 1–2. The MS has music for melody and bass (apparently Morley's) which has been printed with conjectured inner voices by Thurston Dart in ELS, series I, XVI, 66–70.

In XVII, the peddler's wares suggest some indecent double meanings; see the Glossary and *cf.* Autolycus and his "dildos and fadings" (*Winter's Tale*, IV, iv). For other peddlers' songs, see Do1600.XII and note.

In XVIII, the figure anadiplosis links the stanzas and lines (*e.g.* 1–2, 13–14) by repeated words. Puttenham calls it the "Redouble" (p. 200). Sidney uses it frequently; see Ringler, pp. 39, 82, 165. See also the third "Gulling Sonnet" of Sir John Davies (*Poems*, ed. Clare Howard [New York: Columbia University Press, 1941], pp. 224–225).

15 *baine.* This should no doubt read *barre*, as in EMV, p. 631, to rhyme with *starres* (1. 13); *cf.* ELS, series I, XVI, 69.

Robert Jones, *The Second Booke of Songs and Ayres,* 1601

Dedication

Sir Henry Leonard. Sir Henry Lennard or Leonard, twelfth Baron Dacre (1570–1616), was knighted by Essex after Cadiz (1596). (G. E. Cockayne, *Complete Peerage*, s.v. Dacre.) The second *Musica Transalpina* (1597) compiled by Nicholas Yonge was also dedicated to him. (Williams.)

31 *Eagles . . . flyes. Cf.* Tilley E1.

To the Reader

28 *of this fashion. I.e.*, with both mensural and tablature bass.

I.

Cf. the version in Mo1600.X and note. Jones corrects Morley's text in line 8.

II.

This poem may be the work of Thomas Campion. The first stanza was printed in (D) Newman's *Astrophel and Stella* (1591), sig. L3v, among the "Poems and Sonets of sundrie other Noble men and Gentlemen" with other poems by Campion. More significantly, there is a Latin version of this stanza ("In Melleam") in Campion's *Poemata* (1595), sig. E3v:

> Mellea mi si abeam promittit basia septem,
> Basia dat septem, nec minus inde moror.
> Euge licet vafras fugit haec fraus vna puellas,
> Basia maiores ingerere vsque moras.

See also Vivian, pp. 273, 350, 376, and Davis, pp. 9, 424.

Two later copies of the poem are extant in (E) NLS Advocates' MS 5.2.14 (*c.* 1639), fol. 4v, with Jones's tune; and (F) BM MS Add. 29409 (a 19th century transcript of an older Scottish MS), fols. 265v–266. Variants, excluding the Scotticisms of EF, are:

 1 bound] band F
 4 part] passe D
 5 doth not] do no not D (*sic*)
 10 eare] eares F
 19 common] comming F
 20 make] makes EF
 23 would nere] wold never E
 24 the worst] worst F
 27 make] makes E

 11 *kisses were the seales of loue. Cf. Measure for Measure*, IV,i,6.
 20, 27 *make.* EMV, p. 560, emends to *makes.*

IIII.

The treble and bass of Jones's music, with the first stanza of the text, appears in Christ Church, Oxford, MS 439 (*c.* 1620), p. 73; there are no verbal variants.

 12 *stand too. I.e.,* stand to, back up. *Cf.* To the Reader, "I dare not stand to the hazard."

 14 *child that winketh. I.e.,* blind Cupid.

V.

 16 *pish.* As noted in EMV, p. 749, *push,* or *tush,* variants of this exclamation, would rhyme better.
 23–25 *as maidens vse. Cf.* Tilley M34, W660.
 38 *best bloud.* Life's blood, with a secondary sexual meaning; *cf.* Jo1609.V.16.
 53 *Dreams . . . true. Cf.* Tilley D587 and D591.
 53 *thoughts are free.* Tilley T244.

VII.

The dramatic monologue or dialogue of seduction seems to have been a lively sub-genre going back at least to one of the 14th-century Harley lyrics, "My deth I loue, my lif ich hate" (BM MS Harleian 2253, fol. 80v, printed in several modern collections). A particularly idiomatic example is set to music in BM MS Add. 5665, fols. 66v–67, "Be pes, ye make me spille my ale" (*c.* 1510—see John Stevens, *Music and Poetry in the Early Tudor Court* [London: Methuen, 1961], pp. 339–340). *Cf.* also Gr1604, V–VI and Ck1610.V. The tradition continues through the 17th century: see a song from Henry Lawes' MS (BM Loan 35, fol. 7v), "Fye awaye fye what meane you by this" (printed by Cutts in *Seventeenth Century Songs and Lyrics,* p. 119).

The present poem appears in three later MSS: (D) Bod. Douce 280, fol. 68 (copied before 1603?), headed "Mr: Rob: Iones. 2d. booke. For tableture & pricke songe"; (E) BM MS 24665 (*c.* 1615–1626), fol. 40, with the bass of Jones's music and the second stanza only; and (F) Christ Church, Oxford, MS 439 (*c.* 1620), pp. 5–6, with the treble and bass of Jones's music. DF copy most of the repetitions of the words in the musical setting; these repetitions are, as usual, not recorded in the variants, which are:

> 1–9 *omitted in* E
> 1 coile is heere] life is this D
> 2 so] thus F
> 6 so] thus DF
> 8 sweete] Whoe D
>   let] Praye lett D
> 9 or els] Nay then D
>   faith] faith & troth D *in repetition*
>   Ile get me] I will be F
> 10–19 *omitted* D, *but in margin*: Come, &c
> 16 Is] was E
> 17 If . . . flie] to trye if fancie would wyn E
> F *has after* 17: Sweete stand away
> 18 Whoop] See E, Who F
> 19 Naie then] For nowe E
>   doe] You may doe E

D adds this stanza:

> Tush, tush; tush, tush, tush, tush, nowe leaue for shame,
>   My mother comes I pray forbeare.
>   My mother comes I pray forbeare.
> Harke, harke; harke, harke, harke, harke, how shee calls;
>   Harke, harke, harke, how shee calls;
>   Aye me! here's much to doe:
>   Thinke you with kisses, to win loues blisses,
>   O noe, noe, noe, there's more to doe.
> Whoe: quicke dispatch, quicke dispatch, quicke dispatch,
>   I shalbe shent:
>   Now since tis done, now since tis done, ô done,
>   I needes must be content.

4 *nere the neere.* I.e., never the nearer. *Cf.* Do1603.XIII.8.

VIII.

12–15 *Is . . . report.* "Is it not better to love your friend willingly than to owe him love for reporting that you are kind?"

IX.

This poem was first printed in *The Phoenix Nest* (1593), RPN, pp. 98–99; Rollins gives a detailed account on pp. 192–195, with variant readings from Jo1601, *England's Helicon* (1600; see REH, I, 82–83; II, 131–133), and *A Poetical Rhapsody* (2nd ed., 1608; see RPR, I, 291–292; II, 259–260). Jones may have taken his text from *The Phoenix Nest*, but it has several variants (some of which it shares with *A Poetical Rhapsody*).

As Rollins notes (RPN, p. 192), the version in *England's Helicon* was originally signed "S. W. R." (Sir Walter Raleigh), but was covered by a cancel slip reading "Ignoto," the signature printed in the second edition (1614). Francis Davison assigned the poem to Raleigh in BM MS Harleian 280, fol. 99v (See REH, II, 38), but later printed it without ascription in *A Poetical Rhapsody*. The editors of Raleigh, John Hannah (*Poems*, London, 1875, 1892, pp. 78–79) and Agnes Latham (*Poems* [Cambridge: Harvard University Press, 1951], p. 171), are both doubtful of Raleigh's authorship; however, in Miss Latham's first edition of Raleigh (London: Constable, 1929), pp. 191–193, she was more willing to accept the possibility. She also discusses the possible reasons for the cancel slips in *England's Helicon*, and gives variant readings in this 1929 edition.

Other copies of the poem are found in (D) Folger MS V.a.399 (after 1603), fol. 10–10v, headed "Tam arte quam Marte"; (E) BM MS Add. 22601 (*c.* 1604), fols. 104–106 (with 14 extra stanzas); (F) Rosenbach MS 1083/15 (after 1618; described by S. A. Tannenbaum, *PMLA*, XLV [1930], 809–821) pp. 98–100 (with 10 extra stanzas); (G) Thomas Heywood, *The Rape of Lucrece . . . With the severall Songs in their apt places, by* Valerius *the merry Lord . . .* 1638 (first ed., 1608), sigs. C1v–C2. The repetitions (if not the variants) in G suggest that Jones's setting was sung in the play. This version, ascribed to Heywood, was reprinted (according to Rollins) in *Cupids Master-Piece. Or, The Free-School of Witty and Delightful Complements* (*c.* 1650), sig. A6. Rollins also notes that the *Phoenix Nest* version is reprinted with "unimportant changes" in J.O.'s *Venus Looking-Glass or A Rich store-house of choice Drollery* (*c.* 1670), pp. 132–133. Another copy is in (H) *Westminster Drollery* (1672), sig. E1–E1v, largely based on the *England's Helicon* version. It is headed, "The Description of Love, in a Dialogue between two Shepherds, Will and Tom." Finally, a version with Jones's treble and bass and stanzas 1 and 5 is in (I) Christ Church, Oxford, MS 439 (*c.* 1620), p. 35. Variants from D–I are as follows:

    1 Now what is] Shepherd, what's H
      pray thee] will thee G, prethee H
    2 that . . . that] a . . . a EF, the . . . the G
    3 pleasures] pleasure EFGHI
      dwell] dwelles I
    4 that] the G
      sancesing] same sance E, little DF, *and* E *in the margin*
    5 that] which D
      towles] rings DEFG
      all . . . or] to heauen or else to hell D
    6 as] that I
      heare] heard H
    7–28 *omitted* I
    8–13 *stanza 4 in* F, *omitted* G
    8 Now] Yet H
      praie thee] pray thy F, prethee H
    9 on] on a E
    10 match't] mixt D
    11 When] wher D
      blood] Bloods H

12 ten] nine DEF
   their] that F
15–20 *stanza 7 in* E, *stanza 4 in* F
15 thee] be H
   faine] saine E, plain H
16–17 *transposed in* DE
17 gentle pleasing] pleasinge pinchinge E, pleasaunt pinching F, Tooth-ach, or worse H
18–19 A . . . faine] It is a Game, where none doth gain;/ It is a thing turmoils the brain H
20 as I heare] which I doe D
   saine] faine D,F (?)
22–27 *stanza 5 in* DE, *stanza 2 in* F; H *reads*:

> T. Yet Shepherd, what is Love, I pray?
> W. It is a yea, it is a nay,
>   A pretty kind of sporting fray;
>   It is a thing will soon away,
>   For 'twill not long with any stay:
>   And this is Love, as I here say.

22 Yet] Now DF
   praie thee] preythy F
23 pretie] pleasant DEF
24 *after this line,* E *adds*:
> It is an yea it is a nay
> a prety kinde of sportinge play

26 the] youre D
27 And . . . saie] & this is loue &c. D
29–34 *stanza 17 in* E, *omitted* DF
29 Now] Yet H
   I praie thee] I will you G, good Shepherd H
30 A thing] it is a thing I
   it] if it E, and GI
31 prize] toye E, price I
32 one] me GI
33 And . . . so] A kinde of ioye a kinde of woe E
   proues] loues H
34 And . . . know] And Shepherd, this is Love I trow H
   as . . . know] say they that knowe E, sweet friend I tro GI

E has fourteen more stanzas, one of which is in D and eleven in F. With their smack of undergraduate humor, they have every appearance of having been added later. Rollins gives three sample stanzas and says, there is "apparently no reason why the verses should ever have ended" (RPN, p. 194). The new stanzas in E are given here numbered in their original order, with variants from DF.

> [3] Now what is loue I pray thee showe
>   it is a tree of bliss & woe
>   A fruite of all the fruite I knoe

    in shortest time will sonest grow
    It standeth neither high nor lowe   5
    but betwene both as all do knowe

[4] Now what is loue but do not faine
    a coollor tis that soone will staine
    It is a tooth ache or like paine
    a Game it is where none do gaine   10
    The lass saies nay & yet would faine
    and this is loue as I heare saine.

[6] Now what is loue say be not strange
    it is a prety dogg that range
    and like a filthy rotten mange   15
    It is a Coffer of exchange
    Where for dross fair coigne do change
    & this is loue a thinge so strange

[8] Now what is loue I pray thee singe
    it is a finger in a ringe   20
    It is a mopping toothles thinge
    it is a flesh that smells like linge
    It is a morsell for a kinge
    and this is loue as I heare singe.

[9] Now what is loue I pray thee speake   25
    it is a luke warme mutton steake
    It is a thinge that neu'r cries creake
    a thing that maketh stronge things weake
    A thing that maketh most thinges leake
    and this is loue as I heare speake.   30

[10] Now what is loue I pray thee proue
    a thinge beneath & not aboue
    It is a stretchinge cheuerall gloue
    a thinge that holdeth heaue & shoue
    A thinge no thrustinge can remoue   35
    & this is loue as I heare proue.

[11] Now what is loue I pray thee note
    tis lining for a petty cote
    tis armed but for pistoll shote
    it is a semiquauer note   40
    within book fidled & by rote
    and this is loue whereon men dote.

[12] Now what is loue declare I pray
    it is a spiders webb I say
    that weaueth in & out alwaye   45
    to catch the silly fly that playe
    swellinge with feedinge of hir pray
    and this is loue well guess I may

[13] Now what is loue I pray thee thinke
     it is a flowr muche like a pinke   50
     A thinge that stretcheth & will shrinke
     a thing all sweetest still doth stinke
     the sight whereof will make men wink
     & this is loue as I heare thinke

[14] Now what is loue say out of doubt   55
     a thinge holds in a thing holds out
     It is a mark men shoote about
     it is a spill within a clout
     It is a bowle holds rubbers out
     & this is loue I make no doubt.   60

[15] Now what is loue say on say on
     a thinge that can not be alone
     A thinge loues flesh without a bone
     a thinge thats subiect to the stone
     A thing past .40. waxing rone   65
     & this is loue or loue ther's none.

[16] Now what is loue say yet once more
     an open throte that neu'r doth gore
     A thinge no rubbing can make sore
     a nicking tally for to score   70
     An easy timber for to bore
     and this is loue I say no more

[18] Now what is loue say I intreate
     a thinge that neuer fish doth eate
     A thinge that maketh most men sweate   75
     a thinge that sucketh of the teate
     A thinge by suckinge waxeth greate
     & this is loue whereof we treate.

[19] Now to conclude say what loue is
     a thinge of woe a thinge of bliss   80
     a thinge wonn & lost with a kiss
     a firy watry thinge is this
     A thinge that burnes & neu'r cries hiss
     and this is loue or els I miss.

Stanza 3 in EF is stanza 5 in D. Order of stanzas in EF:

E	F
4,6	omitted
8	6
9	7
10	8
11	10
12	omitted
13	13

14	11
15	9
16	14
18	12
19	15

Variants from E in DF:

1 pray thee] prithy F
2 it] loue D
  blisse] weale D
  it . . . woe] a tree of blisse a tree of woe F
3 A] whose D
4 will sonest] doth honest D
6 D *adds* & this is loue &c.
28–29 *transposed in* F
28 a . . . maketh] it is a thing makes F
29 A . . . most] it is a thing make all F
36 I heare] you may F
39 armed] armour F
41 within book] which is both F
51 will] does F
52–53 *transposed in* F
52 all] which (?) F
54 heare] do F
58 spill] spell F
60 this] that F
62,64 *transposed in* F
65 40 . . . rone] sorely grone F
66 or loue] or else F
68 gore] roar F
70 nicking] nickt (?) F
74 fish] flesh F
78 loue . . . treate] the loue that you intreat F
79 Now] Yet F

Lines from the poem were later incorporated into this dialogue from John Gough's *Academy of Complements* (1663 ed.), sigs. G7v–G8, headed "Love-Queries":

> *Bel.* When will love be void of fears?
> *Tel.* When jealousie hath never eyes nor ears?
> *Bel.* When is love most male-content?
> *Tel.* When lovers range and bear their brows unbent.
> *Bel.* Tel me when love is best fed?
> *Tel.* When it hath suck'd the sweet that ease hath bred
> *Bel.* When is loves time ill spent?
> *Tel.* When love doth farm and take no rent.
> *Bel.* When is time well spent in Love?
> *Tel.* When deeds insue, and words work Love.
> *Bel.* What calls't thou Love, I prethee tell

> *Tel.* It is a fountain, and that well
> > Where pleasure and repentance dwell;
> > It is a work on Holy-day,
> > It is *December* match'd with *May*.
> B.   I prethee fair one do not fain.
> T.   It is a Sun-shine mixt with rain;
> > It is a Tooth-ache, or like gaine:
> > It is a yea, it is a nay,
> > A pretty kind of sporting fray.
> B.   Come, come, Ile hear no more, away.

Rollins (RPN, p. 195) lists some analogous definitions of love, to which might be added a poem in Folger MS V.a.162, fol. 50, beginning, "Loue is a freind, a fire, a heauen, a hell,/ Where pleasures, payne, greife, & repentance dwell"; "Aske what loue is? it is a passion," from *A Gorgeous Gallery of Gallant Inventions*, ed. H. E. Rollins (Cambridge, Mass., 1926), pp. 58–59; "Loue what art thou? A vaine thought," from Lady Mary Wroth's *The Countesse of Mountgomeries Urania* (1621), sig. T4v; Cav1598. VI; Jo1601.X and XVII; Jo1605.III; Bt1606.XIIII; Fd1607.II; and Jo1610.I. See also C. R. Baskervill, "Bassanio as an Ideal Lover," in *Manly Anniversary Studies* (Chicago: University of Chicago Press, 1923), pp. 90–103 (esp. p. 95, n. 4).

4 *sancesing bell*. Sanctus bell, loosely used as name for bell announcing church services.

19 *a noe that would full faine*. Cf. Tilley W660.

30 *A thing . . . goe*. Cf. Tilley K49.

XI.

This poem was taken from Sir Philip Sidney's *Arcadia*, Book II, Chapter 17, probably, as Ringler states (p. 567), from one of the editions printed between 1590 and 1599. Variants from Ringler's text (pp. 41–42) are as follows:

> 2   her] their
> 9   breathes] breathe
> 17 sand] sandes
>   tales] paynes
> 18 waters] writer
> 19 streames] streame

Jones's readings in 9 and 17 are shared by other substantive texts (*e.g.*, 1590, 1593, 1598); those in 2 and 18 are apparently Jones's corruptions. Bond unaccountably considers it possible that John Lyly wrote the poem (III, 498).

19–20 Besides summarizing the poem in correlative fashion, these lines emphasize the use of the four elements in the organization of the poem. Cf. Ck1612.IX and Do1597.VII.

XII.

1 *Whither . . . hart*. Cf. Bt1606.XVII.1.

4–5 *haste maketh waste*. Tilley H189.

6 *be gone*. As Fellowes notes (EMV, 2nd ed., p. 623), the rhyme demands *depart*, which in some script might look like *be gone*.

9 *truth.* This should probably be *troth,* since the corresponding lines in the other stanzas have internal rhymes here.

12 *I by thee.* EMV, p. 567, emends this to *I am by thee.*

XIII.

3–5 *proue . . . strike.* The use of these words suggests that double meanings were intended. See Eric Partridge, *Shakespeare's Bawdy* (1948; New York: E. P. Dutton, 1960), where *strike* is defined as "To copulate with."

13 *at best is bad.* EMV, p. 750, suggests *is bad at best* for the sake of the internal rhyme.

XIIII.

14 *fayre.* As noted in EMV, p. 750, the sense and the rhyme demand *true.*

XVII.

Cf. No. IX and note.

There are several later copies of this poem: (D) Folger MS V.a.103 (*c.* 1630–1650), fol. 29, headed "On Love itt selfe"; (E) a MS belonging to Mr. James M. Osborn, MS B.12.5 (housed at Yale; after 1633), fol. 23, one stanza headed "on loue"; (F) BM MS Add. 30012, fol. 143 (a single sheet in a miscellany collection, in what seems to be a 17th century hand; the first three lines of the last stanza are written over in a later hand); (G) Henry Bold, *Latine Songs With their English* (1685), p. 42, with a Latin version of the words; (H) a setting by John Wolfgang Franck, *Remedium Melancholiae* (1690), sig. D1 (error corrected on A1v); and (I) Thomas D'Urfey, *Wit and Mirth: or Pills to Purge Melancholy,* V (1714), p. 104, and VI (1720), pp. 238–239 (sigs. L11v–12), the last headed "A Song. *Set by Mr.* Leveridge." I is also followed by the Latin version of G. The variants are:

1 bable] Bauble FGHI
3 tis this] it is this FGHI
  tis that] that DF
4 tis] It's F, An GHI
  full of] idle GHI
  passions] Passion FGHI
5 of] & E
  sundry] severall DE, such a GHI
  fashions] Fashion FGHI
6 tis like] It's like F, Or itt 'tis D, or it is E
7–27 *omitted* DE
8 Loues] Tis F, *omitted* GHI
  i'th] in the FGHI
9 Foule] Tis fowle F
10 Tis eyther] Always GHI
11 And arrand] *canceled in* F, *then:* A very
  arrand] errant GHI
  lyar] wonder F
12 Fed by desire] Tis here & tis yonder F
13 yet] *omitted* H
16 clad] Cloath'd F
  oft] all GHI

20 No] As noe F
   which waie] where him GHI
   23 That's . . . yonder] Tis here and tis yonder FGI,
'tis here, 'tis yonder H
   24 As] Tis FGHI
      one . . . moe] all men, we know GHI
      as to] and to F
   25 A monstrous] An arrant F, A·very GHI
   26 Euerie mans debter] It's every mans better F,
Ev'ry ones better GI, ev'ry one's beater H
   27 Hang . . . so] Then hang him, and GHI

The Latin version from G reads:

I.

Amor est Pegma;
Merum Aenigma,
Quid sit nemo detegat:
Vejana Passio,
Cui nulla ratio,
Parem natura negat.

II.

Cunis, formosus;
Sella Coenosus,
Calor, aut frigiditas;
Furens Libido,
Dicta Cupido,
Est, & non est entitas.

III.

Amor amasius,
Totus silaceus,
Est Eruca animi;
Deditus malis
Ac praedo, qualis,
Non inventus ullibi.

IV.

Hic & ubique
Compar utrique
Ad stuporem agitat:
Nullus deterior,
Ouovis superior,
In malam rem abeat.

8–9 *fayre . . . sadle*. Tilley C792. The original reading *sable* is probably a foul-case error.

16 *clad oft in yellowe*. Yellow could be symbolic of treachery or jealousy. Marie Linthicum, in explaining Malvolio's yellow stockings in *Twelfth Night*, quotes an "old rhyme":

For he that's jealous of his wife's being bad
Must have his legs in yellow stockings clad.

See *Costume in the Drama of Shakespeare and his Contemporaries* (Oxford, 1936), pp. 47–49.

XVIII.

A copy of this song, with Jones's treble and bass, is in Christ Church, Oxford, MS 439 (c. 1620), p. 100. The text lacks all after *last* in line 4, but there are no variants in the lines that are present.

11 *melte.* I adopt the emendation in EMV, p. 570. The original *meete* was no doubt a misreading of the manuscript *l.*

12, 16 *Mayes.* Two syllables.

XIX.

10 *Two.* Perhaps this should read *To.*

XXI.

7–8 *mirth . . . durance. Cf.* Tilley J90.

15–16 *griefes . . . mournings. Cf.* Tilley P408, 410, 411.

John Dowland, *The Third and Last Booke of Songs or Aires,* 1603

Dedication

John Souch (Zouche or Zowche) of Derbyshire was knighted by James I at Belvoir Castle on April 23, 1603 (see W. A. Shaw, *The Knights of England,* 1906, II, 103). A piece in Dowland's *Lachrimae* (1604, No. 13) is called "Sir Iohn Souch his Galiard."

The Epistle

6–7 *bees . . . drones. Cf.* Do1603.XVIII.

I.

Bond (III, 485), ascribes this poem to Lyly without evidence. But see the note to line 2 following.

2 *discretion . . . swords.* Bond compares Lyly's *Sapho and Phao* (1584), II.iv.110 (Bond, II, 391), "fire to be quenched with dust, not with swordes." See also *Euphues and his England* (1580), "But why goe I about to quench fire with a sword, or with affection to mortifie my loue?" (Bond, II, 90); and *Midas* (1592), V.iii.18, "thou wouldst quench fire with a sword" (Bond, III, 158). But *cf.* Tilley F250.

II.

Thomas Oliphant notes in his *La Musa Madrigalesca* (1837), p. 169, that "These lines must surely have been addressed to Queen Elizabeth. The flattery is too gross for any body but her to have swallowed."

3 *All . . . same. Cf.* Do1603.VII.18–19.

III.

This song was reprinted in Forbes's *Cantus* (1662), sig. T2, without variants.

It is possible that this song may have been part of "A deuice made by the Earle of Essex for the entertainment of the Queene" (Public Records Office, S. P. 12/254, No. 67). This "device" presents before the Queen a blind Indian prince, whose guide explains that he has come on the advice of an oracle to have the Queen cure his blindness. Apparently his blindfold is removed—perhaps to the accompaniment of the song, though there is no such indication in the text—and the prince is revealed to be Cupid, "a prince indeed but of greater territories then all the Indies." The guide apologises for the stratagem and urges the Queen to admit love into her court, for "now that loue hath gotten possesyon of his sight, there can be no error in pollicie or dignitie to receiue him." There is some doubt as to the authorship because of the uncertain relationship of this device to another royal entertainment staged by Essex but known to have been written by Francis Bacon. See James Spedding's *The Letters and the Life*, I (1861), 374–392, and the note to Do1597.V.

V.

9 *the siluer Swanne.* Compare Do1597.XIIII.6 and note, and Orlando Gibbons, *The First Set of Madrigals and Mottets* (1612), No. 1, "The silver swan." The theme is commonplace, especially in musical texts; Arcadelt's "Il bianc'e dolce Cigno," from his *Primo Libro de Madrigali* (1541), No. 1, was particularly popular. See Obertello, pp. 468–469, Tilley S1028, and Sir Thomas Wyatt's "Lyke as the Swanne towardis her dethe," which Miss Agnes Foxwell (*Poems* [London, 1913], II, 219) says is based on a poem by Marcello Filosseno beginning "I voirei ben cantar come fa el cygno."

VI.

This poem was printed in *Poems, Written by the Right Honorable William Earl of Pembroke . . .* [and] *Sir Benjamin Ruddier* (1660), sig. I2. The preface "To the Reader" by John Donne the younger states that the poems were "chiefly preserved by the greatest Masters of Musick, all the Sonnets being set by them," and that he got them from Henry Lawes and "Laneere" (Nicholas?). This account of the origin of the texts and the fact that the volume includes work by several other poets should preclude any hasty ascription of the poem to Pembroke (*cf.* Do1612.I). See MSS E and Q below.

Besides the 1660 volume (D), where it is titled "Apollo's *Oath*," the poem appears in the following sources: (E) Bod. MS Add. B. 97 (after 1609), fol. 18, headed "A songe" and subscribed "Ch: Riues," who may be only the author of the added fourth stanza (but see Q); (F) Bod. MS CCC 328 (*c.* 1650), fol. 74, headed "Apollo's oath A sonnet" with a note in the margin added later, "Pembr. p. 115"; (G) Bod. MS Don. d. 58 (1647), fol. 48v, headed "Vpon younge maides"; (H) Bod. MS Eng. Poet. f. 25 (*c.* 1640–1650), fol. 63v; (I) Bod. MS Rawl. Poet. 199 (after 1635) pp. 86–87; (J) Folger MS V.a.97 (*c.* 1640), p. 53, headed "on Maidens"; (K) Folger MS V.a.124 (*c.* 1657), fols. 21v–22, entitled "Apollo's oath"; (L) Folger MS V.a.319 (mid-17th century), fol. 18, "Apollos oath"; (M) Folger MS V.a.322 (mid-17th century), p. 34, "Apollo's oath"; (N) Folger MS V.a.339 (mid-17th century), fol. 198; (O) Folger MS V.a.345 (*c.* 1630), p. 19, "Apollo's oath"; (P) Rosenbach MS 239/27 (*c.* 1635), p. 58, "Apolloes oath"; (Q) Rosenbach MS 1083/15 (*c.* 1625), p. 23, headed "Of Phoebus & Daphne" and signed "Ch:R" (*cf.* E); (R) Rosenbach MS 1083/16 (dated 1630), pp. 189–190; (S) John Gough, *The Academy of Complements* (1650), sig. H2, "On Maids"; (T) John Cotgrave, *Wits Interpreter* (1655), sigs. O6v–O7, "A Song"; and (U) John Phillips, *Sportive Wit* (1656), sig. E8, "A Song." The variants are:

  1 first did] did fayre E
    Daphne] Dauphne J

2 no meanes might] could no way DFHIJKLMOPQSTU, no way could EGR, nothinge could N

    3 the cause, the cause] acause the cause F, the cause T

      quoth] quod E, saith S

    4 is] on T

      I have vow'd] cause I ha vow'd H, I vowed haue O

    5 Then . . . sware] Then *Phebus* raging, swore DFHIJKLMOPSTU, Then in chase Phebus swore G.

      rage] chafe R

      he sware] he swore ER, Phebe swore NQ

    6 past] 'Bove U

      none] some O

      none but one] *omitted* D–U

      liue] die DEFHKLMNSTU, be IO

    7 shal chance be] perchance are DKOPU, perchance haue F, perchance be N, chance to be HIJQST, by chance are LM

      shal] by EGR

    8 they can scarsly] scarcly they can EQ, they can fittly GR

      Ere . . . head] Ere they can dresse their maiden head K, before that they can dresse their head N

    9 Yet] *omitted* N

      pardon them] pittye them GR, blame them not HIJST

      be] are DEGHIJKLMNOPQRSTU

      loth] wroth F

    10 good *Phoebus*] *Apollo* D–U

    11 And] For S

      twere] it is DR, it were GQ, were HST, tis KLMPU

      child] babe GR

      were borne] vnborne HST

DEFHIJKLMOPSTU contain this third stanza (from D):

> Yet silly they, when all is done,
> Complain our wits their hearts have won;
> When 'tis for fear that they should bee
> Like *Daphne*, turn'd into a Tree:
>   And who her self would so abuse,
>   To be a Tree, if shee could chuse.

Variants in this stanza:

    1 silly they] simple mayds FK

      all is] they have E

    2 our] mens FHIJST

      wits] wiles E, wills FS, iests K

      their . . . have] have their hearts S

    3 that] lest FHIJKLMPT

    4 Like] with HIJKLMOPTU

    5 who . . . abuse] who would so herself abuse HIJTU

E contains a fourth stanza:

> By this they gett sweet mothers name
> And are not barren which were blame,
> Besides by this procure they can,
> The world a child, the prince a man.
> Nowe *Stoick* tell me yf in this,
> That any thinge be done amisse.

1 *Phoebus . . . Daphne.* See Ovid, *Metamorphoses*, I, 452–567.

6 *none but one.* This is an insertion of the composer's. Perhaps the *one* who should live a maid was Queen Elizabeth.

VII.

Cf. Do1603.III; both may possibly have been intended to flatter the Queen.

26 *There . . . she.* As noted in EMV, p. 741, this line occurs in George Mason and John Earsden's *Ayres that were Sung and Played at Brougham Castle* (1618), No. 6, line 12. The texts of these airs have been attributed on fairly good evidence to Campion (Vivian, pp. li–lii; Davis, pp. 447–448).

VIII.

Cf. Do1603.XV. Compare also Ben Jonson's "Slow slow, fresh fount" from *Cynthias Reuels* (1601), I.ii.65–75 (*Works*, IV, 50), set to music by Henry Youll, *Canzonets to three voyces* (1608), No. VIII.

9–10 *My . . . appease.* I.e., "Neither passage of time (season) nor anything else can appease my sorrow."

IX.

According to Rubsamen, p. 278, there is a copy of this song with Dowland's music in four parts in the Taitt MS at U.C.L.A. Diana Poulton tells me that a copy of the song with music for the Cantus is in Edinburgh University MS La III.488.

XI.

5 *rude like to my riming.* As noted in EMV, p. 741, the poet illustrates this phrase in the following two lines.

XII.

David Greer compares Mo1600.XIII, and suggests that the "Queen of May" in line 26 may be Queen Elizabeth.

XIII.

This song seems to have come from a masque or play.

8 *nere the neere.* I.e., *never the nearer*, not nearer to one's purpose. *Cf.* Jo1601.VII.4.

11 *can nothing heare.* This probably means "know nothing here."

XIIII.

Collier (p.76) suggests that this song came from a play. Although it would be appropriate to Jessica in *The Merchant of Venice*, there is no evidence, textual or otherwise, to indicate any connection with this play. See Diana Poulton in *The Musical Times*, CV (1964), 26. Thomas Oliphant (*La Musa Madrigalesca* [1837], p. 173) thinks it is the "effusion of some young gentleman" who has disobeyed his father for his lady's sake.

XV.

Cf. Do1603.VIII and note. Thomas Watson wrote some similar verses for a madrigal by Luca Marenzio in *The first sett of Italian Madrigalls Englished* (1590), No. XII. The original words, Jacopo Sannazaro's Canzone XII, "Venuta era Madonna al mio languire," are not very close to Watson's, which read (Superius, sig. C2v):

> When I beheld the faire face of Phyllis sleeping
> I shewd my ioy by weeping:
> And kissing oft her cheeks with roses stained,
> To my self I thus complained,
> now feed your selues my feeble eies with gazing,
> while her eies with a clowd of sleepe are kept from blazing,
> And thou my hart, whom she hath fired,
> dispaire not of thy desired,
> As now mine eies are pleased,
> So haply when she awakes, thou shalt be eased.

2, 4 *fast . . . waste.* The rhyme is with *fast.* Kökeritz (p. 438) notes Shakespeare's rhyme of *past* with *waste.*

7–8 *That . . . sleeping.* See the Variant Readings. *That* refers to *eyes* (line 5); *lies* is singular because *eyes* could be considered a unit. EMV, p. 436, and most other anthologies give *sleeping* (lines 8 and 16) a separate line to bring out the *eyes-lies* rhyme.

XVI.

8 *now.* Perhaps this should be *not.*

XVII.

This poem is by Thomas Campion, who published his own setting later in 4Camp [1617].XVII (Vivian, p. 183; Davis, pp. 184–185). Campion's version contains three variants:

2 beauties] louely
8 my] mine
9 suters] louers

Two other settings of the poem survive in manuscript, neither of which is like the other or Campion's or Dowland's. The first of these, (D) BM Add. 15117 (after *c.* 1614), fol. 19, is for voice and lute; the other, (E) Christ Church, Oxford, 439 (*c.* 1620), pp. 62–63 and 68–69, for treble and bass: the text of E is printed by John P. Cutts in *Seventeenth Century Songs and Lyrics* (Columbia: University of Missouri Press, 1959), p. 178. In the MS, it is subscribed (p. 69) "fynis quod Mrs Elyzabeth Hampden," who may have been responsible for the music or the third stanza of the text. A third copy, without music, is in (F) Folger MS V.a.339 (mid-17th century), fol. 192v. Another copy of the verses, headed "A sonnet" and without ascription, is in Cambridge MS Add. 7196 (no pagination; not collated). Variants are as follows:

1 yet do] she doth E
2 beauties] bewtious E
3 Thence] hence F
5 forme] frame DF
7–12 *omitted* E

7 agrieu'd then wish] haue greeued and wisht D, haue thought or wisht F
9 admir'd, new] belou'd, fresh F
  suters] lovers DF
  repaire] repaires D
10 That . . . fires] which doth beget in her a new desirē F
11 Rest] cease F
  resolue] conclude F

D and E contain the following stanza (from D):

> Thus my Complaint from her Vntruthe aryse,
> accusinge her & Nature boathe in one
> for Beautie stainde is butt a false disguise,
> a Comon wonder which is quicklye gone,
> A false faire face Cannot with all her feature,
> without a trew hart make a trew faire Creature.

Variants in E:

1 Complaint] complaints
4 which] that
5 face . . . her] soules . . . their

E has still another stanza:

> Whatt need't thou playne, iff thou be still reiectted
> the fayrest creature sumtime may prooue strange
> continuall playntes will make the still reieckted
> if that her wanton mind be giuen to range
> and nothing bettere fitts a mans true partes
> then with dissdayne t'encounter ther false hartes.

As Vivian (p. 370) and Davis (p. 184) note, Campion uses the material in lines 6 and 12 in two of his Latin epigrams, Book II, No. 18, "In Melleam," and No. 116, "Ad Cambricum" (Davis, pp. 426–427, 436–437, gives translations).

XVIII.

This poem survives in no fewer than twenty-eight other 16th- and 17th-century sources, fourteen of which attribute the poem to Robert Devereux, second Earl of Essex. Two sources contain Dowland's music and the three stanzas from Do1603: BM MS Add. 15117 (after *c.* 1614), fol. 21, with music for voice and lute; and Forbes's *Cantus* (1662), sigs. Y1v–Y2. Only Forbes presents variants, which are:

1 It] There
  could] did
4 the] that
7 Then thus] Thus still
  buzd] biss'd
  when] yet
9 this Time] the same
13 Gods] God
14 yet] now

15 Which ... haue] The ... ar
16 And ... when] Yet I cast off, while
17 king] Prince
    but thus] and said
18 bound] made

All of the other sources are in manuscript, and are longer, usually containing fourteen or fifteen stanzas. They are as follows: (D) BM Add. 5495 (*c.* 1606–10) fols. 28v–29, fifteen stanzas headed, "These Verses were pend by Robert late Earle of Essex in his first discontentment in the moneths of July and August"; (E) BM Add. 5956 (after 1601), fols. 23v–24, fourteen stanzas, headed "verses made by the earle of Essex 1598 in his absence from the Courte"; (F) BM Add. 15891 (*c.* 1640–50), fols. 244v–245v, twelve stanzas, written immediately after a copy of a letter from Essex on fol. 243; (G) BM Egerton 923 (*c.* 1640), fols. 5v–7v, headed "A Poem made on Robt Deuorex Earle of Essex by mr Henry Cuff his Chaplaine"; (H) BM Harleian 2127 (*c.* first half of 17th century), fol. 58, title on fol. 59v, "The Bees Songe"; (I) BM Harleian 6910 (*c.* 1601), fols. 167–168, fourteen stanzas without ascription (but on fol. 177 occur "Verses vpon the report of the death of the right Honorable the Lord of Essex"); (J) BM Harleian 6947 (mid-17th century), fols. 230–231v, fifteen stanzas, headed "A Poem made on the Earle of Essex (being in disgrace with Queene Eliz): by mr henry Cuffe his Secretary"; (K) BM Sloane 1303 (1600–02), fols. 71–72v, fifteen stanzas headed "The Earle of Essex his Buzze Which he made vpon some discontentment he received a little before his iourney in to Ireland. Anno Domini 1598," and subscribed "Robert Deuoreux, Earle of Essex and Ewe, Earle Marshall of Englande"; (L) Bod. Ashmole 767 (after 1601), fols. 1–3, fourteen stanzas, headed "The buzzeinge Bees complaynt," and subscribed "E Essex"; (M) Bod. Ashmole 781 (1617–1631), pp. 132–134, subscribed "Essex," and listed in the Table of Contents, p. 168, as "my Lo: of Essex of the Bee"; (N) Bod. Douce 280, fols. 123–124v, fourteen stanzas, marked "E. Essex" (O) Bod. Eng. misc. c. 93, fol. 21v (mid-17th century), fourteen stanzas headed "Verses made by the Erle of Essex"; (P) Bod. Rawl. C. 744 (*c.* 1700), fols. 62v–63 (leaves reversed), fourteen stanzas without ascription, but preceded by other material about Essex; (Q) Bod. Rawl. Poet. 112 (before 1600?), fols. 9–10, fourteen stanzas in a group of poems headed "Verses or English poems written by the lo: the E: of E:"; (R) Bod. Rawl. Poet. 148, fols. 87–88, copied before a poem dated 1598 (the first four stanzas must have been on a leaf now missing; stanzas 5–15 remain), subscribed "quod Mr John Lilly"; (S) Bod. Rawl. Poet. 172 (after 1607), fols. 13v–14, fourteen stanzas, headed "My Lord of Essex his Bee"; (T) Bod. Tanner 76 (18th century copy of an earlier MS), fols. 93–94, fifteen stanzas, headed "Henry Cuff made these following Verses, his Lord and Master the Earl of Essex being then in some Disgrace"; (U) Bod. Tanner 306 (early 17th century), fols. 249–250, fourteen stanzas; a later hand has written in the margin "Rob. Devereux Earl of Essex"; (V) Gonville and Caius College, Cambridge, MS 73/40 C.M.A. 1187 (late 17th century), fols. 157–158, fifteen stanzas, headed "Earle of Essex his Complaint"; (W) Harvard MS Eng. 757 (shortly after 1601), pp. 175–176, thirteen stanzas without ascription, but among papers pertaining to Essex and his execution; (X) Rosenbach MS 240/2 (*c.* 1640–50), pp. 127–131, fourteen stanzas; (Y) Rosenbach MS 1083/15 (*c.* 1625), pp. 61/64, fifteen stanzas headed "honi soit quy mal y pense," and subscribed "R Deuereux. Essex"; (Z) New

York Public Library, Arents MS 115 (*c.* 1600; the only item, no pagination), fourteen stanzas headed "The poor labouring Bee," and subscribed "Essex"; (Dd) Folger MS V.a.339 (mid-17th century), fols. 188v–189, twelve stanzas; (Ee) Folger MS V.a.399 (after 1603), fol. 91–91v, thirteen stanzas; and (Ff) Folger MS X. d. 240 (single sheet dated 1598), fifteen stanzas headed "Carm. Com. Essx" [*sic*].

R. W. Bond prints the entire poem in his edition of Lyly (III, 494–495) from G, with most of the variants from EFHIKLMQRU. Since Dowland uses only the first three stanzas, and since collation of only part of the poem does not seem worthwhile, the reader is referred to Bond. All of the MS versions recorded here differ from Dowland's text in several places. None have the following readings in Dowland: 5 did, 8 should . . . be, 15 fruitlesse Flies haue found to haue a friend.

Bond (III, 445–447) ascribes the poem to Lyly on the basis of R and some rather unconvincing biographical and stylistic evidence. The weight of the manuscript evidence is in Essex's favor. William Browne seems to agree with the ascription to Essex: in *Britannia's Pastorals* (1613), sigs. L4v–M1, he refers to a man who got favor of a "Royall Maide," yet who suffered a wrong which Browne compares to "*Procris heauie Fate.*"

> Hee was a Swaine whom all the *Graces* kist,
> A braue, heroicke, worthy *Martialist*:
> Yet on the Downes he oftentimes was seene
> To draw the merry Maidens of the Greene
> With his sweet voyce: Once, as he sate alone,
> He sung the outrage of the lazy *Drone*,
> Vpon the lab'ring *Bee*, in straines so rare,
> That all the flitting Pinnionists of ayre
> Attentiue sate, and in their kindes did long
> To learne some Noate from his well-timed Song.

3 *Time.* Here and elsewhere there is the common pun on *thyme*.
6 *brought . . . hiue. Cf.* the Epistle to Do1603 and the Dedication to Han1609.

XIX.

This poem was first printed in Francis Davison's miscellany, *A Poetical Rhapsody* (1602), RPR I, 186. Rollins says (II, 164) that this book was Dowland's source; it contains the following variants:

2 sparke his] sparkes their
3 and] The
6 and in] as in
7 waters] riuers

In *A Poetical Rhapsody*, the poem is marked "Incerto," but in a copy in Bod. MS Rawl. Poet, 148, fol. 103, it is ascribed to Sir Edward Dyer, and in Bod. MS Tanner 169, fol. 192v, it is ascribed first to "Mr. Lea," and then to Sir Walter Raleigh. Rollins (RPR, II, 164–167) collates these sources and the following: *The Dr. Farmer Chetham Manuscript*, ed. A. B. Grosart, Chetham Society LXXXIX (1873), 89; BM MS Add. 22602, fol. 19; BM MS Add. 28635, fol. 85v; BM MS Harl. 6910, fol. 140v; Bod. MS Malone 19, fol. 50v; and Forbes's *Cantus* (1682 ed.,), sig. G1v (L2–L2v in 1662 ed.). Hughey (HAH, II, 306–308) gives variants from these sources plus Folger MS V.a.339

(formerly 2071.7), fol. 198v; Folger MS V.a.97 (formerly 1.27), fol. 43; and Folger MS V.a.162 (formerly 452.4), fol. 37. I can add only the following: (D) Rosenbach MS 239/27 (*c.* 1635) p. 182; (E) Rosenbach MS 1083/15 (*c.* 1625), p. 137; (F) Rosenbach MS 1083/16 (dated 1630), pp. 194–195; (G) BM MS Add. 52585 (*c.* 1630), fol. 53v, following a note on fol. 53 saying that "There follow in the 4 leaues ensewinge diuers ditties to be sung & plaid vppon Instruments"; and (H) Inner Temple MS 538. 10 (after *c.* 1630), fol. 3v. Variants from DEFGH are:

1 lowest] smallest E
  trees] shrubbs DF
2 sparke] sparkes E
  his] their E, her G
3 and] the EH
  slender] finest H
5 source] shores F, surges G, courses H
6 and in] as in DE
7 Where] When E
  waters] Riuers E, water G
  run] ronnes G
  foords] floods DF
8 perceiues] perceiue F
9 in the] found in H
10 and yet] but yet H
11 eyes and eares] eares & eyes DG
  tongues] tongue F
12 and see, and sigh] they see, they sigh H

Rollins and Hughey discuss verses written in answer to this poem (*e.g.*, in *A Poetical Rhapsody* and Forbes), and Rollins gives full notes on the appearance of similar phrases in other works. *Cf.* Jo1610.IIII.

1–2 *Ant . . . spleene.* Tilley F393.
2 *little sparke. Cf.* Tilley S714, "Of a little spark a great fire."
3 *haires cast shadowes.* Tilley H25.
4 *Bees haue stings. Cf.* Tilley B211, "Bees that have honey in their mouths have stings in their tails."
6 *loue . . . kings. Cf.* Tilley L519, "Love lives in cottages as well as in courts."
7 *waters . . . foords.* Tilley W123.
8 *diall . . . moue.* Tilley D321.
9 *firmest faith . . . fewest words. Cf.* Tilley W796, "Few words among friends are best," and W828, "Where many words are, the truth goes by."
10 *Turtles. Cf.* Tilley T624, "As true as a turtle to her mate."
11 *hearts . . . speake. Cf.* Tilley H334, "What the heart thinks the tongue speaks."

XX.

A. B. Grosart claimed this poem for Nicholas Breton in his edition of that poet's *Works* (1879), I ("Gleanings"), 9. Grosart based his ascription on the similarity of lines 1 and 2 to a maxim from *Wits Pruiate Wealth* (1611–1670): "Hee that makes beauty a Starre, studies a false Astronomy, and he that is soundly in love, needs no other purgatory" (Grosart, II, item p, p. 7). Grosart may be right, but the evidence is in-sufficient; Breton may have taken the phrase from the song, which antedated *Wits Priuate Wealth*.

10 *it*. This should probably read *them*.

14 *wit . . . wheeles*. *Cf.* Tilley W893, "The world runs on wheels," and T387, "Her tongue runs on wheels."

15 *wit*. EMV, p. 489 emends to *Will*.

XXI.

For other dialogues, see Do1600.XXII and note.

12 *die*. The emendation in EMV, p. 489, *do*, makes better sense.

Thomas Greaves, *Songes of sundrie kindes*, 1604

Dedication

Sir Henry Pierrepont or Perpoint of Holme Pierrepont, Nottinghamshire, married Frances, the daughter of Sir William Cavendish and Elizabeth ("Bess of Hardwick"). Lady Frances' cousin was the composer Michael Cavendish. Pierrepont's sister-in-law, Mary Cavendish, had married Gilbert, Earl of Shrewsbury in 1568, and it was at Shrewsbury's Worksop Manor that James I knighted Pierrepont on April 20, 1603. Moreover, Shrewsbury mentions a servant of his named Thomas Greaves in a letter of 1587; see the Historical Manuscripts Commission, *Appendix to the Fourth Report* (1874), p. 331. See the notes to XVI–XVIII. Pierrepont died in 1615. (G. E. Cokayne, *Complete Peerage*, s.v. Kingston-upon-Hull; DNB, s.v. Talbot, Gilbert; Grove, s.v. Greaves; and T. M., *The True Narration of the Entertainment of his Royal Majesty from . . . Edinburgh till . . . London*, 1603, reprinted in Nichols' *Progresses of James I*, I, 84–88.)

Ad Authorem

6–7 *sweet resounding . . . braines*. *Cf.* the note to XVI.

12 *W. W.* M. C. Boyd (p. 120, n.) thinks this might be William Webbe, who wrote a prefatory poem for Pilkington's *Second Set of Madrigals* (1624).

In home-bred springs, etc.

2 *eare inchaunting*, *I.e.*, "ear-enchanting," with a play on "chanting in the ear."

As once *Appelles*, etc.

This anecdote of the painter and the shoemaker is told by Pliny, *Natural History*, XXXV.85. *Cf.* Tilley, C480.

Said *Pithagor* true

1 *Pithagor*. Pythagoras, whose doctrine of metempsychosis is expounded in Ovid, *Metamorphoses*, XV, 154 ff.

4 *siluer plumed Swanne*. *cf.* Do1603.V.5 and note.

7 *P. B.* These letters are so blurred that no one has agreed on what they are. Ian Spink (ELS, 2nd series, XVIII, ix) reads *F.* or *P. R.* [Philip Rosseter?], while Boyd (p. 114) sees *R. B.* which he thinks might be Richard Barnfield. Fellowes (EM, XXXVI, Greaves, v) gives *I*, *B*, and *E* as possibilities for the first letter.

III.

These verses were reset as a madrigal for three voices by Francis Pilkington in his *Second Set of Madrigals and Pastorals* (1624), No. V (Cantus, sig. B1). There are no variants.

V–VI.

Cf. Jo1601.VII and note.

VI.7 *repentance . . . clap.* Cf. Tilley A57, "Beware an afterclap."

VI.9 *down a down.* The sense and meter of the verse are stretched here to enable the composer to turn *down* into the common nonsense phrase used in refrains and vocal embellishments. *Cf.* Jo1600.XXI.

VII.

These verses were copied, without variants, in Folger MS V.a.124 (mid-17th century), fol. 49v, and entitled "Beauty."

1, 3–4 *beauty but a breath*, etc. Cf. Tilley B165, B169.

X.

This is an imitation of a poem ascribed to Thomas, Lord Vaux in *The Paradise of Dainty Devices* (1576–1606); see the edition by Hyder E. Rollins (Cambridge, Mass.: Harvard University Press, 1927), pp. 19–20, 195–196. Vaux's poem begins: "When I looke backe, and in my selfe beholde,/ The wandring wayes, that youth could not descry." The third stanza ends: "Pardon the faultes committed in my youth." See also HAH, I, 96–97. Hughey gives a long account of this poem (II, 33–38) in which she adds John Harington and D. Sand to the possible authors, and reprints Gr1604.X as a sample imitation. She also mentions William Hunnis' "Alack when I looke backe, vpon my youth thatz paste" (*Paradise*, p. 107) and Thomas Lodge's "When with aduice I weigh my yeares forepast" from *Scillaes Metamorphosis* (1589), sigs. F1v–F2. See also the note to Dan1606.VIII.

The text of this poem on L1v is headed, "*The Dittie of the X. Song.*"

XI.

The text of this song on L1v is headed, "*The Dittie of the XI. Song.*"

6, 12, 17 *woman . . . wo to man.* Tilley W656.

XII.

This is a "song of good life," a type especially favored before the 1590's. *Cf* "My mind to me a kingdom is" and "I joy not in no earthly bliss," both attributed to Sir Edward Dyer, in William Byrd's *Psalmes, Sonets, & songs of sadnes and pietie* (1588), Nos. XIIII and XI.

XIII–XV.

Note the combination of anaphora and correlative verse.

XVI.

When James I visited the Earl of Shrewsbury at Worksop Manor on April 20, 1603 (when Sir Henry Pierrepont was knighted—see the note to the Dedication), he was "nobly received," for "in this place, besides the abundance of all provision and delicacie, there was most excellent soule-ravishing musique, wherewith his Highness was not a little delighted" (T.M., *The true Narration* [1603], reprinted in John Nichols' *Progresses of James I* [London, 1828], I, 84–88). This music may very well have been

Nos. XVI–XVIII. Incidentally, Nicholas Yonge dedicated his *Musica Transalpina* (1588) to Shrewsbury.

XVII–XVIII.

See Cav1598.XXIV and note. Although these madrigals may have been intended for Morley's *Triumphs of Oriana* (1601), it seems more likely that Oriana is here Anne of Denmark, and that they are companion pieces for No. XVI. Ben Jonson, for instance, writes in his *Entertainment at Althorpe* (1603; *Works*, VII, 125):

> Long liue ORIANA,
> To exceed (whom she succeeds) our late DIANA.

See Roy C. Strong, "Queen Elizabeth I as Oriana," *SR*, VI (1959), 258–260.

XIX–XX.

Compare Nicholas Yonge, *Musica Transalpina* (1588), No. XXXI:

> Liquid and watry pearles Loue wept full kindly,
> To quench my heart enflamed,
> But he alas, vnfrindly
> So great a fire had framed,
> As were enough to burne mee,
> Without recomfort and into ashes turne mee.

The original words to the madrigal set by Luca Marenzio begin: "Liquide perle amor da gl'occhi sparse" (Obertello, p. 237). *Cf.* also Thomas Morley, *The First Booke of Ballets* (1595), No. XIV, "Fyer fyer, my hart," and 3Camp[1617].XX (EMV, pp. 151, 402).

XXI.

This piece is a "ballet" rather than a madrigal: it is characterized by homophonic music for the verses alternating with polyphonic "fa la" refrains. See Jo1609.VI and note, and *cf.* Thomas Morley's *First Booke of Balletts to Fiue Voyces* (1595), and John Hilton's *Ayres, Or, Fa las For Three Voyces* (1627).

7 *running in and out.* The music provides a good example of "word-painting" at this point.

Tobias Hume, *The First Part of Ayres*, 1605

A Table

No. 6 *Duke of Holstones Almaine.* See also No. 99. Ulrich, Duke of Holstein, was the brother of Christian IV and Anne of Denmark. He received the order of the Garter in April, 1605 (Nichols, *Progresses of James I*, I, 508).

No. 39 *Duke Iohn of Polland.* This is probably the Swedish Duke John of Östergötland, brother of Sigismund III, king of Sweden and Poland at this time.

Nos. 68 and 95 *Beccus an Hungarian Lord.* Probably one of the Bekes or Bekiesz family, Hungarians living in Poland in the last years of the 16th century (see the *Polski Slownik Biograficzny*).

Dedication

William Earle of Pembrooke. William Herbert, third Earl of Pembroke (1580–1630) had a number of books dedicated to him (see Williams) including the 1623 folio of Shakespeare, Davison's *A Poetical Rhapsody* (1602), and Thomas Tomkins' *Songs of 3.4.5. and 6. parts* (1622). Pembroke, incidentally, took tobacco (DNB; see No. 3).

11 *without the verge of Complement.* I.e., outside the Court. The verge was the area within a twelve mile radius from the Court subject to the Lord High Steward.

To the Reader

Cf. this epistle with that of Hu1607.

8 *no Italian Note to an English dittie.* English words were provided for Italian music by Nicholas Yonge in *Musica Transalpina* (1588 and 1597), Thomas Watson in *The first sett Of Italian Madrigals Englished* (1590), Thomas Morley in *Madrigals . . . Celected out of the best approued Italian Authors* (1598), and in *Canzonets or Little Short Songs* (1597). But see Hume's "French Iigge," "Pollish Vilanell," etc.

10–11 *Carpere . . . tua.* Martial, *Epigrams,* I.91:

> Cum tua non edas, carpis mea carmina, Laeli.
> Carpere vel noli nostra vel ede tua.

14–16 *And from henceforth . . . as the Lute.* See Do1612, To the Reader.

1

Fellowes (EMV, 2nd ed., p. 622) compares this song to Clément Janequin's *La Guerre* (*La Bataille de Marignan, c.* 1525). See M. Brenet, *Musique et musiciens de la vielle France* (1911), pp. 143 ff., and Reese, pp. 295–299. Janequin's piece is edited by H. Expert in *Les Maîtres Musiciens de la Renaissance Française* VII (1898), 31–61. *Cf.* also William Byrd's *Battell* pieces for keyboard in *My Ladye Nevells Booke,* ed. H. Andrews (1926), pp. 20 ff.

14 *Harke . . . shootes.* A direction in the music reads: "Play three letters with your Fingers," referring to three notes to be plucked on the low strings in imitation of "The great Ordenance."

15 *the drums.* A series of rapidly repeated notes in the accompaniment are labeled "Kettle Drumme."

3

The literature on tobacco in the early seventeenth century is extensive. Edward Arber, in reprinting James I's *A Counterblaste to Tobacco* (1604), conveniently surrounds it with accounts of and excerpts from a number of other contemporary books on the subject (see Arber's English Reprints, London, 1869, pp. 81–120). For further information, see the catalog by Jerome E. Brooks, *Tobacco. Its History Illustrated by the Books, Manuscripts and Engravings in the Library of George Arents, Jr.* 5 vols. (New York: Rosenbach, 1937–1952). For tobacco songs, see, for example, Michael East, *The Second set of Madrigales* (1606), No. XXII (EMV, p. 91); Thomas Weelkes *Ayeres or Phantasticke Spirites* (1608), No. VI (EMV, pp. 296–297); and Thomas Ravenscroft, *A Briefe Discourse* (1614), No. XII (EMV, p. 252).

6–8 *tumor . . . humor.* John Gerard says that tobacco dries up the humors, and is good for tumors when applied in a poultice (*Herball,* ed. Marcus Woodward [London: Gerald Howe, 1927], pp. 92–94).

112

This song was copied into BM MS Add. 15117 (after *c.* 1614), fol. 23, with melody and tablature, and without verbal variants.

At the end of the music in Hu1605, there is this note: "You must play one straine with your fingers, the other with your Bow, and so continue to the end."

113

Reprinted in Hu1607, sig. G2v (No. XIV).

114

Since the stanzas are set to different music and the refrain is repeated, the musical form is a rondo; the verse form is technically a carol, with the burden at the beginning (*cf.* Cav1598.XIIII). The song is headed by this note: "The Imitation of Church Musicke, singing to the Organes, but here you must vse the Viole de Gambo for the Organe, playing the burthen strongly with the Bow, singing lowde; your Preludiums and verses are to be plaide with your fingers, singing thereto not ouer lowde, your Bow euer in your hand."

1–2 *why . . . wrong.* Cf. Tilley L260, "Long life has long misery."

13–15 *Thou pinst . . . safetie.* Hume, a former soldier, later suffered paranoid delusions that were intensifications of these feelings. The applicability of these lines and the eccentricity of No. 1 and Nos. I and XXV in Hu1607 suggest at least the possibility that Hume wrote some of his own words.

26 *our . . . deplore.* Perhaps *thats* should be *to*; or the lines may have been intended to mean "music that deplores our sad state." EMV, p. 543, mistakenly reads (or emends) *our* as *out.*

Robert Jones, *Vltimum Vale*, 1605

Dedication

Henrie Prince of Wales. Fer1609 and Han1609 are also dedicated to Prince Henry (1594–1612). See also Coprario and Campion's *Songs of Mourning: Bewailing the vntimely death of Prince Henry* (1613). For Henry's role as a patron, see Elkin C. Wilson, *Prince Henry and English Literature* (Ithaca: Cornell University Press, 1946).

7–10 *Most excellent . . . riper age.* This sentence is corrupt; perhaps a line was dropped after *as neare as to you.*

11–12 *senses . . . are the Soules Intelligencers.* Cf. Sir John Davies, *Nosce Teipsum* (1599), lines 361–368 (*Poems*, ed. Clare Howard [New York: Columbia University Press, 1941], p. 128).

16 *it owne.* A possessive form occasionally used at this time (see OED, *it* III).

16–17 *Musicke in all things.* For an account of the ideas developed in the following passage, see John Hollander, *The Untuning of the Sky* (Princeton University Press, 1961), and Gretchen L. Finney, *Musical Backgrounds for English Literature, 1580–1650* (New Brunswick: Rutgers University Press, n.d., *c.* 1962), especially pp. 28–32.

I.

Vivian (p. liv) suggests, on stylistic grounds alone, that this poem is by Thomas Campion. It is possible that this poem and perhaps others in Jones's books are by Campion, for Jones published settings of three poems before Campion himself did

(Jo1605.X, XVII; 1609.I; see also 1605.IX and note). Dowland (1603.XVII), Ferrabosco (1609.VIII), and Corkine (1610.XI) also published settings earlier than Campion's own. Walter R. Davis (p. 508) cites further evidence: the second stanza resembles 2Camp[1613].VII and 3Camp[1617].VI; and the song appears among other Campion songs in MSS EF described below.

Copies of this song with Jones's music are in (D) BM MS Add. 24665 (1615–1626), fols. 13v–14 (melody and bass); in (E) NLS Advocates' MS 5.2.14 (*c.* 1639), fol. 5 (melody only); (F) NLS MS La. III 490, fol. 31, (from Davis, p. 508), and (G) NLS MS La. III 483, fol. 190 (first line with melody only). The variants, except for Scotticisms in E, are as follows:

    1 prize] praise E
    3 print] prints F
    8 canst] could'st D, can E
    10 Couldst] Could E
    13 *Rozamond . . . as*] Rosamount . . . als E
    16 curse] course F
    17 the] *omitted* F
       do] doth E
    19 seeme] seimes E
    20 Thorowe] through D, in rough [and rue?] F

13 *Rozamond.* Probably the mistress of Henry II and subject of Samuel Daniel's *Complaint of Rosamond* (1592) and Thomas Deloney's ballad "Fair Rosamond" (*Works,* ed. F.O. Mann [1912], p. 297; see also Simpson, pp. 97–99).
17–18 *All . . . obey.* Cf. Tilley T313.

II.

Set also by Pilkington (1605.XVIII) and Corkine (1610.IX). It is almost certainly the work of Anthony Munday, who first printed the poem in his *Famous and Renowned Historie of Primaleon of Greece . . . The Second Booke* (1619), sig. O2v. (The first edition of this book, 1596, exists only in an imperfect copy in the BM; this poem is not in the preserved part.) It was printed again in *England's Helicon* (1600; REH, I, 28–29) with the signature "Sheepheard Tonie" whom Rollins thinks is Munday (II, 31–33). Rollins (II, 91–92) gives variants from the following copies of the poem besides those named so far: BM MS Add. 24665 (1615–1626), fols. 14v–15 (with Jones's melody and bass); BM MS Harleian 4286, fol. 61v; John Cotgrave's *Wits Interpreter* (1655), sig. Q4v (1662, 1671, sig. M1v); BM MS Add. 37492, fol. 39v (a fragment); and Folger MS V.a.103, fol. 29 (formerly MS 1.28, fol. 53).

Rollins did not collate the following versions: (D) BM MS Add. 47111 (*c.* 1646–1649), pp. 48–49, entitled "Sonnet"; (E) Rosenbach MS 1083/16 (formerly Phillipps 9549; *c.* 1630), p. 196, entitled "Beautye"; (F) Rosenbach MS 1083/17 (formerly Phillipps 8270; *c.* 1638–1642), fol. 158v, headed "On Bewty"; (G) Bod. MS Don. d. 58 (*c.* 1647), fol. 29 ("Cant 26"); and (H) King's College, Cambridge, Rowe MS 2 (Turpyn's Book; after 1610), fol. 16v (with Jones's melody and tablature accompaniment). The variants, along with those from (J) *Primaleon* and (K) *England's Helicon,* are as follows:

    2 fairest] *omitted* D
    3 blew] grew D, then G

4 ranne] runne H
5 my] mine EFJK
6 forbidden] hidden J
7 better memory] second thoughts then D
   cride] sayd JK
   fie] fie fie D
8 so] such F
   delights were] delight was D, desire was JK
9–16 *omitted* H
10 But] When EK, and J
14 sometime] sometimes J
15 awakt] walke D
   the] ere D, that J, this K

John Ramsey wrote a curious version of the second stanza in his commonplace book (Bod. MS Douce 280, fol. 35) sometime before 1633—perhaps as early as 1596. Is it possible that this came from Munday's lost *Sweet Sobs and Amorous Complaints of Shepherds and Nymphs* (entered 1583)?

To Alexis.

Montanus. Supprest with cares a sleep I fell,
    my fancye still a workinge:
    where what appear'd I cannott tell
    yet somewhat sure was lurkinge.
    For as I dream't my loue did smile,
    whereat I fell aweepinge:
    But I awakt, as wise this while,
    as when I fell a sleepinge.
    hey Nonnie, Nonnie, &c.

Sheephearde Mountanus.
I: R.

III.

Cf. Jo1601.IX and note.

Other copies occur in (D) BM MS Add. 24665 (*c.* 1615–1626), fols. 15v–16, with Jones's melody and bass; (E) BM MS Add. 15118 (*c.* 1633), fol. 8; and (F) Folger MS V.a.345 (*c.* 1630), pp. 66–67. The variants are:

1 Muze] hart F
3 Though] If E
12 Franzy] frenzie DF, francey E
13 toy] boy F
15 vppon] on F
18 youthes, and] youth then E
23 Then . . . ioyes] Butt leaue and goe to bedd in the sweete Ioue [? *perhaps* Loue] E

10 *baited hookes. Cf.* Tilley B50.

IIII.

Set also by Ferrabosco (1609.XVII). Other copies are found in BM MS Add. 24665 (*c.* 1615–1626), fols. 16v–17, with Jones's melody and bass, without variants; (D) Bod. MS Don. d. 58 (*c.* 1647), fol. 26 ("Cant 16"); and the first stanza only in (E) Henry Lichfild's *First Set of Madrigals of 5. Parts* (1613), No. II. Variants from D and E (Cantus) are:

1 looke] seeke E
5,11,17,23,29 what] Then what D
6–29 *omitted* E
16 Gone] *omitted* D

(Note: in musical repetitions in E, O is added before lines 1, 3, and 5.)

9–10 *Parthian . . . Backward.* This tactic so impressed the Romans, who lost several battles to the Parthians because of it, that it became proverbial. See, *e.g.*, Ovid, *Remedia Amoris,* 224, and Tilley P80.

25, 27 *waste . . . last. Waste* was pronounced to rhyme with *last. Cf.* Do1603.XV.2, 4; see Kökeritz, p. 176.

26 *bloud with sorrow drying.* Melancholy supposedly dried up the humors. *Cf.* Hu1605.3.8–9, Tilley S656, and *Romeo and Juliet,* III.v.57: "Dry sorrow drinks our blood."

V.

Other copies, with Jones's melody and bass, are in (D) BM MS Add. 24665 (*c.* 1615–1626), fols. 17–18, and (E) Christ Church MS 439 (*c.* 1620), p. 67, with these variants:

1 sped] speed DE
2 mist] misse DE
4 tis] it's D
13–36 *omitted* E
18 earth] her *deleted* earth *inserted* D
26 pratling? fye] *cut off after* prat- D
30 stolne] stolen D

3–6 *Ile . . . goes.* "I'll gamble all, and trust my luck; if I keep my meaning to myself, I may win no matter what happens."

26 *blinde man . . . birdes nest.* This seems to be an allusion—perhaps it is related to Tilley B392, "Whist, whist, I smell a bird's nest." *Cf. Much Ado,* II.i.200.

28 *got as in a sleepe. Cf. Lear,* I.ii.15.

32–33 *net That Vulcan set.* Homer, *Odyssey,* VIII, 266–366; Ovid, *Metamorphoses,* IV, 170–189.

VI.

This poem was probably taken from the first edition (1602) of *A Poetical Rhapsody* (RPR, I, 81), where it is headed "Ode V. *His Farewell to his Vnkinde and Vnconstant Mistresse.*" It is in the group of poems assigned to Francis Davison in the first three editions (RPR II, 37, 124). Jones varies thus (probably unintentionally in 13):

8 no] Nor
13 one] mee

14 loues] loue
17 Yet] If

18 *chop and change. I.e.,* to alter. See Tilley C363.
21 *too too late.* Rollins (RPR, II, 124) notes that the repetition of *too* "is an intensive use to indicate 'very much, exceedingly.'" *Cf.* Do1603.XVII.5.

VII.

Copied from Jo1605 without variants in BM MS Add. 24665 (*c.* 1615–1626), fols. 18v–19, with Jones's music for treble and bass.
1–8 *sigh yourselves to death,* etc. On the effect of sighs, *cf.* Donne, "A Valediction: of weeping," lines 26–27. A sigh was supposed to draw a drop of blood from the heart.
3 *liue.* The verb, even though it rhymes with *depriue.* See Kökeritz, p. 213.
11 *Nurse.* Pronounced to rhyme with *course.* See Kökeritz, pp. 467, 235.

VIII.

This poem was printed in the second edition of *A Poetical Rhapsody* (1608) as part of "A Lotterie presented before the late Queenes Maiestie at the Lord Chancellors house. 1601." The whole "Lotterie" is there attributed to "I. D.," probably Sir John Davies (*cf.* Ma1611; see RPR, I, 242–246; II, 42–43, 202–210). A MS formerly in the Conway collection, now Folger MS X. d. 172 (printed in The Shakespeare Society's Papers, II [1845], 65–75), gives a different—and probably correct—occasion and date for the entertainment. The MS is headed (fol. 4v) "In hir Maiesties progresse 1602. The devise to entertayne hir Maiesty att Harfielde, the house of Sir Thomas Egerton Lord keeper and his wife the Countess of Darbye." The Queen visited Harefield in July, 1602. After an opening "humble peticon of a giltles saint" (24 lines), the MS gives the words of No. VIII, with the marginal note: "Sung by 2 mariners presently before the Lottaryes." Now since Jones's book was published in 1605, not 1608, he could not have taken his text from *A Poetical Rhapsody,* as Rollins believed. It is therefore possible that Jones wrote the song used in the entertainment.
   A third copy of the "Lottery," omitting the song (BM MS Add. 22601, fols. 49–52), describes the occasion as "A Lottery Proposed before Supper at the Lord Chief Justice His House . . . 1602." Finally, as Rollins notes, BM MS Harleian 5353, fol. 95, contains "Some of the lotteries which were the last Sumer, at hir Maiesties being with the L. Keeper."
   Variants from (D) the Folger MS, (E) *A Poetical Rhapsody,* and (F) BM MS Add. 24665 (*c.* 1615–1626), fols. 19v–20 (with Jones's melody and bass) are as follows:

8 nor] noe D
  a] the DE
12 her] *omitted* D
14 Which] as E
16 Nor] Noe D
  a] the DE
20 fauoures] fortunes D
21 Such] Some DE
  lot] share DE
22 makes] make F

24 Nor] noe D
   a] the DE

7–8 *there is . . . King.* I.e., there is no fishing like sea-fishing, or service like a king's. See RPR, II, 209–210, and Tilley F336.

IX.

This poem by Thomas Campion was first printed with his music in (D) Ros1601, Part I, No. XIIII (Vivian, p. 13). It was then reprinted in (E) *A Poetical Rhapsody* (1602), RPR, I, 215, entitled "*Vpon his Palenesse,*" and signed "*Th. Campion.*" Jones's text varies thus:

2 into] vnto D
9 within] with E
12 brest] brests DE

X.

Thomas Campion published his own setting of his poem several years later in his (D) *Fourth Booke of Ayres* (c. 1617), No. VII (sig. H2). In the meantime, Richard Alison had published a third setting in (E) *An Howres Recreation in Musicke* (1606), Nos. XIX–XXI (Cantus Primus, sigs. D2–D3). According to Davis (p. 498), BM MSS Add. 17786–17791, No. 20, is a five-part instrumental piece entitled "There is a garden." A MS copy of the treble and bass of Jones's setting is in (F) BM Egerton 2971 (c. 1620), p. 6. The variants from DE are:

4 these] all DE
5 which] that E
  can] may DE
7 These] Those DE
11 no] nor D
   may] can D
15 shaftes] frownes DE
16 presume] attempt D, approch E
17 Those] these E

Davis (p. 174, n.) says that the source of this song may be in Thomas Morley's *First Booke of Balletts to Five Voyces* (1595), No. XVI:

Ladie those Cherris plentie,
Which grow on your lips daintie,
Ere long will fade & languish,
Then now, while yet they last them,
O let mee pull and tast them.

The corresponding verses in the Italian version of Morley's book do not seem to be a source. They begin, "Al primo vostro sguardo" (Obertello, p. 367).

8 *Orient Pearle.* Cf. Do1600.XII.11 and note.

14–15 *browes . . . kill.* A fairly common conceit; cf. Sidney, *Astrophil and Stella*, No. 17 (Ringler, p. 173).

XI.

This poem was taken from *A Poetical Rhapsody* (1602) where it is headed, "Ode I. *Where his Lady keepes his hart*" (RPR, I, 130). As Rollins notes (II, 139–140), it is in the section assigned to Anomos in the first edition, and is ascribed to "A. W." in Davison's list (Rollins reasonably identifies A. W. as "Anonymous Writer." II, 56, 63–71). The only variant is *mine* for *my* in line 1.

9 *vntwined.* Rollins (II, 140) says this should be *entwined.*

XII.

This poem, with Jones's treble and bass, was copied into BM MS 24665, fols. 20v–21, without variants, and dated "1615."

9 *Put it in adventure. I.e.,* take a chance. *Cf.* Tilley H302.

13 *Womens words haue double sence. Cf.* Tilley W660.

14 *Stand away, a simple fence. I.e.,* "Stand away!" is only a parry, a simple defence.

19 *Till the pricke.* The music emphasizes the innuendo here by repeating the phrase and delaying *of conscience.*

XIII.

This poem was taken from *A Poetical Rhapsody* (1602), where it is headed "Ode V. *Petition to haue her leaue to die*" (RPR, I, 148), and assigned to Anomos and A. W., as No. XI. The only variant is *that* for *it* in line 13. The song was copied, with Jones's treble and bass, in BM MS Add. 24665 (*c.* 1615–1626), fols. 21v–22, without variants.

1 *the fountain of my teares. Cf.* Do1603.XV and note.

XIIII.

See Fer1609.XVI for another setting of these verses. A copy of the first stanza of this poem occurs in (D) Folger MS V.b.198, fol. 1; the page is headed "The workes of the Lady Ann Sothwell: Decemb: 2° 1626," and No. XIIII is the first poem, with the title, "Sonnet: 1a." This ascription is weakened by the presence of Raleigh's "The Lie" on fol. 2. Another copy of the poem, (E) Folger MS V.a.339, fol. 192, seems to have been taken from Fer1609 (see variants, line 2); and another copy, (F) Tenbury MS 1018 (after *c.* 1610), fols. 34v–35, has Ferrabosco's music for treble and bass. (G) BM MS Add. 24665 (*c.* 1615–1626), fols. 22v–23, has Jones's melody and bass. The variants are as follows:

    2 sence] soule E
    4 trobling] Tiring EF
    5 O worlde] *omitted* D
      betrayers] betrayer EF
    6 O thoughts] *omitted* D
    7–12 *omitted* D
    7 end] bed E
    8 shipwracke] shipwrackt EFG
    9 strong] strange EF
      lende] send F

5 *betrayers.* EMV, p. 580, emends to *betrayer.*

9–10 *sighes . . . saue.* Several poems use this imagery deriving from Petrarch CLXXXIX, "Passa la nave mia colma d'oblio." See, for example, Sir Thomas Wyatt, "My galley charged with forgetfulness," *Poems,* ed. K. Muir (London, 1949), pp. 22–23.

XV.

See D01597.XVII and note. For other "songs of good life," see Gr1604.XII and note.

Another copy of this poem is in Huntington MS HM 198 (mid-17th century), p. 137, with the following variants:

1 he] the mann
2 who] that
5 who striues] that hopes
8 The] an
9 trauels] pouer
11 so . . . dyes] so got endeth
12 Which] Whose
    by] with
13–18 *omitted*
19–21 All . . . say of me] My only care shalbe they say of me he liud in Piety
22 He] and
23 a] the

5–6 *he who striues . . . fals.* Cf. Tilley P581.
11–12 *fame . . . breath.* Cf. Tilley F46.
17–18 *High trees . . . dwell.* Cf. Tilley C208.
23–24 *On . . . dyes.* As noted in EMV, p. 751, this is a translation of lines 401–403 of Seneca's *Thyestes*:

> illi mors gravis incubat
> qui, notus nimis omnibus,
> ignotus moritur sibi.

XVI.

Another poem taken from (D) *A Poetical Rhapsody* (1602), RPR, I, 156–157, where it is headed "Ode. VIII." As Rollins notes (II, 149), it is in the section of the book ascribed to Anomos; in Davison's list it is ascribed to A. W. See the note to Jo1605.XI. Another setting for four voices by Martin Peerson is in his (E) *Priuate Musicke* (1620), No. IIII (sigs. B1v–B2). A third copy of the poem is in (F) BM MS Harleian 6910 (*c.* 1601), fol. 154. Variants are as follows:

1 me] thee F
7 disdain] dispaire E
11 thy] those DEF
13 smiles] smile DEF
    do] doth DEF
14 frownes] frowne DEF
19 ease] please DEF
20 please] ease DEF

21 *Change is delight.* Cf. Tilley C229.

XVII.

Campion published his own setting of his poem in his *Third Booke of Ayres* (*c.* 1613), No. II (Vivian, p. 161; Davis, pp. 134–135). Pilkington also composed a setting (1605,

VIII), which was copied into BM MS Add. 29291 (18th century) fol. 6v. The texts in Jones and Pilkington probably represent Campion's own early versions. Variants from Campion are:

3 Fained] Fain'd
   so bewitcht] charm'd so
5 desires] ioies
6 desertes] desires
9 heart did attend] cares seru'd
11 the day] t'houre
13 Thou false] False then
15 now so triumphes in] boasts now of
17 Adonis] bright Adonis

As David Greer has shown (*N & Q*, CCX [1965], 333–4), Thomas Heywood parodies this song in *The Rape of Lucrece* (1608), sig. C1v; Valerius sings:

> Let humor change and spare not,
> Since *Tarquins* proud I care not:
> His faire words so bewitch my delight,
> That I dote on his sight.
> Now all is gone new desires embraceing,
> And my deserts disgracing.

For the rhyme "spare not . . . care not," see the English version of a French song by Orlando di Lasso, "Mounsier Mingo," reprinted by F. W. Sternfeld in *Shakespeare Quarterly*, IX (1958), 112, 116; and these lines from No. IV of Nicholas Yonge's *Musica Transalpina* (1588; Obertello, p. 215):

> False Loue now shoot & spare not,
> Now doe thy worst I care not.

See also Thomas Morley, *Madrigalls to Foure Voyces* (1594), No. XII (EMV, p. 141), and Jo1600.XII.16–17.
   11 *True loue abides. Cf.* Tilley L539.

XVIII.

Another poem from (D) *A Poetical Rhapsody* (1602), RPR, I, 178, where it is headed "*Being scorned, and disdained, hee inueighs against his Lady*"; it ends "*Vitijs patienta victa est*" (Ovid, *Amores*, III.xi.1). Assigned to Anomos and A. W. as in No. XI. Also set (E) by Martin Peerson, *Priuate Musicke* (1620), No. VIII (sigs. C1v–C2). The variants are:

4 to too] all too DE *see Variant Readings*
13 as light] are light DE
16 friends] friend E

11–12 *foolish fire . . . night.* On the will-o'-the-wisp, or *ignis fatuus*, Rollins (RPR, II, 157) cites G. L. Kittredge, "The Friar's Lantern and Friar Rush," *PMLA*, XV (1900), 415–441.
   13 *words . . . wind.* Tilley W833.
   15 *broken reed.* Tilley R61; see Isaiah 36:6, and II Kings 18:21.

XIX.

Still another poem from (D) *A Poetical Rhapsody* (1602), RPR, I, 110–111, where it is headed "Ode II. *A dialogue betweene him and his Hart.*" It is in the group of poems assigned to Walter Davison in the first three editions (II, 134). The first two stanzas were later set to music by (E) Martin Peerson in his *Priuate Musicke* (1620), No. IX (sigs. C2v–C3). The variants are:

8 my] mine DE
13 O . . . no] Oh no, no, no, no E
15–42 *omitted* E
16 hath] haue D
22 beare] owe D

Cf. also Jo1600.XII and 1609.VIII.
4 *conuerted.* The spelling of RPR, *conuarted*, suggests the pronunciation.
42 *true loue lasteth euer. Cf.* Tilley L506.

XX.

From (D) *A Poetical Rhapsody* (1602) where it is headed "*Ladies eyes, serue Cupid both for Darts and Fire*" (RPR, I, 137–138). Assigned to Anomos and A. W.; see the note to No. XI. As Rollins notes (II, 142), Samuel Pick included the version from the fourth edition (1621), in (E) his *Festum Voluptatis* (1639), sigs. B3v–B4, as one of his own poems. Variants are:

2 shuld] doth DE
5 sure] since E

8 *bought my wit full deare. Cf.* Tilley W546.
13 *their.* EMV, p. 584, reads *those.*

XXI.

From *A Poetical Rhapsody* (1602), where it is entitled "Ode XIII" and ends with the line "*Scilicet asserui iam me, fugique catenas*" (RPR, I, 177; Ovid, *Amores* III.xi.3). As Rollins notes (II, 156), it was reprinted from the third edition (1611) in the second edition of *England's Helicon* (1614), headed "*A defiance to disdainefull Loue*" (REH, I, 210–211). There are no variants. A late MS note in one of the copies of *A Poetical Rhapsody* (1608) assigns the poem to Raleigh, but Agnes M. C. Latham does not include it in her editions (1929 and 1951).
9 *words . . . winde. Cf.* XVIII.13 and note.
13 *baitst thy hooke. Cf.* Tilley B50.

Francis Pilkington, *The First Booke of Songs or Ayres*, 1605

Dedication
William Earle of Darby. William Stanley, sixth Earl of Derby (d. 1642), also received dedications from Richard Barnfield (*Cynthia*, 1595), Thomas Lodge (*A Fig for Momus*, 1595), and others. He was the son of Henry Stanley, the fourth Earl (1531–1593), and brother of Ferdinando, patron of the dramatic company known as Lord Strange's,

and later fifth Earl (Williams, DNB). Pilkington's *Second Set of Madrigals* (1624) contains "a Pauin made for the orpharion, by the Right Honourable William, Earle of Darbie."

7 *Aristoxenus.* Musical theorist of the 4th century B.C., a pupil of Aristotle, remembered mainly for his classification of the modes and his *Harmonic Elements.* What Pilkington knew of him probably came from later theorists such as Franchinus Gaufurius or Gafurius (*cf.* Thomas Morley's *Plaine and Easie Introduction,* ed. Alec Harman [New York: W. W. Norton, 1952], p. 320) or Gioseffe Zarlino. *Cf.* Zarlino's statement in his *Sopplimenti Musicali* (Venice, 1588), sig. L3v: "Aristosseno . . . disse che l'Anima era Numero, che mouea se stesso."

17 *Quos . . . virtus.* Virgil, *Aeneid,* VI, 129–130.

I.

The four-part version of this song, along with all except No. XXI of the songs in Pi1605, were copied into the four part-books compiled by Thomas Hammond *c.* 1630–40, Bod. MSS Mus. f. 7–10. The songs are clearly attributed to Pilkington, and were probably copied from the printed songbook; compare the title page of Pi1605 with this note in the Tenor partbook (fol. 24v): "Composed by Francis Pilkington, Batchelar of Musicke, & Lutenist, & Chaunter of the Cathedrall Church of Christ, and blessed Mary the Virgin, in Chester." Since this MS has little textual value, only the variants from the part which has the full text will be given. This song appears in the Cantus book, fol. 24, with these variants:

    4 Vnmaskt] Vnmakt
    12 will] must
       kisse . . . Loue] *page trimmed*
    16 eie] eies

10 *farewell faint heart. Cf.* Tilley H302, "Faint heart ne'er won fair lady."

II.

Copied into Bod. Mus. f. 7–10 (see note to I) with these variants (Cantus, fol. 15v):

    4 pleasant] pleasing
    5 sooth] loath
    9 fits] fitt
    22 approued] vnproued

III.

Copied into Bod. Mus. f. 7–10 (see note to I), with these variants (Bassus, fol. 18v):

    7 Am I] I am
    16 loue] *omitted*

3 *Time . . . aproue. I.e.,* time will prove my truthfulness, and compassion will prove hers.

IIII.

Copied into Bod. Mus. f. 7–10 (see note to I), with these variants (Bassus, fol. 19):

    4 loue of] hopes of
    6 that] the
    12 likings] liking

V.

Copied into (D) Bod. Mus. f. 7–10 (see note to I), Cantus, fol. 24v. The first stanza had been set to music by Pilkington's fellow musician at Chester, Thomas Bateson, in (E) *The First Set of English Madrigales* (1604), No. VII (collated from EM, XXI, 39–42, revised by T. Dart and Peter le Huray). Pilkington himself reset the second stanza in his (F) *First Set of Madrigals and Pastorals* (1613), No. IIII (for 3 voices; Cantus, sig. B2v). Variants are:

2 perfumes] perfume E
8 Feare not] Stay Nimph, O stay F
10 water wanton] wanton wanton F
11 springs] springe D
12 murmure rings] mumureing D, murmurings F
21 her] he D
 Phoebe] phoe D

5 *Fortune our friend.* An allusion to the popular song "Fortune my Foe." See Simpson, pp. 225–231.
11 *Strike crochet time. I.e.,* make fast music.
15 *Helitrope.* EMV, p. 634, reads *heliotrope.*
17 *of force. I.e.,* powerful enough.

VI.

Copied into Bod. Mus. f. 7–10 (see note to I), with no variants in the Bassus part, fol. 19v; the Cantus has only the first stanza, and reads *while* in line 3.

VII.

Copied into Bod. Mus. f. 7–10 (see note to I), with these variants in the Cantus, fol. 25:

3 proceeded] proceed
7 low'rs] lower

12 *the thing . . . recouer. Cf.* Tilley T204, "Things past cannot be recalled but may be repented."

VIII.

This poem is by Thomas Campion; see Jo1605.XVII and note. Pilkington's setting was copied into BM MS Add. 29291 (18th century), fol. 6v, and into Bod. Mus. f. 7–10 (see note to I), without variants in the Bassus part, fol. 20, and with the reading *proue* in line 2 in the Tenor part, fol. 17v.

14 *proue.* EMV reads *proves* in the notes (p. 756) but *prove* in the text (p. 636).

IX.

For other poems about Venus and Adonis, see the note to Bt1606.XI.
What seems to be a travesty of this poem was printed in John Phillips' *Sportive Wit* (1656), sigs. Hh2v–3. It begins:

Underneath the Castle wall
 The Queen of Love sits mourning
A tiring of her golden hair,
 Her red-rose cheek adorning;

> With a lilly-white hand she smote her brest,
> And said she was quite forsaken,
> With that the Mountains fell a leaping,
> And the Fidlers fell a quaking.

The six stanzas that follow are not related to Pilkington's text. A version of these lines was printed with a musical setting in Thomas D'Urfey's *Wit and Mirth: or Pills to Purge Melancholy* (1707), IV, 261, with an even more crude travesty upon the travesty beginning, "Underneath the rotten hedge, the Tinkers Wife sat shiting."

Pilkington's version was copied into BM MS Add. 29291 (18th century), fol. 34v, and into Bod. Mus. f. 7–10 (see note to I) with no variants in the Bassus, fol. 20v.

4 *mourne.* Although this could be a noun meaning *sadness,* it is probably a misprint for *bourne,* the result of a foul-case error; *b* and *m* lay close together in the type case.

7 *grast.* Read *graced.*

vnkindnesse. EMV, p. 636, reads *kindness.*

X.

Copied into Bod. Mus. f. 7–10 (see note to I), with these variants from the Bassus (fol. 21):

    17 had] hath
    21 this] thy

1 *William Harwood.* There are at least three contemporary William Harwoods or Harwards, but only one may have died by 1604—if death is indeed the misfortune Pilkington means, and if he is not the same as one of the longer-lived Harwoods. This is the William Harwarde who was made prebendary at Wellington, Lichfield, in 1604 (John Le Neve, *Fasti Ecclesiae Anglicanae* [Oxford, 1954], I, 637).

XI.

Copied into Bod. Mus. f. 7–10 (see note to I), Cantus, fol. 19v, omitting *lyes* in line 8.

XII.

Copied into BM MS Add. 29291 (18th century), fol. 7v; and into Bod. Mus. f. 7–10 (see note to I), Bassus, fol. 22, without variants.

3 *Phenix nest.* Cf. Do1612.II.9.

XIII.

Copied into Bod. Mus. f. 7–10, Cantus, fol. 20v, without variants.

1 *M. Holder.* If the *M.* is not an initial but the abbreviation for "Master," it is probable that this is Clement Holder, who took a B. A. from Caius College, Cambridge, in 1583, and an M. A. in 1586, and was Prebendary of Southwell from 1590 to 1638. He was the father of William Holder (1616–1698), divine, composer, and author of *A Treatise on the Natural Grounds and Principles of Harmony* (1694). See J. and J. A. Venn, *Alumni Cantabrigienses* (1922), and Grove.

12 *T'sore.* EMV, p. 638, reads *To soar,* which is the sense of the passage.

XIIII.

Copied into Bod. Mus. f. 7–10 (see note to I), Tenor, fol. 20v, without variants (the refrains are abbreviated).

6–7 Serpents hisses . . . kisses. As David Greer has shown in *M & L*, XLV (1964), 129, these lines resemble Shakespeare's *Venus and Adonis*, lines 17–18:

> Here come and sit, where never serpent hisses,
> And being set, I'll smother thee with kisses.

11 As noted in EMV, p. 756, a line seems to be missing after this line. It would rhyme with *fyer* and *desire*.

XV.

Copied into (D) Bod. Mus. f. 7–10 (see note to I), Tenor, fol. 21; and into (E) BM MS Harl. 4286 (17th century), fol. 64v (without music). Variants are as follows:

    1 fruit] leafe E
    2–4 *omitted* E
    2 may] will D
    5 flutter] flutters E
    6 frid] feed D
    8 Too . . . mee] To and fro E
    12 sorie] sorrowes E

5 *Flie . . . flame.* Cf. Bt1606.XIII.11–12 and note.
6 *frid.* EMV, p. 756, suggests that this should read *frie*. The MS reading above, *feed*, is also a possibility. With some strain, one could understand the passage to mean that the tears *quench* and *are fried by* the flame.

XVI.

This poem is from (D) Thomas Lodge's *Rosalynde* (1590), sigs. N3v–N4 (sung by Phoebe in reply to Montanus); it was also printed in (E) *England's Helicon* (1600; REH, I, 60–61), where it is assigned to "Thom. Lodge." Pilkington's version was copied into (F) Bod. Mus. f. 7–10 (see note to I), Cantus, fol. 22 (first stanza) and Tenor, fol. 21v (second stanza). Variants are as follows:

    3 oppressed] distressed DE
    4 stong] stung DEF
    5 distressed] oppressed DE
    6–7 with . . . down] With a downe, downe, &c D, with downe a downe, &c. E
    9–22 DE *divide the lines*
    9 mothers] moouers D
    12 brest] breasts E
    15 Chorus . . . downe] Downe a downe./ Thus Phillis sung/ by fancie once distressed, &c. DE
    18 Whilst] Whilest D
    22 mate] make DE
    23 Chorus . . . &c.] DE *repeat the Chorus in full,* D *ending* with downe a downe, adowne downe, adowne a.

Another poem in *England's Helicon* beginning "Hey downe a downe did *Dian* sing" (REH, I, 121–122) is very similar, and also begins with a burden.

XVII.

This poem had been printed in (D) *England's Helicon* (1600; REH, I, 96), headed 'Damelus Song to his Diaphenia," and subscribed "H. C." Rollins (II, 141) takes these initials to stand for Henry Chettle rather than Henry Constable because another poem with these initials comes from a work probably by Chettle, *Piers Plainness* (1595; see REH, I, 83–84; II, 133). Harold Jenkins, in *Henry Chettle* (London, 1934), pp. 46–48 cautiously accepts the poem as Chettle's, and Joan Grundy denies them to Constable in her edition of his *Poems* (Liverpool: University Press, 1960), pp. 50–51. Another copy is in (E) BM MS Harl. 4286 (17th century), fol. 65v, without title or signature. Pilkington's version was copied into (F) Bod. Mus. f. 7–10 (see note to I), Tenor, fol. 22. Variants are:

> 1 *Diaphenia*] Daphne E
> Dafdowndillie] Daffadown-dillie DE
> 6, 12, 18 *omitted* E
> 14 all] *omitted* F

XVIII.

This poem by Anthony Munday is also in Ck1610.IX and Jo1605.II. See the note to Jo1605.II. Pilkington's version was copied into Bod. Mus. f. 7–10 (see note to I), Cantus, fol. 16, without variants.

XIX.

Copied into Bod. Mus. f. 7–10 (see note to I), Cantus, fol. 23, with two small variants:

> 6 wher] weare
> 10 reare] rare

2 *time sporter. I.e.*, music makes sport of time. Or this might possibly read *times porter*.

XX.

This poem was first printed in (D) *The Honorable Entertainement gieuen to the Queenes Maiestie in Progresse, at Eluetham in Hampshire, by the right Honorable the Earle of Hertford* (1591), sig. B4–4v. The song was described as sung by six virgins walking before the Queen "strewing the way with flowers, and singing a sweete song of six parts to this dittie, which followeth." It was reprinted in (E) *England's Helicon* (1600; REH, I, 46–47), headed "The Nimphes meeting their May Queene, entertaine her with this Dittie," and subscribed "Tho. Watson." According to Rollins (II, 37, 102), Watson is also credited with the poem in Francis Davison's MS list of attributions. Watson has a poem with lines similar to the refrain of this poem in his *Italian Madrigalls Englished* (1590), Nos. VIII and XXVIII, beginning "This sweet & merry month of May," and concluding:

> O Beauteous Queene of second Troy,
> Take well in worth a simple toy.

Both settings in Watson's collection are by William Byrd, who reprinted the four-part setting (VIII) as No. IX of his *Psalmes, Songs, and Sonnets* (1611). Hallett Smith, in his *Elizabethan Poetry* (Cambridge, Mass.: Harvard University Press, 1952), p. 269, suggests that Watson rewrote the text, removing the May references so that "With fragrant flowers" could be sung to Byrd's six-part music in the September Elvetham entertainment. Smith thinks the heading of the copy in *England's Helicon* recalls the first version. But the new verses cannot be fitted to Byrd's music without awkwardness. "With fragrant flowers" was rewritten by Anthony Nixon for his *Great Britaines Generall Ioyes* (1613), sig. A4 (printed by Rollins, II, 103). Pilkington's version was copied into Bod. Mus. f. 7–10, Cantus, fol. 23v, omitting the second stanza. Variants from DE are:

2 holy day] holliday D
5, 11 gracious King] beauteous Queene DE
8 Satires] Satyrs D
10 signes] signe D
11–12, 17–18 of second . . . ioy] &c. E
17 gracious King] beauties Queene D, beauteous Queene E

4 *proud.* This should probably be read as *prov'd.* See REH, II, 103, and EMV, p. 642.

XXI.

1 *Thomas Leighton.* As EMV notes, p. 756, Leighton is probably one of the Shropshire Leightons, related to Sir William Leighton, to whose *Teares or Lamentacions of a Sorrowfull Soule* (1614) Pilkington contributed. There were at least two Thomas Leightons, one of whom died in 1606. The other, the son of Richard Leighton of Coates, took a B.A. from Exeter College, Oxford, in 1601 and was in the Middle Temple in 1605. No date is given for his death, but he may be the subject of Pilkington's song. See Joseph Foster, *Alumni Oxonienses* (1891).

John Bartlet, *A Booke of Ayres*, 1606

Dedication
Sir Edward Seymoore, Earl of Hertford (1539?–1621), was made lord lieutenant of Somerset and Wiltshire in May, 1602 (DNB). Several other books were dedicated to him including the English edition of Adrien LeRoy's *A Briefe and Plaine Instruction to Set All Musicke of Eight Diuers Tunes in Tableture for the Lute*, 1574 (Williams).

I.
Psalm 71, verses 22–23; it varies from the lines in *The Whole Booke of Dauids Psalmes Collected into English Metre, by* T. Sternh[old] I.Hopk[ins] W. Whittingham *and others* (1582), sig. I10 (stanzas 23 and 24) thus:

1 O Lord] Therefore
 and] to
2 with viole] both lute and
3 harpe] hart
 and prayse] always
5 wil] shall
7 will] shall

II.
Fellowes (EMV, 2nd ed., p. 607) states that this poem was written "by Mary, Countess of Pembroke, on the death of her brother Sir Philip Sidney." A pencilled

note in the BM copy also asserts that it is "On Sir Philip Sidney." There is no evidence for this guess; moreover, Sir Philip was not the Countess' "onelie brother" (l. 5). Diana Poulton tells me that it seems more like a song from a play.

III.

This song was reprinted, with Bartlet's tune, in (D) Forbes's *Cantus* (1662), sig. V2 ("The Fourtyninth Song"). It is also found with Bartlet's melody and bass in (E) Giles Earle's MS, BM Add. 24665 (1615–1626), fols. 71v–72; and in (F) BM MS Add. 29409, a nineteenth-century transcript of an older Scots MS, fol. 268v (no music). Variants are as follows:

1 lookte] look'd D, look F
    affections] affectioune F
2 vowes] woves D
5 neere] never D
6 but iestingly] bot jest nightlye F
8 loues] loue E
9 Though . . . protest] Though they sweare and protest D,
Yet let them sweir and protest F
    11 theyle all] thay will F
    12 twas] It was D, I was F
    in] *omitted* D

8 *like fethers in the wind.* Tilley F162.

IIII.

This song was reprinted with Bartlet's tune in Forbes's *Cantus* (1662), sig. N1–N1v (1666, E3v), headed "The Thirtie Song," with these variants (excluding the refrain, which Forbes repeats in full for stanzas 1 and 2, and all but the last three words in stanzas 3 and 4):

2 seeth] sayeth
    he] she
8 show] think
    deuoide of] devot of (1666 ed: void of all)
9 kindle] kindles
    strange] strong
10 that] who
14 tender leaues she] comely colours
17 her] the
18 that same] the Sun

VII.

This song, with Bartlet's tune, was copied into (D) William Stirling's Cantus part-book (Edinburgh, NLS, Advocate's MS 5.2.14 [*c.* 1639], fol. 13). The poem appears without music in (E) BM Add. 34064, fol. 23v. This MS dates from around 1596 (see fol. 1: "Anthonie Babington of Warringtonn 1596"), and contains a number of poems by Nicholas Breton, who may have written VII. Grosart prints the poem from (E) in the section of his edition of Breton's *Works* called "Daffodils and Primroses"

(I, 22), reading *witte* in l. 1 and *annexed* in l. 4. (F) BM MS Add. 29291 (*c.* 1762), fol. 6, has a part-song version of Bartlet's music. Variants from DE are:

7 thy] that E
10 Loue . . . to] all the powres on earthe do E
11 in a] will, E
13–18 E *has*:

> looke oh Angell looke vpon me
> see howe I am woe begone me
> of both witt and sence depriued
> but of the to be revived
>
> thow that art the shepperds story [?]
> in thy pittie shewe thy glorye [? *Grosart has* eye]
> I can saie no more but this
> in thie loue my livinge is

16 franzie] frencie D

4 *all . . . mixed.* That is, "All my joys are mixed with love."

VIII.

EMV, p. 727, compares this poem to Sonnet II from Samuel Daniel's *Delia* (1592), "Goe wailing verse, the infants of my loue" (*Poems*, ed. A. C. Sprague [1930], p. 11). Beyond the opening line—a conventional *envoy*—the resemblance is faint, but the two poems may share some remote source. *Cf.* also Francis Davison's poem in *A Poetical Rhapsody* (RPR, I, 90–91), "Goe wayling Accents, goe."
  10 *cheeke bedewed raine.* Hysteron proteron for "rain-bedewed cheek."
  30 *Cupid did mistake her for his mother. Cf.* the third of the little Anacreontic poems between Spenser's *Amoretti* and the *Epithalamion*, and Marlowe's *Hero and Leander*, I, 39–44; the conceit no doubt appears elsewhere.

IX.

The monologue of the maid who wishes to be a maid no longer was a popular sub-genre among the song-writers. Compare 4Camp[1617].IX (set also in Fer1609. VIII) and XXIV, Jo1609.V, Jo1610.XV, and Thomas Vautor, *The First Set* (1619), No. LV. See also the note to Jo1609.IIII, and *cf.* a poem in Richard Johnson's *Golden Garland of Princely pleasures* (1620), sig. G3, beginning "Can any tell me what I aile." See also C. R. Baskervill, *The Elizabethan Jig* (Chicago, 1929), pp. 205–207.

X.

This poem is by George Gascoigne, who published it in his *A Hundreth sundrie Flowres* (1573), sigs. O4–P1, with this heading: "He wrote (at his friends request) in prayse of a Gentlewoman, whose name was Phillip, as followeth." In *The Posies of George Gascoigne* (1575), sig. S4–S4v, it is entitled "The praise of Phillip Sparrowe," which makes the *double-entendre* only slightly less apparent. Both versions conclude with the motto, "Si fortunatus infoelix." Bartlet used five of Gascoigne's nine six-lined stanzas, and made a refrain out of the last two lines of stanza 7. Variants (from both the *Flowers* and the *Posies*, unless noted) are as follows:

3 or sit] or lye
15 merry] chery

18 home] hand
26 new found] newfond *Flowers*

After l. 30, Gascoigne continues (Flowers):

> Hir fethers are so fresh of hew,
> And so well proyned euery day:
> She lacks none 'oyle, I warrant you:
> To trimme hir tayle both tryck and gay.
> And though hir mouth be somewhat wyde,
> Hir tonge is sweet and short beside.
>
> And for the rest I dare compare,
> She is both tender, sweet and soft:
> She neuer lacketh daynty fare,
> But is well fed and feedeth oft:
> For if my phip haue lust to eate,
> I warrant you Phip lacks no meat.
>
> And then if that hir meat be good,
> And such as like do loue alway:
> She will lay lips theron by the-rood,
> And see that none be cast away:
> For when she once hath felt a fitte,
> Phillip will crie still, yit, yit, yit.

32 Hauing] Which had

After 37:

> Wherefore I sing and euer shall,
> To praise as I haue often prou'd,
> There is no byrd amongst them all,
> So worthy for to be belou'd.
> Let others prayse what byrd they will,
> Sweete Phillip shalbe my byrd still.

This poem and others like it probably derive from John Skelton's "Philip Sparrow." Compare Sidney, *Astrophil and Stella*, Sonnet 83, and a song sung by Constance in Richard Brome's *The Northern Lass* (1632), III, ii, beginning:

> A bonny bony Bird I had,
>   A Bird that was my Marrow:
> A Bird whose pastime made me glad,
>   And Philip 'twas my Sparrow.
> A pretty Play-fere: Chirp it would,
>   And hop, and fly to fist,
> Keep cut, as 'twere a Userers Gold,
>   And bill me when I list.
>   Philip, Philip, Philip it cryes,
>   But he is fled, and my joy dyes.

19 *laies on loade.* Deals heavy blows; hence acts vigorously.
28 *fend cut.* The OED notes the possibility of this being a fencing phrase, but sees

it also in relation to the phrase "to keep one's cut," to keep one's distance, be on good behavior. *Cf.* Skelton's "Philip Sparrow," who

> learned after my school
> For to keep his cut,
> With 'Philip, keep your cut!'

(*Complete Poems*, ed. Philip Henderson [London, 1959], p. 63, lines 117–119.) See also Ringler, pp. 298, 482–483.

XI.

This is one of the many poems inspired by Shakespeare's reluctant Adonis in *Venus and Adonis*. See several of the poems in Jaggard's *The Passionate Pilgrim* (1599), "The Sheepheards Song of Venus and Adonis" from *England's Helicon* (REH, I, 174–177), At1622.IV, and Pi1605.IX.

2 *rose checkte Adone.* This almost becomes a Homeric epithet. *Cf.* Marlowe's *Hero and Leander*, I, 93, and Shakespeare's *Venus and Adonis*, l. 3.

18 *heare . . . their.* Read *here . . . there.*

XII.

This poem was first printed in (D) Nicholas Breton's *The Strange Fortunes of Two Excellent Princes* (1600), sig. G3, and consequently ascribed to Breton. Yet it was also printed in (E) J[ohn] H[ind's] *The Most Excellent Historie of Lysimachus and Varrona* (1604), sig. L3, headed "Valentines Song." Hind probably lifted it from Breton; note the similarity of the phrases introducing the song: "She . . . tooke her lute and plaied a note to a dittie, which she sung as followeth" (Breton, sig. G2v). "With that he tooke a Lute in his hand and played a note to a dittie which he sung as follweth" (Hind, sig. L2v). Another version, with the treble and bass of Bartlet's music is in (F) BM MS Add. 29481 (*c.* 1630), fol. 11. The music and first stanza of F was printed in an article by John P. Cutts, "The Strange Fortunes of Two Excellent Princes and The Arbor of amorous Deuises," *RN*, XV (1962), 11. Variants are as follows:

6 sun-like] semlike F
7 but be] be but D
14 grace] Graces DE
    both] *omitted* DE
18 shines] shine D
21 thou were] thou wert DE
22 would I] would D

18 *shines.* EMV, p. 360, reads *shine.*

XIII.

A possible source of this poem may be a song which Diana Poulton has copied for me from the lute MS of Cosimo Bottegari at Modena, Biblioteca Estense MS Mus. C. 311, fol. 47:

> Sta notte m'insognava
> Ch'ero tornato mosca, e che volava
> D'intorn'alla tua vesta
> Mo quà, mo là, con gran piacer e festa.

Poi mi parea volare
Sopra so'bianco petto, e la mi stare
Non poco poco, e poi
Volava sopra quesse trezze toi.

E con fest'e con gioco
Scendev'a s'occhi che son fiamm'e foco;
La dove m'abruciava
L'ali tutte, e in terra poi cascava.

E tu, che mi vedevi
In terra, con le piedi m'uccidevi;
E ti senti a gridare
"A così more che cerca volare."

The conceit of the lover as a fly or moth burned in the flame was common in poetry and emblems. See, for example, Donne's "Elegy VI" ll. 17–19, "The Canonization" ll. 20–21 (Gardner pp. 11, 74; note on p. 203), and the examples discussed by Donald L. Guss in *John Donne, Petrarchist* (Detroit: Wayne State University Press, 1966), pp. 159–164; see also Francis Davison's "Like to the seely flie" in *A Poetical Rhapsody* RPR, I, 87), and No. XXVII of Walter Porter's *Madrigales and Ayres* (1632; EMV, p. 653).

A copy of this song, with the melody and bass of Bartlet's music, is found in Giles Earle's MS, BM Add. 24665 (1615–1626), fols. 51v–52, with these variants:

   4 robe] roabes
   6 soght] tooke
   9 By] &
      new found] suddaine
  12 whereby] by which
  15 moude . . . my] ruthefull of my
  16 And crusht] did crushe
  18 Whose . . . because] Who lost his life because

 10 *feares.* EMV, p. 360, emends to *fear.*
 15 *moude.* EMV, p. 361, emends to *mourned.*

XIIII.

The original source for this poem seems to be (D) George Peele's fragment, *The Hunting of Cupid.* David Horne prints it from the Drummond MSS 7, fols. 352–353, 361, in his *Life and Minor Works of George Peele* (New Haven: Yale University Press, 1952), pp. 204–205. Other versions of the poem are in (E) *The Wisdom of Doctor Dody-poll* (1600), a play attributed to Peele, where it is sung by Cornelia (sig. A4v); (F) Bod. MS Rawl. Poet. 85 (*c.* 1600?), fol. 13, subscribed "M G: Peelle"; and (G) Bod. MS Rawl. Poet. 172, fol. 2v (this MS is a miscellaneous collection covering many years; the leaves containing the poem are probably early seventeenth century), entitled "A description of loue." Variants are as follows:

   1 I pray thee tel] for (wel I wot) loue is a thing D, for sure I am it is a thing E, for sure loue is a thinge FG
   2 it] Loue FG
      prickle] pricke DEG

it] loue FG
sting] thing E
3 it] loue FG
prety prety] prittie G
4 it . . . it] Loue . . . loue FG
6 as] is D
wits] wit D, selfe FG
can] doth D, do E
best deuise] well aduise G
7 loues] His FG
darling lies] dwelling is DEFG

D *continues*:

> from whence do glaunce loves pearcing darts
> that mak such holes into our harts
> and al the world herin accord
> love is a great and mightie lord
> and when he list to mount so hie
> with venus he in heven doth lie
> and ever more heth been a God
> since Mars and sche plaid even and od

FG *vary thus*:

> From whence he shootes his dayntye [painted? G] dartes
> In to the lusty gallants hartes.
> and euer since was [hath been G] calde a god
> That [since G] Mars withe Venus playde euen and odd

For further comment, see John P. Cutts, "Peele's *Hunting of Cupid*," *SR*, V (1958), 121–132; Cutts fits the additional lines from D to Bartlet's music.
Analogous definitions of love are discussed in the note to Jo1601.IX.

XVI.

1 *ascribes*. EMV, p. 361, emends to *ascribe*.
5 *It . . . eye*. Cf. Tilley L501.

XVII.

2 *Whether . . . hart*. Cf. Jo1601.XII.1.
7 *hay ding a ding a ding*. Cf. Mo1600.VI.5.

XIX–XXI.

Songs imitating bird calls are fairly common in the Renaissance. Perhaps the most famous example is Clément Janequin's "Le Chant des oiseaux" (printed in *Les Maîtres musiciens de la Renaissance française*, ed. H. Expert, VII [1898], 1–30). Also compare such pieces as Shakespeare's songs in *Love's Labour's Lost*, V, ii; "In a merry May morn" and the excellent "Cuckoo" song by Richard Nicholson, both printed from BM MS Add. 17797 in Peter Warlock's *Third Book of Elizabethan Songs that were originally composed for one voice to sing and four stringed instruments to accompany* (Oxford, 1926), pp. 4–6 and 15–18. Especially interesting is a song printed in Warlock's *First*

Book, pp. 5–9, the music from BM MSS Add. 17786–91, and the words from Christ Church, Oxford, MS 984. Compare the last line with XIX.9, XX.22, and XXI.9:

> This merry pleasant spring,
> Hark, how the sweet birds sing
> And carol in the copse and on the briar.
> Jug jug jug! the nightingale delivers.
> It it it it, the sparrow sings his hot desire
> The robin he records, the lark he quivers.
> O sweet, O sweet, O sweet, as sweet as ever:
> From strains so sweet, Sweet birds deprive us never!
> (From Warlock.)

XX.7 *flat*. Thus both voice parts, set to a single note. But EMV, p. 362, emends to *flatter* because of the rhyme.

XX.18 *poor Margery*. In this song, the owl; but a hen was sometimes called "Margery-prater" (OED).

XXI.5 *madrigal*. EMV, p. 363, emends to *madrigals*.

John Coprario, *Funeral Teares*, 1606

Vno Sol, etc.

1 *Mountioie*. Charles Blount, Earl of Devonshire and eighth Lord Mountjoy 1563–1606).

6 *Penelope*. Penelope Devereux Rich, who had been Blount's mistress for some years. When he married her in 1605 after her divorce from Lord Rich, it was considered a scandal. (See "In honorable memory," etc. ll. 44ff. and DNB.)

In honorable memory, etc.

Blount's death was also commemorated in poems by John Ford, *Fames Memoriall, or the Earle of Deuonshire Deceased* (1606), and by Samuel Daniel, *A Funerall Poeme vppon the Death of the late noble Earle of Deuenshyre* (1606).

16 *seede of Mnemosine*. The Muses, daughters of Zeus and Mnemosyne.

26–32. The moral nature of Blount's detractors is indicated by the associations of vanity, deceit, stupidity, etc. with the beasts they resemble. This passage should be seen in the light of the long tradition deriving from moral commentary on the Circe legend and culminating in Milton's *Comus*. See especially Spenser, *Faerie Queene*, II.xii.84–87.

61 *pallace*. Read *Pallas'*.

62 *Irish rebels*. In 1601 Blount succeeded the Earl of Essex as the commander of the English forces opposing the Earl of Tyrone, who surrendered in 1602 (DNB).

63 *inuading Spaniard*. Blount had built ships in 1588 to help repel the Armada (DNB).

76–77 *Zepherus . . . His goulden trumpet*. In Chaucer's *House of Fame* (III, 1567–1582, 1637, 1678) Aeolus blows a black brazen trumpet called Sklaundre or a golden trumpet called Clere Laude, depending on the judgment of the goddess Fame.

84 *Omnia . . . Amori*. Virgil, *Eclogues*, X.69; Tilley L527.

IIII.

Lines 1–6 set also by John Dowland, RD01610.X. As Vincent Duckles notes in "The English Musical Elegy of the Late Renaissance," *Aspects of Medieval and Renaissance Music: A Birthday Offering to Gustave Reese* (New York: W. W. Norton, 1966), p. 149, Coprario's bass prelude quotes the opening phrase of the tune to Ophelia's song in *Hamlet*, "He is dead and gone, lady," But see Seng, pp. 135–137.

VII.

For other dialogues, see the note to Do1600.XXII.

Tis true, etc.

1 *Tarantula.* Sir Thomas Browne's skepticism deserts him on the question of the tarantula; see his *Pseudodoxia Epidemica* (1646–1672), ed. Geoffrey Keynes, *Works* (Chicago: 2nd ed., 1964), II, 267.

Quid mortuos, etc.

2 *manticae quod in tergo est.* See the fable of Phaedrus (IV.10); the reference is to the double bagged wallet man carries, with his neighbors' faults in the front bag and his own in the bag behind his back. *Cf.* Catullus XXII.21.

John Danyel, *Songs for the Lute Viol and Voice*, 1606

Dedication

Anne Grene's father, Sir William Grene, had acquired the manor house at Great Milton, Oxfordshire, by 1588, and was still living there in 1611. He had a son named Michael who also was knighted. See the *Victoria History of the County of Oxford*, ed. Mary Lobel (London: Oxford University Press for the Institute of Historical Research, 1962), VII, 120, 126. Sir William and Sir Michael were probably the "Sir Michael Green of Oxfordshire" and "Sir William Green" knighted by James I at Windsor Castle on July 9, 1603 (Nichols, *Progresses of James I*, I, 201).

26–27 *Baucis*, etc. See Ovid, *Metamorphoses*, VIII.

36–37 *him . . . deare to mee.* Danyel's brother, Samuel Daniel the poet. See notes to Nos. IIII and VIII. John Danyel wrote the dedication to the posthumous edition of his brother's *Works* (1623); for further information, see Grove, Warlock, pp. 52–63, and Samuel Daniel's *Works*, ed. Alexander Grosart (1885), I, xxvi, 16.

I.

This poem was reset as a two-part madrigal for four voices by Francis Pilkington in his *Second Set of Madrigals and Pastorals* (1624), Nos. VIII–IX (Cantus, sigs. B2v–B3), with no variants. Answering poems were a popular form; see the note to Do 1603.XIX, and Kerman, pp. 84–85 and note.

1 *Daphne. Cf.* the use of the myth in Do1603.VI.

13 *Greene.* A pun on the name of Anne Greene, suggesting that she or Danyel may have written the two parts of the poem.

II.

EMV, p. 736, cites another version, "Daintie fine Bird," set by Orlando Gibbons, *The First Set of Madrigals And Mottets of 5. Parts* (1612), No. IX, and by Thomas Vautor,

The First Set: Beeing Songs of diuers Ayres and Natures, of Fiue and Sixe parts (1619), No. XVIII. As Obertello (pp. 408, 519) has shown, this is a translation of the source of No. II, Giovanni Battista Guarini's "Auuenturoso augello":

> O Come se' gentile,
> Caro augellino: o quanto
> E'l mio stato amoroso al tuo simile.
> Tu prigion, io prigion: tu canti, io canto,
> Tu canti per colei,
> Che t'ha legato, ed io canto per lei.
> Ma in questo è differente
> La mia [sorte] dolente,
> Che gioua pur à te l'esser canoro.
> Viui cantando, ed io cantando moro.

(From *Rime* [Venice, 1598], sig. L3v, with l. 8 from Obertello.) Obertello (pp. 519–520) lists several similar poems.

IIII.

This poem is from Samuel Daniel's *Delia* sonnets; it was taken from his *Works* of 1601 (or 1602), where it is No. LIIII. See also *Poems and A Defence of Ryme*, ed. A. C. Sprague (Cambridge, Mass., 1930), pp. 34 and 189. Variants from the *Works* (1601, *To Delia*, sig. C2) are:

8 giues] giue
9–10 *These lines follow 11–12 in* Delia
14 sweet] true

V.

Fellowes (EMV, 2nd ed., p. 613), says that the first line of this poem is two syllables shorter than the corresponding lines in the other stanzas; but since in this song the music for the last two stanzas differs from that for the first stanza, the lines do not need to be the same.

11–12 *fire . . . shines. Cf.* Tilley F281, "That Fire which lights us at a distance will burn us when near."

VIII.

This poem is based on a sonnet from Samuel Daniel's *Delia*, No. XXIII, in his *Works* (1601), sig. A6v, and varies thus:

1 canst thou] come and
2 That] Which
4 and] or
6 might] may
7 loue] spare
8 wayes] weies
9–16 *Samuel Daniel has these lines*:

> And yet thou seest thy powre she disobaies,
> Cares not for thee, but lets thee waste in vaine,
> And prodigall of howers and yeares betraies
> Beautie and youth t'opinion and disdaine.
> Yet spare her Tyme, let her exempted bee,
> She may become more kinde to thee or mee.

Fellowes (EMV, 2nd ed., p. 614) speculates that the last eight lines of the song may have been written by Samuel Daniel especially for his brother's use.

A copy of this song, with the treble and bass of Danyel's music, appears in Tenbury MS 1018 (first half of 17th century), fol. 47, with the following variants:

4 decayes] delayes
5–8 *omitted in MS; these lines would be sung to the same music as 1–4.*
9 steeme] esteeme
13–16 *omitted in MS*

The MS gives as a second stanza the first 8 lines of a poem by Thomas, Lord Vaux, "When I looke backe & in my selfe behould," which was printed in *The Paradise of Dainty Devices* (1576–1606; see the edition by H. E. Rollins [Cambridge, Mass., 1927], pp. 19–20).

IX.

Mrs. M. E. and her husband are unknown.

The words to the first part of this song were copied into Bod. MS Eng. Poet. f. 16, fol. 5, with these variants:

3 *MS breaks the line after* shew
6 but from] from but
7 *MS breaks the line after* know
9 And] then
10 That knowes more] wch knows the
11 consume . . . dye] swell, burst, consume, and dye

X.

This second part, with the melody and bass of Danyel's music (though much changed), is found in BM Add. 24665 (1615–1626; Giles Earle's MS), fols. 33v–34, with these variants:

6 niggard] inward
9 knowst more] knowes noe

XIII.–XV.

This three-part song is a virtuoso piece the effect of which cannot be suggested by the words alone. The music is highly illustrative of the text: the words "vnmeasur'd griefes that tyme forget" (XIII.3) are set to syncopated notes; ascending and descending chromatic scales accompany "chromatique tunes" (XIIII.2). Thomas Morley had written that melodies which employ "accidentall motions," that is, with accidental sharps and flats, "may fitlie expresse the passions of griefe, weeping, sighes, sorrowes, sobbes, and such like" (*A Plaine and Easie Introduction to Practicall Musicke* [1597], sig. Aa2). Dowland uses chromaticism in a similar fashion in Do1597.XIV and Do1612.X. See also "Come woeful Orpheus" from William Byrd's *Psalmes, Songs, and Sonnets* (1611), No. XIX (EMV, p. 74).

XV.

These lines are obscure. David Greer (EMV, p. 736) offers the following paraphrase: "Certain uncertainly-remembered melodies, evoking past thoughts, bring back the grief, and then—though the music dies away again—the grief remains." This interpretation takes some liberties with the meanings of *turn*, which at this time does not seem to have had a specifically musical meaning, and with *forecast*, which means *anticipated* or *foreordained*. An even more ingenious explanation, offered to me by my colleague Stewart Baker, is subject to some of the same objections. He suggests that the turn which is "forecast" and which "brings back the same" is like an ornamental turn in music, which is determined by its first note and returns to it (but this idea is not illustrated in Danyel's music); or a rhetorical turn ("vncertain certain") which is determined by its root which it repeats; or an experience which is anticipated and repeats itself. Another paraphrase is possible: "Certain uncertain turns of anticipated thoughts (like uncertain chromatic tunes) occur and recur, then die; but having been set down in song, they will last."

XVI.

19 *nought delights and lastes. Cf.* Tilley J90, H747, and P414.

XVII.

Copies of this poem appear in (D) BM MS Harl. 667 (after 1614), fol. 106v, and in (E) BM MS Add. 24665 (1615–1626; Giles Earle's MS), fols. 23v–24. The latter has the treble and bass of Daniel's music, the melody being ornamented with trills, etc. Variants are as follows:

   1 gate] gates E
   4 misdeeds] miscords E
   5 cleane] cleare E
   7 with-out] within E
   8 neare] faste E
   9 the thoughts] that thought E
  10 That . . . heare] Which with my life is alwaies like to taste E
     their] *omitted* D
  13 refuge] redeemer E
  14 twixt] b twixt D
  17 may be] *omitted* E

XVIII.

This poem is based on two madrigals by G. B. Guarini, found in his *Rime* (Venice, 1598), sigs. L4v–L5. The first stanza corresponds to Madrigal LV, "Mirar mortale":

> Io mi sento morir quando non miro
> Colei ch' è la mia vita.
> Poi se la miro anco morir mi sento,
> Perche del mio tormento
> Non hà pietà la cruda, e non m'aita,
> E sà pur s'i'l' adoro,
> Così mirando, e non mirando, i'moro.

The second stanza adapts Madrigal LIIII, "Amante poco ardito":

> Parlo, misero, o taccio?
> S'io taccio, che soccorso haurà il morire?
> S'io parlo, che perdono haurà l'ardire?
> Taci: che ben s'intende
> Chiusa fiamma talor da chi l'accende.

Parla in me la pietate,
E dice quel bel volto al crudo core,
Chi può mirarmi, e non languir d'amore?

Cf. also Spenser, *Amoretti*, XLIII.

This poem is to be found in a group of MSS dating from the middle of the seventeenth century: (D) BM MS Add. 30982, fol. 36, headed "ii song Jo: Richards"; (E) a MS belonging to Mr. James M. Osborne of Yale, B.12.5, fol. 23v, headed "A despairing louer to his cruell Mris"; (F) Folger MS V.a.319, fol. 28, entitled "A louers passion"; (G) Folger MS V.a.322, p. 53; and (H) Folger MS V.a.103, fol. 33, headed "A despairing Lover to his Cruell Mistresse." The variants are:

2 that] who DEH
3 when] if DEFGH
   yet] not D
5 So that to] for that by E
   wrought] got EH
7–12 *omitted* DE
11 So that . . . one] Soe that to me like misery is wroughte FG
   I see to mee] to mee, I see H
12 Speake . . . vndone] I am vndonne, speake I or speake I not FG

XX.

Although the first line of this poem echoes the first line of Petrarch's "Or che'l ciel e la terra e'l vento tace" (Sonnet CLXIV), the rest of the poem seems closer to Petrarch's "Zefiro torna" (Sonnet CCCX). *Cf.* Cav1598.XXII, XXV and notes. EMV, p. 453, makes line 7 read "When I, when only I, alone" although none of the parts repeat the words in this order. The parts read: "When I alone, when onely I alone, alone" (C1); "Onely I alone, I alone" (B); "When onely I alone, onely I alone, When I alone" (C2); "When onely I alone onely, I alone" (T).

XXI.

The tune which is the basis for this set of variations for the lute bears some resemblance to the tune which William Inglot used for a set of variations, "The Leaves bee greene," in *The Fitzwilliam Virginal Book*, ed. J. A. Fuller Maitland and Barclay Squire (1899, Dover reprint 1963), II, 381–383.

Thomas Ford, *Musicke of Sundrie Kindes*, 1607

Dedication (1)

Sir Richard Weston (1577–1635) was knighted by James I in 1603 and became the first Earl of Portland in 1633 (DNB). See the note to Dedication (2), on Sir Richard Tichborne. Several books were dedicated to Weston, but no other music (Williams).

I.

A copy of this poem in (D) Folger MS V.a.345 (*c.* 1630), p. 33, is entitled "A young mans Epitaph." A note in the margin reads: "He dyed sep 12, 1604, at the age of 23 yeares," and one following the poem says: "These verses above written, were made by one mr Henry Morrice, sonne to mr morrice, Attorney to the Court of awards, who dyed sodenly in milford lane hauing these verses in his pocket." James Morice, Attorney of the Court of Wards, was an important puritan parliamentarian during Elizabeth's reign. He got into trouble during the parliament of 1593 for attacking the bishops and the Court of High Commission. He died in 1597. See J. E. Neale's *Elizabeth I and her Parliaments 1584–1601* (London, 1957), pp. 267–279. Other copies of the poem may be found in (E) Rosenbach MS 239/27 (*c.* 1635), p. 358, with the title "An Epitaph one a yonge man"; in (F) Huntington MS HM 198 (mid-17th century), part II, fol. 7v, headed "Epitaph"; and in (G) Chetham MS 8012, p. 164 (Chetham's Library, Manchester; edited by A. B. Grosart as the *Doctor Farmer Chetham Manuscript* for the Chetham Society Publications, original series, vol. 89 [1873], p. 194). Lines 3–6 were incorporated into a longer elegy published in (H) *The Honour of Vertue. or the Monument erected by the sorowfull Husband, and the Epitaphes annexed by learned and worthy men, to the immortall memory of that worthy gentlewoman, Mrs.* Elizabeth Crashawe. *Who died . . . 1620. In the 24 yeare of her age* (1620; STC 6030), sig. C3. The first six lines of the poem are also in (I) Cambridge MS Add. 4138 (*c.* 1625), fol. 23, headed "of a gent. of the Temple that dyed about the age of 24." The variants are:

> 1–2 *omitted* H
> 1 Not . . . tolde] Twice twelue yeares not full tould FI
> 2 exchangde] exchanged G
> 3 my course] Her time H
>   was] is DE
>   my rest] her rest H
> 6 mirth] ioy H
>   months] yeares H
> 7–10 *omitted* FHI
> 7 cures] endeth all D, cureth E
>   sicknesses] sicknesse E
> 8 Author] Th'author E
>   distresses] distresse E
> 9 O there] Other EG
>   come] comes G

4 *God . . . best.* Tilley G251.
5–6 *for he . . . sorrow.* Cf. Tilley L260, "Long life has long misery."
7 *deth that cures our sicknesses.* Cf. Tilley D141, "Death is a plaster for all ills."
9 *O there.* EMV, p. 521, reads *Other,* as do EG, which is probably the correct reading.

II.

Compare Jo1601.IX and note.

IIII.

Thomas Lodge's poem was printed in (D) *Phillis: Honoured with Pastorall Sonnets, Elegies, and amorous delights* (1593), sig. H3v, where it is entitled "An Ode"; and in (E) *The Phoenix Nest* (1593), sigs. H3v–H4 (RPN, pp. 62–63), where it is subscribed "T. L. Gent." It also appears in (F) BM MS Add. 24665 (Giles Earle's book, 1615–1626), fols. 56v–57, with Ford's melody and bass; (G) Rosenbach MS 239/27 (*c.* 1635), pp. 113–114, headed "A Songe"; (H) Folger MS V.a.345 (*c.* 1630), pp. 137–138, also headed "A song"; (I) Edinburgh, NLS Advocates' MS 5.2.14 (*c.* 1640), fol. 21–21v, with Ford's tune; and (J) Bishop Smith's MS, Carlisle Cathedral (*c.* 1637; see note to Mo1600.XIII), Bassus partbook, p. 92, with Ford's melody and bass. Variants are as follows:

   1 see] find DE
     were] are H
     fained] fainzied I
   3 wethers] weaders I
   4 hart] hearts I
     vnconstant] vnstable DE, inconstant J
   5 sighted] slighted GH
   6 will] loue F
   7 foe] for I
   8 thee] th H
     thy] this DE (D *repeats this variant in the refrain after each stanza except the last,* which reads thy.)
   9–36 *omitted* F
   9 Of] Ô J
     thine] thy I
     eye] eyes DEGHJ
  10 my] mine DE
  11 witty] worthie I
  12 sighes] smiles DE, sights I
     deemed] damned I
     pitty] pritty D
  13 that] which J
     agreeued] greiued GH, so greiued J
  14 trust] heart I
  15, 22, 29, 36 Syren] Sirene pleasant, &c EGI
  16 Fain'de] fainzed I, kind J
  18 but] bot I, with J
  19 trust] faith J
  21 but sorrie] bot sorrow I, but litle J
  23 seemely] beauteous J
  25 shall] sall I
     guide] quitt GH, gall J
  27 pasture] pastyme I
  30–36 *omitted* J
  30 lasts] lusts D
     not] old I, *omitted* G
     will] still D
     follow] fallow I
  31 white . . . yellow] those tresses white now yellowe G, those white tresses yellow H
     those] these DE
  32 lookes] locks H

33 Shall] Sall I
34 shall] sall I
   date] eate D
35 wilt] will I

4 *light as feathers.* Tilley F150; *cf.* F162.
27 *Change . . . pleasure.* Cf. Tilley C230, "Change of pasture makes fat calves."
28 *Beauty . . . treasure.* Cf. Tilley 165, "Beauty does fade like a flower."

VIII.

This poem was reprinted in (D) Richard Johnson's collection, *The Golden Garland of Princely Pleasures* (1620), sigs. G4v–G5, with the title "Loues Constancy." This book is supposedly the third edition, but the first two are not extant. See the article by Allan G. Chester in *MLQ*, X (1949), 61–67. See also the note to IX below. Other copies of the poem may be found in (E) John Cotgrave's *Wits Interpreter* (1655), sig. S5–S5v (also 2nd ed., 1662, sigs. O1v–O2); (F) BM MS Add. 27879 (Bishop Percy's folio, late 17th century), fol. 99v; (G) BM MS Add. 15118 (*c.* 1633), fol. 7v (without music); (H) Folger MS V.a.339 (Joseph Hall's MS; mid-17th century), fol. 193v; and (I) BM MS Add. 29291 (*c.* 1762), fol. 8v, the part-song version of Ford's music. D, E, and F divide each line, and present the poem in quatrains. Variants from all but I are as follows:

1 Since] When FG
  your] thy DEG, her F
  yee] thee FG
2 If now] but if FG
  disdayned] disdaind DE
  my hart] that I FG
  yee] thee FG
3–4 *exchanged with 7–8 in* FG
3 What . . . lou'de] What I have lov'd E, but I that liked F, but you that lik't G
  and you that likte] & you that loude F, if I that lou'd G
  shal wee beginne] is now a time F
4 No] No, no D, O no FG
  my hart is fast] I love thee still E
  fast] fixt DF
  cannot] will not F
  disentangle] now intangle DF
5 admire or prayse] admirde or praisd DG
  fault] fortune F
  you] *omitted* F
  may] might FG
  mee] *omitted* H
6 Or if] or that F, If that G
  hands] hand DFGH
  had] hath F, did G
  stray'd] striue G
  but a] to D, but to FG

touch] teach F
then . . . you] thean might you iustly F
leaue] blame H
7–8 *exchanged with 3–4 in* FG
7 bad] bid EG
  ist] is itt FG
8 No] No, no D, O no FG
  ile loue you] I love thee E, I loue you FH,
I will loue G
  ere] soere G
  betide] betides E
9 are] *omitted* E
  reiecteth] & asketh [?] F, disdaineth G
10 And] *omitted* F, so G
  your] thy D
  sweet] faire FG
  beautie] face F
  past] past all FG
  made] Makes EF
  poore eyes] faint hart F
11 Where] When F
  beautie] fancy
  moues] likes F, is fixt G
  wit] loue G
  signes] showes FG
  kindnes] Loue doe F
  bind] binds D
12 There, O there] there there O there F, There there there G
  where ere] where ever ЭG, whersoeuer F
  I go] it bee G
  ile] I E, I will G

E *continues*:

> If I have wrong'd you, tell me wherein,
>   And I will soon amend it,
> In recompense of such a sin,
>   Here is my heart, I'le send it.
>
> If that will not your mercy move,
>   Then for my life I care not;
> O then, O then torment me still,
>   And take my life and spare not.
>
>   Answer to the third stave.
>
> Art thou so mad to love a Lasse,
>   And leave thy heart behind thee?
> Go learn more wit, green headed asse,
>   For *Cupids* rules will bind thee.

A young Wench loves a Lad that's bold,
 And not a simpring noddy;
Therefore before thou leave thy hold,
 Be sure thou bounce her body.

9 *The Sunne . . . beholder. Cf.* Tilley S985, "The sun shines upon all alike"; but the sense is more like "A cat may look on a king" (C141).

IX.

This poem, like No. VIII, was reprinted in (D) Richard Johnson's *The Golden Garland of Princely Pleasures* (1620), sig. G7, with the title, "*Coridons* Resolution." Another setting (treble and bass) is found in (E) John Gamble's MS (*c.* 1659; New York Public Library Drexel MS 4257), fols. 84v–85. Ford's part-song version was copied into (F) BM MS Add. 29291 (*c.* 1762), fol. 9. There have been several twentieth-century settings of this poem. Variants from DE are:

    1 is] was E
      sweet] faire E
    5 iesture, motion] gestures motions E
    6 wit] witts E
    8 I] Ile E
    9–12 *omitted* D
    9 free . . . winning] desent favour and her E
    11 I . . . I] touch her not oh no ffy fy E
    13 Had] How D
      mine] my E
    14 sports were] sporte noe E
    15 no, no] no D, oh noe E
    16 For I will] And yet I E
    17 Should] Shall E
    18 So] As E
      in] and E
    20 Yet would] And yet E
    21 winged and doth] weaned & will E
    22 Her . . . doth] My Loue her contry now will E

XI.

The words for this dialogue by Francis Davison were probably taken from his *A Poetical Rhapsody* (1602; RPR, I, 92), where it is headed "A Dialogue betweene a Louers flaming Heart, and his Ladies frozen Breast." The only variants from the first edition of *A Poetical Rhapsody* are misprints (in lines 5, 10, and 12 in Ford, and *tha* for *than* in line 12 in Davison), the designation of the voice parts (in Davison, the Altus is "Hart," the Cantus "Breast," and the Chorus is "Both together"), musical repetition of "Shut not" and "Flie not" in Ford (lines 2 & 3), and these:

    11 neuer] n'ere
    15 one] let one

In later editions, Davison changes *Shut* (l. 2) to *Shun*, and makes 14–17 read:

> Let one ioy fill vs, as one greefe did harme vs,
> Let one death kill vs, as one loue doth warme vs.

(RPR, I, 327.) Rollins notes (II, 130) that the poem is a survival of the *debat*-form, refers to his notes to RPR Nos. 138, 220, and 221; *The Paradise of Dainty Devices* (1578), ed. Rollins, p. 106; and to J. E. Wells, *A Manual of the Writings in Middle English* (1916), p. 831. For other musical dialogues, see Do1600.XXII and note.

EMV, p. 527, starts with line 3, so that the parts are out of order until line 6.

Dedication (2)

Sir Richard Tichborne (d. 1657) was knighted in 1603, and became second baronet after his father, Sir Benjamin Tichborne of Tichborne, Hampshire, died in 1629. Sir Benjamin had married an aunt of Sir Richard Weston (see Dedication 1), hence the allusion to Tichborne's and Weston's "neere alliance in blood." (Burke's *Peerage, Baronetage, and Knightage*.) Thomas Goffe's *The Raging Turk* (1631) was also dedicated to Tichborne (Williams).

Tobias Hume, *Captaine Humes Poeticall Music*, 1607

Dedication to Queen Anne

John Dowland dedicated his *Lachrimae* (1604) to Queen Anne. On the blank page facing the dedication in the BM copy, Hume has written: "I doe in all humylitie beseech your Maiestie that you woulde bee pleased to heare this Musick by mee; hauing excellent Instruments to performe itt."

I

"A new Musicke" etc. This piece must be considered free verse. The line divisions follow the musical phrases, but are otherwise arbitrary. The music consists of the vocal line on A2v facing two parts in tablature and a bass viol part, headed by this note: "Three Base Viols and the Voice, with the Meane Lute to play the Ground if you please." Below the bass viol part is this note: "The Viole that playeth this part must bee set fowre Notes lower then the other and he must bee somewhat longer then the two small Basse Viols which play the Tableture being alwaies tuned alike and set as the Lute."

Alwaies thus to the Reader.

Cf. Hu1605, "To the vnderstanding Reader," and note.

The table of the Songes contained in this second booke

1 *The Earle of Shrowsberies fauoret.* This applies to No. XIIII, "What greater griefe." See notes to Gr1604, dedication, XVI–XVIII.

To All Worthy . . . Lordes, etc.

This dedication is in the Manchester copy only, but *cf.* the dedication to the Earl of Arundel, which uses part of the same type-setting. Sir Christopher Hatton, K.B. (d. 1619), was the cousin of Sir Christopher Hatton, lord chancellor (d. 1591), and father of Christopher, first Baron Hatton (d. 1670). Orlando Gibbons dedicated his *First Set of Madrigals and Motets* (1612) to Sir Christopher (DNB, Williams).

To . . . Philip Earle of Arundel

This dedication is in the Folger copy only. Philip Howard, thirteenth Earl of Arundel, died in 1595, so Hume must mean his only son Thomas, the fourteenth Earl (1585–1646). Thomas of Arundel formed a famous art collection, and had several books dedicated to him (DNB, Williams).

XIV.

This song was first published in Hu1605 (No. 113), with tablature for one lyra viol; here it is given with music for two lyra viols and one bass viol.

XXV.

Hunting songs, especially those called generically a "hunt's up," were popular, but the free-wheeling song here, with its cries and dog imitations, seems closer to the later (non-canonic) Italian *caccia*: see Reese, p. 435, and Francis J. Fabry's "The Poetry of the Secular Polyphonic Vocal Forms in England (1588–1627)," University of Texas Ph.D. dissertation, 1964, pp. 74–77. Clément Janequin also wrote an onomatopoetic chanson called "La Chasse" (see note to Hu1605.1; printed in *Les Maîtres musiciens de la Renaissance française*, ed. H. Expert, VII [1898], 62–104). Other English examples may be found in Thomas Ravenscroft's *A Briefe Discourse* (1614), Nos. I, II, and especially IV (EMV, pp. 246–249).

Hume's hunting song, however, probably had a specific occasion, as lines 59–61 would suggest. During his visit to England in July and August, 1606, Christian IV of Denmark went hunting with King James several times. The populace often came out to watch, and it is possible that Hume intruded himself and his song on one of these occasions. Joler or Jowler, the dog who finds the trail (ll. 36–44), was one of King James' favorite dogs. Edmund Lascelles sent the Earl of Shrewsbury this anecdote about Jowler, who turned up while the King was hunting at Royston in 1604 with a note tied to his neck which read: "Good Mr. Jowler, we pray you speake to the King (for he hears you every day, and so doth he not us) that it will please his Majestie to go back to London, for els the country wilbe undoon; all our provition is spent already, and we are not able to intertayne him longer." (Nichols, *Progresses of James I*, I, 464–465.)

Hume's music consists of one line of notes, apparently to be doubled by voice and viol except during the introduction and brief interludes for the viol alone (a few bars of which are in tablature).

Alfonso Ferrabosco, *Ayres*, 1609

Dedication

See the dedication to Jo1605 and note. Ferrabosco was one of Prince Henry's music teachers (Grove).

To My Excellent Friend, etc.

Jonson's poem wittily repeats the commonplaces about music that Ferrabosco refuses to mention in his dedication. Jonson, with whom Ferrabosco collaborated on a number of occasions (see songs III, VI, XI, XVIII–XXIII), also wrote a poem for Ferrabosco's *Lessons for 1. 2. and 3. viols* (1609), and reprinted both poems in his *Epigrammes* (CXXX and CXXXI; *Works*, VIII, 82–83).

4 *building Townes ... tame.* Powers attributed to the music of Amphion and Orpheus.

5–16 For discussions of the ideas presented in these lines, see John Hollander, *The Untuning of the Sky* (Princeton, 1961), pp. 24–36, 162–220, and Gretchen L. Finney, *Musical Backgrounds for English Literature: 1580–1650* (New Brunswick: Rutgers University Press, n.d. [*c.* 1962], pp. 1–20.

To the Worthy Author.

4 *Old Alfonso's Image.* Ferrabosco's father, Alfonso the elder, was in England by 1562, and acquired a great reputation there. A number of his madrigals were printed in Yonge's *Musica Transalpina* (1588 and 1597).

11 *T. Campion.* See the note to VIII below.

Amicissimo, etc.

19 *N. Tomkins.* Probably Nicholas Tomkins, member of the musical Tomkins family, son of Thomas, precentor of Gloucester Cathedral, and brother of Thomas, composer of *Songs of 3. 4. 5. and 6. parts*, 1622 (DNB).

I.

This poem was exceedingly popular during the 16th and 17th centuries. It was first printed in (D) *Britton's Bowre of Delights*, sigs. B4v–C1, but it may have been copied into (E) Sir Edward Hoby's commonplace book (BM MS Add. 38823, fol. 58v) as early as 1585. Sir Walter Raleigh is given as the author in (F) *Today a man, To morrow none: Or, Sir Walter Rawleighs Farewell to his Lady, The night before hee was beheaded* (1644), sig. A4v. Copies may also be found in (G) *The Phoenix Nest* (1593), sig. K3–3v (RPN, pp. 77–78); (H) the Arundel-Harington MS (HAH, I, 240–241); (I) BM MS Harl. 6910 (*c.* 1600), fol. 139v; (J) Bod. MS Rawl. Poet. 85 (*c.* 1600), fol. 25v; (K) Folger MS V.a.169 (formerly 621.1; mid-17th century), Part II, fol. 10v; (L) J. Gough's *Academy of Complements* (1650, also 1663), sig. L1, headed "A song"; and in (M) Lady Catherine Aston's collection of poems (*c.* 1658) printed in *Tixall Poetry*, ed. Arthur Clifford (1813), pp. 115–116. Nicholas Lanier gave it a new musical setting published in (N) John Playford's *Select Musicall Ayres and Dialogues* (1652), sig. B1; another musical setting is in (O) John Gamble's MS, New York Public Library Drexel 4257 (*c.* 1659), fol. 17. Rollins (RPN, pp. 167–171) and Hughey (HAH, II, 313–317) comment fully on the poem and collate between them all copies but L (which reads *pensive place* in line 1 and *ever find* in line 4) and a MS copy mentioned by Agnes Latham (Raleigh's *Poems* [Cambridge, Mass.: Harvard University Press, 1951], p. 104) as being in the Edinburgh University Library, but which no one seems to have seen (*cf.* HAH, II, 315). Ferrabosco's version differs from the earliest versions (DEGHIJ) in that they have eight more lines of text between lines 4 and 5, making the poem a sonnet; versions FKLMNO use the last couplet as a refrain, making the poem three six-line stanzas. The omitted lines are quoted here from D:

> My foode shall be of care and sorrow made,
> My drinke nought else but teares falne from mine eyes,
> And for my light in such obscured shade,
> The flames shall serue that from my heart arise.

> A gowne of griefe my bodie shall attire,
> And broken hope the staff of all my stay,
> Of late repentance linkt with long desire,
> The Couch is made whereon my bones to lay,

As Rollins and others have noted, the poem is a translation of Desportes, *Amours de Diane*, II.8, "Je me veux rendre hermite" (ed. Victor E. Graham, Textes Litteraires Francais [Paris and Geneva, 1959], p. 207). Another translation was made by Thomas Lodge, printed in his *Scillaes Metamorphosis* (1598), sig. E4–E4v.

The ascription of the present translation to Raleigh, accepted by Latham, Rollins, and Hughey, is based on the late version F and on the similarity of some lines (omitted by Ferrabosco) to lines in Raleigh's "The Passionate Man's Pilgrimage" (*Poems*, ed. Latham, pp. 49–51). The case for Raleigh's authorship is weakened, it seems to me, by the fact that *allegoria* is used in "Like Hermit poore" and "The Passionate Man's Pilgrimage" as it is in Cop1606.IV and other poems of the period (Sir John Davies' "Gulling Sonnet" No. 6. parodies the device). Bond's assignment of the poem to John Lyly (III, 470) is (as usual) even more dubious. He speculates that it is the missing song from *Endimion*, III.iv.1. Rollins (RPN, p. 169) cites a number of allusions to the poem which indicate its popularlity.

II.

This song, with the treble and bass of Ferrabosco's music, may be found in (D) Tenbury MS 1018 (first half of 17th century), fol. 33, and (without music) in (E) Folger MS V.a.339 (Joseph Hall's MS, mid-17th century), fol. 192v. Variants are:

    4 her . . . her] theire . . . theire E
    5 come away] *repeated in E as with Ferrabosco's music*
    6 here] her E
      For . . . hopes] *repeated in E as with Ferrabosco's music*

DE continues (from D)

> Bewtie and loue die euen as they were borne,
>   time is theire foe the weakest sex theire guarde/
> ambitious endes, deathes power or fortunes scorne
>   lyke timeless frute withers without rewarde/
> Come then obay this sumons come awaye,
>   for heer vayne hopes must serue you for your paye.

E reads *wither* in line 4. The copyist of D placed *time is* in the first line, *lyke* in the third, and *for heer* in the fifth. This second stanza was added in a late hand to the BM copy of Fer1609, with these words: "added from an Ancient MS." It does not vary from D.

III.

This song is from Ben Jonson's *The Masque of Blackness* (performed 1605; Q. 1608; *Works*, VII, 178), where it is preceded by this note: "One, from the sea, was heard to call 'hem with this *charme*, sung by a *tenor* voyce." The only variants are the omission of the commas at the ends of lines 5 and 6, and the addition of a comma after *land* (line 5). A copy from Royal MS 17. B. XXXI., cited in *Works*, VII, 200, is without variants, as is a copy with Ferrabosco's treble and bass in Christ Church, Oxford, MS 439 (*c.* 1620), p. 31.

IIII.

5–6 *Bird . . . beware. Cf.* Tilley B394, "Birds once snared fear all bushes."

V.

As noted in EMV, p. 745, the first line of this poem resembles the first line of a poem dubiously ascribed to Sir Walter Raleigh (Bod. MS Rawl. Poet. 85, fol. 43v) and to Sir Edward Dyer (BM MS Harl. 7392, fol. 22); see Agnes Latham's first edition of Raleigh's *Poems* (London, 1929) pp. 72–73 and 171, and the revised edition (1951), pp. 172–173. The resemblance does not extend beyond the first line. Another version of the song (with Ferrabosco's treble and bass) in Christ Church, Oxford, MS 439 (*c.* 1620), p. 21, reads *thoughte is* in line 5, and adds this stanza:

> Prayse I would but O how can I:
> prayse her minde her bodye whether:
> prayse them both cryes love If any:
> for best is Shee alltogeether
> Thy speech then thy thoughte is lower
> yet thy thoughtes doth not halfe knowe her.

The words from the MS are printed in John P. Cutts, *Seventeenth Century Songs and Lyrics* (Columbia: University of Missouri Press, 1959), p. 100.

VI.

Ben Jonson's poem first appeared in *Volpone or the Fox* (1607, acted 1605), III.vii (*Works*, V, 82). Volpone sings it as part of his attempt to seduce Celia. The opening eight lines are adapted from Catullus V. 1–6; for other translations *cf.* Campion's "My sweetest Lesbia" (Ros1601.I.I) and Ck1612.XI. Jonson reprinted his poem in *The Forrest*, No. V (*Works*, VIII, 102), where it is entitled "Song. To Celia." Variants from *Volpone* (V) and *The Forrest* (F) are:

2 may] can V
   sweets] sports VF
7 if we once] if, once, we VF
14 Thus] So F
15 fruits] fruit F
16 theft] thefts V

Herford and Simpson collate the *Forrest* version with *Volpone*; (D) BM MS Add. 10309 (*c.* 1630) fol. 117; (E) Bod. MS Rawl. poet. 31, fol. 7; and (F) Bod. MS Rawl. poet. 172 (17th century), fol. 2. Other copies are found in (G) John Cotgrave's *Wits Interpreter* (1655), sig. Y7, headed "Song"; (H) Rosenbach MS 1083/17 (mid-17th century), fols. 91v–92; (I) Folger MS V.a.262 (after 1653), p. 101, headed "A Song"; (J) Folger MS V.a.339 (mid-17th century), fol. 191v, without variants; and (K) BM MS Add. 15117 (after *c.* 1614), fol. 20v, with Ferrabosco's music for voice and lute, without variants. Variants from D–I are:

1 my] sweet DEH
   Celia] Mrs H
2 may] cann EHI
   sweets] sports DEFGHI
4 good] blisse D

7 if we once] when once wee E, if once we FHI
    this] the E
8 tis] It's D
13 Or] and D
    his] hir E
    eares] eyes F
14 Thus] Soe DEFG
    our wile] many a mile DE
15 T'is] It's D
    fruits] fruit FG
16 theft] thefts HI
18 haue] hath D

15–18 *Cf.* Tilley S779, "Sport is sweetest when there be no spectators"; S472, "A sin unseen is half pardoned"; and S473, "Successful sin passes for virtue." Herford and Simpson (*Works*, IX, 719) say the reference is to the "Spartan attitude towards heft."

VII.

This is the first printed version of John Donne's "The Expiration." Gardner (pp. 36–37) gives important variants from ten MS versions and her text, based on the 1633 ed. of Donne's *Poems*, and notes (p. 159) the presence of the poem in fourteen other MSS. Variants from Gardner's text are:

1 leaue] breake
4 happy] happiest
5 aske] ask'd
7 Goe, goe] Goe

Gardner (pp. 242–243) prints the melody of Ferrabosco's setting, as well as that of a different setting (originally with lute accompaniment) from Bod. MS Mus. Sch. 575.
    1 *leaue.* Gardner (p. 159) notes that Ferrabosco's reading agrees with most of the MSS and is "more musical" than *breake.*
    2 *sucks two soules.* Gardner (p. 159) notes Donne's reference in a sermon to the famous epigram ascribed to Plato (*Greek Anthology*, V. 78), about souls meeting in a kiss (*Sermons*, ed. G. R. Potter and Evelyn M. Simpson [Berkeley: University of California Press, 1953–61], III, 320). See also Castiglione's *Courtyer*, Book IV (tr. T. Hoby, 1561), sig. Vv4v.

VIII.

Thomas Campion gave his poem his own setting later in 4Camp[1617].IX, where the words are printed in six-line stanzas (Vivian, pp. 179–180; Davis, p. 177). Variants are:

4 or to] nor to
5–6 *Campion's printer erroneously omits, and repeats 2–3*
11 tis] 'twere

Other versions are as follows: (D) BM MS Add. 24665 (1615–1626), fols. 53v–54, first stanza only, without variants, and with Ferrabosco's treble and bass; (E) BM MS

Harl. 6917 (late 17th century), fol. 61, without variants; (F) Christ Church, Oxford, MS 439 (*c.* 1620), p. 86, with music for treble and bass, subscribed "Mr: Alfonso ferrabosco"; (G) BM MS Harl. 6057 (mid-17th century), fol. 28v, headed "A Songe"; (H) NLS, Advocates' MS 5.2.14 (*c.* 1640), fol. 8v, with music for treble that differs from Campion, Ferrabosco, and Lanier (see LM); (I) Folger MS V.a.245 (*c.* 1640), fol. 17v, headed "A Maydes deliberation," and containing four added stanzas; (J) Rosenbach MS 239/23 (*c.* 1640), pp. 130–133, almost identical to I above; (K) John Gough's *The Academy of Complements* (1650, 1663), sig. I8-8v, headed "A Song"; (L) John Playford's *Select Musicall Ayres & Dialogues* (1652), sigs. Ee1v–Ee2, with music for three voices by "Mr. Nicholas Lanneare"; (M) John Playford's *The Musical Companion* (1673), sigs. Dd2v-3, with music for four voices by "Mr. N. Lannear"; and (N) *Windsor-Drollery* (1672), sig. C12, headed "Song 130." According to Davis (p. 499), the song also appears in BM MS Add. 14934, fol. 192, lacking stanza 2; BM MS Add. 11608 (*c.* 1646–1658), fol. 58, first stanza only, with Lanier's music; and Edinburgh University MS La. III. 483, fol. 194, first line of the text, with music. Still another version in Rosenbach MS 1083/17 (mid-17th century) fols. 141v–142v, 48 lines headed "A Maydes deliberate Resolution," is a very free adaptation of the poem, incorporating the added material from IJ. It begins and concludes thus:

> Although I'me younge, yet not so ignorant am
> but I haue heard of Loue and Cupids name
> . . . .
> If he but dare to chalenge me, shall knowe,
> Ile cope with him, and stand a thrust or two:
> yea, I am confident, I in the ffeild
> Shall fight so well as I shall make him yeeld.

Variants from F–N are:
   1 simple] tender G
   2 doe] *omitted* G
   3 can] doth IJ
      they] men G
   4–6 *omitted* M
   4 foule] fond KLN
      or to] nor to H
   5–6 *same as* 2–3 *in* H
   5 my] these IJ
      lips] lipp G
      them hard] too hard KLN
   6 they] doe G
   7 but a] but my J
   8 Like . . . bide] Like long thirsting, doeth abide IJ,
And thirsty-longing that doth bide KLN
      doth] did F, doe H
      euer] allwayes J
      my] the GJKLN
   9 Where . . . moue] Would my hart would this remove I,
Would my hart could this remooue J, Oh! I feel my heart doth moue KLN
   10 alas] alacke J

11 As . . . needes] ffaith, 'twere good 'twere done & past,/ Since it must IJ
    tis] twere GM, it were KLN
    needes] need'st F
12 Roses] ffor roses IJ
    ouer-blowne] ever blowne G, ouer growne IJ
    then] and IKLN
13 nor Churle] noe churle GIJL, not Churle M
    nor silken] or silken L, or simple I, nor simple J
    maiden] Virgin KN
14 soone] well I, *omitted* J
    would I] I would I G
    could] knew IJ
15 This] But this IJ
    This . . . ere] Yet I'm sure, what ere KLN
    loue hee must] hee shall love IJ

HIJ and the BM copy of Fer1609 (in a 17th century hand) add this stanza (from H):

> Maried wyues may tak or leaue,
> when they list refuse receaue
> we poor mayds may not doe soe,
> we must answere ay with noe.
> we must seame strang coy and curst
> yet do we would faine if we durst

Variants from IJ and the BM copy are:

1 tak] chewsse BM
  or] and IJBM
2 when] wheare BM
  list] please IJ
3 we] But wee IJ
  may] must IJBM
4 with] for BM
5 must] *omitted* BM
  coy] and coy BM
6 yet . . . durst] Yet fayne would doe, if that wee durst IJ, But faine would doe
yf that we durste BM

IJ continue:

> If but a harmeles sparke of love
> Our active spirittes 'gin to move,
> how must wee our passions quell,
> ffor feere our lookes our thoughts should tell:
> A guilty flame dares not appeare,
> O what's a mayden head but feare?
>
> But why should wee be so supprest,
> As not to dare, what men request?
> ffaith the reason I can tell;
> The sport will make our bellies swell,
> But yet the pleasure of the game
> Will quitt the slander of the same [shame J].

> O that our wombes would but conceale,
> What wee ourselves would ne'r reveale!
> Or that the act which wee can smother,
> Would never swell vs to a mother;
> Then might wee enjoy the sport,
> Yet thinck our chastitie vnhurt.

IJ conclude with a quotation from Ovid, *Ars Amatoria*, III, 585–6, 603–4. There is of course no reason to believe that these extra stanzas are by Campion. For similar poems, see Bt1606.IX and note.

IX.

Lines 1–8 of this poem were given another setting for five voices by Francis Pilkington, *Second Set of Madrigals and Pastorals* (1624), No. XX (Cantus, sig. C4v), without variants. Ferrabosco's setting (treble and bass) was copied into (D) Christ Church, Oxford, MS 439 (*c.* 1620), pp. 88–89, and subscribed "Alfonso fferrabosco." A different setting with a highly ornamented treble and bass accompaniment is in (E) BM MS Egerton 2971 (first quarter of 17th century), p. 46, and another is in Cambridge, Fitzwilliam Museum MS 52.D.15, according to Vincent Duckles, "Florid Embellishment in English Song of the Late 16th and Early 17th Centuries," *Annales Musicologiques*, V (1957), 343–344. Variants from DE are:

1 with] my D
3 with . . . lights] those lightes with weeping E
4 thy] this E
9 will we] we will D

X.

This is the first stanza of a six-stanza poem from Bartholomew Yong's translation of Montemayor's *Diana* (1598), Book I, sig. A2v–A3, which varies thus:

1 yet] but
   lou'd] loued
3 yet] but
   mou'd] mooued
Yong continues:

> For euery ill one semblant I doe beare still,
> To day not sad, nor yesterday contented,
> To looke behinde, or go before I feare still,
> All things to passe alike I haue consented:
> I am besides my selfe like him that daunceth,
> And mooues his feete at euery sound that chaunceth:
> And so all like a senselesse foole disdaines me,
> But this is nothing to the greefe that paines me.

> The night to certaine louers is a trouble,
> When in the day some good they are attending:
> And other some doe hope to gaine some double
> Pleasure by night, and wish the day were ending:
> With that, that greeueth some, some others ease them,
> *And all do follow that, that best doth please them:*
> But for the day with teares I am a crying,
> Which being come, for night I am a dying.

> Of Cupid to complaine who euer craue it,
> In waues he writes and to the windes he crieth:
> Or seeketh helpe of him, that neuer gaue it:
> For he at last thy paines and thee defieth.
> Come but to him some good aduise to lend thee,
> To thousand od conceits he will commend thee.
> What thing is then this loue? It is a science,
> That sets both proofe and study at defiance.
>
> My *Mistresse* loued her *Syrenus* deerely,
> And scorned me, whose loues yet I auouched,
> Left to my greefe, for good I held it cleerely,
> Though narrowly my life and soule it touched:
> Had I but had a heauen as he once shining,
> Loue would I blame, if it had bene declining.
> But loue did take no good from me he sent me,
> For how can loue take that he neuer lent me.
>
> Loue's not a thing, that any may procure it,
> Loue's not a thing, that may be bought for treasure;
> Loue's not a thing, that comes when any lure it,
> Loue's not a thing, that may be found at pleasure:
> For if it be not borne with thee, refraine it
> To thinke, thou must be borne anew to gaine it:
> Then since that loue shuns force, and doth disclame it,
> The scorned louer hath no cause to blame it.

Montemayor's verses begin (from *Los Siete Libros de la Diana* [Valencia, 1559], sig. B3v):

> Amador soy, mas nunca fuy amado:
> quisse bien y querre, no soy querido:
> fatigas passo, y nunca las he dado:
> sospiros di, mas nunca fuy oydo:
> quexar me quisse, y no fuy eschuchado:
> huyr quisse de Amor, quede corrido,
> de solo oluido no podre quexarme:
> por que aun no se acordaron doluidarme.

Ferrabosco's treble and bass with the first two stanzas of Yonge's verses appear in Christ Church, Oxford, MS 439 (*c.* 1620), p. 29; the second stanza reads *to such be like* in line 4 and *but that* in line 8. Somewhat similar verses were set by George Kirbye, *The First Set of English Madrigalls* (1597), No. XX, and by John Wilbye, *The Second Set of Madrigales* (1609), No. XIV (EMV, pp. 128, 314).

XI.

This song is from Ben Jonson's *Haddington Masque* (1608; *Works*, VII, 262). Ferrabosco prints only the fifth of a seven-stanza "Epithalamion" which begins, "Vp *youthes* and *virgins*, vp, and praise." Ferrabosco also omits the refrain line in each stanza, "Shine *Hesperus*, shine forth, thou wished *starre*." A copy of this song with bass and ornamented treble is in Christ Church, Oxford, MS 439 (*c.* 1620), pp. 60–61.

6 *mother . . . nobler name*. Jonson's marginal note on this line reads: "A wife, or matron: which is name of more dignity, then *Virgin. D. Heins, in Nup. Ottonis Heurnij. Cras matri similis tuae redibis.*"

XII.–XIIII.

This song was probably addressed to King James; XIII.3 and XIIII.6 (referring to the peaceful union of Scotland and England) point to James. The third part (XIIII) was copied without variants into Christ Church, Oxford, MS 439 (*c.* 1620), p. 90, and subscribed "Mr Allfonso fferrabosco."

XV.

This song, with Ferrabosco's music for treble and bass, was copied without verbal variants into Christ Church, Oxford, MS 439 (*c.* 1620), p. 25, and into Tenbury MS 1018 (first half of 17th century), fol. 34v.

XVI.

See Jo1605.XIIII and note. In addition to the versions described there, a copy of the song with music for Ferrabosco's treble and bass appears in Christ Church, Oxford, MS 439 (*c.* 1620), p. 92. The MS has no verbal variants; it retains the error in line 2, *soule* for *sense*.

XVII.

Ferrabosco may have taken this poem from Jo1605.IIII, which has one more stanza (see note). Ferrabosco's version with music for treble and bass is in Christ Church, Oxford, MS 439 (*c.* 1620), p. 91, subscribed with his name; it has no variants.

XVIII.–XX.

This song in three sections is from Ben Jonson's *Masque of Beautie* (1608; *Works*, VII, 192). Jonson indicates in the masque that XVIII and XIX were sung by "a treble voyce" and XX by a tenor. Variants are as follows:

    XVIII.4 mindes] mind
    XIX.2 pollicie] politie
    .3 although] Albee'
        be] were
    XX.3 beautie] beauties

All three parts were copied, with Ferrabosco's treble and bass, into Christ Church, Oxford, MS 439 (*c.* 1620), pp. 93, 94, and 96. XVIII and XIX are subscribed "Mr alfonso Ferrabosco" and vary only in XVIII.4, where the reading is *minde*. (The plural seems to be Ferrabosco's error).

XVIII.1–3 Jonson has a note on these lines explaining the sighted Cupids: "I make these different from him, which they fayne, *caecum cupidine*, or *petulantem*, as I expresse beneath in the third song [XX], these being chaste *Loues*, that attend a more diuine beautie, then that of *Loues* commune *parent*."

XXI.

This song is from Ben Jonson's *Masque of Beautie* (1608; *Works*, VII, 191). At this point in the masque, the dancers, "standing still, were by the *Musicians*, with a second *Song* (sung by a loud *Tenor*) celebrated." Ferrabosco's text does not vary.

2 *Loue . . . floud.* Jonson's note: "As, in the creation, he is said, by the *ancients*, to haue done." Cf. Spenser, *An Hymne in Honour of Loue*, lines 78–91.

5 *a motion.* Herford and Simpson (*Works*, X, 464), cite Lucian, *De Saltatione*, 7, on the "dance" of the spheres; see Sir John Davies' *Orchestra* (1596), lines 113–154.

7 *which thought was yet.* Jonson's note: "That is, borne since the world, and, out of those duller apprehensions that did not thinke he was before."

8 *loue is elder then his birth.* Herford and Simpson (*Works*, X, 464), cite Spenser, *An Hymne in Honour of Loue*, lines 50–56, and Ficino, *Opera* (1576), II, 1340, "Amor caeteris dijs & antiquior est, & iunior."

XXII.

Another song from Jonson's *Masque of Beautie* (1608; *Works*, VII, 193). The song is introduced thus: "After which songs [Fer1609.XVIII–XX], they danc'd *galliards*, and *coranto's*; and with those excellent graces, that the musique, appointed to celebrate them, shew'd it could be silent no longer: but by the first tenor, admir'd them thus." Jonson's text varies:

> 3 those] these
> 6 their] true

2 *women haue no soule.* Jonson's note: "There hath been such a profane *paradoxe* published." See Tilley W709. Herford and Simpson (*Works*, X, 464) note that this "paradox" was *Mulieres Homines non esse* (Leipzig, 1595), and that the dispute "started from a passage in the spurious Ambrose ('Ambrosiaster') Commentaries on St. Paul, I Corinthians xi.7 and xiv.54." The argument is given in Donne's epistle "To the Countess of Huntingdon" (Grierson, I, 201):

> Man to Gods image; *Eve*, to mans was made,
> Nor finde wee that God breath'd a soule in her.

6 *worlds soule.* Jonson's note: "The *Platonicks* opinion. See also *Mac.* lib. 1. and 2. *Som. Scip.*" *I.e.*, Macrobius, *In Somnium Scipionis*, II.ii.1, 19 quoted in *Works*, X, 464–5. See the translation by W. H. Stahl (New York: Columbia, 1952), p. 193: "Thus the World-Soul, which stirred the body of the universe to the motion that we now witness, must have been interwoven with those numbers which produce musical harmony in order to make harmonious the sounds which it instilled by its quickening impulse. It discovered the source of these sounds in the fabric of its own composition." See also p. 195: "Every soul in the world is allured by musical sounds ... for the soul carries with it into the body a memory of the music which it knew in the sky," *i.e.*, the music of the spheres.

XXIII.

This song is from Ben Jonson's *Masque of Queenes* (1609; *Works*, VII, 315, from holograph in BM Royal MS 18 A.xlv). The song is introduced thus: "When, to giue them [the dancers] rest, from the *Musique* which attended the *Chariots*, by that most excellent *tenor* voyce, and exact Singer (her Maiesties seruant, *mr. Io. Allin*) this Ditty was sung." John Allen also sung in Campion's *Somerset Masque* (1614; see Davis, pp. 266, 280). Jonson's text varies:

> 1 If] When
> 3 and when that] And that, when
> 6 they all] all they

A copy of this song with the music for treble and bass and subscribed with Ferrabosco's name is found in Christ Church, Oxford, MS 439 (*c.* 1620), p. 95; it has no variants.

6 *a Queene.* Queen Anne.

XXV.

This poem is a translation of a madrigal by Giovanni Battista Guarini; see his *Rime* (Venice, 1598), sig. H7v, Madrigal XII, "Nel medesimo soggetto," *i.e.*, "Sogno della sua Donna":

> Occhi, stelle mortali,
>   Ministre de miei mali,
>   Che'n sogno anco mostrate
>   Che'l mio morir bramate;
>   Se chiusi m'vccidete,
>   Aperti che farete?

Francis Davison gives another translation of this poem in *A Poetical Rhapsody* (RPR, I, 267). Ferrabosco composed settings of parts of Guarini's *Pastor Fido*; see the songs edited from MS by Ian Spink in ELS, second series, XIX. A copy of Ferrabosco's setting (voice and lute) with the Italian words under the English is in Tenbury MS 1019 (early 17th century), fol. 2, with these variants:

    4 to kill] and kilst
    6 you'ld] you

Another copy with Ferrabosco's music for treble and bass is in Christ Church, Oxford, MS 439 (*c.* 1620), p. 78; it has no verbal variants.

XXVI.

For other dialogues, see XXVII and XXVIII and the note to Do1600.XXII.

XXVII.

10–11 *Flattery . . . truth. Cf.* Tilley F349, "Flattery gets friends," and T562, "As truth gets hatred so flattery wins love."

XXVIII.

9 *liues.* EMV, p. 520, emends to *livest.*

George Handford, *Ayres*, 1609

Dedication

Jo1605 (see note) and Fer1609 are also dedicated to Prince Henry.
4–5 *I bringe no wax nor hony to the hiue. Cf.* Do1603.XVIII.6.

2.

12 *Cinthias . . . tree. Cf.* Do1597.XXI.15–27.

8.

2 *durst.* EMV, p. 535, reads *dost*; the MS has *dust.*

9.

5 *ahlas.* In the MS, this reads "ah ah las" to fit the music.
7 *ysce. I.e., icy.*

10.

4 *louer.* The MS reads *louell* with an *r* above a caret after *e*. The double *l* was probably miscopied from the preceding word.

11.

There are a number of poems that use the conceit of the salamander; Obertello gives a list of Italian examples on p. 511 (see also p. 387). The notion that the salamander lives unharmed in flames derives from Pliny, *Natural History*, X.lxxxvi and XXIX.xxiii.

4 *my heate.* Perhaps this should read *by heate* or *my hearte.*

12.

This is the final ode from Samuel Daniel's *Delia.* Variants from the *Works* of 1601, *Delia* sig. C3–C3v, are as follows:

  9 Now] *omitted*
  10 the] *omitted*
  15 Doth knowe] Knowes
  21 lyfes] liues
  22 The which] that

John Farmer also gave the first stanza a setting for four voices in his *First Set of English Madrigals* (1599), No. II (Cantus, sig. B1v). This version was copied into the Brussels MS Fetis 3095, pp. 138–139. The only variant in both versions is *by* for *in* in l. 4.

13.

5 *flow flowe my tears.* Cf. 15.1 and Do1600.II.

14.

2 *a.* EMV, p. 538, emends to *an.*
  shall. Perhaps *be* is understood to follow.

15.

Cf. 13.5 and note.

16.

Mall Newberry was a famous prostitute of the time. According to Philip Gawdy, she was carted for three days and imprisoned in Newgate, *c.* 1600. See the Historical Manuscripts Commission, *Appendix to the Seventh Report* (London, 1879), Part I, 528.

18.

7 *then . . . turtledoue.* This arrangement is conjectural. The MS reads: "then wellcome lyfe then welcome lyfe lyfe welcome from my turtledoue." A slight distortion would produce a ten-syllable line, thus: "then wellcome lyfe, lyfe from my turtledoue."

19.

For other dialogues, see Do1600.XXII and note.

20.

1 *Daphne.* This character is male (see l. 17); perhaps the scribe misread a final *-is* (Daphnis) as *-ie.*
  13 *seest.* Perhaps this should be *seekst.*

Robert Jones, *A Musicall Dreame*, 1609

Dedication

Sir John Levinthorpe (or Leventhorpe), was created first Baronet in 1622, and died in 1625 (Burke's *Extinct and Dormant Baronetcies* [London, 2nd ed., 1841]). Five other books, none musical, were dedicated to Levinthorpe (Williams).

To all Musicall Murmurers

18 *descanter . . . Song*. Thomas Morley defines a descanter as "one that can extempore sing a part vpon a playne song" (*Plaine and Easie Introduction*, 1597, sig. K4v).

19–20 *Note aboue Ela*. E la is the last note of the gamut (e"). According to *Andreas Ornithoparcus his Micrologus*, trans. John Dowland (1609), sig. E1v, "It is not lawful for plaine-Song to goe . . . aboue *Ee la*." Thomas Morley is more practical: "Vnder *Gam vt* [G] the voice seemed as a kinde of *humming*, and aboue *E la* a kinde of constrained skricking" (*Plaine and Easie Introduction*, sig. C1).

21 *new come Lutes*. As the century progressed, lutes came to have more and more diapason strings and more complicated tunings; see Thomas Mace, *Musick's Monument* (1676), sig. F4, who writes in 1675 that "we now rest satisfied" with 24 strings.

22 *Diuision*. Varying and embellishing a melody by dividing the long notes into a larger number of short notes.

32 *water wrung out of a Flint*. Tilley W107.

39 *borne with teeth. Cf. Richard III*, II.iv.27–30.

I.

This poem is by Thomas Campion, who gave it his own musical setting in his *Second Booke of Ayres* (c. 1613), No. XVI; nevertheless, a late hand has penciled "Sir Walter Rawleigh" in the Glascow copy. Variants from Campion are as follows:

2 must I not] may not I
4 which] That
6 toy to auoide] shew t'auoid
7–8 *one line in Campion in all stanzas*
9 When . . . sight] Your wisht sight if
10 Suspition] Suspitions
12 Whilst] While
13 Thus . . . say] This a Louer whets you say
18 Youle] You
19 Whilst . . . doth] When my Riuals close doe
25 a] my

Despite the number of variants, Jones's version may represent Campion's own early draft. *Cf.* other settings of Campion poems that antedate Campion's own (*e.g.*, D01603.XVII).

Other copies may be found in (D) New York Public Library, Drexel MS 4175 (c. 1620 or later), fol. 5v, with Jones's melody (Cantus Primus) and bass; (E) Forbes's *Cantus* (1662), sig. N1v–N2 ("The Thirtyone Song"), with Jones's melody; (F) Christ Church, Oxford, MS 439 (c. 1620), p. 26, with Campion's melody and bass (one stanza only); (G) Yale School of Music, Filmer MS A 13a f (c. 1650), three parts of Campion's music, part a (Cantus), fols. 10v–11; (H) BM MS Egerton 2230 (c. 1638) fol. 57–57v (no music); (I) BM MS 33933 (treble part of Campion's music, one line of words only); (J) a version of Campion's setting printed by Dr. John Wilson as his own in *Cheerful Ayres or Ballads* (Oxford, 1660), I (Cantus Primus), sig. F4v–G1; and, according to John P. Cutts, a copy of Wilson's version in (K) Edinburgh University Library, Music MS Dc.1.69, fol. 59; see "Seventeenth-Century Songs and Lyrics," *MD*, XII (1959), 186. Cutts gives variants from Vivian's Campion. Davis (p. 495) also notes that the first line and bass part of Campion's music are in (L) Edinburgh University Library, MS La. iii. 483, the bass counterpart of I. Variants from all but IL are as follows:

> 1 strangenes] Sadnes F
> frets] frett DH
> 2 must] may FGJK
> I not] not I FJK
> 3 tis] it's E
> 4 which] that DFGJK
> must] doth H
> 5 If] When H
> affect] effect E
> 6 tis] it's E
> toy] shew FHJK
> to auoide] t'avoyd JK
> 8 O no] *repeated in* DEF
> 8, 16, 32 is] is alas G
> 9–16 *omitted in* GJK
> 9–32 *omitted in* F
> 9 When . . . I] your wisht sight when I H
> 10 Suspition] Suspitious H
> you] ye E
> 11 you] ye E
> 12 Whilst I] Whiles that I H
> 13 Thus] This H
> 14 Still . . . eager] Stils' made eager H
> 16 O no] *repeated* DE
> 18 Youle] Yet D, You GHJK, Ye'le E
> hold] haue GK
> 19 Whilst] When GK, While E
> riuall] Riualls GJK
> doth] doe GJK
> 20 sit] stand GJK
> 21–28 *omitted* GJK
> 23–24 Is . . . abusing] Is this: &c. H
> 24 O . . . abusing] o no &c. D
> O no] *repeated* E
> 25 Would] Would then E
> a] my H
> 26 Some] Or EH
> your] some your H

27 So] *omitted* H
    lesser] the lesser D, lesse E, less then H
28 so much] in vayne H
29 one] hower D
30 friend] *omitted* D, loue H
31–32 Is . . . abusing] Is this faire: – G
32 O no] *repeated* E
    O . . . abusing] o no &c D

14 *more eager by delay. Cf.* Tilley D213, "Desires are nourished by delay."

II.

Jones's Cantus Primus was reprinted in Forbes's *Cantus* (1662), sig. O1–O1v, with the following variants (lines 13–36 in 6-line stanzas):

3 playning] paining
7 quoth] quod
9 with] for
18 consenting] disdaining
19 quoth] quod
21 haue] will haue
22 attaind] attend
23 they faind] their fain'd
27 in sunder] asunder
30 Kept] keep
31 quoth] quod
35 rough] reugh

8–11 *gladly . . . fitte. Cf. As You Like It,* IV.i.107.
23 *They . . . faind. I.e.,* they reveal that they feigned love.

IIII.

This song was reprinted with Jones's tune in Forbes's *Cantus* (1662), sig. X2–X2v ("The Fiftytwo Song") with the following variants:

3 wot not who] wist not how
6 was] was thus
7 In faith chil] Indeed I'le
12, 27, 42 tis] it's
13, 28, 43 tis] It's
14, 29, 44 belly] belly too
18 But] For
26, 41 There] O there
31 are] be
33 you] ye

Another version in BM MS Sloane 1489 (mid-17th century), fol. 6, varies too much to collate:

> Wille to his mammie said he wold goe woo
> Faine wold he wed but he wist not how
> Nay (quoth she) my Lamme yet a while abide

But like a foole wille then replyde: Nay fake [*sic*]
                Ile have a wyfe a wyfe a wyf
Of what a lyfe haue [I] led for a wyfe in my bed
                I will not tell you.
Wille went a woing, as it was his mynde
And for his bed, a wyfe soone he did fynde
He was not long a doing, ere he won his choice
And like a foole he did then rejoyce. Now haue I
        got a wyfe, ter. [*i.e., three times*]
O what a lyfe shall I leade with a wyfe in my bed
                I wil not tel you
Wille was not wedded full a 12 months space
But he became in a wofull case
Largelye was he headed, tho his cheekes were thin
And to Lament he did then begin. O fye upon a wyfe, ter.
O what a lyfe have I lead with a wyfe in my bed,
                I dare not tell you.
You that are to marrye, learne of crying will
When you are well, to remayne soe still
Better it is to tarrye, & alone to lye
Then like a foole with a foole to crye. O fye upon a wife. thrys
O shees a cracke to my backe, O a smarte to my harte,
                & to my Purse strings too.

A similar song from the feminine point of view appears in the New York Public Library, Drexel MS 4257 (*c.* 1659), fol. 42–42v, with music for treble and bass. For another song on this theme see Jo1609.V and note, and compare line 6 below with Do1603.VI.

There was a mayde this other day sighed sore god wott
& she sayd that wiues might sport & play
but they maidens might not
full fifteene [years?] haue I liud she sayd
since I poore soul was borne
& if I chance for to dye a maide Apollo is forsworne;
oh! oh! oh! for a husband still this was her song
I will haue a husband; a husband be he old or yong

An auncient suitor thither cam his head was almost gray
Though hee was old yet she was yong
And could noe longer stay
But to her Mother went this mayd
And told her presently that a husband she needs must haue
And thus began to cry oh! oh! oh! for a husband &c

Shee had not beene a wedded wife a quarter of a yeare
But shee was weary of her life
And grew in to a feare
ffor the old man hee lay by her side
Could nought but sigh & grone did euer woeman soe abide
'Twere better lye alone; oh! oh! oh! with a husband
Oh! oh! oh! with a husband what a life lead I
Out vpon a husband such a husband; a husband? fye fy fy:

To be a Wedded wife she sayd a 12 month is to long
As I haue beene poore soule she sayd
That am both fayre & yong
When other wiues may haue theire will
That art not like to mee
I meane to goe & try my skill, & find som Remedy
Oh! oh! oh! with a husband what a life lead I
Out vppon a husband such a husband; a husband fy fy fy.

V.

See the note to IIII above, and Bt1606.IX and note.

2 *lead Apes in hell.* Tilley M37. *Cf.* Ck1612.XIIII.4, and Ma1611.XII.2.

10 This line seems to be lacking six syllables, the last rhyming with *me* (l. 9). A conjectural completion might be "since fifteen I did see."

16 *spend my blood. Cf.* Jo1601.V.38 and note.

VI.

The musical form of this song is what Thomas Morley called a "ballet" or "fa-la" modeled after the *ballette* of Gastoldi. See Morley's *Plaine and Easie Introduction* (1597), sig. Aa3v, his *First Booke of Balletts to Five Voyces* (1595) and the separate Italian version (Obertello, pp. 346–372; discussed by Kerman, pp. 136–147). *Cf.* Gr1604.XXI.

The verse is a translation of part of a poem from *Le nouveau recueil des chansons amoureuses . . . non encores imprimees* (Paris, Didier Millot, 1589), fol. 11. The verses Jones uses are as follows:

> Ma complainte n'est que fainte
> Ce sont fables mes amours,
> Je me moque quand j'invoque
> Tant de Dieux à mon secours.
>
> A telle heure que je pleure
> Dans moy-mesme je me ris,
> Et pour rire je souspire,
> Comme si j'estois espris.
>
> Vers les dames j'ay deux ames
> Pour mieux me faindre amoureux,
> En ma face j'ay la glace
> Et la flame quand je veux.

There are six more stanzas, printed by Helen E. Sandison in her edition of *The Poems of Sir Arthur Gorges* (Oxford, 1953), pp. 194–195. Gorges' own translation begins (p. 41):

> When I complayne I doo butt fayne
> my passyon ys noo inwarde griefe
> I sporte withall when I doo call
> The Gods of love to my releefe

Sandison (p. 195) notes that "My complayning is but faining" is in Forbes's *Cantus* (1666), sig. G3–G3v, but does not recognize its source in Jones. Forbes, who prints Jones's tune, varies slightly; I collate the 1662 ed., sig. T1, "The Fourtyfourth Song,"

excluding minor variants in the number of "fa las": 7 Representeth] Representing
12 were] wear

12 *were.* Read *wear,* as in Forbes.

VII.

Cf. Jo1610.XIV.

8, 20 *Cf.* Tilley M34, "Maids say nay and take it," and W660, "A woman says
nay and means aye."

VIII.

Cf. Jo1600.XII and note.

IX.

11 *harde. I.e., heard.*

13 *infants in her eyes. Cf.* Tilley B8, "To look babies in anothers eyes," *i.e.,* to see
one's reflection in the pupil of another's eyes (from a pun on *pupilla,* according to
Gardner, p. 184). *Cf.* Donne, "The Ecstasy," lines 11–12; and At1622.IIII.9.

X.

7 *sease. I.e., sieze.*

10 *Absence . . . liues. I.e., Absence's . . . life's.*

XI.

Cf. Pi1605.XIIII.

XII.

8 *louers eyes are euer blind. Cf.* Tilley L605.

14 *ods. I.e., at odds.*

XIII.

Cf. Petrarch CXXXII (Sonnet 102), the first lines of which are set in No. XXI
below; also *cf.* Fer1609.VIII (poem by Campion).

7–9 *sigh . . . lieth.* This could be a legitimate rhyme; *sigh* was sometimes spelled
sithe and transcribed by early writers on pronunciation with a thorn. See E. J. Dobson,
English Pronunciation 1500–1700 (Oxford, 1957), I, 181–182.

XIIII.

5–7 *life . . . relenting. Cf.* the sentiment in Fd1607.I.9–10. Perhaps here *life* should
read *death,* and *absence, griefe* should be *absence's griefes.* (A reads *griefes,* incidentally.)

XV.

2 *soule . . . limed wings. Cf. Hamlet,* III.iii.68–69.

XVI.

17 *Infused part. I.e.,* the soul, which is infused in the body.

25 *mase.* EMV, p. 595, reads *mass,* as the rhyme demands; but *maze* is a remote
possibility.

26 *grasse. Cf.* Tilley F359, "All flesh is grass."

XVII.

This poem is included in a MS entitled "The Workes of the Lady Ann Sothwell:
Decemb: 2° 1626" (Folger MS V.b.198), where it appears on fol. 1 as "Sonnett 2ª."

The poem is not necessarily by Lady Southwell: see the note to Fer1609.XVI. Variants are as follows:

3 spots] blotts
6–12 *omitted*
13 knowes my fault] showes my Guilt
   what . . . doe] *omitted*
16 griefes] woes
18–19 *omitted*
21 O . . . woes] Yes: Death ends all our woes

XIX.

This song is listed in the table of New York Public Library Drexel MS 4175 (fol. 26), but is missing from the MS. F. W. Sternfeld discusses this and other "Robin" songs in connection with Ophelia's "For bonny sweet Robin is all my joy" (*Hamlet* IV.v.187); see his *Music in Shakespearian Tragedy* (London: Routledge and Kegan Paul, 1963), pp. 68–78. See also Seng, pp. 149–156.

33 *Loue . . . vs. Cf.* Tilley L531, "Love will find a way," and L527, "Love overcomes all."

XX.

Petrarch CLIII (Sonnet 120), lines 1–4. See the *Rime*, ed. Ferdinando Neri, 2nd ed. revised by Ettore Bonora (Turin, 1960), p. 250. Jones or the printer corrupted the text of this and XXI: line 2 should read *pietà contende*. These lines are probably the ultimate source of Do1597.IX.7–12.

XXI.

Petrarch CXXXII (Sonnet 102), lines 1–8 (*Rime*, ed. Neri, p. 225). Simple misprints have been corrected (see Variants) but the following differences remain:

3 *effetto*] l'effetto
5 *Sa'*] s'a
   il] 'l
   el] e
6 *Sa'*] s'a
   vala] vale
7 *dilettose*] dilettoso
8 *no'l*] nol

William Corkine, *Ayres*, 1610

Dedication

Sir Edward Herbert (1583–1648) is of course the first Baron Herbert of Cherbury, philosopher, poet, and brother of George Herbert. A number of other books were dedicated to him. Sir William Hardy does not appear elsewhere as a patron; Williams even puts his title in inverted commas.

6–7 *It was long . . . English Presse.* The first book of tablature printed in England was a translation by J. Alford of a French work of Adrian Le Roy, *A briefe and easye instrution* [*sic*] *to learne the tablature vnto the lute* (1568).

13 *Masters . . . knowledge. Cf.* RD01610, dedication, VI, and note.

II.

Vivian speculates (p. 369) that this poem is by Thomas Campion because of its similarity to 4Camp[1617].XII. Line 4, for instance, is very close to Campion's line 12, "Truth is yet as fayre as shee." Moreover, the phrasing and ideas in the last stanza are somewhat suggestive of these lines from "Rose-cheekt Lawra" (Vivian, p. 50):

> Louely formes do flowe
> From concent deuinely framed;
> Heau'n is musick, and thy beawties
> Birth is heauenly.

The possibility that Campion wrote No. II is increased by our knowledge that early versions of some of his poems differ widely from their final form. See Vivian, pp. 356–357, 366–368, Davis, p. 508, and XI and note below.

23–24 *the sounds . . . firmament.* The music of the spheres.

III.

11, 13 *venture . . . Center.* A perfect rhyme. The *-ure* ending was pronounced like the *-er* of *Center.* (Kökeritz, p. 271).

13–14 *Iust . . . wauers. Cf.* Donne's famous conceit of the compasses in "A Valediction: Forbidding Mourning."

IIII.

Cf. D01600.XI and note.

5 *neare.* Read *ne'er.*

V.

Cf. Jo1601.VII and note.

VI.

This poem appears in BM MS Harl. 6917 (mid-17th century), fol. 31v, entitled "A Sonnet," and varying only in line 6: haue thy] see thy

3 Fellowes (EMV, 2nd ed., p. 612) suspects that two syllables are lacking (*e.g. forsooth* after *bedfellow*).

4 *Lady . . . Ione. Cf.* Tilley J57, "Joan is as good as my lady in the dark."

5 *am.* EMV, p. 436, unnecessarily emends to *are.*

6 *carted. I.e.,* punished as a whore.

VII.

A copy of this poem is preserved in Huntington MS HM 198 (mid-17th century), part II, fol. 111v, with these variants:

1, 6, 11 *omitted*
8 *Which*] that
10 *lie*] lies
12 *sweete*] deare
13 *shale*] spill
15 *Then*] there
    sport] sports

4 *nyer. I.e., nigher.*
10 *all . . . eyes. I.e.,* when they can only look.

VIII.

2 *hopes deceiuing. Cf.* Tilley H608.

IX.

This poem by Anthony Munday was also set in Jo1605.II (see note) and Pi1605. XVIII.

X.

This song is in the stereotyped southwestern dialect used frequently by stage rustics (see Kökeritz, pp. 35–40). It should be compared to the songs in Thomas Ravenscroft's *A Briefe Discourse* (1614), Nos. XVII–XX; see especially the last lines of Nos. XVII and XVIII and the refrain line in the present song. Another (earlier) dialect poem is Thomas Howell's "Jack shows his qualities and great good will to Jone" from *The Arbor of Amitie* (1568), sigs. F4–F5. The sense becomes moderately clear when *f* is substituted for initial *v*, *s* for *z*, some initial *y*'s are dropped (*yend*), and words beginning in *ch*- are seen as contractions of *I* (*ich*); thus *chwore* = *I were.*
7 *Hadds.* Also *Hudds* (10, 14), probably a euphemistic corruption of *God's.*
   woo ma. Probably *wooma'*, woman.

XI.

This poem is by Thomas Campion, but the version in 4Camp[1617]. XVIII differs considerably from Corkine's:

2 *Thinke you*] Think'st thou
    so] then
3 *can . . . voice*] Parats so can learne to prate our speech
7 *hath . . . hide*] courts vs wanting Arte
8 *And . . . he*] Lookes a-squint on his discourse, and
9–12 *omitted in Campion*
Campion continues:

> 3 Skilfull Anglers hide their hookes, fit baytes for euery season;
> But with crooked pins fish thou, as babes doe that want reason,
> Gogions onely can be caught with such poore trickes of treason.

> 4 Ruth forgiue me if I err'd from humane hearts compassion,
> When I laught sometimes too much to see thy foolish fashion:
> But alas, who lesse could doe that found so good occasion?

XII.

4 *shadow make me flie. Cf.* Tilley S261, "To be afraid of a shadow."

Robert Dowland, *A Musicall Banquet*, 1610

Dedication

See Jo1600 dedication and note.

To the Reader.

3 *my collected Lute-lessons.* I.e., Robert Dowland's *Varietie of Lute-lessons* (1610).

16 *such Lettuce.* Cf. Tilley L326, "Like lips like lettuce." Cf. Sir Thomas More, *Latin Epigrams*, ed. Leicester Bradner and C. A. Lynch (Chicago, 1953), No. 143, and Davis, p. 295.

Ad Robertum Doulandum

19 *Henricus Peachamus.* Henry Peacham was one of John Dowland's friends; he wrote an emblem verse about him in *Minerva Britanna* (c. 1612), sig. M1, and gives a biographical explanation of his famous anagram on "Ioannes Doulandus, Annos ludendo hausi," in his *Compleat Gentleman* (1622), sig. Cc3v, saying that "hee had slipt many opportunities in advancing his fortunes."

I.

George Clifford, third Earl of Cumberland (1558–1605) succeeded Sir Henry Lee as Queen Elizabeth's champion. See Do1597.XVIII and note, and No. VIII below. When Do1597.III was reprinted in *England's Helicon*, it was ascribed to Clifford, but Rollins is skeptical (REH, II, 27, 176). For Anthony Holborne, see Do1600.I and note.

II.

For other poems attributed to Essex, see Do1603.XVIII, Do1612.X, and VI below. The appearance of both words and music of this song in (D) Bod. MS Rawl. Poet. 148 (John Lilliat's MS) enables us to date the song more accurately than usual. The first three stanzas of the words appear (without ascription) on fol. 67–67v between poems dated 1596 and 1597 (fols. 63v and 72); the melody and bass of Martin's music (with some variants), headed "Chang thy minde," is on fol. 113 (a poem dated 1599 is on fol. 109). The first stanza with Martin's treble and bass appears also in (E) BM MS Add. 15118 (c. 1633), fol. 2v. The poem appears in (F) Bod. MS Rawl. Poet. 85 (c. 1600), fol. 125; (G) Rosenbach MS 1083/15 (c. 1625), p. 40; and (H) John Cotgrave's *Wits Interpreter* (1655), sig. P4. The variants are:

2 since] sith E
  doth change] is changd E
3 not] not thy D
  still] more E
  abuse] abase H
4 Thy] Thine G
  vntruth] vntruthes F, delayes E
  cannot] will not H
5 When] Since D, Sith E
  doth] may H
  excuse] accuse F
6 and] but H
8–32 *omitted* E
8 Whilst] When FH
9 she hath still delaid] styll she did delay F, still she hath delaid H
11 that] which DF
  deceiu'd] betrayd DFGH
12 although] butt all FH

15 gone] woonne D
16 Being once] hauyng bene F
17 Leaue her] leaue to F, cease to G
    but] and FG
    none] no FH
18 was] is DH
    her] love H
19 but] and H
20–32 *omitted* D
21 preseruest] preseruedste F
22 all ioyes are] thy ioy is FH
23 deseruest] deseruedste F
24–25 Oh . . . offence] They enioy whats iust theyr owne/ happyer lyfe to lyue
alone F
24 my] thy H
25 I] Thou H
    her] their H
26 Dye . . . dye] Yet thus much to ease my mynd F
27 Make] Lett F
28 She . . . lye] She who tyme hath proud vnkynde F
    hopes] hope GH
29 Now is chang'd, I] hauyng changd is F, Changing now is H
30–31 She . . . place] fortune now hath done her worst/ would she had done so
had [*sic*] fyrst F
30 is chang'd] doth change H
    but changed] & change is GH
31 vilde] vile GH

Richard Martin, the composer, was identified by the anonymous author of an article on *A Musicall Banquet* in *The Musical Antiquary*, I (1909), 47, as the Richard Martin (1570–1618) who was recorder of London, M. P., and the wit to whom Ben Jonson dedicated *Poetaster* (1602) and Sir John Davies dedicated *Orchestra* (1596). But even though this Martin was one of the "chief doers and undertakers" in Chapman's *Masque of the Middle Temple and Lincoln's Inn*, presented before the king in 1613, and in which John and Robert Dowland played the lute (*The Records of the Honourable Society of Lincoln's Inn. The Black Books* [1898], II, 156), the composer of No. II may have been the "Rychard Martyn" who became a member extraordinary of the Chapel Royal in February 1596-7 (see *The Old Cheque-Book . . . of the Chapel Royal*, ed. Edward F. Rimbault [London: Camden Society, 1872], p. 37). See the Textual Introduction to Fd1607 for a viol piece called "M. Richard Martins Thumpe."

13 *Loue . . . hate. Cf.* 3Camp[1617].XI, "If Loue loues truth, then women doe not loue."

III.

This poem is found among some poems by Nicholas Breton in (D) BM MS Add. 34064 (*c.* 1596), fol. 7, and may be by him. Alexander Grosart prints the poem from this MS in his edition of Breton's *Works*, I, "Daffodils and Primroses," p. 16. Another copy is in (E) Bod. MS Rawl. Poet. 85 (*c.* 1600), fol. 45.

The first three stanzas of the words and Hales's music for voice and lute are found in (F) King's College, Cambridge, Rowe MS 2 (Turpyn MS; *c.* 1610), fols. 4v–5. The variants are:

    1 O] Myne E
    3 you] yee D
    5 Where] When E
    6 you] yee D
    7 shower] showre E
    8 Hope] tyme F
    9 Though] thoughtes F
    13 But] yitt DE
    14 Where] When F
    15 liues] loues D
        wretchednesse] happines F
    16 Where]When E
        Hope] loue F
    17 Feare] hope F
        is but] but a DEF
    18 Loues happinesse] lyues wrettchednes F
    19–25 *omitted* F
    19 But] yitt DE
    20 Hope and Hap] loue and life DE
DE *continue after line* 24:

> But if I be that louer
> that neuer shall recouer
> but spight shall spill me
> then let thus much suffize mee
> that heaunes this death denist [denyse E] me
> that loue shulde kill me.

For Robert Hales, see D01597.XVIII and note.

IIII.

This poem is the ninth song from Sir Philip Sidney's *Astrophil and Stella.* Ringler (p. 546) says that Robert Dowland "definitely used Q3" for poems by Sidney, that is, *Syr P.S. His Astrophel and Stella . . . Printed for Matthew Lownes* probably by Felix Kingston between 1597 and 1600. Variants from Ringler's text (pp. 221–222), based on the 1598 *Arcadia,* are as follows:

    3 some other] a better
    5 Fro] From
    11 measures] mischiefe's
    17 fayrest] fiercest
    18 Fayrest . . . cruelst] Fiercest . . . fairest
    19 the] ô
        still] do
    25 to vs] eawes
    26 Towards] Toward

29 *Muse*] must
32 then doth she] doth she then
36 hopelesse] helplesse
44 Knowing . . . display] For she knowes, if she display
47 my flocke now] adieu, deere flocke
51 iust] unjust

A different setting of the first stanza only appears in Christ Church, Oxford, MS 439 (*c.* 1620), p. 17, with music for treble and bass ascribed to Robert Taylor. It varies:

3 some other] a better
4 haue] finde (*over cancelled* haue)
5 breast] bright (?)

5 *Fro.* A form of *from.* Ringler notes (p. 486) that *fro* is the reading of the 1598 text (*not* any of the quartos) and Edinburgh MS De.5.96, and reasonably suspects that a tilde was omitted in transmission.

V.

The tenth song from Sidney's *Astrophil and Stella.* See the note to IIII above. The first three stanzas were given a setting for five voices by William Byrd in *Songs of Sundrie Natures* (1589), No. XXXIII, and the last stanza was set for four voices by John Ward, *The First Set of English Madrigals* (1613), No. VIII (Cantus, sig. B4v). Dowland's text (the Lownes quarto) omits three stanzas after line 25; these may be found in Ringler's text (pp. 225–227, from the 1598 *Arcadia*). Detailed collation of the early prints of *Astrophil and Stella*, the Arundel Harington MS, and Bod. MS Rawl. Poet. 85, fols. 107v–108, and the versions already named are given by Hughey (HAH, II, 74–76). Variants from Ringler's text are:

5 hath] have
9 By . . . oft] After parting ought
12 high I] high joyes I (*corrected in text; see Variants*)
14 will I] I will
25 *Dowland lacks three stanzas after this line.*
27 Your] Thy
28 fleetes] melts
30 receiued] revived

VI.

See No. II above and note. It is difficult to avoid seeing Queen Elizabeth in lines 6–7.

Daniel Batchelar, the composer, also contributed two lute pieces to Robert Dowland's *Varietie of Lute-lessons* (1610, sigs. I2v–K1, O1–2v). Batchelar probably served as a page to Sir Philip Sidney, for one of the pages depicted in Thomas Lant's engravings of Sidney's funeral procession, *Sequitur celebritas & pompa funeris* (1587) is labeled "Daniell Batchiler." Batchelar probably got his musical training while in Sidney's service, as did Robert Dowland in the service of Sir Thomas Monson; see the dedication to *Varietie of Lute-lessons* and my note in *RN*, XVIII (1965), 123–124.

This song may be found with Batchelar's melody (highly embellished) and bass in (D) BM MS Add. 24665 (Giles Earle's book, 1615–1626), fols. 48v–50, and with accompaniment for viols arranged from Batchelar by William Wigthorp in (E) BM MSS Add. 17786–17791 (the words are in 17790, fol. 9). Variants are:

    4 wher] which D
    5 yeeld] yeelds DE
    7 can] could D
    9 Is] are DE
    10 you haue] shee hath D
    11 woman-like] woemen-like D
    12 your] her D
       doe] must DE

  8 *hopes*. EMV, p. 504, emends to *hope*.

VII.

This poem is the eighth song from Sidney's *Astrophil and Stella*. See No. IIII above and note; see also the note to At1622.IIII. Ringler (p. 486) notes the similarity of this poem to Fulke Greville's *Caelica* No. 76.

Dowland's source, the Lownes quarto, lacks eight stanzas after l. 69; Ringler gives the complete poem from the 1598 *Arcadia* on pp. 217–221, plus collations from other sources. The variants from Ringler's text are as follows:

    4 in] yong
    9 either in each] each in the
    12 care] cares
    17 reiected] reflected
    19 woe] woes
    28 see] set
    31 Triumphres in] triumpher of
    36 when] where
       are once] once are
    43 the Caracters] each character
    44 sweet face all] face all, all
    45 the] thy
       it] yet
    48 to] ô
    52 proue] love
    53 from] for
       nere] may
    55 apt] more apt (*corrected in text*; *see Variants*)
    59 leaues leaues] the leaues
    68 compelling] repelling
    69 expelling] excelling
Dowland lacks the next 32 lines after line 69
    71 with] so

The composer, Guillaume Tessier, first published the music to this song for four voices in his *Primo Libro Dell'Arie* (Paris, 1582—thus the cantus partbook; the tenor has a French title, *Premier Livre D'Airs*), sig. C2v, as a setting for Ronsard's "Le petit enfant amour" (*Odes*, 1555, IV, xx). Apparently Robert Dowland found that Tessier's tune would fit Sidney's poem, and then fashioned a lute accompaniment from the three lower voices of Tessier's song. The author of the article on RDo1610 in *Musical Antiquary*, I (1909), 48, as well as Warlock (p. 123), Pattison (p. 63), and Ringler (p. 567) assumed that the composer was Charles Tessier, whose *Premier livre de chansons* was published in London in 1597. See my note in *RN*, XVIII (1965), 124–126.

55 *more apt.* Dowland or the compositor had omitted *more.*

VIII.

A note over the Cantus part reads, "For one Voice onely to sing."

Dowland set to music two other poems associated with Lee, 1597.XVIII and 1600. VI–VIII. The occasion for this poem was probably to thank Queen Anne for honoring Lee and his mistress, Anne Vavasour, with a visit in 1608. The Queen later sent Lee a "very fair jewell," perhaps the "starre" referred to in line 12. See E. K. Chambers, *Sir Henry Lee* (1936), p. 211, quoting from *Calendar of State Papers, Domestic*, XXXVI, 40.

4 *he made his pastime story.* That is, he made his former amusements (tilting, etc.) the subject of a story (with connotations of a story to be laughed at). See the OED, s.v. "story," definition 5e.

6 *Goddesse.* Queen Elizabeth.

8 *glorious light.* Queen Anne.

15 *denaid.* From *denay*, a form of *deny.*

22 *Tyme . . . changed.* Compare Do1597.XVIII.1.

with. The sense demands *which*. The compositor may have misread the superscript contraction of the word.

IX.

Dowland probably took this poem from Nicholas Yonge's *Musica Transalpina* (1588); No. 40 (Cantus, sigs. E4v–F1), has the following variants:

3 ouer-cloyed] overjoyed
4 thus ouer-ioyed] and bee destroyed

The original madrigal was composed by Alfonso Ferrabosco the elder, and according to Obertello, pp. 242, 448, the Italian poem was also set by Antonio Orlandini in his *Madrigali* (1598), Horatio Vecchi, *Convito Musicale* (1597), and Benedetto Pallavicino, *Madrigali* (1604). The poem is by Cesare Rinaldi and was printed in his *De' Madrigali* (Bologna, 1588), sig. B1v; it reads:

> Donna, se voi m'odiate,
> A'che si dolci poi baci mi date?
> Forse acciò l'Alma per estrema gioia
> Di dolcezza ne moia?
> Se per questo lo fate,
> Baciate pur baciate;
> Che contento mi fia
> Finir baciando voi, la vita mia.

Ferrabosco's setting, with English words, appears in BM MS Egerton 995, No. 18 (Alto, fols. 31v–32); it is also found in BM MSS Add. 30016–30021, No. 97, with

Italian words. John Wilbye set another translation, "Lady your words doe spight mee," No. 18 of his *First Set of English Madrigals* (1598); compare Thomas Morley's "Lady you think you spite me," No. 15 of his *Canzonets or Little Short Aers* (1597).

Dowland's music was printed as an "Aria" for four instruments in Thomas Simpson's *Taffel-Consort* (1621), No. XIX (Cantus, p. 23).

X.

Another setting, perhaps Dowland's source, is in Cop1606.IIII.

XI.

This song was taken from *Airs de Differents Autheurs, Mis en Tablature de Luth par Gabriel Bataille* (Paris, 1608), sigs. M2v–M3, without variants. Bataille's arrangement, made from a part-song by Pierre Guedron, was reprinted with the music ascribed to Guedron and Bataille, and with an English translation of the words by Sir Edward Filmer in *French Court-Aires* (1629), No. XI (sigs. G1v–G2), as follows:

> IF key of Speach, or locke of Silence,
> Strike vs with errors, or with feares;
> Then let Eies vse their secret stile, whence
> Hearts may bee taught, and yet not Eares.
>   Loue, whose noiselesse wing, by stealth, caught vs,
>   This dumbe discourse, as softly, taught vs.
>
>   Let our Lookes, flying and returning,
>   (Fit secret Posts for close Desires)
>   Whisper each others inward burning,
>   And 'point a time to slake our fires.
>   Loue, whose noiselesse wing, &c.
>
>   But, if our prying riualls mutter
>   To see the language of our Eies,
>   By vnseene Thought our minds wee'll vtter,
>   As messages are done in Skies.
>   Loue, whose noiseless wing, &c.
>
>   Thus, with an armour new-inuented,
>   Breaking the puffes of Enuies lungs,
>   Gard wee our Honors shape vndented,
>   By poison'd shot of Courtiers tungs,
>   Whom in Ignorance wee'll all berrie,
>   And, at their Tombe, bee dumbly merrie.

Filmer gives the French on sig. M2 with these variants, correcting line 9:

> 5 *seulement*] selement
> 9 *des*] de

XII.

This song is also taken from Bataille's *Airs* (see note to XI above), sigs. A4v–B1; Bataille reads *montre* in line 24.

XIII.

This song, like XI and XII, was taken from Bataille's *Airs*, sigs. H3v–H4, which has three minor variants (*pieds* in line 4, *mepris* in line 13, and *entreprise* in line 16) plus three more stanzas:

Cét oeil r'abaissant sa gloire
Vous à blessé de ses traits,
Affin que de sa victoire
Vous vous honnoriez apres.

Bien-heureuse servitude,
Dont le genereux effort
Peut vaincre l'ingratitude
De l'oubli & de la mort.

L'honneur d'un brave adversaire
Honnore vostre trespas,
Heureux qu'en mourant peu faire
Que son nom ne meure pas!

The original song arranged by Bataille is by Pierre Guedron, as acknowledged by Sir Edward Filmer, who prints Bataille's version in his *French Court-Airs*, No. XV (sigs. I1v–I2), with the following translation:

Thou, whome Fortune, now turn'd tender,
With old chaines anew doth greet,
Ioy thy tribute Soule to render
At thy Queenes deseruing feet.

Honour'd, thou, by losse of battell,
With victresse bayes her browes vaile:
Pay, with holocausts of cattell,
Thy new entrance to her jaile.

Blush not, erring, at the glorie
Got by yeelding her thine armes:
Thou alone, in all her storie,
Art found worthy of her harmes.

Her Eie, daigning thee an arrow,
Stoop'd from pitch of wonted glance,
That thy brauely-kindled marrow
Might shine by so rare a chance.

Thy lost Soule, thus new-enchained,
Stile thou her eternall Slaue:
Glorious captaine, who hath gained
Title that defies the Graue.

Thraldome stands on happie pillres,
Whose Fame, Fate-proofe, feares no powres
Of, her ruines strongest willers,
Shakes of Death and *Lethe's* showres,

'Tis a hight worth thy aspiring
To fall by so loftie eies:
Happie hee, whose Soules expiring
His Names birth doth solemnize.

Filmer gives the French text on M2 with these slight variants: 3 *antien*; 4 *pieds*; 6 *Glorieux*; 7 *Honorex*; 12 *veoir*; 13 *mépris*; 15 *Finit*; 16 *l'entreprise*.

XIIII.

Also taken from Bataille's *Airs* (see note to XI above), sigs. K1v–K2, without variants. As Diana Poulton has pointed out (*LSJ*, III [1961], 22), the words are from Book III of Jorge de Montemayor's *Diana* (1558); only lines 1–9 and 40–42 of the 73-line poem were used for the song. Variants from the edition by Enrique Moreno Baez (Madrid, 1955), pp. 164–165, are as follows:

    2 *dessarmado*] desarmado
    4 *Dexaua m'ya*] dexávame ya
    5 *Quam*] Cuán
    6 *deembidiosa*] d'embidiosa
    7 *vays tam*] passáis tan
    8 *ami*] a mi
    9 *enuersé*] en verse
    10 *sta*] está
    12 *ero*] era
    13 *te*] le

Bartholomew Yong translates these verses in his *Diana of George of Montemayor* (1598), sigs. G4–G5 as follows:

> Loue passed by me with his bowe vnarm'd,
>   His eies cast downe, milde, gentle, modest gay,
>   And (carelesse) left me then behind vnharm'd:
> How small a time did I this ioye essaie?
>   For presently enuious Fortune saide,
>   Staie loue, why passest thou so soone awaie?
> Foorthwith the blinde boye turn'd to me, and staide
>   Angry to see himselfe so checkt with blame,
>   For ther's no blame, where his hot fire is laide:
>
>   · · · · ·
>
> O meadowes, groues, and woods of sweete content,
>   Which bred so free a hart as I had heere,
>   So great an ill why did you not preuent?

XV.

As Diana Poulton has pointed out (*LSJ*, III [1961], 24–26), these words are Italian, however corrupt, not Spanish; but she goes on to remind the reader of the dominance of Spain over much of Italy in the early 17th century. The spelling suggests that the words were taken down from dictation by someone who did not know Italian (*medso* = *mezzo*), perhaps a Spaniard, since he avoids double consonants and frequently uses *y* for *i*. Mrs. Poulton cites the following reconstruction and translation made by Michael Morrow:

> Sta notte mi sognava
> Ch'all inferno mestamente me n'andava,
> Non per li miei peccati
> Ma per veder che fanno i dannati.

Stando là mi pareva
Che nel messo Plutone si sedeva
Tra quei spiriti infernali
Chi dan'al'alma tanti stragi mali.

Last night I dreamt
That I was wending my way sadly to Hell,
Not for my sins,
But to see what the damned are doing.

Standing there it seemed to me
That in the midst Pluto was seated
Amongst the infernal spirits
That give to the soul such evil havoc.

This contains some good guesses (*e.g.*, *mestamente*), and although *yaua* might have once been *vaya*, *mi sognava* makes better sense. The substitution of *i dannati* for *lyny* is not necessary, however.

XVI.

This song was taken from Gabriel Bataille's *Airs de Differents Autheurs . . . Second Livre* (Paris, 1609), sigs. Q2v–Q3: Bataille has an important correction for the corrupt phrase in Dowland's line 4, which should read *con tanta aflicion*. Diana Poulton translates the verses in *LSJ*, III (1961), 26, thus:

Your eyes have of love I know not what,
That they freeze me, they rob me, they wound me,
    and by my faith they kill me.
Why do you look at me with so much pain,
That my heart is imprisoned within me?
If you look at me I shall accuse you.

XVII.

This song was taken from Dominico Maria Megli's (or Melli's) *Seconde Musiche* (1602; or 2nd ed., 1609), No. VIII. I have not been able to see this volume, but its contents are described in Johannes Emil Vogel, *Bibliothek der gedruckten Weltlichen Vocalmusik Italiens aus den Jahren 1500–1700* (1892, reprint with additions by A. Einstein, 1962), I, 451.

5,6 *lire. I.e., l'ire.*

XVIII.

This song is from Giulio Caccini's famous *Nuoue Musiche* (Venice, 1602), sig. B4; there are no verbal variants. Caccini gives treble and bass only; Dowland gives a fully realized accompaniment in lute tablature for this and No. XIX below. Another copy of the song is in Tenbury MS 1018 (first half of the 17th century), fol. 39v, with music for treble and bass; it varies thus:

3 *nuouo io miri*] nou'io mira
4 *bramata*] bramate
  de miei martiri] del mio martire
5 *tesoro*] thesore
6 *dirui*] dir

7 *pria*] pri
  moro] mora
9 *poter*] potro

XIX.

Taken (like XVIII) from Caccini's *Nuoue Musiche* (1602), sig. B2–B2v, without verbal variants; Dowland provided the lute part. Another copy, in Tenbury MS 1018, fol. 39 (with Caccini's treble and bass), varies thus:

3 *credi ò*] crede
8 *e'l*] 'l

Diana Poulton has informed me of another copy in BM MS Egerton 2971 (first quarter of the 17th century), p. 94, without tablature. Caccini's melody, with lute accompaniment, is found also in BM MS Add. 15117 (after 1614), fol. 6, with words beginning "Miserere my maker." Peter Philips arranged the music for keyboard; see "Amarilli di Julio Romano" in *The Fitzwilliam Virginal Book*, ed. J. A. Fuller Maitland and W. B. Squire (1899; Dover reprint 1963), I, 329–331.

XX.

Other copies of this song are in BM MS Add. 29481 (*c.* 1650), fol. 13, with music for treble and bass from RD01610, and in BM MS Egerton 2971 (first quarter of the 17th century), p. 84, also with music for treble and bass. Diana Poulton tells me the first has several differences in spelling, as if the copyist did not know Italian; the second, although the spelling is closer to the Italian, has some of the syllables incorrectly divided. Neither have the error *pipiu* in the first line as in RD01610 (see Variants).

4 *mi*. Read *mia*.
5 *mia*. Read *mio*.
7 *mio*. Read *mia*.
8 *fretsa*. I.e., *frezza* or *freccia*, arrow.

Robert Jones, *The Muses Gardin for Delights*, 1610

Dedication

Mary Sidney, daughter of Sir Robert Sidney (Jo1600, dedication), married Sir Robert Wroth in 1604. She was a patroness of some importance—Ben Jonson dedicated *The Alchemist* to her—and was herself the author of *The Countesse of Mountgomeries Urania* (1621). She died after 1640 (DNB, Williams).

I.

For other definitions of love, see Jo1601.IX and note.
28 *thousand eyes*. See the Index for other references to Argus.

III.

Cf. Donne's "The Bait."
4 *Angels*. I.e., *angles*, fish-hooks, with a pun.

IIII.

Cf. Do1603.XIX and note. Bond (III, 490) ascribes this poem to Lyly without evidence, but does note the occurrence of some of the following commonplaces in Lyly's works.

2 *Starres . . . day.* Tilley S826.

6, 12, 18 *Loue . . . secret is.* Cf. Tilley S779, "Sport is sweetest when there be no spectators."

7 *stillest . . . deepe.* Tilley W123.

8 *clearest . . . shower.* Cf. Tilley D92, "No day so clear but has dark clouds." *Cf.* also line 10.

13 *Iewels . . . vertue yeeld.* Gems were believed to have curative and magical powers. See Joan Evans and Mary S. Serjeantson, *English Mediaeval Lapidaries* (London: Early English Text Society, 1933).

14 *sweete . . . gaine.* Cf. Tilley G3, "Gain savors sweetly from anything," and B626, "Stolen bread is ever sweetest."

17 *Cupid is blind.* Tilley L506.

VII.

The use of "L'Envoy" in setting a sonnet to music, while clear in this case, can be confusing: see By1596.V, Dc1600.IX,XX, and Do1612.XVIII and notes.

6 *be thy.* EMV, p. 602, reads *be the.*

VIII.

25 *healt.* Read *heal't.*

IX.

Cf. Mo1600.XIII. H. D. Thoreau quoted the first stanza of this poem in *Walden,* Chapter II. Joseph Leach says that he may have found it in Thomas Evans' *Old Ballads,* I (London, 1810), 248. (*American Notes and Queries,* II [1943], 171.) Evans also includes No. XI on pp. 246–247.

X.

1 *Sea . . . sands.* Tilley S91.

2 *Sunne . . . motes.* Tilley M1192.

10–11 *honies . . . gall.* Cf. Tilley Y40, "A reckless youth makes a gousty age." *Cf.* ll. 17–18 also.

XI.

21 *bracelets made of hayre.* Love tokens. *Cf.* Donne, "The Funerall" and "The Relique."

23 *clothes made out of waxe.* I.e., clothes so scrupulously neat as to seem modeled out of wax. *Cf.* OED, *wax* 3.c., and *Romeo and Juliet,* I.iii.76, "Why he's a man of wax."

XII.

The willow of course signified a forsaken lover. Other "willow" songs have been much discussed in connection with Desdemona's song in *Othello.* See F. W. Sternfeld, "Shakespeare's Use of Popular Song" in *Elizabethan and Jacobean Studies presented to Frank Percy Wilson,* ed. Herbert Davis and Helen Gardner (Oxford, 1959), pp. 154–166; Sternfeld's *Music in Shakespearean Tragedy* (London, 1963), pp. 23–52; and Seng, p. 198.

16 *friends.* This should probably read *fiends.*

30 *Gray hayres . . . fate.* Cf. Tilley H31 and *I Henry VI*, II.v.5, "grey locks, the pursuivants of death."

XIII.

The emphasis here seems to be on the second rather than on the first *entendre*; consequently some of the musical terms are confusing. For example in lines 44–45 the "Long" note refers to duration, the "Gamuet scale" to pitch. See the Glossary and Index.

11 *Didle.* Cf. Mo1600.XVII and note.

41 *without the pricke.* I.e., not in the written (pricked) music.

42–43 *moode . . . three to one.* The measuring of notes by longs and larges is called the *mood.* When three longs are made equal to a large, it is termed the "Great Mood Perfect"; three breves to a long is the "Less Mood Perfect," according to Morley, *A Plaine and Easie Introduction* (1597), sigs. C3v–C4.

XIIII.

25 *you feede, your fancie.* The punctuation here is metrical.

XV.

Cf. Bt1606.IX and note. This poem also appears in BM MS Add. 29409 (a 19th century copy of an older Scotch commonplace book), fols. 267v–268, with these variants:

1 faine] fyne
4 afraide] afeard
10 fourteene] fourtie
12 *cast*] take
16 *chuse*] have
17 *But . . . madde*] Bot a wane maid
19–29 *omitted*
28 *hath*] haue
31 *sung*] sing
32 *must*] might
    doe] did
34 *Though*] Thought
39 *What . . . Nun*] Quhat wald she haue beene he a man
43 *speaketh*] does speak

4 *afraid.* This should probably be *afeard.*

XVI.

2 *to.* Read *too.*

5 *If shee did.* EMV, p. 609, adds *aught* after *did.*

17 *weare.* Read *were.*

19–20 *alter . . . matter.* Shakespeare rhymes *matter* and *water*, and uses *Walter* as a homonym with *water.* The *l* in words like *malt, salt, shalt,* and *halt* was frequently dropped. See Kökeritz, pp. 152, 310–11, 461.

XVII.

This poem by Sir Philip Sidney first appeared among the "certaine Sonnets" appended to the 1598 *Arcadia*, sigs. Ss3v–4, headed "To the tune of a *Neopolitan Villanell*." Other copies are in the Arundel-Harington MS (HAH, I, 239–40), and two MS copies of the *Arcadia*, Folger MS 4009.03, fols. 224v–225 and Bod. MS e. Museo 37, fol. 242–242v. All but the last are collated by Hughey (HAH, II, 311) and all by Ringler (pp. 156–157). Jones's text is corrupt in spots, as the variants from Ringler will show:

5–8, 16–17, 25–26, 34–35, 43–44 *Sidney's refrain reads:*

> Fa la la leridan, dan dan dan deridan:
> Dan dan dan deridan deridan dei:

14 *While . . . stood*] Reason hath thy words removed [*Jones repeats l.9*]
32 *blasphemie*] blaspheme
40 *my*] me
solly] wholly

5–8 *Fa, la, la, etc.* Ringler (p. 432) says these nonsense words once had sexual connotations. *Cf.* Mo1600.VI, XVII.
40 *solly.* I.e., solely; but see variant.
45–46 *And all . . . the lesse*, Puttenham, p. 203, quotes these lines as an example of *prosonomasia*.

XVIII.

1 *the.* Read *thee.*
18 *Like Rauen . . . feind.* David Greer compares the mad song in John Webster's *The Duchess of Malfi*, IV, ii, 65–66 (ed. John R. Brown, Cambridge, Mass., 1964, p. 120):

> As ravens, screech-owls, bulls, and bears,
> We'll bill and bawl our parts.

XIX.

This poem was first printed in *The Speeches and Honorable Entertainment giuen to the Queenes Maiestie in Progresse, at Cowdrey in Sussex, by the right Honorable the Lord Montacute* (1591), a pamphlet reprinted by R. W. Bond in his edition of Lyly's *Works*, I, 423 (the ascription to Lyly is dubious). The song is introduced thus: "On Munday . . . her Highness . . . rode into the Parke: where was a delicate Bowre prepared, vnder the which were placed her Highnes Musitians, and this dittie following song while her Maiestie shot at the Deere." "A Dittie" follows, with these variants (from Bond):

4 *the heauens*] Apollos
5 *miracles*] miracle
worldes] *Bond adds* whole *before* worldes
7 *hopes*] hope
1591 continues after l. 12:

> Goddesse and Monarch of [t]his happie Ile,
> vouchsafe this bow which is an huntresse part:
> Your eies are arrows though they seeme to smile
> which neuer glanst but gald the stateliest hart,

> Strike one, strike all, for none at all can flie,
> They gaze you in the face although they die.

XX.

13 *remooue my lookes. I.e.,* keep me from looking.

XXI.

12–13 *Poet . . . poore.* Ovid, *Metamorphosis* III, 466, "Inopem me copia fecit," translated by Arthur Golding (III, 587; ed. W. H. D. Rouse, New York: Norton, 1966, p. 74) as "my plentie makes me poore." *Cf.* Tilley P427, and Spenser, *Faerie Queene* I,iv.29.

24 *Lazar like.* Luke 16:19–31.

John Maynard, *The XII. Wonders of the World*, 1611

Dedication

Lady Joan Thynne was the wife of Sir John Thynne of Longleat (d. 1623) and daughter of Sir Royland Hayward, who was Lord Mayor of London. Cause Castle, located southwest of Shrewsbury, was part of Lady Joan's dowry. See Ian Harwood's article on Maynard in *LSJ*, IV (1962), 12–13.

I.–XII.

Maynard took this set of twelve poems from the second (1608) edition of *A Poetical Rhapsody* (RPR, I, 239–241), with a few slight changes (II.7 *starue* for *sterue*; V.7 *effects* for *affects*; VI.3 *coasts* for *costs*; VII.2 *Countries* for *Country*; VII.5 *soul* for *sole*; and VIII.4 *which* for *whom*). The version in *A Poetical Rhapsody* is assigned to "Iohn Davys," or Sir John Davies. This attribution is supported by a MS at Downing College, Cambridge, known as the "Wickstede Thesaurus" (1605–1635), in which the poems are headed "Verses giuen to the L: Treasurer vpon Newyeares day vpon a dosen of Trenchers by Mr Davis" (part II, fols. 25v–27). The table of contents to the volume adds "Mr Davies after Sergeant att lawe." A. B. Grosart, in his edition of Davies' *Complete Poems* (London: Early English Poets series, 1876), I, cxvii–cxx, makes a very plausible case for the date of the poems by citing a letter of January 20, 1600 from Davies to one Mr. Hicks: "I have sent you heer inclosed that cobweb of my invention which I promised before Christmas . . . though the imployment be light and trifling, because I am glad of any occasion of being made knowne to that noble gentl. whom I honore and admire exceedingly. If ought to be added, or alter'd, lett me heare from you." Thomas Sackville, first Earl of Dorset, had succeeded Burghley as Lord Treasurer in May, 1599 (DNB), and perhaps the social demands of his new position made him desire a fresh and witty set of trencher-verses. Grosart sees Davies' willingness to alter his verses reflected in the differences between the version in *A Poetical Rhapsody* and the Downing MS, which he takes to be copied from an autograph early version. Variants from (D) the Downing MS are given below.

The trenchers for which the verses were written were thin wooden discs, usually about six inches in diameter, which were painted and inscribed on one side and plain on the other. After a meal, fruit or cheese would be served on the plain side. They were then turned over and the verses read aloud for the amusement of the company. Puttenham discusses them under "Of short Epigrames called Posies" (p. 58): "There be also other like Epigrammes that were sent vsually for new yeares giftes . . . & were made for the nonce, they were called *Nenia* or *apophoreta*, and neuer contained aboue one verse, or two at the most, but the shorter the better, we call them Posies, and do paint them now a dayes vpon the back sides of our fruite trenchers of wood, or vse them as deuises in rings and armes and about such courtly purposes."

Several sets of these trenchers or roundels have survived, and a number have been described in the *Proceedings of the Society of Antiquaries* (of London), *e.g.*, Series 2, X (1885), 207–216 and XII (1888), 201–223. The following sets have Davies verses: (E) 12 trenchers, *c.* 1610, Victoria and Albert Museum, London; these are typically in the "Indian" style (gold and silver on a black ground), with figures of each of the characters surrounded by the verses in concentric circles. Another set (F) is described and the verses quoted (not in the usual order) in a note by G. Blencowe, *N & Q*, Series 1, XIII (1855), 290–291; this set was then at Bradfield Combust Hall, Suffolk, and lacked No. X. John Y. Akerman describes a set similar to E in (G) his "Account of some 'Roundells' or Fruit Trenchers of the time of James the First," *Archaeologia*, XXXIV (1852), 225–230; Nos. V, IX, and XII are missing. H. Clifford Smith, in (H) "Jacobean Painted Platters," *Proceedings of the Society of Antiquaries*, Series 2, XVIII (1916), 78–85, describes both the Victoria and Albert set and a similar one owned by Mr. Henry Howard. Plates of the latter are given facing pp. 79, 80, 82, 83, 84, from which the variants below are taken. A final set (I) belonging to Mr. Henry Nyburg of Caux, Switzerland, was copied by Professor Carroll Camden, who generously allowed me to collate his transcript (and incidentally provided me with several of the references cited above). The poems also appear in the following MSS: (J) BM MS Add. 22601 (*c.* 1603), fols. 40–43; (K) Bod. MS Rawl. poet. 84 (*c.* 1660). fols. 44v–43v (reversed), Nos. XII, IIII, II, III only, in that order; (L) St. John's College, Cambridge, MS U.26 (made by John Cruso, d. 1681; belonged to William Wordsworth), pp. 32, 35–36 (pp. 33–34 lacking), Nos. I–III, X–XII only; and finally, the first two lines of No. X are found in Bod. Eng. poet. d. 152, fol. 103v; Bod. Rawl. poet. 153, fol. 28; and Folger V.a.339, fol. 226, among a group of entries from *Witts Recreations*; see the 1640 ed., sig. F7.

Maynard's book was reprinted without music in a small privately produced edition by E.V. Utterson in 1842.

Variants from D–L are as follows (none, of course, have "A Wonder"):

I *omitted* K
I.2 liude] served DJ
   in] at F
 .3 sell] tell I
   smoake] breath E
   to smile] I smile J
 .5 such as fall] them that fall DJL
   such as rise] them that rise DJL
 .6 a . . . a] my . . . my J
   a rich] my rich D
 .7 Nor] Not GHI
   t'were] it were E

II. *omitted in* I, *after* IIII *in* K
II.2 and . . . sent] one cure doth me contente DJL
(L *has* Care *for* cure)
  .3 no] not E
  .4 kinde true] true kinde DK
  .5 will] *omitted* D
    part it with] change it for L
  .6 Much . . . seeke] Nor followe princes Courts DJL
    Masters] matter L
  .7 while] whilst E
    doth] do EFGHK
    starue] sterue D
III.4 loue] serue L
  .5 oft] hoast EFGHK
    nor often] or often FG
  .6 speaking] talkinge J
    all] doe K
    occasion] occasions DFJK
    shunne] sham F
  .7 loue] live F
    boast] brag DJL
IIII. *after* V *in* DJ, *omitted* L, *second in* K
IIII.2 The . . . is] My practise is the law DJ
    robe] gownd K
  .3 opinion] opinions F
  .4 The] A D
    did] will F
  .5 spunne] spinn F
    in] at GHJK
    length] large K
    wisht] wish E
    an] theire D
  .6–7 D *reads*:
Some say I haue good giftes, and love where I doe take
Yet never tooke I fee, but I advisd or spake.
    .6 nor of] wherof J
    .7 euer] neuer E, ere K
    tooke I fee] took a fee FI, kept I fee J, recd I fee K
V. *before* IIII *in* DJ, *omitted* GKL
V.2 Studie] Suddy E
  vphold] prolonge D
  state] life DJ
  .3 who] Which J
    wee . . . wee] I . . . I D
  .5 receipt] receiptes EJ, receipe H
    or] of DEFH
  .6 Cures] cares EFH

doth] doe E

.7 youth and time] time & youth D

VI. *omitted* KL

VI.3 Discouers] Discouer EFGHIJ

coasts] worldes DJ

countryes] kingdomes D

.6 selling . . . buying] buying and by sellinge E

.7 And] But D

or] and EI

VII. *omitted* HIKL

VII.2 spirits] speech G

praise . . . scorne] the towns and country scorne FG

Countries] country DJ

.3 dwell] liue D

.5 and] nor J

soul] sole DEFGJ

.6 quarrels] quarrell E

not maintaine] and mayntaine J

.7 to] *omitted* EF, t' GJ

VIII. *omitted* KL

VIII.3 The . . . Dog] The horse, the dog, the feild DJ

or] & D

.4 I . . . yet] As yet I haue no wife J

which] whome DEFGHIJ

mine] my E

.6 I . . . thriue] I wish I might not thriue E

.7 tame] rule J

IX. *omitted* GIKL

IX.2 among] amongst DE, amongest J

.3 doe] woulde DJ

wish] seeke J

.4 And] Yea D

did] do E

.5 chance] choise D, happ E

happy] better E

mine] my E

.7 neither] nor D

nor iealous] Ielous EFH, not iealous J

X. *omitted* FK

X.2 our] my D

.3 I . . . am] Thither am I DL

from whence] where firste DL, whence first J

our] my DL

.4–5 DL *read*:

I goe not maskd abroad to visit when I do

My secretes I bewray to none, but one or two

.4 oft] muche J

nor] not E
.5 too] two E
XI. *omitted* IK
XI.2 dying] *omitted* EFGH
　　.4 haue] loue DJL
　　　　must] most J
　　.6 on such as are] such on, as are D, such one, as is L
　　.7 nor younger] No younger GH, Nor richer DJL
　　　　richer will] younger woulde D, younger then J, younger will L
XII. *omitted* GHI, *first in* K
XII.2 I heare] I've heard K
　　.3 shee that] whoso K
　　　　must] shall EK
　　　　in] to E
　　.4 Therefore] Wherefore K
　　　　will] may E, must F
　　　　and] or K
　　.5 on] of DE
　　　　till] while J
　　　　it] all E, I FK
　　　　be driuen] have drove't K
　　.6 yet] but DK

I.3 *sell poore suters smoake.* Tilley S576; see also Rollins' note (RPR, II, 200) in which he quotes Robert Greene and William Mason relating the anecdote of the courtier of Alexander Severus who was choked with smoke for taking bribes. At his execution it was proclaimed: "Fumo pereat qui fumum vendidit" (Mason, *A Handful of Essaies,* 1621, sig. F8v).

II.4–5 *true mother . . . Childe.* See I Kings 3:16–28.

III.7 *loue to doe . . . done. Cf.* Tilley B489, "The greatest boasters are not the greatest doers."

IIII.7 *nor . . . spake. Cf.* Tilley L125, "No fee, no law."

V.6 *The earth . . . see.* Tilley D424.

VIII.7 *tame . . . shrew. Cf.* Tilley M106, "Every man can rule a shrew but he that has her."

IX.4 *my shoe did wring.* Rollins cites several appearances of this expression (RPR, II, 201); see, for example, Chaucer, *Wife of Bath's Prologue,* l. 492 (ed. Robinson, p. 80).

X.5 *in counsaile.* I.e., in confidence. But *cf.* Tilley S196, "Trust no secret with a woman."

　　.6 *sicke in health. Cf.* Tilley W720, "Women weep and sicken when they list."

XI.2, 7 *Cf.* Tilley W342, "Widows are always rich."

　　.4–5 *Cf.* Tilley W340, "The rich widow weeps with one eye and casts glances with the other."

XII.3 *lead an Ape in hell.* Tilley M37; *cf.* Jo1609.V.2, Ck1612.XIIII.4, and Rollins' note (RPR, II, 201–202).

　　.7 *A man that wanteth . . . wants a man.* Rollins (RPR, II, 202) cites Plutarch,

"Themistocles" in *Lives*, trans. A. H. Clough, I (1899), 252; Boccaccio, *Decameron*, V, ix; and Thomas Howell's "Themistocles answer, concerning his Daughter to be maried," in *Newe Sonets, and pretie Pamphlets* (*c.* 1568), sig. D1:

> My daughter deare hath wonne (*quod* he) more wealth than ye do gesse:
> Whom I accompt much better plaste, when truth I truely scan,
> Upon a man that money wants, then money wanting man.

William Corkine. *The Second Booke of Ayres*, 1612

Dedication (1)
Sir Edward Dymmocke (d. 1625), champion at James I's coronation, came from a long line of royal champions beginning with Sir John Dymoke (d. 1381). All or part of four other books were dedicated to him (DNB, Williams).

I.
As one reviewer of EMV (third edition) noted (*TLS*, June 6, 1968, p. 572), this poem is an acrostic spelling ELIZABETH, perhaps in honor of Elizabeth Cope (see Dedication 3 and note). None of Sir Edward Dymoke's three wives or known children was named Elizabeth. See Burke's *History of the Commoners* (1836), I, 35–36.

II.
1 *Truth-trying Time.* Tilley T338.
3–4 *day . . . cleere. Cf.* Tilley D100, "Praise a fair day at night."
9 *peacefull fights. Cf.* Do1612.XXI.7–8.

III.
5–6 *bewraying . . . delaying.* As Fellowes points out (EMV, 2nd ed., p. 612), these words seem to have been transposed.
7 *coth.* I.e., *quoth.*
9 *bewraying.* Perhaps this should be *betraying.*

IIII.
This is the earliest printed version of John Donne's "Breake of Day." In a number of MS sources, this poem is found with Do1612.II (see note), at times as one poem despite the fact (noted by Grierson and Gardner) that the poem in Dowland is spoken by a man and Donne's by a woman. Both poems are in the tradition of the *aube*.

Gardner (pp. 35–36) collates twenty-four MS versions and records the presence of the poem in eighteen more (p. 157); I can add only Rosenbach MS 1083/17, fol. 135v (preceded by lines 1–6 of Do1612.II). She gives Corkine's tune in an appendix (p. 243) and notes that the text "is close to that in the Bridgewater manuscript" (Huntington MS EL 6893). Variants from Gardner's text (the 1633 ed. of Donne's *Poems*) are as follows:

> 1 t'is] 'tis
> 2 and will you] O wilt thou
> 3 What will you] Why should we
> 5 that] which

6 In spight] Should in despight
should] *omitted*
still] *omitted*
11 loue] lov'd
12 hath] had
13 Ist] Must
    that doth you] thee from hence
17 that] which
18 if] when
    should] doth

13–16 *Ist business . . . busied man.* Grierson (II, 23) and Gardner (p. 158) cite Donne's *Sermons* (ed. G.R. Potter and E. M. Simpson [Berkeley, 1953–1956], IV, 121): "It is a good definition of ill-love, that St. *Chrysostom* gives, that it is *Animae vacantis passio*, a passion of an empty soul, of an idle mind. For fill a man with business, and he hath no room for such love."

V.

6 *But . . . loue.* EMV, p. 441, prints this line in the same order as line 12. Corkine repeats "But yet" and "stay" in the music, but in the order given.

VII.

David Greer has called my attention to the similarities between this poem and Ck1610.I; *cf.* especially the alternate version of VII.

VIII.

This poem was printed among the "Posthumi" in (D) Joshua Sylvester's *Complete Works*, ed. Alexander Grosart (1880), II, 341 (Grosart prints from the 1641 folio of *DuBartas his Divine Weekes and Workes*); but since the "Posthumi" also include two poems by Campion (Vivian, pp. 357, 367) and "The Lie," usually attributed to Sir Walter Raleigh (Latham, 1951, p. 128), it is not certain that the poem is Sylvester's. A copy of the poem in (E) Rosenbach MS 1083/16 (*c.* 1630), pp. 54–55, has a modern pencil note ascribing it (without authority) to William Herbert, Earl of Pembroke. Other copies are in (F) BM MS Add. 10309 (*c.* 1630), fols. 133v–134, with a penciled attribution to Sylvester; (G) BM MS 25707 (mid-17th century), fol. 58, with the title "A good Admonicon to yonge Gentelwomen that Liued about the Courte"; (H) BM MS Egerton 923 (*c.* 1630–1640), fol. 16–16v, headed "A cauatt for Maids"; (I) BM MS Egerton 2230 (*c.* 1638), fol. 59v; (J) Bod. MS Eng. poet. f. 25 (mid-17th century), fol. 69; (K) Bod. MS Eng. poet. f. 9 (supposed to have belonged to James I; "1623" on p. 1), p. 25, headed "To yonge gentlewomen at Court"; (L) Bod. MS Rawl. poet. 117 (mid-17th century?) fol. 28v, headed "To yonge Gentelwomen at the Court"; (M) Bod. MS Tanner 169, fol. 199v, with this note: "Thes verses weare geauen to my daughter Kate by Yonge mr Tyffin of wakes hall in Essex. 1622"; (N) Cambridge MS Ee v. 23 (late 17th century), p. 8; (O) Harvard MS Eng. 966.7 (*c.* 1630), fol. 18; (P) Folger MS V.a.245 (*c.* 1640), fol. 10v, headed "To a faire Gentlewoman living at the Court in the tyme of King Henry the 8th"; (Q) Folger MS V.a.339 (mid-17th century), fol. 188; and (R) Folger MS V.a.345 (*c.* 1630), pp. 292–293, headed "To a Gentlewoman" (first stanza only), and p. 312, headed "Good Aduice to a Gentlewoman—being [ling?] at Court" (stanzas 2–4). Yet another copy

(S, not collated) is in Cambridge MS Add. 7196 (no pagination). This last is headed "To young gentlewomen at court" and consists of four stanzas and a couplet as in KL. Verbal variants are:

1–6 *omitted* E

1 Maides] maid DFJPR, mistres I
Musky] Foppish N

2 and] or DHQR

3 fading] vading Q
Clothes] cloaths DK

4 your . . . your] thy . . . thy HJNOPQR
vertues] vertue FHQR
or] or th'of N

5 For . . . once] For once but leave D
you haue] thou hast HNOQ, thou hadst R

6 Who will] Who'le ere F, none will H
regard] respect FHJOQR
your . . . your] thy . . . thy HNOQR, the . . . your K
fortune] fortunes HMQ, fauours J, fauour OPR
or] of K

7 greedy] Ready H
will striue] doth catch EOR, will seek HK, doth striue NQ
to catch] & plucke ER, to plucke HJN,
to spoile O, to cropp P

8 When] where O, But P
none] few P
regards] regard DR, respect P
stalke] stocke ER
growes] grew EOR

9 Each nature] Basenesse D, each man HJ, each creature IO, Each one N, Most natures P
seekes] desires DN, loues EOR, couets FQ, doth striue H, will seek J, striue P
the Fruit still] the fruite F, the fruit for JN, still fruite Q

10 And] But FNR, Yet P
leaue] leaues ILNR, lett O, leavinge Q
Tree] stalk N
fall or stand] grow or fall EN, stand and grow J, fall or grow O, stand or fall PQ

11 Yet] But DJKLNOQ, Then HP
Creatures] Creature DEHIJKLNOPR
of] from EJNOP

12 take Fruit] pull fruite E, touch fruit HQ, pluck fruit JR
he take] hee'll have D, thay take MQ, he pluck R

13–18 *omitted* INP; P *has these lines:*

> If any seeme or striue how to procure
> To stayne thy fame, or blurr thy modestie;
> Say tis thy will, to liue a virgin pure
> And with Dianaes Nimphes doest thus decree,

> Till thou beest bound and ty'de in wedlock bande
> To keepe that fame, whereon thy creditt stande.

13 Beleeue] Credit J
   no] not DKQ
   othes] Vowes EOR
   much] no FHJQ, yet O
14 Credit] Belieue J
   vowes] Oathes ER, words H
   their] a D, noe EFHJKLMQR, yet O
   songs] song DEGOQR
16 Their] The DHQ
   hearts] heart DOQR
   doe] doth DFOQR
   liue] ly ER
   tenne] two O
   their] the DHQ
   tongues] tongue DEGQR
17 For] And HJKLOQR
   they . . . to] and vows they made ye D, thy hart is made to EOR, the hart is
made to H
   thy] the KQ
18 them] ye Q
   least] not O
   for] *omitted* H
19–24 *omitted* I
19 Beware least] Let not E, Take heed lest HMO, Take heed that P, No let not R
   Caesar] Craesus D, Cesars R
   doe] himself E, don't P, selfe R
   minde] hart EHOPQR
20 And] Or DGHJMNOQ, Nor ER, ffor F
   sell] scale EHJN, soile P, stale Q, seale R
   modestie] Chastity JN
21 though] to EHJNOPQR
   a] the EPR
   thou] though J
   euer] even D, only EHOPQR, *omitted* JN
   courteous] vertuous H, constant R
   finde] art EHOPQR, bee & kinde J   art and kind N
22 thine] thy MOQR
   impuritie] impiety O
After 22 in EHJPR, after 24 in KL, and in place of 23–24 in R

> ffor if with one, with thousandes thou't turne whore
> Breake Ice in one place & it crackes in more

These vary:

   ffor if] doe but HKL, If but J, Begin P
   with . . . with] to . . . to J

thou't] thou wilt K
turne] proue J
& it crackes] it will crack HJKLP

23 Beginne] ffor doe EO, If once P
with] to P
King] Kings DHJ
Subiect] subjects DHJ
thou wilt] you will D
24 Lord] Lords JN
Lackey] lacqueys JN
last] length HP
P *concludes*:

> Vos vbi contempti rupistis fraena pudoris,
> Nescitis capti mentis habere modum./ Propert:

9 *nature.* EMV, p. 443, reads *creature.*

Dedication (2)

Sir Robert Rich (1587–1658) was the first son of Robert Rich, first Earl of Warwick, and Penelope Devereux Rich. Sir Robert took part in Ben Jonson's *Masque of
Beauty* in 1608-9. He became the second Earl in 1619. His brother Henry (1590–1649),
later the first Earl of Holland, married Isabel (Elizabeth ?) Cope, daughter of Sir Walter
Cope of Kensington (see Dedication 3). He was executed by the parliamentarians
during the Civil War, despite his brother's attempts to save him. Both brothers had
many books dedicated to them, but no other music (DNB, Williams).

13 *like loues the like.* Tilley L286.

IX.

This poem by Sir Philip Sidney appears both among the "Certaine Sonnets" and
in Book III of the *Arcadia* (1598 ed., pp. 473 and 289). The first version is headed "To
the tune of *Non credo gia che piu infelice amante*," a tune which Professor Francis J.
Fabry, following a lead in Obertello, pp. 74-75, has discovered in a set of MS partbooks at Winchester College, and which he expects to publish soon. In the *Arcadia*,
it appears as a song for five viols and five voices provided by Amphialus for Philoclea.
The poem is found in the Arundel Harington MS (HAH, I, 111–112); Hughey collates
the following versions (II, 66–68): *Arcadia* (1590, 1593, and 1598); Abraham Fraunce's
Arcadian Rhetorike (1588), sig. E1, where the poem is quoted as an example of *polyptoton*;
The Arbor of Amorous Devises (1597), sigs. B3v–B4; Ck1612; Folger MS 4009.03, fol.
216v; Bod. MS Rawl. Poet. 85, fol. 9v; and BM MS Harl. 7392, fol. 39. Ringler
(pp. 136–137) collates these and Cambridge MS Dd v. 75, fol. 27; St John's College,
Cambridge, MS I7, fol. 241v; Bod. MS e. Museo 37; and Cambridge MS Kk. I. 5(2).
As Hughey says, Ck1612.IX probably derives from the 1590 *Arcadia*, for both read
woes in line 1, repeat *turneth* in line 4, and read *ils* in line 8. Variants from the accepted
text, the 1598 ed. (Ringler) are:

1 woes] wrongs
4 his] the
   turneth] keepeth

8 ils] evils
14 thy breath no more] no more thy breath
24 sets by] makes of

Ringler notes (p. 426) the use of the four elements as a basis for invention in one of the *Arcadia* eclogues (Ringler, p. 32), and in Shakespeare's Sonnets 44 and 45. *Cf.* Do1597.VII, which also uses the elements in a *carmen correlativum* as in lines 13–20.
4 *turneth.* EMV, p. 443, reads *keepeth*, as in Ringler.

X.

Cf. these not very original sentiments with Fd1607.I, Jo1609.XVI and XVII.

XI.

Vivian (p. 355) claims this poem for Campion because of its similarity to "My sweetest Lesbia" (Ros1601, part I.I), which (like Fer1609.VI) is an imitation of Catullus V, "Vivamus, mea Lesbia." But Davis (p. 508) seems closer to the truth in thinking it only "a clumsy imitation."

XII.

1–2 *Man . . . paine.* Perhaps there is a remote connection with Tilley C302, "The child was born and cried, became a man, after fell sick and died."

XIII.

Obertello (p. 477) compares this poem to Jo1605.II (Ck1610.IX, Pk1605.XVIII), and "Hard by a Cristal fountaine" from Yonge's second *Musica Transalpina* (1597), No. XXIIII (see Obertello, p. 309; also Morley, *Triumphes of Oriana* [1601] No. XXIII). But neither these poems nor the Italian analogues cited by Obertello are very close—none contain the conceit of the tears in lines 5–6.

XIIII.

4 *Apes in hell.* Tilley M37.

XV.

1 *Lucina cross-legg'd sate.* Lucina prolonged Alcmena's deliverance of Hercules in this manner. See Ovid, *Metamorphoses* IX, 281–315, and Pliny, *Natural History* XXVIII.xvii.

Dedication (3)

Ursula Stapleton married Sir Robert Baynard of Lackham. Her father, Sir Robert, was once sheriff of Yorkshire (Burke's *Extinct and Dormant Baronetage*, s.v. Stapylton of Myton). Elizabeth, or rather Isabel Cope, married Henry Rich, Earl of Holland (see Dedication 2); she was the only child and heiress of Sir Walter Cope of Kensington (d. 1614), who was, among other things, a member of the Society of Antiquaries (DNB). As Lady Rich, Isabel Cope had one other book dedicated to her, John Cope's *A Religious Inquisition*, 1629 (Williams).

XVI.

11 *I must.* EMV (p. 446) reads *must I.*

XVII.

The use of musical terms in the verse is extensive, but the musical setting does not illustrate them as fully as one might expect. *Cf.* Jo1610.XIII, and see the Glossary.
1 *out. I.e.,* out of tune.

XVIII.

4 *coynesse . . . fires. Cf.* Tilley D213, "Desires are nourished by delay."

5 *forbid the baines. I.e.,* forbid the banns, object to a proposed marriage.

Table of Songs

20 *If my Complaints.* Variations for the lyra viol on the tune to Do1597.IIII.

22 *Come liue with me and be my loue.* A version for lyra viol of the tune to which Marlowe's poem was sung. See Simpson, pp. 119–122.

23 *Walsingham.* A version for lyra viol of the ballad tune. See Simpson, pp. 741–743.

24 *Mounsiers Almaine.* See Simpson, pp. 495–496.

John Dowland, *A Pilgrimes Solace*, 1612

Dedication

Theophilus Howard, Lord Walden, later Earl of Suffolk (1584–1640), was Dowland's employer at this time. Thomas Campion addressed a verse epistle to Walden in his *Lord Hayes Maske* (1607; Davis, p. 209). See the note to No. XX below.

To the Reader

5 *Kingly entertainment.* Dowland had been lutenist to Christian IV of Denmark. See Do1600, Textual Introduction.

9–10 *printed in eight most famous Cities, &c.* The following books have been traced so far. Each contains one or more of Dowland's lute pieces. Paris: Antoine Francisque, *Le Trésor d'Orphee* (1600); Cologne: J. B. Besardus, *Thesaurus Harmonicus* (1603); Nuremburg: Valentin Haussman, *Rest von Polnischen und andern Tanzen* (1603); Frankfort: T. Simpson, *Opusculum* (1610); and Hamburg: Zacharias Füllsack, *Auselesener Paduanen und Galliarden* (1607). Dowland apparently did not know of J. van den Hove's *Florida* (Utrecht, 1601), or Rude's *Flores Musicae* (Heidelberg, 1600), which contained some of his music. Pieces by Dowland also appeared in continental imprints in 1612, 1615, 1617, 1621, and 1647. See Thurston Dart in MGG, s.v. "Dowland."

19 *mutation of the Hexachord.* According to Thomas Morley (*Plaine and Easie Introduction*, 1597, sig. ¶4), "Mutation is the leauing of one name of a note and taking another in the same sound." The hexachord is like the first six notes of a modern major scale: that is, a succession of tones with a semitone between the third and fourth notes. But instead of using modern scales, medieval and renaissance musicians thought in terms of a system based on three hexachords. Thus a given note would have a different solmisation name in a different hexachord. See the note to No. XI below.

30 *Booke in defence of the Viol de Gamba.* Hu1605; the quote comes from the address to the reader. *Cf.* Hu1607.

44–45 *Cucullus non facit Monachum.* Tilley H586, "The hood makes not the monk." *Cf. Twelfth Night,* I.v.50–51.

I.

This poem was printed in (D) *Poems, Written by the Right Honorable William Earl of Pembroke . . . Many of which are answered by way of Repartee, by Sir Benjamin Ruddier* (1660), sig. B3, and again on sig. D7. The second version is headed, "That he would not be belov'd." The editor, John Donne the younger, says in his address "To the Reader" that the poems were "chiefly preserved by the greatest Masters of Music, all the Sonnets being set by them," and that he got them from Henry Lawes and one of the Laniers. This collection is not a good authority for attributing the poem to Pembroke, for it contains several poems which are by others. See Do1603.VI and note. Other copies are: (E) BM MS Add. 23229, fol. 52v, is a single leaf in a miscellany volume in a seventeenth-century hand; but since it is not possible to say whether it was copied before or after the 1660 *Poems*, the heading "Verses Made by the Earle of Pembrooke" is not conclusive evidence (a fragment of the poem occurs on fol. 143 of this volume). (F) Bod. MS CCC 328, (*c.* 1640) fol. 78, is headed "A Louer that would not be loud againe," with a later note in the margin reading "Pembr. p. 45" (the page number refers to D, sig. D7). (G) BM MS Add. 22603 (after 1644), fol. 50v, is entitled "Loues Constancie" and subscribed "J. D." (John Donne? John Dowland? John Davies?). (H) Bod. MS Rawl. Poet. 160 (after 1633), fol. 103v, is headed "A Sonnet" and subscribed "J. D." A copy in (I) the Morgan Library in New York, in the Holgate MS (MA1057; late 17th century), p. 139, is headed "That hee would not bee beloued," and follows a poem ascribed to Pembroke. Further copies are in (J) Bod. MS Rawl. Poet. 116 (after 1640), fol. 53v; (K) BM MS Stowe 962 (after 1637), fol. 170v; and (L) Huntington MS HM 198 (mid-17th century), p. 173, and in Part II of the same MS (M), fol. 42v. The variants are as follows:

2 his . . . inioyes] enjoyes his loue J
3 ease] Peace DEFIM
4 And] the F
5 And] Then DGHIJKLM
   frowne . . . say] frown'est, yet J
   thou art] th'art L
6 Ile] I G
   must] most J
7 heate] heat's DEIM
8 and these] for theis EI, for those F
   life and loue] love and life GJKL
   gone] don DEFIJLM
9 nor] & F, or K
   vertue] vertues GHKL
10 baser] basest DIM, brasen GH
   mettals] Mettle DFLM
   too] soe HL
11 woes] owes K
   although I] though I do M
12 with . . . his] if inioys; Its GH
   reward] rewards FIJ

II.

The first stanza of this poem was printed as the first stanza of Donne's "Breake of Day" in (D) the 1669 edition of his *Poems*, sig. C1 (Grierson, I, 432). Grierson says (II, cxlviii), "Mr. Chambers conjectures that the affixing of Dowland's initials to the verse in some collection led to Donne being credited with it, which is quite likely;

but we are not sure that Dowland wrote it, and the common theme appears to have drawn the poems together." There is, however, no good reason to believe that either Donne or Dowland wrote the poem. Gardner prints the poem among the *dubia* (p. 108) and speculates (p. 230) that the poem may be by Dowland; but she notes that the meter and the sex of the speaker are different from "Breake of Day."

Orlando Gibbons set a version of the first stanza to music in (E) *The First Set of Madrigals and Mottets of 5. Parts* (No. XV, sig. C2), printed in the same year as *A Pilgrime's Solace.* In the dedication to Sir Christopher Hatton (sig. A2), Gibbons says that the madrigals "were most of them composed in your owne house . . . the language they speake you provided them." Hatton supplied the texts, but probably did not write them, for Nos. 10–11 are by Spenser, and 3–6 by Joshua Sylvester.

I have seen twenty-seven manuscripts and two other printed versions of this poem, and several more exist: *e.g.,* the Luttrell MS (Sir Geoffrey Keynes), the Osborne MS at Yale, and a setting by Henry Lawes in his autograph MS (BM MS Loan 35), all listed by Gardner, pp. 230, 245. All of those I have seen are considerably later than Dowland's version (mainly *c.* 1630), and most are corrupt. Many of the poems have all or part of Donne's "Breake of Day" (Gardner, pp. 35–36) mixed with the original. In the descriptions that follow, additions from "Breake of Day" and omissions of lines or stanzas will be noted, but will *not* be included in the variants, which are cumbersome enough without them. The other versions are:

F: BM MS Add. 29481 (*c.* 1630), fol. 9, first stanza only, with music (not Dowland's).

G: BM MS Sloane 1792 (after 1626), fol. 12, two stanzas as a separate poem following "Breake of Day."

H: Harvard MS Eng. 686 (*c.* 1633), fol. 94v, two stanzas with four corrupt lines of "Breake of Day" at the end.

I: Bod. MS Eng. poet. f. 9 (*c.* 1623), p. 19, first stanza only, in a group of poems initialed "J. D."

J: Bod. MS Eng. poet. f. 25 (*c.* 1630), fol. 11, first stanza only, followed by the first two stanzas of "Breake of Day."

K: BM MS Stowe 961 (after 1619), fol. 71v, first stanza, followed by three stanzas of "Breake of Day."

L: Bod. MS Rawl. poet. 117 (after 1635), fol. 220v (reversed), headed "Dunne"; the first stanza is followed by the first stanza of "Breake of Day," more of which is copied in the margin.

M: Harvard MS Eng. 966.5, the O'Flaherty MS of Donne's poems (*c.* 1632), fol. 146v (*i.e.,* p. 290), first stanza only, called "Sonnet."

N: BM MS Sloane 542 (after 1624), fol. 11v, two stanzas headed "DD"; between the two stanzas is a corrupt version of the first stanza of "Breake of Day."

O: BM MS Add. 19268 (after 1616), fol. 19, two stanzas mixed with "Breake of Day" as in N; no ascription.

P: Bod. MS CCC 328 (*c.* 1630), fol. 47v, two stanzas and the first stanza of "Breake of Day" as in NO.

Q: Bod. MS Ashmole 47 (after 1635), fol. 73, two stanzas and part of "Breake of Day" as in NOP, headed, "A song Dr Corbet."

R: Bod. MS Don. c. 57 (*c.* 1640), fol. 29v, first stanza only, with music (not by Dowland).

S: BM MS Add. 25707 (after 1633), fol. 18v, first stanza written sideways in the margin next to "Breake of Day."

T: BM MS Add. 10337 (*c.* 1656), fols. 20v–21, first stanza, with music (not Dowland's).

U: Bod. MS Rawl. poet. 214 (late 17th century), fol. 81v (reversed), first stanza, then five corrupt lines of "Breake of Day," then lines 8 and 9—all headed "Verses I had of Mrs. S. L."

V: John Cotgrave's *Wits Interpreter, the English Parnassus* (1655), sigs. O7v and P4v; both copies have the first stanza followed by the first stanza of "Breake of Day."

W: John Gough's *Academy of Complements* (edition of 1650), sigs. I8v–9, has the first stanza, then the first stanza of "Breake of Day," then lines 8–9.

X: Huntington MS HM 198 (mid-17th century), part II, fol. 42v.

Y: Rosenbach MS 1083/17 (mid-17th century), fol. 135, headed "loath to part," first stanza as first stanza of "Breake of Day"; second stanza only on fol. 64v, headed "A wish."

Z: Morgan Library, Holgate MS MA 1057 (*c.* 1630), p. 137.

Dd: Folger MS V.a.319 (mid-17th century), fol. 31v, first stanza, headed "Song," as first stanza of "Breake of Day."

Ee: Folger MS V.a.322 (mid-17th century), p. 55, headed "Song: Dr Donne," text like Dd.

Ff: Rosenbach MS 243/4 (late 17th century), p. 73, first stanza only, following "Breake of Day," and headed, "At the next enjoyment shee quits his rising with an erlyer. His lines."

Gg: Rosenbach MS 239/18 (*c.* 1660), p. 106, first four lines only.

Hh: Rosenbach MS 239/27 (*c.* 1635), pp. 51–52, headed "On his mistresse risinge," with lines 1–6 of "Breake of Day" between the two stanzas.

Ii: Folger MS V.a.262 (after 1653), p. 102, headed "Dr Donne at his Mistris rysing," with lines 1–6 of "Breake of Day" after the first stanza, followed by lines 8–9 and 12–13 of the second stanza.

Jj: Folger MS V.a.97 (*c.* 1640), p. 70, first stanza headed "2 Louers loath to depart," followed by lines 1–6 of "Breake of Day."

Variants are:

2 Sweet . . . rise] Stay, O sweet, and do not rise DIJKLMYDdEeFf, Ah deere hart, why doe you rise E, Ly still my deere why dost thou rise NOPRSTVWGg-HhIi, Stay, sweet, a while, why doest thou rise H, Lye still my deare why wouldst thou rise Q, Ly stil my deare: why shoulds thou rise U, Lie still my loue, why wilt thou rise Jj

     will] doe FG

3 you see] that shines DEHIJKLMNOPQRSTUVWYDdEeFfGgHhIiJj, we see G

     your] thine DHJLNOPRSTUVWFfGgHhIiJj, thy Q, *omitted* G

4 The . . . heart] There breakes not Day but tis my hart K, 'tis not the day breaks tis mine hart O, tis not the day breakes but my heart PVJj

     it is] it breakes R, but tis Y, tis Gg

     my] thy Hh

5 To thinke] Because D, to see R

you] thee HFfJj, thow JOQRSTUVHh

must] should G

6 O . . . dye] O stay a while, or else I dye Z

O] *omitted* DFf

my] those R

must] will DEHIJKLPRSUWYDdEeFfJj

7 And] or RUW, to X

their] my Z

8 Deare] O GHNOPUWYHhIi

dye] lye OPQYIi

in] on GHNOQUWYHhIi

this] that GY, thy NOPQUWXZHhIi

faire] sweet NOPUWHhIi, dear Q

9 Farre . . . the] more sweete then in the P, More sweet then is the NHhIi, more precious then the Q

10 Loue] Loues P

raise] cause PHh, calls Q

desire] desires Hh, is frd P

by] with XZ

his] thy GNOPQXYZ, these H

11 Within . . . armes] And let me die within thy loues armes N, O let me dye within loues armes O, oh let mee ly with in loues armes P, And Lett me dye within Loues armes Hh

this] the QY

thine] these G, those HY, thy Q, her XZ

12 And] Oh HNOPQHh, Thou Ii

let] with XZIi

thy] thes G, me my N, *omitted* P, me yett my Hh

blissefull] blessed Q

cherish] rellish Q

13 Mine . . . perish] Or else my Infant ioyes must perish NPHh, Or els mine Infants ioye must perish O, my infant ioyes or else I needs must perish Q

Mine] My HXZIi

that] which XIi, or Z

must] wold GX, they Z

1 *William Iewel.* William Jewel or Juell matriculated as a gentleman of Devon at Exeter College, Oxford, on June 3, 1603, when he was 17. He took his B. A. February 13, 1606/7, and his M. A. November 17, 1609. In 1626, he was vicar of Rodmersham in Kent.(J. Foster, *Alumni Oxonienses*, s.v. "Juell, William.") He translated *The Golden Cabinet of True Treasure* (1612).

8 *the Phoenix nest.* The nest of the Phoenix was supposedly made of spices.

III.

Fellowes (EMV, 2nd ed., p. 617) says "This poem is by John Donne," and refers to Grierson's edition, I, 449. But Grierson is doubtful about the authorship (II, xcviii–xcix, 268). Gardner does not even include it among the *dubia* of her edition, but prints Dowland's music and text in an appendix (pp. 244–245) because of its similarity to "Love's Infiniteness" (Gardner, pp. 77–78). The O'Flaherty MS (Harvard Eng. 966.5), which according to the compiler (fol. 1) was finished in October, 1632, contains some thirty-eight poems not in the first (1633) edition of Donne, including a copy of No. III (marked "Not Printed" by a later hand) on fol. 158v (*i.e.*, p. 314). It varies thus:

    1 aske] sue
    2 t'were] were
    9 that] who
    14 flower] power
    25 Ile] wee'le

The song appears to be an imitation of Donne's "Loves Infiniteness" which retains some of the wording of the original but simplifies the argument considerably. R. W. Ingram, in "Words and Music" from *Elizabethan Poetry* (1960, Stratford-upon-Avon Studies, No. 2), p. 146, suggests that Donne's poem had been "translated" into a form more suitable for musical setting. This may be true, but we still do not know who wrote the version Dowland used.

IIII.

2–4 *Loue . . . remaine. Cf.* Do1612.VII.12–14.

V.

The music for this song appears in an instrumental version in Dowland's *Lachrimae* (*c.* 1604, No. 14) called "M. Henry Noell his Galiard." (Noel was a colorful courtier who seems to have known a number of musicians—see Morley's memorial canzonet [EMV, p. 158], and the copy of a letter to Dowland signed "your olde Master and Frend" in Folger MS V.a.321, fols. 52v–53.) Lute versions are found in Cambridge University MSS Dd.2.11 and Dd.9.33, with the title "Mignarde," and in Dd.5.78.III. See Diana Poulton, "Dowland's Songs and their Instrumental Forms," *Monthly Musical Record*, LXXXI (1951), 178.

The texts of this poem and No. VI are in a different arrangement from those in EMV, 2nd ed., where lines 9–12 follow line 4, and the poem is in two stanzas with lines 17–20 as a refrain. The songbook is admittedly ambiguous on this point, but each of the three sections of the song is probably repeated (as in Do1597.IIII and V, and Do1600.II) instead of the whole being played through twice. There are no conventional repeat signs in Nos. V and VI, but there are double bars which in No. VII clearly indicate repeats.

VI.

See the note to No. V. A version of Dowland's music arranged for four instruments is found in Thomas Simpson's *Taffel-Consort* (1621), No. X (Cantus, p. 14).

16 *how none knowes.* EMV, p. 742, says that the line read "none knowes how" in the original songbook, but I have seen no copy with this reading.

18–20 *conceit . . . sleight.* It seems that in both words the *ei* could be pronounced as a long *a*. See Kökeritz, pp. 178, 421, and E. J. Dobson, *English Pronunciation 1500–1700* (Oxford, 1957), II, 650, 666.

VII.

14 *I feede by night.* That is, at night he weeps, thus feeding fuel to his sorrows. Compare these two lines with No. IIII, lines 1–4.

VIII.

The tone of the compliment offered in this poem and the fact that the final couplets are sung by a chorus suggest that the song may have been written for some occasion, perhaps a masque.

8 *nor promise debt.* That is, a promise is not held to be binding.

IX.

Both the music and the text of this song hark back to the old songs for one voice and viols, some of which were used in the choirboy plays. See the Introduction, especially the first section.

14 *or teares.* EMV, p. 494, reads *nor teares.*

X.

As I noted in *RN*, XVII (1964), 1–3, this song is made up of stanzas 1, 2, and 11 of a poem of 63 stanzas, which was first printed in 1601 by "V. S. for Iohn Baily" with the title *The Passion of a Discontented Minde.* The poem was reprinted in 1602 and 1621; all editions were anonymous. Dowland's source was probably the 1601 or 1602 edition; all three editions have only one variant from the song, reading "wel-springs" for "well-spring" in line 15.

A copy of the 1602 edition is bound up with several pieces by Nicholas Breton in a volume called "N. Breton's Works" which is now in the Bodleian (Tanner 221). Thomas Corser, *Collectanea Anglo-Poetica* (Manchester: Chetham Society, 1867), Part III, 42, attributed the poem to Breton, since it "has all the marks of Breton's style, and is usually attributed to his pen by competent bibliographers." John Payne Collier reprinted the 1602 edition in his *Illustrations of Old English Literature* (London, 1866), I, No. 6, but doubted Breton's authorship (pp. i–ii) because the poem was not printed by a stationer Breton usually employed. Collier conjectured that Robert Southwell was the author. A. B. Grosart did not include the poem in his edition of Breton's *Works in Verse and Prose* (1879) because the copy he mentions, the 1601 edition, "has neither his name nor initials nor the mint-mark words of the period, whereby the Breton authorship should have been betrayed" (I, lxxiii). But Mrs. Jean Robertson, Breton's latest editor, points out that the printer's of the *Passion* printed other acknowledged Breton pieces; that Grosart accepted other anonymous works as Breton's; and that the *Passion* does indeed contain characteristic phrases which Grosart called "mint-mark words." She compares numerous passages of several of Breton's poems with the *Passion*, and concludes: "I have no hesitation, in the absence of any evidence to the contrary, in assigning *The Passion of a Discontented Minde* to Nicholas Breton, on the strength of the close resemblance in style and subject-matter to his recognized works (*Poems by Nicholas Breton* [Liverpool, 1952], xcii–xcviii).

Mrs. Robertson's evidence is as good as purely thematic and stylistic evidence of this sort can be; yet this is really not very reliable, for the conventions of the penitential style in the later sixteenth century make detection of a personal style almost impossible. A curious confirmation of this difficulty is found in an article by Mary Shakeshaft, "Nicholas Breton's *The Passion of a Discontented Mind*: Some New Problems," *SEL*, V(1965), 165–174. Miss Shakeshaft demonstrates that one G. Ellis, in *The Lamentation of the Lost Sheepe* (1605), adapted and incorporated some fifty stanzas from the earlier poem, and notes that J. P. Collier quoted the same stanza from each poem without noticing Ellis' theft. See *A Bibliographical and Critical Account of the*

Rarest Books in the English Language (New York, 1866), I, 110, 307. More convincing evidence of the authorship is found in three seventeenth-century MSS that ascribe the poem to Robert Devereux, Earl of Essex. The first is in (D) BM MS Sloane 1779, fol. 208v, following accounts of Essex's trial and execution, with the partly obliterated heading, "Es[sex] made . . . the Tower." Another copy, also containing material about the trial, is in (E) Folger MS V.a.164, fols. 134–143, headed "A repentant Poem made by Robert Earle of Essex while he was Prisonner in the Tower. 1601." On fol. 138v, before stanza 30, a note is inserted: "Heere the Earle of Essex paused an howre or twaine, and after some teares, took againe his pen & wrott as followeth: Jo: Aggs report." John Aggs was Warder of the Tower; see Historical Manuscripts Commission, *Salisbury Manuscripts*, XIX (1965), 149. (F) Bod. MS Tanner 76, fols. 114–116v, contains stanzas 22–61, with Tanner's later copy on fols. 89v–92 preceded (fol. 89) by this note:

> A Penitential which I found with other Papers concerning the Earl of Essex's Crimes, and Arraignment in a MS. of that time. Whether made by him, (or for him) in the time of his Confinement to the Ld Keeper's House, from October 1599, to April 1600; Or (as it seems from stanza 36 [i.e., 57] compar'd with Cambden's Annals in fine A. 1600 p. 216) in the Time of his Retirement into the Country or to his own House between the hearing of his Cause by the Queen's Delegates June 5th 1600, and his breaking out into open Rebellion: In both which Intervalls of time he gave himself wholly to Devotion and divine Meditation, as Mr Cambden expressly witnesseth, pp. 187 & 215.

(Tanner's reference to Camden would correspond to sig. Xxx3 of R. Norton's translation of 1630, *The Historie of the Princesse Elizabeth*.) Although Tanner does not mention the period of Essex's imprisonment, parts of the poem, if they concern Essex at all, seem to be appropriate to his stay in the Tower. The ministrations of his chaplain, Mr. Ashton, had reduced Essex to a state of mind very like that described in the poem; for example, the outburst against bad company in stanzas 43–49 may be related to Essex's accusations of his friends in his confession. (See William Barlow's *Sermon Preached at Paules Crosse* [1601], sig. C8, and Camden, tr. Norton, sig. Aaaa2; *cf.* J. E. Neale, *Queen Elizabeth* [London, 1934], p. 375.) Yet it may seem unlikely that Essex, in the short period before his execution, would compose three hundred and seventy-eight lines of verse, even though he had been known to "evaporate his thoughts in a Sonnet" (see Do1597.V note). It is possible that some hack, such as Breton, took advantage of the sensation by writing a poem which was just close enough to actual events to profit from current interest in them. But the evidence of the MSS is at least concrete contemporary evidence, and must have more weight than dubious stylistic analysis and speculation.

Another copy of the poem is in (G) BM MS Egerton 2403 (dated July 10, 1601), fols. 38–48. It is without ascription, but the MS also contains a poem headed "The Sad Complaint of Mary Queen of Scotts, who was beheaded in England in the reign of Queen Elizabeth." Only E and G present variants in the stanzas Dowland used; they are:

    2 moanes] wooes G
    3 sinnes] Syne G
    4 From] My E
      sighes] sigthes G

5 wayling Muse] wofull soule G
6 sad] deep G
8 cause] and Cause E
10 Griefe] Greeue EG
   my . . . griefe] with greefe my greefe is not E
   with . . . not] was not with greefe G
12 cares] Care EG
   grieue] grefe G
13 and sorrow] it is that G
15 spring] springs E
18 mine] my E
   wept] weept G
19 Were . . . kept] Are all to Lyttell yf theye had
bene keept G

1 *Iohn Forster*. Dowland's dedicatee may possibly be the John Forster whom W. H. G. Flood says was the son of Richard Forster and nephew of Sir John Forster, Mayor of Dublin in 1589–1590; see "Irish Ancestry of Garland, Dowland, Campion and Purcell," *M & L*, III [1922], 61. Diana Poulton tells me that Flood's sources are probably John Thomas Gilbert, *Calendar of Ancient Records of Dublin* (1861), and Henry FitzPatrick Berry, *Records of the Dublin Gild of Merchants* (1900). It may be of interest to note that one John Foster was arrested for his part in Essex's rebellion; but the name is common, and there is no indication that he is the Irish Forster. See Historical Manuscripts Commission, *Salisbury Manuscripts*, XI (1906), 44 and 87.

5 *her wofull*. The words under the music read, "her woe, her woe, her wofull," not dividing the word so much as using the first syllable as a separate word.

XI.

Dowland may have meant this song to be a lesson in the "true order of the mutation of the *Hexachord*" for the "simple Cantors" castigated in the address "To the Reader." Diana Poulton has shown me that Dowland puns on the syllables *mi-fa* in the solmisation system, a fairly common conceit among the Italian madrigalists (see Einstein, I, 229). These syllables indicated the semitone of the hexachord, which defined the mode or scale. Thus in the sixth and seventh bars, the hexachord undergoes mutation when the first *mi-fa* is B-natural and C, and the second is A and B-flat.

4, 5 *fa*. EMV, p. 495, reads *fan*.

XII.

2 *wings*. The reading of the other parts, *windes*, may be actually correct, but *wings* is very attractive.

XIII.

William Byrd set a longer version of this poem in his *Psalmes, Sonets, & Songs of Sadnes and Pietie* (1588), No. 30 (Medius, sig. F2v):

> If that a sinners sighes, be Angels food
> or that repentant teares be Angels wine,
> accept ô Lord, in this most pensiue moode,
> these hartie sighes, and faithfull teares of mine :
> That went with Peter forth most sinfullie,
> but not with Peter wept most bitterlie.

2 If I had Dauids crowne to me betide,
or all his purple robes that he did weare,
I would lay then such honor all aside,
and onelie seeke a sackcloth weede to beare:
his Pallace would I leaue that I might show,
and mourne in cell for such offence, my woe.

3 Ther should these hands beate on my pensiue brest,
and sad to death, for sorrow rend my haire,
my voice to call on thee, should neuer rest,
whose grace I seeke, whose iudgement I doe feare:
vppon the ground all groueling on my face,
I would beseech thy fauour and good grace.

4 But since I haue not meane to make the show
of my repentant mind, and yet I see
my sinne to greater heape then Peters grow,
whereby the danger more it is to me,
I put my trust in his most precious bloud,
whose life was payde to purchase all our good.

5 Thy mercy greater is then anie sinne,
thy greatnes none can euer comprehend:
wherefore ô Lord, let me thy mercie winne,
whose glorious name no time can euer end:
wherefore I say all praise belongs to thee,
whom I beseech be mercifull to mee.

Dowland must have known Byrd's work, which, in spite of the variants, was probably his source. Byrd's setting also appears in BM MS Add. 29402, fol. 51; the Medius part contains the words to the first stanza, with no variants from Byrd. According to an article by Philip Brett and Thurston Dart, "Songs by William Byrd in Manuscripts at Harvard," *Harvard Library Bulletin*, XIV (1960), 363, copies of Byrd's song exist in the Christ Church, Oxford, MSS 984–8, No. 72 (words in the second treble book); and in St. Michael's College, Tenbury, MSS 1469–71, fol. 43. The music for four of the parts survives in Harvard MS Mus. 30, fol. 30, but the part-book containing the solo part and the words is apparently missing. An arrangement of Byrd's piece for lute (without words) is in BM MS Add. 31992, fol. 28v. Fellowes (EMV, 2nd ed., p. 618) says that the poem was also set by the elder John Milton in Sir William Leighton's *Tears or Lamentations of a Sorrowfull Soule*, No. 50. But the words from the 1614 edition of Leighton's collection (sig. L2, Cantus) read:

IF that a sinners sighes, sent from a soule with grief
opprest, may thee O Lord to mercy moue, and to compassion,
then pitty me and ease my misery.

XIIII.–XVI.

As I noted in *RN*, XVII (1964), 1, this three-part song is based on a sonnet by Nicholas Breton, printed in his *Soules Harmony* (1602), sigs. C3v–C4. The first two lines of the poem, however, are not Breton's at all, but were adapted by Dowland from the first two lines of stanza 9 of the "Bee" (the first three stanzas of which

Dowland had already set to music in Do1603.XVIII). These lines originally read (from BM MS Harl. 6947, fol. 230v):

> Greate kinge of Bees, that rightest every wronge
> Listen to Patience in her dyinge songe.

See also Bond's *Lyly*, III, 496.

The variants from Breton are:

XIIII.1–3 *omitted*
  .5 asswaged his excessiue] did kill the poyson of his
  .7 comfort] comfortes
XV.3 woes did compasse] crosses compast
  .4 On . . . thought] Yet was his spirit neuer ouer-wrought
  .5 griefes] woes
XVI.2 poore] sore
  .3 yeeres] a yeere
  .4 No . . . set] His heart on Christ no sooner set
  .5 But . . . againe] But teares mou'd grace, and he was well agayne
  .6 No . . . griefe] No Iob, nor Dauid, Cripple more in grief
  .7 Hopes] hope
XV.2 *Dauids life*. I Samuel:19 and 24.
XVI.2 *Criple*. John 5:1–15.

XVII.

These rhymed, accentual verses are imitation sapphics. Compare a similar piece by Fulke Greville, "Eyes, why did you bring vnto me those graces" (*Caelica*, Sonnet VI; Bullough, I, 75–76), which has a different rhyme-scheme. Bullough notes (I, 233) that other rhymed sapphics occur in the *Phoenix Nest* (1593), "I pray thee Loue, say, whither is this posting" (RPN, pp. 109–110); in Sir Philip Sidney's *Arcadia*, Bk. III, "Get hence foule Griefe" (Ringler, pp. 83–84); and in Sidney's *Certain Sonnets*, "O my thoughtes' sweete foode" (Ringler, p. 138). Richard Barnfield, *Greenes Funeralls* (1594), sig. C3, wrote some unrhymed sapphics beginning "Father of Heauen."

XVIII.

This poem was first printed in *Speeches Delivered to Her Maiestie This Last Progresse, at the Right Honorable the Lady Russels, at Bissam, the Right Honorable the Lord Chandos at Sudley, at the Right Honorable the Lord Norris, at Ricorte* (1592), sig. B2, in the description of the pageant at Sudeley, preceded by the following: "This speech ended, her Maiesty sawe Apollo with the tree, hauing on the one side on that sung, on the other one that plaide.

> Sing you, plaie you, but sing and play my truth,
> This tree my Lute, these sighes my notes of ruth:
> The Lawrell leafe for euer shall bee greene,
> And chastety shalbe *Apolloes* Queene.
> If gods maye dye, here shall my tombe be plaste,
> And this engrauen, fonde *Phoebus*, *Daphne* chaste.

After these verses, the song." Variants from the song are:

  2 Th'eldest] The eldest
  6 doth] doeth

10 wordes, nor deedes] deeds nor words
14 Then . . . perfection] Engraue vpon this tree, *Daphnes* perfection

 The poem was reprinted from *Speeches*, without variants, in *England's Helicon* (1600) (REH, I, 122). It is headed "Apollos Loue-Song for faire Daphne," and is followed by a note reading: "This Dittie was sung before her Maiestie, at the right honourable the Lord Chandos, at Sudley Castell, at her last being there in prograce. The Author thereof vnknowne." Rollins (II, 156) calls attention to a remark on the verso of the title-page of the *Speeches* by one "I. B.": "I Gathered these copies in loose papers I know not how imperfect, therefore must I craue a double pardon; of him that penned them, and those that reade them. The matter of small moment, and therefore the offence of no great danger." Without evidence, Bond claimed the pageant for Lyly, and reprinted the 1592 *Speeches* (I, 471–490).
 Dowland's setting may have been the one used for the pageant; but although the song shows no positive characteristics of Dowland's later style, the circumstance of its being printed so many years after the event, and the fact that the poem had appeared in two previous books may make one doubt that Dowland's was the original song.
 Lord Chandos was Giles Bridges, Baron Chandos of Sudeley (1548–1594). See G. E. Cokayne, *Complete Peerage*, III, ed. V. Gibbs (1913), 126–127.

XIX.

 See the note to No. XX following. Sailors were frequent characters in masques: Campion has twelve "skippers" dance in the *Somerset Masque* (1614; Davis, p. 275); there is music for a "Saylers Masque" in BM MS Add. 10444, fols. 27v–28, 79v, which may have been used in Campion's masque or in Ben Jonson's *Neptunes Triumph* (1624; *Works*, VII, 699); see Andrew J. Sobol, *Songs and Dances for the Stuart Masque* (Providence: Brown University Press, 1959), p. 169. Three lost *Masks of Mariners* of 1543, 1554, and 1559 are listed in Alfred Harbage's *Annals of English Drama*, revised S. Schoenbaum (London: Methuen, 1964), p. 265. For other dialogues, see the note to Do1600.XXII.
23 *ratlings*. The rattling of hail on the deck, or the sound of hail in the ratlines (or *ratlings*), the small ropes tied across the shrouds of a ship to serve as a ladder for climbing the rigging.

XX.

 This song and No. XXI (and perhaps No. XIX) may have been used in the wedding festivities of Dowland's current patron, Lord Walden, who married Elizabeth, daughter of the Earl of Dunbar, in March 1611/12. See G. E. Cokayne, *Complete Peerage*, XII, Part I, ed. E. H. White (1953), 467. Although Dowland's book was entered in the Stationers' Register before the wedding (see Textual Introduction), these songs may have been added later; but the wedding itself had been postponed, so the songs may have been completed by the original date (January 1610/11). Moreover, it seems that the marriage was not consummated until the autumn of 1612, for the bride was very young. See the quotations in Cokayne.

XXI.

Compare Nos. XIX–XX and notes.
10 *Marigold*. The marigold opens in the sunshine.

John Attey, *The First Booke of Ayres*, 1622

Dedication

John Egerton (1579–1649), first Earl of Bridgewater, married Frances Stanley, daughter of Ferdinando, Earl of Derby; their children first performed Milton's *Arcades* and *Comus* in 1634. Several other books were dedicated to Bridgewater, but none were musical (Williams, DNB).

22–23 *Phormio ... Hanniball.* Phormio, the Peripatetic philosopher of Ephesus who lectured Hannibal on war, is cited as an example of "prating insolence" in Cicero's *De Oratore*, II. xviii. 75–76. Attey may have found the story in Dowland's translation of Andreas Ornithoparcus' *Micrologus* (1609), sig. P1.

35 *drop ... Ocean. Cf.* Tilley D613.

I.

This poem is a translation of a song first set to music for four voices by Pierre Guedron in his *2ᵉ livre d'Airs de Cour* (1613), fol. 12, and with an arrangement for solo voice and lute in Gabriel Bataille's *4ᵉ livre d'Airs de différents autheurs* (Paris, 1613), fol. 7v. The latter version is included in *Airs de Cour pour Voix et Luth (1603–1643)*, ed. André Verchaly (Paris: Societé Francaise de Musicologie, 1961), pp. 54–55 (notes on p. XLIV). Guedron's music (both versions) with the French words and another translation by Sir Edward Filmer, were included in *French Court-Aires, With their Ditties Englished* (1629), No. IX (sigs. F1v–F2). The French text (sig. M1v) is as follows, corrected from Verchaly in ll. 2 and 20 (Filmer had *disoit* and *plustoſt*).

Vn jour l'amoureuse Siluie
Disait, baise moy je te prie,
Au berger qui seul est sa vie
Et son amour,
Baise moy Pasteur je te prie,
Et te leue, car il est jour.

Regarde la naissante Aurore,
Baise moy Pasteur que j'adore,
Qui veut que je te prie encore
Par nostre amour:
Baise moy Pasteur que j'adore,
Et te leue, car il est jour.

Ma crainte hors d'ici t'appelle,
Baise moy Pasteur ce dit-elle,
O dieux! dit-il, quelle nouuelle
Pour tant d'amour:
Baise moy Pasteur ce dit-elle,
Et te leue, car il est jour.

De cela Pasteur ne me blâme,
Baise moy plustot ma chere ame,
Le secret entretient la flame
D'vn bel amour:
Baise moy doncques ma chere ame,
Et te leue, car il est jour.

Ha! que dis-tu, chere Siluie?
Baise moy Pasteur je te prie,
Le Soleil porte donc enuie
A nostre Amour?
Baise moy Pasteur je te prie,
Et te leue, car il est jour.

  Sa clairté qu'on trouue si belle,
Baise moy Pasteur ce dit-elle,
Se rend importune & cruelle
A nostre Amour:
Baise moy Pasteur ce dit-elle,
Et te leue, car il est jour.

  Mais puis qu'il faut que je te laisse
Baise moy ma chere déesse,
Soulage l'ennuy qui m'oppresse
Par trop d'amour:
Baise moy ma chere déesse,
Et puis adieu, car il est jour.

Filmer's translation is as follows:

Syluia, not long since, halfe-affrighted,
Because loues theft grew vnbenighted,
Wak'd the mate wherein shee delighted,
And thus did say:
With a kisse let all wrongs bee righted,
And get-vp quickly; for tis day.

  See! where young Morne begins to enter:
What early wings haue late bee'n lent her!
Some sleeplesse riuall may haue sent her,
Vs to betray:
Hastily kisse then, to preuent her,
And get-vp quickly; for 'tis day.

  My feare would faine from hence expell thee,
Before this traytresse Light do sell thee
To Shame: then thinke not much I tell thee
Of thy delay;
With a kisse since I must compell thee
To get-vp quickly; for 'tis day.

  My scruple ought not to be blamed:
Loue, by this blow, is no whit lamed:
Stopp'd flame doth rather, more vntamed,
Rage then decay:
With a kisse fairely then bee framed
To get-vp quickly; for 'tis day.

  Syluia! what newes is this doth daunt mee?
(Quoth Shepheard) Canst thou so much scant mee
Of ioy, because the Sunne doth haunt mee
With iealous ray?
But a kisse onely wilt thou grant mee
To get-vp quickly now 'tis day?

His flash, the Worlds beloued wunder,
(To vs like messenger of thunder)
Doth blast Loues arme, and part asunder
His sweetest fray;
With thy kisse (though but enter'd yunder)
Tempting grow'n Flame to fly young Day.

Since then to part I find concerning
Now thy aduice hath taught mee learning,
I will, to shew my sealfe descerning,
Rather then stay,
Take a kisse in pay of loues earning,
And so, farewell; because 'tis day.

II.

These lines are from *Lingua* (1607), attributed to Thomas Tomkis (by Sir John Harington in a note dated 1609; see BM MS Add. 27632, fol. 30). Fellowes (ESLS, 2nd series, IX, 4) had ascribed the words to Anthony Brewer, who was mistakenly thought to have written *Lingua* (see DNB, s.v. Brewer); Fellowes corrected himself in EMV. The context of the poem in the play is amusing: in Act II, sc. ii (sig. D2), Phantastes is reminded of his promise to help a gentleman who "made 19. sonnets of his mistris Busk-point" devise a twentieth; he then produces the poem. Attey's version has no variants, except that he omits the footnote Phantastes inserts between lines 4 and 5: "Then to conclude let him peruert *Catullus* his *zonam soluit diu ligatam* thus, thus." Catullus IIA reads:

Tam gratumst mihi quam ferunt puellae
pernici aureolum fuisse malum,
quod zonam soluit diu ligatam.

Another copy of the poem is found in Bod. MS Ashmole 38 (mid-17th century) p. 146, with these variants:

3 Was] Is   4 faire] hard

1 *gordian knot.* Tilley G375.

III.

A copy of this poem is in BM MS Add. 52585 (*c.* 1630), fol. 19v, headed "Of the vncertaine ioyes of this life." It varies thus:

5 Like] As
6 Like] As
8 Like] As
12 Then] Even then
14 beguile] deceaue

The MS continues:

17 As life what is so sweet   18 What Creature woulde not choose it
19 The wounded hart doth weep   20 When it is forst to loose it.
21 The doue that knowes noe guile   22 Bemones her mate a dying
23 And never blood was spilt   24 But lefte the lover crying.

25 If swans doe sing it is to craue of death
26 He woulde not rob them of there happy breath.

6 *Like ... flow. Cf.* Tilley T284.
7–8 *vncertaine ... range. Cf.* Tilley W412, "As changeable as the wind."

IIII.

Cf. Bt.1606.XI and note for other Venus and Adonis songs. Obertello (pp. 445–446), makes a rather strained comparison of this poem, RDo1610.VII, and "Within a green-wood sweet of mirtle sauour" from Yonge's *Musica Transalpina* (1588), No. XXXIII.

2 *Mirrhas childe.* Myrrha, changed to a myrtle tree (see l. 1) for incest with her father, bore Adonis after her transformation. See Ovid *Metamorphoses*, X. 480–542.
9 *looke Babies in my eyes.* Tilley B8; see Jo1609.IX.13 and note.

V.

This poem by William Browne was printed in his (D) *Britannia's Pastorals* (1616), Book II, song 2 (sigs. F1v–F2). There are two other manuscript versions dating from the mid-17th century: (E) BM MS Harl. 3511, fol. 78–78v, and (F) Harl. 6917, fol. 93, headed "The Choice of a mistris." The variants are:

8 As] that F
9 In as] with so F
   vertues] verses E
10 ere yet imbrac'd] yet ere enricht F
13–18 *follow 19–24 in* F
18 Though] yet F
20 vertues grace] vertue graced F
24 Onely . . . kindle] one whose worth could kindly F
   loue] worth E
25 Such . . . you] Such a one if you doe F
27 browne or faire] faire, or browne F
28 somewhat] somewhile D

VII.

As Fellowes notes (EMV, 2nd ed., p. 606), the first line of this poem resembles that of Sonnet IV ("To the Lady L. S.") from Michael Drayton's *Idea* (1619; *Works*, ed. J. W. Hebel, Oxford, 1932, II, 312), "Bright starre of Beauty, on whose eye-lids sit," but the rest of the poem is different. The opening poem "To his Mistress" in Richard Barnfield's *Cynthia* (1595) also begins "Bright Starre of Beauty, fairest Faire aliue" (*Poems*, ed. Montague Summers, London, 1936, p. 48).

Nos. VII–IX seem to form a group, the ritual flattery of which suggests that they were written for some great lady's formal entertainment.

XII.

This is a much-corrupted version of a poem by Sir Thomas Wyatt. I give the version printed by Kenneth Muir in his edition of the *Collected Poems* (Cambridge, Mass.: Harvard University Press, 1949), p. 19, from Wyatt's own MS (Egerton 2711). For collations with the Devonshire MS (BM Add. 17492, fol. 72) and Tottel's *Miscel-*

lany, see Muir, p. 261, and the edition of Tottel by H. E. Rollins (Cambridge, Mass., 2nd ed., 1965), I, 42 and II, 173.

> RESOUND my voyse, ye wodes that here me plain,
>   Boeth hilles and vales causing reflexion;
> And Ryvers eke record ye of my pain,
>   Which have ye oft forced by compassion
>   As judges to here myn exclamation;
> Emong whome pitie I fynde doeth remayn:
> Where I it seke, Alas, there is disdain.
>
> Oft ye Revers, to here my wofull sounde,
>   Have stopt your course and, plainly to expresse,
> Many a tere by moystor of the grounde
>   The erth hath wept to here my hevenes;
>   Which causeles to suffre without redresse
> The howgy okes have rored in the wynde:
> Eche thing me thought complaynyng in their kynde.
>
> Why then, helas, doeth not she on me rew?
>   Or is her hert so herd that no pitie
> May in it synke, my joye for to renew?
>   O stony hert ho hath thus joyned the?
>   So cruell that art, cloked with beaultie,
> No grace to me from the there may procede,
> But as rewarded deth for to be my mede.

As Rollins notes (II, 173), Wyatt's poem is based on a strambotto by Serafino d'Aquila beginning "Laer che sente el mesto e gran clamore" (*Opere,* 1516, fol. 125).

XIII.
3 *My . . . cloath.* Fellowes (EMV, 2nd ed., p. 606) says that this line seems to lack two syllables, and speculates that the line began with *Adieu,* which the composer did not wish to repeat. The line might just as well have *alas* after *threads.*

XIIII.
A different setting of this song is in BM MS Add. 17786–91 (opening words only), parts 1–4, 6, fol. 13, printed in Peter Warlock's *First Book of Elizabethan Songs . . . for one voice . . . and four stringed instruments* (Oxford, 1926), No. 1, with words from a version (for voice and lute or lyra viol) found in (D) William Ballet's Lute-Book (after 1594?), Trinity College, Dublin, MS D.1.21, p. 76. Another arrangement of this setting is in (E) Bod. MS Mus. f. 7–10 (c. 1630–40; Cantus, fol. 25v), with music for four voices and this note: "The 2. inner parts ware composed by me Tho: Hamond." Diana Poulton tells me that another copy of this version (music for melody and bass) is in BM MS Egerton 2971, p. 10. The variants are:

1] sung] sange D, soong E
2 *Bethelem* was come] Bethlem Iuda Came DE
3 her] a D
4 That] who E
6 quoth] sange D, soong E
7 a] my E

8 Who] which E
  on] an E
11 sang] soonge E
12 sweetly rockt him] rokt him sweetly D, rockt him featly E

Among other nativity lullabies, *cf.* William Byrd, *Psalmes, Sonets, & songs* (1588), No. XXXII, and Martin Peerson, *Priuate Musicke* (1620), No. XII.

Index of First Lines

Glossarial Index

abound, *possess in abundance*, 155

abusion, *deceit*, 153

accord, v. *tune*, 58

Achilles, 364

acquaint, *become acquainted with*, 275

Adams, Thomas, 65, 167, 259, 315, 341

Adonis, 216, 227, 228, 244–245, 417, 537, 545, 622

adventure, n. *chance, risk*, 213; *enterprise*, 317, 334

Aeolus, 411, 548

affect, v. *like, love*, 197, 319

affected, *disposed (with inf.)*, 68

afford, *yield*, 415

after clap, *an unexpected stroke after the recipient has ceased to be on his guard*, 188

Aggs, John, 614

air de cour, 6, 7, 352–354, 587, 588–590, 619–620

Akerman, John Y., 597

Alcmena, 606

Alençon, François, Duke of, 460

Alexander, 415

Alford, J., 580

Alison, Richard, 22, 531

allarum, *call to arms*, 198

Allen, John, 570

Alleyn, Edward, 458

Allot, Robert, 452

allow, *sanction*, 204; *approve*, 350

amate, *to dismay or dishearten*, 407; amated, *confounded*, 410

Ambrose ("Ambrosiaster"), 570

Amis, Kingsley, 1

amisses, *misdeeds*, 92

Amphion, 392, 561

Amyntas, 313

anatamy, *anatomy, analysis*, 169

Andrews, H., 525

angels, *angles, fish-hooks (with a pun?)*, 362

Anne (of Denmark), Queen of England, 282, 283, 524, 559, 570, 587

apayed, *rewarded*, 58, 186

Apollo, 184, 234, 418, 514, 617; *see* Phoebus

Appelles, 184

Apperson's *Proverbs*, 469

approve, *prove, demonstrate*, 80, 130; *make proof of*, 223

Arabella, Lady, *see* Stuart

Arber, Edward, 496, 525; *see also* Stationers' Register

Arbor of Amorous Devises, The, 605

Arcadelt, Jaques, 5, 514

Arents, George, 525

argue, *to evince, indicate*, 392

Argues, *i.e.*, Argus', 140

Argus, 140, 361, 488, 498, 592

Arion, 221

Ariosto, Lodovico, 22, 25, 451

Aristotle, 536

Aristoxenus, 221, 536

Arkwright, G. E. P., 3n

eternished, *made eternal*, 284

Evans, Joan, 593

Evans, Thomas, 593

Evans, Willa McClung, 29n

Euerie Woman in her Humor, 461, 464, 493, 498

except, *unless*, 295

Expert, H., 525, 547

Fabry, Francis J., 560, 605

familiar, *a member of one's household, an intimate friend, or a familiar spirit or demon*, 194

fantastical, *fantastic, irrational*, 114

Farmer, John, 572

Farnaby, Giles, 480

fast, adv. *readily*, 219

fast, *faced*, 82

fat, *rich, complacent*, 211

Faustina, 94

fayned, *feigned*, 75

Fayrfax, Robert, 5

feat, *graceful, pretty*, 87, 94

fell, *cruel, fierce*, 188

Fellowes, Edmund H., viii, 449–624 *passim; see also* EMV

fence, *a defense, parry*, 213

fend cut, *see* note on pp. 544–545

Fenyo, Jane K., 21n

Ferguson, F. S., *see* McKerrow, R. B.

Ferrabosco, Alfonso (I), 2, 7, 292, 561, 587

Ferrabosco, Alfonso (II), 9, 25, 28, 29, 44, 45, 47, 96, 290–303, 441, 472, 475, 486, 527, 529, 532, 543, 560–571, 579, 606

Ferrabosco, Domenico Maria, 45

Ficino, Marsilio, 570

Filmer, Sir Edward, 588, 589, 619–620

fined, *refined, made beautiful*, 212

Finetta, 87

Finney, Gretchen L., 526, 561

fleete, *float, bathe*, 191

Fletcher, John, 475, 482

Fletcher, Giles, 480

flidge, *fledged, having feathers developed enough for flight*, 180

Flood, W. H. G., 615

Flora, 91, 93, 186, 311

Florella, 307

florish, flourish, *prosperity, vigor*, 311

folía, a ground bass formula, 12, 13

fond, *foolish*, 86, 87

fondling, *foolish person*, 102

fondly, *foolishly*, 189

foolish fire, *fool's fire, will-o'-the-wisp, Ignis fatuus*, 217

Forbes, John, 13, 460, 463, 465, 468, 476, 480, 483, 484, 490, 495, 496, 513, 518, 520, 521, 542, 573, 575, 577

forbid, *form of past tense, forbad*, 175

Ford, Thomas, 16, 25, 33, 37, 45, 182, 270–280, 439–440, 486, 548, 553–559, 578, 583, 606

forestall, *to buy up goods in order to raise the price*, 382

Forrest of Fancy, The, 469

Forster, John, 407, 615

forswear, *to deny; to swear falsely; to break an oath*, 392

forward, *ardent*, 74; *bold*, 85

foster, *fosterparent, nurse*, 102

Foster, Joseph, 541, 611

fourteeners, 13, 14, 15, 16, 21, 24, 25

Foxwell, Agnes, 514

foyle, *foil, a repulse, a baffling check*, 121

frame, *to form, produce*, 191, 213

Francisque, Antoine, 607

Franck, John Wolfgang, 511

franke, *free, liberal*, 211

franzy, *frenzy*, 207, 242

Fraser, Russell A., 11n, 12n

Fraunce, Abraham, 451, 605

free mans song, *or* three-mans song, *a simple part-song*, 196

Frere, W. H., 18n

fret, *gnaw, devour*, 421

frid, *see* note on p. 539

Friedman, Albert B., 14

fro, *from*, 345

frottola, Italian verse form; type of song popular in Italy before the madrigal, 5

froward, *adverse, refractory*, 224

Fuller Maitland, John A., 553, 592

Füllsack, Zacharias, 607

Furnival, F. J., 495

Galilei, Vincenzo, 8n

Gamble, John, *see* manuscripts, New York Public Library, Drexel MS 4257: 558, 561

gamut, gam ut, *the lowest note in the medieval scale* (G); *the scale itself*, 53, 185

gan, *past tense of* gin (begin); *used as an auxiliary verb*, 179